M000289203

# MANAGERIAL ECONOMICS

# THE OXFORD HANDBOOK OF

# MANAGERIAL ECONOMICS

*Edited by*

## CHRISTOPHER R. THOMAS

*and*

## WILLIAM F. SHUGHART II

OXFORD
UNIVERSITY PRESS

# OXFORD
## UNIVERSITY PRESS

Oxford University Press is a department of the University of Oxford.
It furthers the University's objective of excellence in research, scholarship,
and education by publishing worldwide.

Oxford   New York
Auckland   Cape Town   Dar es Salaam   Hong Kong   Karachi
Kuala Lumpur   Madrid   Melbourne   Mexico City   Nairobi
New Delhi   Shanghai   Taipei   Toronto

With offices in
Argentina   Austria   Brazil   Chile   Czech Republic   France   Greece
Guatemala   Hungary   Italy   Japan   Poland   Portugal   Singapore
South Korea   Switzerland   Thailand   Turkey   Ukraine   Vietnam

Oxford is a registered trademark of Oxford University Press
in the UK and certain other countries.

Published in the United States of America by
Oxford University Press
198 Madison Avenue, New York, NY 10016

Library of Congress Cataloging-in-Publication Data

The Oxford handbook of managerial economics / [edited by] Christopher R. Thomas and
William F. Shughart II.
p. cm.
Includes bibliographical references and index.
ISBN 978–0–19–978295–6 (cloth : alk. paper)   1. Managerial economics.
2. Managerial economics—Handbooks, manual, etc.   I. Thomas, Christopher R.
II. Shughart, William F.   II. Title: Handbook of managerial economics.
HD30.22.094 2013
338.5024′658—dc23
2012033450

1 3 5 7 9 8 6 4 2
Printed in the United States of America
on acid-free paper

# Contents

## PART VI: ORGANIZATION AND MOTIVATION IN THE MODERN FIRM

## PART VII: FINANCIAL STRUCTURE AND CORPORATE GOVERNANCE

# PART VIII:  PUBLIC POLICY FOR MANAGERS

# Contributors

**Anup Agrawal** is the Powell Chair of Finance at the University of Alabama.

**Leonce Bargeron** is an Assistant Professor of Finance in the Joseph Katz School of Business at the University of Pittsburgh.

**Sunil Chopra** is the IBM Distinguished Professor of Operations Management in the Kellogg School of Management at Northwestern University.

**Massimo G. Colombo** is a Professor of Economics of Innovation in the Department of Management, Economics, and Industrial Engineering at Politecnico di Milano.

**Marco Delmastro** is the Head of Media Competition Office at Agcom.

**Antony W. Dnes** is a Senior Associated Regulatory Scholar at the Mercatus Center in George Mason Law School, and the Editor in Chief of *Managerial & Decision Economics.*

**Luke M. Froeb** is the William C. Oehmig Associate Professor in Entrepreneurship and Free Enterprise in the Owen Graduate School of Management at Vanderbilt University.

**Esther Gal-Or** is the Glenn Stinson Chair in Competitiveness and a Professor of Business Administration and Economics in the Katz Graduate School of Business at the University of Pittsburgh.

**Massimo Garbuio** is a Lecturer at the University of Sydney Business School.

**Michael Gibbs** is a Clinical Professor of Economics and Faculty Director of the Executive MBA Program at the University of Chicago Booth School of Business, as well as a Research Fellow at the Institute for the Study of Labor (IZA).

**Emili Grifell-Tatjé** is a Professor of Management and Business Economics in the Department of Business in the Universitat Autònoma of Barcelona.

**Robert G. Hansen** is the Norman W. Martin 1925 Professor of Business Administration in the Tuck School of Business at Dartmouth College.

**Richard S. Higgins** is the Principal of the Finance Scholars Group.

**Charles A. Ingene** is the Distinguished Professor of Business Administration and a Professor of Marketing in the Department of Marketing at the University of Mississippi.

**Liena Kano** is a Research Associate in the Strategy and Global Management Area in the Haskayne School of Business at the University of Calgary.

**Elif Ketencioglu** is a PhD student at the University of Sydney Business School.

**Thomas J. Kniesner** is the Krishner Professor of Economics and Senior Research Associate in the Center for Policy Research at Syracuse University, a Professor of Economics at Claremont Graduate University, and a Research Fellow at IZA.

**Charles R. Knoeber** is the Alumni Distinguished Undergraduate Professor of Economics at North Carolina State University.

**Praveen K. Kopalle** is a Professor of Marketing in the Tuck School of Business at Dartmouth College.

**John D. Leeth** is a Professor of Economics at Bentley University.

**Kenneth Lehn** is the Samuel A. McCullough Professor of Finance in the Joseph Katz School of Business at the University of Pittsburgh.

**Dan Lovallo** is a Professor of Business Strategy at the University of Sydney Business School.

**C.A. Knox Lovell** is an Honorary Professor at the Centre for Efficiency and Productivity Analysis in the School of Economics at the University of Queensland.

**Thomas P. Lyon** is the Dow Chemical Professor of Sustainable Science, Technology, and Commerce in the Ross School of Business and the School of Natural Resources and Environment at the University of Michigan.

**Robert Maness** is Vice President at Charles River Associates and a Visiting Associate Professor in the Department of Economics at Texas A&M University.

**John W. Maxwell** is the W. George Pinnell Professor in Business, Economics, and Public Policy in the Kelley School of Business at Indiana University.

**David R. Munro** is a PhD student at the University of California in Santa Cruz.

**William S. Neilson** is the J. Fred Holly Chair and a Professor of Economics in the Department of Economics at the University of Tennessee.

**Felix Oberholzer-Gee** is the Andreas Andresen Professor of Business Administration at Harvard University.

**Sharon M. Oster** is the Frederick Wolfe Professor of Economics and Entrepreneurship at the Yale School of Management.

**Mark Perelman** is a Quantitative Analyst at PineBridge Investments.

**David Porter** is the Donna and David Janes Endowed Chair in Experimental Economics, and a Professor of Economics and Mathematics at Chapman University.

**Larissa Rabbiosi** is an Associate Professor in the Department of International Economics and Management at the Copenhagen Business School.

**Stephen J. Rassenti** is the Director of the Economic Science Institute, and the Professor of Economics and Mathematics at Chapman University.

**Paul H. Rubin** is the Samuel Candler Dobbs Professor of Economics at Emory University, and the Editor in Chief of *Managerial & Decision Economics*.

**William F. Shughart II** is the J. Fish Smith Professor in Public Choice in the John M. Huntsman School of Business at Utah State University.

**Oz Shy** is the Senior Economist in the Research Department at the Federal Reserve Bank of Boston.

**ManMohan S. Sodhi** is a Professor of Operations Management and the Head of Operations and Supply Chain Management in the Cass Business School at the City University of London, as well as the Executive Director of the Munjal Global Manufacturing Institute.

**David J. Teece** is Tusher Professor in Global Business and Director of the Institute for Business Innovation in the Haas School of Business at the University of California, Berkeley and Chairman of the Berkeley Research Group, LLC.

**Christopher R. Thomas** is the Exide Professor of Sustainable Enterprise and Associate Professor of Economics at the University of South Florida.

**Alain Verbeke** is a Professor of International Business Strategy and the McCaig Chair in Management, Strategy and Global Management Area in the Haskayne School of Business at the University of Calgary.

**Gregory J. Werden** is the Senior Economic Counsel in the Antitrust Division of the US Department of Justice.

**Lawrence J. White** is the Robert Kavesh Professor of Economics in the Stern School of Business at New York University.

**Steven N. Wiggins** is a Professor of Economics at Texas A&M University.

**Dennis A. Yao** is the Lawrence E. Fouraker Professor of Business Administration at Harvard University.

**Xubing Zhang** is an Assistant Professor of Marketing in the Department of Marketing and Management at the Hong Kong Polytechnic University.

# PART I

# NATURE, SCOPE, AND FUTURE OF MANAGERIAL ECONOMICS

CHAPTER 1

# MANAGERIAL ECONOMICS: INTRODUCTION AND OVERVIEW

CHRISTOPHER R. THOMAS
AND WILLIAM F. SHUGHART II

## 1.1 THE CONCEPT OF THIS HANDBOOK

THE *Oxford Handbook of Managerial Economics* assembles a set of timely and authoritative articles designed to inform scholars, MBA faculty, and professional business consultants about new theoretical and empirical developments in applied business decision making and strategy. The research frontier in managerial economics has moved well beyond applying ideas from microeconomics, capital budgeting, and linear programming to the world of business. Modern managerial economics now integrates concepts from the fields of competitive strategy, marketing, organizational economics, corporate control, and financial structure, among others, in order to explain and inform managers, scholars, and consultants on the issues and challenges of making both short-run operational decisions and long-run strategic plans. The timing and nature of the Oxford University Press handbook series could not be more appropriate in light of the current state of the field of managerial economics. The purpose of Oxford's handbook series, being produced under the general editorship of Michael Szenberg and Lall Ramrattan, is to serve as a forum for summarizing and disseminating the latest scholarly developments in various fields of study and to identify new directions for future research. To our knowledge, this will be the first such handbook in the area of managerial economics.

This *Handbook in Managerial Economics* differs substantially from the many college textbooks in managerial economics that are designed for teaching undergraduate and/ or MBA courses in business schools. Each chapter is written by one or more academics who have done extensive scholarly research in their specialized areas of expertise.

These chapters are written for academics, Ph.D. graduate students, and business consultants who specialize in economics or other academic areas related to business decision making. Consequently, this *Handbook* is not expected to be useful as a *textbook*. In fact, an entire handbook might be warranted to address the pedagogical questions concerning the teaching of managerial economics. For at least the past decade, faculty and administrators at business schools in the United States have been debating whether business students should be required to take a course in managerial economics, and, if so, exactly which topics should/need to be covered in managerial economics courses for undergraduates and MBA students. As this *Handbook* is intended to advance research in managerial economics and serve as a guide for professional consultants, we will largely avoid pedagogical matters in this volume, although we expect that teachers of managerial economics will find much valuable material for classroom presentation and other types of coursework.

## 1.2  WHAT IS MANAGERIAL ECONOMICS (NOW)?

Economists are far more likely to agree on what managerial economics *was* than on what managerial economics has now become. Ponssard and Tanguy (1999) refer to the 1960s as the "golden years" for managerial economics. During this period, economists applied neoclassical analysis of the firm to a "traditional" set of business decisions involving profit maximization, optimal pricing, production analysis, cost minimization, demand forecasting, and capital budgeting. Every kind of quantitative analysis of business decision making constituted a legitimate topic for managerial economists to study and teach. The tool kit for managerial economics seemed extensive at the time, as it included calculus (unconstrained and constrained optimization methods), decision sciences (operations research methods, including linear and dynamic programming and queuing theory models), and statistics (primarily simple and advanced regression analysis). During this golden age, the firm was treated as a black box that, when properly managed, transformed inputs efficiently into outputs, which were then sold for a profit at the optimally set uniform price. In the early days of managerial economics, there seemed to be little interest or motivation to look inside the neoclassical black box to see what might be going on that could be of any interest to business managers. At best, only production engineers could possibly find the internal workings of the black box worthy of inspection or study.

Beginning in the 1970s and reaching full stride by the early 1980s, economists opened the black box and ushered in the current age of the "new" or "modern" managerial economics. Most economists working in the area of managerial economics are likely to agree with Dnes and Rubin's description in the next chapter of this *Handbook*, which characterizes the scope of modern managerial economics not so much as a discrete break with the past but rather as an *augmentation* of traditional managerial economics, focusing on areas such as "globalization, the economics of organization, information economics, strategic behavior, the learning organization, risk management, business ethics, and behavioral economics." The path of this transformation can be clearly traced by examining the topical coverage in several of the prominent academic journals that focus on economic analysis of business: *Managerial and Decision Economics, the Journal of Economic and Management Science*, and *Strategic Management Review*. The dynamic path of managerial economics over the past thirty years has most certainly been shaped by forces of demand and supply: the emerging contemporary issues facing managers during this period created a demand for extending the scope of analysis while the growth of modern industrial organization supplied a rich set of new ideas that promised to advance the economic analysis of business decision making. Modern managerial economics not only developed the new applications but also sped up the delivery of new analytical frameworks to undergraduate business and MBA classrooms. But economists working solely in the field of industrial organization were not the primary suppliers of business applications using game theory, information theory, and advances in organization and behavioral economics.

While a precise definition of (modern) managerial economics is slippery, we think most scholars and professionals whose work involves the application of economics to the formulation and execution of business decisions and strategies will agree that they are employing the tool kit of managerial economics. A look at the table of contents of this *Handbook* also helps define the current scope of managerial economics.[1] We will now describe the architecture of this volume by briefly summarizing the purpose and content of each one of the eight parts of the *Handbook*.

## 1.3  OVERVIEW OF THIS HANDBOOK

### 1.3.1  Nature, Scope, and Future of Managerial Economics

This first handbook in managerial economics opens with an essay by the editors of *Managerial and Decision Economics*, a leading scholarly journal in managerial economics. Antony Dnes and Paul H. Rubin offer their perspective on the present scope and future direction of managerial economics, a perspective forged from the vantage point of many years editing *MDE*. Dnes and Rubin see the "new" managerial economics moving away from the traditional focus on demand and revenue optimization techniques to take up problems associated with the development of "modern" industrial organization: asymmetric information, agency problems, organizational matters, and strategic interactions with rivals. Dnes and Rubin discuss the trends they see in managerial and decision economics, including the complexities introduced by incorporating business ethics, globalization, and new insights from behavioral economics. In their conclusion, Dnes and Rubin identify areas they see as most likely to be fruitful directions for research, suggestions which hold great value coming from the editors of *MDE*.

## 1.3.2  Managing Demand and Cost Conditions

The traditional core of managerial economics has been centered on managing demand and cost conditions to achieve the firm's goal, which is generally assumed to be profit (and value)-maximization. While modern managerial economics broadens and deepens the analysis of business decision making, all aspects of managing both for-profit and nonprofit organizations must build on an understanding of how best to manage the organization's revenues and costs. This first major part of the *Handbook* is composed of four chapters that supply modern viewpoints on several challenging issues currently facing business decision makers and consultants who must understand the complexities of demand and cost in order to control the firm's performance.

Lawrence White leads off by investigating the nature, causes, and measurement of market power. Until 1980, nearly all of the work on market power by economists stemmed from work on public policy matters, especially in the area of antitrust doctrine (competition policy in Europe). Michael Porter (1980) expanded the application of market power analysis from mostly public policy issues to the mainstay issues of executive managers seeking to achieve sustainable competitive advantage over rival firms. White takes advantage of his substantial career in antitrust to lay out clearly the nature and sources of market power in a comprehensive manner that will be extremely useful to practicing business consultants and scholars from fields outside industrial organization. Modern managerial economics now embraces the study of tactical and strategic decisions aimed at creating and protecting "distinctiveness" or "competitive advantage" for the business and its products or services, which, of course, means that managers must find ways to create and hold onto market power without, of course, attracting the attention of the antitrust authorities by abusing that power. Section three of White's chapter may be the most valuable contribution for practicing consultants and applied economists because that section critically analyzes the many methodologies currently employed by consulting firms and antitrust agencies alike to measure market power at either the level of a single firm or a group of firms. Industrial organization scholars will benefit from White's foundation before attempting to master the more advanced work by Perloff et al. (2007) on estimating market power and strategies.

Turning next to the cost side of the profit function, Emili Grifell-Tatjé and C. A. Knox Lovell explain several alternative empirical methods for computing stochastic cost frontiers for individual firms. After briefly reviewing standard cost variance analysis, which is typically carried out by in-house cost accountants, they develop a benchmark cost frontier. In subsequent sections, they modify the benchmark analysis to allow for frontier cost analysis of unit cost, as well as unit labor cost when labor is the only input. Using the methods set forth by Grifell-Tatjé and Knox Lovell, changes in firm-level cost efficiency can be decomposed into both technical components (cost-savings from equiproportionate reductions in the usage of all inputs) and allocative components (cost-savings from changes in relative input usage). In their summary section, the authors present some specific examples of industries where their advanced methods can be applied: financial institutions, regulated utilities, transportation, health, and education.

One source of variation in cost frontiers at the firm level stems from the different strategies managers choose for mitigating disruptive risks in their supply chains, which, in many cases, amounts to employing no strategy at all and fully exposing the firm to small probability, but costly events (e.g., accelerator pedal problems at Toyota, oil spill catastrophes at BP, and Ericsson losing its supply of a key input from a minor fire at a Phillips supply plant). Sunil Chopra and ManMohan Sodhi examine the most recent work by supply chain scholars and engineers on managing the potentially devastating costs of disruptive risks. Drawing on their own research and the recent work of other supply chain scholars, Chopra and Sodhi develop here a number of design and policy recommendations for supply chain designers who face disruptive risks but have no easy way of forecasting the probability of their occurrence or their cost impacts. They remind us that humans tend to underestimate the probability of rare events, and thus managers typically underestimate disruptive risk, which may reinforce their desire to avoid investing in up-front mitigation costs. Chopra and Sodhi also examine the impact of misestimating the likelihood of a disruption, discuss containing the supply chain to localize disruptive impacts, offer general guidelines for what (and how much) reserves to hold (e.g., inventory, redundant supply sources, and flexibility in production or delivery), and describe various response strategies to disruptions.

Auctions nowadays are used widely and are ever more indispensable in the public sector as government agencies rely on all types of auctions not only to procure resources but also to allocate efficiently such things as the wireless radio spectrum and offshore drilling rights. Auctions are now becoming increasingly important in business, not only in the form of business-to-business auctions, but also as a tool for businesses to manage both costs and revenues internally. David Porter, Stephen Rassenti, and David Munro examine the nature and value of a powerful and complex type of auction called a combinatorial auction, one in which bidders place bids on packages or combinations of items—to managers. They carefully explain why this type of auction frequently can improve the efficiency of internal resource allocation, thereby lowering production costs. While Porter, Rassenti, and Munro focus on internal allocations of resources within the firm, combinatorial auctions can also be implemented to increase the firm's total revenue by selling "packages" of the firm's output to buyers willing to pay the most for various combinations of the firm's output. In all cases, the benefit of combinatorial auctions depends on strong complementarity among the items in the packages; bidders value the combination of items more than the sum of their values individually. Significant advances in recent years concerning computational complexities and design issues (see Cramton et al. 2005) now make it possible, according to Porter, Rassenti, and Munro, for any business with a $2,000 computer and a communication network to replace bureaucratic resource allocation decisions with much more efficient combinatorial auction mechanisms.

## 1.3.3    Analytical Foundations of Modern Managerial Economics

Part three of the *Handbook* examines a number of major advances in the analytical foundations of modern managerial economics, many of which follow directly from significant developments in the application of game theory and information economics to modern industrial organization. In addition, a traditional topic in managerial economics—the valuation of future income streams—has benefitted from important new theoretical research on the effects of time, risk, and uncertainty not only by managers, but also by employees, investors, and consumers. And currently, the growing field of behavioral economics appears to be well positioned to add its own transformative impact on managerial economics, as research identifies behavioral patterns that undermine some long-held assumptions about manager, consumer, and shareholder behavior.

The third part of the *Handbook* opens with Esther Gal-Or's examination of recent developments in game and information theory, all of which have advanced the study of managerial economics by forging a richer understanding of the interactions between firms in oligopolistic markets. Gal-Or carefully condenses and summarizes the developments in noncooperative game theory to explore static and dynamic issues including first- and second-mover advantages, strategic commitments and barriers to entry, pricing strategies to enhance profitability, and matters concerning the internal organization of the firm. She then extends the model to allow for incomplete information about demand and cost conditions by utilizing Bayesian-Nash equilibria. This step allows her to cover new areas of interest that involve signaling devices, moral hazard, and adverse-selection problems. In her concluding remarks, Gal-Or discusses the criticism by some business scholars who are skeptical about the value of applying advanced game and information theories to business decision making, and she predicts that behavioral economics will soon influence the direction of managerial economics.

Next, William Neilson surveys the latest advances in the standard model of discounted expected utility, in which an individual evaluates a risky stream of future income by taking the expected value of discounted feature utility values, weighted by the probabilities of occurrence. Uncertainty replaces risk when the probabilities of future outcomes are unknown. This "standard" model depends on several key factors—a constant subjective discount rate, a single utility-of-wealth function, and a unique subjective probability measure—all of which recent research calls into question. Neilson presents and critiques the most significant advances in the analysis of time, risk, and uncertainty from the viewpoint of applied managerial decision making, even though these advances extend into areas involving welfare analysis and government regulation. Neilson presents the experimental evidence that discount factors are likely to increase as the time horizon increases, and that this can cause preferences to be time inconsistent. He then delves into the complex problems that arise when measures of risk aversion are based on the shape of the utility-of-wealth function; yet new theoretical arguments suggest that individuals do not possess single, stable utility functions. Amid all of this complexity, Neilson's goal is to supply a balanced mix of intuition and rigor so that the readers of this *Handbook* can better understand how preferences affect behavior in managerial economics.

Massimo Garbuio, Dan Lovallo, and Elif Ketencioglu argue that the "traditional" approach to modeling the way executive managers make strategic decisions relies too heavily on "false" behavioral assumptions for both the executive managers and the firms' owners. Specifically, they contend that a large number of studies using market-generated and experimentally generated data show that the assumption of rational behavior is "far from a universal truth," and this explains why many predictions about strategic decision making are inaccurate. To make their case—and they do so provocatively—Garbuio, Lovallo, and Ketencioglu examine several key psychological principles and their associated strategic decision outcomes based on three classes of deviations from the rational choice paradigm: nonstandard preferences, nonstandard beliefs, and nonstandard decision making. In each case, they are able to identify compelling examples of strategic decision making in which relying on "more realistic" psychological assumptions leads to impressive improvements in the explanatory power of traditional analysis of managerial decisions. This chapter supports Esther Gal-Or's prediction that behavioral economics is on the way to becoming an indispensable component in the analysis of business decision making.

## 1.3.4 Pricing and Marketing Tactics and Strategies

Managerial economics has always included the study of pricing tactics and strategies. In the early days of "traditional" managerial economics, the emphasis was more on *tactical* pricing decisions designed to extract more of the consumer surplus left behind when firms follow a simple uniform pricing rule, and much of the conceptual and applied research addressed first-, second-, and third-degree methods of price discrimination in situations of perfect information about consumer demand and readily identifiable consumer characteristics. And, in modeling price discrimination, there was scant attention paid to the reaction of rival firms to any particular pricing tactic the firm might choose, even though rival reactions to price changes were certainly a mainstay of *equilibrium* analysis of oligopoly markets. Following the advances in game and information theory associated with modern industrial organization, economists and marketing scholars pushed the sophistication of pricing theory and practice to cover a number of more complicated tactical and strategic pricing methods. In this *Handbook on Managerial Economics* we devote just a single part with two chapters to cover only the most recent areas of progress in pricing theory and research, fully recognizing that so little space cannot possibly cover all of the advancements and refinements, even over the past five or six years. For this reason, we intend for our readers to rely on a sister publication in the Oxford Handbook series to fill this gap, specifically the *Oxford Handbook on Pricing Management*, edited by Özalp Özer and Robert Phillips. A number of other excellent sources on contemporary pricing theory and practice include Phillips (2005), Rao (2009), Shy (2008), and Stole (2007).

While advances in the field of pricing can be attributed to scholars in both economics and marketing, we rely heavily in this volume on the viewpoints of marketing scholars in the two chapters on pricing. In the first pricing chapter, Praveen Kopalle and Robert Hansen argue that managerial economics is most valuable when it is integrative, particularly when combining economics and marketing knowledge on pricing. They believe that economics has contributed a large portion of the theoretical work in pricing while marketing has accomplished most of the work on applying that pricing theory to actual firms and consumers. Kopalle and Hansen begin their chapter with a brief review of fundamental principles for optimal pricing and then spend the rest of their chapter identifying and discussing a large number of recently published papers and books on pricing. They reference and discuss over seventy-five scholarly contributions to the theory and practice of pricing from 2005 to the present. And, given their space constraints, they can tackle only price discrimination, conjoint analysis, dynamic, behavioral, and competitive considerations, and pricing in two-sided markets. In their concluding remarks, Kopalle and Hansen make the case that the availability of consumer- and transaction-level data, coupled with the ability of computers to process more sophisticated pricing models quickly, creates an environment in which retail managers can now adopt and execute successfully much richer pricing tactics and strategies.

In the second chapter on pricing, Charles Ingene and Xubing Zhang focus on retail pricing decisions of various brands within a particular product category. They present a model that allows them to investigate how channel structure and channel pricing policies affect the profit-maximizing number of brands a retailer should carry within a specific product category. Their approach reveals several counterintuitive relations concerning brand pricing and category pricing decisions.

## 1.3.5  Strategy and Business Competition

Michael Porter noted in 1983 that economists working in industrial organization and scholars from management and psychology working in strategic management "viewed each other with suspicion—if they knew each other existed." Since 1983 substantial advances in modern industrial organization have become an integral part of our understanding of business strategy. While many MBA programs still rely on standard case study approaches to teach strategic management, a large and growing number of top programs are either adding to or replacing the case study approach with courses that emphasize game theory, industrial organization models of oligopoly behavior, and organizational economics. The evolution in both the research and teaching of business strategy is immediately visible in the contents of the widely used textbook, *Economics of Strategy* (2010) by David Besanko et al. This evolution has not been entirely attributable to the influence of advances in industrial organization. Today, most economists researching and teaching in the area of strategy and business competition recognize the variance in long-run profitability of firms competing in the same markets and that some meaningful part of this variation in profit is attributable to different strategic decisions made by the firms' executive managers. The chapters in this section of the *Handbook* seek to extend and explain the ongoing evolution—and perhaps convergence—of the overlapping fields of strategic management and the economics of business strategy.

Felix Oberholzer-Gee and Dennis Yao open the strategy section of this *Handbook* with a provocative new way of analyzing and identifying the "holy grail" for strategic management scholars and practitioners: sustainable competitive advantage. In many markets, companies' financial performance varies widely and some of the firms are able to earn positive economic profit in the long run. Oberholzer-Gee and Yao note that currently three schools of thought in the strategy literature supply explanations for why markets remain less than perfectly competitive: one emphasizes the structure of the firms and markets, another focuses on special resources that businesses control, and the third treats the bounded rationality of executive managers as the source of long-run economic profit. Noting that each of these schools of thought on sustainable competitive advantage implicitly ties some form of market imperfection to sustainable profits, Oberholzer-Gee and Yao offer in their chapter a theory of market imperfections as a useful complement to the current views of strategic management. They argue that many of the current frameworks employed by scholars and consulting firms lead executives to see strategic opportunities that do not exist and overlook situations that offer genuinely sustainable competitive advantages. In addition to explaining a process for finding and exploiting strategic opportunities using the lens of market imperfections, Oberholzer-Gee and Yao also point to useful areas of future research by identifying a number of recent examples of cross-pollinating research between the fields of industrial organization and strategic management. They believe that while the majority of research has involved "economics informing strategy rather than vice-versa," strategy has now begun to inform economic research.

The challenge of creating and managing growth is a critical strategic concern for innovation-driven companies. As David J. Teece explains the nature of the challenge, managers must (1) do things right in the short run (i.e., minimize costs and maximize revenues) and (2) do the right things in the long run. He believes that traditional managerial economics provides useful guidance for the first challenge but generally overlooks or even confuses matters on the second challenge. Teece presents a carefully constructed case with several helpful examples from real-world businesses, arguing that modern managerial economics must come to grips with the role of intangible assets and dynamic capabilities if it wishes to supply useful guidance for managing growth and innovation. He points out that only recently has managerial economics begun to investigate and understand the role of dynamic capabilities in building and maintaining competitive advantage. Teece also draws attention to the critical role of the entrepreneurial manager who must sense and seize existing innovation opportunities as well as proactively create opportunities through investments in research and development. To accomplish this, the entrepreneurial manager must understand how the various inputs in the creative process interact in order to ensure that creative resources are deployed and aligned to minimize internal conflict and maximize complementarities. Teece concludes that the "wellspring of the requisite capabilities remains enigmatic and difficult for many firms to harness."

In the next chapter on strategy, Oz Shy lays out the nature of strategic behavior and managerial decision making for firms operating in network industries—a relatively new field in industrial organization—and he identifies the cutting-edge issues facing researchers and business consultants. In network industries, demand is characterized by consumers for whom the utility derived from using a good or service depends largely on the number of other consumers using the same brand or a compatible brand. And, on the supply side, the network firm's profit also depends on the number of rival firms who use the same technology or a compatible technology. He contends that network effects do not change the basic principles of managerial economics, "but rather adds some additional complications." He fully explains all of the critical concepts that are unique to network industries and necessary for sound strategic decisions: critical mass, one-way and two-way compatibility, switching costs and lock-in, and standardization and compatibility considerations. To make it easier to see how dynamic forces arise when network effects influence demand and profits, Shy relies heavily on numerical analysis rather than using more abstract mathematical models. He also ties these ideas to a number of real-world business examples, which include Apple's iPad and Amazon's Kindle Fire, WordPerfect and Microsoft Word, Skype (in VoIP technology) and Adobe (in PDF documents). In recognition of the importance of antitrust analysis in managerial economics—a recurring theme throughout this *Handbook*—Shy discusses the implications for antitrust policy in network industries. Clearly, pricing decisions in network industries require a rather sophisticated skill set, and Shy notes that this may be missing because most MBA programs place too little emphasis on pricing: "Strangely enough, conventional business school curricula do not emphasize teaching students 'how to price.' Thus, typical MBAs are not trained well enough to manage firms seeking strategically to introduce new standards; and in particular they lack the knowledge how a firm's pricing structure can be integrated into the dynamic evolution of a new network of users."

Turning next to recent advances in the strategic management of the multinational enterprise (MNE), Alain Verbeke and Liena Kano explore the theoretical developments of a "new" internalization theory which serves as a general theory of the MNE. Verbeke and Kano argue that the new internalization theory, by adopting a perspective related to Teece's dynamic capabilities paradigm, can now explain how MNEs choose the firm's boundaries, the design of internal governance, and the nature of interactions with the external environment. After they trace the evolution of internalization theory over the past forty years, Verbeke and Kano evaluate its current impact on international business research and forecast where future contributions to the theory will be needed.

In the final chapter of this section, Sharon M. Oster offers considerable insight into the most pressing issues concerning the nature of strategic decision analysis in the non-profit sector—a large and growing sector of the US economy contributing about 5% of GDP. Oster begins her essay by reviewing the recent literature on the objective function of a typical nonprofit organization. She then turns to the task of drawing the connection between strategy and nonprofit production of goods or services. Oster identifies a number of important questions—both theoretical and empirical in nature—that warrant research in the future.

## 1.3.6  Organization and Motivation in the Modern Firm

Organization economics focuses on two fundamental issues: (1) Why organize production in the form of a business firm and (2) how does the organization of a firm affect its performance? The answers to these questions continue to intrigue economists after more than four decades of intensive study. As noted by Gibbons (2005, 201), the make-or-buy decision has become known as the "theory of the firm," and now every modern theory of the firm addresses the motives and consequences of vertical integration. Of course, examining the boundaries of the firm also includes delving into matters of allocating decision rights and information within the internal structure and hierarchy of the organization (i.e., the firm), as well as structuring incentives to manage—and perhaps even resolve—agency problems through the design of employee and executive compensation. In this part of the *Handbook*, our contributors take aim at some of the most pressing issues and conundrums in organizational design.

Massimo Colombo, Marco Delmastro, and Larissa Rabbiosi open this part of the *Handbook* with a critical survey and analysis of current understanding about how the internal organization of firms' activities influence their performance. They pay particular attention to a recent paradigm that involves a delayering of corporate hierarchy in order to open avenues for the adoption of organizational practices which, when implemented as a group with superadditive effects, allegedly can sharply improve the performance of the firm. Columbo, Delmastro, and Rabbiosi show that when these elements are adopted piecemeal—choking off superadditive effects and synergies—the impact on performance is likely to be very small or even negative. In the process of their survey, they highlight recent theoretical and empirical work linking organization to firm performance, and they supply numerous suggestions for future research in the field.

Carefully designed and correctly implemented compensation plans for employees can have a powerful impact on the profitability of a firm by motivating employees to work harder and better. According to Michael Gibbs, the study of incentive compensation has succeeded in producing an immense and rich body of literature that supplies a useful framework for designing and implementing successful pay for performance plans. Gibbs notes that there are a number of excellent surveys of pay for performance— none of which are less than ten years old.[2] He chooses, however, to sidestep adding yet another survey to the incentive compensation literature by presenting a practical and detailed discussion of how to design and implement pay for performance. This novel approach is quite successful and should be valuable to practicing consultants. Scholars in managerial economics and organization theory will value Gibbs's clarity and insight concerning the complexity of the formal, informal, and interrelated parts of incentive plans. Instructors of graduate courses in organization economics may wish to teach pay for performance from this chapter.

Managers notoriously spend a great deal of resources merging and acquiring firms for the purpose of moving important transactions from arm's-length dealings to within the boundaries of the firm. Drawing on their experience in antitrust policy analysis, enforcement, and litigation, Richard Higgins and Mark Perelman critically evaluate current theories of vertical mergers as antitrust authorities and scholars in both the United States and the United Kingdom employ them. The decision to integrate vertically—to make rather than to buy—is a matter of keen interest to managers, and they will make better decisions about merging upstream or downstream by knowing more about how antitrust laws apply to their decisions about integrating production processes through mergers. Higgins and Perelman's insightful and comprehensive explanation of the various theories of vertical merger employed in antitrust leads them to conclude that vertical mergers rarely harm competition but may very likely harm competitors.

Robert Maness and Steven Wiggins wrap up this section on the organization of the firm with a thoughtful essay that evaluates the evolving modern theory of the firm and adds to the important recent contributions by Spulber (2009) and Hart (2011). Maness and Wiggins focus not only on modern theory but also critically review the major empirical work that supports or refutes various aspects of the most prominent theories. They argue that since Coase's original observation about the costs of using markets, economists have made great progress in advancing our understanding of why firms exist in the first place and what forces ultimately limit their size and scope. Nonetheless, Maness and Wiggins conclude that theoretical models still fall short of delivering a single, unified model capable of capturing the numerous conceptual issues concerning whether to use markets or to use internal-to-the-firm governance. Given the reality that multiple factors are likely to interact simultaneously to drive the integration decision, they propose that more nested empirical studies will be needed in order to distinguish between the various modern theories and to identify more clearly the specific factors affecting the choice to rely on markets or vertical integration.

## 1.3.7  Financial Structure and Corporate Governance

Part seven of the *Handbook* rounds out our coverage of traditional forces that influence the profitability of business. Massive theoretical and empirical literatures seek to explain how, when, and why a firm's profit is related to the structure of its financing of assets and the structure of its corporate governance mechanisms. By identifying and concentrating on the most influential recent work on these subjects, the authors of these two chapters not only assist researchers and consultants by condensing matters to a manageable set of principal results, but they also point out where questions and anomalies remain unexplained. While the chapters in this part focus primarily on corporations, many of the results can be readily applied to single proprietorships, partnerships, and even nonprofit organizations.

Modern corporations can finance asset purchases in a number of ways: ordinary debt instruments, common equity, and an assortment of hybrid instruments. Leonce Bargeron and Kenneth Lehn review three alternative but not mutually exclusive theories aimed at explaining the pattern of business financing: trade-off theory, pecking order theory, and market timing theory. Their selective review of recent literature shows that while empirical findings can support important *parts* of the three theories, there remain serious unexplained "puzzles" and anomalies that are creating serious concerns for the contemporary theory of corporate financial decisions. As experienced researchers in these difficult matters, Bargeron and Lehn are able to offer valuable clues and three specific suggestions for new research directions to address the concern expressed by DeAngelo and DeAngelo (2007) that corporate finance is "now left with no empirically viable theory of capital structure."

As with the previous chapters in this part of the *Handbook*, Anup Agrawal and Charles Knoeber distill an enormous literature down to its most important contributions for understanding the contemporary complexities of their subject. Their task is to draw from the literature the most important issues concerning the effects of corporate governance on the performance of firms facing active markets for corporate control (such as the United States and United Kingdom). Agrawal and Knoeber build their selective review around a basic agency problem framework: managers are agents, shareholders are principals, and corporate governance mechanisms attempt to solve the associated principal-agent problem. With this framework in place, they are able to examine a number of critical issues currently challenging scholars and consultants alike. Specifically, how is firm performance related (both conceptually and empirically) to inside ownership, monitoring by large shareholders and boards, and corporate governance regulations? And, is the governance-performance relation different for family firms? Agrawal and Knoeber present a concluding section that is chock-full of intriguing and troubling questions in need of further research—exactly what an *Oxford Handbook* aims to give its readers.

## 1.3.8 Public Policy for Managers

While it would require a dedicated multivolume handbook just to begin addressing the impact on business decision making of government regulatory and social policies, we have nonetheless included in this *Handbook* three chapters that examine several substantial areas of concern for executive managers and business scholars and consultants. These chapters focus primarily on US government policy. However, the analytical methods employed in each chapter apply broadly to most advanced western economies and should also clarify management thinking in developing countries where health and safety concerns in the workplace, design of efficient merger policy, and prospects for profitable investments in corporate environmentalism are emerging topics. And, of course, managers and business consultants in other countries who plan to do business in US markets will find that these chapters offer "policy analysis for managers" not found in many other places.

Thomas Kniesner and John Leeth examine the market incentives for managers to undertake costly investments designed to make their workplaces safer for workers. Even though safety regulations, tort lawsuits, and compensation insurance motivate managers to choose safer working conditions, Kniesner and Leeth argue that the most important factor, based on their assessment of the latest empirical evidence, is the higher cost of worker compensation that less safe businesses must pay in the labor market in order to hire and retain employees. They develop and present a general economic model of production in a workplace characterized by inevitable risks to health and safety. Using this model as a foundation, Kniesner and Leeth proceed to add sequentially a number of factors that complicate a manager's effort to identify and create the optimal level of safety and health in the workplace. These factors include government regulations, mandatory no-fault compensation insurance, and tort liability. In their concluding remarks, Kniesner and Leeth predict that the most important issues on the horizon for managers will be the growing public concern over issues of fairness and equity in workplace health and safety.

Horizontal mergers and acquisitions can offer powerful avenues for increasing profit, either by making collusive pricing easier (explicit or tacit) or by making unilateral (noncooperative) price increases easier. Since cooperative/collusive price increases are illegal and carry prison sentences for guilty executives, there has been substantial recent interest by antitrust agents, scholars, business executives, and consultants in understanding how horizontal mergers can increase the likelihood of profitable, noncooperative price increases (or output and capacity reductions leading to noncooperative price increases). Gregory Werden and Luke Froeb, two leading antitrust experts on the unilateral effects of mergers, lay out in a clear, largely nonmathematical way the cutting-edge theory and antitrust analysis of unilateral effects. While laws and enforcement mechanisms differ across countries, the state-of-the-art analysis set forth by Werden and Froeb in this chapter has been adopted in many antitrust jurisdictions worldwide. Based on their work as antitrust scholars and work experience with US antitrust enforcement agencies, they offer specific recommendations to managers and business consultants concerning the antitrust risks associated with mergers and acquisitions.

Over the past twenty-five years, corporate executives have seen environmental matters move from a fringe concern to a matter of top priority. Of course, firms must comply with environmental laws and regulations, but should they go beyond compliance and engage in acts of corporate environmentalism? In 2005, Einer Elhauge undertook a careful legal analysis of management's fiduciary responsibility to employ corporate resources *only* in value-maximizing ways, and he concluded that business executives do have substantial legal latitude to undertake environmentally beneficial projects, beyond those required by environmental authorities, even when doing so *reduces* the values of their firms. While shareholders will almost certainly wish to replace CEOs who undertake unprofitable environmental projects not required by law, Thomas Lyon and John Maxwell, take a careful look at the prospects for *profitably* engaging in corporate environmentalism (CE). In this chapter, they identify and explain three main sources or drivers of CE. They also examine and critique the most recent empirical evidence and conclude that (a) measuring the profitability of CE is inherently difficult, which makes empirical findings of clearly profitable CE quite elusive, and (b) many of the benefits of CE are related to reputation building, an area in which the economics literature is very thin. From a strategic viewpoint, Lyon and Maxwell warn that CE requires more management "expertise and care" than some other types of strategies, but, when CE does work, it can create a hard-to-imitate competitive advantage.

# 1.4 CONCLUDING REMARKS

As noted at the outset, the new *Oxford Handbook of Managerial Economics* is designed to provide Ph.D. students, scholars, and practitioners in the field with useful summaries of the current state of the literature as well as supply them with directions for future study. Managerial economics has come a long way since it was thought of (and taught) as applied neoclassical economics with "boxes" containing applications of the theory to the business problems managers might actually face. As we have hoped to demonstrate in this volume, the field now combines insights from a variety of disciplines, including, among others, game theory, decision sciences, psychology and behavioral economics, organizational economics, financial economics, industrial organization, marketing, business strategy, and personnel management. While neoclassical economics still is the mother tongue of managerial economics, the decisions reached by the managers of business enterprises, whether operated for-profit or not-for-profit, are now seen to require more than an understanding of how to choose levels of output and the corresponding prices at which profits can be maximized in environments where information is perfect and the behavior of customers, employees, suppliers, stockholders and other groups are fully rational and can be predicted with certainty.

The models of economic theory remain very useful in characterizing the central tendencies of human action, and so, in our judgment, the lessons of those stylized models must be learned by anyone who aspires to be successful (i.e., survive in the long run) in managing a business organization of any size or scope. But, as we have aimed to show herein, that may be necessary but it certainly is not sufficient. Managerial economics may at bottom be applied price theory; in the extended order of markets, however, it also is applied psychology and, more generally, a theory of human behavior, the understanding of which many other social sciences may contribute.

If it achieves nothing else, this *Handbook* should be seen as a call to action, not only for additional scholarly research, but also for a broader and deeper appreciation of the problems business managers face on a daily basis and for further study of those problems. That goal clearly is a moving target, as the contributions that follow amply demonstrate. We nevertheless hope that our readers think that we have come close to the bull's-eye with this first shot at creating a handbook on managerial economics.

## NOTES

1. We should note that not every topic we wished to cover made it into this *Handbook*. Competition from numerous other handbooks on related topics—pricing and decision sciences, for example—made it impossible to recruit worthy contributors in several areas. Specifically, we would have liked to have had additional chapters on the relation between accounting and economics, revenue management, demand forecasting, e-commerce, strategic alliances, and joint ventures.
2. See the surveys by Robert Gibbons (1998), Kevin J. Murphy (1999), and Canice Prendergast (1999).

## REFERENCES

Besanko, David, David Dranove, Mark Shanley, and Scott Schaefer. 2010. *Economics of Strategy*. Hoboken, NJ: John Wiley & Sons.

Cramton, Peter, Yoav Shoham, and Richard Steinberg, eds. 2005. *Combinatorial Auctions*. Cambridge, MA: MIT Press.

DeAngelo, Harry, and Linda DeAngelo. 2007. "Capital Structure, Payout Policy, and Financial Flexibility." Working Paper.

Elhauge, Einer R. 2005. "Corporate Managers' Operational Discretion to Sacrifice Corporate Profits in the Public Interest." In *Environmental Protection and the Social Responsibility of Firms*, edited by Bruce L. Hay, Robert N. Stavins, and Richard H. K. Vietor, 13–76. Washington, DC: Resource for the Future Press.

Gibbons, Robert. 1998. "Incentives in Organizations." *Journal of Economic Perspectives* 12, no. 4:115–32.

——. 2005. "Four Formal(izable) Theories of the Firm?" *Journal of Economic Behavior & Organization* 58:200–245.

Hart, Oliver. 2011. "Thinking about the Firm: A Review of Daniel Spulber's *The Theory of the Firm*." *Journal of Economic Literature* 49, no. 1:101–13.

Murphy, Kevin J. 1999. "Executive Compensation." In *Handbook of Labor Economics*, edited by Orley Ashenfelter and David Card, 3:2485–563. New York: North Holland.

Özer, Özalp, and Robert L. Phillips, eds. Forthcoming. *Oxford Handbook on Pricing Management*. New York: Oxford University Press.

Perloff, Jeffrey M., Larry S. Karp, and Amos Golan. 2007. *Estimating Market Power and Strategies*. New York: Cambridge University Press.

Phillips, Robert L. 2005. *Pricing and Revenue Optimization*. Stanford, CA, Stanford University Press.

Ponssard, Jean-Pierre, and Hervé Tanguy. 1999. "The Future of Managerial Economics." In *Economics Beyond the Millennium*, edited by Alan Kirman and Louis-André Gérard-Varet, 169–83. Oxford and New York: Oxford University Press.

Porter, Michael E. 1980. *Competitive Strategy: Techniques for Analyzing Industries and Competitors*. New York: Free Press.

——. 1983. "The Contributions of Industrial Organization to Strategic Management." *Academy of Management Review* 6, no. 4:609–20.

Prendergast, Canice. 1999. "The Provision of Incentives in Firms." *Journal of Economic Literature* 37 (1): 7–63.

Rao, Vithala R., ed. 2009. *Handbook of Pricing Research in Marketing*. Northampton, MA: Edward Elgar Publishing.

Shy, Oz. 2008. *How to Price: A Guide to Pricing Techniques and Yield Management*. Cambridge: Cambridge University Press.

Spulber, Daniel. 2009. *The Theory of the Firm: Microeconomics with Endogenous Entrepreneurs, Firms, Markets, and Organizations*. Cambridge: Cambridge University Press.

Stole, Lars A. 2007. "Price Discrimination and Competition." In *Handbook of Industrial Organization*, edited by Mark Armstrong and Robert Porter, 3:2221–99. Amsterdam: Elsevier/North Holland.

# CHAPTER 2

........................................................................................

# MANAGERIAL ECONOMICS: PRESENT AND FUTURE

........................................................................................

ANTONY W. DNES AND
PAUL H. RUBIN

## 2.1 INTRODUCTION

........................................................................................

THE purpose of this essay is to clarify the nature and scope of managerial economics and to examine the direction of new work that is currently emerging from applying techniques of analysis drawn from modern mainstream economics. In assessing future directions, we consider the extent to which a convergence may be occurring between the "new managerial economics" and mainstream economics. The new managerial economics is currently developing internationally in a healthy way by moving away from an older focus on modest questions linked to rational decision making, and toward ever wider applications of economics to business questions, frequently based on applications of modern organizational economics.

The new managerial economics incorporates insights from the analysis of problems connected with agency relationships and strategic interaction, and the results of experimental inquiry. It does not so much displace the old managerial economics as augment it. Frequently the focus is on organizational questions related to managing human resources, and an emphasis on applied work that is well-grounded in theory is still very much a requirement. The overall requirement for good work in the field remains the demonstration of an application of economic analysis to significant managerial questions.

## 2.2  TRENDS IN MANAGERIAL AND DECISION ECONOMICS

In assessing the future direction of managerial economics, it is possible to discern themes of inquiry in the context of modern work that are both interesting and generate useful insights for businesses and future inquiry. Managerial economics is unfolding in a healthy fashion, drawing in the new institutional economics in the widest possible sense. One concern, though, is a need to counterbalance a modern tendency spreading from mainstream economics toward an excessively theoretical inquiry that translates economic analysis into brutal mathematical formalism. All modern work requires some degree of rigor for successful completion, but it is not appropriate for an author to make continual recourse to lemmas and complex theorems, especially if with no practical applications, when writing for a managerial economics audience. Extreme formalism appears to be acceptable in writing for the much smaller audience of professional economists.

Managerial economics has generated empirical work that is carried out using a variety of typically, but not always, quantitative methods. Bear in mind in interpreting this statement that modern econometrics has a considerable role for semiquantitative work that models qualities, for example, based on the methods of logit analysis. There remains a strong connection between managerial economics, operations research, and econometrics applications to real world problems, which can be seen in examining classic texts, such as Baumol (1962) and more recent ones such as Salvatore (2006). Typical topics represent a synthesis of economics, decision sciences, and business administration, and interact with each other in a scientific way involving testable predictions and subsequent testing. Recognition of the constraints facing firms is important in this work.

It is notable that leading MBA programs, which have long since included overseas offerings such as the one at Cranfield in the UK as well as the earlier prominent programs like Harvard's, normally include managerial economics courses following the model described above. Often there are variants emphasizing decision sciences or the business environment. Therefore, teaching practice can be seen to some extent as indicating the established ideas in managerial economics. There, developments in recent years have augmented the traditional approach, particularly in areas such as: globalization, the economics of organization, information economics, strategic behavior, the learning organization, risk management, business ethics, and behavioral economics. All of these topics are hot in modern managerial economics and are slowly feeding through into MBA work.

We have identified modern trends as "the new managerial economics." Some modern texts now use the term explicitly (Boyes 2008) and focus on questions of "organizational architecture" (Brickley et al. 2008), particularly including areas such as incentive structures in personnel economics. An increasing volume of specialist work is emerging in these areas and is featured in influential handbooks (Lazear and Oyer 2009). Personnel economics, for example, applies economics to human resources topics, including information interactions, problems of team coordination, morale, and seniority systems. The area has come a long way in a short time. As Lazear (a former Chief Economic Advisor to the US President and a member of the Editorial Board of *Managerial and Decision Economics*) points out, personnel economics now has its own code in the *Journal of Economic Literature*. In managerial terms, this field is a natural development of the economics of organization and of labor economics, and is likely to develop strongly. Many of the lessons to be learned from personnel economics—for example, the purpose behind seniority wages—match well with the experience of personnel management.

Game theory has made a tremendous impact on microeconomics generally, and it is unsurprising that this has spilled over into many field studies, including managerial economics. Game theory has significant managerial implications since there is a natural desire in business to understand strategic interaction. There is no doubt that game theory has brought insights, at least in the understanding of fairly well-contained market situations, such as dominance and pricing, that would be hard to obtain otherwise. Care must be taken, though, because there are dangers in certain applications of game theory. The approach has really been a part of managerial economics from the start, but it can become arid and disconnected from real world issues quite easily. Without drawing attention to individual pieces of work, it is possible to note that a tendency to create ever more detailed models that assume high levels of information for managers may well generate distinct papers, in a technical sense, but may not add much to our knowledge of management. Feet and ground belong together in managerial economics.

Case studies are still useful and show how decisions are made in the real world. Classic areas such as transfer pricing are still of great interest to firms, not just in theoretical terms but also in terms of practices used, not least because transfer pricing practices are often the target of antitrust investigations. Other areas where case studies can be relevant include benchmarking, antitrust cases more generally defined, the characteristics of entrepreneurship, and the development of particular organizational forms. Coase (1988) and Coase and Wang (2012) has famously argued for much more case-study work in economics on the grounds that a great deal of information can be inferred from such observation, encouraging us to ask businessmen about business practice. We might say, ask carefully. There are pitfalls in asking questions so that response biases spoil the information flow. Avoiding problems is often a matter of using common sense and thinking whether there might be adverse incentive structures surrounding the answering of questions. It is now becoming well-known that people filling out questionnaires tend to report themselves as richer, better looking and more interesting than the average person, which is of course impossible in the aggregate. Biases are often ignored by questionnaire designers, and one cannot help being sympathetic to the pleas for less "abominable snowball sampling" that are often encountered within the business community: the value of questionnaires is questionable.

A good example of case-study work is Reid and Jacobsen's (1988) monograph on the small entrepreneurial firm, which used focused observation to make a very careful inquiry into the nature of that highly innovative area of the economy. The papers in Masten (1996) and Ricketts (2008) also give a good flavor of this type of work. Case studies, when carried out carefully in relation to well-identified theoretical questions, are an appropriate way to investigate organizational questions and may be the only means available to do so in some cases. Several recent papers on pricing practices (Levy and Smets 2010; Kwapil et al. 2010) use case-study methods carefully augmented with statistical analysis.

## 2.3  BUSINESS ETHICS AND MANAGERIAL ECONOMICS

A further modern trend is toward incorporating ethics into managerial economics training, or, at least, to juxtapose conventional managerial foci with an ethics focus. Often this will take the form of incorporating concerns about corporate social responsibility, sometimes in terms of social performance and questions of corporate governance, which have generated a series of research questions that show up in the journals. It would be good to see more of this type of work. An argument that managerial economics excludes considerations of ethics has been around for some time (Green and Lopus 2008), but is a little inaccurate. One text with an explicit focus on ethics and corporate social responsibility is Brickley et al. (2008), which also links these topics to organizational questions, and the journals do show a growing amount of work focusing on the area of ethics and performance.

The growth in recent years in research linking business economics with ethics issues is good to see since economics is currently being challenged on this front, often by managerial subjects that simply jump to conclusions over what is virtuous behavior and how good it must necessarily be. Often these conclusions are associated with benefits from teamwork and team spirit (which is not always good: think of Enron). It would be nice to see more hard thinking about business ethics coming through in practical applications to business questions. Notable recent contributions include work by Geoffrey Heal (2005), an environmental economist now working at Columbia in the field of corporate social performance and public policy, examining the purpose of corporate philanthropy, and particularly focusing on externality and distributional questions.

An interesting recent direction of research (Fisman et al. 2009) gives a rigorous demonstration showing how philanthropic gestures may be used to signal quality for a firm in a model of monopolistic competition. The signaling model reveals that it is less costly for quality firms to invest in corporate social responsibility, leading to a separating equilibrium in which low-quality firms do not invest in such efforts, and high-quality firms gain a brand advantage. The signaling model explains the frequent empirical observation that corporate social performance improves profitability performance for many firms (Wood 2010).

In many respects, the recent incorporation of corporate social performance into discussions in managerial economics blends observation with well-developed strategic modeling. The direction of the research suggests that philanthropy is rarely aimed at anything other than improving the fortunes of the firm, and that this is based on sound reasoning. Another interesting recent paper focusing on aspects of social performance is Arruñada et al. (2009) who examine the interaction between franchised firms and institutional constraints.

## 2.4  Is Managerial Economics Converging to the Main Stream?

It can be argued that managerial economics is converging on mainstream economics and losing its separate identity by adopting more and more tools drawn from mainstream economics (Klein 2011). It is true that in the new managerial economics, the demarcation between managerial economics, business strategy, organization theory, personnel, and other applied topics in business administration are increasingly blurred. Klein argues that he could interchange many of the strategy, managerial economics, and standard texts by changing the focus of the courses that he teaches. There is some truth in his claim that much of he modern teaching material is similar across different courses, but, as a matter of judgment, and for the convenience of scholars and practitioners, there appears to be continuing practical value in maintaining a separate subdiscipline focusing on applications of economic analysis to managerial questions.

## 2.5  How Well Does Managerial Economics Fit with Business Practice?

Business consulting firms have grown in recent decades and use the skill sets of modern managerial economics, including the results of work originating in industrial organization. It might be thought that modern developments push the required skill set of the applied business economist to the breaking point. Strategic analysis and decision making focused on product pricing, horizontal and vertical boundaries of the firm, mergers and acquisitions, and forecasting competitor responses have indeed become very complex. While all this is true, it nonetheless is the case that consulting firms working from an economics base occupy a niche in which they supply clients with services going beyond the accounting services and heuristically based consulting often applied in business. This niche is particularly apparent in providing advice in antitrust cases, regulation, and intellectual property (patent infringement) areas. The application of economic analysis tends to highlight valuable economic effects that are not apparent from simple inspection—for example, market responses to patent infringement. Since the application of economics tends to produce net value to firms, it is in demand notwithstanding its costliness.

The difference between economics consulting and other business advisory services does not reflect hostility between disciplines. Rather, the various advisory approaches represent specialism. The difference between accounting and economic cost is well-known, where the accountant focuses on recorded costs, and the economist focuses on opportunity cost including implied costs. It is not that one of them is ignorant, but rather that the purpose of the information is different; standardized business comparison is aided by historic costs, whereas decision making is best approached through recognizing opportunity costs. Extending those reflections to less obvious matters such as whether to use the hedged price of an input or the market price of an input to measure production cost and determine optimal product prices, economic analysis can provide profitable insights. If a firm can economically hedge its costs, it is making poor decisions if it does not do so.

We do see more and more consulting firms emerging who can assemble a team of experts able to increase the profitable use of sophisticated economic analysis. It is an interesting question to ask how complex managerial economics can get and still be an applied area. We think that the need for convincing application in business settings is unlikely to halt technical improvements in analysis, although the communication of ideas and results will keep the in-house or independent business economist's feet on the ground.

## 2.6 INTERNATIONAL GROWTH OF MANAGERIAL ECONOMICS

One gratifying recent trend is the growth in managerial economics around the world. Outside of the United States and Canada, the growth has not simply occurred in Europe, Australia, and New Zealand. Management schools with claims to international prestige have also emerged in India and Southeast Asia, and the world is increasingly opening up intellectually. Managerial economics is in increasingly good shape internationally, largely because globalizing economic development has led to sustained growth in management schools. Also, movement of scholars around the world has supported knowledge transfer. Recent papers reflecting this growing internationalism include Lin et al. (2009), who examine the efficiency of publically traded firms in China.

Journal submissions reflect increasing internationalism. As editors of *Managerial and Decision Economics*, we have marked the recent trend for paper submissions to reflect this growing internationalism, and estimate that around one half of them now originate outside of North America, with around 35% from Europe and 10% from Asia. Articles originate from authors based in diverse locations, including North America, England, France, Germany, Greece, Hong Kong, India, Israel, Italy, the Netherlands, Norway, Singapore, and Spain. Yet, the topics overlap frequently, showing that the same concerns are shared worldwide and that there is also a shared managerial-economics culture. It is not as if, say, the Chinese are doing things differently from the Europeans these days; we also seem to know much the same things and experience similar problems.

## 2.7 BEHAVIORAL AND MANAGERIAL ECONOMICS

An argument has grown in favor of recognition that the behavioral foundations of economics lack realism, and that increases in realism can in fact improve theoretical insights and, ultimately, predictions in managerial and other settings. In practice, the recognition has grown from the results of experimental economics and a certain interaction between economics and psychology. There need be no total rejection of traditional neoclassical economics as a result of these observations, because behavioral economics really just seeks to improve the behavioral foundations of economics. Indeed, there is evidence that from a normative perspective, when individuals (and businesses) are faced with practical problem solving, they do resort to approaches drawn from neoclassical economics that are based on maximization and efficient use of information in a constrained-choice setting (Ariely et al. 2003).

Many of the insights of behavioral economics have arisen in considering problems of rational decision making under uncertainty. Researchers have found, among other things, that the framing of decision making alters decisions, notions of fairness influence behavior, individuals experience loss aversion giving asymmetrically high valuation of losses compared with gains relative to a concave utility function, individuals experience endowment effects over the value of items traded, and that heuristics are frequently involved in making decisions (Thaler and Sunstein 2008). Many of these observations are consistent with approaches to decision making that invoke bounded rationality (Williamson 1985), so there has always been receptiveness to them among economists working on organizational questions. There are practical implications: for example, loss aversion can be cited to explain patterns of change in price elasticities.

The use of heuristics in business needs much more study, not least because heuristics have both good and bad properties. Decision costs are saved, but this can be at the cost of relying on irrational decision making that can go astray. Experimental results emphasizing people's innate sense of fairness leading to loss-making punishment strategies also require more study in business settings. Lazear and Oyer (2009) has suggested that, in the area of personnel economics, deviations from strict reward-based incentive schemes often reflect fairness considerations and are targeted at workplace morale. Recent papers taking an experimental/behavioral approach toward managerial decision making include Rosenboim et al. (2008) who find evidence of regret effects and of status-quo bias. These managerial applications of economic psychology are bound to grow.

# 2.8 CONCLUDING DISCUSSION

Managerial economics has gradually evolved, always reflecting changes within the economics mainstream and some influences from managerial and related studies more widely defined. Contemporary work investigates the nature of corporate social performance, analyzes very detailed issues concerning business administration—so-called "architecture"—in relation to the work of teams and the impact of incentive structures, and draws in behavioral insights in understanding management. It is to be expected that topics of inquiry in managerial economics should mirror wider concerns in the business community. This is healthy, and should make us realize that the emphasis remains very much on applications in the new managerial economics.

We would like to conclude by emphasizing the areas where we believe there are promising prospects for fruitful research. Clearly we are at the very beginning of exploring the behavioral interaction between economic behavior and human psychology in management, and we should expect further work to add productively to our developing knowledge. Together with work on organizational architecture, we might look forward to behavioral work aiding in understanding forensic questions concerning business failure as well as success, including some issues surrounding dysfunctional businesses (such as the incentive failures at Enron that led to fraud). This emphasis should not of course obscure the importance of the continued development of a healthy volume of wide-ranging applications of economics in management, as evidenced by the work showcased in this handbook.

## REFERENCES

Ariely, D., G. Loewenstein, and D. Prelec. 2003 "Coherent Arbitrariness: Stable Demand Curves Without Stable Preferences." *The Quarterly Journal of Economics* 118 (1): 73–105.

Arruñada, B., L. Vázquez, and G. Zanarone. 2009. "Institutional Constraints on Organizations: the Case of Spanish Car Dealerships." *Managerial and Decision Economics* 30:15–26.

Baumol, W. 1962. *Economic Theory and Operations Analysis*. Englewood Cliffs, NJ: Prentice Hall.

Boyes, W. 2008. *The New Managerial Economics*. Mason, OH: Cengage.

Brickley, J., J. Zimmerman, and C.W. Smith. 2008. *Managerial Economics and Organizational Architecture*. Columbus, OH: McGraw-Hill/Irwin.

Coase, R. 1988. *The Firm, the Market and the Law*. Chicago: University of Chicago Press.

Coase, R., and N. Wang. 2012. *How China Became Capitalist*. New York: Palgrave Macmillan.

Fisman, R., G. Heal, and V. Nair. 2009. "A Model of Corporate Philanthropy." Paper presented at the annual meeting of the American Economic Association, San Francisco, January 4. www.aeaweb.org/annual_mtg_papers/2009

Green, S., and J. Lopus. 2008. "Do Managerial Economics Textbooks Cover Ethics and Corporate Social Responsibility?" *International Review of Economics Education* 7:88–93.

Heal, G. 2005. "Corporate Social Responsibility: an Economic and Financial Framework." *The Geneva Papers on Risk and Insurance* 30: 387–409.

Klein, P. G. 2011. "The Future of Managerial Economics." *Organizations and Markets*, January 5. Accessed January 15, 2012. http://organizationsandmarkets.com/2011/01/05/the-future-of-managerial-economics.

Kwapil, C., J. Scharler, and J. Baumgartner. 2010. "How Are Prices Adjusted in Response to Shocks? Survey Evidence from Austrian Firms." *Managerial and Decision Economics* 31:151–60.

Lazear, E. P., and P. Oyer. 2009. "Personnel Economics." In *Handbook of Organizational Economics*, edited by Robert Gibbons and D. John Roberts, 479–519. Princeton: Princeton University Press.

Levy, D., and F. Smets. 2010. "Price Setting and Price Adjustment in Some European Union Countries: Introduction to the Special Issue." *Managerial and Decision Economics* 31:63–66.

Lin, C., Yue Ma, and D. Su. 2009. "Corporate Governance and Firm Efficiency: Evidence from China's Publicly Listed Firms." *Managerial and Decision Economics* 30:193–209.

Masten, S. 1996. *Case Studies in Contracting and Organization*. Oxford: Oxford University Press.

Reid, G., and L. Jacobsen. 1988. *The Small Entrepreneurial Firm*. Edinburgh: Edinburgh University Press.

Ricketts, M. 2008. *The Economics of Modern Business Enterprise*. Cheltenham: Edward Elgar.

Rosenboim, M., I. Luski, and T. Shavit. 2008. "Behavioral Approaches to Optimal FDI Incentives." *Managerial and Decision Economics* 29:601–7.

Salvatore, D. 2006. *Managerial Economics in a Global Economy*. Mason, OH: Cengage.

Thaler, R., and C. Sunstein. 2008. *Nudge*. London: Penguin Books.

Williamson, O. 1985. *The Economic Institutions of Capitalism*. New York: The Free Press.

Wood, D. 2010. "Measuring Corporate Social Performance." *International Journal of Management Reviews* 12:50–84.

# PART II

# MANAGING DEMAND AND COST CONDITIONS

CHAPTER 3

·····································································

# MARKET POWER: HOW DOES IT ARISE? HOW IS IT MEASURED?

·····································································

LAWRENCE J. WHITE[*]

## 3.1 INTRODUCTION

THE nature, causes, and measurement of market power have always been central issues to economists working in the field of industrial organization (IO). Traditional IO approaches market power primarily from a public policy perspective, which supplies the analytical foundation for antitrust policy and enforcement efforts. Indeed, the fundamental concern of antitrust policy—also known outside of the United States as competition policy—is precisely the creation, existence, and exercise of *market power*, as well as possible remedies when market power has been exercised unlawfully or may eventually be exercised unlawfully (e.g., as a consequence of a proposed merger).[1]

Since at least 1980 (e.g., in Porter 1980), IO economists have recognized a second perspective for industrial organization methodology: examining IO issues through the lens of senior managers of a firm that wish to find ways to achieve a sustainable competitive advantage vis-à-vis rival firms, as well as potential new entrants, and thereby maximize the value of the firm and its shareholders' wealth. Attaining and sustaining market power—legally, of course—is a fundamental route to creating that sustained advantage.[2] Furthermore, if senior managers are considering entry into an industry, either through a "fresh start," or "greenfield" effort, or through the acquisition of a company that is already established in that industry, they should want to know if market power is being exercised in that industry and whether and how it can be sustained. Accordingly, senior managers must understand the nature and sources of market power, as well as some practical methods for measuring the degree of market power possessed by their own firms and their rival firms.

[*] The author thanks Christopher Thomas and William Shughart for helpful comments on an earlier draft of this chapter.

Another important reason for managers to understand market power arises when companies inevitably become embroiled in antitrust issues that perforce focus senior managers' attention on market power issues. For example:

- Company A may want to acquire or merge with Company B, but there may be claims by government law enforcement agencies that the merger should be prevented because it will create or enhance market power and is thereby anticompetitive;
- Company A may be accused of being involved in a price-fixing conspiracy, which has the goal of allowing the conspirators jointly to exercise market power;
- Company A may be accused of unilaterally exercising market power, such as charging excessively high prices; or
- Company A may be accused of taking actions that unduly disadvantage rivals and that thereby strengthen its already existing market power: for example, charging prices that are "below costs" and thereby acting in a predatory manner vis-à-vis rivals; or insisting that its distributors/dealers handle only its products and not those of rivals, thereby making it harder for the rivals to find distribution for their products.

Accordingly, issues of market power are not for public policy wonks only. Although it is certainly true that the pioneering work on the nature and measurement of market power has been driven by the demands of public policy and antitrust doctrine, so-called "modern" managerial economics now firmly includes strategic and tactical decision making that is designed to create and protect a high degree of distinctiveness for the company and its products—which, as will be discussed below, implies market power—as the primary path to maximizing the present value of the stream of future economic profits. Nevertheless, there is no escaping the seventy-five or so years of IO history[3] that has largely placed public policy at the center of concerns about market power, and that tradition will unavoidably flavor the discussion in this chapter.[4]

This chapter proceeds as follows. Section 3.2 formally defines market power and discusses current understanding about the sources of market power. Section 3.3 then address the major theme of this chapter, critically analyzing current methodologies for measuring market power and suggesting directions for improvements. Section 3.4 discusses the measurement of market power in three special antitrust contexts: mergers; monopolization; and collusion. Section 3.5 offers concluding remarks and identifies areas for future research.

# 3.2  WHAT IS MARKET POWER? HOW DOES IT ARISE?

## 3.2.1  Defining Market Power[5]

The concept of market power applies to an individual enterprise or to a group of enterprises acting collectively. For the individual firm, it expresses the extent to which the firm has discretion over the price that it charges. The baseline of zero market power is set by the individual firm that produces and sells a homogeneous product[6] alongside many other similar firms that all sell the same product. Since all of the firms sell the identical product (and there are no issues of reliability or other quality differences), the individual sellers are not distinctive. Buyers care solely about finding the seller with the lowest price.

In this context of "perfect competition," all firms sell at an identical price that is equal to their marginal costs, and no individual firm possesses any market power. If any firm were to raise its price slightly above the market-determined price, it would lose all of its customers (since they would quickly switch to the other firms that continue to sell at the market price). If a firm were to reduce its price slightly below the market price, it would be swamped with customers who switch from the other firms (but it would find selling to these new customers unprofitable, since its price would now be below its marginal costs).

Accordingly, the standard definition for market power is the divergence between price and marginal cost, expressed relative to price.[7] In mathematical terms,

$$L = \frac{(P - MC)}{P},$$   (3.1)

where L (the "Lerner Index") is the indicator of market power,[8] P is the price at which the firm sells its output, and MC is the marginal cost of the firm for the volume of output that the firm is selling. When P = MC, as is the case for the outcome when a perfectly competitive firm is selling a homogeneous product, then L = 0. If P > MC, then L > 0.

For the expression of market power (i.e., L > 0), many economists think instinctively of the opposite of competition: monopoly, which is a single seller of a distinct product that is without close substitutes. The monopoly outcome, and the comparison with the perfectly competitive outcome, is best represented geometrically, as in Figure 3.1.[9]

In Figure 3.1, we portray a simple downward-sloping linear market demand curve for a standardized item and a simple horizontal linear unit cost (average cost, or AC) curve for producing that item.[10] If a large number of sellers of this item have these same costs,[11] then the competitive outcome will be $P_C$ = MC (= AVC = AC) with an aggregate market quantity of $Q_C$. If instead a single firm (monopoly) faced the same demand curve and cost conditions (and entry were blockaded), then the monopolist's price[12] would be higher, at $P_M$ (and the monopolist's quantity would be lower, at $Q_M$). In the terms of equation 3.1, $L_M = (P_M - MC)/P_m > 0$, while $L_C = (P_C - MC/)P_C = 0$. Thus, this index would indicate real market power.

As a related matter, this index would also indicate the presence of above-normal profits for the monopolist, and their absence for (perfect) competitors. This is an important point, to which we will return below.

The problem with this rigid use of the Lerner index as an indicator of market power arises as soon as we move away from the simple world of multiple sellers of identical

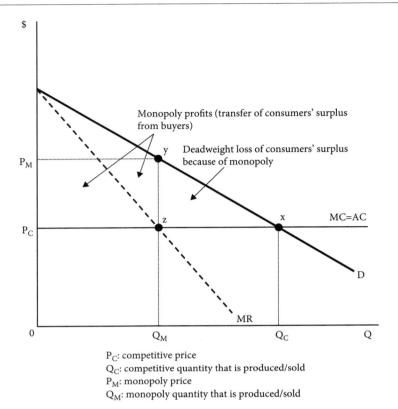

FIGURE 3.1 A Comparison of Monopoly and Competition

homogeneous products—which, at best characterizes only the sellers of primary agri-cultural and mineral commodities. With nonhomogeneous products, the seller is dis-tinctive. In deciding from whom to buy, buyers care about more than just which seller has the lowest price; they care about the attributes of the product and of the seller. The direct implication is that the demand curve that faces each distinctive seller has a nega-tive slope (rather than being horizontal from the perspective of the seller of the homo-geneous product, where only price matters to buyers). In turn, this will mean that the profit-maximizing output for the firm will be at an output where the firm equates mar-ginal revenue (MR) with MC and P > MR = MC, which of course implies P > MC and therefore L > 0.[13]

This result was first recognized by Robinson (1933) and Chamberlin (1933). Robinson termed this market structure "imperfect competition"; Chamberlin termed it "monop-olistic competition." In either case, as Chamberlin's geometry showed—the essence of

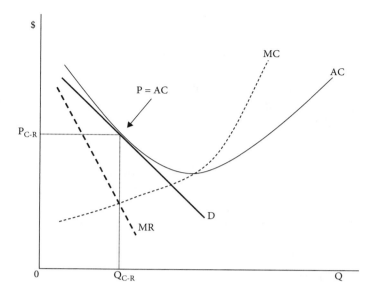

P$_{C-R}$: price charged by a Chamberlin-Robinson seller
Q$_{C-R}$: quantity produced/sold by a Chamberlin-Robinson seller

FIGURE 3.2 The "Tangency" Equilibrium for a Chamberlin-Robinson Competitor

which is reproduced as Figure 3.2—the equilibrium outcome when entry (of distinctive but reasonably close competitors) is sufficiently easy, the typical seller will earn only normal profits,[14] but the equilibrium price will be P = AC > MC.[15] Thus the Lerner index for this firm would register "market power."

However, the landscapes of most market economies are dominated by myriad distinctive firms that produce and sell distinctive products—whether as manufacturers, service providers, or retailers. Although there may be some definitional rigor in attaching the concept of "market power" to such firms, it makes little intuitive sense to identify the corner delicatessen, the neighborhood kitchen remodeler, or a small machine shop with the term "market power." To do so risks either trivializing the concept or—in the context of public policy—greatly overstating the realistic domain of public policy concerns.[16]

Consequently, unless otherwise noted, the remainder of this chapter will describe "market power" as applying to instances where the size of the enterprise (or group of enterprises, in the event of the collective exercise of market power) is large enough to warrant special attention (e.g., from the perspective of public policy)—namely, "significant" market power.[17] We will thus be returning to the traditional notion of "monopoly" that is associated with Figure 3.1 (or with a small-numbers oligopoly over the same domain).

## 3.2.2  How Does Market Power Arise?

What are the sources of market power? If we were to remain consistent with the strict definition of market power as simply any firm that has a positive Lerner index, the answer is easy: distinctiveness of product and/or seller. But for our notion of significant market power, a market of significant size is clearly also necessary; and, beyond size, a more complete and nuanced answer is needed.

### 3.2.2.1  The Single Seller

For a single seller—for the monopolist of Figure 3.1—distinctiveness is certainly not just a starting point; it is a necessary condition. A contradiction in terms would arise if a monopolist were described as one among other firms that are all selling the same product and that are seen as undifferentiated ("homogeneous") by buyers. But more than just distinctiveness is needed.

That "more"—as Bain (1956) recognized—are barriers to entry. Without barriers to entry, the above-normal profits of the monopolist could not persist. Potential sellers of the same or closely similar product would be attracted by the prospects of earning above-normal profits and would continue to enter the industry, so long as those above-normal profits remained as a lure. Only when there are a sufficient number of sellers supplying the quantity that buyers are willing and able to purchase, so that prices (and profits) are at the competitive equilibrium of Figure 3.1 (or the Chamberlin-Robinson outcome of Figure 3.2 is reached with an absence of above-normal profits), would entry cease.

There are fundamentally three categories of barriers:

a. *Ownership of a unique resource.* The ownership of a (sizable) unique resource constitutes one potential barrier to entry. Examples would include: a) a unique mineral deposit; b) a unique government franchise (e.g., the right to be the sole provider of taxicab services within a city); or c) an especially distinctive patent.[18]

b. *Economies of scale.* If the technology of an industry is such that economies of scale prevail over the entire range of possible production volumes, then a single firm—a "natural monopoly"—that supplies the market would be able to do so most efficiently. Even if there is some production volume at which diseconomies of scale prevail, if the relevant market is smaller than that volume, then a monopoly would still be the most efficient framework. The extent to which the monopolist could exploit its market power (i.e., the size of the Lerner index) would be restricted by the extent of the cost disadvantage that smaller entrants would face (which determines the so-called limit-entry price; see Modigliani 1958, and Sylos-Labini 1962), as well as by conjectures by entrants as to how the incumbent would react to their entry.

c. *The size and "sunkenness" of needed investments.* If entry into a market requires a relatively large expenditure and that expenditure has few alternative uses (i.e., the costs are "sunk"), then potential entrants would consider such entry to be quite risky. Examples of such sunk investments include a large investment in specialized machinery that has no alternative use; substantial research and development (R&D) expenditures that may not yield useful results; and large advertising and other promotional expenditures that are lost if unsuccessful. Such required expenditures would constitute barriers to entry. By contrast, if the necessary expenditure is modest and, if spent on a tangible item, that item has a viable secondary market, the barriers to entry would be low. Monopoly would be more likely to arise in the former circumstance than in the latter.

### 3.2.2.2  *A Group of Sellers*

Market power can arise also in the context of a group of firms that act, either explicitly or implicitly, in a joint fashion. The interesting questions arise in the context of "oligopoly": a market structure with a relatively small number of sellers of either a homogeneous product or a differentiated set of products. The crucial feature of oligopoly is that the firms are sufficiently few that they recognize their mutual interdependence: each firm recognizes that what it does affects the others and is in turn affected by what they do.[19]

As authors for almost two centuries have realized, an oligopoly market structure can, in principle, have outcomes that range from the equivalent of a monopoly to a competitive equivalent and thus would be expected to have an index of market power that could be $L_M$, or $L_C$, or anything in between. It all depends on the assumptions that one makes about how the (few) firms in the industry would behave vis-à-vis each other.[20]

At one extreme, if the oligopolists were to collude and coordinate their behavior in a way that maximizes their joint profits, then their Lerner index should approximate $L_M$; in essence, the oligopolists collectively are able to exercise the same degree of market power as could a pure monopolist. This calculation assumes that each oligopolist has the same constant marginal costs as does the monopolist. But if the oligopolists have different costs and/or sell distinctive (differentiated) products, then the calculation of the Lerner index for the group becomes ambiguous: if the product is homogeneous, the price would be uniform and clear-cut; but what should represent "marginal cost" is less clear. The calculations become yet murkier if each seller's product is distinctive. One could, of course, calculate a Lerner index for each member of the oligopoly, but then the group's Lerner index could be represented only by some kind of average of the individual Lerner indexes.

At the other extreme, in a homogeneous good context, if each firm (with identical constant marginal costs) behaves aggressively and prices myopically (i.e., believing that none of the other firms will adjust its price in response to whatever price the first firm selects[21]), then even just two competing oligopolists would drive the equilibrium price down to the level of marginal costs, so that the Lerner index for this two-firm aggressive oligopoly would be $L_C$; in essence, even the two-firm oligopoly would be incapable of exercising market power. If, however, the two firms have differing marginal costs, then the logic of this aggressive pricing would lead to an outcome in which the lower-cost firm sets its price at a level that is just below the marginal costs of the higher-cost firm (and the lower-cost firm sells to all of the buyers in the market), and the Lerner index thus would be positive; in essence, the lower-cost firm enjoys a monopoly, which is limited at the price that is equal to the rival firm's (higher) marginal cost.[22]

Between these two extremes are the possibilities that elements of market structure could influence the extent of the joint exercise of market power. One approach would be to keep the "Bertrand" assumption that each firm myopically sets its price while assuming that the other firms keep their prices unchanged but also to assume that the firms sell differentiated products: the product is not homogeneous, and buyers have preferences among the sellers and their products as well as favoring lower prices.

In this case, the equilibrium price for each firm will exceed its marginal costs. This outcome arises because of the following: With differentiated products, as each firm contemplates (myopically) what would happen if it changes its price, either up or down, the upward change would no longer mean a loss of all customers, and a downward change would no longer attract the entirety of the rival's customers. In essence, differentiating the product "softens" the competition between firms, even for Bertrand competitors. Unless the two firms are symmetric with respect to the buyers' preferences, their equilibrium prices would not be identical; consequently, even if their marginal costs were the same (which they need not be in the case of nonhomogeneous products), the Lerner index for the "industry" would be ambiguous. Again, a Lerner index could be calculated for each firm, but the Lerner index for the industry would have to be some kind of average.

As another possibility, assume that each firm again behaves myopically but this time chooses its output (rather than its price) while assuming that none of the other firms will adjust their outputs in response to its choice.[23] In this case (with a homogeneous product and identical constant marginal costs for all firms) the outcome will be a price that will be between the monopoly price and the purely competitive price, but that will be lower when there are more firms and will asymptotically approach the competitive price as the number of sellers gets very large. Formally, if the market demand curve can be represented as the linear relationship $Q = a - bP$, and each of the n oligopolists has identical constant unit costs of $c < a$, then:

$$P = \frac{(a + nc)}{(n + 1)}. \tag{3.2}$$

And the Lerner index for the n-firm oligopoly would be:

$$L_n = \frac{(a - c)}{(a + nc)}. \tag{3.3}$$

Further, if the firms have different marginal costs, then those with lower marginal costs will have higher Lerner indexes and larger market shares.[24] Again, the Lerner index for the industry will have to be some average of the individual firms' Lerner indexes. If market shares are used as the weights, however, an interesting result arises: the weighted Lerner index can be shown to be equal to the ratio of a) the sum of the squared market shares of all of the sellers in the market—which is often described as the Herfindahl-Hirschman index[25] (HHI) of seller concentration—divided by b) the own-price elasticity of market demand.[26] Finally, if the firms sell differentiated products, the outcome will be an amalgam of the cost differences and the buyers' preferences over the differentiated products.

More generally for an oligopoly, if the analysis moves away from the mechanistic/myopic approaches modeled by Bertrand and Cournot, then one really is in an "it all depends" world with respect to the joint exercise of market power. However, systematic thinking about the structural determinants of the joint exercise of market power can uncover useful insights. The formal name for this systematic thinking is "the structure-conduct-performance" (S-C-P) paradigm:[27] the structure of an industry influences its conduct (or behavior), which in turn influences its performance.[28] In this context, the Lerner index—representing the percentage elevation of price over cost—is primarily a major indicator of an industry's conduct; but since the Lerner index is also an indicator of profits (at least relative to marginal costs), and above-normal profits are associated with allocative inefficiency (consumers are being charged prices that are in excess of the seller's marginal costs), resulting in income transfers (from consumers to the seller), the Lerner index is also an indicator of performance.[29]

One way to motivate the analysis is to begin with the assumption that each firm wants to maximize its own profits. But in an oligopolistic structure the firm's profits will depend not only on its own actions but also identifiably on the actions of its rivals. In that context, each firm faces the following tension:

On the one hand, each firm would recognize that jointly the highest profits that the group could achieve would be the monopoly profits of Figure 3.1 (which would be divided somehow among the group). On the other hand, if all of the others were maintaining that monopoly price, any firm could do even better than its share of the joint monopoly profits by undercutting its rivals' price slightly and stealing their customers and expanding its market share.[30] The longer that it would take the other firms to realize what was happening and to respond, the greater the gain for the first firm would be; conversely, a quick response by the others would mean little gain for the initial price cutter—and hence a weaker incentive to engage in price-cutting in the first place. But, as yet another consideration, each firm may fear that some other firm within the group may cut its price first, so that each firm would be the victim rather than the beneficiary of any price cutting, which would argue for each firm's engaging in price cutting in any event.[31] But if all firms reason in this way, the joint monopoly outcome will quickly unravel, and the Bertrand competitive outcome will prevail.[32]

In this context, then, what are the structural conditions that would tend to make the industry more conducive to the coordination that yields the collusive outcome, and thus the joint exercise of significant market power? Conversely, what are the conditions that would make coordination more difficult, thus being more conducive to a largely competitive outcome?

The tension between the opportunity to share in the joint monopoly profits of the collusive arrangement and the temptation to cut price surreptitiously—to "cheat" on any understanding—but with the likely consequences of an eventual competitive outcome, leads to the consideration of the following structural features as contributing to the likelihood that one or the other of these outcomes, or something in between, eventually will prevail:

- *Can the firms communicate?* Although explicit price fixing—that is, explicit communication and coordination among sellers with respect to prices (or outputs, or market shares) has generally become illegal in most countries—it is nevertheless worthwhile to raise the issue: explicit communication among sellers should make coordination on a joint monopoly outcome easier to achieve.[33] Without explicit communication, the firms instead will have to rely on indirect and implicit understandings, which will make coordination more difficult. The probabilities of being apprehended and convicted for price fixing, as well as the penalties that are attached to conviction, would be important as well.[34]
- *Conditions of mutual monitoring.* If the group of sellers can easily and quickly monitor each others' behavior—e.g., observing each others' sales and prices through industry reports or media stories—they will be able to respond sooner to any firm's "cheating" on an understanding, which will thereby discourage any firm from breaking ranks in the first place. The longer the lag in monitoring, the stronger will be the temptation for a firm to break ranks.
- *The number of sellers.* When the number of sellers is relatively small, it is likely to be easier for the group to monitor each other and to reassure themselves that little or no "cheating" is occurring. Accordingly, fewer sellers would be more conducive to the collusive outcome.
- *The relative sizes of the sellers.* When the sellers are more similar in size, their outlooks (and beliefs about what price level and output quantity would achieve the monopoly outcome) are likely to be more similar, which should make agreement on the collusive outcome easier. However, it is also the case that one firm might dominate the market (because of a superior technology or a superior brand, say), but there are some smaller firms that can survive—albeit with limited capabilities for expansion.[35] In this case, the disparity in sizes need not undermine the exercise of market power, because the superiority of the dominant firm's technology, brand, or both, combines with the limits of the smaller firms to prevent the latter from wholly eroding the former's market power. This "dominant firm" model can be expanded to encompass a few relatively large firms that are dominant (and can coordinate among themselves) in competition with a group of (limited) reactive fringe firms (see Landes and Posner 1981).
- *Conditions of entry.* Analogous to the discussion of simple monopoly, higher barriers to entry would make it easier for a group of firms to reach and maintain an understanding with respect to the joint maintenance of market power. Conversely, easy entry will doom any efforts at the joint exercise of such power, since the

above-normal profits that these efforts would hope to achieve would quickly be eroded by the larger quantities and lower prices that entry would bring.

- *Ease of expansion by smaller firms.* Smaller "fringe" firms may not be part of any oligopolistic understanding, or may believe that they can expand more readily without attracting the attention and response of the larger firms. If they can expand readily—if they are not constrained by production limitations or by the importance of branding—then oligopolistic coordination will be more difficult. Conversely, as was discussed above for the dominant firm or firms, limits on the ability of smaller firms to expand will make the dominance of the larger firms easier to maintain.

- *The cost structures of the sellers.* If the group of sellers all have roughly the same costs, they are more likely to envision the same jointly maximizing industry price; substantial cost differences among industry members may make an understanding harder to reach and maintain, especially with respect to the low-cost producer(s). Further, if the industry is characterized by high fixed costs and low marginal costs, the temptations for an industry member surreptitiously to cut its price would be greater, since the margins (over marginal costs) will be comparatively large. Railroads represent one example of this kind of cost structure, which, in extreme cases, may rule out the existence of a competitive market equilibrium.

- *The buyers' side of the market.* If the buyers of an industry's output are relatively few and knowledgeable and can readily "shop around" among the sellers, their bargaining strength—"My order is sizable and important to you: Give me a special (low) price, or I will take all of my purchases to one of your rivals."—will encourage the unraveling of any oligopolistic understanding among the sellers.[36] By contrast, if the buyers are many and small, they are less likely to shop around as effectively; and in any event, the threat will be far less potent.[37]

- *Industry conditions.* If the industry is relatively stable—e.g., in terms of demand and underlying product and production technologies—the maintenance of an understanding among a group of sellers will be easier. Sharp swings in demand, radical changes in production technologies, or sharp changes in product design or features would make the maintenance of an understanding more difficult.

- *The nature of the product.* If a product is homogeneous, mutual monitoring should be easier; product differentiation should make monitoring more difficult, especially when new products are introduced ("Is the lower price on my rival's new product a reflection of its lower quality? Or is the lower price really a price cut in disguise?"). However, as was discussed above, product differentiation itself tends to "soften" competition among oligopolists. Also, if the demand elasticity with respect to price for the industry's product is relatively low (so that a relatively large price increase will result in only a small decrease in the amount that is purchased), the gains from a coordinated understanding will be greater, which should thereby increase the likelihood that an understanding will develop and be maintained.

- *Industry history and sociology.* An industry in which the senior executives of the various companies have come to know, respect, and trust each other would likely find the development and maintenance of an oligopolistic understanding easier. Rapid turnover of firms and/or senior executives would make maintenance more difficult.

These structural characteristics of an industry should not be seen as individually "make or break" conditions—except, arguably, for conditions of entry, since it is hard to envision that market power could persist when entry is easy—but instead as contributory (so-called "plus") factors to whether a group of oligopolists will be able to maintain an understanding among themselves and thereby jointly to exercise market power.

# 3.3  METHODOLOGIES FOR THE MEASUREMENT OF MARKET POWER

There are a number of methodologies that have been used to estimate and measure market power. This section will discuss their strengths and weaknesses.

## 3.3.1  Cross-Section Regressions to Explain Industry Profit Rates

A direct implication of the monopoly/competition model of Figure 3.1 is the following: Not only will the price that is charged by the monopoly exceed the price that is charged by the otherwise comparable competitive industry (as measured by $L_M$ and $L_C$), but also the profits that are earned by the monopoly will be greater than the profits that are earned by the competitive industry (and, again, the two Lerner indexes will represent the comparative profit rates as well).

For comparisons across two different industries, some additional explanation is needed: The prices across two different industries are not comparable.[38] And information on marginal costs may be difficult to ascertain. But the Lerner index—viewed as a profitability index—avoids both of these problems, since the profit margin (P − MC) is expressed relative to P.[39] Accordingly, if one knew that Industry A was a monopoly and Industry B was competitive, the expectation would be that the Lerner index for the former would be larger than the Lerner index for the latter. Further, one could turn this relationship around and argue that (other things being equal, of course) a higher Lerner index for Industry C as compared with Industry D would provide an inference that the former would more likely be a monopoly than would the latter.

So far we have avoided any discussion of what to do about oligopoly. But the S-C-P paradigm offers some insights, including the argument that the numbers of sellers and their relative sizes (as expressed by market shares) ought to matter; the Cournot model offers a similar insight with respect to numbers and relative sizes, although the Bertrand model for homogeneous products does not.[40] Consequently, there would appear to be a presumption that the relationship between the Lerner index and industry structure should be such that the Lerner index should show higher values—that greater levels of market power would be indicated—when the number of firms in an industry is relatively small or when a few large firms dominate an industry with or without some other, smaller fringe firms. In short, market power should be positively related to seller concentration—although that relationship may well be erratic and nonlinear—with the monopoly outcome as the limiting case.

This, in essence, is the proposition that economists—starting in the 1950s and extending through the 1970s—tested through least-squares regressions on industry-level cross-section data.[41] In these regressions, industry profit rates—as an indicator of market power—were explained by a measure of industry seller concentration.[42] The measure of seller concentration that was used was usually the four-firm concentration ratio (CR4): the fraction of industry sales that are accounted for by the largest four firms. These studies generally found a positive relationship between profits and CR4, which implied that companies in more concentrated industries were more likely to be exercising market power.

Because of the limitations of the CR4 (it ignores all firms beyond the fourth-largest, and it ignores the relative distribution among the first four), the HHI began to replace it when sales shares data for individual firms became available to researchers.[43] In addition to encompassing all firms' shares of sales and thus being more comprehensive, the HHI has the advantage (as was discussed above) of being an indicator of market power in the Cournot model and also in Stigler's (1964) model of the ability of oligopolistic firms to monitor each other.

Also, these studies became more sophisticated over time. In addition to using a measure of seller concentration as an explanation for profit rates, these studies gradually included as explanatory variables more of the measures that the S-C-P paradigm indicate should matter for profitability: for example, barriers to entry (as proxied by advertising rates and measures of economies of scale), competition from imports, measures of risk, and nonlinearities between seller concentration and profit rates. In addition, more sophisticated econometric techniques were employed.

Starting in the late 1960s, however, these studies came under increasing attack. Initially the concern was that the S-C-P paradigm was too simplistic: First, entrants predictably would be attracted to industries with high profit rates, which would affect subsequent observed seller concentration; thus there was an important reverse causality and endogeneity that was being ignored.[44] Next, industries that were concentrated might have higher profits because there were important economies of scale that were being ignored by the S-C-P paradigm.[45] Also, the *national industry* demarcations that were specified in the IRS and Census data might not be the appropriate ones for the measurement of the exercise of market power in product space and/or in geographic space. The appropriate product-space markets might be narrower or broader; also, the appropriate geographic markets might be more local or might be international.

The next wave of criticism argued that the accounting profit rates that were being used were inappropriate for the measurement of "economic profits" and hence for the indication that above-normal profits and the concomitant market power were actually present.[46] Finally, studies in the 1980s indicated that the profit-concentration relationships that appeared to hold for the data for the 1940s through the 1960s were far weaker or nonexistent for the 1970s and early 1980s.[47]

Because of these criticisms—especially with regard to the weaknesses of the accounting data that underlay the profit measurements—these cross-section profit-concentration studies have largely gone out of style as a way of measuring market power and its effects.

## 3.3.2  Price-Concentration Studies

An alternative way of measuring market power is to test directly the relationship between prices and seller concentration. These tests require data on the prices of the same good or service that is sold in different markets where there are differing levels of seller concentration. Almost always this means that the sample involves a good or service that is sold in different geographic areas—such as Metropolitan Statistical Areas (MSAs) for retail goods, or city-pairs for air passenger transportation—where the separate geographic areas are likely to constitute separate markets.[48]

Such studies usually involve regressions of price on seller concentration and other variables that try to control for the other characteristics of the local market on the demand side (e.g., local population size or local average household income) and on the costs of supply (e.g., local wage rates). In essence, the price regressions represent a reduced-form approach to the underlying demand and supply relationships that yield the observed price.[49]

These kinds of studies have been done for railroads, airlines, banking, various categories of retailing, and livestock procurement.[50] The results support the conclusions of the earlier profits-concentration studies (but without relying on accounting data or suffering other drawbacks):[51] higher levels of seller concentration are (controlling for other influences) positively associated with higher prices and thus with greater market power.

## 3.3.3  Auction Data

Auctions can be considered to be markets, and the number of bidders that show up at an auction is an indicator of the extent of competition (and an inverse indicator of the potential for jointly exercised market power) for the item at auction. For example, consider procurement auctions, where a buyer (e.g., a state government) solicits bids for a specified task (e.g., a specific road construction project). The bidders are, in essence, suppliers that are competing on the price (the low bid wins) at which they will supply the item that is desired (the completed road). The number of bidders at the auction are the approximate equivalent of the number of sellers in a market.

Auction theory (building on oligopoly theory) predicts that prices in procurement auctions will be higher (i.e., that market power will be exercised) when fewer bidders are present. Similarly, for an auction where bidders are competing to buy an item, prices will be lower when fewer bidders are present at the auction (which would be an expression of market power on the buying side).[52]

To test this method of measuring market power, one needs to find samples of auctions where different numbers of participants showed up[53] to bid on comparable items or items that are made comparable through the use of suitable control variables. As an example, road construction auctions can be made roughly comparable by including the state highway department's engineers' estimates of the costs of building the road, which should account for the complexity of the project and local cost conditions.[54]

Empirical studies of auction prices and numbers of bidders do indeed find the predicted relationships: fewer bidders at auctions are associated with higher prices in procurement auctions and lower prices at auctions where an item is being sold.[55] Also, instances of collusion at auctions—the joint exercise of market power through price fixing—have been detected empirically.[56]

## 3.3.4  Studies Involving Tobin's Q

For a publicly traded company, the market value of the company's equity shares represents the stock market's estimate of the present discounted value of the company's stream of future net earnings. The total market value of the company would be equal to its equity market value plus the aggregate of its debt (e.g., bonds issued, bank loans, and credit from suppliers). Suppose that the total market value of a company exceeds the replacement costs of its assets. One potential explanation for this situation would be that the firm is earning above-normal profits—namely, is exercising market power.

The ratio of a firm's market value to its replacement costs has come to be known as "Tobin's q" (Tobin 1969). The logic of the previous paragraph indicates that q > 1.0 for a firm should lead to expansion by existing firms, entry by new firms, or both, since either category of firms should be able to sell shares to the public for more than the cost of assembling the assets to replicate the activities (and profits) of that firm. But if there are barriers to entry, then q > 1.0 for the firm may persist.

A crucial element in testing any hypotheses that involve q is the ability by researchers accurately to estimate the replacement cost of the firm's assets. To the extent that the assets are intangible—such as the good will toward a product that is created by advertising or the value that is created by intellectual property, such as patents, copyrights, or trademarks—there may be difficulties in valuation. If these intangible assets are ignored, there will be a tendency for q to be greater than 1.0, even if market power is not present.

The initial study to relate Tobin's q to market power issues (Lindenberg and Ross 1981) used a large sample of publicly traded companies and found a positive relationship between q and the Lerner index for those companies; but the study did not find a relationship between q and the CR4 for these companies. Although there have been a few additional studies in this area,[57] not many efforts to relate Tobin's q to market power have been published—probably because of the measurement problems just discussed.

### 3.3.5 The Panzar-Rosse Approach

A direct implication of profit maximization for a monopoly is that the price-quantity maximization combination will always be in the elastic portion of the monopoly's demand curve.[58] In turn, if the monopolist's costs increase—say, because the price of an input increases—then (holding other things constant) the monopolist's price will increase, but its revenue will fall. Panzar and Rosse (1987) (P&R) expand on this insight to show that the sum of the input price elasticities with respect to the monopolist's revenue must be negative. By contrast, if a firm is operating in a perfectly competitive industry, cost increases will be fully passed through to consumers in the form of higher prices; consequently, for any perfectly competitive firm that can be observed before and after a cost increase, the sum of the input price elasticities with respect to the firm's revenue should be equal to 1.0. Finally, for the Chamberlin-Robinson competitor of Section 3.2, P&R determine that these same elasticities should be equal to or less than 1.0.

Tests of the P&R approach have been done for firms in a few industries, especially in banking[59] and other regulated industries, where data for individual firms usually are readily available and production functions can be expressed with only a few inputs. The studies typically show that only a few firms appear to fall into the category of monopoly or perfect competition, and that most firms appear to be in the category of the Chamberlin-Robinson competitor. However, there are no clear tests for the presence of oligopoly in the P&R approach. More importantly, the approach relies on regressions of firms' revenues against a set of input price variables and other control variables. Unless the input prices are reasonably well measured (which they often are not) and there are good controls for the other influences on a firm's revenues (which there often are not), the tests are not likely to yield useful inferences.

### 3.3.6 The New Empirical Industrial Organization (NEIO) Approach

The "new empirical industrial organization" (NEIO) approach (Bresnahan 1989) arose in the 1980s from a confluence of factors: a) a dissatisfaction with the cross-industry profit-concentration regressions, as discussed above; b) a greater availability of detailed "micro" data on individual products and even on individual transactions, arising from data sources such as the scanner data that are collected from checkout transactions at supermarkets and other large retailers; c) a renewed emphasis on structural rather than reduced-form econometric estimations; and d) improved econometric theory and modeling with respect to structural multi-equation estimation. The NEIO approach has tended to focus on the data within one industry, or sometimes even within one company. Although the NEIO approach can be used to address other IO issues, market power inferences have often emerged from these studies.[60]

The NEIO approach can be illustrated with the following simple example. The demand for a product (for an industry or for an individual firm) can be represented (in inverse form) by:

$$P = f(Q, Z),$$ (3.4)

where Z represents other variables that are likely to influence demand (e.g., income and the prices of substitutes and complements). The marginal revenue for the firm is:

$$MR = \frac{d(P \cdot Q)}{dQ} = \frac{P + Q \cdot dP}{dQ} = P \cdot \left(1 + \frac{1}{\varepsilon}\right).$$ (3.5)

The cost structure for the firm or industry can be represented by:

$$MC = g(Q, W),$$ (3.6)

where W represents variables that are likely to influence costs (such as input prices). The condition for a firm to maximize profits therefore is:

$$MR = MC;$$ (3.7)

or

$$P \cdot \left(1 + \frac{1}{\varepsilon}\right) = g(Q, W).$$ (3.8)

Instead of solving equations 3.4 and 3.8 for P (while eliminating Q) and then estimating a reduced-form regression—which is the general approach of the price-concentration regressions discussed above—the NEIO approach keeps equations 3.4 and 3.8 intact and estimates these two equations jointly (using appropriate econometric techniques). In so doing, not only can the effects of mergers be ascertained,[61] but any influence on the relationships that indicates a change or difference in the price-elasticity of demand can be used to make inferences about market power. Since the prices of a firm with market power should be expected to respond to differences in the elasticity of demand, whereas the perfectly competitive firm's prices are driven solely by costs, this approach provides a means of estimating market power.

It appears likely that the NEIO approach is the wave of the future for estimating market power.[62]

# 3.4  MARKET POWER ESTIMATION IN ANTITRUST CONTEXTS

Market power estimations are especially important in three antitrust contexts: mergers, allegations of monopolization, and the calculation of damages from price fixing. All three will be discussed.[63]

## 3.4.1  Mergers[64]

The goal of modern antitrust policy with respect to mergers is to prevent mergers (or to require sufficient divestitures, spinoffs, or other ameliorations) that would otherwise create or enhance market power. The updated (2010) US DOJ-FTC *Horizontal Merger Guidelines* (HMG) recognize that a merger might create or enhance market power in either of two ways:

- *Coordinated effects.* By reducing the number of sellers in an industry and increasing the market share of the merged entity, a merger may create or enhance the oligopolistic conditions that are conducive to the joint exercise of market power, as was discussed in Section 3.2.
- *Unilateral effects.* When two firms that previously sold somewhat similar but differentiated and competing products consummate a merger, the presence of each firm as a check on the other firm's ability to raise prices is eliminated. If appreciable numbers of one firm's customers see the other firm as their next best alternative (and other firms' products are a sufficiently distant third), then the merged firm will possess enhanced market power and be able to increase the price of one or both products accordingly.

Each potential route for a merger to create or enhance market power will be addressed.

### 3.4.1.1  *Coordinated Effects*

If the fear is that a merger will create or enhance an oligopolistic joint exercise of market power, then a "market" must be defined (delineated); otherwise, there is no basis for the determination of "market shares."[65] The HMG adopt the following paradigm: a market is a collection of sellers that are selling a specific product that, if they coordinated their behavior so as to act like a monopoly, could profitably (and sustainably) raise the price above the current prevailing price. In essence, a market is a collection of firms that can exercise market power; equivalently, a market is something that can be monopolized.[66]

The specific question is whether a group of firms, if they acted as a monopoly (the "hypothetical monopolist test") with respect to a specific product, could sustain a "small but significant and non-transitory increase in price" (the "SSNIP test"). If the answer is "yes" (because only a sufficiently small percentage of sales would be lost), then that group of firms that are selling that product constitutes a relevant market;[67] if the answer is "no," then the market must be expanded to include more firms (either in geographic space or in product space) until the answer becomes "yes." Generally, the smallest group of sellers that satisfy the SSNIP test will constitute the relevant market; the SSNIP is usually 5%.

The crucial information for ascertaining the answer to the SSNIP test is the price-elasticity of demand ($\varepsilon$) for the product in question and the price-cost margin (PCM) on the product. The critical question in the SSNIP test is whether the percentage reduction in sales (PRS) will be sufficiently small, so that the proposed price increase for the hypothetical monopolist is profitable. This "critical loss" in sales can be shown to be:

$$|\text{PRS}^\wedge| < \frac{\text{SSNIP}}{(\text{PCM}+\text{SSNIP})}. \tag{3.9}$$

Since the price-elasticity of demand ($\varepsilon$) is the percentage change in quantity that is brought about by (i.e., divided by) a percentage change in price, if both sides of inequality 3.8 are divided by SSNIP, the result is:

$$|\varepsilon^\wedge| = \frac{|\text{PRS}^\wedge|}{\text{SSNIP}} < \frac{1}{(\text{PCM}+\text{SSNIP})}. \tag{3.10}$$

$\varepsilon^\wedge$ is often termed the "critical elasticity."

Data for these calculations can come from company information on PCMs and on NEIO-type data and econometric estimations to ascertain elasticities.[68]

Once the relevant market has been delineated, the HMG then turn to the oligopoly and market structure considerations that were discussed in Section 3.2 to try to ascertain whether the proposed merger likely would create or enhance market power. Because market shares are the most readily quantifiable, the postmerger HHI and the change in the HHI brought about by the merger tend to receive prominent attention.[69] However, the conditions of entry, the buyers' side of the market, whether the merged firm would likely become more aggressive or less aggressive vis-à-vis the other firms in the market, etc., also are considered. Finally, the potential efficiencies—i.e., reductions in costs—that may accompany the merger are also considered as a potential offset; however, because cost reductions are easy to promise but may be difficult to deliver, prospective cost-reduction claims usually require considerable substantiation.[70]

### 3.4.1.2. Unilateral Effects

If the prospective merger partners each sell a differentiated product, then the merger eliminates the presence of both to act as a check on the other's ability to raise its price, and the merged firm may be able to raise prices unilaterally.

Consider each firm's behavior prior to the merger: Each firm has set its price on its product so as to maximize its profits, in accordance with equation 3.8. It doesn't want to set a higher price, because (at that profit-maximizing price) the prospective loss of customers (and the margins that are being earned on them) more than offsets the higher profit margins on the customers that would remain with the firm at the higher price. If, however, any of those lost customers would have switched to the prospective merger partner, then the merged firm would recapture some profit margins on those diverted customers. Hence, the merged firm would find a higher price to be profitable for this product than did the premerger firm; in essence, the merged firm can exercise more market power. And this effect can operate for both firms' products.

The strength of the postmerger "upward pricing pressure" (UPP)[71] would depend on the extent to which the merged firm is able to recapture the diverted customers that were otherwise lost to the premerger firm (the "diversion ratio") and the profit margins on the "companion" product to which the customers are diverted. The more that the customers of the one firm see the product of the other as their next-best alternative, and the wider are the margins on that next-best product, the greater will be the postmerger price increase. An offset to this UPP would be any efficiencies—specifically, reductions in marginal costs of the first product—that might occur as a consequence of the merger. Consequently, if the diversion ratio from Firm A's product to Firm B's product is labeled $D_{AB}$ and the merger-connected reduction in Firm A's marginal costs is $\Delta MC_A$, the net $UPP_A$ will be positive—i.e., the merged firm will be able to exercise greater market power with respect to product A—if:

$$\text{net } UPP_A = D_{AB} * PCM_B - \Delta MC_A > 0. \tag{3.11}$$

It is worth noting that this determination of UPP does not require a process of market delineation. Instead, it requires only the finding that one or the other (or both) of the two firms' products have significant numbers of customers that find the other firm's product to be their next best alternative (and, of course, the finding that the magnitudes are nontrivial from a policy perspective). Or, if it were felt that there must be a delineation of a market in order for there to be a finding that the postmerger firm has been able to exercise greater market power, then (tautologically) the finding of a positive net UPP (if it exceeds some threshold) must mean that the two prospective merger partners comprise a relevant market for that product.

The analysis thus far has ignored the possible responses by other firms. If entry would occur in response to the net UPP, or if other firms would reposition their products so that the diversion ratio decreases, the net UPP would decrease.

The data that are needed for a net UPP calculation are the relevant PCMs, measures of own-price elasticity and cross-price-elasticity of the products, and the postmerger reductions in MCs, as well as information on the possibilities of entry and of product repositioning. As usual, the PCMs are the easiest to gather, since they may be available from accounting data (if AVC is considered to be a tolerable stand-in for MC). The demand elasticities will require NEIO-type data and econometric estimation. Indeed, since the introduction of unilateral effects into merger analysis in the early 1990s, there has come into existence a "cottage industry" of "merger simulation" efforts.[72] And, finally, as is true for a "coordinated effects" analysis, the prospective cost reductions are often the hardest to evaluate, since they are easy to promise but may be difficult to deliver.

Although modern merger analysis has been pioneered by the US antitrust enforcement agencies, the approaches that have been discussed above are now generally employed by comparable enforcement agencies around the world.

## 3.4.2 Monopolization[73]

In a monopolization case, the plaintiff often alleges that the defendant undertook specific actions that disadvantaged the plaintiff and reduced competition; the plaintiff is usually an actual or potential (or former) rival. Or the customer-plaintiff may allege that the defendant charged above-competitive prices, which harmed the plaintiff. Or the US Government sues the defendant on behalf of the general public.

As a preliminary matter, the plaintiff will need to establish that the defendant has substantial market power; and the defendant will want to try to deny that this is so. Accordingly, the plaintiff will want to try to establish that the relevant market is relatively narrow, and the defendant has a large or dominant market share and thus can exercise substantial market power; and the defendant will want to claim that the relevant market is broad, and the defendant has only a small market share of that broad market and hence cannot exercise substantial market power.

A famous example of this type of issue arose in the DOJ's antitrust suit against du Pont in the 1950s, alleging the monopolization of cellophane.[74] The DOJ alleged that the relevant market was narrow: only cellophane; du Pont argued that the relevant market was much broader and encompassed all flexible wrapping materials. More recently, in the DOJ's monopolization suit against Microsoft in the late 1990s,[75] the DOJ argued that the relevant market was operating systems for Intel-compatible personal computers; Microsoft argued for a wider definition that would have encompassed software on all platforms for computing (including applications running on servers). Yet more recently, in the DOJ's antitrust suit against Visa and MasterCard in the early 2000s alleging monopolization of credit card issuance,[76] the DOJ argued for a narrow market of credit and charge cards; Visa and MasterCharge argued for a broader payments market that also encompassed debit cards, checks, and cash.

If the plaintiffs' views of the relevant markets were valid, the defendants clearly possessed market power, and the trials would then turn to the allegations of monopolization and whether they were valid; if the defendant's views of the relevant markets were valid, the defendants had little or no relevant market power, and the cases should be dismissed. Which views were valid?

Unfortunately, the market definition paradigm that works well for the HMG approach to "coordinated effects" merger cases generally does not apply to such monopolization cases. Recall that the HMG's market definition paradigm is used to assess a *prospective* merger and the possibility that this merger might create or enhance market power in the future. The paradigm can thus ask, for market definition purposes, "Could a hypotheti-cal monopolist raise the price significantly above where it is currently?"

By contrast, in the context of a monopolization case, the goal is to try to determine whether the defendant *currently* has market power. The use of a SSNIP test—i.e., asking "Could the defendant profitably raise its price by 5% from current levels?"—ought to be useless, because the answer should always be "no," regardless of whether the defendant does or does not possess market power.[77] If the defendant is maximizing profits in accor-dance with equation 3.8, its current price should be its profit-maximizing price, and any increase above the current level would be unprofitable, even for a monopolist, because the firm would lose too many sales.[78]

If profits were considered to be a reliable indicator of the exercise of market power, they might help address the market power issue. Recall that the monopolist of Figure 3.1 can be expected to earn above-normal profits, whereas the perfect competitors of Figure 3.1 and the Chamberlin-Robinson competitors of Figure 3.2 can be expected to earn only normal profits. But, as was discussed in Section 3.4, since the early 1980s, econo-mists have generally looked with disfavor on the use of profit rates as evidence that can help measure the presence of market power; and the use of Lerner indexes alone won't help, since both the Chamberlin-Robinson competitors of Figure 3.2 and the monopo-list of Figure 3.1 have Lerner indexes that exceed 1.0.

Unfortunately, there have been no generally accepted market definition paradigms for monopolization cases that would solve this conundrum.[79] The development of an appropriate paradigm remains a serious need for antitrust policy and jurisprudence. And, again, this need is not confined to just the US experience but applies to enforce-ment regimes worldwide.

## 3.4.3 Collusion (Price-Fixing)

When competing firms formally collude in a "horizontal" price-fixing arrangement,[80] the firms' collective goal is to elevate their prices above what competition would other-wise generate. In essence, the goal is the joint exercise of market power.

As was noted above, in the United States price fixing among competitors is a "per se" offense: the plaintiff or prosecutor must simply prove that the effort to fix prices occurred in order to win the case; there is no need to show the extent of the effect, or even that there was any effect. In essence, there is no need to demonstrate or measure the exercise of market power in order to win the case—only that there was an explicit effort jointly to exercise market power.[81]

However, if the plaintiff hopes to win damages from the price fixers, then the plaintiff must demonstrate that the price-fixing did have some effect: that market power was exer-cised. This demonstration usually involves the following: a) determining the period of time during which the price fixing occurred; b) determining the actual prices that were charged during this period; c) determining the "but for" prices—the prices that would have otherwise been charged in the absence of the price-fixing conspiracy—during this period; d) determining the volume of transactions that occurred during the period; and e) multiplying the volume of transactions times the "overcharge" (the difference between the actual price charged and the "but for" price) so as to determine the aggregate damages.[82]

The interesting issue with respect to the damages calculation is almost always the determination of the "but for" price, and to a lesser extent the determination of the time period during which the conspiracy occurred.[83] The "but for" price is another instance where NEIO modeling and data can prove useful.[84]

# 3.5  CONCLUSION

Market power—how it arises, and how it is measured—is an interesting and important topic for managerial economics as well as for the field of industrial organization (IO). The topic is surely worthy of further study by managers and by those who instruct and advise them.

Much of this future study will surely have a strong empirical flavor, with detailed microlevel data on products, prices, consumers, and firms being analyzed through the use of sophisticated econometrics and careful modeling. This is all to the good.

As scholars undertake research—in managerial economics as well in traditional IO—that touches on issues of market power, there are a few areas that are especially worthy of attention. First, as was indicated in the discussion of antitrust policy, there is still no paradigm for the delineation of markets in monopolization cases that is comparable to the paradigm that has been quite successful in the analysis of mergers. This void is important, because judicial decisions in monopolization cases as to whether defendants possessed and exercised market power are consequently likely to be erratic, which is not an encouraging prospect for the long-run efficiency of the US economy (or for other economies where similar judicial issues arise).

Next, developing incentive-compatible methods for merger proponents to describe the prospective efficiencies that would flow from proposed mergers would surely have high social value. Enforcement officials usually adopt skeptical attitudes toward claimed prospective efficiencies, because the efficiencies are so easy to promise beforehand but may be difficult to deliver afterward. This may well mean that prospective mergers that may increase market power but that would also have more-than-offsetting efficiencies are rejected. Again, this is not an encouraging prospect for long-run efficiency.

Finally, the concept of market power itself needs a nuanced reassessment, especially from the IO side. Although the "price equals marginal cost" standard for allocative efficiency is surely a useful place to start, the ready identification of "market power" with any positive deviation of price from marginal cost carries real dangers, especially since "market power" too often carries a pejorative connotation because it is readily associated with "monopoly" and the allocative (and possibly distributional) drawbacks of the latter. Yet the development of distinctiveness by a seller for its product is a well-recognized path toward greater competition and innovation and better satisfaction of buyer demands, even if this distinctiveness almost always means that price is likely to exceed marginal costs in equilibrium.

The real issue that accompanies distinctiveness, as Spence (1976) and Dixit and Stiglitz (1977) demonstrated, is the tradeoff between the economies of scale that might be better exploited for surviving products if there were fewer distinctive products that were being sold versus the decreased buyer satisfaction (reduced consumer surplus) that would also accompany fewer distinctive choices. This is the same type of issue that arises in standardization controversies (such as whether an industry should adopt a common technological standard). The issues are real; but they are not helped by the identification of distinctiveness with market power and its pejorative connections.

Given the long use of the Lerner index and its association with "market power," there may be no good remedy for this conundrum. It is nevertheless worth some careful thought, as well as careful usage.

## Notes

1. Some forms of regulation—e.g., "public utility regulation"—also have as their goal the limiting of companies' ability to exercise market power. Market power, per se, is not unlawful. The antitrust laws come into play only when such power is acquired illegally or existing power is abused.

2. It is noteworthy, however, that the term "market power" does not appear in the index of Porter (1980).

3. Industrial organization appears to have developed as a separate, recognizable field in economics in the late 1930s; see White (2010a, 2010b) for a discussion of the origins and development of the IO field.

4. In that sense, this chapter will be complementary to the chapters in Part 8 ("Public Policy for Managers") of this volume.

5. Unless otherwise indicated, this chapter will focus on issues of market power as they apply to sellers. Roughly comparable issues of the exercise (and measurement) of market power can also apply to buyers ("monopsony"); but, although they are not wholly absent, these issues arise less often in policy concerns.

6. This is frequently described as a "commodity."

7. See, for example, Motta (2004, 41), Carlton and Perloff (2005), Perloff et al. (2007), and Tremblay and Tremblay (2012).

8. Since Lerner (1934) was the first to popularize this formulation of market power, this is often called the Lerner index; for some historical perspective, see Elzinga and Mills (2011). Lerner also popularized the relationship by showing that $L = (P - MC)/P = -1/\varepsilon$, where $\varepsilon$ is the own-price elasticity of demand for the firm's product. This last relationship can be derived from the first-order condition for a firm to maximize its profits. It is worth noting that it appears that Lerner's derivation was apparently preceded by a similar derivation of this relationship by Amoroso (1930); see Keppler (1994) and Giocoli (2012).

9. This geometric portrayal is a standard demonstration that can be found in most microeconomics textbooks.

10. If the long-run AC cost is horizontal, then long-run AC, average variable cost (AVC), and MC are all identical. Also, AC is defined to include a normal profit on invested capital.

11. As standard texts demonstrate, the linear horizontal line of long-run AVC = AC = MC could arise from a large number of identical sellers that each have a U-shaped AC curve, the bottom of which is at the level of the AC = AVC = MC line in Figure 3.1, combined with easy entry and exit.

12. This assumes that the monopolist is not able to practice price discrimination and thus can charge only a simple uniform price to all of its customers.

13. The perfectly competitive firm also chooses an output at which MR = MC; but in that case P = MR, and hence P = MC.

14. Recall that a normal profit on invested capital is embodied in the AC curve.

15. If entry is not sufficiently easy—if the seller is sufficiently distinctive—then the seller may be able to earn above-normal profits, as a return on its distinctiveness; this would imply an equilibrium outcome in Figure 3.2 where the DD demand curve is displaced up and to the right and isn't tangent to the AC curve. Also, the AC curve need not be U-shaped but could instead embody economies of scale (i.e., lower unit costs at higher volume) over the entire range of output.

16. See Pepall et al. (2008, 53–54) for similar concerns over the use of the Lerner index as a misrepresentation of "market power."

17. This recognition that there must be some relative size threshold for realistic considerations of "market power" can also be found in Fisher (2008) and Baker (2008). It is possible, however, that even with a size threshold, a large firm with a positive Lerner index might be just a large-scale version of the Chamberlin-Robinson firm of Figure 3.2. Areeda and Hovenkamp (2002, 133) state that "Market power need not trouble the antitrust authorities unless it is both substantial in magnitude and durable." However, their subsequent discussion indicates that "magnitude" refers to the deviation between price and marginal cost, and not the size of the enterprise.

18. With respect to patents, there is a long and unfortunate legal history of describing all patents (and other forms of "intellectual property," such as copyrights and trademarks) as "monopolies." Since the United States alone currently issues almost 200,000 patents each year (and has issued over 8 million patents since the beginning of the US patent system in 1789), "monopoly" cannot be a useful descriptor for all patents. Instead, recognizing them as distinctive pieces of *property*—some (probably only a relative few) of which each year are sufficiently distinctive that "monopoly" may be a useful descriptor for those patents—is a superior framework. Patents define a product, but not necessarily a market; the class of cholesterol-lowering statin drugs provides an apt example.

19. For an overview, see, e.g., Shapiro (1989).

20. In slightly more formal terms, the outcome depends on the "conjecture" that each firm holds as to how the other firms will react to the first firm's actions.

21. This is usually labeled "Bertrand competition," since it was first suggested by Bertrand (1883).

22. This "limit pricing" outcome assumes that the higher-cost firm, even if it isn't selling anything, remains a constant threat to reenter the market, or there are equally situated firms that could enter. If, instead, the higher-cost firm could be driven permanently from the market, never to return, and there were no other firms that could enter, then an initial period of limit pricing could allow the lower-cost firm subsequently to achieve a monopoly, with the appropriate Lerner index.

23. This is usually labeled "Cournot competition," since it was first suggested by Cournot (1838).

24. Even with a homogeneous product, the lowest-cost firm does not drive out the others, because of the "choose output" Cournot assumption.

25. See Herfindahl (1950) and Hirschman (1945; 1964).

26. It appears that Cowling and Waterson (1976) were the first to discover this relationship between the sales-share-weighted Lerner index and the HHI. We will return to the use of the HHI in Section 3.3.

27. Pieces of the discussion that follow can be found in Fellner (1949), Chamberlin (1956, app. B), and Stigler (1964). The paradigm is usually summarized in IO textbooks; see, for example, Scherer and Ross (1990); Carlton and Perloff (2005); and Pepall et al. (2008). See also Jacquemin and Slade (1989).

28. Critiques of the S-C-P paradigm will be delayed until Section 3.3.

29. In the geometry of Figure 3.1, the triangle yxz represents the allocative inefficiency (deadweight loss) of market power: the accumulated difference between the seller's marginal costs and buyers' willingnesses to pay that are above marginal costs but below the price that the monopolist charges; the rectangle $P_M yz P_C$ represents the transfer from buyers to the monopolist: the excess (over the competitive price) that buyers pay times the quantity that is bought by the buyers at the monopoly price.

30. This temptation for expansion, of course, assumes that the firm can readily increase output and doesn't quickly confront bottlenecks or other impediments to expansion.

31. In the language of game theory, in these circumstances cutting the price below the joint monopoly level is the dominant strategy for each firm: regardless of what the other firms do, it is always in each one's interest (at least in the short run) to cut its price. This is the essential lesson of the classic game theory problem of the "prisoner's dilemma."

32. Or, if one thinks that the "undercutting" occurs through a Cournot-oriented expansion of output, then the Cournot equilibrium would be the "noncooperative" result.

33. And, indeed, despite its illegality, explicit communication to achieve price fixing and market allocation continues to occur, as the US Department of Justice's (DOJ) videotapes of the lysine conspiracy of the 1990s vividly illustrate; see, for example, http://www.youtube.com/watch?v=ytNI56yzbQg. For a longer description of the lysine conspiracy, see Eichenwald (2000); for a wider discussion of price fixing conspiracies more generally, see Connor (2008). Because prosecutors must prove that an agreement to fix prices has been negotiated, but do not need to show that the agreement actually was implemented or caused prices to rise, Posner (1976, 25–26), for one, argues that law-enforcement resources have been misallocated toward conspiracies that are easy to uncover but result in little or no economic harm.

34. Also, so-called "leniency programs" by antitrust enforcers—the willingness of an antitrust agency to waive penalties for the first member of a price-fixing conspiracy to step forward, confess, and provide useful evidence against the other members—surely help enforcers detect already-in-place price fixing conspiracies and probably deter their formation, since potential conspirators might thereby fear that the conspiracy would be more likely to be detected. See Polo and Motta (2008) and Spagnolo (2008) for overviews.

35. This model is generally attributed to Stigler (1940), with revivals by Saving (1970) and Landes and Posner (1981). However, it appears that Amoroso (1938) preceded even Stigler; see Giocoli (2012).

36. This buyer-side bargaining should not be confused with "monopsony," which is the exercise of market power by a single buyer (vis-à-vis a group of competitive sellers that collectively

have a rising supply curve). The monopsonist can drive down its purchase price by buying less than would a competitive group of buyers (just as the monopolist in Figure 3.1 is able to sell at a higher price by supplying less than would the group of competitive sellers).

37. A straightforward example of the effect of the buyers' side of the market can be found in the automobile industry: Large fleet buyers (e.g., auto rental agencies, large corporations, and governments that buy fleets of vehicles for on-the-job use by their employees) pay far less than do individual buyers; see White (1971, 133–35; 1977; 1982). For a discussion of a similar phenomenon in pharmaceuticals (large hospitals versus prescription-based individual purchasers), see Elzinga and Mills (2004).

38. This, of course, is the traditional problem of "comparing apples with oranges."

39. Because marginal costs are usually difficult to measure, average variable costs are usually used as a stand-in.

40. However, versions of the Bertrand model with differentiated products can yield the inference that the number of sellers and their relative sizes matter.

41. The first such study appears to have been by Bain (1951). Dozens of studies followed, for the United States and then for other countries. Summaries can be found in Weiss (1971; 1974; 1989), Bresnahan (1989), Schmalensee (1989), Scherer and Ross (1990, chap. 11), Waldman and Jensen (2001, chap. 16), Martin (2002, chap. 7), Newmark (2006), Carlton and Perloff (2005, chap. 8), and White (2008b).

42. The sources of the data were usually the US Internal Revenue Service's annual *Statistics of Income* for industry profits and the US Census Bureau's periodic *Census of Manufactures* and annual *Survey of Manufactures* for seller concentration. Sometimes the profit variable in the regressions would be the Lerner index or a variant of it, and sometimes the dependent variable would be the ratio of profits to owners' equity. This latter variable could be argued to be what the owners of companies would want to maximize, and it also would be the basis for calculating the opportunity cost of equity capital and measuring the allocative distortion that above-normal profitability from the exercise of market power would yield.

43. It probably also helped that the 1982 DOJ *Merger Guidelines* used HHIs in discussing the seller concentration levels that would trigger antitrust concerns.

44. These criticisms can be found, for example, in Brozen (1971; 1974), Demsetz (1973; 1974) and Mancke (1974). The issue of the endogeneity of seller concentration was subsequently reemphasized by Sutton (1991; 1998).

45. The profit regressions implicitly assumed—following Bain (1956) and Kaysen and Turner (1959)—that economies of scale were not important for most industries and thus were not salient in explaining observed concentration levels.

46. See Benston (1982); Fisher et al. (1983); Fisher and McGowan (1983); and Fisher (1987). Carlton and Perloff (2005) and Perloff et al. (2007, chap. 2) offer eight reasons why accounting data are inappropriate and misleading for these kinds of studies.

47. See Domowitz et al. (1986a; 1986b; 1987; 1988).

48. The data often arise as a consequence of antitrust cases or regulatory proceedings.

49. See Rubinfeld (2008) for a discussion.

50. See, for example, Weiss (1989) and Audretsch and Siegfried (1992) for some of the studies and summaries of others. See also Dalkir and Warren-Boulton (2009), Ashenfelter et al. (2006), Baker (1999), and Busse and Rysman (2005).

51. For a critique, however, see Newmark (2006).

52. Surveys of auction theory can be found in McAfee and McMillan (1987), Klemperer (2004), Milgrom (2004), and Hendricks and Porter (2007).

53. The number of bidders that show up may be endogenous, and thus this potential endogeneity may need to be taken into account in any empirical testing.

54. See, for example, De Silva et al. (2009). Similarly, when the auction involves bidders that are bidding for an item that is being sold—e.g., when the US Government auctions the rights to harvest lumber or to drill for oil on federal lands—the government's estimates of the likely resources on the land provide the basis for rough comparability.

55. See, for example, Brannman et al. (1987), Brannman and Klein (1992), Athey and Levin (2001), and Hendricks and Porter (2007).

56. See Hendricks and Porter (2007) for an overview; see also Porter and Zona (2009). For a criticism of the latter approach, see McChesney and Shughart (2007).

57. See, for example, Salinger (1984) and Smirlock et al. (1984).

58. Recall from Section 3.2 that the first-order condition for maximizing profits yields the result that $L = (P - MC)/P = -1/\varepsilon$. If $MC > 0$, then $|\varepsilon| > 1.0$ for $L > 0$.

59. As well as adding to those studies, Bikker et al. (2012) review thirty-two applications of the P&R approach to banking alone.

60. Summaries of NEIO studies that provide estimates of market power, including Lerner indexes, can be found in Bresnahan (1989), Perloff et al. (2007, chap. 3), Einav and Levin (2010), and Tremblay and Tremblay (2012, chap. 12).

61. See Whinston (2007) for an overview.

62. Kumbhakar et al. (2012) offers an alternative that is similar in spirit to the NEIO approach but instead uses a production function approach and does not require the information on input prices that is often needed for NEIO studies. The Kumbhakar et al. approach is relatively new, and its widespread practicability has yet to be shown.

63. For general overviews, see Baker and Bresnahan (2008) and Rubinfeld (2008).

64. Overviews of the effects of mergers can be found in Whinston (2007), Werden and Froeb (2008a; 2008b), Kuhn (2008), Ordover (2008), Werden (2008), and Leonard and Zona (2008); see also the *Review of Industrial Organization* 39 (August–September 2011) for a special issue that is devoted to the 2010 U.S. DOJ-FTC *Horizontal Merger Guidelines*. It is worth noting that most competition policy agencies worldwide have adopted approaches that are similar to the US-oriented approaches that are described in the text below.

65. For a dissenting view, which argues that market delineation is wholly unnecessary, see Kaplow (2011).

66. Although this paradigm was first used in the DOJ 1982 *Merger Guidelines*, the concept appears to have first been developed by Adelman (1959); see Werden (2003).

67. Although the HMG focus on sellers in the delineation of a relevant market, if a group of sellers can practice price discrimination (market segmentation) toward a group of customers that are located in a specific geographic area or that are in a specific line of trade, then the sales by those sellers to those customers would also constitute a relevant market.

68. See, for example, Rubinfeld (2008).

69. The HMG assume, on a "pro forma" basis, that the postmerger market share of the merged firm will be the sum of the two merger partners' premerger shares. It is then readily shown that the change between the pre- and postmerger HHIs must be equal to twice the product of the two premerger market shares.

70. If the promised cost efficiencies fail to occur after the merger has been consummated, it may be difficult to undo the merger: The merged firm is likely to integrate personnel and systems, eliminate brands and offices, etc., and thus an effort to undo the merger would require "unscrambling the egg."

71. This is the phrase that Farrell and Shapiro (2010) have popularized.

72. Summaries can be found in Werden (2008), Leonard and Zona (2008), Werden and Froeb (2008a; 2008b), and Rubinfeld (2008).

73. A more complete discussion can be found in White (2008a).

74. See *U.S. v. E.I. du Pont de Nemours & Co.*, 351 U.S. 377 (1956); for discussion, Stocking and Mueller (1955) is apt.

75. See *U.S. v. Microsoft Corp.*, 253 F.3d 34 (2001); for discussion, see, e.g., Rubinfeld (2009).

76. See *U.S. v. Visa U.S.A., Inc. Visa International Corp., and MasterCard International Inc.*, 344 F.3d 229 (2003); for discussion, see Pindyck (2009).

77. Unfortunately, as White (2008a) documents, this has not stopped judges in monopolization cases—and even some expert economists—from asking a SSNIP-type of question in these cases. In the du Pont cellophane case, the US Supreme Court asked it, and the majority concluded that du Pont did not have market power because the company could not increase its price of cellophane profitably from current levels—that du Pont was too constrained by competition from other flexible wrapping materials. This inappropriate use of a SSNIP-type of question has since come to be known in antitrust discussions as the "cellophane fallacy."

78. As Werden (2000) has pointed out, a SSNIP test would be appropriate if the issue that was under litigation was a *prospective* action (e.g., an exclusionary act) by the defendant against which the plaintiff was seeking an anticipatory injunction; but few monopolization cases involve prospective actions.

79. White (2008a) offers some suggestions.

80. The term "horizontal" is important, so as to distinguish price fixing among competitors from a "vertical" agreement between, say, a manufacturer and a distributor as to what the latter's resale price of the manufacturer's product should be. These latter types of arrangements do not carry the automatic presumption of socially detrimental behavior. See, for example, Elzinga and Mills (2008).

81. This "per se" approach reflects the belief that such behavior is almost always adverse to the public interest, so that just the evidence that the effort was undertaken is sufficient for conviction.

82. In the United States, private parties are entitled to treble damages from the defendant: a tripling of the actual economic damages that are proved at trial.

83. For example, for varying views on the lysine price-fixing conspiracy of the 1990s, see Connor (2001) and White (2001).

84. See, for example, Rubinfeld (2008).

## REFERENCES

Adelman, Morris A. 1959. "Economic Aspects of the Bethlehem Opinion." *Virginia Law Review* 45:684–96.

Amoroso, Luigi. 1930. "La Curva Statica di Offerta." *Giornale degli Economisti* 45:1–26. Translated by G. Forrest and W.M. Shepard as "The Static Supply Curve." In *International Economic Papers*, vol. 4, edited by Alan T. Peacock, Wolfgang F. Stolper, Ralph Turvey, and Elizabeth Henderson, 39–65. London: Macmillan, 1954.

——. 1938. *Principii di Economica Corporativa*. Bologna: Zanichelli.

Areeda, Phillip E., and Herbert Hovenkamp. 2002. *Fundamentals of Antitrust Law*, vol. 1. New York: Aspen Law & Business.

Ashenfelter, Orley, David Ashmore, Jonathan B. Baker, Suzanne Gleason, and Daniel S. Hosken. 2006. "Empirical Methods in Merger Analysis: Econometric Analysis of Pricing in FTC v. Staples." *International Journal of the Economics of Business* 13:265–79.

Athey, Susan, and Jonathan Levin. 2001. "Information and Competition in U.S. Forest Service Timber Auctions." *Journal of Political Economy* 109:375–417.

Audretsch, David B., and John J. Siegfried, eds. 1992. *Empirical Studies in Industrial Organization: Essays in Honor of Leonard W. Weiss*. Dordrecht: Kluwer.

Bain, Joe S. 1951. "Relation of Profit Rate to Industry Concentration: American Manufacturing, 1936–1940." *Quarterly Journal of Economics* 65:293–324.

——. 1956. *Barriers to New Competition*. Cambridge, MA: Harvard University Press.

Baker, Jonathan B. 1999. "Econometric Analysis in FTC v. Staples." *Journal of Public Policy & Marketing* 18:11–21.

——. 2008. "Market Definition." In *Issues in Competition Law and Policy*, vol. 1, edited by Wayne D. Collins, 315–51. Chicago: American Bar Association.

Baker, Jonathan B., and Timothy F. Bresnahan. 2008. "Economic Evidence in Antitrust: Defining Markets and Measuring Market Power." In *Handbook of Antitrust Economics*, edited by Paolo Buccirossi, 1–42. Cambridge, MA: MIT Press.

Benston, George J. 1982. "Accounting Numbers and Economic Values." *Antitrust Bulletin* 27:161–215.

Bertrand, Joseph. 1883. Review of "Theorie Mathematique de la Richesse Sociale" and "Recherches sur les Principes Mathematiques de la Theorie des Richesses." *Journal des Savantes* 67:499–508.

Bikker, Jacob A., Sherrill Shaffer, and Laura Spierdijk. 2012. "Assessing Competition with the Panzar-Rosse Model: The Role of Scale, Costs, and Equilibrium." *Review of Economics and Statistics* 94:1025–44.

Brannman, Lance, and J. Douglas Klein. 1992. "The Effectiveness and Stability of Highway Bid-Rigging." In *Empirical Studies in Industrial Organization: Essays in Honor of Leonard W. Weiss*, edited by David B. Audretsch and John J. Siegfried, 61–75. Dordrecht: Kluwer.

Brannman, Lance, J. Douglas Klein, and Leonard W. Weiss. 1987. "The Price Effects of Increased Competition in Auction Markets." *Review of Economics and Statistics* 69:24–32.

Bresnahan, Timothy F. 1989. "Empirical Studies of Industries with Market Power." In *Handbook of Industrial Organization*, vol. 2, edited by Richard Schmalensee and Robert D. Willig, 1011–157. Amsterdam: Elsevier.

Brozen, Yale. 1971. "Concentration and Structural and Market Disequilibria." *Antitrust Bulletin* 16:241–48.

——. 1974. "Concentration and Profits: Does Concentration Matter?" *Antitrust Bulletin* 19: 381–99.

Busse, Meghan, and Mark Rysman. 2005. "Competition and Price Discrimination in Yellow Pages Advertising." *Rand Journal of Economics* 36:378–90.

Carlton, Dennis W., and Jeffrey M. Perloff. 2005. *Modern Industrial Organization*, 4th ed. Boston: Pearson.

Chamberlin, Edward H. 1933. *The Theory of Monopolistic Competition*. Cambridge, MA: Harvard University Press.

——. 1956. *The Theory of Monopolistic Competition*, 7th ed. Cambridge, MA: Harvard University Press.

Connor, John M. 2001. "Our Customers Are Our Enemies: The Lysine Cartel of 1992–1995." *Review of Industrial Organization* 18:5–21.

——. 2008. *Global Price Fixing*, 2nd ed. Berlin: Springer.

Cournot, Augustin A. 1838. *Researches sur les Principes Mathematique de la Theorie des Richesses.* Paris: Hachette.

Cowling, Keith, and Michael Waterson. 1976. "Price-Cost Margins and Market Structure." *Economica* 43:267–74.

Dalkir, Serdar, and Frederick R. Warren-Boulton. 2009. "Prices, Market Definition, and the Effects of Merger: Staples-Office Depot (1997)." In *The Antitrust Revolution: Economics, Competition, and Policy*, 5th ed., edited by John E. Kwoka, Jr., and Lawrence J. White, 178–89. New York: Oxford University Press.

Demsetz, Harold. 1973. "Industry Structure, Market Rivalry, and Public Policy." *Journal of Law & Economics* 16:1–9.

——. 1974. "Two Systems of Belief about Monopoly." In *Industrial Concentration: The New Learning*, edited by Harvey J. Goldschmid, H. Michael Mann, and J. Fred Weston, 164–83. New York: Columbia University Press.

De Silva, Dakshina G., Thomas D. Jeitschko, and Georgia Kosmopoulou. 2009. "Entry and Bidding in Common and Private Values in Auctions with an Unknown Number of Rivals." *Review of Industrial Organization* 35:73–93.

Dixit, Avinash K., and Joseph E. Stiglitz. 1977. "Monopolistic Competition and Optimum Product Diversity." *American Economic Review* 67:297–308.

Domowitz, Ian, Glenn R. Hubbard, and Bruce C. Petersen. 1986a. "Business Cycles and the Relationship between Concentration and Price-Cost Margins." *Rand Journal of Economics* 17:1–17.

——. 1986b. "The Intertemporal Stability of the Concentration-Margins Relationship." *Journal of Industrial Economics* 35:13–34.

——. 1987. "Oligopoly Supergames: Some Empirical Evidence on Prices and Margins." *Journal of Industrial Economics* 35:379–98.

——. 1988. "Market Structures and Cyclical Fluctuations in U.S. Manufacturing." *Review of Economics and Statistics* 70:55–66.

Eichenwald, Kurt. 2000. *The Informant*. New York: Random House.

Einav, Liran, and Jonathan Levin. 2010. "Empirical Industrial Organization: A Progress Report." *Journal of Economic Perspectives* 24:145–62.

Elzinga, Kenneth G., and David E. Mills. 2004. "The Brand Name Prescription Drugs Antitrust Litigation." In *The Antitrust Revolution: Economics, Competition, and Policy*, 4th ed., edited by John E. Kwoka, Jr., and Lawrence J. White, 301–20. New York: Oxford University Press.

——. 2008. "The Economics of Resale Price Maintenance." In *Issues in Competition Law and Policy*, vol. 3, edited by Wayne D. Collins, 1841–58. Chicago: American Bar Association.

——. 2011. "The Lerner Index of Monopoly Power: Origins and Uses." *American Economic Review* 101:558–64.

Farrell, Joseph, and Carl Shapiro. 2010. "Antitrust Evaluation of Horizontal Mergers: An Economic Alternative to Market Definition." *B.E. Journal of Theoretical Economics: Policies and Perspectives* 10 (1):1–39.

Fellner, William J. 1949. *Competition among the Few*. New York: Knopf.

Fisher, Franklin M. 1987. "On the Mis-Use of the Profits-Sales Ratio to Infer Monopoly Power." *Rand Journal of Economics* 18:384–96.

———.2008. "Detecting Market Power." In *Issues in Competition Law and Policy*, vol. 1, edited by Wayne D. Collins, 353–71. Chicago: American Bar Association.

Fisher, Franklin M., and John J. McGowan. 1983. "On the Misuse of Accounting Rates of Return to Infer Monopoly Profits." *American Economic Review* 73:82–97.

Fisher, Franklin M., John J. McGowan, and Joen E. Greenwood. 1983. *Folded, Spindled, and Mutilated: Economic Analysis and U.S. v. IBM*. Cambridge, MA: MIT Press.

Giocoli, Nicola. 2012. "Who Invented the Lerner Index? Luigi Amoroso, the Dominant Firm Model, and the Measurement of Market Power." *Review of Industrial Organization* 41:181–91.

Hendricks, Ken, and Robert H. Porter. 2007. "An Empirical Perspective on Auctions." In *Handbook of Industrial Organization*, vol. 3, edited by Mark Armstrong and Robert H. Porter, 2073–143. Amsterdam: Elsevier.

Herfindahl, Orris C. 1950. *Concentration in the U.S. Steel Industry*. PhD diss., Columbia University.

Hirschman, Albert O. 1945. *National Power and the Structure of Foreign Trade*. Berkeley: University of California Press.

———. 1964. "The Paternity of an Index." *American Economic Review* 54:761–72.

Jacquemin, Alexis, and Margaret E. Slade. 1989. "Cartels, Collusion, and Horizontal Merger." In *Handbook of Industrial Organization*, edited by Richard Schmalensee and Robert D. Willig, 1:415–73. Amsterdam: Elsevier.

Kaplow, Louis. 2011. "Market Definition and the Merger Guidelines." *Review of Industrial Organization* 39:107–25.

Kaysen, Carl, and Donald F. Turner. 1959. *Antitrust Policy: An Economic and Legal Analysis*. Cambridge, MA: Harvard University Press.

Keppler, Jan H. 1994. "Luigi Amoroso (1886–1965): Mathematical Economist, Italian Corporatist." *History of Political Economy* 26:589–611.

Klemperer, Paul. 2004. *Auctions: Theory and Practice*. Princeton: Princeton University Press.

Kuhn, Kai-Uwe. 2008. "The Coordinated Effects of Mergers." In *Handbook of Antitrust Economics*, edited by Paolo Buccirossi, 105–44. Cambridge, MA: MIT Press.

Kumbhakar, Subal C., Sjur Baardsen, and Gudbrand Lien. 2012. "A New Method for Estimating Market Power with an Application to Norwegian Sawmilling." *Review of Industrial Organization* 40:109–29.

Landes, William M., and Richard A. Posner. 1981. "Market Power in Antitrust Cases." *Harvard Law Review* 94:937–96.

Leonard, Gregory K., and J. Douglas Zona. 2008. "Simulation in Competitive Analysis." In *Issues in Competition Law and Policy*, vol. 2, edited by Wayne D. Collins, 1405–36. Chicago: American Bar Association.

Lerner, Abba P. 1934. "The Concept of Monopoly and the Measurement of Monopoly." *Review of Economic Studies* 1:157–75.

Lindenberg, Eric B., and Stephen A. Ross. 1981. "Tobin's Q Ratio and Industrial Organization." *Journal of Business* 54:1–32.

Mancke, Richard B. 1974. "Causes of Interfirm Profitability Differences: A New Interpretation of the Evidence." *Quarterly Journal of Economics* 88:181–93.

Martin, Stephen. 2002. *Advanced Industrial Economics*, 2nd ed. Malden, MA: Blackwell.

McAfee, R. Preston, and John McMillan. 1987. "Auctions and Bidding." *Journal of Economic Literature* 25:699–738.

McChesney, Fred S., and William F. Shughart. 2007. "Delivered Pricing in Theory and Policy Practice." *Antitrust Bulletin* 52:205–28.

Milgrom, Paul. 2004. *Putting Auction Theory to Work*. Cambridge: Cambridge University Press.

Modigliani, Franco. 1958. "New Developments on the Oligopoly Front." *Journal of Political Economy* 66:215–32.

Motta, Massimo. 2004. *Competition Policy: Theory and Practice*. New York: Cambridge University Press.

Newmark, Craig M. 2006. "Price-Concentration Studies: There You Go Again." In *Antitrust Policy Issues*, edited by Patrick Moriati, 9–42. New York: Nova Science.

Ordover, Janusz A. 2008. "Coordinated Effects." In *Issues in Competition Law and Policy*, vol. 2, edited by Wayne D. Collins, 1359–83. Chicago: American Bar Association.

Panzar, John C., and James N. Rosse. 1987. "Testing for 'Monopoly' Equilibrium." *Journal of Industrial Economics* 35: 443–56.

Pepall, Lynne, Dan Richards, and George Norman. 2008. *Industrial Organization: Contemporary Theory and Empirical Applications*, 4th ed. Malden, MA: Blackwell.

Perloff, Jeffrey M., Larry S. Karp, and Amos Golan. 2007. *Estimating Market Power and Strategies*. New York: Cambridge University Press.

Pindyck, Robert S. 2009. "Governance, Issuance Restrictions, and Competition in Payment Card Networks: *U.S. v. Visa and MasterCard* (2003)." In *The Antitrust Revolution: Economics, Competition, and Policy*, 5th ed., edited by John E. Kwoka, Jr., and Lawrence J. White, 507–29. New York: Oxford University Press.

Polo, Michelle, and Massimo Motta. 2008. "Leniency Programs." In *Issues in Competition Law and Policy*, vol. 3, edited by Wayne D. Collins, 2219–28. Chicago: American Bar Association.

Porter, Michael E. 1980. *Competitive Strategy: Techniques for Analyzing Industries and Competitors*. New York: Free Press.

Porter, Robert H., and J. Douglas Zona. 2009. "Bidding, Bid Rigging, and School Milk Prices: *Ohio v. Trauth*." In *The Antitrust Revolution: Economics, Competition, and Policy*, 5th ed., edited by John E. Kwoka, Jr., and Lawrence J. White, 329–50. New York: Oxford University Press.

Posner, Richard A. 1976. *Antitrust Law: An Economic Perspective*. Chicago: University of Chicago Press.

Robinson, Joan. 1933. *The Economics of Imperfect Competition*. London: Macmillan.

Rubinfeld, Daniel L. 2008. "Quantitative Methods in Antitrust." In *Issues in Competition Law and Policy*, vol. 1, edited by Wayne D. Collins, 723–42. Chicago: American Bar Association.

——. 2009. "Maintenance of Monopoly: *U.S. v. Microsoft* (2001)." In *The Antitrust Revolution: Economics, Competition, and Policy*, 5th ed., edited by John E. Kwoka, Jr., and Lawrence J. White, 530–57. New York: Oxford University Press.

Salinger, Michael A. 1984. "Tobin's q, Unionization, and the Concentration-Profits Relationship." *Rand Journal of Economics* 15:159–70.

Saving, Thomas R. 1970. "Concentration Ratios and the Degree of Monopoly." *International Economic Review* 1:139–46.

Scherer, F. M., and David Ross. 1990. *Industrial Market Structure and Economic Performance*, 3rd ed. Boston: Houghton-Mifflin.

Schmalensee, Richard. 1989. "Inter-Industry Studies of Structure and Performance." In *Handbook of Industrial Organization*, vol. 2, edited by Richard Schmalensee and Robert D. Willig, 951–1009. Amsterdam: Elsevier.

Shapiro, Carl. 1989. "Theories of Oligopoly Behavior." In *Handbook of Industrial Organization*, vol. 1, edited by Richard Schmalensee and Robert D. Willig, 329–414. Amsterdam: Elsevier.

Smirlock, Michael, Thomas Gilligan, and William Marshall. 1984. "Tobin's q and the Structure-Performance Relationship." *American Economic Review* 74:1051–60.

Spagnolo, Giancarlo. 2008. "Leniency and Whistleblowers in Antitrust." In *Handbook of Antitrust Economics*, edited by Paolo Buccirossi, 259–303. Cambridge, MA: MIT Press.

Spence, A. Michael. 1976. "Product Selection, Fixed Costs, and Monopolistic Competition." *Review of Economic Studies* 43:217–35.

Stigler, George J. 1940. "Notes on the Theory of Duopoly." *Journal of Political Economy* 34:521–41.

——.1964. "A Theory of Oligopoly." *Journal of Political Economy* 72:55–69.

Stocking, George W., and Willard F. Mueller. 1955. "The Cellophane Case and the New Competition." *American Economic Review* 45:29–63.

Sutton, John. 1991. *Sunk Costs and Market Structure*. Cambridge, MA: MIT Press.

——.1998. *Technology and Market Structure*. Cambridge MA: MIT Press.

Sylos-Labini, Paolo. 1962. *Oligopoly and Technological Progress*. Cambridge, MA: Harvard University Press.

Tobin, James. 1969. "A General Equilibrium Approach to Monetary Theory." *Journal of Money, Credit and Banking* 1:15–29.

Tremblay, Victor J., and Carol H. Tremblay. 2012. *New Perspectives on Industrial Organization: Contributions from Behavioral Economics and Game Theory*. New York: Springer.

Waldman, Don E., and Elizabeth J. Jensen. 2001. *Industrial Organization: Theory and Practice*, 2nd ed. New York: Addison Wesley Longman.

Weiss, Leonard W. 1971. "Quantitative Studies of Industrial Organization." In *Frontiers of Quantitative Economics*, edited by Michael D. Intrilligator, 362–403. Amsterdam: North-Holland.

——. 1974. "The Concentration-Profits Relationship and Antitrust." In *Industrial Concentration: The New Learning*, edited by Harvey J. Goldschmid, H. Michael Mann, and J. Fred Weston, 184–233. New York: Columbia University Press.

——. 1989. *Concentration and Price*. Cambridge, MA: MIT Press.

Werden, Gregory J. 2000. "Market Delineation under the Merger Guidelines: Monopoly Cases and Alternative Approaches." *Review of Industrial Organization* 16:211–28.

——. 2003. "The 1982 Merger Guidelines and the Ascent of the Hypothetical Monopolist Paradigm." *Antitrust Law Journal* 71:253–76.

——. 2008. "Unilateral Effects of Horizontal Mergers I: Basic Concepts and Model." In *Issues in Competition Law and Policy*, vol. 2, edited by Wayne D. Collins, 1319–41. Chicago: American Bar Association.

Werden, Gregory J., and Luke M. Froeb. 2008a. "Unilateral Competitive Effects of Horizontal Mergers." In *Handbook of Antitrust Economics*, edited by Paolo Buccirossi, 43–104. Cambridge, MA: MIT Press.

——. 2008b. "Unilateral Effects of Horizontal Mergers II: Auctions and Bargaining." In *Issues in Competition Law and Policy*, vol. 2, edited by Wayne D. Collins, 1343–57. Chicago: American Bar Association.

Whinston, Michael D. 2007. "Antitrust Policy Toward Horizontal Mergers." In *Handbook of Industrial Organization*, vol. 3, edited by Mark Armstrong and Robert H. Porter, 2369–440. Amsterdam: Elsevier.

White, Lawrence J. 1977. "The Automobile Industry." In *The Structure of American Industry*, 5th ed., edited by Walter Adams, 165–220. New York: Macmillan.

——. 1982. "The Automobile Industry." In *The Structure of American Industry*, 6th ed., edited by Walter Adams, 136–90. New York: Macmillan.

———. 2001. "Lysine and Price Fixing: How Long? How Severe?" *Review of Industrial Organization* 18:23–31.

———. 2008a. "Market Power and Market Definition in Monopolization Cases." In *Issues in Competition Law and Policy*, vol. 2, edited by Wayne D. Collins, 913–24. Chicago: American Bar Association.

———. 2008b. "Horizontal Merger Antirust Enforcement: Some Historical Perspectives, Some Current Observations." In *Corporate Mergers: Modern Approaches*, edited by P.L. Jayanthi Reddy, 88–99. Hyderabad, India: Icfai University Press.

———. 2010a. "Economics, Economists, and Antitrust: A Tale of Growing Influence." In *Better Living through Economics*, edited by John J. Siegfried, 226–48. Cambridge, MA: Harvard University Press.

———. 2010b. "The Growing Influence of Economics and Economists on Antitrust: An Extended Discussion." *Economics, Management, and Financial Markets* 5:26–63.

# CHAPTER 4

# ADVANCES IN COST FRONTIER ANALYSIS OF THE FIRM[1]

EMILI GRIFELL-TATJÉ AND
C. A. KNOX LOVELL

## 4.1 INTRODUCTION

FOLLOWING the global economic downturn that began in 2008, firms responded in various ways, but primarily through efforts to match declining revenue with cost reductions so as to maintain or improve profitability. Examples culled from media reporting include, and are not limited to, workforce reductions, rewriting labor contracts to reduce wages and benefits, increasing reliance on outsourcing and offshoring, undertaking efficiency initiatives and "transformative" changes to the cost structure, adopting cost-saving new technologies, restructuring, and reducing service quality. Some of these actions are attempts to reduce waste, others involve downsizing, or "rightsizing," and others are attempts to reduce the levels of efficient costs. Borenstein and Farrell (2000) assign these and more strategies to either of two categories: (i) trimming fat, and (ii) reoptimizing in response to changes in exogenous factors. This background invites an investigation of controllable cost as a financial performance indicator, and productivity as a cost driver.

From a managerial perspective, cost accounting provides the information that enables management to control internal plant operations and direct business operations and financial affairs, and facilitates the allocation of costs across product lines and strengthens forecasting efforts that underlie budgeting and product pricing policies (Gold 1955, 1971; Johnson 1972, 1975).[2] Cost accounting also provides (most of) the raw data used in variance analysis, which can direct managerial attention to where it is most needed, and can be used in management performance evaluation. These uses are internal, focused on a single firm or plant. Cost accounting also provides the raw data used by economists, who conduct external examinations of (preferably large) samples of firms with very different objectives in mind. The estimation of cost-output relationships in a sample of firms sheds light on the nature of economies of scale (Nerlove 1965; Christensen and Greene 1976) and scope (Baumol et al. 1982), as well as the nature of technical change (Ohta 1974), all of which informs competition and regulation policy. Conversion of a cost function to a theoretically preferred cost frontier enables the estimation of cost efficiency (Førsund and Jansen 1977; Schmidt and Lovell 1979), which has the additional benefit of bringing the economic analysis of cost behavior closer to the managerial accounting approach.

In this chapter we explore the relationship between productivity performance and financial performance in an environment that ignores the revenue half of the picture. In such an environment financial performance depends on cost, and productivity performance depends on output and input quantities, and also on input prices. We begin in Section 4.2 with a brief discussion of standard cost variance analysis, which identifies essentially the same cost drivers as economic analysis does, although from a different perspective and under different assumptions. Indeed a central tenet of variance analysis is that input-oriented productivity change is a key driver of cost change. This discussion helps motivate subsequent analysis in Section 4.3, where we introduce a cost frontier as a benchmark, and we estimate and decompose the contribution of productivity change to cost change. In Section 4.4 we convert the financial performance indicator from cost to unit cost, and we employ a unit cost frontier. In Section 4.5 we narrow the financial performance indicator from unit cost to unit labor cost. We discuss alternative empirical techniques available for the estimation of cost frontiers in Section 4.6. In the concluding Section 4.7 we discuss some relevant empirical applications of cost efficiency analysis, and we suggest what we believe are promising new opportunities for research and application.

The terminology of variance analysis suggests that output quantities and input prices are not entirely under management control. Economic analysis concurs, and is more explicit: reliance on a cost frontier is appropriate when firms treat output quantities and input prices as exogenous. If some input quantities are temporarily fixed, the relevant frontier becomes a variable cost frontier. The appropriateness of a cost frontier is enhanced if firms seek to adjust endogenous inputs in an effort to minimize operating cost, total or variable. Scholars have used cost functions to estimate, and occasionally to decompose, productivity change for decades, and it is a short but potentially informative step from a cost *function* to a cost *frontier*.

Primal approaches to productivity analysis are based exclusively on input and output quantity data, with a production frontier bounding, or enveloping, the data from above. They introduce technical efficiency change as a potential driver of productivity change, and hence change in financial performance. The dual approaches we develop in this chapter are based on input and output quantity data, and also on input price data, with a cost frontier enveloping the data from below. An advantage of dual cost frontiers is that, being based on price as well as quantity data, they introduce change in the efficiency with which inputs are allocated as a new potential driver of productivity change.

Thus emphasis shifts from technical efficiency to the broader concept of cost efficiency, which has both technical and allocative components.

Focusing analysis on the cost half of the picture is easily motivated and widely practiced.

(i) In some sectors output prices are missing, particularly in services such as education and health care. In these sectors the analysis of financial and productivity performance usually takes on a cost perspective.

(ii) In some sectors output prices are distorted, by market power or cross-subsidy, for example. This leaves two options. One is to replace distorted output prices with allocated unit costs. Depending on the difficulties surrounding the cost allocation exercise, it may be preferable to ignore the revenue half of the picture.

(iii) In other sectors firms lack control over output quantities and output prices. This occurs under incentive regulation, in which firms must satisfy consumer demand and the regulator sets prices so as to provide firms with an incentive to increase productivity in order to contain or reduce cost. In this context performance analysis naturally focuses on the cost half of the picture.

(iv) Unit cost and unit labor cost are widely reported performance indicators, particularly in international competitiveness comparisons. In some circumstances unit labor cost, despite its obvious drawback, is the best available indicator.

We suggest four strategies for analyzing financial and productivity performance from a cost perspective. The first is standard cost variance analysis. The second is cost efficiency analysis based on a cost frontier, the dual to the production frontier. The third is a variant of the second, and is based on a unit cost frontier, which has the same theoretical foundation as a cost frontier and decomposes similarly. The fourth is based on a unit labor cost frontier, and is appropriate when labor is the only variable input, in which case unit labor cost is unit variable cost, or when labor is the only input for which reliable comparable data are available.

We conclude this introductory section with a guide to notation. Input quantity and price vectors are $x = (x_1, \ldots, x_N) \geq 0$ and $w = (w_1, \ldots, w_N) > 0$, and operating cost $C = \Sigma_n w_n x_n = w^T x$. An input quantity index $X = w^{tT}x^1/w^{tT}x^0$ is a Laspeyres index $X_L$ if $t = 0$ and a Paasche index $X_P$ if $t = 1$. An input price index $W = x^{tT}w^1/x^{tT}w^0$ is a Paasche index $W_P$ if $t = 1$ and a Laspeyres index $W_L$ if $t = 0$. Output quantity and price vectors are $y = (y_1, \ldots, y_M) \geq 0$ and $p = (p_1, \ldots, p_M) > 0$, and revenue $R = \Sigma_m p_m y_m = p^T y$. An output quantity index $Y = p^{tT}y^1/p^{tT}y^0$ is a Laspeyres index $Y_L$ if $t = 0$ and a Paasche index $Y_P$ if $t = 1$. An output price index $P = y^{tT}p^1/y^{tT}p^0$ is a Paasche index $P_P$ if $t = 1$ and a Laspeyres index $P_L$ if $t = 0$. Superscripts "1" and "0" on variables refer to situations 1 and 0. In variance analysis situations 1 and 0 refer to actual and budgeted, and differences are variances. In benchmarking situations 1 and 0 refer to the benchmarking firm and the benchmark. In economic analysis situations 1 and 0 typically refer to intertemporal comparisons, and differences are changes, although they apply equally to interfirm comparisons. An input distance function $D_i(y,x) = \max\{\theta: x/\theta \in IL(y)\}$ scales an input vector $x$ to an input isoquant $IL(y)$, and the technical efficiency of that input vector is $D_i(y,x)^{-1}$. Operating cost $C \geq c(y,w) = \min_x\{w^Tx: D_i(y,x) \geq 1\}$, a minimum cost frontier, and cost efficiency is $c(y,w)/C \leq 1$. This weak inequality is key; we want to know why management allows operating cost to exceed its minimum value, why the magnitude of the inequality varies, both across firms and through time, and why it can persist.[3]

## 4.2 STANDARD COST VARIANCE ANALYSIS

In this section, situations "1" and "0" refer to actual and budgeted situations, and the budget is the standard, or benchmark, against which actual outcomes are evaluated. In sharp contrast to the economic approach based on best practice frontiers, there is no sense of optimality about the budget.[4]

The objective of cost variance analysis is to explain the variance of actual from budgeted cost, which we write $w^{1T}x^1 - w^{0T}x^0$. Three drivers come to mind. Output quantities can differ from their budgeted amounts; this is referred to as a sales activity (or volume) variance. Input quantities can differ from their budgeted amounts, independently of the activity variance; this is referred to as a productivity (or efficiency) variance. Finally, input prices can differ from their budgeted values; this is referred to as a price variance.

An important feature of variance analysis is the procedure by which budgeted input quantities are established. Input requirements are determined by fixed input/output ratios $\alpha_{nm}$, $n = 1, \ldots, N$, $m = 1, \ldots, M$, and so a Leontief technology underlies the budget. Thus if the budgeted amounts of outputs $y_m$ are $y_m^0$, $m = 1, \ldots, M$, the budgeted amount of input $x_n$ is $x_n^0 = \Sigma_m x_{nm}^0 = \alpha_{n1}y_1^0 + \ldots + \alpha_{nm}y_m^0 + \ldots + \alpha_{nM}y_M^0 = \Sigma_m\alpha_{nm}y_m^0$. If the budgeted prices of inputs $x_n$ are $w_n^0$, $n = 1, \ldots, N$, the cost budgeted for the production of output $y_m$ is $C_m^0 = w_1^0\alpha_{1m}y_m^0 + \ldots + w_n^0\alpha_{nm}y_m^0 + \ldots + w_N^0\alpha_{Nm}y_m^0 = y_m^0\Sigma_n w_n^0\alpha_{nm}$, and the unit cost budgeted for output $y_m$ is $c_m^0 = C_m^0/y_m^0 = \Sigma_n w_n^0\alpha_{nm} = \Sigma_n w_n^0 x_{nm}^0/y_m^0$. Variance analysis thus offers a procedure for cost allocation. Although variance analysis allocates *budgeted* cost, and in Section 4.3 we allocate *actual* cost, the Leontief procedure adopted in variance analysis can also be used to allocate actual cost.

We can now decompose the cost variance $w^{1T}x^1 - w^{0T}x^0$ into its three drivers by means of

$$w^{1T}x^1 - w^{0T}x^0 = \Sigma_m\Sigma_n w_n^0\alpha_{nm}(y_m^1 - y_m^0) \qquad \text{sales activity variance}$$
$$+ \Sigma_n w_n^0[x_n^1 - \Sigma_m\alpha_{nm}y_m^1] \qquad \text{productivity variance} \qquad (4.1)$$
$$+ \Sigma_n x_n^1(w_n^1 - w_n^0). \qquad \text{price variance}$$

The sales activity variance is the sum of M individual output activity variances, and measures the cost impact of a departure of the actual output vector from what was originally budgeted. It can be rewritten as $\Sigma_m c_m^0(y_m^1 - y_m^0) = c^{0T}(y^1 - y^0)$, which values output variances at their budgeted unit costs. The productivity variance is the sum of N individual input productivity variances. Since $\Sigma_m\alpha_{nm}y_m^1 = \Sigma_m\alpha_{nm}y_m^0(y_m^1/y_m^0) = x_n^0(y_m^1/y_m^0)$, the productivity variance can be rewritten as $\Sigma_n w_n^0[x_n^1 - x_n^0(y_m^1/y_m^0)]$, and so measures the cost impact of a departure of actual input use from budgeted input use *for the output vector actually produced*. It can be simplified further to $\Sigma_n w_n^0 x_n^1 - \Sigma_m c_m^0 y_m^1 = w^{0T} x^1 - c^{0T} y^1$, and so the productivity variance values actual inputs by their budgeted prices and actual outputs by their budgeted unit costs. The price variance is also the sum of N individual input price variances, and measures the cost impact of a departure of actual input prices from their budgeted values. The price variance uses actual input quantities to weight input price variances. Each variance is said to be favorable if it reduces the cost variance. The sales activity variance, the productivity variance and the price variance sum to the original cost variance. The use of budgeted unit cost and price weights in the sales activity and productivity variances in combination with actual input quantities in the price variance prevents the embarrassing appearance of a joint variance term discussed by Weber (1963) and Bashan et al. (1973) in a cost variance context, and by Balk (2003) in a productivity change decomposition context.

The information required to implement variance analysis is minimal: budgeted quantities $y^0$, $x^0$ and prices $w^0$, and ex post quantities $y^1$, $x^1$ and prices $w^1$. However the fixed proportions assumption that generates budgeted input quantities $x^0$ is hardly innocuous. It is often criticized for not allowing varying input proportions in response to changing input prices, and consequently for providing the wrong incentives to management. Variance analysis models with totally flexible budgets, flexible with respect to output quantities as in traditional variance analysis, and also with respect to input prices, have been proposed, but the fixed proportions assumption survives.[5] In Section 4.3 we develop an economic alternative to variance analysis that allows, even encourages, input substitution. However dispensing with the fixed proportions requirement comes at a cost: the need to estimate the structure of the underlying technology. Management can conduct an informative variance analysis with a sample of size one, while estimating the structure of technology requires a somewhat larger sample. Thus variance analysis assumes a fixed proportions technology, and economic analysis estimates the structure of the technology.

# 4.3  COST FRONTIER ANALYSIS

In this Section, situations "1" and "0" refer to a comparison period and a base period. We use a theoretical cost frontier to establish a best-practice standard, or benchmark, against which to analyze operating cost change and its drivers. We propose two alternative techniques for estimating this cost frontier in Section 4.7.

Alexander Alexandrovich Konüs (1895–1991) was a Russian, later Soviet, scholar. In his 1939 paper, Konüs developed a theoretical input price index that we use to compare operating cost at two input price vectors. His *index* is the *ratio* of two cost frontiers $c(y,w^1)/c(y,w^0)$, and if this ratio is greater (less) than unity, the minimum cost of producing output vector y when input prices are $w^1$ is greater (less) than when input prices are $w^0$. The Konüs concept can be extended to generate a decomposition of cost change between base and comparison periods expressed in ratio form. This decomposition begins with

$$\frac{w^{1T}x^1}{w^{0T}x^0} = \frac{c^1(y^1,w^1)}{c^1(y^1,w^0)} \times \left[ \frac{w^{1T}x^1 / c^1(y^1,w^1)}{w^{0T}x^0 / c^1(y^1,w^0)} \right] \qquad (4.2)$$

The first term on the right side of (4.2) is an input price index that holds technology and output quantities fixed at comparison period levels in order to isolate the impact of the input price change from $w^0$ to $w^1$. $c^1(y^1,w^1)/c^1(y^1,w^0) \gtreqless 1$ signals that input prices increase, remain unchanged or decline. The second term is an input quantity index, which decomposes as

$$\left[ \frac{w^{1T}x^1 / c^1(y^1,w^1)}{w^{0T}x^0 / c^1(y^1,w^0)} \right] = \left[ \frac{w^{1T}x^1 / c^1(y^1,w^1)}{w^{0T}x^0 / c^0(y^0,w^0)} \right] \times \frac{c^1(y^0,w^0)}{c^0(y^0,w^0)} \times \frac{c^1(y^1,w^0)}{c^0(y^0,w^0)} \qquad (4.3)$$

The first component of the input quantity index is a *cost efficiency index* that allows technology, output quantities, and input quantities and prices to vary between periods and compares actual with minimum feasible expenditure in the two periods. $[w^{1T}x^1/c^1(y^1,w^1)]/[w^{0T}x^0/c^0(y^0,w^0)]$, is $\lesseqgtr 1$ as cost efficiency improves, remains unchanged or declines. The second component of the input quantity index is a *technical change index* that holds output quantities and input prices fixed at base period levels to isolate the impact of a change in technology, with $c^1(y^0,w^0)/c^0(y^0,w^0) \lesseqgtr 1$ as technical change reflects progress, stagnation, or regress. The final component of the input quantity index is an *activity index* that holds technology fixed at its comparison period level and input prices fixed at base period levels in order to measure the impact of the output change from $y^0$ to $y^1$. $c^1(y^1,w^0)/c^1(y^0,w^0) \gtreqless 1$ signals that output quantities increase, remain unchanged, or decline.

The Konüs framework identifies four drivers of cost change, two of which (the activity index and the cost efficiency index) can be decomposed further. It is also possible to base the analysis on a base period Konüs price index, or on the geometric mean of the two. Either would require offsetting adjustments to the remaining effects identified in (4.3).

We can translate the Konüs input price index into an *indicator*, the *difference* between two cost frontiers $[c(y,w^1) - c(y,w^0)]$. If this difference is positive, the minimum cost of producing output vector y when input prices are $w^1$ is higher than when input prices are $w^0$. With this background we provide an initial decomposition of cost change as[6]

$$\begin{aligned} w^{1T}x^1 - w^{0T}x^0 &= [c^1(y^1,w^1) - c^1(y^1,w^0)] &\text{price effect} \\ &+ \{[w^{1T}x^1 - c^1(y^1,w^1)] - [w^{0T}x^0 - c^1(y^1,w^0)]\} &\text{quantity effect} \end{aligned} \qquad (4.4)$$

The quantity effect in (4.4) decomposes as

$$[w^{1T}x^1 - c^1(y^1,w^1)] - [w^{0T}x^0 - c^1(y^1,w^0)] \quad \text{cost efficiency effect}$$
$$[w^{1T}x^1 - c^1(y^1,w^1)] - [w^{0T}x^0 - c^0(y^0,w^0)] \quad \text{technology effect}$$
$$+ [c^1(y^0,w^0) - c^0(y^0,w^0)] \quad \text{activity effect} \quad (4.5)$$
$$+ [c^1(y^1,w^0) - c^1(y^0,w^0)]$$

If the monetary value of cost inefficiency declines from base period to comparison period, the value of wasted or misallocated resources declines, and the cost efficiency effect is negative. If technical change induces progress, it makes input savings possible, the cost frontier shifts downward, and the technology effect is also negative. If output quantities increase, a costly increase in resource use is required, and the activity effect is positive.[7]

A comparison of (4.2)–(4.5) with (4.1) shows that, despite their different methodologies and terminologies, variance analysis and economic analysis identify the same drivers of cost change/variance. The only difference is that (4.3) and (4.5) contain a cost efficiency effect and a technology effect that (4.1) aggregates into a productivity effect.

Now recall the fixed proportions assumption used to determine $x^0$ in variance analysis. If the fixed proportions are set not just by engineers but also with $w^0$ in mind, then we expect that the budgeted cost $w^{0T}x^0 \approx c^0(y^0,w^0)$. If there is a price variance, $w^1 \neq w^0$, and we expect management to substitute inputs in an effort to minimize $[w^{1T}x^1 - c^1(y^1,w^1)]$. This effort puts downward pressure on the cost efficiency effect in (4.5), but it is penalized in (4.1), where the productivity variance values $[x_n^1 - \Sigma_m a_{nm} y_m^1]$ at $w_n^0$ $\forall n$. An unfavorable productivity variance is built into variance analysis because it penalizes input substitution in response to a price change.

We now illustrate the decomposition of cost change in (4.4) and (4.5), with the assistance of Figure 4.1, in which a base period cost frontier $c^0(y,w^0)$ lies above a comparison period cost frontier $c^1(y,w^1)$, which in turn lies above a mixed-period cost frontier

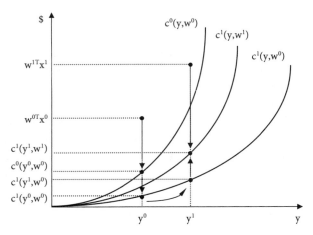

**FIGURE 4.1** Decomposing Productivity Change Using a Cost Frontier

$c^1(y, w^0)$, all on the assumption that the cost-reducing benefits of technical progress are partly offset by an increase in input prices.

A firm's expenditure increases from $w^{0T}x^0$ to $w^{1T}x^1$. Part of the cost change is attributable to a change in cost efficiency, as indicated by the two arrows pointing down from $w^{0T}x^0$ to $c^0(y^0, w^0)$, and from $w^{1T}x^1$ to $c^1(y^1, w^1)$. A second part of the cost change is due to technical progress, as measured by the arrow pointing down from $c^0(y^0, w^0)$ to $c^1(y^0, w^0)$. A third part of the cost change is attributable to expansion, as indicated by the arrow from $c^1(y^0, w^0)$ to $c^1(y^1, w^0)$. This completes the decomposition of the quantity effect. The remaining source of cost change appears as the vertical distance between $c^1(y^1, w^0)$ and $c^1(y^1, w^1)$. This is the price effect. Each source of cost change has its ratio counterpart in (4.2) and (4.3).[8]

Summarizing the decomposition of cost change, the Konüs framework can be expressed in either index or indicator form. In both forms it uses a cost frontier to decompose cost change into four drivers. In both forms the four drivers are input price change (the price effect in (4.4)), output quantity change (the activity effect in (4.5)), and cost efficiency change and technical change (the cost efficiency and technology effects in (4.5)).

The Konüs approach to decomposing cost change can be extended to a decomposition of profit change that is quite different from those in the literature (e.g., Grifell-Tatjé and Lovell 1999). We begin by decomposing profit change in a new way as

$$\pi^1 - \pi^0 = (p^{1T}y^1 - w^{1T}x^1) - (p^{0T}y^0 - w^{0T}x^0)$$
$$= [p^{0T}(y^1 - y^0) + y^{1T}(p^1 - p^0)] - (w^{1T}x^1 - w^{0T}x^0). \tag{4.6}$$

The first component of profit change combines a Laspeyres output quantity indicator with a Paasche output price indicator to generate a revenue change indicator. The second component is cost change. Inserting (4.4) and (4.5) into the cost change component and rearranging terms generates a new cost-oriented decomposition of profit change

$$\pi^1 - \pi^0 = y^{1T}(p^1 - p^0) \qquad \text{output price effect}$$
$$+ [c^1(y^1, w^0) - c^1(y^1, w^1)] \qquad \text{input price effect}$$
$$+ p^{0T}(y^1 - y^0) - [c^1(y^1, w^0) - c^1(y^0, w^0)] \qquad \text{profit activity effect} \tag{4.7}$$
$$+ \{[w^{0T}x^0 - c^0(y^0, w^0)] - [w^{1T}x^1 - c^1(y^1, w^1)]\} \qquad \text{cost efficiency effect}$$
$$+ [c^0(y^0, w^0) - c^1(y^0, w^0)] \qquad \text{technology effect}$$

The revenue change indicator in (4.6) is divided into a Paasche output price effect and part of an augmented activity effect we call a profit activity effect because, unlike the activity effect in (4.5), it measures the contribution of output change to profit change. All the nonprice drivers of profit change do so through their impacts on cost, enabling us to take a cost-oriented approach to the analysis of profit change.

Every effect in (4.2)–(4.7) involves cost frontiers with varying superscripts, and so quantifying the effects requires estimating a cost frontier and evaluating it at various combinations of base period and comparison technology, output quantities and input prices. Implementing (4.7) also requires information on output prices, whether or not they are under control of management. We discuss estimation in Section 4.7.

# 4.4  Unit Cost Frontier Analysis

Bliss (1923) advocates the use of two ratios, unit cost and the expense (or operating) ratio C/R, to evaluate business financial performance, and he notes that the former is likely to be more volatile than the latter because price fluctuations influence only the numerator of the former but both numerator and denominator of the latter. An appealing feature of unit cost as a financial performance indicator is its independence of firm size; it is a meaningful way to compare financial performance of firms of varying size. A corresponding difficulty is the definition of "unit." This is not an issue for a single product firm, but it does arise for a firm producing a range of products, for which an output quantity index is required.

Gold (1971) considers total cost, unit cost, and what he calls cost proportions and we call cost shares. He expresses the belief that having timely and accurate information on all three cost concepts is essential to all areas of managerial decision making, including budgeting, the allocation of resources among product lines, pricing policies, and forecasting. He analyzes the term "unit" in some detail, and discusses the construction of a "nonexistent composite product." He decomposes change in unit cost, using base period cost proportions to weight change in individual input unit costs; this analysis is a precursor to our analysis below. He discusses cost cutting and the pressure to "keep costs down," and he notes that keeping unit costs down does not require keeping *all* unit costs down, and that unit cost policies cannot ignore unit revenues. Finally, he echoes Davis (1955) in viewing cost components as representing "the distribution of returns from production" or the "proportional allocation of the change in average product price among the unit cost (and profit) categories."

## 4.4.1  Decomposition by Economic Driver

We develop a simple model that initially decomposes unit cost change into the impacts of changing input prices and productivity change. We express this model in ratio form and also in difference form. Because "output" is the divisor in unit cost, we adopt the following convention. A firm produces output vector $y^t = (y_1^t, \ldots, y_M^t)$, t = 0,1, and has output quantity index given by the scalar $Y = Y^1/Y^0$, where $Y^0$ and $Y^1$ aggregate $y^0$ and $y^1$, respectively. Unit cost is $UC^t = C^t/Y^t$, t = 0,1.

The change in nominal unit cost from base period to comparison period is, in ratio form

$$UC^1/UC^0 = (C^1/Y^1)/(C^0/Y^0) = (C^1/C^0)/(Y^1/Y^0) = W/(Y/X), \qquad (4.8)$$

where W and X are input price and quantity indexes, Y is an output quantity index, and the third equality invokes the product test, which requires $WX = C^1/C^0$. Expression (4.8) states that unit cost change is entirely determined by two drivers: input price change reflected in the input price index W, and productivity change captured by the productivity index Y/X. Increases in input prices raise unit cost, and productivity growth reduces unit cost. Maintaining cost competitiveness requires management to keep input price rises in line with productivity gains.

We do not assign functional forms to the indexes in (4.8). However if we specify a Konüs input price index $W_K = c^1(y^1,w^1)/c^1(y^1,w^0)$, the product test requires $C^1/C^0 = [c^1(y^1,w^1)/c^1(y^1,w^0)]XI_K \Rightarrow XI_K = [C^1/C^0]/[c^1(y^1,w^1)/c^1(y^1,w^0)]$, an implicit Konüs input quantity index. Substituting $XI_K$ into (4.8) and rearranging terms yields a second expression for unit cost change

$$\frac{UC^1}{UC^0} = \frac{c^1(y^1,w^1)}{c^1(y^1,w^0)} \times \left[ \frac{w^{1T}x^1 / c^1(y^1,w^1)}{w^{0T}x^0 / c^1(y^1,w^0)} \frac{Y^0}{Y^1} \right]$$

$$= \frac{c^1(y^1,w^1)}{c^1(y^1,w^0)} \times \left[ \frac{w^{1T}z^1 / ac^1(y^1,w^1)}{w^{0T}z^0 / ac^1(y^1,w^0)} \right]$$

(4.9)

in which we replace total cost $w^Tx$ with unit cost $w^Tz$, where $z_n = x_n/Y$, $n = 1, \ldots, N$, are input-output ratios, and $w^Tz \geq c(y,w)/Y = ac(y,w)$, minimum unit cost. Expression (4.9) states that unit cost change is the product of a Konüs input price index and a reciprocal productivity index $XI_K/Y$. Although (4.9) places unit cost change in a Konüs framework, cost efficiency change plays no role. However since $UC = w^Tz \geq ac(y,w)$, an alternative expression for unit cost change is

$$UC^1/UC^0 = \{[ac^1(y^1,w^1)]/[ac^0(y^0,w^0)]\} \div (CE^1/CE^0),$$

(4.10)

which is a third expression for unit cost change, in which $CE^t = c^t(y^t,w^t)/w^{tT}x^t \leq 1$, $t = 0,1$, is cost efficiency. Expression (4.10) states that unit cost change is the ratio of change in efficient unit cost to change in cost efficiency.

Expressions (4.9) and (4.10) are both based on the concept of a unit cost frontier $ac(y,w)$. Although they have different structures and different interpretations, both lead directly to the following decomposition of unit cost change

$$UC^1/UC^0 = [ac^1(y^1,w^1)/ac^1(y^1,w^0)] \times [ac^1(y^0,w^0)/ac^0(y^0,w^0)]$$
$$\times [ac^1(y^1,w^0)/ac^1(y^0,w^0)] \div CE^1/CE^0.$$

(4.11)

Change in unit cost is driven by a shift in the unit cost frontier, attributable to either a change in input prices $ac^1(y^1,w^1)/ac^1(y^1,w^0)$ or technical change $ac^1(y^0,w^0)/ac^0(y^0,w^0)$, and by a movement along a unit cost frontier due to a change in output quantities $ac^1(y^1,w^0)/ac^1(y^0,w^0)$, and by a change in cost efficiency $(CE^1/CE^0)$. The input price effect, the technology effect, and the cost efficiency effect are identical to their cost frontier counterparts in (4.2) and (4.3), although the size effect is not. The product of the final three components of (4.11) is the reciprocal implicit Konüs productivity effect $XI_K/Y$.

We now explore a difference version of (4.11). We adapt the theoretical cost frontier model of Section 4.3 to a unit cost context, and we replace the cost frontier $c(y,w)$ with a unit cost frontier $ac(y,w)$ as above. We also replace total cost $w^Tx$ with unit cost $w^Tz$, where $w^Tz \geq ac(y,w)$. This yields the decomposition of unit cost change

$$
\begin{aligned}
w^{1T}z^1 - w^{0T}z^0 &= [ac^1(y^1,w^1) - ac^1(y^1,w^0)]. & \text{price effect} \\
&+ [w^{1T}z^1 - ac^1(y^1,w^1)] - [w^{0T}z^0 - ac^1(y^1,w^0)] & \text{productivity effect}
\end{aligned}
\tag{4.12}
$$

in which the price effect is the difference version of a Konüs input price index and the productivity effect is the difference version of the implicit Konüs productivity effect in (4.9). The productivity effect decomposes as

$$
\begin{aligned}
[w^{1T}z^1 - ac^1(y^1,w^1)] - [w^{0T}z^0 - ac^1(y^1,w^0)] & \quad \text{technology effect} \\
[ac^1(y^0,w^0) - ac^0(y^0,w^0)] & \quad \text{size effect} \\
+ [ac^1(y^1,w^0) - ac^1(y^0,w^0)] & \quad \text{cost efficiency effect} \\
+ [w^{1T}z^1 - ac^1(y^1,w^1)] - [w^{0T}z^0 - ac^0(y^0,w^0)] &
\end{aligned}
\tag{4.13}
$$

The technology effect values a shift in $ac(y,w)$, the size effect values a movement along $ac(y,w)$, and the cost efficiency effect values a movement toward or away from $ac(y,w)$.[9]

In Figure 4.2 the cost efficiency effect is given by the two arrows connecting $w^{1T}z^1$ with $ac^1(y^1,w^1)$, and $w^{0T}z^0$ with $ac^0(y^0,w^0)$, respectively. The technology effect is given

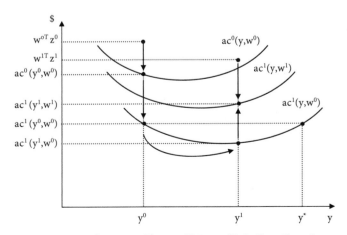

**FIGURE 4.2** Decomposing Productivity Change Using a Unit Cost Frontier

by the arrow connecting $ac^1(y^0,w^0)$ with $ac^0(y^0,w^0)$. The size effect is given by the arrow connecting $ac^1(y^0,w^0)$ with $ac^1(y^1,w^0)$. This completes a decomposition of the productivity effect. The decomposition of unit cost change is completed by the price effect, which is given by the arrow connecting $ac^1(y^1,w^0)$ with $ac^1(y^1,w^1)$. An improvement in cost efficiency $\{[w^{1T}z^1 - ac^1(y^1,w^1)] < [w^{0T}z^0 - ac^0(y^0,w^0)]\}$ and technical progress $[ac^1(y^0,w^0) < ac^0(y^0,w^0)]$ both increase productivity and reduce unit cost. Moving along a unit cost curve changes unit cost [in this case $ac^1(y^1,w^0) < ac^1(y^0,w^0)$]. Finally, input price increases $[ac^1(y^1,w^1) > ac^1(y^1,w^0)]$ increase unit cost. Empirically all that is required is the estimation of a unit cost frontier, on which the four points identified in Figure 4.2 are located. This strategy decomposes unit cost change into price and productivity effects, the latter including a size effect as well as cost efficiency and technology effects. All effects have Konüs structure, expressed in indicator rather than index form.[10]

## 4.4.2 Decomposition by Individual Input Quantities & Prices

We now switch from a theoretical unit cost frontier $ac(y,w)$ to an empirical approach based on indicators and indexes. We begin with $w^{1T}z^1 - w^{0T}z^0$, and we decompose this unit cost difference into a productivity effect and a price effect. We specify a Laspeyres quantity indicator and a Paasche price indicator to obtain

$$w^{1T}z^1 - w^{0T}z^0 = w^{0T}(z^1 - z^0) + z^{1T}(w^1 - w^0)$$
$$= w^{0T}z^1(1 - Z_L^{-1}) + z^{1T}w^0(W_P - 1). \qquad (4.14)$$

The first equality decomposes unit cost change into a quantity indicator and a price indicator. The second equality converts the quantity and price indicators into (equivalent) expressions in index form, in which $Z_L = w^{0T}z^1/w^{0T}z^0$ is a Laspeyres quantity index and $W_P = z^{1T}w^1/z^{1T}w^0$ is a Paasche input price index. However since the quantities in the Laspeyres quantity index are $x_n/Y$, this quantity index is also a reciprocal Laspeyres productivity index, with $Z_L^{-1} = Y_L/X_L$. Productivity growth ($Z_L < 1$) causes unit cost to decline, and an increase in input prices ($W_P > 1$) causes unit cost to increase. The monetary value of productivity growth is $w^{0T}z^1(1 - Z_L^{-1})$, and the monetary value of input price growth is $z^{1T}w^0(W_P - 1)$. If productivity and input prices change at the same rate, $Z_L^{-1} = W_P$, the two effects cancel and unit cost remains unchanged. This is a satisfying result not available from most other index number pairings.[11]

Expression (4.14) decomposes unit cost change into an *aggregate* productivity effect and an *aggregate* price effect. It is possible to decompose the aggregate productivity indicator by variable, since $w^{0T}(z^1 - z^0) = \Sigma w_n^0[(x_n^1/Y^1) - (x_n^0/Y^0)] = \Sigma w_n^0 z_n^1[(1 - (z_n^0/z_n^1)]$ to generate N *partial* productivity effects with partial productivities $z_n^0/z_n^1$. It is also possible to decompose the aggregate input price indicator by variable, since $z^{1T}(w^1 - w^0) = \Sigma(x_n^1/Y^1)[w^1 - w^0] = \Sigma w_n^0 z_n^1[(w_n^1/w_n^0) - 1]$ to generate N *partial* input price effects with partial price changes $w_n^1/w_n^0$.

Suppose the nth input is labor. Labor's partial productivity change in indicator form is

$$w_L^o[(L^1/Y^1) - (L^o/Y^o)] = ULC^1_0 \times \{1 - [(Y^1/L^1)/(Y^o/L^o)]\}, \qquad (4.15)$$

which values the contribution of labor productivity change to aggregate productivity change and, using (4.14), to unit cost change. The impact of labor productivity change on unit cost change depends on deflated comparison period unit labor cost $ULC^1_0 = w_L^o L^1/Y^1$, which acts as a multiplier that converts labor's productivity change to unit cost change.

Again focusing on labor, its partial price change in indicator form is

$$(L^1/Y^1)[w_L^1 - w_L^o] = ULC^1_0 \times [(w_L^1/w_L^o) - 1], \qquad (4.16)$$

which values the contribution of a change in labor's wage to aggregate input price change and, using (4.14), to unit cost change. A change in labor's wage is scaled by $ULC^1_0$ to value its contribution to unit cost change, and this multiplier is the same as the multiplier in (4.15).

Adding (4.15) and (4.16) yields an expression for labor's net contribution to unit cost change

$$\begin{aligned}(w_L^1 L^1/Y^1) - (w_L^o L^o/Y^o) &= w_L^o[(L^1/Y^1) - (L^o/Y^o)] + (L^1/Y^1)(w_L^o - w_L^1) \\ &= ULC^1_0 \times \{(w_L^1/w_L^o) - [(Y^1/L^1)/(Y^o/L^o)]\}.\end{aligned} \qquad (4.17)$$

Thus, labor's net contribution to unit cost change depends on the difference between labor's partial productivity change and wage change, scaled by an index of labor's importance. As in the aggregate expression (4.14), if $(Y^1/L^1)/(Y^o/L^o) = (w_L^1/w_L^o)$, then labor's net contribution is zero.

Summing (4.15) and (4.16) over all inputs, unit cost change can be expressed as

$$w^{1T}z^1 - w^{oT}z^o = \Sigma\{UC_{no^1} \times \{(w_n^1/w_n^o) - [(Y^1/x_n^1)/(Y^o/x_n^o)]\}\}, \qquad (4.18)$$

in which $UC_{no^1} = w_n^o x_n^1/Y^1$ is the deflated unit cost of the nth input. Expression (4.18) scales the differences between individual price changes and partial productivity changes by their deflated comparison period unit costs.

Expressions (4.14) and (4.18) provide complementary decompositions of unit cost change, the former into *aggregate* productivity and price effects and the latter into weighted sums of *partial* productivity and price effects. Although neither expression quantifies the contributions of the economic drivers of productivity change, that is not the objective of this Section. In Section 4.4.1 we use a unit cost frontier to identify the economic drivers of unit cost change. Here we use index numbers and indicators to identify the individual input quantities and prices most responsible for the behavior of unit cost.[12]

# 4.5  UNIT LABOR COST ANALYSIS

Businesses engage in the practice of outsourcing, particularly of the offshoring variety, in an effort to reduce cost and enhance their competitiveness. Since most offshoring involves jobs, we anticipate that its impact works through a reduction in unit labor cost, and then unit cost, via (4.17) and (4.18), which demonstrate that if offshoring is to reduce unit cost it must put downward pressure on wages, raise labor productivity, or both, and the magnitude of the net effect depends on real unit labor cost $ULC^1_0$. Limited empirical evidence suggests that offshoring does reduce unit cost, through both channels.[13]

We begin by acknowledging that in some circumstances unit labor cost may provide an acceptable approximation to unit cost. The relationship between the two is

$$ULC = (w_L L/C) \times (C/Y) = S_L \times UC, \tag{4.19}$$

where ULC and UC are unit labor cost and unit cost, respectively, $w_L L$ is labor expense and $S_L = w_L L/C$ is labor's cost share. The closer $S_L$ is to unity, the better the approximation of ULC to UC.

Now consider change in unit labor cost, given by

$$ULC^1/ULC^0 = (S_L^1/S_L^0) \times (UC^1/UC^0), \tag{4.20}$$

and so change in ULC provides a relatively good approximation to change in UC when labor's cost share is relatively stable. This result does not require labor's cost share to be large. Although we prefer (comprehensive) unit cost to (partial) unit labor cost as a financial performance indicator, often we must satisfice, and (4.20) offers cause for optimism when we must.[14]

We now turn to the decomposition of change in unit labor cost. Substituting (4.11) into (4.20) generates the decomposition

$$ULC^1/ULC^0 = (S_L^1/S_L^0) \times \{[ac^1(y^1,w^1)/ac^1(y^1,w^0)] \times [ac^1(y^0,w^0)/ac^0(y^0,w^0)]$$
$$\times [ac^1(y^1,w^0)/ac^1(y^0,w^0)] \div CE^1/CE^0\}, \tag{4.21}$$

and so unit labor cost has the same drivers as unit cost, with their joint impact weighted by $S_L^1/S_L^0$. The impact is magnified if technical change is labor-saving, or if the allocative efficiency change component of cost efficiency change reduces labor misallocation.[15]

We continue with an alternative, more conventional, decomposition

$$ULC^1/ULC^0 = (w_L^1/w_L^0) / [(Y^1/L^1)/(Y^0/L^0)], \tag{4.22}$$

which states that unit labor cost is driven up by wage increases and down by labor productivity gains. Suppose next that the production relationship can be expressed as

$Y = Af(K,L)$, where $f(K,L)$ is a production frontier satisfying constant returns to scale and A is a productivity index. Then $Y/L = Af(K/L)$ and, using (4.22),

$$ULC^1/ULC^0 = (w_L^1/w_L^0) / \{(A^1/A^0) \times [f(K^1/L^1)/f(K^0/L^0)]\}, \qquad (4.23)$$

which states that unit labor cost is raised by increases in labor's wage, and reduced by productivity growth and by capital deepening (provided that $f(K/L)$ is an increasing function). We can incorporate change in technical efficiency relative to the production frontier by rewriting the production relationship as $Y = Af(K,L)\theta$, with $\theta \leq 1$ reflecting technical inefficiency. This generates

$$ULC^1/ULC^0 = (w_L^1/w_L^0)/\{(A^1/A^0) \times [f(K^1/L^1)/f(K^0/L^0)] \times (\theta^1/\theta^0)\}, \qquad (4.24)$$

which introduces technical efficiency change as an additional driver of unit labor cost change. Increases in technical efficiency reduce unit labor cost. If we make the further assumption that $f(K,L) = K^\alpha L^{1-\alpha}$, then

$$ULC^1/ULC^0 = (w_L^1/w_L^0) / \{(A^1/A^0) \times [(K^1/L^1)/(K^0/L^0)]^\alpha \times (\theta^1/\theta^0)\}, \qquad (4.25)$$

which specifies the magnitude of the impact of capital deepening as depending on the unobserved (and presumed constant) output elasticity of capital $\alpha$, which is frequently proxied by the observed cost share of capital $S_K$ (because if K and L are allocated in a cost-efficient manner, then $S_K = \alpha$). The denominator is a familiar decomposition of labor productivity change practiced around the world, here embedded in a unit labor cost context.[16]

Expression (4.25) decomposes change in unit labor cost in ratio form, and has a somewhat different structure than previous decompositions of cost change and unit cost change. It is easily extended from a value added framework to a gross output framework, provided that the assumption of constant returns to scale is maintained.

The analysis can be extended to international comparisons, in which productivity is invariably defined as labor productivity and financial performance is defined as unit labor cost. Unit labor cost in, say, Spain, expressed in its domestic currency, is

$$ULC^\epsilon = w_L^\epsilon / (Y/L). \qquad (4.26)$$

Spain's international competitiveness depends on its domestic wages and its labor productivity, but also on the exchange rates between the euro and other currencies. Since many traded commodities are valued in USD, we transform $ULC^\epsilon$ to $ULC^{USD}$ to obtain

$$ULC^{USD} = [w_L^\epsilon / (Y/L)] \times E^{\epsilon/USD}, \qquad (4.27)$$

where E is the exchange rate that converts euros to USD. Converting (4.27) into a change format, and expressing change as "$\Delta$" rather than as the explicit ratio of comparison period to base period values, generates

$$\Delta ULC^{USD} = [\Delta w_L^{\epsilon} / \Delta(Y/L)] \times \Delta E^{\epsilon/USD}. \qquad (4.28)$$

Spain's international competitiveness is enhanced by an increase in its labor productivity, and retarded by an increase in its domestic wages, over which it presumably has some control, and also by a strengthening euro, over which it presumably has little control. The impact of exchange rate movements on international competitiveness can be dramatic.[17]

# 4.6 EMPIRICAL TECHNIQUES

Most of this chapter is based on a cost frontier $c(y,w)$ or a unit cost frontier $ac(y,w)$. Estimation of either can be implemented with a linear programming technique known as Data Envelopment Analysis (DEA) (Charnes et al. 1978) or with an econometric technique called Stochastic Frontier Analysis (SFA) (Aigner et al. 1977). Fried et al. (2008) offer an accessible introduction to both techniques. Commercial software and freeware are widely available for both techniques. Here we sketch the essentials, with the assistance of Figure 4.3.

Figure 4.3 shows a sample of firms incurring cost $w^T x$ in the production of output y. The data show a positive cost-output relationship, although they also exhibit considerable dispersion in the relationship. A cost *function* fitted by least squares regression would *intersect* the data, with positive slope. A cost *frontier envelops* (most or all of) the data from below. Two such frontiers are depicted, one labelled DEA and the other SFA.

DEA being a linear programming technique, the DEA cost frontier envelops *all* of the data from below, as tightly as possible, subject to the restrictions that it have nonnegative slope and that the feasible cost-output set bounded below by the DEA cost frontier be a convex set. The DEA cost minimization linear program is

$$\min_{x,\lambda} w^T x$$
$$\text{s.t. } Y\lambda \geqq y$$
$$x \geqq X\lambda \qquad (4.29)$$
$$\lambda \geqq 0$$
$$\Sigma\lambda_i = 1,$$

where now Y and X are data matrices rather than index numbers. The objective is to select an input vector that minimizes expenditure, given input prices w. The first two sets of linear constraints require that the firm under evaluation (i) produce no more of each output than a convex combination of other firms does ($Y\lambda \geqq y$), (ii) using no less of each input than the same convex combination of other firms does ($x \geqq X\lambda$). The final constraints require the combinations to have nonnegative weights summing to unity. In Figure 4.3 firms defining the DEA cost frontier are cost-efficient, and the cost efficiency of the remaining firms located above the DEA cost frontier is measured by the ratio of their cost to the minimum cost of producing the same output vector, and so $w^T x^{CE}/w^T x \leqq 1$, with $w^T x^{CE}$ located on the DEA cost frontier.[18]

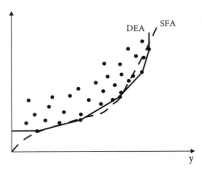

**FIGURE 4.3** SFA and DEA Cost Frontiers

Construction of an SFA cost frontier begins with the understanding that actual cost is at least as great as minimum cost, and so $w_i^T x_i \geqq c(y_i, w_i; \beta)$, where i indexes firms and $\beta$ is a parameter vector characterizing the structure of the SFA cost frontier. In the belief that the relationship is stochastic, we allow for random shocks by writing $w_i^T x_i \geqq c(y_i, w_i; \beta) + v_i$, in which $v_i$ is a normally distributed random error term with zero mean and constant variance. The SFA stochastic cost frontier in Figure 4.3 is $c(y_i, w_i; \beta) + v_i$, but all that is visible is the deterministic component $c(y_i, w_i; \beta)$. Firms having $v_i > 0$ lie above $c(y_i, w_i; \beta)$, and firms having $v_i < 0$ can (not must) lie beneath $c(y_i, w_i; \beta)$. Finally, converting the inequality into an equality is achieved by adding an additional error term, and so the SFA cost frontier regression is

$$w_i^T x_i = c(y_i, w_i; \beta) + v_i + u_i, \qquad (4.30)$$

in which $u_i \geqq 0$ captures the cost inefficiency of firm i relative to the stochastic cost frontier $c(y_i, w_i; \beta) + v_i$. The cost inefficiency error component thus has a one-sided distribution, usually but not necessarily the nonnegative part of a normal distribution.

DEA and SFA cost frontiers are likely to tell similar stories about cost efficiency in a sample of firms. The only essential difference between the two techniques is that DEA is deterministic (the inequalities in (4.29) do not allow for random shocks), while SFA is stochastic, and allows random events to influence cost efficiency estimation via the random error component $v_i$.

# 4.7 SUMMARY, EMPIRICAL APPLICATIONS, AND NEW DIRECTIONS

We have presented four strategies for analyzing financial and productivity performance from a cost perspective, and we have provided an introduction to a pair of empirical techniques widely used to implement the strategies. Each presentation is skeletal, and can be fleshed out with the assistance of the references we provide. Rather than do so ourselves, we provide evidence on the empirical usefulness of these cost-oriented performance evaluation strategies. Since cost variance analysis is an internal technique developed generations ago, and remains widely practiced by firms around the world, we omit it from our discussion. We discuss the use of cost frontier analysis in a variety of contexts; we discuss a single recent study in each context, leaving to the reader the task of following the paper trail. We include a benchmarking application that has more general relevance. We conclude by suggesting what we believe to be some promising new opportunities for research and application.

(i)  Financial Institutions: Academic journals publish literally hundreds of bank efficiency studies annually. Occasionally a consultancy gets involved. Arthur D. Little (2007, 2008) studied the cost efficiency of fifty-one major European banks. They defined cost efficiency in terms of the cost/income ratio, a popular ratio readily available from bank income statements, so no estimation of a cost frontier was required. They found a wide variation in cost efficiency, ranging from 38% to 86%. They found the most cost-efficient banks to share important features such as a cost-conscious culture, a flat hierarchy that minimizes bureaucracy, heavy investment in IT that reduces cost and enhances service quality, and a broad focus on profitability rather than a narrow focus on cost-cutting that might actually reduce cost efficiency.

(ii)  Regulation: Because regulators set service prices, and consumer demand is unlikely to be under management control, interest centers on what management can control, the cost of service provision. Because so many services are regulated around the world, this is a popular, and important, application of productivity and cost efficiency analysis. Abrate et al. (2011) used econometric techniques in their study of the cost efficiency of local Italian water service authorities. They found unobserved heterogeneity across authorities to be the main source of cost variation, a common finding in economic research. They also found evidence of technical regress, which they attributed to the cost of implementing mandated quality improvements, and of improvements in cost efficiency, an intended consequence of regulation. Nonetheless they concluded that regulatory reform failed to meet expectations.

(iii)  Transport: rail, trucking, and air. In most cases government agencies collect and make public sufficient financial and operating data to support studies of economic and financial performance, and all three industries have been studied extensively. Since rates are typically regulated, interest centers on productivity and cost. Eakin et al. (2010) used econometric techniques to examine the productivity and cost performance of US freight rail transport since deregulation in 1980. They found a rapid and sustained increase in the rate of productivity growth, which contributed to a steep decline in the unit cost of delivery. The benefits have been shared unequally, with shippers gaining more in terms of reduced real rates than railroads have gained in terms of improved margins.

(iv) Education and health care: In these two sectors output prices are missing for all but the most gross output measures (e.g., student-years in education), and so performance analysis typically centers on the relationship between productivity performance and the cost of providing various education and health care services. Gronberg et al. (2012) used econometric techniques to compare the cost efficiency of public schools and charter schools in Texas. They found that charter schools have a lower cost frontier than public schools, but that they exhibit greater cost inefficiency relative to their own lower cost frontier than public schools have relative to their higher cost frontier. Thus charter schools have failed to fully exploit the cost advantage they enjoy as a result of facing fewer regulations.

(v) Benchmarking: Benchmarking is widely practiced, but rarely within an analytical cost-efficiency framework. Grifell-Tatjé and Lovell (2000) used a cost decomposition model similar to that in (4.4) and (4.5) to conduct a benchmarking exercise. They converted the cost change decomposition exercise into a cost gap decomposition exercise, the gap being the difference between the cost of a producer (say $w^{1T}x^1$) and that of a target firm ($w^{0T}x^0$). They proposed two ways of selecting the target firm. In one exercise firms benchmark their performance against that of the firm having the lowest unit cost in the sample, which requires either $M = 1$ or an output quantity index. In the other exercise the target firm is a cost-efficient firm, which requires estimation of a cost frontier. In both exercises the cost gap can be decomposed into an input price effect and a quantity effect. Since the sample is cross-sectional, the quantity effect contains only a cost efficiency effect and an activity effect, because in a cross-section it is possible to estimate only a single best practice technology, so there is no technology component. The exercise can be conducted in a panel setting (with the benefit of being able to identify a technology effect), and the target firm(s) can be selected in additional ways.

Grifell-Tatjé and Lovell used DEA to construct two sets of cost gaps for a sample of US electric power generating companies. The low-cost benchmark had unit generating cost less than half the sample mean, and so mean cost gaps are large. However, barely 10% of the mean cost gap is attributable to the input price effect, so benchmarking firms are not unduly disadvantaged by relatively high input prices. The activity effect and the quantity effect each accounted for about 45% of the mean cost gap. The activity effect may reflect exogenous size differences over which benchmarking firms have no control, but the productivity effect is entirely endogenous, and reveals a lot of waste and misallocation. If benchmarking managements have little influence over the input prices they face, and if they cannot control the demand they face, they can direct their efforts at improving their cost efficiency. Turning to the cost-efficient benchmark, the mean cost gap is very large, and negative because the cost-efficient benchmark was one of the largest firms in the sample. Consequently the activity effect dominated the cost gap, with benchmarking firms having a negative mean activity effect reflecting their smaller size. The negative price effect implies that the cost-efficient benchmark was disadvantaged by relatively high input prices. Once again, benchmarking firms may have little to learn from these two components of the cost gap. However the positive productivity effect suggests, once again, that benchmarking utilities can narrow the cost gap primarily, if not exclusively, through improvements in cost efficiency.

In the introduction we noted the different uses made of cost accounting by management and economists. This difference, and our survey of analytical approaches to the cost-productivity relationship, suggest some promising new directions for research and application. Perhaps the most promising new direction involves benchmarking against the best, as we do above, rather than against an average or a target. This practice would implement a common business practice with the economist's cost frontier. Another involves management evaluation of the performance of outlets, of which Walmart currently has nearly 10,000 worldwide. The economist's cost frontier provides an analytical framework within which to conduct the evaluation. Both directions can be enhanced by refinements to the cost frontier. One incorporates the possibility of synergies, or cost complementarities, across the product line, which would provide valuable information to management. Another incorporates the concept of capacity and its rate of utilization, which would require additional information from management. Perhaps the most important refinement incorporates information on features of the operating environment into the cost frontier, which would reflect an attempt to create a level playing field in the exercises just mentioned, and others as well. These and additional new directions and analytical refinements require a degree of cooperation between management and economists, which itself would constitute a significant advance.

## NOTES

1. This research has been supported by the Spanish Ministry of Science and Technology (ECO2010–21242–C03–01) and the *Generalitat de Catalunya* (Autonomous Government of Catalonia) (2009SGR 1001).
2. By way of contrast, Levenstein (1991) reports that, at the Dow Chemical Company at the beginning of the 20th century, unit cost information played a secondary role in monitoring, control and planning, while physical productivity data played the primary role, partly because it was deemed too risky to disseminate cost information that might leak to competitors, and partly because physical productivity information was more timely.
3. Kumbhakar and Lovell (2000, chap. 2) provide the analytical details underpinning cost frontiers and cost efficiency.
4. Our model of variance analysis is generic, and can be found in any number of cost accounting textbooks. We follow Horngren et al. (2008).
5. Totally flexible variance analysis models inspired by economic theory were proposed as far back as the 1980s by Mensah (1982), Marcinko and Petri (1984) and Darrough (1988).
6. The difference expression (4.4) is related to the ratio expression (4.2) by means of

$$w^{1T}x^1 - w^{0T}x^0 = c^1(y^1,w^0)\{[c^1(y^1,w^1)/c^1(y^1,w^0)] - 1\}$$
$$+ [c^1(y^1,w^1)\{[w^{1T}x^1/c^1(y^1,w^1)] - 1\} - c^1(y^1,w^0)\{[w^{0T}x^0/c^1(y^1,w^0)] - 1\}],$$

in which the price indicator is a scaled input price index, and the quantity indicator is the difference between a pair of scaled input quantity indexes. Each scaling factor converts an index into a monetary value. The quantity effect decomposition in (4.5) can also be expressed in scaled ratio form.

7.  The cost efficiency effect in (4.5) decomposes into the sum of a technical efficiency effect and an allocative efficiency effect. The former captures the cost of pure waste, and the latter captures the cost of a misallocation of resources in light of their relative prices.

8.  The activity effect captures the cost impact of moving from $y^0$ to $y^1$, a move that has radial and nonradial components. Isolating the nonradial component can identify the productivity gains or losses associated with changing the product mix or product diversification. Schoar (2002) investigates the impacts of diversification and product switching on firm performance, and she finds a positive impact on productivity, but a negative impact on shareholder returns. Although diversified firms create more value than single-segment firms, they distribute it differently, with a smaller share going to stockholders and a larger share going to labor.

9.  As in Section 4.3, each effect in the unit cost change decomposition (4.12)–(4.13) can be rewritten as a scaled index. For example, the Konüs price effect $[ac^1(y^1,w^1) - ac^1(y^1,w^0)] = ac^1(y^1,w^0)\{[c^1(y^1,w^1)/c^1(y^1,w^0)] - 1\}$, in which $c^1(y^1,w^1)/c^1(y^1,w^0)$ is a Konüs input price index.

10.  A zero size effect does not imply that the technology is characterized by locally constant returns to scale. In Figure 4.2 expansion from $y^0$ to $y^*$ along $ac^1(y,w^0)$ makes the size effect zero, even in the absence of constant returns to scale.

11.  We obtain similar results if we reverse the Laspeyres/Paasche structure of (4.14).

12.  Many years ago Gold (1955) noted that unit cost change can be expressed as a share-weighted sum of unit input cost changes, and wrote something like $\Delta UC = \Sigma S_n^0 \Delta(w_n x_n/y)$, from which (4.18) can be derived.

13.  The *McKinsey Quarterly* has published several offshoring studies. Themes common to many studies include (i) the practice is beneficial to both countries, (ii) it reduces unit labor cost at offshoring companies, and (iii) the reduction in unit labor cost opens up additional opportunities to increase revenue, although these opportunities are frequently overlooked. Amiti and Wei (2009) provide evidence on the impact of offshoring on labor productivity in US manufacturing over the period 1992–2000. They find that service offshoring has contributed 10% of labor productivity growth over the period, and materials offshoring another 5%.

14.  The US Bureau of Labor Statistics reports that labor's cost share in the US private nonfarm business sector has averaged 68% since 1948, which discourages the use of ULC as a proxy for UC, but that it has rarely moved outside a 66%–70% range, which encourages the use of $ULC^1/ULC^0$ as a proxy for $UC^1/UC^0$. The OECD reports slightly greater variability, with a generally downward trend, in labor's cost share in the manufacturing sector of OECD member countries since 1993. Variation across member countries is far larger, ranging from over 80% in the UK down to 30% in Ireland.

15.  Expression (4.21) implies that labor use efficiency is measured relative to the same cost frontier as cost efficiency is measured.

16.  Scholars stress the empirical significance of capital deepening as source of labor productivity growth, and the US Bureau of Labor Statistics reports that capital deepening and multifactor productivity growth have each contributed 1% point toward a 2.3% point

labor productivity growth in the US private business sector since 1987. An additional, increasingly popular, wrinkle is to decompose K into its information technology (IT) and non-IT components, and to decompose L into its hours and composition components. BLS reports roughly equal contributions of IT and non-IT capital to labor productivity growth in the US manufacturing sector since 1987, and roughly equal contributions of hours and labor composition to the labor input in the private business sector since 1987.

17. Annual consolidated statements of income in annual reports of all major multinational corporations contain a line titled something like "foreign exchange gain (loss), net." If this line is positive for Airbus, it is negative for Boeing.

18. Since (4.29) is a linear program, it has a dual linear program that provides information on the structure of the DEA cost frontier. In the SFA cost frontier below, this information is conveyed by the parameter vector $\beta$.

# REFERENCES

Abrate, G., F. Erbetta, and G. Fraquelli. 2011. "Public Utility Planning and Cost Efficiency in a Decentralized Regulation Context: The Case of the Italian Integrated Water Service." *Journal of Productivity Analysis* 35:227–42.

Aigner, D. J., C. A. K. Lovell, and P. Schmidt. 1977. "Formulation and Estimation of Stochastic Frontier Production Function Models." *Journal of Econometrics* 6:21–37.

Amiti, M., and S.-J. Wei. 2009. "Service Offshoring and Productivity: Evidence from the US." *The World Economy* 33:203–20.

Arthur D. Little. 2007. *Cost Efficiency of Leading European Banks.* Accessed January 11, 2013. http://www.adlittle.de.

——. 2008. "Five Habits of Highly Efficient Banks." Accessed January 11, 2013. http://www.adl .com/uploads/tx_extthoughtleadership/ADL_Five_Habits_of_Highly_Efficient_Banks.pdf.

Balk, B. M. 2003. "The Residual: On Monitoring and Benchmarking Firms, Industries, and Economies with Respect to Productivity." *Journal of Productivity Analysis* 20:5–47.

Bashan, O., Y. Goldschmidt, G. Levkowitz, and L. Shashua. 1973. "Laspeyres Indexes for Variance Analysis in Cost Accounting." *Accounting Review* 48:790–93.

Baumol, W. J., J. C. Panzar, and R. D. Willig. 1982. *Contestable Markets and the Theory of Industry Structure.* New York: Harcourt Brace Jovanovich.

Bliss, J. H. 1923. *Financial and Operating Ratios in Management.* New York: The Ronald Press Co.

Borenstein, S., and J. Farrell. 2000. "Is Cost-Cutting Evidence of X-Inefficiency?" *American Economic Review* 90:224–27.

Charnes, A., W. W. Cooper, and E. Rhodes. 1978. "Measuring the Efficiency of Decision-Making Units." *European Journal of Operational Research* 2:429–44.

Christensen, L. R., and W. H. Greene. 1976. "Economies of Scale in U.S. Electric Power Generation." *Journal of Political Economy* 84:655–76.

Darrough, M. N. 1988. "Variance Analysis: A Unifying Cost Function Approach." *Contemporary Accounting Research* 5:199–221.

Davis, H. S. 1955. *Productivity Accounting.* Philadelphia: University of Pennsylvania Press.

Eakin, B. K., A. T. Bozzo, M. E. Meitzen, and P. E. Schoech. 2010. "Railroad Performance Under the Staggers Act." *Regulation* 33:32–38.

Førsund, F. R., and E. S. Jansen. 1977. "On Estimating Average and Best Practice Homothetic Production Functions via Cost Functions." *International Economic Review* 18:463–76.

Fried, H. O., C. A. K. Lovell, and S. S. Schmidt, eds. 2008. *The Measurement of Productive Efficiency and Productivity Growth.* Oxford: Oxford University Press.

Gold, B. 1955. *Foundations of Productivity Analysis.* Pittsburgh: University of Pittsburgh Press.

———. 1971. *Explorations in Managerial Economics: Productivity, Costs, Technology and Growth.* New York: Basic Books.

Grifell-Tatjé, E., and C. A. K. Lovell. 1999. "Profits and Productivity." *Management Science* 45:1177–93.

———. 2000. "Cost and Productivity." *Managerial and Decision Economics* 21:19–30.

Gronberg, T. J., D. W. Jansen, and L. L. Taylor. "The Relative Efficiency of Charter Schools: A Cost Frontier Approach." *Economics of Education Review* 31:302–17.

Horngren, C. T., G. Foster, S. M. Datar, M. Rajan, and C. Ittner. 2008. *Cost Accounting, 13th ed.* Englewood Cliffs, NJ: Prentice Hall.

Johnson, H. T. 1972. "Early Cost Accounting for Internal Management Control: Lyman Mills in the 1850s." *Business History Review* 46:466–74.

———. 1975. "Management Accounting in an Early Integrated Industrial: E. I. du Pont de Nemours Powder Company, 1903–1912." *Business History Review* 49:184–204.

Konüs, A. 1939. "The Problem of the True Index of the Cost of Living." *Econometrica* 7:10–29.

Kumbhakar, S. C., and C. A. K. Lovell. 2000. *Stochastic Frontier Analysis.* Cambridge: Cambridge University Press.

Levenstein, M. 1991. "The Use of Cost Measures: The Dow Chemical Company, 1890–1914." In *Inside the Business Enterprise: Historical Perspectives on the Use of Information*, edited by Peter Temin, 71–112. Chicago: University of Chicago Press.

Marcinko, D., and E. Petri. 1984. "Use of the Production Function in Calculation of Standard Cost Variances—An Extension." *Accounting Review* 59:488–95.

McKinsey & Company. *McKinsey Quarterly.* Accessed January 11, 2013. http://www.mckinseyquarterly.com/home.aspx.

Mensah, Y. M. 1982. "A Dynamic Approach to the Evaluation of Input-Variable Cost Center Performance." *Accounting Review* 57:681–700.

Nerlove, M. 1965. *Estimation and Identification of Cobb-Douglas Production Functions.* Chicago: Rand McNally & Company.

Ohta, M. 1974. "A Note on the Duality Between Production and Cost Functions: Rate of Return to Scale and Rate of Technical Progress." *Economic Studies Quarterly* 25:63–65.

Organization for Economic Co-operation and Development (OECD). *Stat Extracts.* Accessed January 11, 2013. http://stats.oecd.org/Index.aspx.

Schmidt, P., and C. A. K. Lovell. 1979. "Estimating Technical and Allocative Inefficiency Relative to Stochastic Production and Cost Frontiers." *Journal of Econometrics* 9:343–66.

Schoar, A. 2002. "Effects of Corporate Diversification on Productivity." *Journal of Finance* 57:2379–403.

United States Department of Labor, Bureau of Labor Statistics. "Overview of BLS Productivity Statistics." Accessed Janurary 11, 2013. http://www.bls.gov/bls/productivity.htm.

Weber, C. 1963. "The Mathematics of Variance Analysis." *Accounting Review* 38:534–39.

# CHAPTER 5

# SUPPLY CHAIN DESIGN FOR MANAGING DISRUPTIVE RISKS

SUNIL CHOPRA AND MANMOHAN S. SODHI[1]

## 5.1 INTRODUCTION

THE first decade of the 21st century witnessed a sharp increase in risks faced by global supply chains. The economic downturn of 2009 saw GDP and demand in the United States and Europe shrink while GDP in China and India continued to increase. The dollar fluctuated between a high of 124 yen in 2007 and a low of 81 yen in 2010. The US dollar reached a low of 0.63 euro in 2008 and a high of 0.83 euro in 2010. The Brazilian Real reached a high of $0.64 and a low of about $0.40. Freight and fuel costs also have moved up and down dramatically in the recent past. In 2010, the Baltic Dry Index, which measures changes in the cost of shipping raw materials, such as metals, grains, and fossil fuels, fluctuated between a high of 4187 in May and a low of 1709 in July. Crude oil prices were as low as $31 per barrel in February 2009 and increased to $104 per barrel by January 2012. At Toyota, a faulty accelerator that was common to many vehicles sold across the world led to a recall of millions of vehicles in China, Europe, and the United States. Each of these examples highlights the risks which supply chains have had to face. For each of the four quarters of 2010 in the MFG Watch survey (www.mfg.com), over a third of US manufacturers reported at least one significant supply chain disruption in the previous three months.

These fluctuations and disruptions had significant impacts on supply chain performance. It has been reported that every one-cent drop in the dollar relative to the euro costs European automakers about $75 million each year. Toyota's recall caused by defective parts cost it billions of dollars in repairs and lost sales, resulting in an immeasurably large negative impact on its brand. Thus, a supply chain disruption can cause significant sales losses or cost increases.

Many companies have invested too little toward alleviating the threat of such risks to their supply chains (Rice and Caniato 2003; Zsidisin et al. 2000, 2004). According to a study conducted by Computer Sciences Corporation in 2003, 43% of 142 companies, ranging from consumer goods to healthcare, reported that their supply chains are vulnerable to disruptions; yet, at the same time, 55% of these companies had no documented contingency plans (c.f., Poirier and Quinn 2003). According to another survey conducted by CFO Research Services, 38% of 247 companies acknowledged that they have too much *unmanaged* supply chain risk (c.f., Eskew 2004). A possible reason for this "apprehension without action" (c.f., Sodhi and Tang 2012) could be that without accurate estimates of the (rare) likelihood of the occurrence of a major disruption, companies cannot perform cost-benefit or return-on-investment analyses to justify investment in risk-reduction programs or contingency plans (Rice and Caniato 2003; Zsidisin et al. 2000). As such, it is worthwhile understanding the importance of accurately estimating the likelihood of a disruption.

This chapter focuses on two fundamental questions related to disruptive risk: (1) Given the difficulty of estimating the probability of a disruption, what guidance can we provide for supply chain design, and (2) What fundamental design strategies can best help deal with disruptive risks? While our answers to these two questions are obtained from stylized models, they are nonetheless robust across a variety of settings. After discussing the difference between more common recurrent risks and rare disruptive risks in Section 5.2, we look at supply chain design for managing disruptive risk from four different angles Section 5.3 examines the impact of misestimating the likelihood of a disruption. Section 5.4 discusses designing supply chains so that the impact of a disruptive incident can be localized. Section 5.5 provides general guidelines for how much reserve to use in a particular situation and describes general principles for tailoring. Then Section 5.6 describes response to disruptions as comprising detection of the incident, designing a response, and deploying the response: this too has implications for supply chain design. Finally, Section 5.7 summarizes the implications for managers and offers concluding thoughts on directions for future research.

# 5.2  Recurrent and Disruptive Risks

Before we discuss how to manage disruptive risks, we need to distinguish between two categories of risks in the supply chain, recurrent and disruptive, with our focus in this chapter being on the latter. *Recurrent risks* refer to fluctuations that are ongoing and faced by a supply chain on a regular basis. Changes in demand, freight prices, exchange rates, and minor fluctuations in supply lead times are examples of recurrent risks. Recurrent risks display some degree of independence across time and geography—if one region has low demand, another region may have high demand—and, in the short term, display small fluctuations with small impacts on supply chain performance. *Disruptive risks* refer to events that potentially shut down the supply chain or some part of it. Product recalls, fire at a supply plant, or collapse of suppliers because of lack of availability of capital, are examples of disruptive risks. Disruptive risks tend to have correlated impacts on the supply chain. A defective part affects all cars using that part. A disrupted supply source impacts all demand points that it supplies.

Recurrent and disruptive risks require fundamentally different analytical approaches. Whereas demand or lead-time fluctuations can effectively be handled by building an inventory reserve, fire at a supply plant or the bankruptcy of a supplier cannot be addressed simply by holding inventory: the company may have to develop an extra or a more reliable supplier despite the potential additional cost. In the last decade, supply chains have become much better at dealing with recurrent risks but in the process have often left themselves more vulnerable to disruptive risks. In 2008, the World Economic Forum said in a report that, "Extended supply chains, which have allowed global economic integration to flourish in the last two decades, may be concealing increased vulnerability of the global system to disruptive risks" (World Economic Forum 2008). Whereas the building of operational reserves, such as production capacity and inventory, has mitigated recurrent risks, the concentration of these reserves in sole-source suppliers, common parts, or centralized inventories has often left the supply chain more vulnerable to disruption.

Toyota's recalls in 2010 are an example of this phenomenon. The use of common parts produced by a single supplier for vehicles sold around the world allowed Toyota to reduce production costs and inventories while dealing very effectively with demand fluctuations. This phenomenon of pooling production and inventory by utilizing common parts, however, left it extremely vulnerable to a disruption related to any particular part. When a quality defect was highlighted for such a part, millions of cars across the globe had to be recalled by Toyota.

Disruptive risks are challenging not only because of their potential impact but also because they occur rarely and therefore are difficult to estimate. Estimates of the likelihood of recurrent-risk events can be based on history, as assumed by inventory models, for instance, and are therefore easy and acceptably accurate. In contrast, estimates of the likelihood of a disruptive risk may be purely subjective given that events are rare—they may not even have occurred at all in the past—and may have many different triggers that could lead to the same type of disruption. Whereas it is relatively easy to use past data to estimate recurrent risks such as demand uncertainty, it is almost impossible to estimate the probability of a supplier going bankrupt or a quality problem arising with a common part. Adding to the problem is the tendency of humans to underestimate the probability of rare events the further removed they are from the previous time such an event occurred (Taleb 2007). This creates a natural bias among supply chain designers and managers towards underestimating disruptive risk when crafting mitigation strategies. This tendency gets exacerbated because the cost of any mitigation strategy is incurred upfront, or on an ongoing basis, while the benefits are realized only on the rare occasion a disruption actually occurs.

# 5.3 Supply Chain Design with Misestimated Likelihood of Disruptive Risk

Traditional risk assessment comprises estimating the likelihood and the expected impact of a risk incident (Sodhi and Tang 2012, chap. 3). In the context of disruptive risks, it is very difficult to come up with reasonable estimates of failure probability: there could have been no reasonable way for Toyota to estimate the probability of a part failure or for Ericsson to predict the probability of a supply plant completely shutting production for an extended period of time because of a minor fire incident. In such settings it may even be attractive for decision makers to underestimate the probabilities because it avoids having to invest in upfront mitigation costs. It is thus important to understand the impact of misestimating disruptive risks when designing supply chains.

Lim et al. (2012) argue that it is worth spending time and effort to obtain estimates of disruptive risk and underestimation can be expensive when dealing with such risk. We present a simple model used by them and show some of the results obtained. Although this is a stylized model, the results are quite robust under a variety of simulation scenarios. Their findings are: (1) As long as supply chains are designed for disruptive risk, the total (expected) cost of the "optimal" robust supply chain is not very sensitive to small errors in estimating the likelihood (probability) of disruption, and (2) Underestimating disruption probability is, on average, more expensive than overestimating it.

Our model assumes a geographical region $\Omega$ with a sufficiently large area $A$ on a plane. Consumer (or customer) demand is assumed to be distributed uniformly with density $\rho$ over the entire region. The supply-chain network designer can either build *unreliable* facilities or *reliable* facilities to satisfy all demand. Unreliable facilities are cheaper to build (cost = $f_U$) but can fail with disruption probability $q$. Reliable facilities cost more to build (cost = $f_R$) but do not fail at all. The demand at any point in $\Omega$ is served from the closest facility (which could be either unreliable or reliable). In the event supply from the closest unreliable facility is disrupted, demand is served from the closest *reliable* facility (which has unlimited capacity).

To simplify the analysis, we tile the region $\Omega$ into subregions $\Omega_0$ of area $A_0$ as shown in Figure 5.1. Each region $\Omega_0$ is assumed to have one reliable facility at its center along with $n_0-1$ unreliable facilities. All distance is measured using the Manhattan metric—i.e., the distance along a square grid between any two points on a plane without being able to move on a diagonal, reflecting the path of a car in Manhattan—to simplify the analysis.

The model's objective is to design a network that minimizes the total cost of locating $n_R$ reliable facilities and $n_U$ unreliable facilities plus the expected transportation cost to meet all demand. If $c$ is the transportation cost per unit distance per unit demand, the *expected total cost* ($E[TC]$) is obtained as:

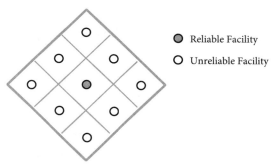

**FIGURE 5.1:** Sample tiling to surround a reliable facility with unreliable ones for subregion $\Omega_o$ of area $A_o$ with one reliable facility at its center along with $n_o-1$ unreliable facilities

$$E[TC] = f_R n_R + f_U n_U + q\gamma \sqrt{\frac{1}{n_R}} + (1-q)\gamma \sqrt{\frac{1}{n_R + n_U}}, \text{where } \gamma = \frac{\sqrt{2}}{3}\rho A^{3/2} c$$

Noting that the expected total cost is convex in $n_R$ and $n_U$, we can set the first partial derivatives with respect to $n_R$ and $n_U$ to zero and obtain the optimal facility deployment policy as follows:

Proposition 1: *The optimal network is determined by the disruption probability q relative to the threshold* $q_{th} = \dfrac{f_R - f_U}{f_R} = 1 - \dfrac{f_U}{f_R}$. *Furthermore, if* $q \le q_{th}$, *the optimal network has both reliable and unreliable facilities with*

$$n_R^* = \left(\frac{g q}{2(f_R - f_U)}\right)^{2/3} \text{ and } n_U^* = \left(\frac{g(1-q)}{2f_U}\right)^{2/3} - \left(\frac{g q}{2(f_R - f_U)}\right)^{2/3}$$

*and if* $q > q_{th}$, *the optimal network has reliable facilities only with*

$$n_R^* = \left(\frac{g}{2 f_R}\right)^{2/3} \text{ and } n_U^* = 0.$$

We omit the proof and refer the reader to Lim et al. (2012).

In practice when designing a supply chain, we expect $q_{th}$ to be close to 1 because unreliable facilities are likely to have a much lower fixed cost than reliable ones—that is, $f_U \ll f_R$. At the same time, for disruption we expect $q$ to be small (disruptions occur rarely) with a value close to zero. Thus, the condition $q \le q_{th}$ will hold in most situations.

It follows from the proposition that the ratio $U^*$ of the number of unreliable facilities relative to reliable ones when the network is optimal is given by

$$U^* = \frac{n_U^*}{n_R^*} = \left(\frac{1-q}{q}\right)^{2/3} \left(\frac{q_{th}}{1-q_{th}}\right)^{2/3} - 1$$

for $q \leq q_{th}$ and 0 otherwise. From this expression and from the expression for $n_R$ in the proposition, observe that for small values of the disruption probability $q$, a small change in $q$ has a significant impact on the optimal proportion $U^*$ of unreliable to reliable facilities. At the same time, the number of reliable facilities $n_R$ grows only slightly sublinearly with $q$ so that the sensitivity to $q$ is almost proportional.

*As a result, misestimating the disruption probability $q$ can have a significant impact on the optimal number of reliable facilities $n_R$ and especially so when $q$ is small.* Figure 5.2 reflects the percentage change in the (miscalculated) optimal number of reliable facilities when there is a small misestimation of the true value of $q$—the effect is larger for smaller values of the true value.

This raises the question of how the misestimation of the true value of $q$ impacts the *total expected cost* of the network. For any supply chain consistent with Figure 5.1 using, as per Proposition 1, (a) the optimal ratio $U^*$ of the number of unreliable to reliable facilities and (b) the optimal number of reliable facilities, the (expected) total cost is given by

$$E\left[TC(n_R^*, U^*)\right] = f_R n_R^* + \left(1 + (1-q_{th})U^*\right) + q\gamma \sqrt{\frac{1}{n_R^*}} \left(1 + \frac{1-q}{q\sqrt{1+U^*}}\right)$$

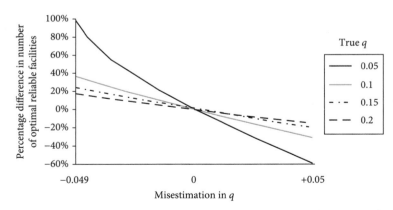

FIGURE 5.2. Misestimating disruption likelihood $q$ by a small amount can result in a miscalculated number of reliable facilities (for the case $q < q_{th}$); the percentage difference in the number of reliable facilities is greater when $q$ is smaller (say, 0.05) than when it is larger (say, 0.20).

Source: Lim et al. (2012)

for the case $q < q_{th}$. This expression can be used to determine the sensitivity of expected total cost to the misestimation of $q$: If $q$ erroneously is estimated to be $q_e$, the supply network would be incorrectly optimized with the number of reliable facilities $n_R^e$ and unreliable facilities as per the ratio $U^e$ (as determined from Proposition 1 using the misestimated value $q_e$). For the case $q < q_{th}$, the expected total cost would then be higher than the optimal value by the proportion

$$\frac{E\left[TC(n_R^e, U^e)\right] - E\left[TC(n_R^*, U^*)\right]}{E\left[TC(n_R^*, U^*)\right]}$$

with the actual value of failure $q$ being used to compute the expected value in both cases.

Supposing the erroneously estimated value of failure probability has a percentage error $\alpha$ over the true value so that

$$q^e = (1+\alpha)q$$

We then obtain the (incorrectly) optimized values of $n_R^e$ and $U^e$. Now we can use the above expression to obtain the percentage difference in expected cost from optimizing the supply network incorrectly as a function of $\alpha$ and $q$, given the values respectively of $\gamma, f_R$ and $q_{th}$. Figure 5.3 provides the percentage increase in the total expected cost as a result of the estimation error $\alpha$ and the true value. This figure is largely unchanged in shape for a wide range of values of $\gamma, f_R$ and $q_{th}$.

Table 5.1 does the same for sample values of $f_R/f_U$, $q_e$ and $q$ to show the percentage increase in total (expected) cost as we vary the values of $q$ and $q_e$. In Table 5.1 observe that a $\pm 50\%$ error in estimating disruption probability causes a total expected cost error of less than 2.28% even when a reliable facility is five times more expensive than an unreliable one. In other words, as long as the error is not too large, the expected total cost is

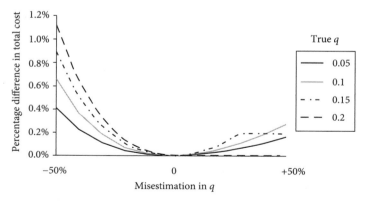

**FIGURE 5.3:** Percentage increase in the *total expected cost* when the disruption probability is misestimated by a percentage $\alpha$, for different levels of $q$ indicated by the legend, for the case $q < qth$.

Source: Lim et al. (2012)

Table 5.1: Percentage increase in total expected cost on misestimating the disruption probability when q is misestimated as qe, for different levels of q and different ratios of the fixed costs of reliable facilities ($f_R$) to those of unreliable facilities ($f_U$). Source: Lim et al. (2012)

| True Probability $q$ | | 0.01 | q = 0.05 | | q = 0.10 | | | | q = 0.15 | |
| --- | --- | --- | --- | --- | --- | --- | --- | --- | --- | --- |
| Estimated Probability $q_e$ | | 0.1 | 0.01 | 0.10 | 0.01 | 0.05 | 0.15 | 0.20 | 0.10 | 0.20 |
| Percentage increase in E[TC] (%) | $f_R/f_U = 1.25$ | 2.48 | 2.04 | 0.50 | 6.14 | 0.66 | 0.27 | 0.87 | 0.32 | 0.19 |
| | $f_R/f_U = 1.5$ | 2.70 | 16.75 | 0.51 | 20.11 | 0.89 | 0.26 | 0.91 | 0.39 | 0.78 |
| | $f_R/f_U = 2$ | 3.36 | 56.16 | 0.52 | 71.51 | 1.62 | 0.26 | 1.02 | 0.69 | 0.17 |
| | $f_R/f_U = 5$ | 5.07 | 65.47 | 0.76 | 78.20 | 2.28 | 0.37 | 1.40 | 0.94 | 0.23 |

relatively insensitive to the misestimation of disruption probability. When the error is large, however, the situation changes. For example, when the true disruption probability $q$ is 0.10 and the (under)estimated probability $q_e$ is 0.01 (a 90% underestimate), the error in total expected cost can be as large as 78%! More importantly, there is an asymmetry: an overestimation of the disruption probability appears to be much less expensive relative to an underestimation: using an estimate of 0.20 instead of a true disruption probability of 0.10, a 100% overestimate, causes a total cost error of only 1.4%.

From Figure 5.3 and Table 5.1, we can make the following observations that are also supported analytically by the model:

Observation 1: *Reasonable bounds for misestimating the disruption probability significantly reduce the increase in total expected cost owing to this misestimation.*

Observation 2: *The increase in total expected cost from* underestimating *the disruption probability is greater than the increase in total cost from* overestimating *the disruption probability.*

In a different setting, Tomlin (2006) observed similar results from misestimating the duration of a disruption. He found that underestimating the duration of a disruption typically led to significantly larger increases in cost than overestimating the duration of a disruption.

Our results indicate that the supply chain designer should never ignore the disruption probability—this amounts to significant underestimation with $\alpha = -100\%$—because the resulting increase in expected total cost owing to the misestimation is large (Observation 2). It is therefore worth spending time and effort to set reasonable bounds for the disruption probability (Observation 1). If no such bounds can be determined or if these bounds are large, the supply chain designer should work with a reasonable *overestimate* of the disruption probability, that is, with $\alpha > 0$.

These results can be extended to the cases when demand is correlated across geographic regions and/or when reliable facilities have limited capacity. Observations 1 and 2 continue to hold in these settings, although the difference in cost between under- and overestimation diminishes somewhat. This is because both correlated demand and limited capacity lead to a requirement of a larger number of reliable facilities to mini-mize the expected total cost.

# 5.4  SUPPLY CHAIN DESIGN AND CONTAINMENT TO REDUCE FRAGILITY

Supply chain *fragility* is a measure of the impact of a disruption on supply chain perfor-mance. Fragility measures the difference in operating costs and sales for a network with and without disruption. In case of disruption, operating costs may go up and sales may go down so networks with high fragility can have a large drop in profits as a result. For example, while the use of a single supply source at a Phillips plant in Albuquerque, New Mexico, allowed Ericsson to reduce its costs and deal effectively with recurrent demand risk, it also increased supply chain fragility. When the Phillips plant ceased production because of a fire, Ericsson reportedly lost $400 million in revenue in the first quarter of 2000 alone. In contrast, Nokia had alternate supply sources that it brought online quickly, thus limiting the impact of the disruption. The high fragility of its supply chain significantly hurt Ericsson. The lower fragility of the Nokia network allowed it to deal more effectively with a disruption.

The design of oil tankers provides one of the earliest examples of fragility consider-ations. The first oil tankers were built by Branobel, a company founded by two brothers of Alfred Nobel;[2] these tankers stored their cargo in two iron tanks linked together by pipes. Having large storage tanks caused stability problems and the oil sloshing from side to side caused ships to capsize. The solution was to build many smaller holds rather than one or two large holds for the oil. The new design was more expensive to build but eliminated the stability problem by reducing the impact of sloshing oil, which was the source of the fragility in the previous design.

Having a single supply source or storing inventory in a single centralized facility can be compared to an oil tanker with a single large cargo hold. Such a design is cheaper but is more fragile and is more vulnerable to disruption. The design with multiple holds "contains" the impact of sloshing oil to a smaller hold, ensuring that the ship as a whole stays stable. Lim et al. (2010) show that for most types of disruption, some degree of *con-tainment* is effective in lowering fragility when designing supply chain networks.

Supply chains often deal with recurrent risks by "pooling" through the use of central-ized inventory or common parts. More pooling lowers the supply chain cost incurred to mitigate recurrent risks. The marginal benefit of pooling recurrent risks, however, falls as they are pooled to a greater extent, as shown in Figure 5.4. Thus, for example, when an auto manufacturer has no common parts across different models of cars, building some degree of commonality has significant benefits. Increasing commonality, however, provides diminishing benefits. In other words, while the total benefit of pooling may be increasing, the marginal benefit is decreasing.

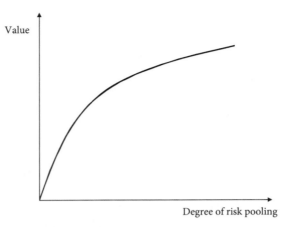

**FIGURE 5.4:** Value from Pooling Reserves

The observation on the marginal benefit of pooling above is also significant because more extensive pooling or coverage makes the supply chain more vulnerable to disruption risk. The fragility of a network measures the impact that a disruption has on its performance. For example, while the use of common parts (produced by a single supplier) across many models at Toyota increased the amount of pooling provided by the common part and the common supplier, it increased the fragility of the network to quality disruptions. The disruption ended up costing Toyota billions of dollars in lost sales and increased costs.

It is thus important to design networks that are effective in dealing with recurrent risks (e.g., by pooling inventory or some other resource) but at the same time not to make the supply chain vulnerable to disruptions. A *containment* strategy seeks to limit the impact of a disruption to only a section of the supply chain. Having more than one supply source can be viewed as a form of containment that would have been very helpful for Ericsson in the example cited above. Containment in this case would have required Ericsson to develop alternate supply sources so that the impact of one supply plant being disrupted is "contained" to only some plants or some product lines that source from this particular supply plant. Likewise, a containment strategy at Toyota would have resulted in the automaker having multiple supply sources for common parts or limiting the extent of commonality. In either case, the impact of a recall would be controlled and losses reduced.

We can examine containment using a stylized model where the underlying supply chain network is a *chain* as presented by Jordan and Graves (1995). Such a chain has the same number of supply and demand nodes, each supply node supplying two demand points and each demand node sourcing from two supply nodes; all of the nodes together thus form a ring. Fragility of this or any other network can be measured in terms of the increase in sales lost as the result of a disruption. Lim et al. (2010) have considered both link and node failures in a network of this type. From their results on the impact of the size of a chain on its fragility vis-à-vis random disruption, we have:

Observation 3: *When there is a single link failure, the fragility of a chain* increases *as the size of the chain increases. In other words, longer chains are* more *fragile in the face of a single link failure.*

Observation 4: *When there is a single node failure, the fragility of a chain* decreases *as the chain increases. In other words, longer chains are* less *fragile when facing a single node failure.*

These two results indicate that when a supply chain network faces a single link failure, containment (limiting the size of a chain) is an effective strategy. When facing a single node failure, however, containment by itself is not effective.

Given these contradictory indicators, Lim et al. (2010) also study the impact of simultaneous multiple failures on both nodes and links on supply chain fragility using simulation. From their findings, we have:

Observation 5: *When a supply chain network is subject to multiple node and link failures, fragility generally increases with the size of the chain. In other words, smaller (shorter) chains are less fragile when subject to multiple node and link failures.*

This implies that, rather than fully integrating a supply chain (either through completely common parts or a single supplier), it is better to design supply chains with limited integration so that the *chain* is smaller in size.

Observations 3 through 5 together indicate that when facing the possibility of disruption, containment—whether by redundancy of nodes or links, or by keeping the supply chain short—may be the best overall approach for designing supply chains to limit the impact of disruption.

# 5.5 Supply Chain Design by Tailoring Reserves

Supply chain risks can be countered by building reserves, such as inventory, redundant supply sources and flexibility in production or delivery (Chopra and Sodhi 2004). But how much reserve should we use? That depends on the specific situation, but general guidelines can be developed for "tailoring" the extent of reserves.

Just as an insurance company holds cash reserves to pay claims, top manufacturers maintain supply-chain reserves that include excess inventory, excess capacity, and redundant suppliers. The big challenge for supply chain designers is to mitigate risk by smart positioning and sizing of supply-chain reserves without compromising profitability. So while stockpiling inventory may shield a company against delivery delays by suppliers, building reserves willy-nilly also drives up costs and reduces profit. The managers' role here is akin to a stock portfolio manager: achieve the largest achievable profits for varying levels of supply-chain risk and do so cost-effectively by operating on an "efficient frontier" (Chopra and Sodhi 2004). This means that the manager must seek additional profits for any level of risk protection and preparedness, or increase prevention

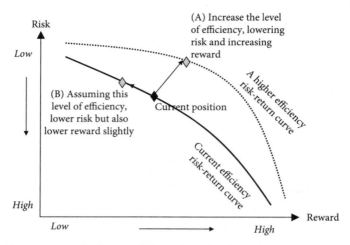

**FIGURE 5.5:** Choosing supply-chain risk/reward trade-offs — Choice (A) entails moving to a higher level of efficiency (with a better trade-off), reducing risk while increasing rewards. Choice (B) entails remaining at the current level of efficiency (same trade-off) and therefore reducing risk, which also consequently means reducing the reward. Source: Chopra and Sodhi (2004)

and preparedness without reducing profits. Figure 5.5 shows the efficient frontier as the solid line—any point below this curve is "inefficient" and the manager can certainly do better. Success at this task requires a good understanding of supply chain risks and remedies, both in general and tailored to the context of the manager's own company. Even greater success can come from pushing out the efficient frontier itself by a different supply chain design or policy. Figure 5.5 shows how from a current point on the efficient frontier, the manager may seek to go to Choice A on another efficient frontier that offers better trade-offs, or moving to a different Choice B that is on the same efficient frontier.

Just as a generic portfolio strategy needs to be tailored for any given portfolio, we need to tailor the portfolio of reserves for any given company's supply chain risk. There are four aspects to a company's situation that are useful to understand tailoring:

- Cost of the "reserve"
- Impact of centralizing versus decentralizing the reserve in question
- The level of risk (high or low), and
- High-volume stable demand (low risk) versus low-volume uncertain demand (high risk).

Given these four aspects, three key relationships influence how much of the reserve to use in a particular context:

(1) Using inventory to cover a high level of demand risk costs proportionately more than covering a low level of risk.

(2) Pooling forecast risk (stemming from the forecast error), receivables risk, or some other risk reduces the amount of reserve required for a given level of risk coverage. For example, the level of inventory required to ensure a given fill (replenishment) rate decreases when the demand forecasts at different locations are pooled.

(3) The benefit of pooling grows with the level of risk covered: the benefit of pooling inventory is large if the product has high forecast or inventory risk.

Therefore, as shown in Figure 5.6, managers need to keep in mind that: (a) Covering a high level of demand risk using inventory is proportionally much more expensive than covering a low level of risk in that way, (b) The required level of inventory needed to mitigate forecast risk falls as this risk is pooled (say, by combining the forecasts of a number of facilities with a single inventory pool), and (c) The benefit of pooling inventory is large only if the product has high forecast or inventory risk.

Managers can balance these relationships to tailor their response to risk with a surer grasp of the size and type of reserve, along with rules of thumb to tailor risk-mitigation strategies. First, when the cost of building a reserve is low, reserves should be decentralized so that decentralized backups would enable a local entity to respond faster to risk incidents. Second, when the cost of the reserve is high, reserves should be pooled to

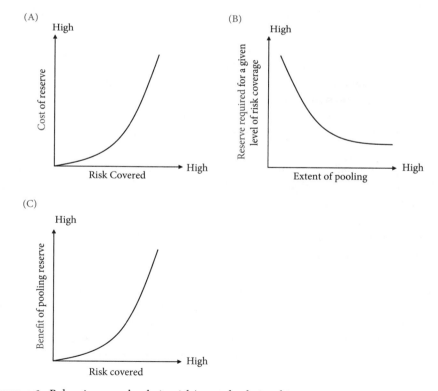

FIGURE 5.6: Balancing supply-chain risk/reward relationships.

Source: Chopra and Sodhi (2004)

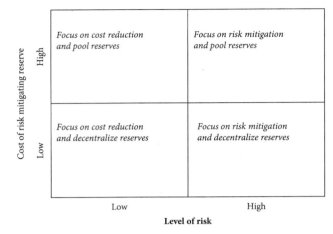

**FIGURE 5.7:** Rules of thumb for tailored risk management for reasoning with the level of risk and the cost of the reserve to mitigate the risk

manage supply chain risk at affordable costs. Third, if the level of risk is low, focus on reducing costs. Finally, if the risk is high, focus on risk mitigation. Figure 5.7 reflects these four rules of thumb in a two-by-two matrix summarizing the level of risk and the cost of the reserve needed to mitigate the risk.

Besides the cost of building the reserve, companies must consider product volumes. Fast-moving standard products, with low margins and low forecast risk, call for different types of reserves than slow-moving specialized products with high margins and greater forecast risk. When planning capacity, managers should select a low-cost supplier for supplying high-volume stable demand (low-risk and low-margin) items. In contrast, a more responsive supplier (even if the supplier is expensive) is better suited for supplying low-volume uncertain demand (high-risk and high-margin) items. For instance, Cisco tailors its response by manufacturing high-volume products with stable demand in specialized, inexpensive but not-so-responsive Chinese plants. Low-volume items with uncertain demand and with high margins get assembled in responsive, flexible and more expensive US plants. Sony exploits a similar strategy using flexible but high-cost plants in Japan and low-cost but specialized plants in Malaysia and China.

A specialized and decentralized approach offers the best way to maintain capacity for *high-volume* commodity items with *low forecast risk*. Doing so should produce greater responsiveness and lower transportation costs—but only if doing so adequately exploits economies of scale. In contrast, capacity for *low-volume, short life-cycle products* with *high* forecast risk should be made more flexible and centralized to pool demand. That helps explain why automakers, for example, build specialized plants in each major market for fast-moving products. But plants for high-end, slower-selling cars are centralized and more flexible.

When capacity is expensive, managers can reduce supply-chain costs by centralizing capacity to pool risk. As costs decline, capacity can be decentralized further to be more responsive to local markets. Consider the personal computer industry. PCs can be assembled to order in two different ways: One is the way Dell used to assemble with centralized capacity. The other is a model widely used in India whereby companies sell component kits to local assemblers for assembly on demand. Given the low cost of assembly capacity in India, it is economical to decentralize capacity, even though this action reduces pooling and increases the overall size of assembly capacity across the supply chain. In contrast, given the higher cost of capacity in the United States, centralizing buffer capacity is more effective.

In addition to separating products with different risk characteristics, managers must also consider separating capacity for the low-risk and high-risk aspects of each product. Utility companies use this strategy by employing low-cost, coal-fired power plants to handle predictable base demand, and utilizing responsive but high-cost gas- and oil-fired power plants to handle uncertain peak demand. Similarly, General Electric (GE) ships light bulbs by sea on a weekly basis from its plant in China to cover the predictable portion of demand. But the company also maintains an inventory of bulbs in the United States, or flies them in from China, to cope with unpredictable demand. Table 5.2 summarizes these different strategies.

## Table 5.2: Tailoring reserves for a given company's context

| General Risk Mitigation Strategy | Tailored Strategies |
| --- | --- |
| Increase capacity | Focus on low-cost, decentralized capacity for predictable demand. Build centralized capacity for unpredictable demand. Increase decentralization as cost of capacity drops. |
| Get redundant suppliers | More redundant supply for high-volume products with stable demand, less redundancy for low-volume products with uncertain demand. Centralize redundancy for low-volume products with uncertain demand in a few flexible suppliers. |
| Increase responsiveness | Favor cost over responsiveness for commodity products. Favor responsiveness over cost for short-lifecycle products. |
| Increase inventory | Decentralize inventory for low-value products with stable demand. Centralize inventory for high-value products with uncertain demand. |
| Increase flexibility | Favor cost over flexibility for predictable, high-volume products. Favor flexibility for low-volume unpredictable products. Centralize flexibility in a few locations if it is expensive. |
| Pool or aggregate demand | Increase aggregation as unpredictability grows. |
| Increase capability | Prefer capability over cost for high-value, high-risk products. Favor cost over capability for low-value commodity products. Centralize high capability in flexible source if possible. |

# 5.6 Supply Chain Design for Effective Response to Disruptions

Responding to risks has not received much attention in the supply chain, risk-management literature thus far, although Sodhi and Tang (2009, 2012) have presented a three-stage model of response time: detecting, designing a solution, and deploying the solution to reduce response time and thus recovery time.

Consider the following two examples: First, immediately after the 9/11 attacks, Chrysler was the first automaker to request its logistics providers to switch the mode of transportation from air to ground. Speedy deployment of this strategy enabled Chrysler to get the parts from suppliers, such as TRW, via ground. Ford was unable to deploy the same strategy because, by the time Ford decided to switch to ground shipping, all ground transportation capacity had been taken up. Facing parts delivery problems, Ford had to shut down five of its US plants for weeks and reduce production volumes by 13% in the fourth quarter of 2001.

Second, in the Ericsson example we mentioned earlier from March 2000, both Ericsson and Nokia were facing the same supply shortage of a critical cellular phone component (radio frequency chips) after a key supplier, Phillips Electronics, shut down its semiconductor plant in New Mexico. Nokia recovered quickly by doing the following. First, Nokia immediately sent an executive team to visit Phillips in New Mexico so as to assess the situation. Second, Nokia reconfigured the design of its basic phones so that the modified phones could accept (slightly different) chips from other Phillips plants; and, third, Nokia asked Phillips to produce these alternative chips immediately at other locations. Consequently, Nokia satisfied customer demand smoothly and obtained a stronger market position mainly due to the speedy deployment of its recovery plan. In contrast, Ericsson was unable to deploy a similar strategy later because Nokia and other existing customers had taken up all of Phillips's production capacity at other plants.

Therefore, any organization must develop adaptive capabilities for quick responses to risk incidents; that is, reduce *response time*. This response time comprises: (1) the time to detect a risk incident ($D1$), (2) the time to design one or more solutions as well as selecting one solution in response to the incident ($D2$), and (3) the time to deploy the solution ($D3$). Companies can reduce the impact of supply chain risk incidents by shortening these three elements of time and, hence, the total response time ($R1 = D1 + D2 + D3$). After deployment, the time it takes to restore operations is the *recovery time*.

The three "D" components of time can be illustrated by using the failed relief efforts associated with Hurricane Katrina. Despite live TV coverage of Katrina's aftermath in late August 2005, it took three days for FEMA director Michael Brown to learn of 3000 evacuees stranded at New Orleans' Convention Center. In our terminology, the detection lead-time $D1 =$ three days. Communication and coordination between FEMA and local authorities reportedly were poor: it took days to sort out who should do what, when, and how. For example, it took two days for Louisiana Governor Blanco to decide on the use of school buses to remove the stranded evacuees, so the design time D2 then was two days. However, most school buses were marooned in the flooded parking lots. FEMA requested over 1000 buses to help out but only a dozen or so arrived the day after; hence, the deploy lead time D3 was quite long. As a result, New Orleans had not fully recovered even after six years, with displaced people continuing to live in temporary accommodations; the recovery time R2 thus exceeds six years. The Katrina fiasco suggests that one can reduce the impact—number of deaths, costs, and recovery time R2—associated with a disruption by reducing the total response lead time D1 + D2 + D3.

There are various ways of shortening the following time elements:

1 Detection time (D1) can be reduced by developing mechanisms to discover a risk incident quickly when it occurs or even to predict it before it occurs. Companies must also identify ways to share the information with their supply-chain partners. Monitoring and advance warning systems can enable firms to reduce detection time. For instance, many firms have various IT systems for monitoring material flows (delivery and sales) and information flows (demand forecasts, production schedule, inventory level, quality) along the supply chain on a regular basis. For example, Nike has a "virtual radar screen" for monitoring its supply chain operations; Nokia monitors the delivery schedules of suppliers; and Seven-Eleven Japan monitors the production/delivery schedules of its vendors (suppliers) as well as point of sales data from different stores throughout the day. Such monitoring systems typically use various types of control charts to oversee operations and to issue alerts should any anomaly occur. Advance warning systems, by contrast, are intended to detect an undesirable event before it actually occurs, thus reducing detection time to a minimum. For example, smart alert systems enable GE to conduct remote sensing and diagnostics so that it can deploy engineers to service turbines before catastrophic failures occur.

2 Design time (D2) can be reduced if a company and its partners can develop contingent recovery plans for different types of disruptions in advance. Many organizations seek to do so through business continuity efforts. For example, Li & Fung has a variety of different contingent supply plans to enable it to switch from one supplier in one country to another supplier in a different country. Seven-Eleven Japan has developed contingency delivery plans to enable switching from one transportation mode (trucks) to another (motorcycles), depending on traffic conditions. A company may find it useful to use decision analysis tools, such as decision trees, to refine and select a recovery plan.

3 Once a recovery plan has been selected, deployment time (D3) can be shortened by improving communication and coordination between supply chain entities within the company or among supply chain partners. Van Wassenhove (2006) has suggested three forms of coordination: (1) by command (central coordination), (2) by consensus (information sharing), and (3) by default (routine communication). In the event of a major disruption, coordination by

command seems to be more appropriate during the design phase of a recovery plan and its deployment. Once the recovery plan is in place, coordination by consensus would seem appropriate, especially when each party has a clear role and responsibility has been assigned in advance.

In addition to good design of response procedures, good placement of reserves is necessary to reduce each of the three time elements.

## 5.7  SUMMARY AND CONCLUSION

We have discussed four different aspects of supply chain design to manage disruptive risks. First we looked at the problem of misestimating the likelihood of a disruption and found that while small errors do not matter, there is a large asymmetry in that underestimating the likelihood can result in much higher expected cost than overestimating the likelihood by the same amount. Second, we looked at containing the supply chain so that the impact of a disruptive incident can be limited to a section of it. Through analytical and simulated results, our conclusion was that, overall, it makes sense to contain the supply chain by using such reserves as inventory, redundant suppliers, and redundant capacity. Third, we looked into general guidelines for how much reserve to use in a particular situation and described general principles for tailoring. Finally, following Sodhi and Tang (2009), we described actual response to disruptions as comprising detection of the incident, designing a response, and deploying it. Supply chain design must ensure that the times for these are as short as possible so the impact can be contained in time.

With respect to the future, one research topic is to investigate how companies assess supply chain risk, given what we noted the impact of misestimating disruption probability. A related question is how they *should* assess supply chain risk, given that much of the necessary information is hard to come by and the different entities along the supply chain may not be willing to disclose private information. Just as we discussed fragility, we need more research on practical measures of *robustness* at an operational level in different parts of the supply chain and along the supply chain overall. While many *stylized* models now exist, we also need to look at *practical* models of supply chains in different sectors to see how different containment strategies can be tailored for different circumstances. This will require the development of practical procedures for measuring the impact of avoiding a disruption on the additional costs of the containment strategy as well as the potential benefits of the strategy. Finally, future research should also focus on expanding the framework for supply-chain analyses. In Sodhi and Tang (2012, chap. 17), several such areas for attention are examined: multicase studies, behavioral research, event studies, and scenario planning.

Designing and redesigning supply chains is ever more important in today's world as supply chains become more global in scope and character. We hope that this chapter helps further the theory and practice of managing supply-chain disruptions.

## NOTES

1. Sunil Chopra is IBM Distinguished Professor of Operations Management at the Kellogg School of Management, Northwestern University. ManMohan S. Sodhi is Professor in Operations & Supply Chain Management at Cass Business School and Executive Director of the Munjal Global Manufacturing Institute at the Indian School of Business.
2. See, for instance, Wikipedia, accessed July 27, 2011, http://en.wikipedia.org/wiki/Oil_tanker#cite_ref-hub05_15-0.

## REFERENCES

Chopra, S., and M. S. Sodhi. 2004. "Managing Risk to Avoid Supply Chain Breakdown." *Sloan Management Review* 46:53–61.

Eskew, M. 2004. "Mitigating Supply Chain Risk." *CEO* (April): 25–26.

Jordan, W. C., and S. C. Graves. 1995. "Principles on the Benefits of Manufacturing Process Flexibility." *Management Science* 41 (4): 577–94.

Lim, M., A. Bassamboo, S. Chopra, and M. S. Daskin. 2010. "Flexibility and Fragility: Use of Chaining Strategies in the Presence of Disruption Risks." Working Paper, Northwestern University.

Lim, M., M. S. Daskin, A. Bassamboo, S. Chopra. 2012. "Facility Location Decisions in Supply Chain Networks with Random Disruptions and Imperfect Information." *Manufacturing & Service Operations Management* (forthcoming).

Poirier, C. and F. Quinn. 2003.*Calibration Supply Chain Management.* El Segundo, CA: Computer Sciences Corporation Report.

Rice, B., and F. Caniato. 2003. "Building a Secure and Resilient Supply-Chain." *Supply Chain Management Review* 7 (5): 22–30.

Sodhi, M. S., and C. S. Tang. 2009. "Time-Based Disruption Management: A Framework for Managing Supply Chain Disruption." In *Managing Supply Chain Risk and Vulnerability: Tools and Methods for Supply Chain Decision Makers,* edited by J. Blackhurst and T. Wu, 29–40. New York: Springer.

———. 2012. *Managing Supply Chain Risk.* New York: Springer.

Taleb, N. 2007. *The Black Swan: The Impact of the Highly Improbable.* New York: Random House.

Tomlin, B. 2006. "On the Value of Mitigation and Contingency Strategies for Managing Supply Chain Disruption Risk." *Management Science* 52:639–57.

Van Wassenhove, L. 2006. "Humanitarian Aid Logistics: Supply Chain Management in High Gear." *Journal of the Operational Research Society* 57:475–89.

World Economic Forum. 2008. *Global Risks 2008: A Global Risk Network Report.* Geneva, Switzerland: January.

Zsidisin, G., L. M. Ellram, J. R. Cater, and J. L. Cavinato. 2004. "An Analysis of Supply Risk Assessment Techniques." *International Journal of Physical Distribution & Logistics Management* 34 (5): 397–413.

Zsidisin G., A. Panelli, and R. Upton. 2000. "Purchasing Organization Involvement in Risk Assessments, Contingency Plans, and Risk Management: An Exploratory Study." *Supply Chain Management: An International Journal* 5 (4): 187–97.

# CHAPTER 6

·······································································································

# COMBINATORIAL AUCTIONS

·······································································································

DAVID PORTER, STEPHEN J. RASSENTI
*WITH* DAVID R. MUNRO

## 6.1 INTRODUCTION

·······································································································

AN important task for any business manager is to select appropriate mechanisms for allocating resources efficiently. Such mechanisms can be used to allocate inputs in order to
efficiently produce goods and services as well as outputs in order to satisfy consumers in
profit-maximizing ways. Solving resource allocation problems is often a nontrivial task
because it involves the aggregation of decentralized information, myriad substitution possibilities, and competing interests within a business organization. In order to introduce
the characteristics of the resource allocation problems that we will focus on in this chapter,
we consider the management task associated with allotting scarce productive resources to
competing business projects. Some examples of these limited resources include machine
time, software licensing time, meeting rooms, and organizational budgets, to name but
a few. Typically these resource allocation problems are solved in a bureaucratic fashion
through a series of internal negotiations between department heads or in one or more
argumentative committee meetings. This process can be a costly and inefficient one.

One such example of a contentious resource allocation process materialized during the
planning for NASA's Cassini mission to Saturn. Planetary missions are undertaken to collect scientific measurements in deep space. In order to take these measurements, various
telemetry instruments are proposed by instrument teams, selected, and then funded for
development at a cost of millions of dollars per fiscal year. The instruments must be integrated into a spacecraft that defines the constraints, such as mass in kilograms, energy in
watts, data transmission rates in kilobytes per second, within which the teams must work
to design their instruments. One problem encountered during the design process was
creeping resource growth, requiring more resources from NASA over time to complete
instrument and spacecraft development. Solving this problem demanded the convening
of endless meetings in which instrument teams made presentations as to the legitimacy of

their resource requests and to debate the scientific trade-offs imposed by engineering constraints. Initial meetings were followed by more meetings to present supporting data and to evaluate all alternatives. This became a very time-consuming and contentious process.

In order to arrest this costly resource growth, NASA decided to provide a predetermined portfolio of resources to the various Cassini instrument teams so that each would be forced to trade off its instrument's capabilities in order to stay within its resource portfolio. Moreover, to facilitate instrument development the Cassini project's managers also introduced a system that allowed instrument teams to trade resources among themselves in order to reconfigure their initial resource portfolios. In such an environment, trades are not so simple! Efficient trading often involves multiple teams simultaneously exchanging multiple resources. A new trading mechanism to simplify decision making in that environment was designed and tested experimentally by Ledyard et al. 1994.[1] This mechanism created a decentralized market whereby instrument teams could offer to trade bundles of instrument development resources by submitting bids and asks. In particular, a bid was a vector $b_{ij} = (x_1^{ij}, x_2^{ij}, ...., x_n^{ij})$, where i denoted the bid number, j the instrument team, and $x_k$ the amount of resource k included in the bid. If $x_k^{ij} < 0$ that amount resource k was being offered by the bid, while $x_w^{ij} > 0$ meant that that amount of resource w was being asked for in that same bid.

Experimental economists have shown that decentralized decision-making mechanisms work remarkably well for resource allocation problems. These mechanisms are typically executed in the form of an auction where participants bid for the use of resources knowing only their own private resource values. The competition amongst participants helps the resources to be allocated in an efficient manner, such that those who value them the most obtain them.[2] Certain auctions are better suited for certain kinds of economic environments. For the Cassini mission, the system devised was a combinatorial electronic barter exchange. One of the main problems with barter is the double coincidence of wants. Specifically, valuable trades often require a series of simultaneous bargains called a *chain* to be executed. In the Cassini market a computer algorithm was used to find all possible chains so that instrument teams could locate potentially valuable trades and execute them easily. This is not a simple problem because the minimum

number of computations required to find all chains with n bids is: $\sum_{k=2}^{n} \dfrac{n!(2^n-1)^k}{(n-k)!k!}$ . This

combinatorial barter mechanism certainly improved on NASA's old bureaucratic allocation process because it allowed the bidders (different instrument teams within NASA) to manage resources more effectively through the discovery of value-improving trades. It also importantly avoided protracted internal negotiations which created strong incentives to hide relevant information from other instrument teams in order to drive a hard bargain for self-gain that compromised the overall efficiency of the mission. Ledyard et al.'s 1994 combinatorial barter market facilitated the discovery of mutually satisfactory combinations of trades that helped solve a management problem.

For the remainder of this chapter, we will be examining the design of combinatorial auctions. These auctions are resource allocation processes that can be implemented when packages of multiple resources must be allocated simultaneously amongst competing uses and when information concerning the values of the various possible resource uses and the constraints affecting those uses is decentralized. The reason combinatorial auctions were first proposed was to limit the financial risk associated with unsuccessful attempts to assemble valuable packages of goods under a traditional bureaucratic process or a simple "nonpackage" auction. Suppose a 24/7 firm has decided to allocate workdays-off to employees using simultaneous online sealed bid auctions, one for each day of the month ahead. Because of complementarities between items (e.g. "I want to take off for a four-day jaunt to Vegas"), a simple "nonpackage" auction may lead a bidder to offer amounts well above his private values for individual items in the hope of winning all of the complementary items of a particular valuable package (four consecutive days off). High premiums paid for the individual items of the package (the particular days off) can be more than offset by the aggregate value of the package (four sequential days off). However, this strategy always leaves the bidder at risk of not assembling his high-valued package of items and still paying above value for whatever individual items he does acquire in his failed attempt to aggregate. This financial risk is known as the *exposure problem*.[3] Combinatorial auctions avoid this problem because the bidding message space allows bidders to express alternative values for various packaged and unpackaged items without any financial risk.

In addition to the NASA spacecraft resource example outlined above, there are many other examples of economic environments where item complementarities exist. They include, but are not limited to, transportation networks, wireless broadcast spectrums, real estate, emissions credits, energy networks, and all scheduling problems. Given the prevalence of such environments and the computational prowess with which every organization with a $2000 computer and networked communications is now endowed, we view combinatorial auctions as an essential tool for any business practitioner. In this chapter we will review the allocation problems tackled by combinatorial auctions, some of the important combinatorial auction mechanisms proposed to date, and the benefits and potential concerns with those mechanisms.

## 6.2  SET PACKING PROBLEM

Consider another real world example. The demands for landing and takeoff "slots"[4] at New York's LaGuardia Airport exceed the aircraft servicing constraint of forty-five arrivals per hour. The Port Authority of New York requires airlines to have in their possession a designated takeoff or landing slot prior to the time of use. Now imagine that congested airspace becomes a simultaneous reality at many major airports and that the slot-based regime is enforced by all airport authorities. One can easily see how a sequential auction for these slots would either a) leave bidders with the financial risk associated with the exposure problem, or b) raise much less revenue than a combinatorial auction because of bidders' attempts to avoid the risks associated with that problem.

For example, if an airline was looking to purchase the combination of a 9:00 a.m. takeoff slot from La Guardia Airport and an 11:45 a.m. landing slot at Chicago's O'Hare field what would they bid in a sequential auction for the La Guardia departure time by itself? Bidding half its value for the combination could leave the airline vulnerable to financial risk should they fail to win the 11:45 a.m. arrival time at O'Hare. Allowing for package bids in a combinatorial auction, "I'll take La Guardia 9:00 a.m. and O'Hare 11:45 a.m. or nothing," avoids this exposure problem.[5]

Without an auction mechanism in which bidders can reveal their private values for certain packages of items, a central authority would have to determine the efficient (value-maximizing) allocation of landing and takeoff slots to competing airlines across the country. This would require solving the following optimization problem with added logistical constraints:[6]

Maximize:

$Z = \Sigma_j \pi_j x_j \rightarrow$ Maximize the value of the allocated packages (of slots) (1)

Subject to:

$\Sigma_j a_{ij} x_j \leq b_i \ \forall i \rightarrow$ Maximum number of slots available (imposed by airports) (1a)
$\Sigma_j d_{kj} x_j \leq e_k \ \forall k \rightarrow$ Logical constraint on its package bids (imposed by airlines) (1b)
$x_j \in \{0,1\} \rightarrow$ Either the whole package is accepted or not

Where:

$i = 1, \ldots, N$ subscripts some particular takeoff or landing slot at some particular airport;
$j = 1, \ldots, J$ subscripts some package of slots that has value for some particular airline;
$k = 1, \ldots, K$ subscripts some particular logistical constraint imposed on a set of packages by some airline or by the optimizing center;[7]
$a_{ij} = 1$ if package j includes slot i
0 otherwise;
$b_i$ = the number of planes that can takeoff (land) in slot i at some airport;
$d_{kj} \in \{-1, 0, 1\}$ if package j appears in logistical constraint k;[8]
$e_k$ = an integer;
$\pi_j$ = the value of obtaining slot package j to the airline that seeks it.

We refer to this optimization problem as the *set-packing problem*. While this is a difficult (but manageable) integer programming problem, the critical issues are that $\pi_j$ (the value of package j to the airline that seeks it), $a_{ij}$ (whether a particular slot is included in package j), and $d_{kj}$ (whether package j is part of some logistical constraint k), and all of the parameters are *not* known to the "allocation center" but privately known to the competing airlines. That is, the center needs to solve a resource allocation problem wherein information on the coefficients in the objective function and constraints both is decentralized and unknown to a hypothetical planner. In these complex resource environments a salient auction mechanism is an extremely valuable information-gathering tool for any manager insofar as it aggregates the decentralized information and produces high efficiency and high revenue allocations.

# 6.3  COMBINATORIAL AUCTION DESIGNS

Numerous designs of combinatorial auction mechanisms have been suggested in the past three decades. In this section we will describe some of the more important of them, the real world environments for which they are best suited, and the potential concerns for business managers in their selection and use of these mechanisms.

## 6.3.1  Sealed-Bid Combinatorial Auction

A combinatorial auction was first proposed by Rassenti, Smith, and Bulfin (RSB) 1982 to solve the allocation problem of airport and landing slots outlined above. This auction was a sealed bid auction where bidders were free to submit offers for any item or package of items. In the case of the airport slot problem these package bids might consist of a set of takeoff and landing slots a particular aircraft could use on a given day. The integer-programming problem outlined in the previous section was solved to determine the optimal (revenue maximizing) allocation given the bids received. An important issue for any auction is to determine the prices each seller (airport) received for the items sold (takeoff and landing slots). Integer programs do not typically allow the dual program to find linear shadow prices for each resource that separate winning from losing bids fully.[9] The RSB design incorporated two pseudo-dual programs for the integer optimization to calculate two prices, high and low, for each slot. If the submitted bid for a package exceeded the sum of the prices for the slots in that package then that bid was definitely accepted, and if the submitted bid was less than the sum of the prices for the slots in that package, then that bid was definitely rejected. Bids in between were accepted or not depending on how well they fit with other accepted bids. This allowed price feedback between auctions, and determined appropriate payments to airports.[10]

The main concern with this sealed bid format is that it does not give any price feedback to bidders during an auction and therefore creates considerable bidding complexity for the participants.[11] For example, in an auction with just six items there are $2^6 - 1$ (or 63) possible combinations of items on which to bid. In addition to the complexity of submitting all possible bids, the cost of value elicitation is typically nontrivial and thus places considerable financial burden on the auction's participants. However, some circumstances exist when a sealed bid combinatorial auction might be appropriate. Consider an environment where there are many substitutable items among those being offered. A one-shot sealed bid combinatorial auction might be more resistant to implicitly collusive behavior on the part of competitors.[12] For example, in forestry auctions where each competitor is interested in obtaining the cutting rights to multiple tracts, some of which are close substitutes, sealed bid auctions are often favored.

## 6.3.2  Combinatorial Auctions with Package Price Feedback

An iterative auction with price feedback on individual items greatly reduces the computational burden for bidders in a combinatorial environment. Prices signal to bidders what bid they must submit in order to become the provisionally winning bidder on any item/package. Iterative price vectors guide bidders toward their most profitable items/packages, greatly reducing the computational burden associated with bidding on all combinations of items with positive value, and attempting to determine how to fit one's bid with other submitted bids to get it accepted. For example, imagine the items offered in an auction to be the working shifts (day, evening, night) on particular days (M, T, W, . . . ) that must be covered by a type of hospital employee (resident, nurse, orderly, . . . ), and a bid to be what a particular employee would be willing to pay or be paid to be assigned to a schedule of her design. Clearly schedules can interfere with each other in a very complicated way and there are many possibilities to be explored by the auction.

Banks et al. (1989) proposes an ascending combinatorial English auction, where the auction has multiple rounds of bidding. In each round bidders are given new information regarding the prices of packages of items for sale. This new information is the revenue-maximizing allocation given the bids submitted to the auction up to that point. In order to unseat a standing winning bid, a new bid must be submitted to the system that fits with other bids in a way that adds to the auctioneer's current revenue. The auction is over when there are no new bids that unseat standing winning bids. In each round this auction reports the current standing bids and the amount the standing winner is willing to pay for the package of items in that bid. However, this format does not report the individual item prices, only the prices for the combination of items in a package. This leaves it to bidders to compute how their values for items and packages fit with other bids in a way that can unseat a provisionally winning bid. For auctions with only a few items, this is a very manageable task. However, larger auction environments place a significant computational burden on bidders. Specifically, the bidders must solve the optimization problem outlined in (1) to determine what bids will combine with the other nonstanding (or queue) bids to displace current standing bids. Table 6.1 below outlines an example of the process of the combinatorial English auction:

Ledyard et al. 2002 proposed a slight variant of this combinatorial English auction to Sears Logistics Services (SLS) as a revenue improving solution to their procurement of transportation contracts. SLS is a company that specializes in supply-chain services, connecting vendors, distribution centers, retail outlets, and cross-dock facilities. Prior to the implementation of a combinatorial English auction, SLS would contract trucking services through a series of sequential bilateral negotiations. Because of the sheer number of lanes (single transportation paths, for example, from Chicago to Los Angeles) required to fulfill their transportation needs, negotiation was a time-consuming and expensive process. In addition, the providers of truckload services could not coordinate their schedules to minimize "deadheading"[13] and other inefficient

## Table 6.1: Combinatorial English Auction

| Standing Bids (Contract 1) | | | |
|---|---|---|---|
| Bidder | Item X | Item Y | Bid ($) |
| 1 | 15 | 2 | 50 |
| 4 | 1 | 10 | 75 |
| 5 | 4 | 8 | 100 |
| | 20 | 20 | 225 |
| | ↓ | | |

| Standby Queue | | | | → | Current Displacement Required | | | |
|---|---|---|---|---|---|---|---|---|
| Bidder | Item X | Item Y | Bid ($) | | Bidder | Item X | Item Y | Bid ($) |
| 8 | 5 | 4 | 40 | | 1 | 15 | 2 | 50 |
| | ↓ | | | | 4 | 1 | 10 | 75 |
| New Potential Bid | | | | | | 16 | 12 | 125 |
| Bidder | Item X | Item Y | Bid ($) | | | | | |
| 6 | 11 | 8 | 120 | | | | | |
| | ↓ | | | | | | | |

| Combined 8+6 Value | | | | → | New Standing Bids (Contract 2) | | | |
|---|---|---|---|---|---|---|---|---|
| Bidder | Item X | Item Y | Bid ($) | | Bidder | Item X | Item Y | Bid ($) |
| 8 | 5 | 4 | 40 | | 8 | 5 | 4 | 40 |
| 6 | 11 | 8 | 120 | | 6 | 11 | 8 | 120 |
| | 16 | 12 | 160 | | 5 | 4 | 8 | 100 |
| | | | | | | 20 | 20 | 260 |

Table 6.1 Caption: The system has 20 units of X and 20 units of Y available for sale. Currently bidder 1 has a bid for 15 units of X and 2 units of Y and is willing to pay $50 for that package. Bidders 4 and 5 also have standing bids for packages. The current bids exhaust the available resources. Bidder 8 submits a bid for 5 units of X and 4 units of Y for $40. This cannot displace any of the standing bids alone unless Bidder 8 raises his bid to $125. Thus, his bid is sent to the standby queue. Bidder 6 sees Bidder 8's bid and tenders a bid for 11 units of X and 8 units of Y for which he is willing to pay $120. Together Bidders 6 and 8 displace Bidders 1 and 4 since their combined bid is higher and fits within the just-released resources. The new set of bids now becomes the standing bids.

itinerary configurations. Adopting a combinatorial English auction allowed transportation providers to bid and compete for combinations of freight contracts (truckloads and lanes). The result for SLS was a significant cost savings, from $190 million to $165 million.

While the combinatorial English auction is an improvement on the RBS design because it gives bidders some guidance as to which packages are being demanded and at what prices, it still leaves bidders with a significant computational burden to determine how their bids may fit with bids placed by other auction participants.

## 6.3.3  Combinatorial Auctions with Item Price Feedback

In 1994, the Federal Communications Commission (FCC) developed the Simultaneous Ascending Auction (SAA) for the sale of wireless spectrum licenses.[14] The FCC sells wireless spectrum licenses that have defined geographic boundaries and specified bandwidths. Complementarities can exist between these licenses for reasons pertaining to economies of scale (advertising, technological infrastructure) and the value to the end-user from having access to a network without geographical gaps. The FCC was concerned with developing an auction that would be computationally manageable for the participants and computationally manageable for the auctioneer, while limiting the concerns associated with the exposure problem. After mulling several alternatives, the FCC adopted the SAA.

The SAA is not truly a combinatorial mechanism because bidders are unable to submit "all or none" package bids, but under certain environments it can function very well. It works as follows: prices on all items start at levels predetermined by the auctioneer, bidders are free to submit new (higher) bids on any item, all items remain active until the auction is complete, and when a round goes by with no new bids the auction is over. In addition, the SAA typically includes bid activity rules and bid withdrawal rules. Bid activity rules are used to ensure that bidders reveal their interest in items, and not sit on the sidelines until later in the auction when they start competing actively. The bid withdrawal rules are used to ease the burden of the exposure problem. As mentioned, the SAA does not accept bids for packages of items. Therefore, any bidder who has complementary value for a package of items needs to bid on every individual item in the hope of winning all of them, and aggregating the desired package. However, because of the complementarities between them, a bidder may bid well past his value for any one item so as to obtain an aggregate package higher value. But in this process, a bidder may fail to win all items in the desired package and be stuck paying for those he does win at prices exceeding his private value. The bid withdrawal rule is used to allow bidders to back out of failed aggregations and protect themselves from financial exposure. However, there was a potential cost to withdrawing bids. The bidder whose bid is withdrawn must pay the difference between the price at which he withdrew his bid and the final price of that item (if it is below his withdrawn bid). Laboratory experiments with this withdrawal rule revealed a trade-off in using the rule: efficiency and revenue increase, but individual losses are larger. Furthermore, the greater efficiency does not outweigh the higher prices paid so buyers' surplus falls in the presence of the withdrawal rule (Porter 1999).

In practice, the bid withdrawal rule is more frequently used strategically because it allows bidders to misrepresent their interests, drive up prices for competitors, and use retaliatory bidding to signal collusion (see Cramton and Schwartz 2000). To prevent this strategic behavior, a limit of three bid withdrawals per auction was proposed. This limits, though, the purpose of the bid withdrawal rules in the first place: to encourage bidders to pursue package aggregations without fear of financial exposure. While elegantly simple at its core, when the SAA is altered to function in environments with strong complementarities it loses that simplicity and creates the opportunity for strategic bidding behavior. Therefore, while we view it as a useful auction mechanism, careful consideration must be made regarding the strength of the complementarities between items to ensure that the SAA is well suited for the economic environment in question.[15]

In an attempt to select prices for each item to help guide bidders in a multiround combinatorial auction, Kwasnica et al. 2005 devised a set of prices, one for each item, that determine whether a bid submitted in a given round is acceptable. This auction is called the Resource Allocation Design (or RAD). It was motivated in an attempt to improve the noncombinatorial auction process used by the FCC to auction off spectrum licenses. When prices are posted for each individual item, it becomes easy for a bidder to calculate the minimum bid required for a package to be acceptable by simply summing the prices for each item in the package. Returning to (1), the task is to find a set of prices $v_i$, one for each slot i = 1,..., m, that can guide bidders and move the auction forward.[16] RAD proposed three properties that prices must satisfy if bidders were to pay them: (a) all accepted bids would receive price signals with aggregate costs totaling less than or equal to what they bid; (b) all rejected bids would receive price signals that resulted in aggregate costs totaling more than what they bid; and (c) new bids signaling a willingness to pay more than the aggregate price of the package should have a good opportunity to become provisionally winning (that is, prices ought to "guide" new bids to packages that will increase revenues). As discussed in RSB, (a) and (b) are generally impossible to solve simultaneously, so these guidelines can only be executed in an approximate manner. Because the RAD pricing mechanism is solved using a linear program instead of a mixed integer program it does not produce unambiguous price signals, since a losing bid can exceed the sum of the prices of items of that package. In addition, RAD is still faced with the computational burden of solving the optimization problem stated in (1) for each round.

In another attempt to deal with the bidding complexity associated with combinatorial auctions, Goeree and Holt 2007 propose the Hierarchical Package Bidding (HPB) auction. This auction removes computational complexity for the auctioneer by prepackaging the items on offer. For example, in a wireless auction, one could break up the "packages" into three levels, the first level would simply be the individual licenses, the second level could contain nonoverlapping geographical groupings of individual items, and the highest level could contain the global (all-license) package for a particular bandwidth. The nonoverlapping structure of this hierarchy simplifies the set packing problem outlined in (1) to a linear program since winners at any level can be compared to the sum of the winning bids at the lower level. The pricing algorithm works quite simply; at any given round the auctioneer determines the current revenue maximizing bids, and the prices for the next round are equivalent to price levels at each hierarchy plus a "tax" that would in the aggregate unseat the provisionally winning bids.

This auction mechanism was tested against a version of the SAA and the flexible package bidding combinatorial environment (MPB) in a laboratory setting with financially motivated subjects.[17] The results show that the HPB performs consistently better than both the SAA and MPB.[18] Based on these findings the FCC decided to use the

HPB auction for licensing the 700MHz spectrum. One would expect the HPB mechanism to perform best in environments where the prepackaged items correspond to the highest induced package values of the laboratory subjects.[19] While cases exist wherein the auctioneer can prepackage items reliably, and thus profit from the simplicity and effectiveness of the HPB, not all economic environments are conducive to the use of this mechanism because of the diversity and complexity of the desired item aggregations.[20] This is a useful auction for a practitioner to have in her tool kit, but again, a careful understanding of the economic environment is crucial before it should be put into practice.

In a unique environment, Ishikida et al. 2001 develop an auction mechanism for a two-sided combinatorial market, where participants are involved in both the bid and ask sides of the market. This mechanism is known as the Two-Sided Combinatorial Auction (TSC) and was designed as a market mechanism to enable efficient trading of pollution credits in Southern California's South Coast Air Quality Management District. The Regional Clean Air Incentives Market Program (RECLAIM) works by establishing property rights for emissions of industrial polluters in the Los Angeles area. Once these rights were established, participants were free to trade these emission credits using the RECLAIM market. To begin, factories were assigned an emission allowance for nitrogen oxide (NO) and sulfur dioxide ($SO_2$) based on their past three years' of emissions. These emission allowances were gradually reduced each year, 8.3% per year for NO and 6.8% per year for $SO_2$, between 1994 and 2003. Complementarities arise in this environment because most manufacturers produce both types of emissions in the course of their production runs; an unbundled emission credit for $SO_2$ only thus is of very little value. In addition, a firm contemplating investing in pollution abatement equipment must determine the trade-off between the investment cost of and the value of the emission credits it could sell in the market to cover that cost. The auction proceeded in rounds in which participants submitted bids and offers on packages of pollution credits. At the end of a round, an algorithm was run that would maximize the total surplus for exchanges based on the submitted bids and offers. Then, a set of prices for each pollutant and year was derived so that at these prices the surplus-maximizing trades would voluntarily be consummated and no deficits occurred. The trades for that round then became the standing orders for the next round that could be displaced.

There are two important deficiencies with iterative auctions where participants are allowed select a bid $\pi_j$ for package j. The first is the fact that they do not know what bids to submit in order not to overshoot the competitive prices. McCabe et al. 1988 found jump bidding behavior in their testing of English auctions for multiple units. This led them to the conclusion that allowing bidders to announce bid prices from the floor is not a good design feature in multiple unit auction environments as it can lead impatient bidders to overshoot competitive prices or aggressive bidders to deliver implicit signals to competitors.

The second deficiency is that bidders can use this freedom to select a bid as a signaling technique to enable buyer collusion. This is accomplished by submitting a bid with a trailing sequence of digits that delivers some information to other bidders. Cramton and Schwartz 1999 highlight evidence from FCC wireless spectrum auctions where large bids (which one would expect to end in zeros) included such information.[21]

## 6.3.4 Combinatorial Auctions with Clock Prices

To help mitigate these issues, Porter, Rassenti, Roopnarine, and Smith (PRRS) 2003 extend the notion of a clock auction to a combinatorial environment (this process is referred to as the Combinatorial Clock Auction, CCA). Using clocks to move the price upward in an automated fashion on items with excess demand reduces the bid message space, and thus prevents bid overshooting and bid signaling, and leaves bidders with a much simpler bidding task. Specifically, returning to the maximization in (1), there is a posted price $^t v_i$ for each item $i = 1, \ldots, m$ in each round $t = 1, 2, \ldots$. During each round, participants must choose the packages/items on which they wish to bid, given the posted prices in that round. The auction proceeds as follows:

i Calculate the current excess demand $^t q_i$ for each item $i$[22]
ii If $^t q_i > b_i$, set $^{t+1} v_i \leftarrow {}^t v_i + {}^t \varepsilon_I$; otherwise, set $^{t+1} v_i \leftarrow {}^t v_{i\backslash}$

In other words, the clock price for an item i ticks up by $^t \varepsilon_I$ in round $t + 1$ if total demand ($^t q_i$) for that item is larger than supply ($b_i$). The price increment $^t \varepsilon_i$ that is selected by the auctioneer can be different for different items, and can change during the auction. The magnitude of the price increment can affect the auction's performance. A small increment typically will lead to a more efficient allocation of items because allocation possibilities will be more thoroughly explored, but smaller increments lead to more auction rounds and an appropriate balance must be found between auction time and auction efficiency.

As the rounds proceed and clock prices tick upward, a bidder can observe the new clock prices and submit any new vector of package/item bids and constraints along with stating which of his bids from previous rounds he wishes to keep active in the system. This process continues until a round where there is not explicit excess demand for any item being offered ($^r q_i <= b_i \; \forall \; i$), and the auction enters the closeout phase.

If in round r the explicit demand at the current clock prices exactly equals the supply of all resources, then the auction has drawn to a successful conclusion and all items are awarded at current clock prices without the need to solve (1). If, however, at least one item is undersubscribed at the final prices (quantity demanded is less than quantity supplied) then a winner-determining maximization algorithm must be run to find the revenue maximizing allocation. If the solution to this maximization problem does not include all standing bids at the final auction prices, then there exists implicit competition for certain items. The prices for all items that have implicit competition are raised, a new round of bids is solicited, and the winner-determining algorithm is run again. This process continues until there is no implicit competition for any item at the final clock prices. Thus, the final allocation always includes all standing bids at the final clock

## Table 6.2: Combinatorial Clock Calculations

| Round | Item Prices | | | Package Bids Submitted | | | Aggregate Item Demand | | |
|---|---|---|---|---|---|---|---|---|---|
| | A | B | C | {AB} | {BC} | {A} | A | B | C |
| 1 | 100 | 100 | 100 | √ | √ | √ | 2 | 2 | 1 |
| 2 | 120 | 120 | 100 | √ | | √ | 2 | 1 | 0 |
| 3 | 140 | 120 | 100 | √ | | | 1 | 1 | 0 |
| 4 | 160 | 140 | 100 | | | | 0 | 0 | 0 |

prices, but also may include bids placed in previous rounds to allocate items undersubscribed at the final prices.

For example, suppose that there are three single items for sale (A, B, and C) and three bidders: the first wants to win only package AB, the second only package BC, and the third only wants item A. Suppose the bidding proceeds as in Table 6.2.

Notice that in round 3 there is only one standing bid remaining, {AB}, at a total price of 260, but because there are previous bids, {BC} at 200 from round 1 and {A} at 120 from round 2, that can be combined for generating more revenue to displace the standing {AB} bid, the auctioneer raises the prices on items A and B because of the implicit competition. In this example, the prices of A and B in round 4 are raised, causing the first bidder to stop bidding on {AB}, and in the next round {BC} and {A} are declared the winners.

In the CCA auction the cognitive costs of bidding are low relative to the ones outlined for previous mechanisms; bidders need only to know their private values for packages and do not need to estimate what it might take for a package bid to be acceptable. Also, like the other forms of iterative auctions mentioned above, bidders need not bid on all packages in early rounds of the auction, and can let prices guide them toward their most profitable packages.

Generally, experiments with CCA have found it to be an efficient and computationally manageable auction in relatively small test environments with various ranges of complementary item values; however, the robustness of the CCA has been questioned. Specifically, the optimization in (1) can create unacceptably long computation times in larger environments.[23] Second, the fact that the CCA allows bidders to employ a "wait and see" approach to bidding can result in efficiency losses. This latter matter will be discussed in further detail below.

Recent testing of CCAs by Kagel et al. 2010 and Scheffel et al. 2012 find two important characteristics: bidders tend to bid on a small subset of available packages, and because of this behavior, certain environments produce low efficiency allocations.[24] As mentioned above, the use of iterative auctions allows bidders not to submit all profitable bids early in the auction, and instead let prices guide them toward their best package.[25] This myopic bidding strategy wherein bidders observe the vector of prices in each round and pursue only their most profitable bid limits the information (bids) the auctioneer has available when solving for the optimal allocation. But more importantly, a bidder using this strategy ("only bid on your best package") may find herself blocked by high item prices from delivering a bid on other lower-valued packages when her high valuation packages become overpriced.

If an auction has a unique efficient goods assignment, there exist unique efficiency relevant bids for packages/items. Specifically, an auction that is efficient is one where the sum of the private values for the winners of the items available is the highest possible sum given the private values of *all* auction participants. If an auction allocates items such that the sum of private values for the winners of an auction is not the maximum, the result is subefficient, and the auction mechanism is lacking in its ability to elicit relevant bids. The myopic bidding behavior found in Kagel et al. 2010 and Scheffel et al. 2012 can result in numerous packages receiving no bids throughout the course of an auction. This suggests that in some circumstances the CCA mechanism can struggle to elicit efficiency relevant bidding, and the corresponding efficient allocation.

## 6.3.5  Descending Clock Prices

To reduce the computational burden and resolve the efficiency problems created by myopic bidding, Munro and Rassenti 2011 (MR) propose a Descending Price Combinatorial Auction (DPCA). Intuitively, descending prices reduce the computational burden because the objective function in the allocation optimization, (1), will be simpler as only the most competitive bids are submitted. Conversely, with ascending prices, nearly all bidders will be able to submit bids for packages/items at lower prices, and depending on what mechanism rules are being used, most if not all of those bids need to be included in the objective function for winner determination optimization. In addition, bidders employing a myopic bidding strategy are never blocked from submitting bids on lower-valued items because prices are descending. This feature allows bidders to see the item prices that stop at high levels, and enables them to refocus their bidding efforts on packages/items that still have prices falling.

The DPCA works as follows:

1. Prices start at predetermined levels above the expected selling prices.
2. Prices begin to decrement uniformly until a bid is submitted in some round.
3. Once a bid (or multiple) bids are submitted in a round, the revenue maximizing optimization in (1) is run to see if a market clearing condition exists in which all items are sold.
4. If a market clearing condition exists (all items are sold), the auction is over; otherwise "dummy" bids for all single items available in the auction are added

to the objective function in (1) at each item's next lower price level, and the optimization is solved again.[26]

5. Prices for all dummy bids that are included in the revenue maximizing allocation in step 4 are the only ones actually lowered for the next round.

6. Steps 4 and 5 continue until a market clearing condition exists.

In the testing of the DPCA against the CCA using simulations, MR find meaningful improvements both in average efficiency and the number of auctions reaching 100% efficiency in the face of myopic bidding. Specifically, all eight environments simulated with deterministic bidding agents showed statistically significant ($p < 0.01$) improvements in efficiency for the DPCA. As a robustness check, MR also test the CCA with deterministic bidding agents against the DPCA with errors incorporated into the bids of programmed agents and found that the DPCA produced statistically significant ($p < 0.05$) improvements in efficiency in seven out of eight environments. In addition, the average computational time required to complete an auction was reduced considerably when using the DPCA. As one might expect, auctions with myopic bidding agents produce little difference in computational times between the CCA and DPCA. However, with fully revealing bidding agents, the difference in computation time becomes stark. In environments with the fewest participants (three bidders), the CCA computational time goes from a minimum of 0.156 seconds for a four-item auction to a maximum of 90.38 seconds for a twelve-item auction, an increase by a factor of 580. In the same environment, on the other hand, the DPCA goes from a minimum of 0.055 seconds for the four-item auction to a maximum of 0.818 seconds in the twelve-item auction, a fifteen-fold increase. With six participating bidders, computation time in the CCA ranges from a minimum of 0.304 seconds for the four-item auction to a maximum of 571.55 seconds for the twelve-item auction, an increase by a factor of 1880. In the same setting, computational time for the DPCA increases twenty-three-fold, from a minimum of 0.067 seconds when four items are auctioned to a maximum of 1.526 seconds for twelve items. Of course, only some of the computational times reported above pose much concern to an auctioneer, but the results indicate that the time required for computations grows exponentially in the CCA with the number of participants and the number of items being auctioned. In, for example, FCC wireless auctions, having hundreds of bidders and thousands of licenses on offer, computation time in a combinatorial auction might become an extremely important consideration.

In addition to improvements in efficiency and computation time, the DPCA shares desirable features with other multi-unit descending auctions. These include the inability to collude through bid signals, and the inability to use retaliatory bidding tactics. Both are what Brown et al. 2009 highlight as the important reasons why tacit collusion breaks down, or fails to develop in multiunit descending auctions. Because of the desirable features of the DPCA we view it as a improvement over the CCA, and recommend its use for environments with strong item complementarities, decentralized package information, and a large number of items, all of which lead to computational complexity for both the bidder and the auctioneer.

# 6.4 CONCLUSION

Managers are constantly faced with resource allocation problems where the trade-off information about choices is held by decentralized agents. One basic method for obtaining such trade-off information is through the use of auctions that solicit the values from those agents. However, when the choices to be made are affected by strong complementarities and logistic constraints, the design of the auction becomes crucial. In particular, the financial exposure associated with nonpackage auctions is significant enough that business practitioners aiming to maximize efficiency and output need to design it away. There has been a wealth of work completed on the topic of combinatorial auctions over the past three decades: there are many resource allocation problems for which resource complementarities and logistic problems exist. A few examples discussed in this chapter include payload resources on NASA spacecrafts, personnel scheduling, landing and takeoff slots at congested airports, transportation networks, wireless spectrum networks, and pollution credit markets. This short list of examples illustrates the potential diversity of economic environments where a combinatorial auction may be the allocation method of choice. However, the diverse nature of these environments gives rise to varying constraints and incentives in each case that require detailed engineering of the most suitable combinatorial auction. This chapter has outlined what we view as some of the most important combinatorial auction mechanisms for business practitioners to have in their tool kit.

The progression of combinatorial auction designs outlined above highlights some of the main concerns with these mechanisms: manageable bidding processes with salient price feedback, resistance to collusion, computational efficiency, allocative efficiency, and revenue maximization. When well designed and implemented in the appropriate economic environment, the results are marked. Sears Logistic Services implemented a combinatorial English auction to replace bilateral negotiations used in the procurement of transportation contracts. Its change to a decentralized allocation mechanism resulted in a savings of $25 million. In the field of emissions trading the independent Automated Credit Exchange in southern California utilized a two-sided combinatorial market to trade millions of dollars worth of pollution credit portfolios in the RECLAIM market. Since 1999 the Chilean government has been conducting sealed bid combinatorial auctions for the procurement of meals for school children in the various territorial units of the country, with over $3 billion in multi-territory contracts awarded to meal providers since then.[27] In an even more valuable market, the Federal Communications Commission has utilized several combinatorial auction institutions in the sale of rights to the wireless spectrum. These institutions include the Simultaneous Ascending Auction, variants of Combinatorial Clock Auction, and the Hierarchical Package Bidding auction. Over the past few decades the use of these auctions has resulted in revenues in the billions of dollars for the FCC.

While combinatorial auctions can be notionally complex, we encourage business managers not to be intimidated by them. Technology that was practically impossible to implement a decade ago is now within the grasp of every firm that must bring decentralized information to bear in order to effectively allocate scarce resources. This chapter is an introduction to the wealth of information currently available on combinatorial auctions. Where needed, there are countless additional sources that can provide further insight in the operation, attributes, and concerns surrounding these mechanisms. Once the incentives and constraints governing the use of resources in a business environment are appropriately understood, implementation of a combinatorial auction can often improve business efficiency and revenues, an ever-growing requirement of successful business management in a globally competitive economy.

## Notes

1. For more detail on this market, see Wessen and Porter 1997.
2. Efficiency is a common way of evaluating the desirability of a resource allocation. It can be measured precisely in experiments where participants' values for various resources are induced by cash payoffs from the experimenter.
3. See Bykowsky et al. 2000 for more on financial exposure in noncombinatorial auctions.
4. A takeoff/landing slot is usually thought of as a fifteen-minute interval during which a maximum number of airplanes can safely take off and/or land.
5. As in the NASA example above, a takeoff or landing slot alone is not of much value to an airline interested in combinations (packages) of slots to optimize their own flight resources. Furthermore, a particular aircraft is most efficiently used when it cycles through a series of takeoffs and landings in a given day or set of days. If slots were not allowed to be sold in useful combinations but had to be procured piecemeal (slot by slot and airport by airport), an airline would face the considerable financial exposure of paying too much for a noncomplementary sets of slots
6. One can think of the vector $<\pi j, aij, dkj, ek>$ as a bid submitted by an airline.
7. For example, suppose an airline has one airplane and a value $\pi_z$ for using it with the cycle of slots in package z, and $\pi_y$ for using it with the cycle of slots in package y, which occurs 30 minutes later. Then the airline would specify its interest in obtaining package z or y but not both, by submitting the logical constraint $x_z + x_y \leq 1$ to the center. Similarly, the center might wish to impose constraints on allocations to potential users: for example, user u should not be allocated the rights to any more than s slots at airport a.
8. As an example of a logical constraint suppose we have $e_k = 2$ and $d_{k1} = -1; d_{21} = 1; d_{31} = 1$ for some k so that we have a constraint $-x_1 + x_2 + x_3 \leq 1$. This means that a necessary condition for both packages 2 and 3 to be part of the solution is that package 1 must also be part of the solution; otherwise, only one of packages 2 or 3 can be included.
9. There are infrequent exceptions that occur when the linear solution to (1) happens to correspond to an integer solution and a competitive equilibrium exists with separating prices.
10. For a detailed description of this process, see Rassenti et al. 1982.
11. Banks et al. 1989 shows that price feedback helps achieve more efficient allocations.
12. Klemperer 2002 points out that Open English auctions are susceptible to tacit collusion because of the ability to signal and punish, while sealed bid auctions do not afford such strategies. Brown et al. 2009 show in experiments that ascending bid auction for

multi-objects allow for collusion, while descending bid auctions, that are essentially sealed bids, are not.

13. "Deadheading" is a term used in the trucking industry for trucks traveling without cargo on an outbound or inbound trip.

14. For a summary of the work done on Simultaneous Ascending Auctions see Cramton 2006.

15. In addition to concerns with complementarities between items, the practitioner must also be concern with collusive behavior emerging in multi-unit simultaneous ascending auction mechanisms; see Brown et al. 2009 for more information.

16. Recall that RSB found a pseudo dual envelope of prices for a single-round sealed bid. These prices could also be used in a multiround auction.

17. The SAA is referred to as the SMR in Goeree and Holt 2007. Participants in the SMR were limited to withdrawing bids in two rounds of the auction with associated financial penalties for bid withdraws.

18. Goeree and Holt 2007 also test environments where only half of the regional bidders can bid for their preferred packages and found that the HPB still out performed MPB. This was attributed to the difficulty of fitting packages together in the MPB, commonly referred to as the *threshold problem*.

19. Goeree and Holt 2007 find the performance of the HPB to be robust to some degree of "mis-packaging."

20. Typically one would expect that combinatorial environments where the auction is for geographically adjacent items, the auctioneer could reliably prepackage items. However, there are numerous other environments, such as takeoff and landing rights, where prepackaging would simply be infeasible for the auctioneer.

21. For example, In a FCC spectrum auction McLeod submitted a bid of $62,378 for license 283E topping US West's currently winning bid, and a bid of $313,378 for license 452E where US West was also currently winning to signal US West to stop competing against McLeod on license 378 (Cramton and Schwartz 1999)

22. PRRS counts a bidder's overlapping packages as contributing multiple units of demand on the overlapped resources. This tends to lead bidders to avoid competition with themselves through round by round submission of the profit maximizing nonoverlapping vector of packages and items.

23. This is especially true in CCA mechanisms where provisional winners are announced at the end of each round. Some preprocessing of the objective function may be completed to eliminate some of the unnecessary bids from the CCA, and thus reduce computation time (e.g., remove bid improvements from the same bidder), but the amount of information removed from the objective function depends on the mechanism's rules.

24. The version of the CCA tested in Kagel et al. 2010 uses a XOR rule. This rule restricts the auctioneer to assigning a bidder only one of his bids as a winning bid. For example, if a bidder submitted a total of five bids in the course of an auction, the auctioneer can select only one of them as part of the solution to (1). Also, the Kagel et al. 2010 CCA uses a different rule for determining which prices to adjust in each round. Specifically, the pricing algorithm looks at the set of provisionally winning bids in the previous round and the set of new bids in the current round, and if an item attracts new bids from two or more bidders, or if it is identified as a provisionally winning new bid, the price on that item is raised. What is important to note is that these CCA rule changes produce different incentives for bidding.

25. This strategy is especially useful in the face of costly value elicitation.
26. When current price levels are $^tv_i$, dummy prices therefore equal $^tv_i - {}^t\varepsilon$.
27. See Bichler et al. 2005.

# REFERENCES

Banks, Jeffrey S., John Ledyard, and David Porter. 1989. "Allocating Uncertain and Unresponsive Resources: An Experimental Approach." *Rand Journal of Economics* 20 (1): 1–25.

Bichler, M., A. Davenport, G. Hohner, J. Kalagnanam. 2005. "The Design of Combinatorial Auctions for Procurement: An Empirical Study of the Chilean School Meals Auction." In *Combinatorial Auctions*, edited by P. Cramton, Y. Shoham, R. Steinberg, 593–612. Cambridge, MA: MIT Press.

Brown, Alexander L., Charles Plott, and Heidi J. Sullivan. 2009. "Collusion Facilitating and Collusion Breaking Power of Simultaneous Ascending and Descending Price Auctions." *Economic Inquiry* 47 (3): 395–424.

Bykowsky, Mark M., Robert J. Cull, and John O. Ledyard. 2000. "Mutually Destructive Bidding: the Federal Communications Commission Auction Design Problem." *Journal of Regulatory Economics* 17 (3): 205–28.

Cramton, Peter. 2006. "Simultaneous Ascending Auctions." In *Combinatorial Auctions*, edited by P. Cramton, Y. Shoham, and R. Steinberg, 99–114. Cambridge, MA: MIT Press.

Cramton, Peter, and Jesse A. Schwartz. 1999. "Collusive Bidding in the FCC Spectrum Auctions." Working Paper, University of Maryland.

———. 2000. "Collusive Bidding: Lessons from the FCC Spectrum Auctions." *Journal of Regulatory Economics* 17:229–52.

Goeree, Jacob K., and Charles A. Holt. 2007. "Hierarchical Package Bidding: A 'Paper & Pencil' Combinatorial Auction." *Games and Economic Behavior* 70 (1): 146–69.

Ishikida, Takashi, John O. Ledyard, Mark Olson, and David Porter. 2001. "Experimental Testbedding of a Pollution Trading System: Southern California's RECLAIM Emissions Market." *Research in Experimental Economics* 8:185–220.

Kagel, John H., Yuanchuan Lien, and Paul Milgrom. 2010. "Ascending Prices and Package Bidding: A Theoretical and Experimental Analysis." *American Economic Journal: Microeconomics* 2:160–85.

Klemperer, Paul. 2002. "What Really Matters in Auction Design." *The Journal of Economic Perspectives* 16:169–89.

Kwasnica, Anthony M., John O. Ledyard, David Porter, and Christine DeMartini. 2005. "A New and Improved Design for Multi-object Iterative Auctions." *Management Science* 51 (3): 419–34.

Ledyard, John O., Mark Olson, David Porter, Joseph A. Swanson, and David P. Torma. 2002. "The First Use of a Combined-Value Auction for Transportation Services." *Interfaces* 32 (5): 4–12.

Ledyard, John O., David Porter, and Antonio Rangel. 1994. "Using Computerized Exchange System to Solve a Project Management Problem." *Journal of Organizational Computing* 4 (3): 271–96.

McCabe, Kevin, Stephen Rassenti, and Vernon Smith. 1988. "Testing Vickrey's and Other Simultaneous Multiple Unit Versions of the English Auction." *Research in Experimental Economics*, edited by R. M. Isaac, 4:45–79. Greenwich, CT: JAI.

Munro, David R., and Stephen Rassenti. 2011. "Combinatorial Clock Auctions: Price Direction and Performance." Working Paper, Chapman University.

Porter, David. 1999. "An Experimental Examination of Bid Withdrawal in a Multi-object Auction." *Review of Economic Design* 4 (1): 73–97.

Porter, David, Stephen Rassenti, Anil Roopnarine, and Vernon Smith. 2003. "Combinatorial Auction Design." *Proceedings of the National Academy of Sciences* 100 (19): 11153–57.

Rassenti, Stephen J., Vernon L. Smith, and Robert L. Bulfin. 1982. "A Combinatorial Auction Mechanism for Airport Time Slot Allocation." *The Bell Journal of Economics* 13: 402–17.

Scheffel, Tobias, Georg Ziegler, and Martin Bichler. 2012. "On the Impact of Package Selection in Combinatorial Auctions: An Experimental Study in the Context of Spectrum Design." *Experimental Economics* 15 (4): 667–692.

Wessen, Randii, and David Porter. 1997. "A Management Approach for Allocating Instrument Development Resources." *Space Policy* 13 (3): 191–201.

# PART III

ANALYTICAL FOUNDATIONS OF MODERN MANAGERIAL ECONOMICS

CHAPTER 7

·······································································

# GAME AND INFORMATION THEORY IN MODERN MANAGERIAL ECONOMICS

·······································································

ESTHER GAL-OR

## 7.1 INTRODUCTION

·······································································

THIS chapter examines the areas where recent developments in game and information theory have advanced the study of managerial economics. Applying concepts developed in this field has proven to be extremely helpful in understanding the interaction of firms competing in a market, especially if the structure of this market is oligopolistic. Using the basic framework of noncooperative game theory and applying the concept of Nash equilibrium, researchers developed static and dynamic models of competition to address a broad set of issues that confront marketplace rivalry. Some examples include: first- and second-mover advantages, long-term strategic commitments versus short-term tactical choices made by competitors, erection of entry barriers to secure market power, choices of product-mix, special pricing mechanisms to enhance profitability, and issues related to vertical control and the internal organization of the firm. While the earlier studies of these topics were conducted in environments where participants have complete information about demand and cost conditions, more recent studies utilize the Bayesian Nash Equilibrium approach to understand more realistic settings where firms face incomplete information about some aspects of the environment. In this context, researchers have investigated the incentives of competing firms to gather and/or share information about uncertainties, signaling devices utilized by firms to reduce uncertainties, and the role of incomplete information in generating moral-hazard and adverse-selection problems. In this chapter I will discuss the manner in which the various models of competition have been incorporated in the study of managerial economics. In my experience teaching this subject, I have found that MBA students appreciate the intuitive appeal of game theory and its "real world" relevance in spite of the mathematical rigor sometimes necessary in applying this methodology.

This chapter is organized as follows. In the next section, I derive models of price formation in oligopoly markets in environments characterized by both complete and incomplete information. Section 7.3 investigates the distortions introduced in markets due to incomplete information regarding the quality of products produced. In section 7.4, I investigate such distortions in the context of the vertical structure of firms, and section 7.5 offers concluding remarks.

## 7.2 STATIC MODELS OF OLIGOPOLY

When teaching managerial economics in the 1970s the topic of price formation in markets was discussed using models of perfect competition and monopoly. In these extreme cases of market structure, there is no need to incorporate issues related to the behavior or expectations of competitors. In case of perfect competition, each firm is assumed to be so small that it can pretty much ignore how competitors react to its behavior; and in case of (pure) monopoly, there are no competitors to incorporate given that they do not exist. However, many industries consist of a relatively small number of competing firms dominating significant shares of the market.

In such industries the traditional models of price formation are likely to be misleading, given the close attention that competitors pay to each other's behavior. To understand such markets, tools and methodologies developed in the field of game theory are more apt, given the focus of the field on strategic decision making. Models of noncooperative game theory are especially relevant given the competitive nature of markets, even when they are less than perfectly competitive. Applying the Nash equilibrium concept to the earlier models of Cournot and Bertrand led to a better understanding of the implications of those classical theories of imperfect competition (Cournot 1838; Bertrand 1883).

### 7.2.1 One-Stage Cournot and Bertrand Models

To illustrate these models, assume a market that consists of $n$ differentiated firms each facing constant returns to scale technology. The unit cost of each firm is designated by $c$. The inverse demand facing firm $i$ is linear and expressed as follows:[1]

$$p_i = a - bq_i - d\sum_{j \neq i} q_j \quad i, j = 1, n; b \geq d > 0; a > 0. \tag{7.1}$$

The parameter $a$ is the vertical intercept and the parameters $b$ and $d$ are the slopes of the demand, measuring own and cross effects, respectively, of output levels on prices. At the extremes, when $b = d$ the products produced by the firms are homogenous and when $d \to 0$ the products are completely independent. For intermediate values of $d \in (0, b)$

the products are strictly differentiated with the degree of differentiation declining as the parameter $d$ approaches the value of the parameter $b$.

It is possible to obtain the direct demand function facing firm $i$ by inverting the system of equations (1) to express $q_i$ in terms of prices as follows:

$$q_i = \frac{a(b-d)-(b+(n-2)d)p_i + d\sum_{j\neq 1}p_j}{(b-d)(b+(n-1)d)} \quad i,j=1,n; b\geq d>0; a>0. \quad (7.2)$$

Equation (1) can be interpreted as each individual firm independently choosing its level of production and prices being set by a market auctioneer to equate the quantity demanded of each product with that supplied by the firm producing it. In contrast, equation (2) can be interpreted as each individual firm independently setting its price and consumers responding by choosing the quantities they demand of the different products. Applying the Nash equilibrium concept in this setting would depend on whether the strategy space of each firm is the choice of quantity or price. In the former case, each firm chooses $q_i \in R^+$ and equation (1) determines prices; and in the latter case $p_i \in R^+$ and equation (2) determines quantities of output. The outcome derived in the first case is the Cournot equilibrium and in the second is the Bertrand equilibrium. The specification of the model yields a unique equilibrium in each case, which is symmetric given the assumptions of the model. Table 7.1 summarizes the Cournot and Bertrand equilibria. We designate by $q$, $p$, and $\pi$ the common quantity, price, and profit of each firm at the equilibria.

Note that the two outcomes coincide only in the boundary case where $d = 0$, namely when each firm acts as a local monopoly. In this case, the predicted quantity produced by each firm is $\frac{a-c}{2b}$ and its profit is $\frac{(a-c)^2}{4b}$, corresponding indeed to the monopoly outcome. In contrast, when $d > 0$ the two equilibria differ, with the outcome predicted in the Bertrand game being more competitive than in Cournot. Specifically, $q_B > q_C, p_B < p_C$ and $\pi_B < \pi_C$. In particular, when the products are homogenous (i.e., $d = b$), the Bertrand

## Table 7.1  Cournot and Bertrand Outcomes

|  | $q$ | $p-c$ | $\pi$ |
|---|---|---|---|
| Cournot | $\dfrac{(a-c)}{[2b+(n-1)d]}$ | $\dfrac{b(a-c)}{[2b+(n-1)d]}$ | $\dfrac{b(a-c)^2}{[2b+(n-1)d]^2}$ |
| Bertrand | $\dfrac{[b+(n-2)d](a-c)}{[b+(n-1)d][2b+(n-3)d]}$ | $\dfrac{(b-d)(a-c)}{[2b+(n-3)d]}$ | $\dfrac{(b-d)[b+(n-2)d](a-c)^2}{[b+(n-1)d][2b+(n-3)d]^2}$ |

outcome yields marginal cost pricing and zero profits, even with only two competitors. In contrast, the Cournot outcome yields prices above marginal cost and positive profits for any finite number of firms. The equilibrium converges to the perfectly competitive outcome of marginal cost pricing only when $n$ is infinitely large.

Given this divergence in predictions, a question arises as to which solution concept is more appropriate and how the answer to this question depends on the environment considered. Kreps and Scheinkman (1983) provide an answer by demonstrating that the Cournot equilibrium can be interpreted as an environment where firms confront capacity constraints. Specifically, they show that in a two-stage game, where firms choose irreversible levels of capacity first and prices subsequently, the unique equilibrium is the Cournot outcome. Hence, the Cournot equilibrium is the sensible description of an oligopolistic market whenever the industry is confronted with capacity constraints that are common knowledge to market participants. In contrast, in an environment with significant excess capacity or when firms utilize a flexible technology that allows them easily to adjust production levels, the Bertrand equilibrium is the sensible solution concept for oligopolistic markets. While Kreps and Scheinkman provide this intuition for a deterministic environment, Gal-Or (1984) extends the result to an environment where firms face uncertainty about demand conditions.

## 7.2.2 Multistage Cournot and Bertrand Models

The underlying assumption of the Cournot and Bertrand equilibria is that all firms choose their strategies simultaneously, once, and for all. Such an assumption is inconsistent with the evolution of many industries, where firms become established in the market at different points in time. With sequential entry, a natural question arises as to whether sequence matters in determining the relative profitability of firms. In particular, does early entry into an industry award an advantage to the firm? To answer this question, two-stage models of competition, both in the Cournot and Bertrand settings, can be considered. In such Stackelberg, two-stage games, the firm that moves first (in stage 1) is designated as the Leader and the firm that moves second (in stage 2) is designated as the Follower. Consider, as earlier, an industry facing linear demand with only two competing firms and, for simplicity, normalize unit cost to zero. Designate the Leader as firm 1 and the Follower as firm 2. Given that at the Stackelberg equilibrium the choice of output levels or prices (Cournot and Bertrand, respectively) is done sequentially, the strategies $s_i$ of the firms are: $s_1 \in R^+$ and $s_2 : R^+ \to R^+$. Hence, while the Leader chooses its strategy as a scalar, the Follower chooses its output (price) as a function of the observed choice made by the Leader. Implicit in this specification is the assumption that the choice of the Leader is fully observable to the Follower and completely irreversible. If either one of these two assumptions is violated the model collapses to the simultaneous-move game I considered previously. Table 7.2 summarizes the Stackelberg outcomes when quantities and prices are the relevant strategy choices of the firms.

Table 7.2 Stackelberg Equilibria

| | Quantities | Prices | Profits |
|---|---|---|---|
| Quantity is the strategy space | $q_1 = \dfrac{a(2b-d)}{2(2b^2-d^2)}$ <br><br> $q_2 = \dfrac{a(4b^2-2bd-d^2)}{4b(2b^2-d^2)}$ <br><br> $q_1+q_2 > 2q_c$ | $p_1 = \dfrac{a(2b-d)}{4b}$ <br><br> $p_2 = \dfrac{a(4b^2-2bd-d^2)}{4(2b^2-d^2)}$ | $\pi_1 = \dfrac{a^2(2b-d)^2}{8b(2b^2-d^2)}$ <br><br> $\pi_2 = \dfrac{a^2(4b^2-2bd-d^2)^2}{16b(2b^2-d^2)^2}$ <br><br> $\pi_2 < \pi^c < \pi_1, \quad \pi_1+\pi_2 < 2\pi_c$ |
| Price is the strategy space | $q_1 = \dfrac{a(2b+d)}{4b(b+d)}$ <br><br> $q_2 = \dfrac{a(4b^2+2bd-d^2)}{4(b+d)(2b^2-d^2)}$ <br><br> $q_1+q_2 < 2q_B$ | $p_1 = \dfrac{a(b-d)(2b+d)}{2(2b^2-d^2)}$ <br><br> $p_2 = \dfrac{a(b-d)(4b^2+2bd-d^2)}{4b(2b^2-d^2)}$ | $\pi_1 = \dfrac{a^2(b-d)(2b+d)^2}{8b(b+d)(2b^2-d^2)}$ <br><br> $\pi_2 = \dfrac{a^2(b-d)(4b^2+2bd-d^2)^2}{16b(b+d)(2b^2-d^2)^2}$ <br><br> $\pi_B < \pi_1 < \pi_2$ |

The results reported in Table 7.2 illustrate the existence of a first-mover advantage with quantities as strategies and a second-mover advantage with prices as strategies. When quantity is the strategy choice, the Leader can preempt the Follower by expanding its production and obtaining a larger market share. In contrast, when price is the strategy choice, the second mover takes advantage of being able to observe the price of the Leader and then undercut it in order to expand its market share. Gal-Or (1985a) generalizes this result to demonstrate that first- versus second-mover advantages depend upon the signs of the slope of reaction functions in a sequential move game. When reaction functions are downward-sloping (as in the Cournot model when quantity is the strategy choice) the Leader has an advantage over the Follower, and when reaction functions are upward-sloping (as in Bertrand's model when price is the strategy choice) the Follower has an advantage over the Leader. The table also illustrates that leadership models need not always yield improved coordination among firms in enhancing industry profits. In fact, introducing sequential move to Cournot results in an expansion of aggregate industry output, in comparison to the regular simultaneous move environment and, as a result, aggregate industry profits decline.[2] Hence, even though the Leader benefits from preemption, the loss to the Follower exceeds this benefit. In Bertrand's model, however, leadership does yield improved coordination among firms. In fact, even though the Follower has an advantage over the Leader in this environment, even the Leader earns higher profits than in the simultaneous move environment.[3]

The importance of the signs of reaction functions in multistage environments has been analyzed extensively in the literature. In this context, a distinction between long-term commitments and short-term tactical decisions of competing firms has been introduced (see Bulow et al. 1985; and Besanko et al. 2010, chap. 9, for instance). In the context of the Cournot and Bertrand models, the choice of output levels (Cournot) and prices (Bertrand) is considered to be a short-term tactical decision. Decisions related to the internal structure of the firm (Baye et al. 1996; or Chen and Ross 2000), managerial compensation (Fershtman and Judd 1987), binding long-term contracts (Singh and Vives 1984), or the financial structure of the firm (Brander and Lewis 1986) are considered to be long-term strategic decisions. This literature demonstrates that in an environment with downward-sloping reaction functions (as in Cournot), firms seek long-term commitments aimed at achieving an aggressive posture vis-à-vis the competitor. In contrast, in an environment with upward-sloping reaction functions (as in Bertrand), firms seek long-term commitments aimed at achieving a soft posture vis-à-vis the competitor. Table 7.3 summarizes the taxonomy that has been introduced to distinguish among the different types of long-term commitments.

In this table, the term used to describe the long-term strategy reflects the objective of the firms in modifying the nature of competition in the short-term. For instance, "Puppy Dog" implies that firms cut back on aggressive long-term strategies in order to appear less threatening when price competition (upward-sloping reaction functions) materializes. Examples of such Puppy Dog behavior may include reducing investment in capacities, reducing investment in automation that is likely to lower marginal cost, or reducing leverage in financing the everyday operation of the firm.

| Table 7.3 Taxonomy of Business Strategies | | |
| --- | --- | --- |
| | Long-Term Commitment Yields | |
| | Aggressive Posture | Soft Posture |
| Reaction functions upward sloping | Underinvest **Puppy Dog** | Overinvest **Fat Cat** |
| Reaction functions downward sloping | Overinvest **Top Dog** | Underinvest **Lean and Hungry** |

## 7.2.3  Incorporating Incomplete Information in Oligopoly Models

As most market participants are confronted with great uncertainties about demand and cost conditions, incorporating such uncertainties into models of oligopoly is essential for understanding producers' behavior. Moreover, firms may have access to different sources of information regarding the uncertainties they face, thus transforming the deterministic environment I have considered thus far to a game with incomplete information. Such games are characterized by a state of the world that is stochastic, with players having access to private information about the fluctuations in relevant market data. The solution concept employed in predicting the outcome of such games is the Bayesian Nash equilibrium. In such an equilibrium, each player conditions her strategy on the available information and chooses the "best response," given her expectations about the behavior of other players in the game. Expectations have to be rational in the sense that they abide by the Bayesian rule for updating beliefs.

Consider, once again, linear demand with zero expected unit cost and two differentiated competitors. Also consider two types of stochastic shocks to the environment: A "common value" shock affecting the intercept of the demand function, designated by $u$ and distributed normally with $E(u) = 0$, $Var(u) = \sigma_u$, and a "private value" shock designated by $c_i$, affecting the unit cost of firm $i$, with $c_1$ and $c_2$ independently and normally distributed with $Ec_i = 0$, $Var(c_i) = \sigma_c$ and $Cov(c_1, c_2) = 0$. I will show the predicted Bayesian Nash Equilibrium for the two types of stochastic shocks only in Cournot's model.

### 7.2.3.1  Common Value Shock to Demand

Modifying equation (1) to correspond to the new stochastic environment yields:

$$p_i = a + u - bq_i + dq_j, \quad i, j = 1, 2, i \neq j. \tag{7.3}$$

Assume that each firm has access to a private signal about $u$ and designate this signal by $y_i$ for firm $i$, where $y_i = u + l_i, l_i \sim N(0, m_u)$. Assume that conditional on $u$, $l_1$

and $l_2$ are independently distributed. In contrast to the Cournot outcome in the deterministic environment, where the output level is chosen as a scalar, in the environment with private information about demand the output level is chosen as a function of the private signal available to each firm. Hence, in maximizing its profits each firm has to form expectations not only about the state of the demand $E(u \mid y_i)$ but also about the stochastic behavior of the competing firm $E[q_j(y_j) \mid y_i]$. As mentioned earlier, these expectations have to be rational in the sense that they abide by Bayesian rule. Using this reasoning yields the following equilibrium decision rules for each firm.

$$q_i(y_i) = \frac{a}{2b+d} + \frac{\sigma_u y_i}{[2b(\sigma_u + m_u) + d\sigma_u]} \tag{7.4}$$

Hence, in expectation each firm produces as much as it would in a deterministic environment. However, better realizations of the state of the demand lead to expansion of output.

### 7.2.3.2  *Private Value Shock to Cost*

Let $z_i$ designate firm's $i$ private signal about its unit cost, where $z_i = c_i + f_i; f_i \sim N(0, m_c)$; $Cov(f_i, c_i) = Cov(f_i, f_j) = 0$. Using Bayesian updating leads to the decision rules used in the Cournot quantity-setting game as follows:

$$q_i(z_i) = \frac{a}{2b+d} - \frac{\sigma_c z_i}{(\sigma_c + m_c)2b}. \tag{7.5}$$

Hence, output declines as the firm observes a signal of higher unit cost.

Extending the derivation of the equilibria to an environment with incomplete information gave rise to an extensive literature related to the role of private information in a competitive environment. The following are three examples of questions addressed. Will firms have incentives to share information about uncertainties even if they cannot coordinate on choosing quantities or prices (Crawford and Sobel 1982; Noveshek and Sonneshein 1982; Clarke 1983; Gal-Or 1985b; Vives 1984; and Gal-Or 1986)? Does being better informed always offer an advantage to the firm (Gal-Or 1988)? Can the existence of private information reverse the advantage of moving first or second in the game (Gal-Or 1987)?

To answer the first question, suppose that the firms in the stochastic environment described above have the capacity to precommit to truthfully revealing the realization of their private signals to competitors. Such revelation can be accomplished, for instance, under the auspices of a trade association that shares the information among all participants in the market. If information sharing arises in spite of no coordination in setting quantities, the new decision rules followed by the firms are:

$$q_i(y_1, y_2) = \frac{a}{2b+d} + \frac{\sigma_u(y_1 + y_2)}{(2\sigma_u + m_u)(2b+d)};$$

$$i = 1,2 \text{ for a common shock to demand,} \qquad (7.6)$$

$$q_i(z_1, z_2) = \frac{a}{2b+d} - \frac{\sigma_c 2bz_i}{(\sigma_c + m_c)(4b^2 + d^2)} +$$

$$\frac{\sigma_c dz_j}{(\sigma_c + m_c)(4b^2 - d^2)}; \quad \begin{matrix} i, j \\ i \neq j \end{matrix} = 1,2 \text{ for private shocks to unit cost.} \qquad (7.7)$$

Hence, each firm uses not only its own private signal but that of its competitor as well in choosing how much to produce. With improved information about the uncertainty, information sharing has the potential to increase firms' expected profits. However, when comparing the decision rules in (6) and (7) with those in (4) and (5), it is apparent that information sharing affects also the extent of correlation between the strategies chosen by competitors. Specifically, note that when information sharing regards a common shock to demand, correlation between strategies increases, and when it regards a private shock to unit cost, correlation declines. Whether such a change in the extent of correlation benefits the firms depends on the environment in which they compete. Recall that, at Cournot, reaction functions are downward-sloping. In such an environment, greater correlation between the decision rules of competitors can hurt the individual firms. Indeed, in such an environment, sharing information about common-value uncertainties is never an equilibrium. In contrast, sharing information about private value types of uncertainty arises as an equilibrium, both because it improves the accuracy of the information that is available for decision making and reduces the extent of correlation between the decision rules of the firms. This result is reversed in the Bertrand model (Gal-Or 1986), and if the products produced by firms are complements instead of substitutes (Vives 1984).

Related to the last two questions mentioned earlier, the literature has demonstrated that the existence of private information can give rise to counterintuitive predictions about the value of information in competitive settings. In particular, market conditions exist under which less informed firms can gain an advantage over better informed competitors. In Gal-Or (1988), competitors are uncertain about their unit costs and gain improved information about their technologies from experience. Specifically, greater experience gained from producing larger volumes of the product improves information about the realization of cost. In such an environment, a less informed firm can gain an edge over better informed one(s), because it has stronger incentives to expand output in order to reduce its relative ignorance. Ignorance, in this case, serves as a precommitment device by the firm to expand its output and steal market share from the competitor. Similarly, in Gal-Or (1987) it is demonstrated that the "first-mover advantage" present in the Stackelberg game with quantities as strategies may disappear and even reverse if the Leader is better informed than the Follower about the state of uncertain demand. While a firm that is established in an industry early on may have the advantage of pre-empting potential entrants, it is usually also better informed than these entrants about existing consumer demand. In its attempt to mislead potential entrants, it cuts output in order to signal a bad state of demand. Sophisticated entrants are not easily fooled and may take advantage of the cut in output of the established firm in order to grab market share from it.

## 7.3 INCOMPLETE INFORMATION ABOUT PRODUCT QUALITY

The discussion so far focused primarily on the choice of price and/or quantity of production by an oligopolistic firm. Another important dimension of such a firm's strategy is its choice of product mix. In this regard, firms select the quantities and characteristics of products to offer to consumers (Lancaster 1966). In this section, I evaluate the effect of incomplete information regarding the attributes of products on the market equilibrium. In particular, the focus primarily will be on the role of incomplete information regarding product quality.

In an environment where consumers can fully evaluate the quality of the products available in the market, firms choose quality in a manner similar to the choice of any other attribute aimed at differentiating their products from those of competitors. If consumers have heterogeneous preferences, with differing willingness to pay for higher quality, the equilibrium is likely to be characterized by competing firms offering different quality levels, even if a priori all firms have access to the same technologies. In particular, high-quality products may coexist with low-quality products so as to target different segments of consumers and, as a result, alleviate price competition. Gabszewicz and Thisse (1979) and Shaked and Sutton (1982) derive such equilibria for an environment where the strategy space of each firm consists of *price* and quality level (Bertrand), and Gal-Or (1985c) derives the equilibrium when *quantity* and quality defines the strategy space (Cournot).

When consumers cannot evaluate quality before purchasing the product, producers may have incentives to take advantage of consumers' ignorance to lower quality in order to save on costs. The market failure that might result because of such incentives is described in Akerlof's (1970) seminal article analyzing the market for "lemons." To illustrate, consider the used car market. Potential sellers own cars that vary in terms of quality levels. The prior distribution of quality in the population of used cars is uniform on the unit interval. While each owner of a used car can observe the quality of the car he owns, prospective buyers cannot. Buyers can, however, form expectations about quality based upon assessments of potential sellers' incentives and their ex ante assessment of the distribution of product quality. If $q$ is actually the quality of a given used car, the seller receives utility $\alpha q$ if he keeps the car or the price of a used car in the market, designated by $p$, if he sells it. The buyer receives a net utility of $\beta q - p$, with $\beta > \alpha$, if she buys a car of quality $q$. Given this scenario, the seller will offer the car to the market only if $\alpha q < p$, or if $q < \frac{p}{\alpha}$. Buyers correctly rationalize, therefore, that cars of relatively low quality (i.e., less than $\dfrac{p}{\alpha}$) are the only ones available for purchase. Given the prior uniform distribution of used car quality, the buyer estimates the quality of a used car on offer as $\dfrac{p}{2\alpha}$. She will thus purchase a used car only if $\left(\dfrac{\beta p}{2\alpha} - p\right) > 0$, namely as long as $\beta > 2\alpha$.

In particular, when $\alpha < \beta < 2\alpha$, the used car market breaks down completely, because there is no price that can support trade between potential buyers and sellers. Given that buyers always value a used car of certain quality more highly than sellers do $(\beta > \alpha)$, it follows that buyers' incomplete information about quality leads to inefficiencies due to lost opportunities for mutually beneficial trades.

It is important to note that the possible collapse of the market discussed in Akerlof is not simply the result of uncertainty regarding the quality of used cars in the population. Rather, it is the different levels of information about quality that is available to sellers and buyers. For instance, if both buyers and sellers were equally ignorant about the quality of a used car, they would both assess average quality as $\dfrac{1}{2}$ and any price $p \in \left[\dfrac{\alpha}{2}, \dfrac{\beta}{2}\right]$ would support trade. This type of uncertainty in the environment has been referred to in the literature as a game with imperfect, but complete, information. Because there is uncertainty about quality, the game is characterized by imperfect information. However, because all players are equally informed (or uninformed) about this uncertainty, the game is with complete information. When players have private information about the uncertainty, as sellers do in the used car market, the environment is designated as a game with incomplete information. Market failures and inefficiencies are usually the result of such incompleteness.

Given the inefficiencies that incomplete information about product quality may generate, markets have developed mechanisms to overcome such inefficiencies. Two such mechanisms that I will discuss are the buildup of reputation (goodwill) by firms and the use of various vehicles to signal quality.

## 7.3.1 Reputation as a Mechanism to Maintain Quality

To illustrate the role of reputation, consider a perfectly competitive market where each firm acts as a price taker. At the time of purchase, consumers cannot observe the quality of the product. Instead, they rely on the reputation of the firm in assessing quality. Following the assumptions of Shapiro (1983), the reputation of the firm in a given period $t$ is determined by the quality of its product in period $(t-1)$. Hence, after some consumers purchased the product in period $(t-1)$ and assessed its quality from the experience gained by using it, the information about quality is immediately disseminated to all other consumers in the market. Using the notation in Shapiro (1983), $R_t = q_{t-1}$, where $R_t$ designates the reputation of the firm in period $t$ and $q_{t-1}$ designates the quality of the product produced by the firm in period $(t - 1)$. The unit cost of producing a product of quality $q$ is $c(q)$, where $c'(q) > 0$ and $c''(q) > 0$. In addition, a minimum quality $q_0$ can be found below which it is illegal to produce. This minimum restricts the extent to which firms can reduce quality when contemplating "milking" their reputation in order to cut cost. Consumers value higher-quality products but their marginal utilities from higher quality differ. In every period each firm has a choice between maintaining its current reputation or "milking" it by offering the lowest quality that is legally feasible. The benefit from lowering quality amounts to a saving in production costs of $c(q) - c(q_0)$ and the cost of cutting quality is the deteriorated reputation of the firm.

Given that $q_0$ is the minimum quality allowed, every potential entrant into this industry has to offer a product of quality level at least as high as $q_0$. Competitive pressure from potential entrants implies, therefore, marginal cost pricing of the lowest quality permitted, namely $p(q_0) = c(q_0)$. Considering a stationary equilibrium in a dynamic setting, a firm producing quality level $q$ will continue to maintain its reputation if the benefit from "milking" its current reputation, $c(q) - c(q_0)$, falls short of the lost future stream of discounted profits that such reputation guarantees, namely $\dfrac{p(q) - c(q)}{r}$, thus yielding the following inequality necessary for firms to have incentives to maintain their reputation.

The incumbent has no incentive to deviate to $q_0$ if:

$$p(q) \geq c(q) + r(c(q) - c(q_0)). \tag{7.8}$$

A new entrant wishing to offer quality $q$ can expect a discounted stream of profits amounting to $p_e - c(q) + \dfrac{p(q) - c(q)}{r}$, where $p_e$ is the price a new entrant receives for its product. It is sensible to assume that $p_e = c(q_0)$, namely that new products are perceived by consumers to be of the lowest quality level permitted. Consumers are justifiably suspicious of new products, given that the absence of entry barriers can potentially attract fly-by-night sellers who can overrun the market with items of the lowest quality if $p_e > c(q_0)$. Hence, the following inequality is necessary to guarantee that new entrants have no incentive to enter and offer products of quality $q$.

Additional entry with quality $q$ is not worthwhile if:

$$p(q) \leq c(q) + r(c(q) - c(q_0)). \tag{7.9}$$

Combining inequalities (8) and (9) implies that the price schedule that arises at the stationary equilibrium with free entry satisfies the equation:

$$p(q) = c(q) + r(c(q) - c(q_0)). \tag{7.10}$$

Hence, in spite of the perfectly competitive environment assumed, prices have to exceed marginal cost in order to motivate firms to maintain their reputation. More specifically, in the early period of its operation (the first period in the current model) a firm offering quality $q$ loses money, while building up its reputation (since $p_e - c(q) = c(q_0) - c(q) < 0$). Once its reputation is established, however, it can charge a price above marginal cost to compensate for such losses (since $p(q) > c(q)$ in (10)). The premium above marginal cost is larger the greater is the per-period interest rate $r$ and the smaller is $q_0$. In the context of the model, $r$ rises when it takes longer for consumers to assess deteriorations in the quality of the product offered by the firm or, put differently, when firms have greater opportunities to "milk" their reputations. A smaller value of $q_0$ implies a lower minimum standard imposed on the industry, thus raising, once again, the benefit from cutting quality in order to save on cost. When one of these variables change to provide stronger incentives for firms to offer less quality, the gap between price and marginal cost widens. Recall that if quality were fully observable to consumers, price would equal marginal cost in a perfectly competitive market. Hence, the existence of incomplete information about quality (i.e., sellers know more than consumers do which quality is offered) implies that some consumers (those having lower willingness to pay) are priced out of the market in comparison to an environment with complete information. As a result, while reputation is a mechanism that can alleviate some of the problems of incomplete information, it does not eliminate altogether the opportunities of mutually beneficial trade foregone as the result of unobservable quality.

The modeling approach of reputation buildup that was developed by Shapiro (1983) has been further extended in the literature. Allen (1984), for instance, allows for greater sophistication on the part of consumers in evaluating quality based upon observed prices and cost schedules of the sellers. Even with such greater sophistication, though, the general result derived in Shapiro (1983) remains valid. Namely, price has to exceed marginal cost even in a perfectly competitive market in order to provide incentives for firms to maintain their reputations for high quality. As a result, some trading opportunities are lost.

## 7.3.2 Signaling as a Mechanism to Reveal Quality

The main idea behind the existence of mechanisms for signaling quality is derived from the seminal work of Spence (1973). Spence proposes that education can serve as a means for workers successfully to signal their productivities to potential employers. The environment considered in Spence (1973) is similar to that arising when quality cannot be observed by customers. Specifically, workers vary in their potential productivities (talents) but employers cannot distinguish between high- and low-productivity workers. To illustrate, assume that there are two types of workers in the market, high and low productivity. Designate their contributions, measured in dollars, to a potential employer by $T_H$ and $T_L$, with $T_H > T_L$. The proportion of high- and low-productivity workers in the population is $z$ and $(1 - z)$. Assuming fierce competition among employers for workers implies that in the absence of any signaling, wages are determined by the weighted average of a worker's contribution as follows:

$$W_{NS} = zT_H + (1-z)T_L. \tag{7.11}$$

While low-productivity workers benefit from employers' confusion, given that they are paid a wage above their contribution, high-productivity workers have a strong incentive to identify a mechanism to reveal credibly to employers their type, given that they otherwise will be paid wages below their contributions. Spence (1973) demonstrates that investment in education can provide such a signaling device.

The main idea is that while the actual out-of-pocket expenses, in terms of tuition and room and board, of either type of worker are the same, more-talented individuals have to exert less effort than the less talented in order to attain the required standards of any educational program. Assume, for instance, that the cost of this effort is $\frac{y}{2}$ and $y$ per unit of education for the more-talented and less-talented workers, respectively. At a signaling equilibrium, the two types of workers choose different levels of education. This different behavior, which is observable from the resumes of candidates, allows employers to distinguish between the two types of workers and pay them accordingly; $T_H$ to the high type and $T_L$ to the low type.

Suppose that the more-talented workers choose to invest in $E_H$ units of education and the less talented in $E_L$ units, then a signaling equilibrium should satisfy the following two inequalities:

$$T_H - \frac{y}{2} E_H \geq T_L - \frac{y}{2} E_L, \ (IC_H) \tag{7.12}$$

$$T_L - y E_L \geq T_H - y E_H. \ (IC_L) \tag{7.13}$$

Inequality (12) guarantees that a more-talented worker does not have an incentive to deviate from the larger investment in education $E_H$ to the lower investment $E_L$, in which case her educational spending declines along with her wages, from $T_H$ to $T_L$. Inequality (11) guarantees that the less-talented person does not have a similar incentive to mimic the more-talented in order to attain the higher wage, $T_H$. The two inequalities have been referred to in the literature as Incentive Compatibility constraints necessary to support the signaling (separating) equilibrium. The inequalities yield the following restrictions on the gap between the investments in education for the high- and low-productivity types:

$$\frac{2(T_H - T_L)}{y} \geq E_H - E_L \geq \frac{T_H - T_L}{y}. \tag{7.14}$$

Multiplicity of equilibria is possible with different investment levels that support signaling. If one assumes that education does not enhance the productivity of workers and its sole purpose is to serve as a signaling device, the most efficient outcome arises when each type invests the minimum level necessary in the feasible range described in (14); specifically, when $E_H = \frac{T_H - T_L}{y}$ and $E_L = 0$. The net payoff to the two types of workers is then $\frac{T_H + T_L}{2}$ and $T_L$, respectively. The high-productivity workers' net payoff is less than their full contribution $T_H$ because they have to incur the cost of investment in order to be identified as high-productivity types. In the context of the example, their net payoff with signaling exceeds their payoff at the equilibrium without signaling (equation (11)), if $z < 0.5$, namely if the population of workers comprises more low-type than high-type individuals.

The main reason investment in education can serve as a signaling device is that the cost of investment in the signal varies across different types of workers. In the literature related to signaling of unobservable quality, the proposed mechanisms have a similar property; namely the net benefit of investing in the mechanism to signal high quality is larger for a high-quality producer than for a low-quality producer. The greater net benefit may be the result of lower costs of investment in the signaling mechanism, as in the labor market example considered by Spence (1973), or the larger net revenues that accrue to the high-quality producer, if identified as such. The literature proposes a variety of vehicles through which firms can signal the quality of their products to consumers. Some examples include advertising levels (Kihlstrom and Riordan 1984), prices (Milgrom and Roberts 1986, and Bagwell and Riordan 1991), warranties (Gal-Or 1989), and product return policies (Shieh 1996, and Che 1996). I will discuss these proposed vehicles next.

Kihlstrom and Riordan (1984) consider a model where advertising messages are completely uninformative, in the sense that they cannot credibly communicate the characteristics of the product. Specifically, the message communicated in an ad does not allow consumers to distinguish between high- and low-quality products, given that the producer of either type of product has incentives to communicate high quality. However, the authors demonstrate that if consumers can observe the level of advertising expenditure of different producers, there are conditions under which a signaling equilibrium might arise. At such an equilibrium, high-quality producers spend more money on advertising than low-quality producers, and consumers can infer, therefore, based upon the level of advertising, which are the higher-quality products.

To illustrate the conditions necessary to support a signaling equilibrium, consider a perfectly competitive market that consists of both high- and low-quality producers. The prices of high- and low-quality products are $P_H$ and $P_L$ with $P_H > P_L$. The gap in prices $(P_H - P_L)$ falls short of the premium consumers are willing to pay for high quality, and producers take the prices as given. Assume that there are only two quality levels possible. The cost functions of producing $x$ units of a given product are:

$$TC_H(x) = F_H + \frac{x^2}{4}, MC_H(x) = \frac{x}{2}$$

$$TC_L(x) = F_L + \frac{x^2}{2}, MC_L(x) = x, \text{ and } F_H > F_L. \tag{7.15}$$

Hence, while the fixed cost of producing high-quality products exceeds that of low-quality products, the marginal cost of producing those of the former is less than that of the latter. It is sensible to assume, though, that the average cost of producing high-quality products is greater than lesser quality ones, namely that $F_H - F_L \geq \frac{x^2}{4}$ for all feasible levels of output.

Given that the market is perfectly competitive, firms maximize profits by choosing output levels where price equals marginal cost. Hence, if a high-quality firm is perceived by consumers to be, indeed, of high quality, it produces $x_H^* = 2P_H$ and earns net profits equal to $\pi_H^* = P_H^2 - F_H$. In contrast, if it is perceived to be of low quality it produces $\hat{x}_H = 2P_L$ and earns net profits equal to $\hat{\pi}_H = P_L^2 - F_H$. A low-quality firm that is identified correctly by consumers produces at the level $x_L^* = P_L$ and earns $\pi_L^* = \dfrac{P_L^2}{2} - F_L$, and if it is perceived as high quality, it produces $\hat{x}_L = P_H$ and earns $\hat{\pi}_L = \dfrac{P_H^2}{2} - F_L$. Using the approach proposed in Spence (1973), in a signaling equilibrium with advertising serving as a signal of quality, firms that produce different qualities choose different levels of advertising, namely $A_H \neq A_L$. The following incentive compatibility constraints guarantee that neither firm has an incentive to deviate:

$$P_H^2 - F_H - A_H \geq P_L^2 - F_H - A_L \quad (IC_H),$$

$$\frac{P_L^2}{2} - F_L - A_L \geq \frac{P_H^2}{2} - F_L - A_H \quad (IC_L).$$

Combining the two inequalities yields:

$$P_H^2 - P_L^2 \geq A_H - A_L \geq \frac{P_H^2 - P_L^2}{2}. \tag{7.16}$$

As in Spence (1973), multiple advertising levels are possible, which can support the signaling equilibrium. As advertising is wasteful in this example, the most efficient equilibrium is characterized by $A_H = \dfrac{P_H^2 - P_L^2}{2}$ and $A_L = 0$.

The characteristic of the example that is essential to support advertising as a signaling device in this environment is the nature of the cost functions facing high- versus low-quality production. Specifically, even if high-quality products lead to higher average cost, it is necessary that the marginal cost of producing them is lower. With a lower marginal cost, a high-quality producer benefits more than a low-quality producer when consumers are willing to pay a higher price for its product. Such a producer increases its output to a greater extent when it can fetch the price $P_H$ rather than $P_L$ ($2(P_H - P_L)$ for a high-quality producer versus $(P_H - P_L)$ for a low-quality producer). Being perceived as high quality, therefore, is more valuable to a firm that produces high quality than one that produces low quality. Such a differential benefit from being recognized as high quality is essential to support the separating equilibrium.

Kihlstrom and Riordan (1984) show that the property of declining marginal cost for high-quality products (assumed in the example above) has to be valid more generally for any setting in which firms act as price takers in order to support the separating equilibrium with advertising. Milgrom and Roberts (1986) consider an environment where firms have the power to set introductory prices as well as levels of advertising and consumers learn about quality both from experience with the product over time and by observing the selected prices and advertising levels of the firm. The conditions they derive for the existence of a signaling equilibrium relate to the profit functions of the firms instead of the shape of the cost functions only (as in Kihlstrom and Riordan 1984). However, the conditions are still derived from the incentive compatibility constraints of high- versus low-quality producers.

Bagwell and Riordan (1991) investigate whether the price schedule of the firm over time can by itself, without any other signaling device, communicate to consumers whether the firm produces a high- or low-quality product. In this model, a fraction of the population is fully informed about product quality. This group of consumers does not have to rely on any signal to infer quality. Moreover, the size of the group increases over time, as more consumers gain experience with the product. The authors find that high introductory prices, combined with a time-wise declining schedule of prices, serve as vehicles to signal quality. The intuition here, once again, relates to the differential benefit from investing in the signal across different quality levels. Specifically, in order to signal quality, the high-quality firm sets a price above that which maximizes its profit in a world with complete information. The low-quality firm does not have an incentive to mimic such pricing because its lost profits from raising the price are greater than the lost profits of the high-quality firm (in this model, the variable costs of low-quality production are less than those of high-quality production). As before, the model exhibits differential benefits derived from investment in the signal (i.e., raising price). As the population of informed consumers rises over time, the high-quality producer can reduce its reliance on the signal and bring its price closer to the level that maximizes profits in an environment with complete information.

The articles by Gal-Or (1989), Shieh (1996), and Che (1996) investigate conditions under which offering to consumers warranties of longer duration or adopting more flexible product return policies can support a signaling equilibrium. In contrast to the earlier models with advertising or price as signals, in these articles the investment in the signals (either warranty or return policy) affects the characteristics of the product consumed and, as a result, the utility consumers derive from it. Hence, a warranty of longer duration enhances the utility of the consumers, in addition to possibly communicating higher quality. Gal-Or (1989) demonstrates that this additional attribute of quality can make a signaling equilibrium more difficult to reach.

## 7.4 INCOMPLETE INFORMATION AND THE VERTICAL STRUCTURE OF FIRMS

The discussion so far centered on horizontal competition of firms in markets. However, a very important component of the study of managerial economics relates to the vertical structure of firms. In this regard, issues pertaining both to the structure of a vertically integrated firm and the relationship between a firm and its outside suppliers and retailers are relevant. The basic framework utilized to address these issues is the principal-agent model, where the existence of incomplete information is an important ingredient of the analysis. Incomplete information arises within a firm when managers have access to more precise knowledge than do its owners regarding the competitive environment (demand or cost) or because owners cannot fully observe the actions taken by managers. In the relationship with outside entities, similar asymmetry of information regarding the environment or the behavior of different parties may also exist. The literature uses the concept of *adverse selection* to characterize the existence of asymmetry of information ex ante regarding stochastic shocks to the environment. The notion of *moral hazard* characterizes asymmetry of information regarding the ex post behavior of agents in a vertical relationship.

### 7.4.1 Models of Adverse Selection

The seminal paper of Baron and Myerson (1982) served as the building block for many agency models with adverse selection. While Baron and Myerson developed their model in the context of a regulated public utility, the basic paradigm they proposed has been adopted in many different applications. In my own work, I have utilized their approach to study so-called vertical restraints[4] between manufacturers and their retailers (Gal-Or 1991c), and the vertical structure of firms operating in an oligopolistic market (Gal-Or 1990, 1991a, 1991b, 1992, 1995, 1997).

To illustrate the approach, consider a monopolist that faces a deterministic linear demand function, $p = a - bq$, and a stochastic unit cost, $c$. The prior distribution of unit cost is binomial. Specifically, $c \in \{C_L, C_H\}$ $C_L < C_H$, where the probability of each realization is the same. Top management makes decisions concerning the level of production (or pricing). However, production managers usually have access to more precise information about potential cost realizations. Using the terminology of agency models, the top manager can be considered as the principal and the production manager as the agent. The principal has to design a mechanism to induce the agent truthfully to reveal his information about cost in order for decisions to be more closely aligned with the state of the technology. The production manager may have incentives to distort his report in order to retain "informational rents." The top manager designs the mechanism to guarantee truthful reporting while minimizing the extent of rents secured by the production manager.

Consider a mechanism that consists of two instruments: quantity of output to produce, $q$, and budget allocated to the agent to cover the costs of production, $J$. Both instruments can be selected contingent upon the report delivered by the agent about unit cost, namely $\{q(\hat{c}), J(\hat{c})\}$. Further assume that the principal has the commitment power to sign an agreement prior to actually communicating with the agent. Specifically, reversing the agreement after communication is extremely costly for the principal. The optimization problem of the principal is constrained by two types of restrictions: First, the agent should have an incentive truthfully to reveal his type (incentive compatibility, IC, constraint). Second, irrespective of the cost realization, the agent can never incur losses (limited liability, LL, constraint). Specifically, the budget allocated to the agent should be sufficient to cover production costs. Such limited liability on the part of the agent implied, possibly by imperfect credit markets or limited wealth, yields the individual rationality, IR, constraint confronting the principal in optimizing the firm's profits. The following is the constrained optimization problem solved by the principal.

$$\max_{q_i, J_i} \left\{ \frac{1}{2} \left[ \left( a - bq_1 \right) q_1 - J_1 \right] + \frac{1}{2} \left[ \left( a - bq_2 \right) q_2 - J_2 \right] \right\}$$

Subject to: $J_i - q_i c_i \geq J_j - q_j c_i \quad j \neq i, i, j = L, H.$   (IC)

$$J_i - q_i \, c_i \geq \text{(IR)}.$$

In two-type adverse selection models, of the kind I consider in this example, only one individual rationality constraint and one incentive compatibility constraint are binding. Specifically, the individual rationality constraint pertaining only to the agent facing high cost (the "bad" type), and the incentive compatibility constraint pertaining only to the agent facing low cost (the "good" type) are binding. As a result,

$$J_H = q_H c_H,$$

$$J_L = q_L c_L + q_H (c_H - c_L).$$   (7.17)

Hence, the "bad" type receives a budget just sufficient to cover costs and the "good" type receives a budget in excess of production costs. The larger budget is necessary to eliminate the incentive of the "good" type to mimic the "bad" type. In fact, the excess budget, beyond production costs, that the low-cost manager receives is just sufficient to eliminate his incentives to misrepresent the state of the technology.

Solving the constrained optimization yields the quantity of output selected by top management as follows:

$$q_H = \frac{a - c_H - (c_H - c_L)}{2b} \quad \text{and} \quad q_L = \frac{a - c_L}{2b}.$$   (7.18)

In a world with complete information, when top management can observe production costs, $q_i = \dfrac{a - c_i}{2b}$ for $i = L, H$. Hence, incomplete information on the part of top management results in underproduction in the "bad" state and "optimal" production in the "good" state. Thus, in spite of communication between top and production managers, suboptimal levels of production arise in equilibrium, leading to lower expected profits accruing to the firm in comparison to an environment with complete information.

At the "second best" solution that arises with vertical separation between the two layers of management, the reduction in the firm's output level, in comparison to the "first best" outcome, can be interpreted as an additional "informational cost" incurred by the firm. In the context of the example, this additional "informational cost" per unit is equal to $\frac{(c_H - c_L)}{2}$, an amount that increases with the gap between the two possible cost realizations. A wider gap provides stronger incentives for the manager facing low cost to mimic the reporting behavior of a manager facing high cost, thus raising his "informational rents" and leading to a more significant distortion in the production decision of top management.

The distortion illustrated in the above example arises in many different types of vertical relationships characterized by adverse selection. The existence of asymmetric information results in suboptimal behavior in the comparison to the "first best." The size of the "informational cost" is tied to the inverse of the hazard rate function of the uncertainty confronting the firm, namely $\left( \frac{1 - F(c)}{f(c)} \right)$. It is interesting to note that irrespective of the vertical restraints utilized by the principal, eliminating the "informational cost" may not be feasible. In particular, the literature on vertical restraints in the relationship between manufacturers and their retailers (or suppliers) has demonstrated that utilizing restraints such as retail price maintenance (RPM) or quantity forcing (QF) can restore optimality in a world with complete information (Matthewson and Winter 1983, 1984; Rey and Tirole 1986). In contrast, such restraints may be insufficient to eliminate distortions arising from having to induce truthful reporting. While RPM contracts can achieve the "first best" outcome when the agent (retailer or supplier) observes private information only about demand, when the agent can also observe private information about cost, informational distortions persist (Gal-Or 1991c).

Even though the basic framework of the principal-agent model with adverse selection has been developed in a setting with a single principal and a single agent, the literature expanded this framework to allow for competition among firms in the market (multiprincipal setting) and for multiple agents serving a single principal (multiple retailers serving a manufacturer or multiple managers reporting to the owner). Examples of studies that tie the vertical structure of the firm to the extent of competition in product markets (horizontal structure) include Caillaud et al. (1995), Gal-Or (1991a, 1991b, 1992, 1993, 1995), Hermalin (1992), and Nalebuff and Stiglitz (1983). These studies obtain contradictory results on the effect of product market competition on the magnitude of agency costs. Examples of studies considering multiagent settings include Demski and Sappington (1984), Gal-Or (1991b), Katz (1991), and Martimont (1996). These studies illustrate that when the private information that is available to multiple agents is correlated, the principal can design the vertical relationship to reduce agency costs.

## 7.4.2  Models of Moral Hazard

To illustrate the agency costs that arise due to lack of observability of actions taken by agents (moral hazard models), I will use a framework utilized widely in the literature

(by Holmstrom and Milgrom 1987, 1991; and Itoh 1992, for instance). In this framework the principal is risk neutral and the agent is risk averse, with his utility over wealth
exhibiting a constant degree of risk aversion, $r$. The uncertainty underlying the environment is governed by a normal distribution. Specifically, if "a" designates the unobserved
effort taken by the agent, the principal observes a signal of this effort $x = a + \varepsilon$, where
$\varepsilon$ is normally distributed with mean zero and variance $\sigma^2$. The contract with the agent
can be specified as a function of the observable performance measure $x$ but cannot be
specified contingent upon the unobservable effort level "a." The agent incurs the private
cost $\frac{1}{2}a^2$ when exerting the effort level "a."

It is easy to show that the above specification simplifies significantly the maximization
problem of the principal. The functional form of the utility of the agent, combined with
the normal distribution of the uncertainty, imply that the expected utility of the agent
depends only on the mean and variance of his compensation schedule. Specifically,
he chooses effort to maximize the objective $\left[ E(y) - \frac{1}{2}rVar(y) - \frac{1}{2}a^2 \right]$, where $y$ is the
agent's compensation schedule. Suppose that the principal specifies the compensation
of the agent to consist of two components: a fixed salary, $\gamma$, and a performance based
sharing rule, $\alpha$, so that $y = \gamma + \alpha x$. To maximize the profits of the firm the principal
solves the following constrained optimization:

$$\max_{\alpha, \gamma} \pi = E_\varepsilon \left[ (1-\alpha)(\hat{a}+\varepsilon) \right] - \gamma$$

Subject to: $\hat{a} = \arg\max_a \left\{ E_\varepsilon \left[ \alpha(a+\varepsilon) + \gamma \right] - \frac{1}{2}rVar\left[ \alpha(a+\varepsilon) + \gamma \right] - \frac{1}{2}a^2 \right\},$

$$E_\varepsilon \left[ \alpha\left(\hat{a}+\varepsilon\right) + \gamma \right] \geq 0.$$

The maximization of the principal is constrained by the self-interested behavior of the
agent and the need to guarantee him a nonnegative payoff (assuming that the outside
option of the agent is normalized to zero). It is easy to show that the solution to the above
maximization problem is:

$$\alpha = a^* = \frac{1}{1+r\sigma^2}. \tag{7.19}$$

In a world with complete information, when the principal can observe the agent's
behavior "a," or alternatively, when the two layers of the vertical structure are integrated,
the optimal effort level maximizes the net benefit function $\left[ a - \frac{1}{2}a^2 \right]$, namely $a^* = 1$.
Hence, lack of observability of "a" yields suboptimal levels of effort exerted by the agent.
The distortion is greater the more risk averse the agent (larger values of r) and the less
accurate the performance measure used by the principal to estimate the agent's effort

level (larger values of $\sigma^2$ ). In particular, when either r or $\sigma^2$ are infinitely large, $\alpha = 0$, and the compensation of the agent consists of a fixed salary only. As a result, the agent finds it optimal to exert no costly effort aimed at improving the performance of the company.

As is the case with models of adverse selection, in moral hazard models as well, incomplete information leads to distortions in the behavior of the firm. The source of the distortion is the suboptimal sharing rule that the firm follows in order to provide incentives to the agent to exert appropriate effort. Specifically, given that the agent is more risk averse than the principal, optimality would require that the agent's compensation consists only of a fixed salary so that he is not exposed to any risk. However, when effort is unobservable, the principal has to expose the agent to some risk ($\alpha > 0$) in order to provide him incentives to exert positive levels of effort.

The literature has proposed a variety of tools in order to reduce distortions generated by moral hazard in agency relationships. Holmstrom (1982), for instance, proposes identifying additional outside signals to supplement the performance measures used by the principal in assessing the agent's behavior. For instance, shareholders may use the profits of the firm or its stock price in evaluating and compensating the CEO, given that the actions of the CEO affect these performance measures. However, according to Holmstrom (1982), supplementing these performance measures with additional signals that are determined outside of the control of the CEO can reduce distortions due to agency costs. While decisions made by the CEO do affect the stock price of the company, there are additional factors beyond his control that contribute to fluctuations in the stock price. One example, for instance, is the overall state of the economy, as measured by the rate of growth of GDP. Using this variable in compensation reduces the variance $\sigma^2$ in the above formulation, and as a result, the extent of distortion due to moral hazard.

In organizations with multiple agents, the existence of correlation in the performance measures of different agents can also reduce the extent of uncertainty in compensating them and, as a result, reduce distortions (Demski and Sappington 1984; Katz 1991; and Varian 1990). Relative performance evaluation and tournaments are especially useful in this respect (Lazear and Rosen 1981; and Green and Stokey 1983). However, if the firm can benefit from inducing cooperation among its employees, relative performance evaluation may eliminate the incentive of workers to help each other. Itoh (1992) proposes that the optimal compensation rule should incorporate, therefore, both the need to reduce the uncertainty facing the agents and foster cooperation among them. With this dual objective in mind, Holmstrom and Milgrom (1991) consider an environment in which the principal has to allocate tasks among multiple agents. They show that it is not only the compensation scheme but the design of the job itself that is important in controlling incentives. They find, for instance, that each task should be the responsibility of just one agent. Moreover, tasks should be grouped into jobs in such a way that tasks in which performance is relatively easy to measure (small $\sigma^2$ in the above example) are assigned to one worker and tasks in which performance is more difficult to measure (large $\sigma^2$ ) are assigned to a different worker.

## 7.5  Concluding Remarks

This chapter described how methodologies developed in the field of game and information theory can assist in understanding the interaction of competitors in markets.
The chapter highlighted, in particular, the role of incomplete information in generating
market failures, and provided examples of mechanisms that can alleviate such failures.
While the discussion focused primarily on the study of managerial economics, the concepts described in this chapter have been applied extensively in other fields of study in
business schools. In accounting, agency models are used to design incentive schemes
that induce truthful financial reporting of managers; in finance, signaling models have
been developed to understand capital structure and the behavior of stock markets; and
in marketing, models of incomplete information are used to understand distribution
channels and compensation of sales personnel. In spite of this widespread applicability,
the field has its share of critics who consider the approach of game theory unrealistic
and lacking in predictive power. With research and teaching interests derived primarily from behavioral disciplines, such as sociology and psychology, some scholars in
business schools question two basic premises of the field: that behavior is motivated
solely by self-interest and that individuals are perfectly rational. These critics argue, for
instance, that social responsibility to the community and not profits alone guide producers' choices, and that even in the era of supercomputers, it is unlikely that individuals
can process the large amounts of information necessary to support the rational expectations assumption of the field. While I agree with some aspects of this criticism, I believe
that the methodologies and rigor developed in the field of game theory are flexible
enough to accommodate alternative assumptions regarding objectives of individuals or
their ability to process information. In fact, the growing field of behavioral economics incorporates, indeed, concepts related to fairness, altruism, and bounded rationality in game theoretic models. It is only a question of time before such modified models
are also incorporated in the study of managerial economics. If the alternative modeling
specification yields theoretical predictions concerning the behavior of producers that
are different from those implied by the traditional framework, it is up to empiricists to
determine which approach has the stronger predictive power.

## Notes

1. This inverse demand function is implied by a quadratic utility function of a representative
   consumer expressed as follows:

$$U(q_1 \ldots q_n) = a \sum_{i=1}^{n} q_i - \frac{b}{2} \sum_{i=1}^{n} q_i^2 - d \sum_{i \neq j} q_i q_j + T$$

   with $T$ designating a numeraire consumption good produced outside of the industry.
2. This result can be generalized to any environment with downward sloping reaction functions.

3. This result can be generalized to any game with upward-sloping reaction functions.
4. Examples of vertical restraints include: retail price maintenance, exclusive territories, and quantity forcing.

## References

Akerlof, G. 1970. "The Market for 'Lemons': Quality Uncertainty and the Market Mechanism." *The Quarterly Journal of Economics* 84:488–500.

Allen, F. 1984. "Reputation and Product Quality." *Rand Journal of Economics* 15:311–27.

Bagwell, K., and M. Riordan. 1991. "High and Declining Prices Signal Product Quality." *American Economic Review* 81:224–39.

Baron, D., and R. Myerson. 1982. "Regulating a Monopolist with Unknown Costs." *Econometrica* 50:911–30.

Baye, M., K. Crocker, and J. Ju. 1996. "Divisionalization, Franchising, and Divestiture Incentives in Oligopoly." *American Economic Review* 86:223–36.

Bertrand, J. 1883. Review of *Theorie Mathematique de la Richesse Sociale* and of *Recherches sur les Principles Mathematiques de la Theorie des Richesses* by A. A. Cournot. Translation by James W. Friedman. *Journal de Savants* 67:499–508.

Besanko, D., D. Dranove, M. Shanley, and S. Schaefer S. 2010. *Economics of Strategy*. New Jersey: John Wiley & Sons.

Brander, J. A., and T. R. Lewis. 1986. "Oligopoly and Financial Structure: The Limited Liability Effect." *American Economic Review* 21:956–70.

Bulow, J., J. Geanakpolus, and P. Klemperer. 1985. "Multimarket Oligopoly: Strategic Substitutes and Complements." *Journal of Political Economy* 93:488–511.

Caillaud, B., B. Julien, and P. Picard. 1995. "Competing Vertical Structures: Precommitment and Renegotiation." *Econometrica* 63:621–46.

Che, Y. 1996. "Customer Return Policies for Experience Goods." *Journal of Industrial Economics* 44:17–24.

Chen, Z., and T. Ross. 2000. "Strategic Alliances, Shared Facilities, and Entry Deterrence." *Rand Journal of Economics* 31:326–44.

Clarke, R. 1983. "Collusion and the Incentives for Information Sharing." *Bell Journal of Economics* 14:383–94.

Cournot, A. A. 1838. *Researches into the Mathematical Principles of the Theory of Wealth*. Translated by Nathaniel T. Bacon. New York: Macmillan Company.

Crawford, V., and J. Sobel. 1982. "Strategic Information Transmission." *Econometrica* 50:1431–51.

Demski, J., and D. Sappington. 1984. "Optimal Incentive Contracts with Multiple Agents." *Journal of Economic Theory* 33:152–71.

Fershtman, C., and K. Judd. 1987. "Equilibrium Incentives in Oligopoly." *American Economic Review* 77:927–40.

Gabszewicz, J., and J. Thisse. 1979. "Price Competition, Quality and Income Disparities." *Journal of Economic Theory* 20:340–59.

Gal-Or, E. 1984. "Price Dispersion with Uncertain Demand." *International Economic Review* 25:441–57.

———. 1985a. "First Mover and Second Mover Advantages." *International Economic Review* 26:649–53.

——. 1985b. "Information Sharing in Oligopoly." *Econometrica* 53:329–43.

——. 1985c. "Differentiated Industries without Entry Barriers." *Journal of Economic Theory* 37:310–39.

——. 1986. "Information Transmission-Cournot and Bertrand Equilibria." *The Review of Economic Studies* 53:85–92.

——. 1987. "First Mover Disadvantages with Private Information." *Review of Economic Studies* 54:279–92.

——. 1988. "The Advantages of Imprecise Information." *Rand Journal of Economics* 19:267–75.

——. 1989. "Warranties as a Signal of Quality." *Canadian Journal of Economics* 22:50–61.

——. 1990. "Excessive Retailing at the Bertrand Equilibria." *Canadian Journal of Economics* 23:294–304.

——. 1991a. "Optimal Franchising in Oligopolistic Markets with Uncertain Demand." *International Journal of Industrial Organization* 9:343–64.

——. 1991b. "A Common Agency with Incomplete Information." *Rand Journal of Economics* 22:274–86.

——.1991c. "Vertical Restraints with Incomplete Information." *The Journal of Industrial Economics* 39:503–16.

——. 1992. "Vertical Integration in Oligopoly." *Journal of Law, Economics, & Organization* 8:377–93.

——. 1993. "Internal Organization and Managerial Compensation in Oligopoly." *International Journal of Industrial Organization* 11:157–83.

——. 1995. "Correlated Contracts in Oligopoly." *International Economic Review* 36:75–100.

——. 1997. "Multiprincipal Agency Relationships as Implied by Product Market Competition." *Journal of Economics & Management Strategy* 6:235–56.

Green, J., and N. Stokey. 1983. "A Comparison of Tournaments and Contracts." *Journal of Political Economy* 91:349–64.

Hermalin, B. 1992. "The Effects of Competition on Executive Behavior." *Rand Journal of Economics* 23:350–65.

Holmstrom, B. 1982. "Moral Hazard in Teams." *Bell Journal of Economics* 13:324–40.

Holmstrom, B., and P. Milgrom. 1987. "Aggregation and Linearity in the Provision of Intertemporal Incentives." *Econometrica* 55:303–28.

——. 1991. "Multiple Principal-Agent Analysis: Incentive Contracts, Asset Ownership and Job Design." *Journal of Law, Economics & Organization* 7:24–52.

Itoh, H. 1992. "Cooperation in Hierarchical Organizations: An Incentive Perspective." *Journal of Law, Economics & Organization* 8:321–45.

Katz, M. 1991. "Game-Playing Agents: Unobservable Contracts as Precommitments." *Rand Journal of Economics* 22:307–28.

Kihlstrom, R., and M. Riordan. 1984. "Advertising as a Signal." *Journal of Political Economy* 93:427–50.

Kreps, D., and J. Scheinkman. 1983. "Quantity Precommitment and Bertrand Competition Yield Cournot Outcomes." *Bell Journal of Economics* 14:326–37.

Lancaster, K. J. 1966. "A New Approach to Consumer Theory." *Journal of Political Economy* 74:132–57.

Lazear, E., and S. Rosen. 1981. "Rand-Order Tournaments as Optimum Labor Contracts." *Journal of Political Economy* 89:841–64.

Martimont, D. 1996. "Exclusive Dealing, Common Agency, and Multiprincipal Incentive Theory." *Rand Journal of Economics* 27:1–31.

Mathewson, G., and R. Winter. 1983. "The Incentives for Resale Price Maintenance under Imperfect Information." *Economic Inquiry* 21:337–48.

——. 1984. "An Economics Theory of Vertical Restraints." *Rand Journal of Economics* 15:27–38.

Milgrom, P., and J. Roberts. 1986. "Price and Advertising Signals of Product Quality." *Journal of Political Economy* 94: 796–821.

Nalebuff, B. J., and J. E. Stiglitz. 1983. "Information, Competition, and Markets." *American Economic Review: Papers and Proceedings* 73:278–83.

Noveshek, W., and H. Sonneshein. 1982. "Fulfilled Expectations Cournot Duopoly with Information Acquisition and Release." *Bell Journal of Economics* 13:214–18.

Rey, P., and J. Tirole. 1986. "The Logic of Vertical Restraints." *American Economic Review* 76:921–39.

Shaked, A., and J. Sutton. 1982. "Relaxing Price Competition Theory Product Differentiation." *The Review of Economic Studies* 49:3–13.

Shapiro, C. 1983. "Premiums for High Quality Products as Returns to Reputations." *The Quarterly Journal of Economics* 98:659–80.

Shieh, S. 1996. "Price and Money-Back Guarantees as Signals of Product Quality." *Journal of Economics and Management Strategy* 5:361–77.

Singh, N., and X. Vives. 1984. "Price and Quantity Competition in a Differentiated Duopoly." *Rand Journal of Economics* 15:546–54.

Spence, M. 1973. "Job Market Signaling." *Quarterly Journal of Economics* 87:355–74.

Varian, H. R. 1990. "Monitoring Agents with Other Agents." *Journal of Institutional and Theoretical Economics* 146:153–74.

Vives, X. 1984. "Duopoly Information Equilibrium: Cournot and Bertrand." *Journal of Economic Theory* 34:71–94.

# CHAPTER 8

# ISSUES IN THE ANALYSIS OF TIME, RISK, AND UNCERTAINTY

### WILLIAM S. NEILSON

## 8.1 INTRODUCTION

THE studies of time, risk, and uncertainty provide the underpinnings for one of the most fundamental tasks in managerial economics, the valuation of future income streams. Remarkably, for the most part this literature has promoted a single model as its standard.

Let $\tilde{x}$ denote a lottery with outcomes $x_1, \ldots, x_n$ occurring with probabilities $p_1, \ldots, p_n$ and at times $t_1, \ldots, t_n$ periods from today. According to the standard model, discounted expected utility (DEU), the individual evaluates such lotteries according to the formula

$$DEU(\tilde{x}) = \sum_{i=1}^{n} p_i \, \delta^{t_i} u(x_i).$$

The individual evaluates the potential outcome $x_i$ according to the contemporaneous utility function $u$, discounts it into current utility using the discount factor $\delta$, and then takes the expected value of these discounted utility values by weighting them according to the probabilities with which they occur. Time preferences are captured by the exponential discounting term $\delta^t$, an idea that traces back at least to Samuelson (1937). Risk occurs when the probabilities are known while uncertainty (also called ambiguity) occurs when the probabilities are unknown, a dichotomy introduced by Knight (1921). The expected utility form $\sum p_i u(x_i)$ was first introduced by Bernoulli (1954) in 1738, and axiomatized by von Neumann and Morgenstern (1944) for the case of risk where the decision maker knows the underlying probabilities. Anscombe and Aumann

(1963) and Savage (1954) provided axiomatic foundations for the formation of subjective probabilities in the case of uncertainty. The literature has long rested on firm axiomatic underpinnings.

The study of preferences over time has concentrated on the term $\delta^t$, where the discount factor $\delta \leq 1$ reflects the decision maker's impatience. The closer $\delta$ is to one, the more patient the individual is and the less she discounts future payoffs when comparing them to current payoffs. On the other hand, as $\delta$ moves closer to zero, the less patient the individual is and the less weight future payoffs receive in the discounted expected utility computation. From the standpoint of time preferences, the key assumption in the discounted expected utility model has the discount factor $\delta$ independent of the time horizon $t$. Experimental and other evidence suggests that the discount factor increases with the time horizon, which can lead to time inconsistent preferences. These topics are taken up in Section 8.2.

In expected utility theory, the shape of the utility function $u(x)$ governs risk attitudes, with a concave function corresponding to risk aversion and a convex function corresponding to a preference for increasing risk. An implicit assumption of the model, though, is that an individual has only a single, stable utility function, and there are good theoretical reasons why this might not be the case. Section 8.3 presents these arguments and provides some insight from the exploding literature on how risk attitudes vary with demographics, choice context, and other factors. A single utility function is not the only implicit assumption pertaining to risk, though. The discounted expected utility model also assumes that utility values are weighted by the probabilities when taking the expected value, and Section 8.3 also describes the leading alternative model which transforms the probability distribution before taking the expectation.

The discounted expected utility model makes no real distinction between risk and uncertainty. Either way, the individual forms a well-behaved probability distribution and takes the mathematical expectation of utility according to that distribution. Individuals might exhibit aversion to uncertainty beyond their aversions to risk, but the discounted subjective expected utility model cannot accommodate uncertainty aversion. Section 8.4 presents some evidence of this and reviews the alternative ways that theorists think about uncertainty aversion.

Time, risk, and uncertainty are all entities that have value to individuals. To be more precise, they all have negative values, and individuals are willing to pay to avoid delays, risk, and uncertainty. It is important for managers, and also for researchers in managerial economics, to have a thorough understanding of these negative values because they have major implications for how firms deal with their customers, their suppliers, and their employees. For example, writing a contract with a supplier who must bear up-front costs in return for future payment on delivery involves time (the delay for the payment), risk (because the costs might have a random component), and uncertainty (if the distribution of that random component is not fully understood). The firm writing the contract must compensate the supplier for each of these factors, and the nuances of preferences determine how much the firm must pay. All of these important applications are covered elsewhere in this book, and one goal of this chapter is to provide enough intuition along with enough rigor for readers to determine how preferences impact behavior in managerial economics.

## 8.2  TIME

The standard problem in the study of choice over time concerns an individual comparing alternative consumption streams. Notationally, let $(c_0, c_1, \ldots, c_T)$ denote a consumption stream in which the individual consumes the amount $c_0$ in the current period, consumes $c_1$ one period in the future, $c_2$ two periods in the future, and so on through $T$ periods in the future. The standard model evaluates this consumption stream according to the discounted utility model

$$DU(c_0, \ldots, c_T) = \sum_{t=0}^{T} \delta^t u(c_t), \tag{8.1}$$

where $\delta \in (0,1)$ is the individual's *subjective discount factor*. The subjective discount factor is a component of the individual's preferences reflecting her degree of patience, and it is the primary subject of this section. The subjective discount factor has a corresponding *subjective discount rate* $\rho > 0$ given by

$$\delta = \frac{1}{1+\rho},$$

which acts much like an interest rate in that the individual discounts consumption that arrives in the future according to the "interest rate" $\rho$. The utility-of-consumption function $u(c)$ typically is assumed to be concave to reflect diminishing marginal utility of consumption.

Consider an individual who lives for two periods, has no bequest motive, gets utility from consumption only, earns $y_0$ in the current period, and earns $y_1$ in the final period. The market interest rate, at which she can either borrow or save, is $r$. She must choose a consumption path $(c_0, c_1)$ to maximize $DU(c_0, c_1)$ subject to the budget constraint

$$c_1 = (y_0 - c_0)(1 + r) + y_1,$$

which is easily interpreted. If the individual consumes less than her income in the current period, so that $y_0 - c_0 > 0$, she saves the remainder at interest rate $r$. After one period she has $(y_0 - c_0)(1 + r)$ in her account. She empties her account in period 1, combines it with her period-1 income $y_1$, and consumes the combined amount. If, on the other hand, she consumes more than her income in the current period, she must borrow $c_0 - y_0$ to finance her spending. She borrows at interest rate $r$ and must repay $(c_0 - y_0)(1 + r)$ in period 1. She subtracts this amount from her period-1 income and consumes the rest, yielding consumption $c_1 = (y_0 - c_0)(1 + r) + y_1$.

The consumer's problem reduces to choosing $c_0$ to maximize

$$DU(c_0, c_1) = u(c_0) + \frac{1}{1+\rho}(u(y_0 - c_0)(1+r) + y_1).$$

The first-order condition is

$$\frac{u'(c_1)}{u'(c_0)} = \frac{1+\rho}{1+r}.$$

Holding the market interest rate $r$ constant, and keeping in mind that the concavity of $u$ implies that $u'(c)$ is a decreasing function, increases in the subjective discount rate imply that the individual skews consumption toward the present and away from the future, that is, it increases the ratio $c_0/c_1$. This fits perfectly with the intuition that higher subjective discount rates reflect lower levels of patience, because the formula implies that a less-patient individual consumes more now and less later. Furthermore, the formula also shows that the two consumption levels are equal when the subjective discount rate exactly matches the market interest rate.

To determine people's tendencies to skew consumption toward the present it becomes necessary to measure the subjective discount rate and compare it to the market interest rate. Warner and Pleeter (2001) do just this through clever exploitation of a natural experiment. In 1991 the US Department of Defense was authorized to reduce the armed forces' active duty strength by 25%, with the reduction to come from every rank and every experience level. The military accomplished this by offering early separation incentives, and they offered everyone in the military a choice between a lump-sum payment or an annuity, both of them tied to the individual's current pay and years of service. For each instance one can compute an interest rate that makes the annuity have the same present value as the lump-sum payment, and the average interest rate that equalizes the two values was 18%. This equalizing interest rate was much higher than the prevailing market interest rate of 7%. Still, if the individual making the choice had a subjective discount rate greater than 18% she should take the lump sum, and if she had a subjective discount rate less than 18% she would be better off with the annuity.

More than 90% of the enlisted personnel who elected to leave the military chose the lump-sum separation payment. In the United States, enlisted personnel tend not to have college educations, but officers do. More than 50% of the officers who chose to separate also took the lump sum. Warner and Pleeter estimated an average subjective discount rate of 20% for officers and 26% for enlisted personnel. Perhaps the most striking feature of their analysis is how profitable exploiting impatience was for the military. If the government had made only the annuity option available, and if the same set of individuals had left the military, the payments would have cost the government a present value of $4.2 billion. By offering the lump sum as an alternative the government spent only $2.5 billion. Offering the lump-sum option proved to be a win-win situation as it improved the well-being of those who chose it and it saved the taxpayers a substantial sum of money.

## 8.2.1  Decreasing Impatience

The standard discounted utility model (8.1) has considerable appeal because it is simple to analyze and it has only a single parameter, the subjective discount factor $\delta$ or, equivalently, the subjective discount rate $\rho$. It has proven to be too simple, though. In the standard discounted utility model the discount factor is assumed to be independent of the time horizon, but experimental and other evidence suggests that this independence fails.

To set a running example, consider the following pair of choices. The first choice is between \$95 today and \$100 in four weeks, and many people would prefer the immediate sum, \$95. According to the discounted expected utility model where $\delta$ is the weekly discount factor, the individual chooses \$95 today if $u(95) > \delta^4 u(100)$, which reduces to

$$\delta^4 < \frac{u(95)}{u(100)}. \tag{8.2}$$

This condition has the simple interpretation that the subject chooses \$100 today if she is sufficiently impatient. If one assumes a linear functional form for $u$, condition (8.2) yields a weekly discount factor no higher than 0.987, which translates into an annual subjective discount factor no higher than 0.513 and an annual subjective discount rate $\rho$ no lower than 94.9%. The individual must be very impatient to be unwilling to delay the payment by four weeks in order to earn an extra \$5.

The second choice pair is between a \$95 payment in 26 weeks or a \$100 payment in 30 weeks. According to the discounted expected utility model they choose \$95 in 26 weeks if $\delta^{26} u(95) > \delta^{30} u(100)$, which reduces to exactly expression (8.2) for choosing the immediate \$95 payment. If the individual chooses the earlier payment in the first choice task, the model predicts that she will choose the earlier payment in the second. This prediction has not held up to experimental evidence, though. Subjects tend to choose the later \$100 payment when both payments are delayed, but they choose the earlier \$95 payment when there is no delay in receiving it.

The evidence is consistent with discount factors that increase with the length of the time horizon or, equivalently, subjective discount rates that decrease with the time horizon. For the example, choosing \$95 today requires an annual discount factor below 0.513, but declining \$95 in 26 weeks requires an annual discount factor above 0.513. The discount factor that applies to payments delayed by half a year seems higher than the one that applies to instant payments. Impatience appears to lessen as all payments are moved farther into the future.

Researchers have proposed several variants of the discounted utility model to account for this declining impatience, but two of them deserve special notice. Ainslie (1992) proposes *hyperbolic discounting*, which takes the general discounted utility form

$$GDU(c_0,\ldots,c_T) = u(c_0) + \sum_{t=1}^{T} \left( \prod_{s=1}^{t} d(s) \right) u(c_t).$$

The discount factor $\delta(s)$ is used to discount a payment delayed from period $s - 1$ to period $s$ and the standard model of equation (8.1) assumes that $\delta(s) = \delta$ for all $s$. This constant discounting model is often referred to as the *exponential discounting model* because $\prod_{s=1}^{t} \delta(s) = \delta^t$. Hyperbolic discounting, on the other hand, allows for declining impatience by assuming that

$$\delta(s) = \frac{1+(s-1)h}{1+sh}.$$

This formula has several desirable features. First, when $s = 1$ so that the individual is discounting the future from the present, the discount factor reduces to $1/(1 + h)$, so $h$ plays the role of a subjective discount rate for discounting one period from the present. Second, $\delta(s)$ increases with $s$, eventually converging to one, so it allows for lessening impatience. Finally, and importantly, it has only a single parameter $h$, with the value of $h$ being determined entirely by how much the individual discounts when comparing current payments to payments delayed by one period.

Another alternative to exponential discounting is Laibson's (1997) quasi-hyperbolic discounting, a model sometimes referred to as $(\beta,\delta)$ preferences. An individual with these preferences has the discounted utility form

$$QHDU(c_0,\ldots,c_T) = u(c_0) + b\sum_{t=1}^{T} \delta^t u(c_t).$$

In this model payments made one period in the future are discounted by the factor $\beta\delta$, payments made two periods in the future are discounted by $\beta\delta^2$, and so on. The key to the quasi-hyperbolic discounting model is that it treats delays from the current period to the future differently than it treats delays from a future period to one farther in the future. This can be seen by considering the running example: the individual chooses \$95 now over \$100 in four weeks if $u(95) > \beta\delta^4 u(100)$ but chooses \$100 in 30 weeks over \$95 in 26 weeks if $\beta\delta^{30}u(100) > \beta\delta^{26}u(95)$ which reduces to $\delta^4 u(100) > u(95)$. The two choices are no longer contradictory.

The appeal of the quasi-hyperbolic discounting model is its utter simplicity. The model looks just like the standard exponential discounting model except that all future payments are discounted by an additional factor of $\beta < 1$. The parameter $\beta$, then, reflects the individual's present-bias, and smaller values of $\beta$ translate into a stronger preference for immediate payments over delayed payments, regardless of how long the payments are delayed.

## 8.2.2  Time Inconsistency

Declining impatience, whether represented through hyperbolic discounting, quasi-hyperbolic discounting, or something else entirely leads to a time inconsistency problem, an issue first noted by Strotz (1955). Continuing with the running example, suppose that an individual prefers $95 now to $100 in four weeks, but prefers $100 in 30 weeks to $95 in 26 weeks. If she is given a chance to reconsider this second choice after half a year, she faces a choice between $95 now and $100 in four weeks. Unless her preferences change, 26 weeks from now she will choose something different than she would have chosen for herself today. The time inconsistency problem arises because the individual is more patient when determining now allocations that will take place in the future than she will be when the future actually arrives.

Individuals can be classified into three types depending on whether their discount factors increase with the time horizon and whether they are time inconsistent. The first type has ordinary exponential discounting and these individuals are automatically time consistent. The other two types have increasing discount factors. Sophisticated agents realize that they have time-inconsistent preferences and correctly forecast their future choices. Naive agents do not recognize their time inconsistency problem and so believe that they really will be less impatient when the future arrives. In the example, a sophisticated agent understands that 26 weeks from now she will choose the immediate $95 payment over the delayed $100 payment. A naive agent does not, and believes that 26 weeks from now she will prefer the delayed $100 payment. This leads to very different behavior.

Gilpatric (2009) explores how this works for rebates. The consumer goes to the store and sees that the item she is considering offers a mail-in rebate. To collect the rebate she must purchase the item, send in the receipt along with a UPC code from the package, and then some time later will receive a check or a debit card in the amount of the rebate. Assume that the consumer values the item at $V$, the before-rebate price is $P$, and the rebate amount is $R$. The purchase takes place in period 0, the consumer submits the rebate information at cost $C$ in period 1, and the consumer receives the rebate check in period 2, with the delays between periods of equal length to simplify the discussion.

First think how a time consistent exponential discounter approaches the problem. In period 0 she must consider three different paths. The first path comes from not purchasing the item, in which case her payoff is zero. The second path comes from purchasing the item and submitting the rebate form, in which case her discounted payoff is $V - P - \delta C + \delta^2 R$. The third path entails purchasing the item but not redeeming the rebate coupon, in which case her discounted payoff is simply $V - P$. If she selects path 2 it implies that $V - P - \delta C + \delta^2 R > V - P$, which reduces to $\delta R > C$, exactly the condition that governs her period-1 choice of whether to submit the rebate request. Consequently, if she chooses path 2 in period 0 she really will file for the rebate in period 1, and her plans are time consistent.

Contrast this with the decisions of a naive customer with quasi-hyperbolic discounting. At time 0 she considers the same three paths, but values the rebate path at $V - P - \beta\delta C + \beta\delta^2 R$. The quasi-hyperbolic consumer discounts both the filing cost $C$ and the rebate $R$ more than the exponential discounter does. She chooses the rebate path over the purchase-but-no-rebate path if $V - P - \beta\delta C + \beta\delta^2 R > V - P$, which reduces to $\delta R > C$ just as in the exponential discounting case. In particular, she behaves as if at time 1 she will discount the time-2 rebate by $\delta$. This is not how she actually behaves at time 1, though, because at time 1 she values claiming the rebate at $-C + \beta\delta R$, which is less than the projected time-0 value of $-C + \delta R$. If $\beta\delta R < C < \delta R$ the quasi-hyperbolic consumer believes that she will redeem the rebate (the second inequality) but when it comes time to actually mail in the rebate form she will choose not to. She therefore ends up paying the full price $P$ for the item, and if $P > V$ she will regret buying it because it was not worth the price she paid. She bought it because of the rebate, but did not follow through.

A sophisticated consumer with quasi-hyperbolic preferences behaves differently again. The sophisticated agent looks ahead to period 1 to determine whether she will file for the rebate or not. If not, she deduces that the rebate path is not feasible, and restricts the choice to either the no-purchase path or the purchase-but-no-rebate path. Consequently, if she will not file for the rebate because $\beta\delta R < C$, she will purchase the product only if it is worthwhile when paying full price, that is, when $V > P$. Because of this, a sophisticated agent cannot regret her original purchase.

We end up with three very different behavioral predictions for the three types, the most interesting of which occur when $-C + \delta R > 0$ and $V - P < 0 < V - P - \beta\delta C + \beta D^2 R < V - P - \delta C + D^2 R$. The exponential discounter buys the item and collects the rebate. The naive quasi-hyperbolic discounter buys the item with the intention of collecting the rebate but never collects it and therefore regrets her purchase. The sophisticated quasi-hyperbolic discounter thinks that the item would be worth purchasing if she collected the rebate but knows that she will not do so, so she refrains from purchasing the item. Present-bias hurts both naive and sophisticated quasi-hyperbolic consumers, but the time inconsistency only hurts the naive ones. O'Donoghue and Rabin (1999) use the same ideas to look at procrastination of a project that must be performed only once. They find that naive agents are hurt when there are immediate costs and delayed rewards, as with the decision to redeem a rebate coupon, but that sophisticated agents are hurt in situations with immediate rewards and delayed costs. As for implications of the preferences, Gilpatric (2008) looks at declining impatience and time inconsistency in a contracting setting, and shows that naive present-biased agents might sign contracts that they later will not wish to fulfill, and he derives the optimal contract for that setting. He finds that optimal contracts do not always contain penalties sufficient to force agents to overcome their self-control problems, but instead sometimes use penalties small enough that the naive present-biased agents will choose to pay them. In this way a principal can exploit the present-biasedness and naiveté of agents. Laibson (1997) looks at savings behavior and argues that the abundance of financial instruments that attach penalties to early liquidation, such as retirement accounts or home purchases, might constitute a market response to savers' time inconsistency problems. He also notes, however, that most recent financial innovations have moved to increase liquidity, not decrease it, and these innovations might explain the drop in the US savings rate.

# 8.3  RISK

In its earliest incarnation, expected utility took the form

$$EU(\tilde{x}) = \sum p_i u(w + x_i), \tag{8.3}$$

where $w$ denotes initial wealth, $x_i$ denotes income from the gamble, and the decision maker chooses among gambles $\tilde{x}$ to maximize $EU(\tilde{x})$. This functional form leads to a number of conveniences. Risk aversion, or a preference for the expected value of a gamble over the gamble itself, is implied by a concave utility function $u$, and more concave functions are more risk averse. Furthermore, since wealth is always nonnegative (presumably), one can use convenient functional forms for $u$ such as the natural logarithm or the square root.

An individual's degree of risk aversion impacts some important choices. For example, more risk-averse individuals invest less in high-risk/high-return assets and more in low-risk/low-return ones. Risk aversion also leads to less bargaining power. To connect risk aversion and bargaining, consider an alternating offers game in which two players bargain over how to divide a surplus. Player 1 proposes a division to player 2, who can either accept or reject. If she accepts they allocate the surplus according to the proposed division and the bargaining process is over, but if she rejects then with some probability $p$ the game ends and they both walk away with nothing. With probability $1 - p$, though, the game continues, in which case player 2 proposes a division to player 1, who either accepts or rejects. If 1 rejects then, once again, the game can end with probability $p$ and both walk away with nothing; otherwise player 1 makes the next offer. The degree of risk aversion impacts the lowest offer players will accept when it is their turn to accept offers, with a more risk-averse player willing to settle for a smaller certain payoff to avoid the lottery.

A third type of choice impacted by the degree of risk aversion is search behavior. Consider an individual seeking an attractive match, such as one that would arise from a higher-paying and more prestigious job, from a more appealing spouse, or from a lower price for a planned purchase. Every time the individual conducts a market search, she bears a cost. After taking a draw from the market, she must compare the value of the match she observes against the expected utility of a new random draw, less the search cost. A more risk-averse searcher values the future random draw less, so is likely to stop sooner, ending up with a less attractive match.

All three of these consequences of greater risk aversion—less aggressive financial investing, less aggressive bargaining, and less aggressive search—have important implications for an individual's income and wealth. Because more risk-averse individuals search less and have less bargaining power, they tend to be paid less in their jobs and they tend to pay more for big-ticket items like cars or houses. Because they also invest less in high-risk/high-return assets like equities, they tend to accumulate less wealth than more risk-tolerant individuals.

## 8.3.1 Arguments against the Existence of a Single Utility Function

The expected utility representation makes discussions of risk aversion simple, because everything is driven by the concavity of the utility function $u$. Two separate lines of inquiry suggest that the expected utility representation in (8.3), with a single utility function defined over wealth levels, may not be appropriate. One approach, taken by Rabin (2000), shows that, theoretically, if an individual with a preference representation as given in (8.3) is averse to the same small-stakes gamble at every wealth level, then she must be implausibly averse to large-stakes gambles. For example, consider the 50:50 gamble in which the bettor can win $110 or lose $100 based on the toss of a fair coin. If the individual in (8.3) turns down this gamble at every wealth level, that is, for every value of $w$, then that person would necessarily turn down any 50:50 gamble that involves a loss of $1000 or more, regardless of how large the gain is. Rabin argues that people cannot possibly be this risk averse, and researchers have come to know this result as the *Rabin calibration theorem*.

The method of proving the assertion points to where the problem lies. Start at, say, wealth level $w = 1000$ and consider a 50:50 win $110:lose $100 gamble. Turning down the gamble puts a constraint on the concavity of $u$ over the [900,1110] interval. Turning down the gamble when wealth is 1210 restricts the concavity over the [1110,1320] interval. Pasting together these concave segments yields a very concave utility function over a large interval, and after pasting together all of the segments one is left with a function so concave that no gain can make up for a 50% chance of losing $1000.

A second line of inquiry is based on experimental evidence, and it traces back to Kahneman and Tversky's (1979) original prospect theory paper. They find, for example, that an individual would prefer a sure $3000 payment to an 80% chance of $4000 (and nothing otherwise), but that the same individual would prefer an 80% chance of losing $4000 to a sure loss of $3000. A utility function defined over final wealth levels cannot accommodate their evidence, because the first choice implies risk aversion but the second implies risk seeking. Kahneman and Tversky propose instead that the utility function should instead be defined over gains and losses from some reference wealth level. Put differently, the function $u(w + x)$ in equation (8.3) should be replaced by a function of the form $u(x; w)$, where $w$ denotes reference wealth and $x$ is the change in wealth, yielding

$$EU(\tilde{x}) = \sum p_i u(x_i; w). \tag{8.4}$$

Moreover, the utility function would be S-shaped over changes in wealth—namely, concave over gains and convex over losses, in order to accommodate the evidence. Such a utility function is shown in Figure 8.1.

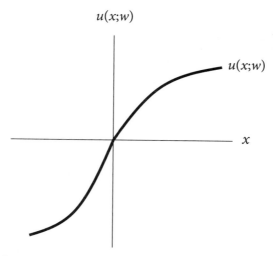

FIGURE 8.1: The S-shaped reference-dependent utility function

These two lines of inquiry, the Rabin calibration theorem and Kahneman and Tversky's reference-dependent utility, are compatible. In particular, reference-dependent utility offers one solution to overcome Rabin's critique. Proving his assertion required moving initial wealth around and then pasting together concave portions of a single utility function. Reference dependence assumes that the individual has different utility functions corresponding to different reference wealth levels, though, so one cannot use Rabin's thought experiment to trace out an entire utility function.

## 8.3.2 Measuring Risk Attitudes

Because risk attitudes play an important role in many economic outcomes, it becomes important to measure them. One way to do this would be to look at economic data from the pertinent economic problem, such as from financial, insurance, or labor market decisions, and use the data to infer levels of risk aversion. Although valuable, such an approach begs the question of whether levels of risk aversion correlate with the decisions, because the approach assumes the correlation and then backs the degree of risk aversion out of the choices. To identify the correlation properly, one would have to measure risk aversion directly and then determine whether the measured level of risk aversion correlates with the behaviors of interest. This allows one to see if more risk-averse people do, in fact, invest in lower-risk/lower-return portfolios, but it requires measuring risk aversion for a sample whose economic decisions are also observable.

One promising method inserts questions designed to gauge risk attitudes into a survey. The following provides an example of a common survey question from the Health and Retirement Study (see Anderson and Mellor 2009).

Suppose you are the only income earner in the family, and you have a good job guaranteed to give you your current (family) income every year for life. You are given the opportunity to take a new and equally good job, with a 50–50 chance it will double your (family) income and a 50–50 chance it will cut your (family) income by a third. Would you take the new job?

A risk neutral respondent would take the new job because if $w$ denotes current income then the new job has expected income of $\frac{4}{3}w$. A sufficiently risk-averse respondent, on the other hand, would stay with the current job. This methodology for assessing risk attitudes directly has good external validity. For example, Barsky et al. (1997) use data from the Panel Study of Income Dynamics (PSID) to find that respondents whom the survey reveals as more risk tolerant are more likely to smoke, more likely to drink, more likely to be self-employed, and more likely to be uninsured. They also hold a larger share of their wealth in stocks. Similarly, Schmidt (2008) finds that women who are more risk tolerant according to the survey marry later and are more likely to either have children earlier or delay them indefinitely.

As noted in the previous subsection, there are both theoretical and experimental reasons to believe that a single individual's risk attitudes vary with both circumstances and the type of risk being evaluated. This issue can be addressed using a set of survey questions rather than a single one. When the survey is designed appropriately, the responses have implications for the coefficient of relative risk aversion when the utility function is specified to have the power function form $u(z) = z^{1-r}$. These augmented survey designs provide empirical evidence supporting the conjecture of situation-specific utility functions, and the extent of context-dependence and the magnitude of the individual risk attitude swings can be surprising. For example, one would believe that insuring a car and insuring a home would constitute such sufficiently similar situations that they would be governed by the same utility function. After all, the reference wealth for both should be about the same, and both involve large, unlikely losses. Barseghyan et al. (2011) determine whether individuals could use the same coefficient of relative risk aversion $r$ in making their deductible choices for three types of insurance coverage: auto collision, auto comprehensive, and all home perils. Because customers are offered menus of deductibles and premium rates, the choice task is able to provide a fairly fine partition of risk aversion coefficients. Barseghyan et al. rule out identical risk aversion coefficients in 77% of cases, with households being more risk averse in home deductible choices than in automobile deductible choices. In terms of magnitude, the house insurance risk aversion coefficients suggest that a household would be willing to pay more than $45 to avoid a 50:50 chance of winning or losing $100, but the car insurance coefficients suggest that the same household would be willing to pay less than $30 to avoid the same lottery. These are significant differences in behavior from subtle differences in context.

Prior experiences also impact risk attitudes. One example of this is for so-called Depression babies, people who grew up during the Great Depression and had their attitudes toward saving and thriftiness changed by the experience. Malmendier and Nagel

(2011) take the idea of Depression babies seriously and look at the financial investment behavior of people who have experienced low market returns. They found that individuals who had experienced low stock market returns throughout their lives were less willing to take financial risks, less willing to participate in the stock market, invested smaller proportions in stocks when they did participate in the market, and were more pessimistic about future stock returns. The same held true for bond markets, with people who had experienced low bond returns less likely to own bonds. More recent experiences had stronger effects, a finding further documented by Liu et al. (2010), who use Taiwan Stock Exchange data to compare individual investors' afternoon trading to their morning gains. Their data show that morning gains lead investors to take above-average afternoon risks.

This last effect, that past experiences affect current risk attitudes, may operate through reference wealth changes. Reference wealth plays an important role in these context-specific utility functions, but it has a second role as well because it anchors the point around which the individual becomes loss averse. Loss aversion occurs when an individual's utility falls more when $x is lost than it rises when $x is gained, and loss aversion is a key feature of prospect theory (Kahneman and Tversky 1979). It implies that individuals forego mean-zero gambles around the reference point. Reference points become doubly important because researchers have reached a consensus that individuals tend to be risk averse over gains but risk tolerant over losses as in Figure 8.1. Consequently, it becomes important to have an idea of how reference points are formed and, more importantly, how they change over a sequence of decisions.

Kahneman (1992) provides a thought experiment that illustrates all of the difficulties with reference points. Suppose that you have good reason to expect a $5,000 raise, but in the end receive only $3,000. Is this a gain or a loss? If you integrate the anticipated raise into your reference point, then the actual raise constitutes a $2,000 loss. On the other hand, if you segregate the anticipated raise from current income, the actual raise constitutes a $3,000 gain. Anything in between is also possible. The same issue arises in stock holdings. Suppose that you purchased the stock for $10,000. The price then rose as high as $15,000, but has since fallen to $13,000. Does the current price represent a $3,000 gain or a $2,000 loss?

Baucells et al. (2011) explore exactly this question, and their results provide insight into the dynamics of reference points. They present subjects with a stock price history beginning with the hypothetical purchase price, and ask subjects for the price which would generate zero experienced utility, that is, neither a gain nor a loss, which they consider the reference price. They found that if the subject purchased the stock at price $p_0$ and then observed subsequent prices $p_1, \ldots, p_n$, with $p_n$ the most recent price, then the primary factors influencing the reference point are the original price $p_0$ and the most recent price $p_n$. If the subject observes one more price, $p_{n+1}$, then the importance of the next-most recent price $p_n$ falls dramatically, but the importance of the purchase price $p_0$ does not. Greatly simplified, the reference price can be captured by the weighted average $\alpha p_0 + (1 - \alpha)p_n$, where $p_n$ is the most recent observed price. Moreover, weights close to ½ fit the data well.

While this analysis provides an easy answer to Kahneman's thought experiment—the $3,000 raise is considered a $500 gain because the reference point already included half of the anticipated $5,000 raise—it does not explain the Liu et al. finding that morning gains lead to increased afternoon risk taking on the Taiwan Stock Exchange. Neilson (1998) shows that such behavior is more readily explained if one segregates the reference point into two components, original wealth and the gains so far. This two-component reference wealth model easily allows for a house-money effect, where investors who have experienced a gain become more risk tolerant over asset positions that do not jeopardize the entire experienced gain, as well as the breakeven effect, where investors who have experienced a loss become more risk tolerant over asset positions that allow for a possibility of recouping the losses.

Explicit modeling of reference points for utility functions remains an ongoing research topic with much still to learn. Furthermore, risk attitudes seem to change with circumstances, as seen from the discussion of deductibles for different types of insurance and from the discussion of Depression babies. Future research will continue to document patterns in risk attitudes. However, evidence also suggests that the reference-dependent utility function alone may not be enough to capture all of the relevant patterns in risk attitudes. Put differently, experimental evidence has called into question the expected utility model itself, and the next section explores alternative formulations.

## 8.3.3  Probability Transformations

That the expected utility formulation in (8.4) cannot accommodate all patterns in behavior toward risk has become well accepted among economists. The first evidence traces back to Maurice Allais' famous paradox. Letting ($x,p_x$; $y,p_y$; $z,p_z$) denote a lottery which pays $x$ with probability $p_x$, $y$ with probability $p_y$, and $z$ with probability $p_z$, the Allais paradox involves two separate pairwise decisions. When given a choice between A = ($1M, 1.00) and B = ($5M, 0.10; $1M, 0.89; $0, 0.01) where M denotes millions, a majority of respondents prefer A. Lottery B has a larger expected payoff, but it also has a slight chance of not winning anything, and many people would rather have the sure $1 million than risk getting nothing. When given a choice between C = ($1M, 0.11; $0, 0.89) and D = ($5M, 0.10; $0, 0.90), a majority of respondents prefer D. Lottery D has a higher expected payoff, a much higher payoff conditional on winning, and only a slightly smaller probability of winning. Furthermore, neither C nor D offers much chance of winning anything at all. The most common pair of choices is [A,D]. The "paradox" comes from the fact that this pair violates expected utility.

More precisely, there is no utility function $u$ in (8.4) for which $EU(A) > EU(B)$ and $EU(D) > EU(C)$. One can prove this quite easily. Writing out the expected utility representation (and dropping the initial wealth term for notational simplicity) one finds that

$$EU(A) - EU(B) = u(1) - [0.10u(5) + 0.89u(1) + 0.01u(0)]$$
$$= 0.11u(1) - 0.10u(5) - 0.01u(0),$$

(8.5)

where the arguments of the utility function correspond to millions of dollars for notational ease. Similarly,

$$EU(D) - EU(A) = [0.10u(5) + 0.90u(0)] - [0.11u(1) + 0.89u(0)]$$
$$= 0.10u(5) + 0.01u(0) - 0.11u(1). \qquad (8.6)$$

The individual prefers A to B if the expression in (8.5) is positive and prefers D to C if the expression in (8.6) is positive. But this provides a contradiction, because if (8.5) is positive then (8.6) must be negative, and vice versa.

The decade of the 1980s saw theorists devoting attention to offering alternatives to expected utility in response to this empirical challenge. Experimentalists responded with new evidence challenging the new choice theories. To the extent that this process spawned a "winner," that winner is Tversky and Kahneman's (1992) *cumulative prospect theory*, itself based on Quiggin's (1982) rank-dependent expected utility theory. To explain the model, consider lotteries with three or fewer outcomes, as in the Allais paradox lotteries, restrict all of the outcomes to be gains, again as in the Allais paradox lotteries, and order the gains $x_1 < x_2 < x_3$. For the Allais paradox lotteries the corresponding values are $x_1 = 0$, $x_2 = 1M$, and $x_3 = 5M$. The preference representation combines a utility function $u(x)$, defined over gains and losses as discussed above, and a probability transformation function $g(p)$ into

$$CPT(x) = g(p_1)u(x_1) + [g(p_1 + p_2) - g(p_1)]u(x_2) + [1 - g(p_1 + p_2)]u(x_3). \qquad (8.7)$$

The cumulative prospect theory representation in (8.7) differs from the expected utility representation in (8.4) by transforming the probability distribution before computing the expectation of the utility values of the payoffs. Figure 8.2 illustrates how this works. The horizontal axis shows the original probabilities, and the vertical axis shows the transformed probabilities. The diagonal dashed line is the 45° line. In an expected utility world, the individual would weight the utility value $u(x_1)$ by $p_1$, weight $u(x_2)$ by $p_2 = (p_1 + p_2) - p_1$, and weight $u(x_3)$ by $p_3 = 1 - (p_1 + p_2)$. In a cumulative prospect theory world, the individual weights $u(x_1)$ by $g(p_1)$ instead of $p_1$, weights $u(x_2)$ by $g(p_1 + p_2) - g(p_1)$ instead of $(p_1 + p_2) - p_1$, and weights $u(x_3)$ by $1 - g(p_1 + p_2)$ instead of $1 - (p_1 + p_2)$.

Probability transformation functions are restricted to be strictly increasing with $g(0) = 0$ and $g(1) = 1$. The one depicted in Figure 8.2 is typical, with an inverted S shape. This shape has an interpretation. The fact that $g(p_1)$ is above the 45° line means that a cumulative prospect theory individual overweights that outcome relative to an expected utility maximizer. Given that $x_1$ is the least desirable of the three outcomes, this contributes another source of risk aversion beyond the shape of the utility function $u(x)$, and it can be thought of as pessimism: The cumulative prospect theory individual behaves as if the worst outcome is more likely than an expected utility maximizer facing exactly the same lottery.

As documented by Neilson (2003), cumulative prospect theory leads to two primary behavioral differences compared to expected utility. One is that *CPT* maximizers tend to overweight unlikely, extreme outcomes. In Figure 8.2 the cumulative prospect theory individual places considerably more weight on $u(x_1)$, considerably less weight on $u(x_2)$,

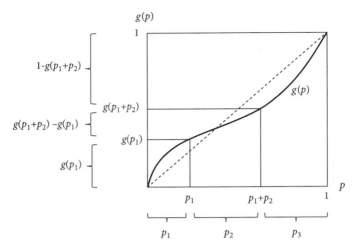

**FIGURE 8.2:** Probability transformation function

and slightly more on $u(x_3)$ than an expected utility maximizer would. Consequently, the cumulative prospect theory individual shown in the figure places more weight on the tails of the distribution than an expected utility maximizer would. This overweighting of unlikely, extreme outcomes has important behavioral implications, the most obvious of which is that it leads individuals to both buy lottery tickets for small chances of large gains and insure against unlikely losses.[1] Cumulative prospect theory is not the first model to account for this pattern. Friedman and Savage (1948) accommodate purchases of both insurance and lottery tickets using the nonreference-wealth-dependent expected utility model of equation (8.3), and Markowitz (1952) does the same using the reference-wealth-dependent expected utility model of equation (8.4). Both of these explanations, based only on the shape of the utility function, can allow for some insurance purchases and some lottery ticket purchases, but only when the payoffs are in the "right" range. Cumulative prospect theory, in contrast, links the pattern to the probabilities and allows it to exist irrespective of the size of the payoffs.

Relative to expected utility theory, cumulative prospect theory creates inertia around certainty, and this is the second behavioral difference between the models. In other words, cumulative prospect theory individuals prove much more difficult to entice away from sure things than expected utility maximizers are. To see this, consider a comparison between (a) a sure gain of $x$ or (b) a $p:1 - p$ chance of gaining $x - \varepsilon$ or gaining $x + \varepsilon$, where $\varepsilon > 0$. An expected utility maximizer compares $EU(a) = u(x)$ to $EU(b) = pu(x - \varepsilon) + (1 - p)u(x + \varepsilon)$. A cumulative prospect theory individual, in contrast, compares $CPT(a) = g(1)u(x) = u(x)$ to $CPT(b) = g(p)u(x - \varepsilon) + [1 - g(p)]u(x + \varepsilon)$. If $g(p) > p$, it becomes possible for

$$pu(x - \varepsilon) + (1 - p)u(x + \varepsilon) > u(x) > g(p)u(x - \varepsilon) + [1 - g(p)]u(x + \varepsilon),$$

in which case the expected utility maximizer would choose the gamble (b) whereas a cumulative prospect theory individual would prefer the sure thing (a). This tendency manifests itself in greater propensity to buy full insurance with no deductible, and greater propensity to take no position, either long or short, in a given financial asset. In contrast, expected utility predicts that individuals buy full insurance only when the premium exactly equals the expected benefit payment, and that investors take some non-zero position in every undominated financial asset. Thus, cumulative prospect theory allows for some prominent real-world behavioral patterns.

# 8.4  UNCERTAINTY

The difference between risk and uncertainty can be illustrated with the three-color Ellsberg problem (Ellsberg 1961). The decision maker must draw a ball from an urn containing 90 balls in a mixture of red, yellow, and black. The decision maker knows that exactly 30 of the balls are red, but has not been provided any information regarding the color composition of the remaining 60 balls. The decision maker is given a choice between a bet that pays $100 if she draws a red ball (and nothing otherwise) or a bet that pays $100 if she draws a yellow ball. Most people would bet on red.

The primary difference between the bet on red and the bet on yellow is that the individual knows the probability that she will win with red, but not the probability that she will win with yellow. We use the term *risk* to describe a setting in which the decision maker knows the probability distribution over outcomes, and the terms *uncertainty* or *ambiguity* to describe one in which she does not know the probability distribution. The bet on red, then, is a risky bet, but the bet on yellow is uncertain with a probability of winning somewhere between 0 and 2/3. People tend to be averse to uncertainty, consistent with their tendency to choose the bet on red. Further evidence of uncertainty aversion arises from another pair of bets, where the individual chooses between a bet that pays $100 if she draws a red or black ball and a bet that pays $100 if she draws a yellow or black ball. People tend to bet on yellow or black. They know that there are exactly 60 yellow or black balls, but the number of red or black balls could lie anywhere between 30 and 90. Once again they prefer the risky alternative of betting on yellow or black with its known 2/3 probability of winning over the uncertain alternative with an unknown probability of winning lying somewhere between 1/3 and certainty.

## 8.4.1  Subjective Probabilities

The first step in thinking systematically about uncertainty and unknown probabilities requires defining a set of objects to think about. In expected utility theory and behavior under risk, these objects are probability distributions or, equivalently, random variables. Because uncertainty rules out knowing probability distributions, something else must be used. Savage's (1954) pioneering work provided a foundation on which to build a theory of choice under uncertainty.

The model begins with a set of states of the world, $s_1, \ldots, s_n$. In the three-color Ellsberg urn, the three states of the world correspond to drawing a red, yellow, or black ball, respectively, and these can be denoted by $s_R$, $s_Y$, and $s_B$. The next step is to define an act as a mapping from the state of the world into an outcome, typically a monetary payoff, and acts are denoted by the function $f(s)$. For the three-color Ellsberg problem, the act corresponding to a bet on red is $f(s_R, s_Y, s_B) = (100, 0, 0)$ and the act corresponding to a bet on red or black is denoted is $g(s_R, s_Y, s_B) = (100, 0, 100)$. Decision makers have preferences over acts, just as decision makers over risks have preferences over probability distributions.

The key feature of an act is that it assigns payoffs, but not probabilities, to states. A probability distribution, on the other hand, assigns both, so that in a situation of risk the decision maker can compute the expectation of the utility values of the payoffs, as in expression (8.4). Savage (1954) and Anscombe and Aumann (1963) showed that if the set of acts is sufficiently rich and if the preferences over them satisfy key axioms, the decision maker forms a subjective probability distribution over states. More precisely, and ignoring reference wealth issues, there exists a utility function $u(x)$ and a probability distribution $\mu(s)$ assigning probabilities to states such that the individual's preferences over acts $f$ can be represented by the subjective expected utility formulation

$$SEU(f) = \sum u(f(s_i))\mu(s_i).$$

$$(8.8)$$

The intuition behind this formula is that when the individual chooses act $f$ and state $s_i$ occurs, her payoff is $f(s_i)$. She evaluates that according to the utility function $u(x)$, and then weights the utility value by the subjective probability of that state, $\mu(s_i)$. The result is an expected utility value, but the probabilities are subjective because of the uncertainty as opposed to objective as they would be for decisions under risk.

Subjective expected utility is attractive because it retains the basic form of expected utility and so all of the results from the expected utility analysis of risk carry over to the subjective expected utility analysis of uncertainty. In particular, if two individuals form the same subjective probabilities then their comparative risk attitudes are governed entirely by the utility function $u(x)$, and the researcher retains a large body of literature by presuming that individuals form subjective probabilities when the likelihood of different states of nature is unknown.

Subjective expected utility cannot handle the three-color Ellsberg setup, however. Suppose that the same individual bets on red instead of yellow, and also bets on yellow or black instead of on red or black. Because all of the bets are for $100, we have

$$SEU(\text{bet on red}) = \mu(s_R)u(100)$$

$$SEU(\text{bet on yellow}) = \mu(s_Y)u(100)$$

$$SEU(\text{bet on red or black}) = [\mu(s_R) + \mu(s_B)]u(100)$$

$$SEU(\text{bet on yellow or black}) = [\mu(s_Y) + \mu(s_B)]u(100).$$

$$(8.9)$$

The individual bets on red if $\mu(s_R) > \mu(s_Y)$, and bets on yellow or black if $\mu(s_Y) + \mu(s_B) > \mu(s_R) + \mu(s_B)$. These two inequalities are contradictory, regardless of the specific values of $\mu(s_R)$, $\mu(s_Y)$, and $\mu(s_B)$. Subjective expected utility, by its very nature, implies uncertainty neutrality, and cannot allow for uncertainty aversion. Because of this, researchers began looking for a useful alternative model. Unlike the case of preferences toward risk, no broad consensus has formed over which alternative model to use.

## 8.4.2  Uncertainty Aversion

One way to think about the Ellsberg paradox is that people behave as if, somehow, there are some missing balls. They know that 60 balls are either yellow or black, but they behave as if fewer than 30 are yellow and fewer than 30 are black. Taking this idea seriously leads to an alternative model of choice under uncertainty, Schmeidler's (1989) *Choquet expected utility*.

Consider the following set of "probabilities" for draws from the Ellsberg urn.

$$\begin{array}{ll}
\mu(\emptyset) = 0 & \mu(s_R \text{ or } s_Y) = 7/12 \\
\mu(s_R) = 1/3 & \mu(s_R \text{ or } s_B) = 7/12 \\
\mu(s_Y) = 1/4 & \mu(s_Y \text{ or } s_B) = 2/3 \\
\mu(s_B) = 1/4 & \mu(s_R \text{ or } s_Y \text{ or } s_B) = 1
\end{array} \tag{8.10}$$

These obviously violate the laws of probability. For example, the laws of probability dictate that, because $s_Y$ and $s_B$ are mutually exclusive, $\mu(s_Y \text{ or } s_B) = \mu(s_Y) + \mu(s_B)$. In the set of probabilities given in (8.10), though, $\mu(s_Y) + \mu(s_B) = 1/2 < 2/3 = \mu(s_Y \text{ or } s_B)$. Because the "probabilities" in the array (8.10) violate the laws of probability, it becomes prudent to call them something else, and we use the term *capacities*. Applying the subjective expected utility formula with capacities instead of probabilities yields the Choquet expected utility model. If one computes Choquet expected utility for the Ellsberg bets according to formula (8.8) using the capacities in (8.10), the calculations yield

$$SEU(\text{bet on red}) = (1/3)u(100)$$

$$SEU(\text{bet on yellow}) = (1/4)u(100)$$

$$SEU(\text{bet on red or black}) = (7/12)u(100)$$

$$SEU(\text{bet on yellow or black}) = (2/3)u(100)$$

According to these computations, the individual bets on red and also bets on yellow or black.

Strict uncertainty aversion arises in Choquet expected utility when the capacities are *superadditive*, that is, when $\mu(E_i \text{ or } E_j) > \mu(E_i) + \mu(E_j)$ for any two disjoint events $E_i$ and $E_j$. With this in mind, it becomes clear from expression (8.9) why subjective expected utility cannot accommodate uncertainty aversion: It assumes that $\mu(s_i \text{ or } s_j) = \mu(s_i) + \mu(s_j)$ in the last two lines of (8.9). The interpretation of superadditive capacities is basically one of missing probability. When facing the choice between a bet on red and a bet on yellow, the decision maker assigns too little probability to either of the uncertain states $s_Y$ and $s_B$, so that $\mu(s_R) + \mu(s_Y) + \mu(s_B) < 1$. When making the choice between a bet on red or black and a bet on yellow or black, she assigns too little probability to the uncertain events ($s_R$ or $s_B$) and $s_Y$, so that $\mu(s_R \text{ or } s_B) + \mu(s_Y) < 1$. For the Ellsberg gambles, this amounts to the individual behaving as if there are 60 yellow or black balls but fewer than 30 yellow and fewer than 30 black. While these capacities provide troubling violations of the laws of probability, they do allow for uncertainty averse preferences.

An alternative way of thinking about behavior in the Ellsberg paradox arises from the following thought process. The decision maker knows that there are 60 yellow or black balls in the urn, but not how many yellow or how many black. She thinks for some reason that there are no fewer than 10 and no more than 50 yellow balls, and the corresponding number of black balls, yielding 41 possible combinations of yellow and black balls. She is also pessimistic. When choosing between a bet on red and a bet on yellow, she evaluates the yellow bet according to the worst-case scenario in which the urn has only 10 yellow balls, yielding a 1/9 probability of winning the bet on yellow but a 1/3 probability of winning the bet on red. She chooses to bet on red. When choosing between a bet on red or black and a bet on yellow or black, she again evaluates according to the worst-case scenario, this time the one in which the urn contains only 10 black balls, yielding a 4/9 probability of winning the bet on red or black but a 2/3 probability of winning the bet on yellow or black. She bets on yellow or black.

The reasoning again violates the laws of probability, not because of issues with additivity, but because the decision maker uses different probability distributions to evaluate different lotteries. Taking the reasoning seriously, though, leads to Gilboa and Schmeidler's (1989) *maxmin expected utility*. In this model the individual forms a set $P$ of priors, which are objective probability distributions over states, and a typical prior $p$ assigns probability $p_i$ to state $s_i$. She evaluates the act $f(s)$ according to the maxmin expected utility function

$$MEU(f) = \min_{p \in P} \sum p(s_i)u(f(s_i)).$$

When the state $s_i$ is realized the decision maker receives a payoff of $f(s_i)$, and she evaluates that payoff according to the utility function $u$. The probability she assigns to the state $s_i$ is $p(s_i)$, and summing over the states of nature yields expected utility. Each prior in $P$ yields a different expected utility measure, and she evaluates the act $f$ according to whichever probability distribution in $P$ yields the lowest expected utility for that act. Uncertainty aversion arises because the decision maker evaluates different acts according to different probability distributions over states of nature, always assigning to an act its worst possible probability distribution. If she used the same distribution to evaluate every act, she would have subjective expected utility preferences as in (8.8).

A newer approach to uncertainty aversion is found in Klibanoff et al. (2005) and Neilson (2010). As with maxmin expected utility, these models begin with a set of priors, but this time rather than using a single prior to evaluate the act, the individual has a probability distribution over the possible priors. In the case of the Ellsberg urn, the different priors would correspond to different numbers of yellow balls, and the individual would have a distribution over the possible numbers of yellow balls. This representation requires a bit more notation than the others. As before, let $P$ denote the set of priors, which are objective probability distributions over states of nature, and let $f(s)$ denote an act mapping states into payoffs. Preferences are again defined over acts. This time, though, the individual possesses a subjective probability distribution defined over priors. Recalling that a prior $p$ is an $n$-vector $p = (p_1, \ldots, p_n)$, assume that the set of priors is finite and distinguish between them with superscripts so that $p^j$ and $p^k$ are two distinct $n$-vectors of probabilities over states. Let $q(p)$ be the subjective probability the individual assigns to prior $p$. Finally, let $EU(f; p)$ denote the expected utility of the act $f(s)$ when the probabilities of the states are given by the vector $p$:

$$EU(f; p) = \sum_{i=1}^{n} p_i u(f(s_i)).$$

According to the new model, preferences over acts are represented by the *second-order expected utility* function

$$SOEU(f) = \sum_{p^k \in P} q(p^k) v(EU(f; p^k)).$$

In this model attitudes toward ambiguity are governed by the curvature of $v$ in exactly the same manner as risk attitudes are governed by the curvature of $u$. When $v$ is linear the individual is ambiguity neutral, because the model reduces to subjective expected utility, and if $v$ is concave the individual is ambiguity averse because of Jensen's inequality.

Both maxmin expected utility preferences and second-order expected utility preferences rely on sets of priors, in the former case relying on the worst prior for each act and in the second relying on the entire distribution of priors. The two classes of preferences are related, but in a surprising way. Strzalecki (2011) demonstrates that the intersection of the set of maxmin expected utility preferences and the set of second-order expected utility preferences is precisely the set of subjective expected utility preferences. In other words, the only way the two models are compatible is if the individual is ambiguity neutral. This might seem to suggest that the Choquet expected utility preferences would provide a way out of this tangle, but Gilboa and Schmeidler (1989) show that Choquet expected utility preferences are a special case of the maxmin expected utility preferences, so once again they are incompatible with the second-order expected utility preferences. Further research must be done to determine which, if any, of these models will become the standard for describing uncertainty averse preferences.

The primary contribution of the second-order expected utility approach is that it brings all of the results from risk aversion into the setting of uncertainty aversion. In essence, uncertainty aversion leads to changes in behavior in the same direction as risk aversion, only more so. Take, for example, an insurance situation. A customer who is both risk and uncertainty averse considers buying insurance against an unknown risk and we wish to know the largest premium she will pay for the insurance. Risk aversion moves the premium above the expected benefit payment, and uncertainty aversion moves it up even more.

# 8.5  CONCLUSION

The standard model of discounted expected subjective expected utility has both guided intuition and produced theoretical results for decades. It relies on several key factors, namely a constant subjective discount rate, a single utility-of-wealth function, and a unique subjective probability measure with which to weight alternative utility values. Recently, though, research has called each of these three factors into question. Evidence now points to levels of impatience that are not constant, but instead decline with the consumption horizon. Evidence also points to the use of different utility functions for different tasks and under different circumstances. Finally, evidence not only points to the nonexistence of a unique set of subjective probabilities, but it suggests that these probabilities cannot be used as weights in the first place.

Theoretical research has concentrated on finding alternative functional forms. For behavior under risk, the winner appears to be cumulative prospect theory. For choice over time, the most results have come from the quasi-hyperbolic discounting model. For choice under uncertainty, the future is less clear, and researchers continue to struggle with which model holds the most promise. The task is important because how people behave toward time, risk, and uncertainty has important implications for many managerial tasks. The models will play important roles in determining optimal employee compensation schemes, in understanding demand for goods and services, and in understanding how regulators will behave.

The long-term research agenda on time, risk, and uncertainty has, for the most part, concentrated heavily on how best to represent preferences. Research applying those preferences to common economic settings is much less abundant. Most applied problems, including contracts, pricing, bargaining, and auctions, have only been addressed using standard discounted expected utility, and not the alternative choice models. One major open avenue for research, then, involves extending these lines of inquiry to include the more realistic preferences. A more difficult avenue for research, and one with potentially greater impact, involves welfare analysis. Government regulation, including tax and international trade policies, begins with the foundation of maximizing a social welfare function. The research discussed in this chapter suggests that individuals have attitudes toward risk that depend on their pasts and on the nature of the choices they face, they have attitudes toward time that may be time inconsistent, and they have attitudes toward uncertainty that rely on what information they have about the details of the distribution they face. A regulator or policy analyst must make modeling choices about all of these factors in setting the social welfare function, and for the most part the literature is silent on how these choices should be made. This is an open, important, and hopefully fruitful research topic.

## Notes

1. The S-shaped utility function in Figure 8.1 is convex over losses, ruling out insurance against losses, and concave over gains, ruling out buying lottery tickets. If the individual overweights unlikely, extreme losses, though, the extra weight attached to the utility of the loss may outweigh the convexity of the utility function and lead to insurance. The individual would not insure against a likely loss, though, because the probability transformation function in Figure 8.2 does not overweight large probabilities. For exactly the same reasons, an individual who is otherwise risk averse over gains might choose to play a lottery with a small chance of winning a large prize, because the probability transformation function in Figure 8.2 underweights the low outcome (not winning the lottery) and so must overweight the high outcome (winning the lottery). If the probability transformation function overweights the high outcome enough, the otherwise risk-averse individual buys the lottery ticket.

## References

Ainslie, George W. 1992. *Picoeconomics*. Cambridge: Cambride University Press.

Anderson, Lisa R., and Jennifer M. Mellor. 2009. "Are Risk Preferences Stable? Comparing an Experimental Measure with a Validated Survey-based Measure." *Journal of Risk and Uncertainty* 39:137–60.

Anscombe, Francis J., and Robert J. Aumann. 1963. "A Definition of Subjective Probability." *Annals of Mathematical Statistics* 34:199–205.

Barseghyan, Levon, Jeffrey Prince, and Joshua C. Teitelbaum. 2011. "Are Risk Preferences Stable across Contexts? Evidence from Insurance Data." *American Economic Review* 101:591–631.

Barsky, Robert B., Thomas Juster, Miles S. Kimball, and Matthew D. Shapiro. 1997. "Preference Parameters and Behavioral Heterogeneity: An Experimental Approach in the Health and Retirement Study." *Quarterly Journal of Economics* 112:537–79.

Baucells, Manel, Martin Weber, and Frank Welfens. 2011. "Reference-point Formation and Updating." *Management Science* 57:506–19.

Bernoulli, Daniel. 1954. "Exposition of a New Theory on the Measurement of Risk." Translated by Louise Sommer. *Econometrica* 22:23–36. Originally published as "Specimen Theoriae Novae de Mensura Sortis" (St. Petersburg: *Commentarii Academiae Scientiarum Imperialis Petropolitanae*, 1738).

Ellsberg, Daniel. 1961. "Risk, Ambiguity, and the Savage Axioms." *Quarterly Journal of Economics* 75 (4): 643–69.

Friedman, Milton, and Leonard J. Savage. 1948. "The Utility Analysis of Choices Involving Risk." *Journal of Political Economy* 56:279–304.

Gilboa, Itzhak, and David Schmeidler. 1989. "Maxmin Expected Utility with a Non-unique Prior." *Journal of Mathematical Economics* 18:141–53.

Gilpatric, Scott M. 2008. "Present-biased Preferences, Self-awareness and Shirking." *Journal of Economic Behavior and Organization* 67:735–54.

——. 2009. "Slippage in Rebate Programs and Present-biased Preferences." *Marketing Science* 28:229–38.

Kahneman, Daniel. 1992. "Reference Points, Anchors, Norms, and Mixed Feelings." *Organizational Behavior and Human Decision Processes* 51:296–312.

Kahneman, Daniel, and Amos Tversky. 1979. "Prospect Theory: An Analysis of Decision under Risk." *Econometrica* 47:263–91.

Klibanoff, Peter, Massimo Marinacci, and Sujoy Mukerji. 2005. "A Smooth Model of Decision Making under Ambiguity." *Econometrica* 73 1849–92.

Knight, Frank H. 1921. *Risk, Uncertainty, and Profit*. Boston and New York: Houghton Mifflin.

Laibson, David. 1997. "Golden Eggs and Hyperbolic Discounting." *Quarterly Journal of Economics* 112:443–77.

Liu, Yu-Jane, Chih-Ling Tsai, Ming-Chun Wang, and Ning Zhu. 2010. "Prior Consequences and Subsequent Risk Taking: New Field Evidence from the Taiwan Futures Exchange." *Management Science* 56:606–20.

Malmendier, Ulrike, and Stefan Nagel. 2011. "Depression Babies: Do Macroeconomic Experiences Affect Risk Taking?" *Quarterly Journal of Economics* 126:373–416.

Markowitz, Harry. 1952. "The Utility of Wealth." *Journal of Political Economy* 60:151–58.

Neilson, William S. 1998. "Reference Wealth Effects in Sequential Choice." *Journal of Risk and Uncertainty* 17:27–47.

——. 2003. "Probability Transformations in the Study of Behavior Toward Risk." *Synthese* 135:171–92.

——. 2010. "A Simplified Axiomatic Approach to Ambiguity Aversion." *Journal of Risk and Uncertainty* 41:113–24.

O'Donoghue, Ted, and Matthew Rabin. 1999. "Doing It Now or Later." *American Economic Review* 89:103–24.

Quiggin, John. 1982. "A Theory of Anticipated Utility." *Journal of Economic Behavior and Organization* 3:323–43.

Rabin, Matthew. 2000. "Risk Aversion and Expected-Utility Theory: A Calibration Theorem." *Econometrica* 68:1281–92.

Samuelson, Paul A. 1937. "A Note on the Measurement of Utility." *Review of Economic Studies* 4:155–61.

Savage, Leonard J. 1954. *Foundations of Statistics*. New York: Wiley.

Schmeidler, David. 1989. "Subjective Probability and Expected Utility without Additivity." *Econometrica* 57:571–87.

Schmidt, Lucie. 2008. "Risk Preferences and the Timing of Marriage and Childbearing." *Demography* 45:439–60.

Strotz, Robert H. 1955. "Myopia and Inconsistency in Dynamic Utility Maximization." *Review of Economic Studies* 23:165–80.

Strzalecki, Tomasz. 2011. "Axiomatic Foundations of Multiplier Preferences." *Econometrica* 79:47–73.

Tversky, Amos, and Daniel Kahneman. 1992. "Advances in Prospect Theory: Cumulative Representation of Uncertainty." *Journal of Risk and Uncertainty* 5:297–323.

von Neumann, John, and Oskar Morgenstern. 1944. *Theory of Games and Economic Behavior*. Princeton, NJ: Princeton University Press.

Warner, John T., and Saul Pleeter. 2001. "The Personal Discount Rate: Evidence from Military Downsizing Programs." *American Economic Review* 91:33–53.

# CHAPTER 9

........................................................

# BEHAVIORAL ECONOMICS AND STRATEGIC DECISION MAKING

........................................................

## MASSIMO GARBUIO AND DAN LOVALLO
## *WITH* ELIF KETENCIOGLU

## 9.1 INTRODUCTION

........................................................

A large part of economic theory has been developed by considering a firm's strategic decision making to occur within a "black-box" in which a firm is portrayed as a unitary and representative actor somehow motivated purposefully to advance the goals of the firm itself. Strategic decision-making theory evolved by opening the black box to understand how strategic decisions are made as well as to predict the ultimate effect of these decisions on the firm's performance (e.g., Schwenk 1985; Hambrick and Mason 1984; Dean and Sharfman 1996). Modern strategic decision theory focuses on the actions taken by general managers on behalf of the owners of the business, as these decisions dictate how the firm's resources will be used to enhance the firm's performance given the constraints imposed by the external environment (Nag et al. 2007). These decisions are considered strategic by strategy scholars, as well as executives, since they commit substantial resources, set precedents, and create waves of less important decisions (Mintzberg et al. 1976). In contrast, short-term price competitions between rival firms are not considered strategic decisions for strategy scholars or executives, even if they are strategic decisions in economic theory. Despite some differences, through most of the twentieth century, strategic decision making maintained a fundamental relationship with economic theory (Schendel et al. 1980; Rumelt et al. 1994) by relying heavily on models of rational decision makers maximizing either utility or profits. Reliance on the traditional assumptions of economic theory forcefully shaped the early evolution of strategic theories, frameworks, and analytical tools.

This early approach was appealing given its straightforward and sometimes simple methodology, and it would indeed have remained persuasive if its assumptions and predictions had been confirmed in the data. However, after years of research using both market-generated data and experimental data, it is now clear that the assumption of rationality is far from a universal truth for the behavior of both executives and the firm's owners, and predictions based on the assumption of rational decision making frequently are inaccurate. In recognition of this problem, a number of neighboring disciplines successfully have incorporated alternative behavioral assumptions into the core areas of their theories. As a consequence and indicator of the success of this new behavioral approach, several of the leading areas of study—behavioral economics, behavioral finance, and behavioral corporate finance—are no longer considered just novel or curious twists but now stand as relevant "branches" of their respective fields (Camerer et al. 2005; Thaler 1999). It is important to recognize that these particular branches each possessed clear theoretical foundations anchored in rationality, self-interest, and market efficiency (Rabin 2002; Camerer and Loewenstein 2003; Della Vigna 2009; Thaler 1999; Schleifer 2000; Barberis and Thaler 2003; Baker et al. 2006). In sharp contrast to these fields, however, business strategy faces the challenge of having neither a dominating conceptual paradigm nor a clear set of assumptions upon which scholars could build behavioral models (Mintzberg et al. 1998).

Despite these difficulties, scholars over the past two decades have been inspired by the advances in research on behavioral decision making. In the areas of behavioral economics and finance (Kahneman and Tversky 2000; Gilovich et al. 2002; Kahneman 2011), researchers have investigated heuristics and biases in strategic decisions, successfully answering some questions while raising many more (Powell et al. 2011). Their work focuses on three fundamental characteristics that make strategic decisions, such as market entry and exit decisions or mergers and acquisitions (M&As), particularly challenging moves. First, these strategic decisions are both rare and complex decisions, and they absorb significant portions of corporate resources. Second, these decisions take time, both because of the effort required to evaluate their costs and benefits and the process of reaching a managerial consensus. Finally, feedback, in terms of profits and losses realized, is delayed and ambiguous, making it difficult to isolate cause-and-effect mechanisms that can be applied in future similar decisions.

This chapter will examine the key heuristics and biases affecting strategic decision makers operating in an organizational environment.[1] We frame our discussion by distinguishing among three classes of deviation from the standard strategic decision-making assumptions of economic theory, known as "nonstandard assumptions": nonstandard preferences, nonstandard beliefs, and nonstandard decision making. *Nonstandard preferences* explain how decisions are evaluated from a time and risk perspective. *Nonstandard beliefs* explain how systematic biases form expectations about a company's resources, its external environment, and the causes of performance. *Nonstandard decision making* explains how the framing of decisions affects outcomes.[2] This framework considers the peculiar characteristics of strategic decisions identified above: they hardly are routine decisions (thus diminishing the potential for learning) and they leverage internal resources that affect the external environment in the quest for superior performance.

This chapter proceeds as follows. The next three sections illustrate, respectively, non-standard preferences, beliefs, and decision making. For each of these, we discuss key psychological principles and their strategic consequences. We then conclude with a discussion of the topics presented in this chapter. We hope that our account will provide insights into how behavioral economics can be applied to strategic decisions in organizational settings and, moreover, how asking questions that are unique to the role of executives making strategic decisions can enrich it.

## 9.2  NONSTANDARD PREFERENCES

Preferences refer to how a decision maker ranks a series of alternatives on the basis of specific characteristics, for example, a series of investment opportunities or set of alternative actions. A particularly important set of preferences for decision making involves a decision maker's attitude toward risk, as these preferences determine how the decision maker ranks risky alternatives. Also critical for decision making are time preferences that describe whether a decision maker is impatient regarding the income stream anticipated from an investment opportunity. For example, will a decision maker favor investments with short-term benefits over those with long-term benefits, or vice versa?

Risk and time preferences are two key ingredients in any strategic decision. When executives are called upon to choose among alternative strategic investment opportunities, a straightforward procedure is to discount future uncertain cash flows and to select the opportunity that offers the highest expected return. Since future cash flows are inherently uncertain (Laverty 1996), determining whether to approve or reject a project requires attention to both the time at which the investment pays off and the probability that the uncertainty is resolved favorably.

This section examines how the evaluation of gains and losses is not as straightforward as one might think. Often, the evaluation of long-term investments is influenced by the experience of short-term results: the exploitation bias will illustrate how executives tend to underinvest in long-term projects (Jacobs 1991) and to fail to explore new opportunities (Teece 2007). Moreover, the ownership of an asset should not affect value judgments. However, because of the endowment effect (Thaler 1980), executives exhibit a tendency to ask more in selling an asset than what they would be willing to pay to purchase it. Finally, if an investment portfolio is augmented with nonpreferred options, preferences for the original options should not change. However, because of extremeness aversion (Simonson and Tversky 1992), executives may change their preferences over the original set and invest in options that would not be justified from a value perspective.

### 9.2.1  Exploitation Bias

Most individuals—and executives in particular—tend to employ narrow frames of reference in searching out and seizing opportunities (Kahneman and Lovallo 1993; Levinthal and March 1993; Lovallo and Kahneman 2003; Teece 2007). The *exploitation bias*, which refers to the strategic decision maker's tendency to focus narrowly on the short term (e.g., by exploiting available technologies and innovation) rather than long-term growth opportunities (e.g., by exploring new innovative ideas), may be a possible explanation.

In sensing opportunities—a process referred to as "exploration"—strategic decision makers in incumbent firms tend to pay too much attention to "local search" rather than to the periphery of the ecosystem (Teece 2007; Levinthal 1997; Levinthal and March 1993). In particular, search is affected by assets in hand and by existing customers' needs, especially those of powerful customers (Teece 2007; Christensen 1997). As a result, new entrants rather than incumbent firms often are the sources of innovation. For example, in the computer industry it has been argued that no leading computer manufacturer has been able to replicate its initial success when subsequent innovative technologies appeared and corresponding markets emerged (Christensen 1997).

Exploitation takes place once new opportunities have been sensed and they become available to any reasonably alert manager. Strategic decision makers seem to frame opportunities for innovation in ways that are consistent with the firm's current knowledge base, assets, and established problem-solving heuristics and business model (Teece 2007). If the current way of doing business has been successful in the past, executives seem to find little reason for changing it. As a result, executives have a bias toward incremental, competency-enhancing improvements rather than radical, competency-destroying innovation (Teece 2007). Even if incumbent firms are exposed to innovative business opportunities, they often fail to invest in them. Also of note is the fact that executives are more likely to commit financial resources to support investments whose cash flows confidently can be projected (Teece 2007). They prefer to invest in "old" technology rather than to exploit recently discovered technology or search for new ones for which markets are not yet established and expected returns are more difficult to predict. As a result, firms tend to overinvest in exploitation rather than in exploration.

This bias toward exploitation has been explained by Levinthal and March (1993) in terms of the availability of feedback. According to these scholars, exploitation generates clearer, earlier, and more immediate opportunities for feedback than exploration. It corrects itself sooner and provides more positive returns in the near term. Psychologically, exploitation bias results from a combination of narrow framing—that is, new investment opportunities are evaluated in isolation rather than in combination with preexisting investments in a portfolio—and risk propensity. The closer is the distance between current (or expected) performance outcomes and aspirations for them, the greater the focus tends to be on exploitation rather than exploration. This means that when aspirations and outcomes are close (e.g., because the aspiration level is based on current or past performance), decision makers tend to be risk-averse and therefore focus on the less-risky activity, which is exploitation. In contrast, when aspirations and outcomes are far apart (e.g., because the aspiration level is the superior performance of a competitor in the industry), decision makers tend to be risk seeking and therefore focus on exploration rather than exploitation.[3]

Clarifying how the exploitation bias operates in strategic decision making is of critical importance if we want to understand how executives' attentions can be redirected from existing and sometimes underperforming technologies and assets toward becoming comfortable with exploring and promoting new and innovative alternatives.[4]

## 9.2.2 Endowment Effect

From a rational point of view, willingness to pay (i.e., the maximum amount a person is willing to offer or exchange for a good) and willingness to accept (that is, the maximum amount a person is willing to receive in order to give up a good) should be the same (Willig 1976; Freeman 1979). This is also addressed by the Coase theorem, according to which the allocation of resources will be independent of the initial assignment of property rights when there are no transaction costs or income effects (Coase 1960). Thaler (1981), however, argued that goods an individual already possesses will be valued more than other goods. In business, M&As are largely affected by this pattern: the willingness to accept the price offered for an asset often exceeds the willingness to pay to acquire the same asset.

Kahneman et al. (1990) show the presence of the *endowment effect* in an experiment where half of the participants were given a coffee mug, which sells for $6.00 at a local bookstore. When offered the chance to exchange the coffee mugs for money, very few participants accepted, and this pattern persisted over four trials. The median owner was unwilling to sell for less than $5.25, while the median buyer was unwilling to pay more than $2.25–$2.75. Also, given normal distributions of preferences across the conditions, economic theory predicts that one-half of the goods should be traded voluntarily, yet the observed volume was always less than half. To assess whether reluctance to buy and sell were potential alternative explanations, a third group of individuals were introduced in successive experiments: "choosers" were asked to choose between a mug and cash. The results confirmed significantly different and higher valuations from sellers as compared to both buyers and choosers. Finally, as participants were involved in several trials, learning has been shown not to undermine the endowment effect (Kahneman et al. 1991).

In a company setting, the endowment effect may result in overestimation of resource values by executives, since such resources are owned by their firms rather than being rented or available through alliances and joint ventures. As a result, executives are expected to attribute excessive value to what is already in the firm's portfolio, independent of the expected profitability of the resources. This implies that portfolio decisions may involve holding onto owned resources for too long, and thus not freeing up funds to pursue the acquisition and accumulation of potentially more valuable resources. Most importantly, it can help explain the presence of thin markets for business assets.

## 9.2.3 Extremeness Aversion

When executives consider a set of alternative resources that could be acquired in factor markets, they are asked to make judgments with respect to several common attributes of those resources. The size of the initial outlay and distance of the new plant to company headquarters are examples of these attributes. In an ideal world, decisions would consider all of this information and the best alternative, according to some efficiency-based criteria (e.g., net present value), would be chosen. However, evaluations are often not this smooth. All else being equal, any resource of moderate value possessing at least one attribute that is "more extreme" than the attribute of another comparable resource tends to be viewed as less attractive than it. This pattern is defined as *extremeness aversion* (Simonson and Tversky 1992) and affects choices in many settings, from the political to the strategic.

In one of the experiments proposed by Simonson and Tversky (1992), subjects were asked to choose from three cameras with varying prices and qualities. When an extreme option was introduced, people tended to choose the intermediate option, which is referred to as the compromise effect. More specifically, the popularity of the intermediate option rises when extreme options (e.g., much higher quality and price) are introduced. The same results were observed even when the extreme option was presented but not available for purchase.

A recent example of extremeness aversion in a political strategic context is provided by President Obama's 2009 request for advice on the number of troops to deploy in Afghanistan. General McChrystal's report outlined three options for slightly different types of missions: sending 80,000 more troops to conduct a robust counterinsurgency campaign throughout Afghanistan; 40,000 troops to reinforce the southern and eastern areas of the country where the Taliban were most active; or 10,000 to 15,000 troops with the primary aim of training Afghan troops. However, the *New York Times* reported that a White House official was surprised by the numbers, assuming that there should be an option representing a middle ground between 10,000 and 40,000. "Why wasn't there a 25 number?" the official asked in an interview. He then answered his own question, "It would have been too tempting." The presence of a 25,000 troops option would have made that number the middle option and thus much more likely to be chosen (Baker 2009).

In decisions regarding a firm's assets, executives are likely to fall victim to extremeness aversion. They may be more likely to allocate funds to resources with values closer to the status quo than to more extreme alternatives, regardless of their value. This may be particularly evident in decisions regarding expanding in the domestic market, entering adjacent geographical markets, or entering faraway markets. Executives may be tempted to prefer adjacent over domestic markets when the option to invest in faraway markets is included in the option set, even if a risk-reward analysis would advise against it (Garbuio et al. 2011a). Empirical evidence is sought in the context of internationalization strategy, but this is, of course, only one of the situations in which extremeness aversion can be present.

## 9.3 NONSTANDARD BELIEFS

Executives' strategic choices respond to a company's internal and external situations. The internal situation is defined by a company's internal resources and capabilities

(R&C) (e.g., Wernerfelt 1984; Rumelt 1984; Barney 1986, 1991). The external situation embraces the broader "business 'ecosystem'—the community of organizations, institutions, and individuals that impact the enterprise and the enterprise's customers and suppliers" (Teece 2007, 1325).

In strategy scholarship, the importance of internal and external environments is recognized in two prominent theoretical traditions: the *resource-based view* of the firm (Wernerfelt 1984; Rumelt 1984; Barney 1986, 1991) and the *positioning approach* to strategy (Porter 1980). Both traditions have generated explanations for strategic choices that underpin a firm's success. In the first tradition, the key factors are resources—such as technological assets, locations, people, and proprietary knowledge—and capabilities—the unique combination of resources, such as R&D, marketing, and so on, allowing a firm to take specific actions—that are valuable, rare, and constitute the basis of a company's ability to create and capture value in the marketplace (Barney 1991). In the positioning approach, a company's advantage is based on the industry in which the company operates, and especially its competitors' R&C as well as their actions (Porter 1980; Rumelt 1984). However, for a long time, no questions arose as to whether decision makers' perceptions of the external and internal situations are affected by cognitive biases.

In strategic decision making, beliefs are used to explain how people form future expectations using available information. In the rational world of mainstream strategy, expectations are not a problem. Executives are assumed to have correct expectations about future events due to their complete and unambiguous understanding of i) the internal situation of the company, its R&C; ii) the external situation, particularly regarding competitors and competitors' responses to the company's actions; and iii) how the internal and external situations contribute to a company's performance. A psychological account of strategic decision making challenges these key assumptions and acknowledges that decision makers have selective and inaccurate perceptions of their organization and its environment (Hambrick and Mason 1984; Mezias and Starbuck 2003).

## 9.3.1  Beliefs about a Firm's Resources and Capabilities

A company's ability to achieve and sustain competitive advantage depends on how well the bundle of valuable resources—such as assets, capabilities, organizational processes, company attributes, and knowledge (neither perfectly imitable nor substitutable)—at the company's disposal are utilized (Wernerfelt 1984; Rumelt 1984; Barney 1991). However, if executives have only an ambiguous understanding of the causes of competitive advantage (Reed and DeFilippi 1990; King and Zeithaml 2001; Powell et al. 2006; King 2007), they will be unable to leverage internal R&C and overcome barriers to transferring competencies inside the organization. Overconfidence, causal ambiguity, and endowment anchoring are among the more persistent psychological underpinnings of belief formation in understanding a firm's set of resources (Hayward and Hambrick 1997; Zajac and Bazerman 1991; Reed and DeFilippi 1990).

### 9.3.1.1 Overconfidence

There is overwhelming evidence that people are overconfident about their abilities. Moore and Healey (2008) explain overconfidence in three distinct ways. First, people *overestimate* their actual abilities, performances, levels of control, or chances for success. As examples, students overestimate their own performances on exams (Clayson 2005) and, more generally, people overestimate the speed at which they can get work done (Buehler et al. 1994). Second, people *overplace* their own performance relative to other people's performances, such as ranking themselves above the median. Known also as the *above-average effect* (and could be called the Lake Wobegon effect, after Garrison Keillor's fictional Minnesota town where "all the children are above average"), the best-known empirical example is the sample of American and Swedish drivers rating themselves as more skillful than the median driver in their own country (Svenson 1981). This tendency to see one's own performance as "above average" is exacerbated by the ambiguity of the traits being measured (*ambiguity effect*). For example, soccer players rated themselves significantly higher on ambiguous dimensions (such as soccer ability) than relatively unambiguous ones (such as heading the ball; see, e.g., Van Yperen 1992). Finally, overconfidence has been studied as *excessive precision* in one's own beliefs. These studies usually ask for numerical answers (e.g., the length of the Nile River) and then estimate the confidence interval around the answers, which usually shows how people are overconfident about the precision of their own responses (e.g., Alpert and Raiffa 1982; Soll and Klayman 2004).

In a company setting, overconfident executives tend to overestimate their chances of success and, thus, enter markets more frequently than otherwise. Contrary to standard theory, overconfidence predicts that agents will be risk seeking, because when risk is high overconfidence might lead them to prefer riskier contracts, apparently thinking that they can beat the odds. Camerer and Lovallo (1999) showed that when the payoffs to market entry depended on abilities, decision makers overestimated their chances of success and entered markets more often than justified. This may be particularly common in startup ventures, as entrepreneurs are thought to have different overconfidence levels than other managers (e.g., Dosi and Lovallo 1997; Busenitz and Barney 1997). Also, overconfidence and hubris (defined as exaggerated self-confidence) may be especially insidious when it comes to M&As, explaining why acquirers tend to overpay for their targets (Roll 1986) and also why M&As often take place, despite the fact that such transactions often fail (Malmendier and Tate 2005). When executives rely heavily on revenue synergies in decisions to pursue acquisitions, this should signal the presence of an overconfidence problem, since revenue synergies are less likely to be realized than cost synergies (Sirower 1997).

### 9.3.1.2 Causal Ambiguity

The above-average and ambiguity effects that explain overconfidence are also crucial parts of an important strategic phenomenon: *causal ambiguity*. Causal ambiguity refers to executives' ambiguous understanding of the link between a company's resources and its competitive advantages (Reed and DeFilippi 1990; Barney 1991). Powell et al. (2006) propose an explanation of causal ambiguity as a property of management perception rather than as a property of resources and capabilities, as others have suggested previously. According to this definition, executives may systematically overestimate their own firms' competencies (the above-average effect), especially in cases of ambiguous competencies (ambiguity effect). These effects are likely to be more pronounced in emotive situations, when attribution is poorly verifiable, when the true degree of competence is higher, when the attributor's achievement motivation and self-efficacy are greater, and when neglect of competition is more extensive (Powell et al. 2006).

Important implications of causal ambiguity are observed through the difficulty of leveraging internal resources and capabilities. When the sources of competitive advantage are basic characteristics, such as a low-cost structure, high product quality, or economies of scale and scope from company size, there is little reason to believe that misperceptions will be rampant or that competitors will have a hard time imitating them. However, when resources and capabilities are more complex to evaluate—e.g., when competencies are tacit or firm-specific or when a large number of competencies interact—imitation by rivals will be more difficult, if not impossible, and the source of competitive advantage is protected, at least in the short run. However, this also has important implications for the ability of a firm to leverage its competencies. In fact, in poorly performing companies, the intrafirm causal ambiguity was found to be greater overall than in successful firms (King and Zeithaml 2001). This inability to identify the causes of competitive advantage hinders the process of transferring competencies inside the organization to the external environment and, as such, it is an important area for future research endeavors.

### 9.3.1.3 Endowed Anchoring

Anchoring is a heuristic in which a decision maker starts with a rough reference point (an anchor) and then makes adjustments relative to that anchor to reach a target estimate (Tversky and Kahneman 1974). Anchoring occurs unintentionally and unconsciously, and is difficult to avoid even among experts (Diekmann et al. 1996) and even when an individual is aware that an anchor has been generated randomly.

In a classic study of anchoring, Tversky and Kahneman (1974) showed that when asked to guess the percentage of African nations that also are members of the United Nations, people who were first asked "Was it more or less than 10%?" guessed lower values (25% on average) than those who had been asked if it was more or less than 65% (45% on average). A similar pattern was observed in a natural setting when Northcraft and Neale (1987) gave amateurs and experts in real estate comprehensive information regarding a property, including either a high or low list price, before anyone toured it. When participants were asked to estimate the actual value of the property, the final estimates were elevated for those who received the high price list, including both amateurs and experts in real estate. Anchoring bias has also been demonstrated in a number of judgmental tasks, such as rating simple gambles (Carlson 1990; Chapman and Johnson 1994), answers to factual questions (Jacowitz and Kahneman 1995), preference judgments (Chapman and Johnson 1994), as well as forecasts of economic trends and estimates of historical facts (Russo and Shoemaker 1989). In all of these studies, higher starting points led to higher final answers.

In the context of strategic decisions and resource allocation decisions within a firm, in particular, anchoring is likely to be based not on random cues, but rather on the most recent allocation decision. This circumstance is referred to as *endowed anchoring* and is due to a combination of the endowment effect from ownership of previous entitlements—e.g., the share of the capital budget received in the previous round—and anchoring from previous allocations (Garbuio et al. 2011a). These allocations are likely to create suboptimal decisions because endowed anchoring limits efficient allocation that would incorporate the most current information about the expected profitability of resources.

## 9.3.2 Beliefs about the External Environment: Competition Neglect

In strategic decision making, a crucial component of Porter's (1980) prescriptive framework for industry and competitor analysis is the identification of each competitor and their actions with respect to the focal firm's strategic-positioning decisions. Needless to say, executives' ability to perform such analyses may be less than perfect, as identified by Porter (1980, 59) himself.

The psychological pattern that is likely to emerge during such evaluations of competitive positioning is called *competition neglect*. It refers to the tendency to focus on one's own plans, resources, and capabilities while ignoring objective predictors of success, such as the quality of competitors and previous success rates in comparable environments (Lovallo 2008; Moore et al. 2007; Camerer and Lovallo 1999). Lovallo (2008) designed an experiment to show competition neglect at work and the benefits of taking an outside view of the problem. Sixty first-year associates at a professional services firm were asked to predict their chances of making partner. Half of the associates were encouraged to adopt an "inside" view by reflecting on how qualified, suited to the job, and competent they perceived themselves to be. The other half were instead encouraged to adopt the "outside" view by reflecting on the historical probability of success and how qualified, suited to the job, and competent were their peers. Only later were they asked to compare themselves with their peers on several dimensions. The associates invited to adopt an inside view had a mean response for the probability of being elevated to partner status of 34.6%, whereas those who were invited to adopt an outside view had a mean response equal to 19.8%, which, while still mildly optimistic, was considerably lower.

The implications of competition neglect in strategic decision making are related mainly to survival in the environment. For example, Zajac and Bazerman (1991) developed several propositions regarding the consequences of competitive blind spots, a special case of competition neglect where decision makers fail to consider the contingent responses of competitors to their actions. They argued that competitive blind spots lead to premiums in acquisition decisions, failure of entry decisions, and overcapacity in case of capacity-expansion decisions. Camerer and Lovallo (1999) argue that when competing on skills, agents will be insufficiently sensitive to the quality of competition and amount of risk. In addition, Radzevick and Moore (2008) suggest that firms need to invest in intelligence regarding competitors, and that to succeed new entrants ought to devote as much time to understanding their future competitors as they do to understanding their own capabilities.

## 9.3.3  Beliefs about the Causes of a Company's Performance

Being able to correctly identify the causes of positive or negative performance outcomes means being able to learn from past experience by interpreting signals accurately, taking the most appropriate corrective strategies, and, ultimately, enhancing future firm performance. However, strategic actions may be affected by the attribution of performance rather than by the actual causes of that performance. One possible explanation is related to fundamental attribution error.

In explaining the causes of human behavior, the fundamental attribution error describes the tendency to overestimate personality traits as a causal factor in regard to actions involving oneself, while downplaying the influence of environmental constraints on other people's actions (Jones and Harris 1967; Ross 1977). In an early experiment, Jones and Harris (1967) presented subjects with pro- or anti-Castro essays that supposedly had been written under high-choice conditions (the writer freely decided to take the essay's position) or low-choice conditions (the debate-team advisor told the writer to prepare a particular position statement). The task of the subjects was to infer the "true attitude" of the person who wrote the essay. Despite their knowledge of the high- or low-choice condition, subjects disregarded situational constraints in their evaluation of a writer's attitude toward Castro, but instead overestimated personality or dispositional causes of behavior.

In strategic decision making, executives look at a firm's performance outcome and ascribe it to internal and external causes. As a result of fundamental attribution error, executives are victims of a tendency to take credit for good outcomes and lay blame upon the environment or chance for less favorable outcomes (Bowman 1976; Bettman and Weitz 1983; Staw et al. 1983; Salancik and Meindl 1984; Clapham and Schwenk 1991). Common external factors to blame include governmental regulations, demand shocks, weather, and output prices; all are an attempt to make sense of the disappointing performance and develop a better understanding of the variables affecting it (Schwenk 1985). If outcomes are good, the most available explanation is the actions taken by management in achieving the performance goal. However, if outcomes are bad, the focus is directed to external events that negate the effect of otherwise sound decisions. The attribution of performance has consequences for the selection of future actions. Empirical evidence shows that executives tend to select internal strategies (e.g., operative and administrative fixes) or external strategies (e.g., defense, improvement, creation, or abandonment of market share) in response to downturns, disregarding the actual causes of underperformance (Ford 1985).

# 9.4 NONSTANDARD DECISION MAKING

Standard economic theory assumes that individuals will seek utility- and profit-maximizing decisions. However, executives are also particularly busy individuals who need to use shortcuts to navigate information and make decisions for their company. In fact, research has also shown that decision makers tend to use suboptimal heuristics when solving complex maximization problems (Tversky and Kahneman 1974). Here we discuss two heuristics—naive diversification and the familiarity effect—that prevent executives from allocating resources to the best investment opportunities.

## 9.4.1 Naive Diversification and Partition Dependence

According to rational choice theory, when asked to allocate a scarce resource, for example money, to a fixed set of investment opportunities and/or consumption options, individuals should not be affected by the number of possibilities available or how those possibilities are presented (Arrow 1963). Instead, the possibilities should be weighted according to preestablished criteria and the allocation should follow. However, individuals facing a complex choice may use heuristics to simplify the decision.

According to one of these heuristics—the *naive diversification*, or $1/n$, heuristic (Simonson 1990; Read and Loewenstein 1995)—decision makers tend to diversify equally among $n$ available alternatives. For example, observing choice behavior among college students, Simonson (1990) showed that when faced with simultaneous choices regarding seven consumer products, the students tended to diversify rather than commit to specific options. Read and Loewenstein (1995) found similar behavior in a Halloween experiment in which children chose among different types of candy. In a study of 401(k) investments, Benartzi and Thaler (2001) also showed that some investors follow the naive diversification heuristic, dividing their contributions evenly across the funds offered in the plans.

In strategic decision making, the periodic allocation of resources to business units is a typical example in which naive diversification may happen. In an experiment that considered managerial settings, Bardolet et al. (2011) held hypothetical firm characteristics constant and manipulated the partition of the options over which experienced executives were asked to allocate capital. In one condition of these experiments, the firm was organized on the basis of geography, and each geographic division was organized along product lines. In another condition, the firm was organized on the basis of products, and each product division was organized along geographic lines. The results revealed a strong degree of *partition dependence*: the capital allocation was influenced significantly by whether allocations were first made by geography or by product. When the numbers of regions and products differed (e.g., two regions and five product lines), the allocation of funds to regions and to products varied considerably according to how the partition was presented to the participant (i.e., whether the first allocation was made to regions or products). The result of this experiment has been confirmed using secondary data from COMPUSTAT.[5] Taken together, these two pieces of evidence show that current partitioning interferes with decision makers' capacities to efficiently allocate in ways that reflect the most current information about the existing and potential value of a firm's resource portfolio.

Of course, endowment anchoring and partition dependence in resource-allocation decisions may take place simultaneously. Future empirical work is required to disentangle their combined effect.

## 9.4.2 Familiarity Effect

Another impediment to allocating resources to their highest valued uses is related to the familiarity of the decision maker with those uses. In fact, decision makers' familiarity with the situation at hand may affect their preferences.

Heath and Tversky (1991) conducted a series of experiments to compare people's willingness to bet on clear chance events or on their uncertain beliefs. In one study, subjects were asked to choose among bets based on three sources of uncertainty: the results in various US states of the 1988 presidential election, the results of various professional and college football games, and the results of a random draw from an urn with a known composition of colored balls. Participants were preassigned to two groups on the basis of their expertise (e.g., participants who were experts in politics and nonexperts in football, and participants who were experts in football but not in politics). Participants who were knowledgeable about politics but not about football preferred betting on political events rather than on chance events that they considered equally probable. In addition, they preferred betting on chance events rather than football events that they considered equally probable. Similarly, students who were preselected for their knowledge of football preferred betting on football rather than chance, and preferred chance to politics. The study revealed that people prefer to bet on their vague beliefs in situations where they feel especially competent and knowledgeable but prefer to bet on chance when they do not feel competent or knowledgeable. A similar preference for the familiar has been described in the finance literature in terms of investors' preferences for local versus national equities and domestic versus international ones (French and Poterba 1991).

In a firm setting, Garbuio et al. (2011a) argue that executives tend to bet on resources with which they are most familiar, thus generating a portfolio that may not have an optimal composition for producing successful returns. Familiarity may come from the accumulation of experience in a particular industry or field, or contact with a particular type of resource (e.g., patents versus plants). Once called to make allocation decisions across resources of a different nature, executives will tend to favor the resources they have primarily been exposed to during their careers. Because of the familiarity effect with the resources of the company itself, executives may also be inclined to make allocation decisions to internal resources rather than acquiring resources from the factor market, regardless of whether acquisitions are important vehicles for growth or whether the expansion of a company's existing businesses is not necessarily apt to be less successful than expansion through M&As (Garbuio et al. 2011b; Lovallo et al. 2007; Lubatkin 1987).

## 9.5 SUMMARY AND CONCLUSION

This chapter has examined a number of important areas in which behavioral economics can be applied to strategic decision making. These applications enrich behavioral economics by asking questions that are unique to the role of executives making strategic decisions.[6] We examined key psychological principles and their strategic consequences on the basis of three classes of deviation from the traditional, rational-choice way of looking at strategic decisions: nonstandard preferences, nonstandard beliefs, and nonstandard decision making. For each deviation, we identified key assumptions on which strategy scholarship has been based and showed that by accounting for realistic psychological assumptions, research in strategic decision making has been able to improve the explanatory power of its theories and models, and ultimately the effectiveness of executives' choices.

Because of nonstandard preferences, executives tend to evaluate long-term investments by looking at their short-term results. Because of exploitation bias, executives tend to underinvest in long-term investments (Jacobs 1991) and in exploring new opportunities (Teece 2007). Also, because of endowment effects (Thaler 1980), executives show a tendency to ask more when selling an asset than what they would be willing to pay when buying the same asset, which may explain distorted behavior in M&A decisions. Finally, because of extremeness aversion (Simonson and Tversky 1992), executives may distort their internationalization strategies, preferring adjacent over domestic markets only when the option to invest in faraway markets is introduced to the option set (regardless of risk-reward analysis considerations).

We examined nonstandard beliefs on the basis of executives' expectations about three aspects of a company's decisions. First is the internal situation of the company and the inability to understand the causes of competitive advantage and to leverage internal capabilities (causal ambiguity). We also discussed endowed anchoring, which grounds capital allocation decisions on past decisions, thereby missing chances to incorporate the latest information. Second is the external situation of a company and, in particular, the inability to examine competitors' actions and reactions, resulting in too many market entries. Third, we explained executives' tendency to overweight internal causes of success and external causes of failures, resulting in distorted subsequent decisions.

Finally, we illustrated nonstandard decision making and the use of heuristics to facilitate complex decisions. Because of naive diversification and partition dependence, we saw how the allocation of corporate resources is affected by the way in which options are presented to the decision maker. Also, because of the familiarity effect, executives will tend to favor the resources they have been exposed to most during their careers or to make allocation decisions by focusing on internal resources rather than acquiring resources from external factor markets, regardless of profitability considerations.

For researchers who plan to investigate any of the points illustrated in this chapter and strategic decision making more broadly, we offer two further considerations that are specific to the strategy field. First, the study of heuristics and biases in strategic decisions needs to take into account that executives are embedded in a hierarchical organizational structure that probably has an impact on their preferences, beliefs, and choices. In fact, evidence already exists showing that individuals at different levels of an organization are affected by behavioral impediments in different ways. In King and Zeithaml's (2001) study of causal ambiguity, top executives and middle managers appeared to experience causal ambiguity differently. In their study of managerial perceptions of strength and weakness indicators as well as perceived environmental uncertainty, Ireland et al. (1987) found support for the hypothesis that those perceptions were level-specific. In their account, managers at the top, middle, and technical levels use information that they more easily recall in making decisions (i.e., the information that is "available"—see Tversky and Kahneman 1973). In fact, managers at the same level are exposed to similar information and experiences, driving them to form common understandings of their company's strengths and weaknesses as well as those in the external environment. Thus, depending on the scope of the study, there is a need to explore research questions at different levels in the organization and to consider how the overall organizational context (e.g., organizational routines and politics) may impact available information and, ultimately, decisions. Teece (2007) provides guidance on how the two levels of analysis can fruitfully be considered simultaneously in theory development.

Finally, some critics point out that much of the evidence in behavioral economics as applied to strategic decision making stems from experimental studies. However, many works in behavioral economics (Della Vigna 2009) and behavioral finance (Barberis and Thaler 2003) have now been extended beyond the laboratory. More importantly, in behavioral disciplines as well as strategic decision-making scholarship, experimental evidence is not used in isolation. Experimental results complement theorizing and other research strategies rather than substituting for them. Through multimethod approaches—for example, by combining experimental evidence with large sample surveys or archival studies as well as neuroscience studies—researchers can address both internal and external validity while also gaining multiple perspectives on the same phenomenon (e.g., Flynn and Staw 2004; Powell et al. 2011; Bardolet et al. 2011).

As a result of the fungibility of financial resources and the large volume of transactions consummated daily, the assumption that capital markets can reverse misguided choices may have some credibility in economics or finance. However, strategic decision making has several challenges that render these assumptions less relevant. The inherent size, singularity, and path dependence (David 1994) of many strategic decisions leave less room for executive learning or for error correction. Incentives may surely help to attenuate biases, but violations of rationality do not disappear by simply strengthening incentives (Camerer and Hogarth 1999, 7). Stock options, a favorite prescription of agency theorists for promoting managerial risk taking, have been found to make CEOs place high-variance bets rather than simply larger bets, and especially to favor options that in the end deliver more large losses than gains (Sanders and Hambrick 2007). Some risks that accompany strategic initiatives are external, such as unpredictable actions by competitors, and cannot be hedged against. However, some strategic initiatives, such as managing the resource-allocation process, fall largely within the control of top management teams. Identifying and correcting psychological impediments to sound decision making by executives presents a rather straightforward path for increasing the value creation potential of a company.

## NOTES

1. We clearly take the decision makers—that is, executives—as the unit of analysis. The firm as the unit of analysis, and in particular a *representative* firm, is the approach taken by another behavioral tradition in strategic management, the behavioral theory of the firm (Cyert and March 1963).
2. Similar distinctions have been previously examined in behavioral finance (Barberis and Thaler 2003) and behavioral economics (Della Vigna 2009).
3. In explaining the balance between exploration and exploitation, it is very likely that other psychological mechanisms come into play. Overconfidence and optimism are likely to have a role in explaining preference for exploration. Overconfident and optimistic individuals may be more likely to invest in the most risky activities. Entrepreneurs are thought to have different risk attitudes, optimism, and overconfidence levels in comparison to other executives (e.g., Gary et al. 2008; Busenitz and Barney 1997). Studies that compare entrepreneurs with some other types of managers are likely to provide interesting insights.
4. If the exploitation bias is confirmed in empirical studies, it may provide a behavioral explanation to the existence of x-inefficiencies (for a summary of the debate on the existence of x-inefficiency between Leibenstein, 1978, and Stigler, 1976, see Hay and Morris, 1991, 44–47). A further behavioral explanation to the presence of x-inefficiencies is provided by managerial errors that are recognizable ex ante and not explained by cognitive or other market failures (Powell and Arregle, 2007).
5. Bardolet, Fox and Lovallo (2011) use a nineteen-year period (1979–97), which spans the beginning of the COMPUSTAT segment database until the industry code designations were changed in 1998. They also limit their sample to nonfinancial business units so that the final dataset has 7432 business unit years from 638 multibusiness firms. The authors established a comparison between the multibusiness firms in their sample and their stand-alone peers, using two samples. The first sample, which is called "Real," is made up of multibusiness firms in the COMPUSTAT files in the years mentioned. The second sample, "Virtual," was obtained by randomly selecting, for each of the business units in the Real sample, a COMPUSTAT single-segment firm of similar size in the same industry.

6.  Two topics that we did not discuss are social preferences and the impact of emotions on decision making. In fact, in standard economic models individuals are self-interested in order to maximize their utilities. However, in many cases individuals will make decisions that involve others' interest as well (Charness and Rabin 2002), including instances in which a decision maker's wealth is sacrificed to the benefit of someone else (Fehr and Schmidt 1999). There is also evidence that in some instances the decision maker's utility is an increasing function of the fairness of a distributional outcome (e.g., Andreoni and Miller 2002; Charness and Rabin 2002). In addition, emotions may play an important role of decision making (Loewenstein and Lerner 2003; Vohs et al. 2007). Social preferences and emotions in strategic decision making are two areas of research that, to the best of our knowledge, have not been explored yet deserve further attention.

# References

Alpert, Marc, and Howard Raiffa. 1982. "A Progress Report on the Training of Probability Assessors." In *Judgment under Uncertainty: Heuristics and Biases*, edited by Daniel Kahneman, Paul Slovic, and Amos Tversky, 294–305. Cambridge: Cambridge University Press.

Andreoni, James, and John Miller. 2002. "Giving According to Garp: An Experimental Test of the Consistency of Preferences for Altruism." *Econometrica* 70 (2): 737–53.

Arrow, Kenneth J. 1963. "Social Choice and Individual Values." New Haven: Yale University Press.

Baker, Malcom, Richard S. Ruback, and Jeffrey Wurgler. 2006. "Behavioral Corporate Finance." In *Handbook of Corporate Finance: Empirical Corporate Finance*, edited by B. Espen Eckbo, 146–63. Amsterdam: Elsevier Science.

Baker, Peter. 2009. "How Obama Came to Plan for 'Surge' in Afghanistan." *New York Times*, December 5. Accessed 7 January 2013. http://www.nytimes.com/2009/12/06/world/asia/06reconstruct.html.

Barberis, Nicholas, and Richard H. Thaler. 2003. "A Survey of Behavioral Finance." In *Handbook of the Economics of Finance*, edited by G. M. Constantinides, M. Harris, and R. M. Stulz, 1053–1128. Amsterdam: Elsevier Science B.V.

Bardolet, David, Craig Fox, and Dan Lovallo. 2011. "Corporate Capital Allocation: A Behavioral Perspective." *Strategic Management Journal* 23 (13): 1465–83.

Barney, Jay B. 1986. "Strategic Factor Markets—Expectations, Luck, and Business Strategy." *Management Science* 32 (10): 1230–41.

——. 1991. "Firm Resources and Sustained Competitive Advantage." *Journal of Management* 17:99–120.

Benartzi, Shlomo, and Richard H. Thaler. 2001. "Naive Diversification Strategies in Defined Contribution Saving Plans." *American Economic Review* 91 (1): 79–98.

Bettman, James R., and Barton A. Weitz. 1983. "Attributions in the Board Room—Causal Reasoning in Corporate Annual Reports." *Administrative Science Quarterly* 28 (2): 165–83.

Bowman, Edward H. 1976. "Strategy and the Weather." *Sloan Management Review* 17 (2): 49–62.

Buehler, Roger, Dale Griffin, and Michael Ross. 1994. "Exploring the 'Planning Fallacy': Why People Underestimate Their Task Completion Times." *Journal of Personality and Social Psychology* 67 (3): 366–81.

Busenitz, Lowell W., and Jay B. Barney. 1997. "Differences between Entrepreneurs and Managers in Large Organisations: Biases and Heuristics in Strategic Decision Making." *Journal of Business Venturing* 12 (1): 9–30.

Camerer, Colin F., and Robin M. Hogarth. 1999. "The Effects of Financial Incentives in Experiments: A Review and Capital-Labor-Production Framework." *Journal of Risk and Uncertainty* 19 (1–3): 7–42.

Camerer, Colin F., and George Loewenstein. 2003. "Behavioral Economics: Past, Present, Future." In *Advances in Behavioral Economics*, edited by Colin F. Camerer, George Loewenstein, and Matthew Rabin, 3–52. Princeton: Princeton University Press.

Camerer, Colin F., George Loewenstein, and Drazen Prelec. 2005. "Neuroeconomics: How Neuroscience Can Inform Economics." *Journal of Economic Literature* 43 (1): 9–64.

Camerer, Colin F., and Dan Lovallo. 1999. "Overconfidence and Excess Entry: An Experimental Approach." *American Economic Review* 89 (1): 306–18.

Carlson, Bruce W. 1990. "Anchoring and Adjustment in Judgments under Risk." *Journal of Experimental Psychology-Learning Memory and Cognition* 16 (4): 665–76.

Chapman, Gretchen B., and Eric J. Johnson. 1994. "The Limits of Anchoring." *Journal of Behavioral Decision Making* 7 (4): 223–42.

Charness, Gary, and Matthew Rabin. "Understanding Social Preferences with Simple Tests." *Quarterly Journal of Economics* 117 (3): 817–69.

Christensen, Clay M. 1997. "The Innovator's Dilemma: When New Technologies Cause Great Firms to Fail." Boston: Harvard Business School.

Clapham, Stephen E., and Charles R. Schwenk. 1994. "Self-Serving Attributions, Managerial Cognition, and Company Performance." *Strategic Management Journal* 12 (3): 219–29.

Clayson, Dennis E. 2005. "Performance Overconfidence: Metacognitive Effects or Misplaced Student Expectations?" *Journal of Marketing Education* 27 (2): 122–29.

Coase, Ronald H. 1960. "The Problem of Social Cost." *Journal of Law and Economics* 3: 1–44.

Cyert, Richard M., and James G. March. 1963. *A Behavioral Theory of the Firm*. Engelwood Cliffs, NJ: Prentice-Hall.

David, Paul A. 1994. "Why Are Institutions the 'Carriers of History'?: Path Dependence and the Evolution of Conventions, Organizations and Institutions." *Structural Change and Economic Dynamics* 5 (2): 205–20.

Dean, James W., Jr., and Mark P. Sharfman. 1996. "Does Decision Process Matter? A Study of Strategic Decision Making Effectiveness." *Academy of Management Journal* 39 (2): 368–96.

Della Vigna, Stefano. 2009. "Psychology and Economics: Evidence from the Field." *Journal of Economic Literature* 47 (2): 315–72.

Diekmann, K. A., A. E. Tenbrunsel, P. P. Shah, H. A. Schroth, and M. H. Bazerman. 1996. "The Descriptive and Prescriptive Use of Previous Purchase Price in Negotiations." *Organizational Behavior and Human Decision Processes* 66 (2): 179–91.

Dosi, Giovanni, and Dan Lovallo. 1997. "Rational Entrepreneurs or Optimistic Martyrs? Some Considerations on Technological Regimes, Corporate Entries, and the Evolutionary Role of Decision Biases." In *Technological Innovation: Oversights and Foresights*, edited by Raghu Garud, Preveen Rattan Nayyar, and Zur Baruch Shapira, 41–68. New York: Cambridge University Press.

Fehr, Ernst, and Klaus M. Schmidt. 1999. "A Theory of Fairness, Competition, and Cooperation." *Quarterly Journal of Economics* 114 (3): 817–68.

Flynn, Francis J., and Barry M. Staw. 2004. "Lend Me Your Wallets: The Effect of Charismatic Leadership on External Support for an Organization." *Strategic Management Journal* 25 (4): 309–30.

Ford, Jeffrey D. 1985. "The Effects of Causal Attributions on Decision Makers' Responses to Performance Downturns." *Academy of Management Review* 10 (4): 770–86.

Freeman, Myrick A. 1979. "Approaches to Measuring Public-Goods Demands." *American Journal of Agricultural Economics* 61 (5): 915–20.

French, Kenneth R., and James M. Poterba. 1991. "Investor Diversification and International Equity Markets." *American Economic Review* 81:222–26.

Garbuio, Massimo, Adelaide King, and Dan Lovallo. 2011a. "Looking Inside: Psychological Influences on Structuring a Firm's Portfolio of Resources." Special issue, *Journal of Management* 37 (5): 1444–63.

Garbuio, Massimo, Dan Lovallo, and John Horn. 2011b. "Overcoming Biases in M&A: A Process Perspective." In *Advances in Mergers and Acquisitions*, edited by Cary L. Cooper and Sydney Finkelstein, 9:83–104. Bingley, UK: Emerald Group Publishing Limited.

Gary, Shayne Michael, Giovanni Dosi, and Dan Lovallo. 2008. "Boom and Bust Behavior: On the Persistence of Strategic Decision Biases." In *The Oxford Handbook of Organizational Decision Making*, edited by Gerard P. Hodgkinson and William H. Starbuck, 33–55. New York: Oxford University Press.

Gilovich, Thomas, Dale Griffin, and Daniel Kahneman. 2002. *Heuristics and Biases: The Psychology of Intuitive Judgment*. Cambridge: Cambridge University Press.

Hambrick, Donald C., and Phyllis A. Mason. 1984. "Upper Echelons—the Organization as a Reflection of Its Top Managers." *Academy of Management Review* 9 (2): 193–206.

Hay, Donald A., and Derek J. Morris. 1991. *Industrial Economics and Organization: Theory and Evidence*. Oxford: Oxford University Press.

Hayward, Mathew L. A., and Donald C. Hambrick. 1997. "Explaining the Premiums Paid for Large Acquisitions: Evidence of CEO Hubris." *Administrative Science Quarterly* 42 (1): 103–27.

Heath, Chip, and Amos Tversky. 1991. "Preference and Belief: Ambiguity and Competence in Choice under Uncertainty." *Journal of Risk and Uncertainty* 4:5–28.

Ireland, R. Duane, Michael A. Hitt, Richard A. Bettis, and Deborah A. Deporras. 1987. "Strategy Formulation Processes—Differences in Perceptions of Strength and Weakness Indicators and Environmental Uncertainty by Managerial Level." *Strategic Management Journal* 8 (5): 469–85.

Jacobs, Michael T. 1991. *Short-Term America: The Causes and Cures of Our Business Myopia*. Boston: Harvard Business School Press.

Jacowitz, Karen E., and Daniel Kahneman. 1995. "Measures of Anchoring in Estimation Tasks." *Personality and Social Psychology Bulletin* 21 (11): 1161–66.

Jones, Edward E., and Victor A. Harris. 1967. "The Attribution of Attitudes." *Journal of Experimental Social Psychology* 3 (1): 1–24.

Kahneman, Daniel. 2011. *Thinking, Fast and Slow*. New York: Farrar, Straus and Giroux.

Kahneman, Daniel, Jack L. Knetsch, and Richard H. Thaler. 1990. "Experimental Tests of the Endowment Effect and the Coase Theorem." *Journal of Political Economy* 98:1325–48.

———. 1991. "Anomalies: The Endowment Effect, Loss Aversion, and Status Quo Bias." *Journal of Economic Perspectives* 5 (1): 193–206.

Kahneman, Daniel, and Dan Lovallo. 1993. "Timid Choices and Bold Forecasts: A Cognitive Perspective on Risk-Taking." *Management Science* 39:17–31.

Kahneman, Daniel, and Amos Tversky. 1982. "Subjective Probability: A Judgment of Representativeness." In *Judgment under Uncertainty: Heuristics and Biases*, edited by Daniel Kahneman, Paul Slovic, and Amos Tversky, 32–47. New York: Cambridge University Press.

———. 2000. *Choices, Values, and Frames*. New York: Cambridge University Press, 2000.

King, Adelaide W. 2007. "Disentangling Interfirm and Intrafirm Causal Ambiguity: A Conceptual Model of Causal Ambiguity and Sustainable Competitive Advantage." *Academy of Management Review* 32 (1): 156–78.

King, Adelaide W., and Carl P. Zeithaml. 2001. "Competencies and Firm Performance: Examining the Causal Ambiguity Paradox." *Strategic Management Journal* 22:75–99.

Laverty, Kevin J. 1996. "Economic 'Short-Termism': The Debate, the Unresolved Issues, and the Implications for Management Practice and Research." *Academy of Management Review* 21 (3): 825–60.

Leibenstein, Harvey. 1978. "X-Inefficiency Xists: Reply to an Xorcist." *American Economic Review* 68 (1): 203–11.

Levinthal, Daniel A. 1997. "Adaptation on Rugged Landscapes." *Management Science* 43 (7): 934–50.

Levinthal, Daniel A., and James G. March. 1993. "The Myopia of Learning." Special issue, *Strategic Management Journal* 14:95–112.

Loewenstein, George, and Jennifer S. Lerner. 2003. "The Role of Affect in Decision Making." In *Handbook of Affective Sciences*, edited by Richard J. Davidson, Klaus R. Scherer, and Hill H. Goldsmith, 619–42. Oxford: Oxford University Press.

Lovallo, Dan. 2008. "Competition Neglect and the Inside View: Experimental and Field Evidence." Working paper, University of Sydney Business School.

Lovallo, Dan, and Daniel Kahneman. 2003. "Delusions of Success: How Optimism Undermines Executives' Decisions." *Harvard Business Review* 81 (7): 56–63.

Lovallo, Dan, Patrick Viguerie, Robert Uhlaner, and John Horn. 2007. "Deals without Delusions." *Harvard Business Review* 85 (12): 92–99.

Lubatkin, Michael. 1987. "Merger Strategies and Stockholder Value." *Strategic Management Journal* 8 (1): 39–53.

Malmendier, Ulrike, and Geoffrey Tate. 2005. "CEO Overconfidence and Corporate Investment." *Journal of Finance* 60 (6): 2661–700.

Mezias, John M., and William H. Starbuck. 2003. "Studying the Accuracy of Managers' Perceptions: A Research Odyssey." *British Journal of Management* 14 (1): 3–17.

Mintzberg, Henry, Bruce Ahlstrand, and Joseph Lampel. 1998. *Strategy Safari: A Guided Tour through the Wilds of Strategic Management*. New York: Free Press.

Mintzberg, Henry, Duru Raisinghani, and Andre Theoret. 1976. "The structure of 'Unstructured' Decision Processes." *Administrative Science Quarterly* 21 (2): 246–75.

Moore, Don A., and Paul J. Healy. 2008. "The Trouble with Overconfidence." *Psychological Review* 115 (2): 502–17.

Moore, Don A., John M. Oesch, and Charlene Zietsma. 2007. "What Competition? Myopic Self-Focus in Market-Entry Decisions." *Organization Science* 18 (3): 440–54.

Nag, Rajiv, Donald C. Hambrick, and Ming-Jer Chen. 2007. "What Is Strategic Management, Really? Inductive Derivation of a Consensus Definition of the Field." *Strategic Management Journal* 28 (9): 935–55.

Northcraft, Gregory B., and Margaret A. Neale. 1987. "Experts, Amateurs, and Real-Estate- an Anchoring and Adjustment Perspective on Property Pricing Decisions." *Organizational Behavior and Human Decision Processes* 39 (1): 84–97.

Porter, Michael E. 1980. *Competitive Strategy*. New York: The Free Press.

Powell, Thomas C., and Jean-Luc Arregle. 2007. "Firm Performance and the Axis of Errors." *Journal of Management Research* 7 (2): 59–77.

Powell, Thomas C., Dan Lovallo, and Carmina Caringal. 2006. "Causal Ambiguity, Management Perception, and Firm Performance." *Academy of Management Review* 31 (1): 175–96.

Powell, Thomas C., Dan Lovallo, and Craig R. Fox. 2011. "Behavioral Strategy." *Strategic Management Journal* 32:1369–86.

Rabin, Matthew. 2002. "A Perspective on Psychology and Economics." *European Economic Review* 46 (4–5): 657–85.

Radzevick, Joseph R., and Don A. Moore. 2008. "Myopic Biases in Competitions." *Organizational Behavior and Human Decision Processes* 107 (2): 206–18.

Read, Daniel, and George Loewenstein. 1995. "Diversification Bias: Explaining the Discrepancy in Variety Seeking between Combined and Separated Choices." *Journal of Experimental Psychology: Applied* 1 (1): 34–49.

Reed, Richard, and Robert J. DeFilippi. 1990. "Causal Ambiguity, Barriers to Imitation, and Sustainable Competitive Advantage." *Academy of Management Review* 15 (1): 88–102.

Roll, Richard. 1986. "The Hubris Hypothesis of Corporate Takeovers." *Journal of Business* 59 (2): 197–206.

Ross, Lee. 1977. "The Intuitive Psychologist and His Shortcomings: Distortions in the Attribution Process." In *Advances in Experimental Social Psychology*, edited by Leonard Berkowitz, 173–220. New York: Academic Press.

Rumelt, Richard P. 1984. "Toward a Strategic Theory of the Firm." In *Competitive Strategic Management*, edited by Robert Boyden Lamb, 556–70. Englewood Cliffs, NJ: Prentice-Hall.

Rumelt, Richard P., Dan E. Schendel, and David J. Teece, eds. 1994. *Fundamental Issues in Strategy*. Boston: Harvard Business School Press.

Russo, J. Edward, and Paul Shoemaker. 1989. *Decision Traps*. New York: Doubleday.

Salancik, Gerald R., and James R. Meindl. 1984. "Corporate Attributions as Strategic Illusions of Management Control." *Administrative Science Quarterly* 29: 238–54.

Sanders, Gerard W. M., and Donald C. Hambrick. 2007. "Swinging for the Fences: the Effects of CEO Stock Options on Company Risk Taking and Performance." *Academy of Management Journal* 50 (5): 1055–78.

Schendel, Dan, Igor Ansoff, and Derek Channon. 1980. "Statement of Editorial Policy." *Strategic Management Journal* 1 (1): 1–5.

Schleifer, Andrei. 2000. *Inefficient Markets: An Introduction to Behavioral Finance*. New York: Oxford University Press.

Schwenk, Charles R. 1985. "Management Illusions and Biases—Their Impact on Strategic Decisions." *Long Range Planning* 18 (5): 74–80.

Simonson, Itamar. 1990. "The Effect of Purchase Quantity and Timing on Variety-Seeking Behavior." *Journal of Marketing Research* 27 (2): 150–62.

Simonson, Itamar, and Amos Tversky. 1992. "Choice in Context: Tradeoff Contrast and Extremeness Aversion." *Journal of Marketing Research* 29 (3): 281–95.

Sirower, Mark L. 1997. *The Synergy Trap*. New York: Free Press.

Soll, Jack B., and Joshua Klayman. 2004. "Overconfidence in Interval Estimates." *Journal of Experimental Psychology: Learning, Memory and Cognition* 30 (2): 299–314.

Staw, Barry M., Pamela I. McKechnie, and Sheila M. Puffer. 1983. "The Justification of Organizational Performance." *Administrative Science Quarterly* 28:582–600.

Stigler, George J. 1976. "The Xistence of X-Efficiency." *American Economic Review* 66 (1): 213–16.

Svenson, Ola. 1981. "Are We All Less Risky and More Skillful Than Our Fellow Driver?" *Acta Psychologica* 47 (2): 143–48.

Teece, David J. 2007. "Explicating Dynamic Capabilities: The Nature and Microfoundations of (Sustainable) Enterprise Performance." *Strategic Management Journal* 28 (13): 1319–50.

Thaler, Richard H. 1980. "Toward a Positive Theory of Consumer Choice." *Journal of Economic Behavior and Organization* 1:39–60.

——. 1981. "An Economic Theory of Self-Control." *Journal of Political Economy* 89 (2): 392–406.

——. 1999. "Mental Accounting Matters." *Journal of Behavioral Decision Making* 12 (3): 183–206.

Tversky, Amos, and Daniel Kahneman. 1973. "Availability: a Heuristic for Judging Frequency and Probability." *Cognitive Psychology* 4:207–32.

——. 1974. "Judgment under Uncertainty: Heuristics and Biases." *Science* 185 (4157): 1124–31.

Van Yperen, Nico W. 1992. "Self-Enhancement among Major-League Soccer Players: The Role of Importance and Ambiguity on Social-Comparison Behavior." *Journal of Applied Social Psychology* 22 (15): 1186–98.

Vohs, Kathleen D., Roy F. Baumeister, and George Loewenstein. 2007. *Do Emotions Help or Hurt Decision Making?: A Hedgefoxian Perspective.* New York: Russell Sage Foundation.

Wernerfelt, Birger. 1984. "A Resource Based View of the Firm." *Strategic Management Journal* 5 (2): 171–80.

Willig, Robert D. 1976. "Consumers Surplus without Apology." *American Economic Review* 66 (4): 589–97.

Zajac, Edward, and Max Bazerman. 1991. "Blind Spots in Industry and Competitor Analysis: Implications of Interfirm (Mis)Perceptions for Strategic Decisions." *Academy of Management Review* 16:37–56.

# PART IV

# PRICING, MARKETING TACTICS AND STRATEGIES

# CHAPTER 10

························································································

# ADVANCES IN
# PRICING STRATEGIES
# AND TACTICS

························································································

## PRAVEEN K. KOPALLE AND
## ROBERT G. HANSEN

## 10.1 INTRODUCTION

THIS chapter examines the recent literature on pricing with a focus on blending an economics approach with that of marketing. We believe that the field of managerial economics is at its best when it is integrative, and the combination of economics and marketing expertise in pricing is an ideal place for this integration to occur. While economics as a field has done much of the fundamental work in pricing theory, the marketing domain shows how that theory can be used with actual firms and consumers.

One way to approach pricing is to consider the logical bounds to the price in any transaction—marginal cost on one hand and economic value on the other. Economic value is the maximum amount a customer would be willing to pay for the product and is the sum of the reference value (price of the perceived closest substitute) and the value differential between the product offering and that of the closest substitute. The more tricky aspect is to figure out optimal price points and to move from a uniform price across customers to one of personalized pricing. Pricing an entire product line only complicates the situation, as does the inclusion of competitive effects and the dimension of time.

The rest of this chapter is organized as follows. In Section 10.2, we briefly discuss the fundamental principles of optimal pricing, which serves as the foundation for more advanced pricing methods. This is followed by summaries of price discrimination in Section 10.3, pricing using conjoint analysis in Section 10.4, dynamic, behavioral, and competitive considerations in Section 10.5, and pricing in two-sided markets in section 10.6. Section 10.7 offers concluding remarks.[1]

# 10.2 PRICING BASICS

The nature of more advanced pricing strategies and tactics can best be seen by noting the imperfections of simple uniform pricing. Consider a monopolistic seller facing a linear, downward sloping demand function. The simple uniform price that maximizes profit, $P^*$, satisfies the well-known first-order condition given by the following relation:

$$\frac{P^* - MC}{P^*} = -\frac{1}{\varepsilon} \tag{10.1}$$

where $MC$ is the marginal cost of production and $\varepsilon$ is the own-price elasticity of demand ($<0$). Rather than the familiar "marginal revenue equals marginal cost" formula, expression (10.1) restates the first-order condition for profit maximization as: *The profit maximizing markup of price over marginal cost is inversely proportional to the elasticity of demand.*[2]

Figure 10.1 shows the two sources of imperfection associated with simple uniform pricing: consumer surplus from units that are purchased at prices less than marginal value (Area A); and additional net surplus from units currently not sold but for which marginal value exceeds marginal cost (Area B). To appropriate these potential additional profits, the seller will have to use more sophisticated pricing schemes, under the general heading of price discrimination. According to Stigler (1987), price discrimination occurs when two or more *similar* goods are sold at prices in different ratio-to-marginal cost. With first-degree discrimination, the perfectly discriminating monopolist would "walk down the demand curve" and sell the efficient quantity and extract the maximum potential profit. Second-degree discrimination, or more generally nonlinear pricing, is any pricing scheme for which the amount paid by a consumer is not strictly proportional to quantity. A simple nonlinear scheme that can achieve maximum profit potential with

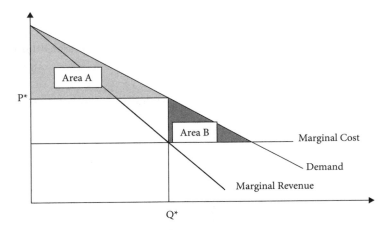

**FIGURE 10.1** Imperfection of Simple Uniform Pricing

homogeneous consumers is a two-part tariff with a per-unit price of MC and an "entry fee" set at the level of total consumer surplus. Third-degree discrimination will price differentially to submarkets that differ in terms of elasticity, with equation (10.1) guiding the optimal third-degree price discrimination policy.

## 10.3  PRICE DISCRIMINATION

While most recent work in price discrimination—both theoretical and empirical—has been on second-degree price discrimination, there is also a continuing literature on two fundamental questions concerning price discrimination: when and how profitable is it; and what are its impacts on quantity and social welfare? Malueg and Snyder (2006) suggest that the profitability of third-degree price discrimination can be as much as $N$ times the profitability of a nondiscriminating seller, under reasonable conditions, where $N$ is the number of independent markets served. Aguirre et al. (2010) generalize much of the earlier work on the welfare impact of price discrimination and conclude that, "In many cases discrimination reduces welfare, but our analysis has shown that the conditions for discrimination to raise welfare are not implausible" (Aguirre et al. 2010, 1611; Robinson 1933).

Relatively little empirical work has been done on third-degree discrimination, but one example is Cabolis et al. (2007), who find evidence of large price differences in international textbook pricing, suggesting that third-degree price discrimination leads publishers to price higher in more inelastic markets. On first-degree price discrimination, there is a literature on discrimination in automobile pricing; see, for example, Harless and Hoffer (2002), who conclude that auto dealers engage in extensive price discrimination based on age and cash payment.

### 10.3.1  Second-Degree Price Discrimination/Nonlinear Pricing

The basics of nonlinear pricing are found in Oi (1971), Schmalensee (1981), Maskin and Riley (1984), Tirole (1992) and Wilson (1993).[3] Taking Oi's classic example of theme park pricing with an entry fee and a per-unit price as the elements of a nonlinear pricing scheme, we can see the profit potential of that strategy, as well as the complications, once we introduce the idea of consumer heterogeneity. If all consumers are identical, the optimal two-part tariff is, as mentioned before, simply a per-unit price equal to the marginal cost of production coupled with a per-consumer fixed or entry fee equal to the consumer surplus generated when the consumer buys the efficient quantity.

With heterogeneous consumers, the optimal, single, two-part tariff will however be different from this. With consumer heterogeneity, some customers will choose not to buy at all (the entry fee exceeds their possible surplus from buying at $MC$) while other consumers will be left with excess surplus. The case of pricing with a single, two-part tariff in the face of heterogeneous consumers is covered by Varian (1989). Varian notes that the optimal *per-unit price* can be expressed as a variant of Equation (10.1), with an adjustment based on the demand of the *marginal* consumer relative to the *average* consumer. If the average consumer demands more than the marginal consumer, then the optimal per-unit price is still above marginal cost; but if the average consumer demands less than the marginal consumer, then the optimal per-unit price will be less than marginal cost. This points out a key issue in designing multipart pricing schemes: the self-selection of consumers as to participation and as to choice of tariff or product version (e.g., quality). This issue arises in all the most interesting pricing schemes, be they nonlinear pricing, bundling, versioning, dynamic pricing, or revenue management.

## 10.3.2  Second-Degree Price Discrimination with "Menu Pricing" and Consumer Self-Selection

Suppose there are two "types" of consumers, one type with high and elastic demand, who will purchase a large quantity if the per-unit price is relatively low; and a second type with low and inelastic demand. If restricted to a single two-part tariff, the seller would set (as in Varian 1989) a per-unit price above marginal cost and the entry fee equal to the consumer surplus of the marginal/low-demand consumer. A single per-unit price above marginal cost inefficiently restricts consumption, while the single entry fee leaves consumer surplus with the inframarginal consumer. However, if the seller offers two multipart pricing schemes, and allows consumers to self-select which one they desire, profit will increase. Think of offering two tariff choices of the form $(e_i, p_i)$, where $e_i$ is the entry fee in tariff $i$ and $p_i$ is the per-unit price in tariff $i$. For the high demand, elastic consumer, we will target a tariff with low $p_i$ (generally in fact equal to MC; see Varian 1989, 613) and a high $e_i$ to extract consumer surplus. The lower-demand, less-elastic consumer will face a higher per-unit price and a lower entry fee. The key point is to make sure that the *self-selection* constraints are met: that each consumer type *prefers* the tariff targeted at him/her. Many pricing schemes use multipart pricing with self-selection among tariffs. Cellular telephone pricing is a great example, but the method is also inherent in many satellite and cable TV pricing policies (combinations of monthly charge plus surcharges for additional channels); financial platforms such as credit cards and banking/trading accounts (annual fees and per-transaction or interest charges); rental cars (different combinations of daily rates and mileage charges); and even health insurance (different annual premiums plus per-visit charges).

Maskin and Riley (1984, 171) provide a general model of optimal nonlinear pricing where consumers' utility function is:

$$U_i(q,-T) = \int_0^q p(x, v_i)dx - T. \tag{10.2}$$

$U_i$ is consumer $i$'s utility given consumption of $q$ units and total payment of $T$; $p(x; v_i)$ is the marginal value ("demand price") for unit $x$ given consumer $i$'s demand parameter $v_i$. This is a standard approach based on consumer surplus, with no income effects on demand from the payment of $T$. Note that the two-part tariff $(e_i, p_i)$ fits this framework, in that faced with an $(e_i, p_i)$ tariff, a consumer will have an implied quantity demanded of $q$ and a total payment $T$. Maskin and Riley describe the economics behind optimal nonlinear pricing, and they go further to characterize the optimal tariff design: The optimal scheme will generate inefficiency, with almost all consumers not buying the efficient amount; and generally, the optimal scheme will involve quantity discounts, with high-volume purchasers paying a lower average price. Note that this fits our above examples, where, for instance, the rental car driver who selects an optimal tariff assuming that she will drive a lot will pay a lower average price per mile.

Recent papers have extended this basic theory, tested it with real-world data, and discussed implementation of optimal schemes (see Iyengar and Gupta 2009 for a review). Essegaier et al.'s (2002) analysis in service industries (online services, telecom, fitness and health clubs, and so on) indicates that multipart pricing may not be optimal in an environment of constrained capacity. Sundararajan (2004) allows for transaction costs associated with usage fees and shows that when the marginal cost of producing additional units of some goods is essentially zero (information goods), an optimal pricing scheme may involve only a per-period flat fee. More recently, Goettler and Clay (2011) explore consumer selection of flat-rate versus usage-sensitive tariffs, applying a Bayesian learning model that explains the "flat-rate bias." Given the rise in importance of behavioral decision making in economics, marketing, and even finance, this is a promising research area.

Other papers bring the theory of nonlinear pricing closer to meeting the data, typically with structural model estimation. Lambrecht and Skiera (2006) consider what happens if consumers aren't strict utility-maximizers but also care about other aspects of the tariff—preferring, for example, a flat-rate tariff even if it is not the best for them. On the basis of empirical work using European internet service tariffs, choices, and usage, they find that any bias in favor of flat rates does not significantly affect the seller's profit, but that a bias toward pay-per-use (probably due to underestimation of usage) creates "churn" and lowers profit. Lambrecht et al. (2007) examine three-part tariffs (access fees, usage prices, and usage allowances) based on data from a German internet service provider on tariff choices and consumption, allowing them to estimate underlying preference parameters and demand elasticities. Their key findings suggest that a preference for flat-rate plans and consumer uncertainty over likely usage rates drive much of the choice patterns (with high uncertainty leading to selection of plans with greater usage allowances). Iyengar et al. (2011) use data from a field experiment for a subscription-based telecom service to test explicitly if consumers have inherent preferences for different tariff plans (e.g., flat rates). They find that consumers prefer pay-per-use plans over two-part pricing schemes, but that even with the consequences of reduced usage and more churn, the two-part tariff still yields higher profit.

## 10.3.3  Second-Degree Discrimination through Versioning and Product-Line Pricing

The practice of *versioning* extends consumer self-selection to product choice as well as tariff choice, and fits into Stigler's (1987) definition of price discrimination as charging prices in different proportion to *MC* for *similar* goods. The core idea of versioning is to strengthen the seller's ability to use self-selection to extract profit by creating slight product (quality) differences between the choices offered to consumers. The differences do not have to encompass only physical product characteristics, but can extend to time and place of availability (e.g., timing of movie releases on DVD, publication dates for paperback versions of new books, locations of outlet stores for clothing and other goods). A classic example is airline seating between business class and coach: while all passengers are on the same plane and flight, the disparity in material comfort is obvious, with the business class and coach seats being wider or narrower versions of the same underlying product. A key issue with versioning is the self-selection constraint; with airline seats, we can think of price differences between coach and business class as creating the potential for a form of "arbitrage" or cannibalization—with large price differences, some business class customers will move to coach. To control this, the airline has two sets of instruments, the price difference and the comfort difference, and to maximize total revenue, each instrument needs to be used. As we tell our MBA students, the next time you are in coach and wonder why the airline cannot give the coach customers just a little more legroom (how much would it cost to remove one row of seats?), realize that the answer lies not in incremental cost from lost coach class revenue but in the lost *business class revenue* from the marginal business customer who would shift to coach if the legroom were greater.[4]

As Varian (1989) points out, the analytics of the quality-pricing problem are similar to the nonlinear pricing model of Maskin and Riley (1984), with quality simply substituted for quantity. Varian (1997) and Shapiro and Varian (1999) are more recent classics in the versioning literature, especially with respect to information goods. Deneckere and McAfee (1996) popularize the term "damaged goods" to refer to a manufacturer purposely and at cost reducing the quality of a product in order to effect indirect price discrimination. Examples are computer printers (print engine slowed down to create low quality); computer chips (internal clock slowed in low-end chips); and auto companies repurchasing cars initially sold to rental car companies (almost-new, "program" vehicles). We should not be surprised that it might be profitable for a manufacturer to pay to reduce the quality of its product, as this is just one way to produce a product line of multiple versions of essentially the same thing. McAfee (2007) characterizes more fully the situations when damaging goods might be profitable; one key finding is that the strategy cannot be profitable if the value of the damaged product is a constant proportion of the value of the undamaged product. For versioning to be profitable, Anderson and Dana (2009, 980) add that "the percentage change in social surplus from product upgrades is increasing in consumers' willingness to pay."

In marketing, the question of versioning is phrased in terms of product-line design and pricing (Chen 2009; Moorthy 1984). The problem of choosing an optimal product line is one of optimal versioning and can be stated as choosing the set of products and prices to maximize profitability, where a product is seen as a set of underlying attributes and is therefore infinitely variable. Guiltinan (2011), summarizing research on product-line pricing, argues that the issue of cannibalization—deriving from self-selection—is overemphasized and that research should bring different approaches to bear. Belloni et al. (2008) focus on computational efficiency in designing an optimal product line, while Schön (2010) extends Belloni et al. by including third-degree price discrimination, applying the technique to a large-scale conjoint study of an IT infrastructure provider and showing improved profitability.

Structural modeling and estimation allows simulating policy and pricing experiments in this area—see Leslie's (2004) application to a Broadway play where the quality/price data arise from different seats sold at different prices. It turns out that the optimal set of ticket prices come quite close to the actual prices and the profitability of discrimination appears to be about a 5% improvement with negligible effect on welfare. Draganska and Jain (2006) estimate a structural model, with consumers choosing over quality, price, and flavor in the retail yogurt market. The authors conclude that price discrimination at the product-line level only (not across flavors) is optimal, as consumer preferences differ more across lines than flavors.

## 10.3.4  Bundling

Another form of price discrimination is commodity bundling. Typical examples are options packages on new autos; packages of cable TV channels; McDonald's "value meals"; vacation packages; and the "Big Deal" offered to research libraries by academic journal publishers (Nevo et al. 2005; Edlin and Rubinfeld 2005). We begin with the basic monopoly models of bundling and then discuss key extensions. We note immediately that there has been little systematic empirical work on bundling. Stigler (1963) was perhaps the first academic treatment of bundling, and Adams and Yellen (1976) gave a more theoretical analysis, as did Schmalensee (1984) and McAfee et al. (1989). Stemersch and Tellis (2002) give a synthesis with economic, marketing, and legal perspectives. Standard treatment compares the extreme case of pure bundling where only the bundled offering is available to mixed bundling where both the package and separate products are made available (Ansari et al.1996; McCormick et al.2006; Mulhern and Leone 1991; Venkatesh and Mahajan 1993).

The basic idea behind bundling is as follows. Bundling increases revenue extraction because low or negative correlation between reservation values for the individual products reduces variance in the sum of the bundled values (see Schmalensee 1984). As we have already seen from nonlinear pricing, an essential problem in revenue extraction is consumer heterogeneity: if some parts of a bundle are valued highly by some consumers but valued less so by others, a la carte pricing tends to favor an optimal price close to the "average" value, thereby deterring some consumers from buying at all, while leaving others with excess surplus. With bundling, given low or negative correlation among reservation values, the variance of the sum of the values (value of the bundle) is reduced, allowing for better revenue extraction. In a case with perfect negative correlation of values, all consumers would assign the same value to the bundle, and revenue extraction would be perfect. Negative correlation in values can often be induced by the peculiarities of the specific product. For instance, with TV channels, given that most consumers are going to watch a limited number of hours of programming per day, if they value one kind of channel highly they are almost bound to value another kind of channel less highly. Fixed budgets of research libraries can also induce negative correlation in values for scientific journal subscriptions.

Consider a simple cell phone pricing example for two add-on services: voice mail and text messaging. As seen in Table 10.1, let's say there are four customer segments each with a different willingness to pay per month.

For simplicity, assume that the variable costs are zero. If we priced the services separately as in pure components, the optimal price for voice mail is $8.00, $8.50 for text messaging, yielding a total profit of $33. By bundling both services at $10.50, the profit is $42. However, offering a mixed bundle (voice mail and text messaging prices of $9 each and a bundle price of $13) is the most profitable ($44) strategy as it extracts the most consumer surplus, as seen in Figure 10.2. Broadly speaking, mixed bundling is generally the optimal solution.

There have been a few key extensions. One is incorporating competition. Matutes and Regibeau (1992) examine the impact of competition on bundling strategies and show there is a prisoner's dilemma-type situation where both firms end up providing discounts on the bundled offering. While mixed bundling generally dominates pure bundling, Kopalle et al. (1999) show that in a competitive setting, mixed bundling is the subgame perfect Nash equilibrium when there is scope for market expansion; selling components on a standalone basis is the equilibrium solution otherwise. Balachander et al. (2010) suggest that due to greater customer loyalty, competitors benefit by offering bundle discounts relative to price reductions on individual products.

Extending bundling to the digital arena where the marginal cost of products or services is low, Bakos and Brynjolfsson (2000) suggest that the large-scale bundling of digital products creates economies of aggregation and discourages entry in the

### Table 10.1 Bundling Example

| Customer Segment | Voice Mail | Text Messaging | Both |
|---|---|---|---|
| 1 | 9.00 | 1.50 | 10.50 |
| 2 | 8.00 | 5.00 | 13.00 |
| 3 | 4.50 | 8.50 | 13.00 |
| 4 | 2.50 | 9.00 | 11.50 |

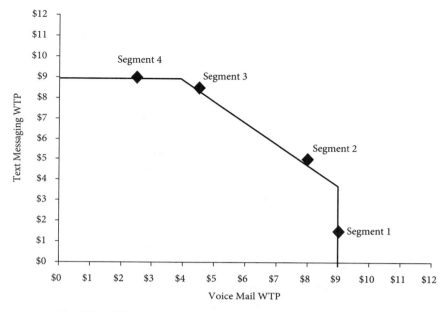

FIGURE 10.2 Mixed Bundling Strategy

bundler's markets. Hitt and Chen (2005) and Shin-yi et al. (2008) extend the analysis for digital products, and show the optimality of customized bundling strategy of customers self-selecting up to $M$ goods drawn from a larger pool of $N$ at a fixed price. Nalebuff (2004) and Peitz (2008) also argue that a firm with market power in two products can, by bundling, create an entry barrier to a new entrant with only one of the products.

There is an emerging research stream that links, through the operation of product complementarity, bundling with auctions (Popkowski Leszczyc and Häubl 2010; Subramaniam and Venkatesh 2009). Other extensions include examining the impact of customers' knowledge of the usefulness of a product to them on the optimal bundling strategy (Basu and Vitharana 2009). Prasad et al.'s (2010) results indicate that when there is asymmetry in network externalities and costs across two products, mixed bundling needs to be refined further such that one product is available only in a bundle. Banciu et al. (2010) show the suboptimality of mixed bundling when the two products are vertically differentiated and their production is capacity constrained.

From a psychological standpoint, it is interesting that bundling of season tickets—such as for sporting events and theater performances, where consumption is spread over time—"decouples" transaction costs and benefits, and thus decreases a consumer's likelihood of using a service that was paid for up-front (Soman and Gourville 2001). For a further review of the bundling literature, see Stremersch and Tellis (2002) and Venkatesh and Mahajan (2009). Finally, we conclude this section with a remark that most of the bundling literature has been theoretical in nature and, going forward, there is much scope for testing the analytic results empirically.

## 10.3.5 Revenue Management

Revenue (or yield) management comprises a set of practical techniques based on pricing theory to allocate limited resources (e.g., bucketing airfares into multiple classes and managing seat inventory) among a variety of customer types and, hence, to optimize revenue. Situations where it is expensive or impossible to store excess resources, future demand is uncertain, and firms can differentiate among customer segments with differing elasticities are appropriate for revenue management, which is just another form of price discrimination. What is new is that the decision-making process is a technologically sophisticated, operations-research-based approach. It is driven by advances in information technology that provide the capability to automate transactions, capture and store vast amounts of data, and quickly execute complex algorithms (see Kimes 2009; Talluri and Van Ryzin 2005; and Talluri 2012, for recent advances in revenue management).

We begin with a simple illustration that highlights the intuition behind this technique and consider a hotel with 210 rooms and two types of customers: a leisure segment wherein buyers are more price sensitive and purchase in advance, and a business segment that is less price sensitive and does not purchase in advance (Netessine and Shumsky 2002). The respective prices charged are $105 and $159. Say, it is February and the hotel is taking reservations for the night of March 29 and a leisure customer wants a room for that night. The issue is whether the hotel should continue to sell at the leisure price of $105 or hold the room for a business traveler at a later (but not too much later) date. The booking limit is the maximum number of rooms sold to leisure customers and the corresponding protection limit is the number of rooms held for business customers. All rooms are categorized as either "protected" or "available" at a discount. Let the current protection level be $Q + 1$ rooms. Whether this should be reduced to $Q$ depends on two factors: (1) the relative full and discount prices and (2) the anticipated demand for a full price room. (See Figure 10.3 for an illustration of the hotel's options.)

Protecting room $Q + 1$ has an expected revenue of  probability(demand for full fare $> Q$)($159$) + probability(demand for full fare $<=Q$)($0$). Therefore, the protection level should be lowered to $Q$ as long as probability(demand for full fare $> Q$) ($159$) $< $105$.

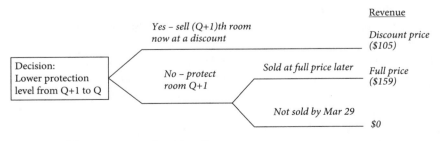

**FIGURE 10.3** Yield Management Decision Tree

*That is, probability (demand for full farte* $> Q) < \dfrac{\$105}{\$159} = 0.66$

*Or, probability (demand for full fare* $\leq Q) \geq 1 - 0.66 = 0.34 = \dfrac{p_H - p_L}{p_H}$  (10.3)

To find the probability of selling the room at full price, one can look at historical data and determine, for a given number of rooms ($Q$), the cumulative fraction of days when the demand for rooms at full price is at or below $Q$. Then figure out the smallest $Q$ (say $Q^*$) with a cumulative fraction that is greater than or equal to 0.34, giving the corresponding optimal protection level; the booking limit is given by 210- $Q^*$. Note that the right-hand side in Equation (10.3) is similar to the critical ratio in the newsvendor problem[5]. The optimal protection level is the smallest $Q$ such that the probability of demand for a full-price room less than or equal to $Q$ is greater than or equal to the critical ratio.

Consumers who are either sure of their travel plans in advance or are more price sensitive, self-select by booking early (or stay that extra Saturday night) and take advantage of lower room prices while others may wait until later (or not stay an extra night) and pay a premium. While typical revenue management models acknowledge such consumer self-selection, more recent research takes into consideration the possibility of price decreases closer to an expected departure date. This raises the issue of the impact of strategic (or forward-looking) consumers on revenue management as they time their purchases to obtain lower prices (Jerath et al. 2010; Shen and Su 2007). The typical result is that the presence of such strategic customers may exert a negative influence on firm revenues (Anderson and Wilson 2003; Levin et al. 2009). In this regard, section 10.5.4 below on dynamic structural models is also relevant here but more importantly, there is little empirical research on the impact of strategic consumer behavior on revenue management and this problem therefore points in a fruitful direction for future research.

## 10.4  Pricing Using Conjoint Analysis

While managers typically have good knowledge of their costs, competitor prices, key product differentiators, etc., they have little knowledge of consumer price response (Simon 1989). In terms of researching price sensitivity, Table 10.2 provides a good summary of the various tools used; we believe that the emphasis should be on conjoint surveys, price experiments, and use of historical data.[6] For example, price elasticities for existing products are estimated using historical data (Simon 1989). A review of 337 published studies shows that the average price elasticity across both consumer and industrial products is -2.5 (Tellis 1988; Bijmolt et al. 2005) and consumer products are better understood than industrial products (Noble and Gruca 1999). For consumer products, most of the effect of a price change appears to be brand switching—25% primary product demand-related and 75% caused by brand switching (Bell et al.1999); see

**Table 10.2 Tools Used in Estimating Price Elasticity**

| Criterion | Method | Expert Judgment | Customer Surveys | | Price Experiments | Historical Market Data |
|---|---|---|---|---|---|---|
| | | | Direct | Conjoint | | |
| Validity | Medium | low | medium-high | | medium-low | high |
| Reliability | medium-high | uncertain | medium-high | | high | high |
| Costs | very low | low-medium | medium | | medium-high | depends on availability and accessibility |
| Applicability to New Products | Yes | questionable | yes | | yes | no, except by analogy |
| Applicability to Established Products | Yes | yes | yes | | yes | yes |
| Overall Evaluation | useful for products, new situations | questionable | very useful | | useful | useful for new established products |

also Section 10.5.4. Also, categories that are less perishable have larger own-price elasticities, as do those accounting for greater shares of household budgets; so-called necessities have smaller elasticities (Blattberg and Neslin 1990; Blattberg and Briesch 2012; Shankar and Bolton 2004; Shankar and Krishnamurthi 1996). Finally, there seems to be an asymmetric price effect between higher-price/higher-quality tier brands and lower-price/lower-quality tier brands, where the premium brands draw more significantly from the lower-priced brands selling at a price discount than vice-versa (Blattberg and Wisniewski 1989; Sethuraman and Srinivasan 2002).

While historical data are useful in determining price elasticities for existing products, they are not useful for new products. For new products, conjoint analysis is widely used both in industry and academia to determine price elasticities and willingness-to-pay, and to conduct pricing simulations (Green and Srinivasan 1978, 1990; Mahajan et al. 1982; McCullough 2002). The conjoint analysis framework views products and services as bundles of attributes. For example, a personal computer (PC) is a bundle that consists of a CPU, RAM, disk drives, audio/video features, brand name, and price, to name a few, and consumers place value on the attributes. The PC's overall value is given by $\theta_1 X_1 + \theta_2 X_2 + \dots + \theta_k X_K$, where $X_i$, $X_{i+1}$, $X_{i+2}$, etc., are levels for attribute $i$ and $\theta$s denote the value of the attribute levels. The question is, how can we learn about the value of product attributes? One way is to ask people directly for their values. Alternatively, we could ask them questions designed to elicit their values. For example, when MBA students at a top business school were asked to rate various job attributes in terms of how important they are to them, they ranked salary as sixth, US region as second, job location as fifth, people/culture as number one, functional area as third, firm growth as seventh, business travel as eighth, and opportunity to advance as fourth. However, the respective ranking of these attributes based on a conjoint with the same group was actually one through eight!

In a conjoint study, respondents are shown a set of products composed of different mixes of attributes and asked their purchase likelihood for each product. Importance weights that best predict purchase likelihood are then inferred. Consider an example of automobile pricing using conjoint analysis. Say that an automobile company, P, plans to introduce a new model of its SUV. Respondents are given a set of purchase situations with three or four vehicles where each vehicle is described in terms of product attributes. Respondents choose the vehicle they are most likely to purchase in each scenario and the product attributes are changed from one scenario to another. Figure 10.4 provides a screenshot of a conjoint survey instrument.

Consumers make trade-offs based on competing products and the attributes and their levels in each product. We can then construct a model of choice as a function of product attributes including the price. The probability of an individual choosing product j from a set of J products is given by the logit model (Ben-Akiva and Lerman 1994) with price as one of the independent variables.

The $\theta$s are estimated simply by dummy variable regression or techniques such as Hierarchical Bayes (Andrews et al. 2002). Attributes with levels that show a wider range of $\theta$s are more important relative to those with a smaller range. The $\theta$s are also useful in conducting simulations to determine price elasticities. Figure 10.5 is example of a price simulation based on conjoint analysis. This chart depicts the effect of changing Product P's (e.g., RX 330) price on the choice share of P as well-competing vehicles. For example, a 10% increase in P's price decreases its choice share by 28.2% (i.e., elasticity = -2.82). Similarly, a 10% increase in P's price would increase H's choice share by 11.5% (cross price elasticity of 1.15).

Table 10.3 shows the effect of a 1% price increase of the vehicles in the columns. For example, automobile P's column gives the effect of a 1% increase in its price on its choice

| Which vehicle would you be most likely to purchase? | | | |
|---|---|---|---|
| Lexus RX 330 3.3 liter V-6 engine | BMW X5 3.0i 3.0 liter I-6 engine | Mercedes Benz ML 320 3.2 liter V-6 engine | Acura MDX 3.5 liter V-6 engine |
| No Moonroof | Moonroof (wide) | No Moonroof | No Moonroof |
| Third Row Seating | Third Row Seating | Third Row Seating | Third Row Seating |
| Navigation System | Navigation System | No Navigation System | Navigation System |
| No Rear Seat Entertainment | No Rear Seat Entertainment | Rear Seat Entertainment | Rear Seat Entertainment |
| Manual Rear Door | Power Rear Door | Power Rear Door | Power Rear Door |
| Sport Package | No Sport Package | Sport Package | Sport Package |
| $45,000 | $40,000 | $42,500 | $37,500 |
| Make your selection by touching the box with your stylus | | | |

FIGURE 10.4  Screen Shot of a Pricing Conjoint Study

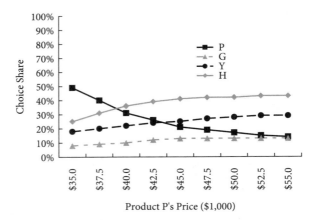

**FIGURE 10.5** Conjoint Simulation: Effect of Price on Choice Share

**Table 10.3 Clout and Vulnerability Matrix**

| Effect On | Product P | Product G | Product H | Product Y |
|---|---|---|---|---|
| Product P | −2.82 | 2.17 | 0.30 | 1.11 |
| Product G | 1.29 | −3.33 | 0.30 | 0.31 |
| Product H | 1.15 | 1.18 | −4.46 | 2.43 |
| Product Y | 1.08 | 1.46 | 1.10 | −3.15 |

share as well as those of its competitors. In other words, a drop in $P$'s price will harvest buyers from $G$, $H$, and $Y$. From $P$'s row, we can see that a drop in $H$'s price will hurt $P$'s share less than a drop in $Y$'s or $G$'s price. $P$ is more susceptible to a drop in $G$'s price than a drop in $Y$'s price. Regarding the willingness to pay, assume that model $P$ is the most preferred model. Relative to $H$, the most an individual is willing to pay for $P$ is given by equating the value of $P$ with that of $H$ and simplifying for the price of $P$, that is, $1/\theta_{price}$ [brand value of $P$ – brand value of $H$ + value of quality attributes of $P$ – value of quality attributes of $H$ + $\theta_{price}$ (price of $H$)].

While conjoint analysis was first used in industry in 1971, its commercial application has taken off both in the United States and Europe with about 80% of the applications in consumer and industrial goods and about 50%–60% of the projects having a pricing purpose (Cattin and Wittink 1982; Wittink and Cattin 1989; Wittink et al. 1994). More recent developments in this area have focused on uncovering heterogeneous reservation prices for products and bundles and using them in optimal product-line pricing (Jedidi et al. 2003), integrating conjoint with economic theory to uncover consumer reservation prices (Jedidi and Zhang 2002), and incorporating statistical machine learning for more accurate parameter estimates (Evgeniou et al. 2007). Recent research in this area has further focused on three key issues: (1) Learn as much as possible about a consumer's preference by choosing the right question using polyhedral (deterministic or probabilistic) choice-methods (Toubia et al. 2007); (2) include the right incentives into conjoint studies so participants respond truthfully (Ding 2007); and (3), ensure that the predicted market shares in the base case conjoint scenario closely match actual market shares (Gilbride et al. 2008). For a discussion of recent developments in conjoint analysis, see Rao (2008).

# 10.5 Dynamic, Behavioral, and Competitive Considerations

## 10.5.1 Dynamic Pricing

Dynamic pricing considers multiple periods wherein today's prices impact future profitability (Kopalle et al. 1999; Krishnan et al. 1999; Seetharaman 2009), in particular, how the current pricing decision affects future variable costs and/or future consumer behavior. One example of dynamic pricing is that of experience curve effects whereby marginal cost decreases over time with cumulative production. The implication is that firms may want to sacrifice some profit today for a larger profit in the next period. The total profit now and in the future is given by:

$$profit = \sum_{t=1}^{T} (p_t - c_t) * (b_0 + b_1 * p_t) - FC_t \qquad (10.4)$$

To capture the experience curve effect, the variable cost in period $t$ is given by:

$$c_t = c_I [\text{cumulatives } sales_t]^{\frac{-1}{4}} \qquad (10.5)$$

Consider two periods and let the variable cost in period 1 be $c_1$ = \$10 and $c_2$ = $c_1{}^*$(Cumulative Sales)$^{-1/4}$. Assuming $b_0$ = 200 and $b_1$ = -10, static optimization gives $p_1^*$ = \$15 and $p_2^*$ = \$11.88 , yielding a total profit of \$859. Simultaneously maximizing profits from both periods, we get:

$$\frac{dy}{dp_1} = (300 - 20p_1) - 25(200 - 10p_2)(200 - 10p_1)^{-5/4} = 0$$

$$\frac{dy}{dp_2} = (-10) * \left[ p_2 - 10(200 - 10p_1)^{-1/4} \right] + (200 - 10p_2) = 0 \qquad (10.6)$$

Accordingly, $p_1^*$ = \$14.34 and $p_2^*$ = \$11.82 , with a total profit of \$865, higher than in the static case.

## 10.5.2  Price Psychology (Reference Prices) and Dynamic Pricing

A reference price is an internal standard against which observed prices are compared (Winer 1986) and is typically modeled as an exponentially smoothed average of past prices. Buying decisions are affected significantly by the difference between the actual price and the reference price, where the impact on sales of a price decrease could be greater or less than that of a corresponding price increase. Prior research (Greenleaf 1995; Kopalle et al. 1996) suggests that it is optimal for a firm to have high-low pricing cycles over time when the impact on sales of a gain is greater than that of a corresponding loss; and maintain constant prices otherwise. Intertemporal linkages such as these can be solved using a dynamic programming approach (Kopalle et al. 2012). Dynamic programming is a mathematical technique and a systematic procedure for optimizing a sequence of interrelated decisions (Bertsekas 1987). It is primarily about thinking ahead and reasoning backwards. Prices are the decision variables and since past prices impact current and future reference prices, the state variable is reference price. The dynamic programming approach suggests that, from a given reference price in a period, the profit consideration to the next period and onwards is composed of two additive components: (1) profit to get to a state in the next period, and (2) the maximum profit from that state onwards. This is solved by backward induction, starting in the last period. At each state, we then determine the most profitable option going forward. In Section 10.5.5, we provide an algorithm for backward induction that incorporates price dynamics in a competitive framework.

## 10.5.3  Personalized Pricing

Personalized pricing refers to individual-level pricing that is time and product specific. The main driver of personalized (targeted) pricing is technology. Firms collect detailed information about consumers' shopping behavior and preferences, estimate price sensitivities at the individual level, and then determine dynamic prices which are sent to targeted consumers (Cheng and Dogan 2008) over the Internet, through email messages, or at the point of purchase. Membership clubs such as Costco, BJ's, Sam's Club, and firms such as Tesco and CVS that have strong loyalty programs, are in a good position to implement this type of customized pricing. Tesco has been particularly successful in mining its customer database and delivering customized promotions (Humby et al. 2005).

More recent work (Kopalle et al. 2012) considers household level heterogeneity in price responsiveness and determines optimal dynamic pricing strategies. Using consumers' purchase history data and Bayesian estimation of household level parameters, Kopalle et al. estimate household level heterogeneity in price response and dynamic reference price effects and then use the parameter estimates to conduct price optimization over time. Their results show that total profit was 81% higher relative to the case that ignores household heterogeneity. Rossi et al.'s (1996) results indicate that there can be a significant improvement in revenues (50% to 250%) by using targeted coupons (or other promotions) to households compared to providing price discounts to all households.

Zhang and Krishnamurthi (2004) provide a decision-support system of personalized promotions for online stores. Using household level data, they model joint purchase incidence, brand choice, and purchase quantity to optimize price discounts for each household. The analysis of a holdout sample showed significant ($p < .001$) profit improvement with the customized approach, particularly with previous-period buyers. Acquisti and Varian (2005), noting that the rapid advances in information technology allow firms to base their prices on consumers' purchase histories, deduce that firms will, in general, find it profitable to condition prices on purchase history. Zhang and Wedel (2009) demonstrate empirically that the profit potential with customized promotions is higher than with optimal undifferentiated promotions in online stores. Shaffer and Zhang (2002) find that personalized pricing leads to more vigorous price competition but has a positive effect of increasing market share, implying that a firm offering a product of higher quality might gain from personalized pricing.

Finally, given that greater access to information about individual customers and their purchase histories leads to growth in targeted prices and promotions, this might lead to situations where brand-loyal customers and brand-switchers receive different price discounts. Feinberg et al. (2002) examine this issue from a behavioral standpoint using experimental data from the laboratory (to calibrate a stochastic model) and a corresponding game-theoretic analysis. The authors find that offering lower prices to switchers may not be a sustainable practice; this is consistent with Amazon.com's experiment with DVDs back in 2000. For a good discussion of customized pricing, see Phillips 2012.

## 10.5.4  Dynamic Structural Pricing Models

This section extends the structural models discussed in Section 10.3 (consumer self-selection, versioning, and revenue management) to dynamic pricing models based on scanner panel data. Early research on price response estimation methods and dynamic price optimization algorithms (including personalized pricing) assumes that consumers are not forward-looking. This was improved by structural models of pricing that consider consumers' future price expectations in current brand choice and purchase quantities (Chan et al. 2009). Erdem and Keane (1996) and Gönül and Srinivasan (1996) demonstrate that dynamic structural models are important in explaining how consumers take into consideration future expectations of promotional activity in deciding when, what, and how much to buy in the current period. Sun et al. (2003) conclude that brand-switching elasticity estimates (due to price promotions) may be overstated in reduced-form models and that dynamic structural models are better suited for addressing such a bias. Sun (2005) proposes a dynamic structural model to examine the impact of price promotions on consumption behavior and finds endogenous consumption response to promotion due to consumers' forward-looking and stockpiling behavior.

Using a dynamic structural model, Chan et al. (2008) find that when sales of a brand increase due to a price promotion during a week, 29% of that increase is due to increased consumption in that week, 28% is due to consumers switching from other brands, and 43% is due to consumer stockpiling for consumption in future weeks. From a normative standpoint, Chen and Zhang's (2009) analytic results suggest that personalized promotions would still benefit competing firms even when consumers behave strategically.

Dynamic structural models have been applied to frequency reward programs as well (Lewis 2004; Kopalle et al., 2012). Frequency reward programs are of the type, "Buy $n$, get $n + 1$ free" and are essentially a form of discriminatory price promotion. Both Lewis (2004) and Kopalle et al. (2012) find that reward programs increase sales and find strong evidence for a "points pressure" effect where consumers increase purchase rates as they get closer to a reward, thus increasing overall sales.

Finally, note that there has also been some debate in the marketing literature with respect to the Lucas critique[7] (Franses 2005). Accordingly, van Heerde et al. (2005) report that even for substantial policy changes (typically studied in macroeconomics), there is little empirical evidence supporting the critique. Further, they argue that if supermarket shoppers do not have a good knowledge of the price they just paid (Dickson and Sawyer 1990), consumers cannot be expected to notice price changes and to revise their future expectations accordingly. Therefore, it is our belief that while dynamic structural models of pricing are an important advance in their own right (as they somewhat alleviate the Lucas critique), they do not really undercut the contribution of price optimization mechanisms where we first estimate market response and then determine optimal dynamic prices (Hall et al. 2010; Dubé et al. 2008).

## 10.5.5 Game Theoretic Contributions: Pricing under Nash Equilibrium

In a competitive environment, it is not enough for a firm to know its own-price elasticity. Competitors' price reactions due to the cross-price effect on sales will change the net volume response that a price change produces. Thus, the net effect of a price change will depend on: (i) own-price elasticity, (ii) cross-price elasticity, and also (iii) competitive reactions.

The normative pricing research with competition focuses on determining Nash equilibrium prices (Tirole 1992). The basic approach to arrive at the Nash equilibrium in a two-firm setting is to differentiate each rival's profit function with respect to its price and solve the first-order conditions simultaneously. From these equilibrium prices, neither firm will have an incentive to change their prices unilaterally. With competition, the optimal price goes down and profitability decreases; this Nash equilibrium is a "prisoner's dilemma" where both firms are better off pricing high, but each has a unilateral incentive to defect and charge a lower price. Shaffer and Zhang's (1995) analysis suggests that targeting rival firm's customers via coupons would also result in a prisoner's dilemma situation.

Empirically, there has been much research showing a significant impact of competitor prices on the sales of a target product. Using weekly scanner data from multiple stores and brands in five US markets, Shankar and Bolton (2004) suggest that competition across brands within a store is an important determinant of retail prices. Further, a more recent time-series analysis of fifty-five Denver area supermarkets covering forty-three categories over 123 weeks indicates that competitive prices across stores account only for less than 10% of the variation in retail prices (Nijs et al. 2007). On the other hand, a study of the Dutch grocery retailing industry suggests that when the market leader reduced prices in 2003 to stem its declining market share, intense price competition quickly emerged across stores (van Heerde et al. 2008). Ailawadi et al. (2010) examine how incumbent stores in the United States reacted to Wal-Mart's entry and find that no reaction is common, despite a significant decline in sales! Interestingly, it turns out that there are asymmetric competitive effects across different store formats; that is, price competition is more intense within store formats (e.g., discount store, regular super-market, large supermarket) than across store formats (Gonzalez-Benito et al.2005). Chu et al. (2007) also find an asymmetric pattern of cross-price elasticities across different channels in the personal computer industry. From a structural standpoint, other empir-ical research relies on the "new empirical industrial organization" literature and disen-tangles the impact of competition on prices from that of the demand and cost effects (Sudhir 2001; Vilcassim et al. 1999).

Compared to static games, dynamic competitive pricing games yield richer insights as they consider the future impact of current pricing decisions (Aviv and Vulcano 2012; Fudenberg and Tirole 1991; Kopalle and Shumsky 2012). Rao and Bass (1985) solve the dynamic experience curve problem under competition and show that competitive dynamic pricing strategies dominate the myopic ones.

The usefulness of the Nash equilibrium idea in a managerial context is most relevant when the demand specification captures the underlying complex consumer behavior. Let's now add competition to the consumer psychology-based reference price problem mentioned earlier. Assume that the demand for product $i$ in time $t$ is given by: $q_{it} = b_0 + b_1 p_i + b_2 p_j + g(r_i - p_i)$, where $g = \delta$, if $r_i > p_i$; $\gamma$ otherwise, and where reference price, $r_{it} = \alpha r_{it-1} + (1-\alpha)p_{it-1}$. The firms maximize their profit over a long-term horizon and so the objective function for firm $i$ is to maximize the sum of profit over a time horizon $(0, T)$: $\max_{p_{it}} \sum_{t=1}^{T} \beta^{t-1}(p_{it} - c)q_{it}$. This can be restated as the Bellman principle of optimality:

$$V_{it} = \max_{p_{it}} \left[ \pi_{it} + \beta V_{it+1}(r_{it+1}) \right].$$

In this problem, each period is a subgame wherein the two firms set prices by con-sidering the future impact of current prices on sales and profitability, and Kopalle et al. (1996) develop Markov Perfect Nash Equilibrium (Fudenberg and Tirole 1991) prices in each subgame. The problem is solved via a backward induction algorithm (see Appendix 1). The results of implementing the algorithm show that the two competitors follow an in-phase high-low pricing policy when the impact of a gain ($\delta$) on demand is greater than that of a corresponding loss ($\gamma$) and a constant pricing policy otherwise. More recent research in this area combines both empirical analysis and analytic mod-eling of competitive pricing decisions in the context of packaged-goods giant Procter

& Gamble's (P&G's) "value pricing strategy" (Ailawadi et al. 2005)—see Section 10.5.6. Finally, for a full coverage of game theoretic models and the terminology, see Fudenberg and Tirole (1991), Gal-Or (this *Handbook*) and Kopalle and Shumsky (2012).

## 10.5.6  Game-Theoretic Contribution: Pricing under Manufacturer/Retailer Interactions

While the previous section assumes that firms make simultaneous moves, here we consider situations where firms make sequential decisions and evaluate the corresponding equilibrium. In a pricing context, a manufacturer moves first and sets the wholesale price, the retailer sets the retail price, and, finally, consumers decide whether or not to buy the product (Choi 1991; Kim and Staelin 1999; Kopalle et al. 1999). Such sequential moves are called Stackelberg games. Ailawadi et al. (2005) consider this game in the context of P&G's value pricing strategy. They find that a game-theoretic model combined with strong empirical input can significantly predict directional changes in wholesale prices, retail prices, and wholesale deal amounts provided by manufacturers to retailers.

Let's consider competition both at the retailer and the manufacturer levels. In the first stage, the two manufacturers 1 and 2 set their respective wholesale prices, Retailer *A* maximizes his/her category profit and sets retail prices for the two products, Retailer *B* simultaneously maximizes his/her category profit and also sets two retail prices; customers then make purchase decisions regarding the two retailers and the two products (see Appendix 2 for the demand functions; the first subscript denotes the product and the second the retailer). Note that sales are now sensitive to prices of other products at the same store as well as the competing store. The first step is to write the profit functions for the two manufacturers and the retailer (Appendix 2). The retailer follows a category profit maximization perspective (Hall et al. 2010; Tellis and Zufryden 1995) while each manufacturer maximizes their respective profits from the two retailers.

The next step is to differentiate retailer 1's profit with respect to $p_{1A}$ and $p_{2A}$ and set each derivative equal to zero; then differentiate retailer 2's profit with respect to $p_{1B}$ and $p_{2B}$ and again set each equal to zero. Solving the four equations for $p_{1B}$, $p_{2B}$, $p_{1B}$, and $p_{2B}$ simultaneously, we can express them as functions of $w_1$ and $w_2$; this provides each retailer's Nash equilibrium response to both manufacturers' actions. We can then substitute the output from this step into the manufacturers' profit functions so that the respective profits can be expressed as functions of $w_1$ and $w_2$ alone. Differentiating manufacturer $i$'s profit with respect to $w_i$, setting it equal to zero, and solving for $w_i$ will, implicitly, yield manufacturer $i$'s reaction to manufacturer $j$'s wholesale price. Solving the two equations for $w_1$ and $w_2$ will give us the Nash equilibrium wholesale prices. As seen in Table 10.4, retail competition improves manufacturer profit and customer surplus but hurts retailers. Manufacturers under competition are better off with retail competition, but retailer profit is lower; finally, consumers also benefit.

Sudhir (2001) provides a structural analysis of a Stackelberg pricing game in the auto market where the estimates are used to conduct market share simulations and address

Table 10.4 Manufacturer/Retailer Stackelberg Equilibrium: Prices and Profits

|  | Only manufacturer competition | Manufacturer + Retailer Competition |
|---|---|---|
| Manufacturer Price | $9.33 | $9.48 |
| Manufacturer Profit | $142.22 | $242.95 |
| Retailer Price | $14.67 | $13.91 |
| Retailer Profit | $284.44 | $196.67 |

issues such as what price to charge when a new product is introduced or when an existing product's characteristics are changed (see Sudhir and Datta 2009 for pricing in a manufacturer/retailer channel).

# 10.6 PRICING IN TWO-SIDED MARKETS

An important aspect of pricing that has not yet made it into most managerial economics textbooks concerns pricing in two-sided markets, or platform pricing. Two-sided markets involve much of the pricing theory covered in this chapter but they force us to bring in other considerations, in particular so-called *network externalities* (see Shy 2013, this volume).

Two-sided markets exist frequently but we focus on situations where some kind of *platform* exists on which more than one set of economic agents interacts, and where all agents potentially pay fees to the platform's owner. The volume of business depends on the level of prices charged to the agents, and the demand on the part of agents depends upon the number or usage of other agents. This latter point establishes the externalities aspect of two-sided markets. To make pricing by the owner of the platform the main problem of interest, we suspend the Coase Theorem so that the agents do not bargain away the network externalities.

Rochet and Tirole (2006), Klein et al. (2006), Rysman (2009), and Evans (2010) provide an excellent review of two-sided markets. Payment card systems (e.g., Visa and Mastercard) are classic two-sided markets, with consumers and merchants interacting over the platform and both agents pay fees to the platform owner. Similarly, a newspaper gets revenue from readers and from advertisers, usage on each side affects demand by the other side, and there are costs to serve each set of agents. Drawing on Klein et al. (2006), using their newspaper setting, we can write total profit for the newspaper as:

$$\text{Total Profit} = (p_R Q_R - C_R) + (p_A Q_A - C_A), \tag{10.7}$$

where the subscript $R$ or $A$ refers to Reader or Advertiser; $p_i$ is price; $Q_i$ quantity of either readers or advertisers; and $C_i$ is the total cost of serving either readers or advertisers.

The key interactions/externalities are modeled by noting that $p_i = p_i(Q_A, Q_R)$; that is, the (inverse) demand curve for readers is a function of the quantity of readers and of advertisers, and similarly for the advertisers' demand. Doing the usual calculus, the first-order conditions for profit maximizing prices and quantities are:

$$p_R(1 + 1/\varepsilon_R) = MC_R - (\partial P_A/\partial Q_R)Q_A$$
$$p_A(1 + 1/\varepsilon_A) = MC_A - (\partial P_R/\partial Q_A)Q_R, \tag{10.8}$$

where $\varepsilon_i$ is the own-price elasticity, e.g., the elasticity of reader demand with respect to $p_R$. The left-hand sides of (10.8) are marginal revenues for either readers or advertisers, respectively; the equations are just a more elaborate version of $MR = MC$, and inform that for optimal pricing in a two-sided market, we can essentially think of a positive network externality as reducing the marginal cost of production. In Equation (10.8), if $\partial P_A/\partial Q_R$ is positive, readers create a positive externality regarding advertisers' demand, and that externality is equivalent to thinking that the marginal costs of readers are lower.

If the two partial derivatives in Equation (10.8) were zero, there would be no network externalities present and the two equations would reduce to our earlier equation giving the optimal price for a product as a function of its own demand elasticity and its marginal cost. With positive cross-partial derivatives, prices depend not only on own elasticity and own marginal cost, but also on the strength of network externalities.

In some cases, the relative strength of network externalities will cause a profit-maximizing platform owner to bring one price to zero. For the newspaper example, it is likely that $\partial p_A/\partial Q_R$ is very high (advertisers benefit a lot from readers) but that $(\partial p_R/\partial Q_A)$ is low or even negative (readers don't benefit much, or even don't value, advertising). This would tend to cause a low price to readers, maybe even zero, and a higher price to advertisers.

Rochet and Tirole (2006) consider a more complex model and elicit key pricing principles for two-sided markets. Empirical work in two-sided markets is scarce but growing. Rysman (2004) is one of the first to deal with the simultaneous nature of demands in a structural fashion, estimating three equations: consumer demand for information, advertiser demand, and the first-order condition for profit-maximization. Rysman finds significant network effects, with consumer usage positively affecting advertising and advertising positively affecting consumer usage. Given structural estimates, he is also able to conduct a policy simulation on the effects of competition, finding that a more competitive network is preferred. Kaiser and Wright (2006) estimate a structural model for magazines in Germany, again finding significant evidence of network effects between readers and advertisers. The estimates are in line with the standard prescription in the media industry to price "low" to readers and "high" to advertisers. Song (2011) estimates a more general structural model for a different set of magazines in Germany, finding that magazines generally set reader prices below marginal cost, consistent with strong network effects, and the author concludes that, in that industry, mergers are less of a problem for efficiency and may even be welfare-improving.

# 10.7  SUMMARY

There has been much interest in pricing strategies and tactics both in the research and practice domains (Levy et al. 2004). Developments in the world of pricing continue to occur at a fast pace, particularly as the availability of consumer- and transaction-level data interacts with economic theory and the ability of computers to quickly process more complex models. Combined with quantitatively trained senior managers with an analytical orientation, these changes provide a nice opportunity for pricing managers and researchers to have an impact on the bottom line. In this spirit, this chapter aims to bridge the gap between theory and practice and nudge retail managers towards a more quantitative analysis in their pricing decisions at both tactical and strategic levels. We argue that the time is now ripe for managers to take an analytic perspective on pricing decisions by using data and estimating demand models with foundations in economics and marketing.

In essence, what is really needed are analytic strategies and methods in pricing that account for complex interactions within and across product categories, taking into consideration both controllable factors (such as promotions) and uncontrollable ones (such as seasonality, time trends, competition, and uncertainty in consumer preferences). Going forward, both researchers and practitioners need to be mindful of four factors. One is to incorporate the psychological aspect of consumers when developing pricing models. Modeling complex, adaptive systems that mimic the marketplace is tough to do as this involves embedding humanlike properties in the intelligent system created by an analyst. Second is scalability. For example, in retailing, a typical grocery store may have 30,000 stock-keeping units. Given the many decision variables for each SKU, this could result in millions of variables! Third is parameter estimation. A large model increases the possibility for instability in the parameter estimates. Fourth, in developing a price optimization plan, the objective function should include a more general maximization function rather than including simply the profit, the dollar sales, or the unit sales. Instead, it could place different weights on each of the above three factors. The function could also include the activity cost—for example, the cost of changing prices. Thus, although work remains to be done, the idea of elasticity-based price optimization seems viable and worthy of the effort required to understand it more fully (Grewal et al. 2011).

## APPENDIX 10.1

### Dynamic Programming Algorithm

For $t = T$ to 1
For each possible combination of state variables, $(r_1, r_2)$
For each combination of prices $(p_1, p_2)$
Compute profit for the two firms in period $t$, $\pi_1$, and $\pi_2$

Compute reference price in period $t+1$, $r_{1t+1}$, $r_{2t+1}$

Recall future maximal profit for the two firms, $V_{1,t+1}(r_{1,t+1}, r_{2,t+1})$ and $V_{2,t+1}(r_{1,t+1}, r_{2,t+1})$. If $t=T$, then $V_{1T} = V_{2T} = 0$.

Compute $U_{1t} = \pi_1 + V_{1,t+1}$ and $U_{2t} = \pi_2 + V_{2,t+1}$

Prices $p_1$ and $p_2$ constitute a subgame perfect Nash equilibrium $\vec{P_1}$ and $\vec{P_2}$ in time $t$ iff:

$U_{1t}(p_1^*, p_2^*) \geq U_{1t}(p_1, p_2^*)$ and

$U_{2t}(p_1^*, p_2^*) \geq U_{2t}(p_1^*, p_2)$

Store $V_{1t}(r_1, r_2) = U_{1t}(p_1^*, p_2^*)$ and $V_{2t}(r_1, r_2) = U_{2t}(p_1^*, p_2^*)$ and the equilibrium prices, $\vec{p_1}$, $\vec{p_2}$ as functions of reference prices $r_1$ and $r_2$ and time $t$.

Increment to next combination of state variables, $(r_1, r_2)$

Decrement to next $t$

## APPENDIX 10.2

# TWO MANUFACTURERS (1, 2)/TWO RETAILERS (A, B) STACKELBERG EQUILIBRIUM

Demand Functions:

Unit sales of product 1 at store A = $50 - 10p_{1A} + 5p_{2A} + 3p_{1B}$

Unit sales of product 2 at store A = $50 - 10p_{2A} + 5p_{1A} + 3p_{2B}$

Unit sales of product 1 at store B = $50 - 10p_{1B} + 5p_{2B} + 3p_{1A}$

Unit sales of product 2 at store B = $50 - 10p_{2B} + 5p_{1B} + 3p_{2A}$

Profit functions for the manufacturers (assuming variable cost=\$4) and retailers:

$$\pi_{M1} = (w_1 - 4)\{(50 - 10p_{1A} + 5p_{2A} + 3p_{1B}) + (50 - 10p_{1B} + 5p_{2B} + 3p_{1A})\}$$

$$\pi_{M2} = (w_2 - 4)\{(50 - 10p_{2A} + 5p_{1A} + 3p_{2B}) + (50 - 10p_{2B} + 5p_{1B} + 3p_{2A})\}$$

$$\pi_{RA} = (p_{1A} - w_1)(50 - 10p_{1A} + 5p_{2A} + 3p_{1B}) + (p_{2A} - w_2)(50 - 10p_{2A} + 5p_{1A} + 3p_{2B})$$

$$\pi_{RB} = (p_{1B} - w_1)(50 - 10p_{1B} + 5p_{2B} + 3p_{1A}) + (p_{2B} - w_2)(50 - 10p_{2B} + 5p_{1B} + 3p_{2A})$$

First order conditions for the four retail prices:

$$\frac{d\pi_{R1}}{dp_{1A}} = 50 - 20p_{1A} + 3p_{1B} + 10p_{2A} + 10w_1 - 5w_2 = 0$$

$$\frac{d\pi_{R1}}{dp_{2A}} = 50 - 20p_{2A} + 3p_{2B} + 10p_{1A} + 10w_2 - 5w_1 = 0$$

$$\frac{d\pi_{R2}}{dp_{1B}} = 50 - 20p_{1B} + 3p_{1A} + 10p_{2B} + 10w_1 - 5w_2 = 0$$

$$\frac{d\pi_{R2}}{dp_{2B}} = 50 - 20p_{2B} + 3p_{2A} + 10p_{1B} + 10w_2 - 5w_1 = 0$$

Solving the above equations, we get:

$$p_{1A} = 7.143 + 0.635w_1 + 0.079w_2$$

$$p_{2A} = 7.143 + 0.079w_1 + 0.635w_2$$

$$p_{1B} = 7.143 + 0.635w_1 + 0.079w_2$$

$$p_{2B} = 7.143 + 0.079w_1 + 0.635w_2$$

Substituting optimal retail prices in the manufacturers' profit, we get:

$$\pi_{M1} = 0.4762(w_1 - 4)(150 - 17w_1 + 11w_2)$$
$$\pi_{M2} = 0.4762(w_2 - 4)(150 - 17w_2 + 11w_1)$$

Differentiating these equations and solving for the two wholesale prices, we have:

$$\frac{d\pi_{M1}}{dw_1} = 0.4762(218 - 34w_1 + 11w_2) = 0$$

$$\frac{d\pi_{M2}}{dw_2} = 0.4762(218 - 34w_2 + 11w_1) = 0$$

$$\rightarrow w_1 = \$9.478, w_2 = \$9.478$$

## Notes

1. We readily admit that there is no way to cover all the advances in pricing theory in a single chapter. Indeed, more complete treatments can be found in the *Oxford Handbook on Pricing Management* (2012) and the *Handbook of Pricing Research in Marketing* (2009), both of which provide dozens of chapters on various pricing topics. We have also benefitted from excellent surveys by Varian (1989) and Stole (2007).
2. This formula is sometimes referred to as the Lerner Index of market power, as one can calculate the implied elasticity of demand from observed prices and estimates of marginal cost.
3. Varian (1989, 612) points out that earlier work in nonlinear pricing was focused primarily on public utility pricing. Wilson's (1993) excellent book on nonlinear pricing is in that vein.
4. Varian (1989, 640) quotes Jules Dupuit's description of early train travel:

   "It is not because of the few thousand francs which would have to be spent to put a roof over the third-class carriages or to upholster the third-class seats that some company or other has open carriages with wooden benches. What the company is trying to do is to prevent the passengers who can pay the second class fare from traveling third class; it hits the poor, not because it wants to hurt them, but to frighten the rich. And it is again for the same reason that the companies, having proved almost cruel to the third-class passengers and mean to the second-class ones, become lavish in dealing with first-class passengers. Having refused the poor what is necessary, they give the rich what is superfluous."

5. The newsvendor problem is a situation where a vendor must decide how many copies of newspaper to stock given that demand is uncertain and unsold copies are worthless (Silver et al. 1998, 385).

6. Historical data are widely available for packaged goods, such as detailed consumer panel data (Levy et al. 2004). These data allow the use of advanced statistical methods, have high validity as they rely on observations of real customer behavior under real market conditions, and estimate price elasticities while controlling for other factors, such as promotional activity and competition (Chintagunta 2002)—see Section 10.5.

7. In a nutshell, the Lucas critique implies that consumers would be forward looking and therefore their response (e.g., the coefficients in a regression model) could change in reaction to a policy change (e.g., modifications in a firm's pricing strategies based on the regression coefficients).

# REFERENCES

Acquisti, Alessandro, and Hal R. Varian. 2005. "Conditioning Prices on Purchase History." *Marketing Science* 24 (3): 367–81.

Adams, William James, and Janet L. Yellen. 1976. "Commodity Bundling and the Burden of Monopoly." *The Quarterly Journal of Economics* 90 (3): 475–98.

Aguirre, Inaki, Simon Cowan, and John Vickers. 2010. "Monopoly Price Discrimination and Demand Curvature." *The American Economic Review* 100 (4): 1601–15.

Ailawadi, Kusum L., Praveen K. Kopalle, and Scott A. Neslin. 2005. "Predicting Competitive Response to a Major Policy Change: Combining Game-Theoretic and Empirical Analyses." *Marketing Science* 24 (1): 12–24.

Ailawadi, Kusum L., Jie Zhang, Aradhna Krishna, and Michael W. Kruger. 2010. "When Wal-Mart Enters: How Incumbent Retailers React and How This Affects Their Sales Outcomes." *Journal of Marketing Research* 47 (4): 577–93.

Anderson, C. K., and J. G. Wilson. 2003. "'Wait or Buy?' The Strategic Consumer: Pricing and Profit Implications." *Journal of the Operational Research Society* 54 (3): 299–306.

Anderson, Eric T., and James D. Dana, Jr. 2009. "When Is Price Discrimination Profitable?" *Management Science* 55 (6): 980–89.

Andrews, Rick L., Asim Ansari, and Imran S. Currim. 2002. "Hierarchical Bayes versus Finite Mixture Conjoint Analysis Models: A Comparison of Fit, Prediction, and Partworth Recovery." *Journal of Marketing Research* 39 (1): 87–98.

Ansari, Asim, S. Siddarth, and Charles B. Weinberg. 1996. "Pricing a Bundle of Products or Services: The Case of Nonprofits." *Journal of Marketing Research* 33 (1): 86–93.

Aviv, Yossi, and Gustavo Vulcano. 2012. "Dynamic List Pricing." In *Handbook of Pricing*, edited by Özalp Özer and Robert Phillips. Oxford: Oxford University Press, 522–584.

Bakos, Yannis, and Erik Brynjolfsson. 2000. "Bundling and Competition on the Internet." *Marketing Science* 19 (1): 63–82.

Balachander, Subramanian, Bikram Ghosh, and Axel Stock. 2010. "Why Bundle Discounts Can Be a Profitable Alternative to Competing on Price Promotions." *Marketing Science* 29 (4): 624–38.

Banciu, Mihai, Esther Gal-Or, and Prakash Mirchandani. 2010. "Bundling Strategies When Products Are Vertically Differentiated and Capacities Are Limited." *Management Science* 56 (12): 2207–23.

Basu, Amiya, and Padmal Vitharana. 2009. "Research Note—Impact of Customer Knowledge Heterogeneity on Bundling Strategy." *Marketing Science* 28 (4): 792–801.

Bell, David R., Jeongwen Chiang, and V. Padmanabhan. 1999. "The Decomposition of Promotional Response: An Empirical Generalization." *Marketing Science* 18 (4): 504–26.

Belloni, Alexandre, Robert Freund, Matthew Selove, and Duncan Simester. 2008. "Optimizing Product Line Designs: Efficient Methods and Comparisons." *Management Science* 54 (9): 1544–52.

Ben-Akiva, Moshe, and Steven R. Lerman. 1994. *Discrete Choice Analysis: Theory and Application to Travel Demand*. Cambridge: MIT Press.

Bertsekas, Dimitri P. 1987. *Dynamic Programming: Deterministic and Stochastic Models*. Englewood Cliffs, NJ: Prentice Hall.

Bijmolt, Tammo H. A., Harald J. van Heerde, and Rik G. M. Pieters. 2005. "New Empirical Generalizations on the Determinants of Price Elasticity." *Journal of Marketing Research* 42 (2): 141–56.

Blattberg, Robert C., and Richard Briesch. 2012. "Sales Promotion." In *Handbook of Pricing*, edited by Özalp Özer and Robert Phillips. Oxford: Oxford University Press, 585–619.

Blattberg, Robert C., and Scott A. Neslin. 1990. *Sales Promotion: Concepts, Methods, and Strategies*. Englewood Cliffs, NJ: Prentice Hall.

Blattberg, Robert C., and Kenneth J. Wisniewski. 1989. "Price-Induced Patterns of Competition." *Marketing Science* 8 (4): 291–309.

Cabolis, Christos, Sofronis Clerides, Ioannis Ioannou, and Daniel Senft. 2007. "A Textbook Example of International Price Discrimination." *Economics Letters* 95 (1): 91–95.

Cattin, Philippe, and Dick R. Wittink. 1982. "Commercial Use of Conjoint Analysis: A Survey." *The Journal of Marketing* 46 (3): 44–53.

Chan, Tat, Vrinda Kadiyali, and Ping Xiao. 2009. "Structural Models of Pricing." In *Handbook of Pricing Research in Marketing*, edited by Vithala R. Rao, 108–31. Northampton, MA: Edward Elgar Publications.

Chan, Tat, Chakravarthi Narasimhan, and Qin Zhang. 2008. "Decomposing Promotional Effects with a Dynamic Structural Model of Flexible Consumption." *Journal of Marketing Research* 45 (4): 487–98.

Chen, Yuxin. 2009. "Product Line Pricing." In *Handbook of Pricing Research in Marketing*, edited by Vithala R. Rao, 216–31. Northampton, MA: Edward Elgar Publications, Inc.

Chen, Yuxin, and Z. John Zhang. 2009. "Dynamic Targeted Pricing with Strategic Consumers." *International Journal of Industrial Organization* 27 (1): 43–50.

Cheng, Hsing Kenneth, and Kutsal Dogan. 2008. "Customer-Centric Marketing with Internet Coupons." *Decision Support Systems* 44 (3): 606–20.

Chintagunta, Pradeep K. 2002. "Investigating Category Pricing Behavior at a Retail Chain." *Journal of Marketing Research* 39 (2): 141–54.

Choi, S. Chan. 1991. "Price Competition in a Channel Structure with a Common Retailer." *Marketing Science* 10 (Fall): 271–96.

Chu, Junhong, Pradeep K. Chintagunta, and Naufel J. Vilcassim. 2007. "Assessing the Economic Value of Distribution Channels: An Application to the Personal Computer Industry." *Journal of Marketing Research* 44 (1): 29–41.

Deneckere, Raymond J., and R. Preston McAfee. 1996. "Damaged Goods." *Journal of Economics & Management Strategy* 5 (2): 149–74.

Dickson, Peter R., and Alan G. Sawyer. 1990. "The Price Knowledge and Search for Supermarket Shoppers." *Journal of Marketing* 54 (3): 42–53.

Ding, Min. 2007. "An Incentive-Aligned Mechanism for Conjoint Analysis." *Journal of Marketing Research* 44 (2): 214–23.

Draganska, Michaela, and Dipak C. Jain. 2006. "Consumer Preferences and Product-Line Pricing Strategies: An Empirical Analysis." *Marketing Science* 25 (2): 164–74.

Dubé, Jean-Pierre, Gunter J. Hitsch, Peter E. Rossi, and Maria Ana Vitorino. 2008. "Category Pricing with State Dependent Utility." *Marketing Science* 27 (3): 417–29.

Edlin, Aaron S., and Daniel L. Rubinfeld. 2005. "The Bundling of Academic Journals." *American Economic Review* 95 (2): 441–46.

Erdem, Tulin, and Michael P. Keane. 1996. "Decision-Making under Uncertainty: Capturing Dynamic Brand Choice Processes in Turbulent Consumer Goods Markets." *Marketing Science* 15 (1): 1–20.

Essegaier, Skander, Sunil Gupta, and Z. John Zhang. 2002. "Pricing Access Services." *Marketing Science* 21 (2): 139–59.

Evans, David S. 2010. *Essays on the Economics of Two Sided Markets.* Boston: Competition Policy International.

Evgeniou, Theodoros, Massimiliano Pontil, and Olivier Toubia. 2007. "A Convex Optimization Approach to Modeling Consumer Heterogeneity in Conjoint Estimation." *Marketing Science* 26 (6): 805–18.

Feinberg, Fred M., Aradhna Krishna, and Z. John Zhang. 2002. "Do We Care What Others Get? A Behaviorist Approach to Targeted Promotions." *Journal of Marketing Research* 39 (3): 277–91.

Franses, Philip Hans. 2005. "On the Use of Econometric Models for Policy Simulation in Marketing." *Journal of Marketing Research* 42:4–14.

Fudenberg, Drew, and Jean Tirole. 1991. *Game Theory.* Cambridge: MIT Press.

Gal-Or, Esther. 2013. "Game and Information Theory in Modern Managerial Economics." In *Handbook of Managerial Economics*, edited by Christopher Thomas and William Shughart. Oxford: Oxford University Press.

Gilbride, Timothy J., Peter J. Lenk, and Jeff D. Brazell. 2008. "Market Share Constraints and the Loss Function in Choice-Based Conjoint Analysis." *Marketing Science* 27 (6): 995–1011.

Goettler, Ronald L., and Karen Clay. 2011. "Tariff Choice with Consumer Learning and Switching Costs." *Journal of Marketing Research* 48 (4): 633–52.

Gönül, Füsun, and Kannan Srinivasan. 1996. "Estimating the Impact of Consumer Expectations of Coupons on Purchase Behavior: A Dynamic Structural Model." *Marketing Science* 15 (3): 262–79.

Gonzalez-Benito, Oscar, Pablo A. Munoz-Gallego, and Praveen K. Kopalle. 2005. "Asymmetric Competition in Retail Store Formats: Evaluating Inter-and Intra-Format Spatial Effects." *Journal of Retailing* 81 (1): 59–73

Green, Paul E., and V. Srinivasan. 1978. "Conjoint Analysis in Consumer Research: Issues and Outlook." *Journal of Consumer Research* 5 (2): 103–23.

——. 1990. "Conjoint Analysis in Marketing: New Developments with Implications for Research and Practice." *The Journal of Marketing* 54 (4): 3–19.

Greenleaf, Eric A. 1995. "The Impact of Reference Price Effects on the Profitability of Price Promotions." *Marketing Science* 14 (1): 82–104.

Grewal, Dhruv, Kusum L. Ailawadi, Dinesh Gauri, Kevin Hall, Praveen K. Kopalle, and Jane R. Robertson. 2011. "Innovations in Retail Pricing and Promotions." *Journal of Retailing* 87:S43–52.

Guiltinan, Joseph. 2011. "Progress and Challenges in Product Line Pricing." *Journal of Product Innovation Management* 28 (5): 744–56.

Hall, Joseph M., Praveen K. Kopalle, and Aradhna Krishna. 2010. "Retailer Dynamic Pricing and Ordering Decisions: Category Management versus Brand-by-Brand Approaches." *Journal of Retailing* 86 (2): 172–83.

Harless, David W., and George E. Hoffer. 2002. "Do Women Pay More for New Vehicles? Evidence from Transaction Price Data." *The American Economic Review* 92 (1): 270–79.

Hitt, Lorin M., and Pei-yu Chen. 2005. "Bundling with Customer Self-Selection: A Simple Approach to Bundling Low-Marginal-Cost Goods." *Management Science* 51 (10): 1481–93.

Humby, Clive, Terry Hunt, and Tim Phillips. 2005. *Scoring Points: How Tesco Is Winning Customer Loyalty.* Philadelphia: Kogan Page Business Books.

Iyengar, Raghuram, and Sunil Gupta. 2009. "Nonlinear Pricing." In *Handbook of Pricing Research in Marketing,* edited by Vithala R. Rao, 355–83. Northampton, MA: Edward Elgar Publications, Inc.

Iyengar, Raghuram, Kamel Jedidi, Skander Essegaier, and Peter J. Danaher. 2011. "The Impact of Tariff Structure on Customer Retention, Usage, and Profitability of Access Services." *Marketing Science* 30 (5): 820–36.

Jedidi, Kamel, Sharan Jagpal, and Puneet Manchanda. 2003. "Measuring Heterogeneous Reservation Prices for Product Bundles." *Marketing Science* 22 (1): 107–30.

Jedidi, Kamel, and Z. John Zhang. 2002. "Augmenting Conjoint Analysis to Estimate Consumer Reservation Price." *Management Science* 48 (10): 1350–68.

Jerath, Kinshuk, Serguei Netessine, and Senthil K. Veeraraghavan. 2010. "Revenue Management with Strategic Customers: Last-Minute Selling and Opaque Selling." *Management Science* 56 (2): 430–48.

Kaiser, Ulrich, and Julian Wright. 2006. "Price Structure in Two-Sided Markets: Evidence from the Magazine Industry." *International Journal of Industrial Organization* 24 (1): 1–28.

Kim, Sang Yong, and Richard Staelin. 1999. "Manufacturer Allowances and Retailer Pass-Through Rates in a Competitive Environment." *Marketing Science* 18 (1): 59–76.

Kimes, Sheryl E. 2009. "Pricing and Revenue Management." In *Handbook of Pricing Research in Marketing,* edited by Vithala R. Rao, 477–87. Northampton, MA: Edward Elgar Publishing.

Klein, Benjamin, Andres V. Lerner, Kevin M. Murphy, and Lacey L. Plache. 2006. "Competition in Two-Sided Markets: The Antitrust Economics of Payment Card Interchange Fees." *Antitrust Law Journal* 73:571–626.

Kopalle, Praveen K., P. K. Kannan, Lin Bao Boldt, and Neeraj Arora. 2012. "The Impact of Household Level Heterogeneity in Reference Price Effects on Optimal Retailer Pricing Policies." *Journal of Retailing* 88 (1): 102–14.

Kopalle, Praveen K., Aradhna Krishna, and João L. Assunção. 1999. "The Role of Market Expansion on Equilibrium Bundling Strategies." *Managerial and Decision Economics* 20 (7): 365–77.

Kopalle, Praveen K., Carl F. Mela, and Lawrence Marsh. 1999. "The Dynamic Effect of Discounting on Sales: Empirical Analysis and Normative Pricing Implications." *Marketing Science* 18 (3): 317–32.

Kopalle, Praveen K., Ambar G. Rao, and João L. Assunção. 1996. "Asymmetric Reference Price Effects and Dynamic Pricing Policies." *Marketing Science* 15 (1): 60–85.

Kopalle, Praveen K., and Robert A. Shumsky. 2012. "Game Theory Models of Pricing." In *Handbook of Pricing,* edited by Özalp Özer and Robert Phillips. Oxford: Oxford University Press, 381–414.

Kopalle, Praveen K., Yacheng Sun, Scott A. Neslin, Baohong Sun, and Vanitha Swaminathan. 2012. "The Joint Sales Impact of Frequency Reward and Customer Tier Components of Loyalty Programs." *Marketing Science* 31 (2): 216–35.

Krishnan, Trichy V., Frank M. Bass, and Dipak C. Jain. 1999. "Optimal Pricing Strategy for New Products." *Management Science* 45 (12): 1650–63.

Lambrecht, Anja, Katja Seim, and Bernd Skiera. 2007. "Does Uncertainty Matter? Consumer Behavior under Three-Part Tariffs." *Marketing Science* 26 (5): 698–710.

Lambrecht, Anja, and Bernd Skiera. 2006. "Paying Too Much and Being Happy about It: Existence, Causes, and Consequences of Tariff-Choice Biases." *Journal of Marketing Research* 43 (2): 212–23.

Leslie, Phillip. 2004. "Price Discrimination in Broadway Theater." *The Rand Journal of Economics* 35 (3): 520–41.

Levin, Yuri, Jeff McGill, and Mikhail Nediak. 2009. "Dynamic Pricing in the Presence of Strategic Consumers and Oligopolistic Competition." *Management Science* 55 (1): 32–46.

Levy, Michael, Dhruv Grewal, Praveen K. Kopalle, and James D. Hess. 2004. "Emerging Trends in Retail Pricing Practice: Implications for Research." *Journal of Retailing* 80 (3): xiii–xxi.

Lewis, Michael. 2004. "The Influence of Loyalty Programs and Short-Term Promotions on Customer Retention." *Journal of Marketing Research* 41 (3): 281–92.

Mahajan, Vijay, Paul E. Green, and Stephen M. Goldberg. 1982. "A Conjoint Model for Measuring Self- and Cross-Price/Demand Relationships." *Journal of Marketing Research* 19 (3): 334–42.

Malueg, David A., and Christopher M. Snyder. 2006. "Bounding the Relative Profitability of Price Discrimination." *International Journal of Industrial Organization* 24 (5): 995–1011.

Maskin, Eric, and John Riley. 1984. "Monopoly with Incomplete Information." *The Rand Journal of Economics* 15 (2): 171–96.

Matutes, Carmen, and Pierre Regibeau. 1992. "Compatibility and Bundling of Complementary Goods in a Duopoly." *The Journal of Industrial Economics* 40 (1): 37–54.

McAfee, Preston. 2007. "Pricing Damaged Goods." *Economics: The Open-Access, Open-Assessment E-Journal* 1. Accessed December 29, 2012. http://www.economics-ejournal.org/economics/journalarticles/2007-1.

McAfee, R. Preston, John McMillan, and Michael D. Whinston. 1989. "Multiproduct Monopoly, Commodity Bundling, and Correlation of Values." *The Quarterly Journal of Economics* 104 (2): 371–83.

McCormick, Robert E., William F. Shughart, and Robert D. Tollison. 2006. "A Theory of Commodity Bundling in Final Product Markets: Professor Hirshleifer Meets Professor Becker." *International Review of Law and Economics* 26 (2): 162–79.

McCullough, Dick. 2002. "A User's Guide to Conjoint Analysis." *Marketing Research* 14 (2): 18–23.

Moorthy, K. Sridhar. 1984. "Market Segmentation, Self-Selection, and Product Line Design." *Marketing Science* 2 (4): 288–307.

Mulhern, Francis J., and Robert P. Leone. 1991. "Implicit Price Bundling of Retail Products: A Multiproduct Approach to Maximizing Store Profitability." *The Journal of Marketing* 55 (4): 63–76.

Nalebuff, Barry. 2004. "Bundling as an Entry Barrier." *The Quarterly Journal of Economics* 119 (1): 159–87.

Netessine, Serguei, and Robert A. Shumsky. 2002. "Introduction to the Theory and Practice of Yield Management." *INFORMS Transactions on Education* 3 (1): 34–44.

Nevo, Aviv, Daniel L. Rubinfeld, and Mark McCabe. 2005. "Academic Journal Pricing and the Demand of Libraries." *American Economic Review* 95 (2): 447–52.

Nijs, Vincent, Shuba Srinivasan, and Koen Pauwels. 2007. "Retail-Price Drivers and Retailer Profits." *Marketing Science* 26 (4): 473–87.

Noble, Peter M., and Thomas S. Gruca. 1999. "Industrial Pricing: Theory and Managerial Practice." *Marketing Science* 18 (3): 435–54.

Oi, Walter. 1971. "A Disneyland Dilemma: Two-Part Tariffs for a Mickey Mouse Monopoly." *The Quarterly Journal of Economics* 85 (1): 77–96.

Özer, Özalp, and Robert Phillips, eds. 2012. *Oxford Handbook on Pricing Management*. Oxford: Oxford University Press.

Peitz, Martin. 2008. "Bundling May Blockade Entry." *International Journal of Industrial Organization* 26 (1): 41–58.

Phillips, Robert. 2012. "Customized Pricing." In *Handbook of Pricing*, edited by Özalp Özer and Robert Phillips. Oxford: Oxford University Press, 465–491.

Popkowski Leszczyc, Peter T. L., and Gerald Häubl. 2010. "To Bundle or Not to Bundle: Determinants of the Profitability of Multi-Item Auctions." *Journal of Marketing* 74 (4): 110–24.

Prasad, Ashutosh, R. Venkatesh, and Vijay Mahajan. 2010. "Optimal Bundling of Technological Products with Network Externality." *Management Science* 56 (12): 2224–36.

Rao, Ram C., and Frank M. Bass. 1985. "Competition, Strategy, and Price Dynamics: A Theoretical and Empirical Investigation." *Journal of Marketing Research* 22 (August): 283–96.

Rao, Vithala R. 2008. "Developments in Conjoint Analysis." In *Handbook of Marketing Decision Models*, edited by Berend Wierenga, 23. New York: Springer.

Rao, Vithala R., ed. 2009. *Handbook of Pricing Research in Marketing*. Northampton: Edward Elgar Publishing.

Robinson, Joan. 1933. *The Economics of Imperfect Competition*. London: Macmillan and Company.

Rochet, Jean-Charles, and Jean Tirole. 2006. "Two-Sided Markets: A Progress Report." *The Rand Journal of Economics* 37 (3): 645–67.

Rossi, Peter E., Robert E. McCulloch, and Greg M. Allenby. 1996. "The Value of Purchase History Data in Target Marketing." *Marketing Science* 15 (4): 321–40.

Rysman, Marc. 2004. "Competition between Networks: A Study of the Market for Yellow Pages." *Review of Economic Studies* 71 (2): 483–512.

——. 2009. "The Economics of Two-Sided Markets." *Journal of Economic Perspectives* 23 (3): 125–43.

Schmalensee, Richard L. 1981. "Output and Welfare Implications of Monopolistic Third-Degree Price Discrimination." *The American Economic Review* 71 (1): 242–47.

——. 1984. "Gaussian Demand and Commodity Bundling." *The Journal of Business* 57 (1): S211–30.

Schön, Cornelia. 2010. "On the Optimal Product Line Selection Problem with Price Discrimination." *Management Science* 56 (5): 896–902.

Seetharaman, P. B. 2009. "Dynamic Pricing." In *Handbook of Pricing Research in Marketing*, edited by Vithala R. Rao, 384–93. Northampton, MA: Edward Elgar Publications, Inc.

Sethuraman, Raj, and V. Srinivasan. 2002. "The Asymmetric Share Effect: An Empirical Generalization on Cross-Price Effects." *Journal of Marketing Research* 39 (3): 379–86.

Shaffer, Greg, and Z. John Zhang. 1995. "Competitive Coupon Targeting." *Marketing Science* 14 (4): 395–416.

——. 2002. "Competitive One-to-One Promotions." *Management Science* 48 (9): 1143–60.

Shankar, Venkatesh, and Ruth N. Bolton. 2004. "An Empirical Analysis of Determinants of Retailer Pricing Strategy." *Marketing Science* 23 (1): 28–49.

Shankar, Venkatesh, and Lakshman Krishnamurthi. 1996. "Relating Price Sensitivity to Retailer Promotional Variables and Pricing Policy: An Empirical Analysis." *Journal of Retailing* 72 (3): 249–72.

Shapiro, Carol, and Hal R. Varian. 1999. *Information Rules: A Strategic Guide to the Network Economy.* Cambridge: Harvard Business School Press.

Shen, Zuo-Jun M., and Xuanming Su. 2007. "Customer Behavior Modeling in Revenue Management and Auctions: A Review and New Research Opportunities." *Production and Operations Management* 16 (6): 713–28.

Shin-yi, Wu, Lorin M. Hitt, Chen Pei-yu, and G. Anandalingam. 2008. "Customized Bundle Pricing for Information Goods: A Nonlinear Mixed-Integer Programming Approach." *Management Science* 54 (3): 608–22.

Shy, Oz. Forthcoming. "Strategies for Network Industries." In *Oxford Handbook in Managerial Economics,* edited by Christopher R. Thomas and William F. Shughart II. Oxford: Oxford University Press.

Silver, Edward A., David F. Pyke, and Rein Peterson. 1998. *Inventory Management and Production Planning and Scheduling.* New York: John Wiley.

Simon, Hermann. 1989. *Price Management.* Amsterdam: North-Holland.

Soman, Dilip, and John T. Gourville. 2001. "Transaction Decoupling: How Price Bundling Affects the Decision to Consume." *Journal of Marketing Research* 38 (1): 30–44.

Song, Minjae. 2011. "Estimating Platform Market Power in Two-Sided Markets with an Application to Magazine Advertising." Working Paper, University of Rochester Simon School.

Stigler, George J. 1962. "United States v. Loew's Inc.: A Note on Block-Booking." *Supreme Court Review* 1962:152–57.

Stigler, George J. 1987. *The Theory of Price.* New York: Macmillan.

Stole, Lars A. 2007. "Price Discrimination and Competition." In *Handbook of Industrial Organization,* 3rd ed., edited by Mark Armstrong and Robert Porter, 2221–99. Amsterdam: North Holland.

Stremersch, Stefan, and Gerard J. Tellis. 2002. "Strategic Bundling of Products and Prices: A New Synthesis for Marketing." *The Journal of Marketing* 66 (1): 55–72.

Subramaniam, Ramanathan, and R. Venkatesh. 2009. "Optimal Bundling Strategies in Multiobject Auctions of Complements or Substitutes." *Marketing Science* 28 (2): 264–73.

Sudhir, K. 2001. "Competitive Pricing Behavior in the Auto Market: A Structural Analysis." *Marketing Science* 20 (1): 42–60.

Sudhir, K., and Sumon Datta. 2009. "Pricing in Marketing Channels." In *Handbook of Pricing Research in Marketing,* edited by Vithala R. Rao, 319–54. Northampton, MA: Edward Elgar Publications, Inc.

Sun, Baohong. 2005. "Promotion Effect on Endogenous Consumption." *Marketing Science* 24 (3): 430–43.

Sun, Baohong, Scott A. Neslin, and Kannan Srinivasan. 2003. "Measuring the Impact of Promotions on Brand Switching When Consumers Are Forward Looking." *Journal of Marketing Research* 40 (4): 389–405.

Sundararajan, Arun. 2004. "Nonlinear Pricing of Information Goods." *Management Science* 50 (12): 1660–73.

Talluri, Kalyan T. 2012. "Revenue Management." In *Handbook of Pricing*, edited by Özalp Özer and Robert Phillips. Oxford: Oxford University Press, 655–678.

Talluri, Kalyan T., and Garrett Van Ryzin. 2005. *The Theory and Practice of Revenue Management*. New York: Springer.

Tellis, Gerard J. 1988. "The Price Elasticity of Selective Demand: A Meta-Analysis of Econometric Models of Sales." *Journal of Marketing Research* 25 (4): 331–41.

Tellis, Gerard J., and Fred S. Zufryden. 1995. "Tackling the Retailer Decision Maze: Which Brands to Discount, How Much, When and Why?" *Marketing Science* 14 (3): 271–99.

Tirole, Jean. 1992. *The Theory of Industrial Organization*. Cambridge: MIT Press.

Toubia, Olivier, John R. Hauser, and Rosanna Garcia. 2007. "Probabilistic Polyhedral Methods for Adaptive Choice-Based Conjoint Analysis: Theory and Application." *Marketing Science* 26 (5): 596–610.

Van Heerde, Harald J., Marnik G. Dekimpe, and William P. Putsis, Jr. 2005. "Marketing Models and the Lucas Critique." *Journal of Marketing Research* 42 (1): 15–21.

Van Heerde, Harald J., ELS Gijsbrechts, and Koen Pauwels. 2008. "Winners and Losers in a Major Price War." *Journal of Marketing Research* 45 (5): 499–518.

Varian, Hal R., 1989. "Price Discrimination." In *Handbook of Industrial Organization*, edited by Richard Schmalensee and Mark Armstrong, 597–654. Amsterdam: North Holland.

——. 1997. "Versioning Information Goods." Unpublished Paper, University of California, Berkeley.

Venkatesh, R., and Vijay Mahajan. 1993. "A Probabilistic Approach to Pricing a Bundle of Products or Services." *Journal of Marketing Research* 30 (4): 494–508.

——. 2009. "The Design and Pricing of Bundles: A Review of Normative Guidelines and Practical Approaches." In *Handbook of Pricing Research in Marketing*, edited by Vithala R. Rao, 232–57. Northampton, MA: Edward Elgar Publications, Inc.

Vilcassim, Naufel J., Vrinda Kadiyali, and Pradeep K. Chintagunta. 1999. "Investigating Dynamic Multifirm Market Interactions in Price and Advertising." *Management Science* 45 (4): 499–518.

Wilson, Robert B. 1993. *Nonlinear Pricing*. Oxford: Oxford University.

Winer, Russell S. 1986. "A Reference Price Model of Brand Choice for Frequently Purchased Products." *Journal of Consumer Research* 13 (2): 250–56.

Wittink, Dick R., and Philippe Cattin. 1989. "Commercial Use of Conjoint Analysis: An Update." *Journal of Marketing* 53 (3): 91–96.

Wittink, Dick R., Marco Vriens and Wim Burhenne. 1994. "Commercial Use of Conjoint Analysis in Europe: Results and Critical Reflections." *International Journal of Research in Marketing* 11 (1): 41–52.

Zhang, Jie, and Lakshman Krishnamurthi. 2004. "Customizing Promotions in Online Stores." *Marketing Science* 23 (4): 561–78.

Zhang, Jie, and Michel Wedel. 2009. "The Effectiveness of Customized Promotions in Online and Offline Stores." *Journal of Marketing Research* 46 (2): 190–206.

# CHAPTER 11

# PRODUCT DISTRIBUTION AND PROMOTION: AN ANALYTICAL MARKETING PERSPECTIVE

CHARLES A. INGENE AND
XUBING ZHANG

## 11.1 INTRODUCTION

ACADEMIC marketers who employ analytical models rely on tools and techniques that are well-known to microeconomists, but marketers typically examine the world through glasses with a different prescription than economists use. Marketers distinguish between research that underlies product development; manufacturing that generates physical products; promotion that informs (some would say persuades) potential customers of product attributes and brand differences; distribution that makes a brand available for purchase; and pricing that generates rewards for distributors, promoters, manufacturers, and researchers. Marketers also discriminate between brands and product categories; the former comprises multiple product variants under a common label, while the latter usually is composed of multiple brands.

In this chapter we focus on the distribution and pricing of brands within a product category. Our concern is with the profits earned by retailers and manufacturers, and the surplus obtained by consumers. We then explore how brand differentiation and brand promotion affect profits. To reify our analysis, we focus on frequently purchased consumer goods (FPCGs). These items are sold widely in grocery stores, drugstores, and discount stores; we offer specific illustrations of FPCGs in the next section.

Our primary focus is on how channel structure and channel pricing policies influence the decision on how many brands a manufacturer should produce in a category and how many brands a retailer should carry within a specific product category. We demonstrate that the use of *category pricing* (CP) encourages a channel to distribute more brands than does *brand pricing* (BP). We define a category as a set of brands that is related in demand, either as substitutes or as complements. With CP, the prices of brands in a category are jointly set to maximize profits from the entire category. With BP the price of each brand is set to maximize profit of that brand without consideration of the demand interaction with other brands in the category. If there is only one brand in a category, BP and CP are indistinguishable; but, with more than one brand, BP and CP lead to different prices. Intuitively, CP should generate higher profit than does BP; however, we will show highly plausible conditions for which intuition is upended.

We will also establish three points that may not be well-known. First, a manufacturer-direct-to-consumers model (also known as a vertically integrated model) yields distinctly different results than does a decentralized-distribution model in which the manufacturer sells through a retail intermediary. In particular, CP is both the equilibrium and the optimum in a direct-to-consumers model, and is the global equilibrium in the decentralized model; but manufacturer and retailer are trapped in a prisoners' dilemma in a decentralized channel, for over much of parameter space they would both be better off using BP. The prisoners' dilemma disappears only when brands in the category are *little* differentiated from each other. Second, we will establish that when the pricing policy is CP, there are often more (and are never fewer) brands in a category than occurs when the pricing policy is BP. Third, when BP is used, we will show that parametric values exist for which a decentralized channel generates more consumers' surplus than does a vertically integrated channel. This result, which is due to the decentralized channel offering a broader range of brands in a category than does a vertically integrated channel, counters the conventional wisdom that a vertically integrated channel produces higher consumers' surplus than does an uncoordinated, bilateral-monopoly channel.[1]

We base our analysis on linear demand derived from a representative consumer's quasi-linear utility function. We make this derivation so for several reasons. (1) For FPCGs, the income effect is apt to be minor, so setting this effect aside is unlikely to cause much distortion of what presumably occurs in practice. (2) It allows us easily to compare a one-brand channel with a multibrand channel over the BP and CP policies. (3) Consumers' surplus can be readily determined. (4) It is compatible with any degree of product differentiation. (We only discuss substitutes, but the extension to complements is straightforward.) (5) A change in the representative consumer's product-interaction term affects own-price and cross-price sensitivities as well as demand intercepts; this becomes consequential when we discuss the use of promotion to enhance demand or to differentiate products. (6) Last, but hardly least, the mathematics is tractable, so closed form solutions generally are obtainable.

We use our derived demand curves to analyze the distribution of either one or two brands in a vertically integrated channel that uses either BP or CP. Because BP ignores the effect of the *j*th brand's price on demand for substitute brands, it imposes excessive *price competition* relative to CP. While this can be avoided by selling a single brand, selling multiple brands augments *aggregate demand*, though the demand increase is less the more similar the brands are.

We also examine decentralized channels with one or two manufacturers selling through a single retailer. With two manufacturers, the retailer alone makes the category breadth decision—will it, or will it not, carry two brands? In the single manufacturer case, for two brands to be produced and distributed requires manufacturer and retailer both to benefit from a wider category breadth. We treat the interaction between manufacturer(s) and retailer as a vertical-Nash game.

We restrict the manufacturer(s) to a constant per-unit wholesale price; this imposes *double marginalization*: prices are above the level that would maximize the sum of retailer plus manufacturer profit (aka channel profit). Of course, two-part tariffs could be used to replicate the performance of a vertically integrated channel, but this would miss the critical fact that few channels are coordinated in practice. A one-part tariff is a parsimonious method of studying a lack of channel coordination. Finally, we do not consider intrabrand pricing issues because, for many FPCGs, all product variants within a brand are priced identically.

This chapter proceeds as follows. In the next section we offer stylized facts to support our assertion that BP was the historic norm, but that it largely has been displaced by CP for FPCGs. In the ensuing sections we present our model and assumptions, we analyze the performances of a manufacturer-direct-to-consumers model and a decentralized, vertical-Nash model. Then we briefly investigate demand-enhancing and brand-differentiating promotions. We conclude with a few managerial implications and suggestions for further research.

## 11.2  STYLIZED FACTS

Four stylized facts motivate our investigation; they relate to historic changes in manufacturing, retailing, and pricing. To reify our analysis, we focus on frequently purchased consumer goods (FPCGs). These items are sold widely in grocery stores, drugstores, and discount stores; we offer specific illustrations below.

First, large corporations control more brands within the same product category than was once the case; we illustrate with the beverage category. PepsiCo, which focused originally on Pepsi-Cola, acquired Mountain Dew in 1964, Tropicana in 1998, and Gatorade (via Quaker Oats) in 2001. It has also developed brands in-house: Sierra Mist (2000) and AMP Energy (2001) are two examples. PepsiCo's US website indicates twenty-one beverage brands encompassing soft drinks, energy drinks, juices, tea and coffee, and water. Its main rival, Coca-Cola, owns or distributes some 500 brands worldwide; until 1960 it had only one brand. The phenomenon of a large number of brands being controlled by a company is not unique to beverages—as walking down the cereal aisle in any grocery store readily indicates.

Second, brands commonly contain more variants than they did a few decades ago. As a consequence, most products have close substitutes within the brand (e.g., diet colas and decaffeinated colas) as well as across brands (e.g., Coke and Pepsi). For example, the Coca-Cola brand consisted solely of Coca-Cola until Diet Coke was added in 1982 and Caffeine-Free Coca-Cola in 1983. Today there are sixteen Coke variants sold in the United States. More dramatically, their Powerade sports drink comes in twenty-nine flavors while their low-calorie Powerade Option is available in five flavors. Most FPCG categories have experienced an explosion in product variants over roughly the same time frame; that is, the past thirty years or so.

Third, individual brand managers in a multibrand company historically were pitted against each other as they battled for market share; as such, they used BP. And, of course, many companies had only one brand in a category (e.g., Coca-Cola until the 1960s when it acquired Minute Maid and developed Fanta). But by the 1990s, many consumer goods manufacturers had switched to category managers who simultaneously set the prices of all brands under their control: CP pricing. The shift from brand management to category management, combined with more brands being controlled by large companies—by acquisition, by internal development, or both—means that CP has been replacing BP at the manufacturing stage, at least in most FPCGs categories.[2]

Fourth, stores whose main focus is the sale of FPCGs are dramatically larger than they once were. To illustrate, the very first supermarket (King Kullen) was constructed in 1930 with approximately 3000 square feet; grocery stores at that time were distinctly smaller. Today, Kroger's average supermarket is 60,500 square feet. Of course, store sizes did not jump twenty-fold overnight; growth has been gradual. The same phenomenon holds true for drugstores and discount stores. For example, in 1998 CVS Pharmacy stores ranged from 8000 to 10,000 square feet; by 2011 CVS's stores ranged up to 25,000 square feet. Today, Wal-Mart's discount stores (not supercenters) range from 30,000 to 219,000 square feet, with an average of 106,000 square feet. Twenty years ago the comparable figures were 10,000–126,000, with an average of 70,700 square feet.[3] With substantial increases in store size, grocery stores, drugstores, and discount stores today sell more product categories, carry a wider assortment of brands within FPCG categories, and stock a broader inventory of product variants within a brand than was the case twenty, forty, or eighty years ago. And, at the retail level, the use of CP is now common at most mass merchandise stores (Zenor 1994), often because one brand is appointed as a "category captain" to coordinate pricing and promotion for the retailer (Subramanian et al. 2010).

In sum, compared to the historic norm, stores are larger and carry more brands; the brands are purchased from fewer manufacturers; and there is a higher degree of cross-brand (and intrabrand) substitutability. Further, the shift from BP to CP at both manufacture and retail levels indicates that brands are more apt to be priced with an eye to their demand interactions than was once the case. In what follows we begin from an initial position of a retailer selling a single brand that is produced by a single manufacturer. We then increase the number of available brands, but set prices according to BP. Finally, we examine CP. We believe that this is the sequence of events that transpired in FPCGs categories.

# 11.3 THE MODEL

We make five assumptions:

(1) A manufacturer can produce any number of substitutable brands, but in a decentralized channel it can sell only those brands that the retailer is willing to distribute. Therefore, category breadth (i.e., number of brands in a category) is a joint decision in a bilateral monopoly. When manufacturers produce a single brand, but retailers buy from multiple manufacturers, category breadth is solely a retailer decision.

(2) All decision makers are profit-maximizers with full information about demand and costs.

(3) Each brand has a nonnegative, per-unit cost of production ($C_k$) and of distribution ($c_k$), $k \in \{i, j\}$, where $k$ denotes a brand. Later we introduce costs of promotion.

(4) When multiple brands are sold the manufacturer charges constant per-unit wholesale prices $W_k$, $k \in \{i, j\}$; when one brand is sold it charges a constant per-unit wholesale price $W_k^{One}$. Hence, our analysis is restricted to one-part tariffs.

(5) The representative consumer selects optimal quantities of the brand(s) that are available for purchase. When N brands are available, the quasi-linear utility function is:

$$U = \sum_{k \in \{1,N\}} \left( A_k Q_k - B_k Q_k^2 / 2 - p_k Q_k \right) - \sum_{\substack{k \in \{1,N\} \\ i \neq j}} T_{ij} Q_i Q_j, \qquad (11.1)$$

where $Q_k$ is the quantity purchased of the $k$th brand; $p_k$ is its price; $A_k$ and $B_k$ are nonnegative parameters. $T_{ij} > 0$ indicates the degree of substitutability between the $i$th and $j$th brands. The closer $T_{ij}$ is to zero, the more differentiated are the $i$th and $j$th brands. At $T_{ij} = 0$, brands are unrelated in demand—that is, they belong to different product categories.

For simplicity going forward, we focus on either one brand (the $i$th) or two brands (the $i$th and $j$th). We set $B_i = B_j \equiv B$, so we drop the subscripts on $T_{ij} \equiv T$. When only one brand is sold, utility is calculated from (11.1) by setting the quantities of nondistributed brands to zero.

Demand for a single brand is:

$$Q_k^{One} = \left( A_k - p_k \right) / B, \qquad k \in \{i, j\}. \qquad (11.2)$$

The second-order condition (SOC) for a maximum is: $-\left( 1/B \right) < 0 \Rightarrow B > 0$.
When two brands are distributed, the demand system is:[4]

$$Q_i^{Two} = \left[\left(BA_i - TA_j\right) - Bp_i + Tp_j\right]/\left(B^2 - T^2\right)$$
$$Q_j^{Two} = \left[\left(-TA_i + BA_j\right) + Tp_i - Bp_j\right]/\left(B^2 - T^2\right). \tag{11.3}$$

SOCs for a maximum are $B^2 > T^2$.

Own-price and cross-price sensitivity are $-B/(B^2 - T^2) < 0$ and $T/(B^2 - T^2) > 0$. The $i$th brand's demand intercept is $(BA_i - TA_j)/(B^2 - T^2)$; reversing $i$'s and $j$'s gives the $j$th brand's maximal demand; we will also refer to these terms as the "base levels" of demand. Notice that a change in $B$ or $T$ affects own-price sensitivity, cross-price sensitivity, and both demand intercepts. We will make use of this property when we discuss how promotion affects profitability. Both demand intercepts are positive only if:

$$A_i > \chi A_j > \chi^2 A_i, \tag{11.4}$$

$$\text{s.t.} \quad \chi \equiv T / B \in [0,1]. \tag{11.5}$$

We assume that inequalities (11.4) hold. The ratio of the cross-price effect to the own-price effect ($\chi$) is the standardized measure of brand differentiation as seen by the representative consumer.

When the $i$th brand is distributed initially, and then the $j$th brand is added to the category, aggregate demand rises to:

$$\left(\sum_{k \in \{i,j\}} Q_k^{Two} - Q_i^{One}\right) = (1-\chi)Q_j^{Two} > 0. \tag{11.6}$$

Thus, sales of the $j$th brand come, in part, from cannibalizing the $i$th brand:

$$\left(Q_i^{Two} - Q_i^{One}\right) = -\chi Q_j^{Two} < 0. \tag{11.7}$$

The $j$th brand augments category demand (11.6), but it lowers demand for the $i$th brand when brands are substitutes (11.7). The less differentiated are the brands (the larger is $\chi$), the smaller is demand augmentation.

## 11.4 MANUFACTURER-DIRECT-TO-CONSUMERS MODELS

Consider a vertically integrated channel that sells the $i$th brand. Should it add the $j$th brand? The answer pivots on each brand's base level of demand; the pricing policy that is used; and, in the case of BP, the degree of brand differentiation.

It is straightforward that a single-brand, vertically integrated channel earns a profit:

$$\Pi_i^{VI,One^*} = B\left(Q_i^{One^*}\right)^2 / 4,$$

(11.8)

where

$$Q_i^{One^*} \equiv \left(A_i - c_i - C_i\right)/B > 0.$$

(11.9)

$Q_i^{One^*}$ is the quantity that would be sold at marginal cost pricing; this is the socially optimal output when only one brand is sold. The optimal quantity and margin for a vertically integrated channel are $Q_i^{VI,One^*} = Q_i^{One^*}/2$ and $\mu_i^{VI,One^*} = BQ_i^{One^*}/2$.

Should the vertically integrated channel expand the product category by adding the $j$th brand? To answer this question, and at no loss of generality, we assume that $Q_i^{One^*} \geq Q_j^{One^*}$. For ease of presentation, we define the ratio of socially optimal quantities as:

$$0 < Q^* \equiv Q_j^{One^*} / Q_i^{One^*} = \left(A_j - c_j - C_j\right) / \left(A_i - c_i - C_i\right) \leq 1.$$

(11.10)

The inequalities needed for positive demand intercepts for both brands (see (11.4)) may now be rewritten as $1 > \chi Q^* > \chi^2$. Since $1 > \chi Q^*$ by $Q^* \in (0,1]$, and $1 > \chi$ by the second-order conditions, the binding constraint is $Q^* > \chi$; if this is violated, only the $i$th brand is sold.

We now assess the profitability of selling one brand versus selling both brands when pricing with BP. The $k$th brand manager maximizes $\Pi_k^{VI,BP} = \mu_k Q_k^{Two}$; thus, he/she ignores the effect of the $k$th price on prices charged by other brand managers. Whether it is advantageous to introduce a second brand pivots on the parametric values of $\chi$ and $Q^*$. At low $\chi-$ values it is intuitive that there is minimal cannibalization, so that it should be optimal to sell both brands. In contrast, at high $\chi-$ values there is substantial cannibalization, so that it should be non–optimal to sell both brands. The question is where in-between is the "one-*versus*-two" boundary? A profit comparison gives the parametric values for which a BP-using, vertically integrated channel offers one *versus* two brands in a product category:

$$\Delta\Pi^{VI,BP-One} = B\left(Q_i^{One^*}\right)^2 \left\{\frac{4\left(4-3\chi^2+\chi^4\right)\left(Q^*\right)^2 - 16\left(2-\chi^2\right)\chi Q^* + \left(12-5\chi^2+\chi^4\right)\chi^2}{4\left(4-\chi^2\right)^2\left(1-\chi^2\right)}\right\} \gtrless 0,$$

(11.11)

where $\Delta\Pi^{VI,BP-One} \equiv \left(\Pi^{VI,BP^*} - \Pi_i^{VI,One^*}\right)$. The numerator of (11.11) must be positive for both brands to be offered; only one brand is sold when the numerator is negative. There is a straightforward logic to offering two brands: (i) $\Pi_i^{VI,One^*}$ is $\chi$–invariant. (ii) At $\chi = 0$, the BP-margin on the $i$th brand when both brands are sold is the same as when only the $i$th brand is sold. Since the channel also earns profit from the $j$th brand, an additional brand always makes BP more profitable at $\chi = 0$. (iii) As $\chi$ increases, cannibalization rises, so margins decrease on both brands. It is better to sell two brands with BP (only the $i$th brand) below (above) the critical $\{\chi, Q^*\}$ – values given by (11.11). The essence of this argument is that the benefit of demand augmentation must be balanced against the harm of cannibalization with its associated decline in per-unit margins.

Figure 11.1 shows in $\{\chi, Q^*\}$ –space the values for which one or two brands should be sold.[5] The horizontal axis is the ratio of the socially optimal outputs of the $j$th to the $i$th brand $(Q^* \equiv Q_j^{One*} / Q_i^{One*})$; the vertical axis measures brand differentiation ($\chi$); together they form a unit square. In the shaded, upper-left triangle, the demand intercept for the $j$th brand is negative $(Q^* < \chi)$, and so this region is labeled "Only $i$, $j$ is Infeasible." In the lightly shaded portion of Figure 11.1 (labeled $i$), profit is maximized by selling only the $i$th brand, *even though there is positive demand* for the $j$th brand (by construction, base demand for the $i$th brand is greater than for the $j$th brand). In the unshaded portion of Figure 11.1 it is more profitable to sell both brands priced with BP than it is to sell a single brand. For a vertically integrated channel, the profit-equilibrating value between one and two brands is $\chi = 0.612$ at $Q^* = 1$; it is $\chi = 0.323$ at $Q^* = 0.5$; at $Q^* = 0.25$, profit equality occurs at $\chi = 0.165$; and, as $Q^* \to 0$, profit equality goes to $\chi = 0$.

Now consider the adoption of category pricing (CP). Under CP, the category manager simultaneously maximizes profit from both brands:

$$\max_{\mu_i, \mu_j} \ \Pi^{VI,CP} = \mu_i Q_i^{Two}\left(\mu_i, \mu_j\right) + \mu_j Q_j^{Two}\left(\mu_j, \mu_i\right). \tag{11.12}$$

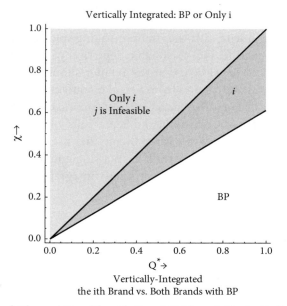

Vertically Integrated: BP or Only i

Vertically-Integrated
the ith Brand vs. Both Brands with BP

FIGURE 11.1  Optimal Channel Breadth with Brand Pricing: A Vertically Integrated Channel

Optimization leads to the conclusion that a broader product category is more profitable than a narrower category when the pricing policy is CP (i.e., $\Pi^{VI,CP^*} > \Pi^{VI,One^*}$). Since CP considers the effect of each brand's price on sales of the rival brand (which BP does not), we also find that $\Pi^{VI,CP^*} \geq \Pi^{VI,BF}$ (the equality holds only for $\chi = 0$). Thus, CP never leads to fewer brands in a category, and often leads to more brands, no matter how similar the brands are. The logic is that there is neither double marginalization nor excessive price competition in a vertically integrated channel. In summary, when a vertically integrated channel adopts CP in lieu of BP, its decision calculus shifts from (a) balancing demand augmentation against price competition to (b) producing a wider range of substitute brands. This does not deny that other factors drive category breadth; it is to say that, *ceteris paribus*, CP encourages more brands in a category. Since CP generates more profit than BP whenever two brands are offered, CP supplants BP in a vertically integrated channel. We now ask whether this logical deduction also holds in a decentralized channel.

## 11.5 Decentralized, Vertical-Nash Models

In this section we examine a decentralized channel that is organized as vertical Nash and we contrast its results with those obtained in a vertically integrated model. With linear demand there is vertical strategic substitutability, so a vertical-Nash game is likely when no channel member is powerful enough to become a Stackelberg leader (e.g., PepsiCo and Wal-Mart). We assume that the retailer has made the credible commitment required for vertical-Nash stability.

Once again we begin with only the $i$th brand being sold. We think a single-brand bilateral-monopoly channel is a reasonable depiction of the introductory stage of the product life cycle. We ask whether the retailer should expand its offerings by stocking a second, substitute brand from a *rival* manufacturer. A two-manufacturer scenario is indicative of a mature market with interbrand competition from competing manufacturers (such as Coca-Cola and Pepsi-Cola when they both had a single brand). We undertake this analysis when the retailer uses BP and when it uses CP. Then we turn to purchasing two brands from a single manufacturer. We end with an analysis of consumers' surplus in a vertically integrated versus a vertical-Nash channel.

### 11.5.1 Two Manufacturers, Each with One Brand

The retailer will buy from a second manufacturer (the $j$th) in order to offer a substitute brand when doing so is profit-enhancing. Simple calculation reveals that when the retailer uses a BP policy, its profit gain from a second brand is:

$$\Delta\pi^{VN,BP-One} = B\left(Q_i^{One^*}\right)^2 \left( \dfrac{\begin{array}{l} 9\left(9-11\chi^2+4\chi^4\right)\left(Q^*\right)^2 - 36\left(3-2\chi^2\right)\chi Q^* \\ \quad +2\left(27-26\chi^2+8\chi^4\right)\chi^2 \end{array}}{9\left(1-\chi^2\right)\left(9-4\chi^2\right)^2} \right) \gtreqless 0, \qquad (11.13)$$

where $\Delta\pi^{VN,BP-One} \equiv \left(\pi^{VN,BP^*} - \pi^{VN,One^*}\right)$ is the retailer's profit gain from the $j$th brand. It is optimal for the retailer to sell both products if the numerator of (11.13) is positive. This requires that the brands be at least moderately differentiated. Only the $i$th product is sold if the $i$th and $j$th brands are minimally differentiated. As with a vertically integrated channel, availability of a second brand does not automatically induce category expansion. Figure 11.2 details this information graphically. The profit-equilibrating value is $\chi = 0.807$ at $Q^* = 1$; as $Q^* \to \chi$, the point of equality goes to $\chi = 0.721$. Contrasting Figures 11.1 and 11.2 makes apparent that the decentralized channel will have a product category with more brands than does a vertically integrated channel over a nontrivial portion of parameter space; however, the fundamental message remains the same: unless brands are sufficiently differentiated, only one brand will be distributed.

Now consider a world in which the retailer uses CP—this is a plausible characterization of the way FPCGs are priced today. The additional profit of the second brand is:

$$\left(\pi^{VN,CP^*} - \pi^{VN,One^*}\right) = B\left(Q_i^{One^*}\right)^2 \left( \dfrac{\begin{array}{l} 9\left(9+7\chi^2\right)\left(Q^*\right)^2 + 18\left(15+\chi^2\right)\chi Q^* \\ \quad +\left(162-19\chi^2+\chi^4\right)\chi^2 \end{array}}{9\left(1-\chi^2\right)\left(9-\chi^2\right)^2} \right) > 0. \qquad (11.14)$$

The retailer prefers more brands with CP since the second brand augments profit at any level of differentiation. This result has the same flavor as with vertical integration: CP drives out BP.

There is another feature of the model that is of some interest. When one brand is distributed, the manufacturer and the retailer share profit equally in a vertical-Nash game with linear demand. When the retailer sets prices according to BP and sells two brands, the $k$th manufacturer and the retailer earn equal shares of the profit generated by the $k$th brand. But, when the retailer employs CP, the retailer's profit share from the $k$th brand is one-half only at $\chi = 0$; it rises to 100% as the brands become more similar (as $\chi \to 1$). Thus, at any given $\chi$−level, manufacturer remuneration falls when the retailer switches from BP to CP. It follows that $\pi^{VN,CP^*} > \pi^{VN,BP^*}$ (and $\pi^{VN,CP^*} > \pi^{VN,One^*}$). Single brand manufacturers were clearly disadvantaged when retailers switched from BP to CP. As we show below, a multibrand manufacturer splits channel profit equally with the retailer in a vertical-Nash channel whether both channel members use BP or they both employ CP. Thus, producing multiple brands provided manufacturers with some protection from retailer power. This *may* be one reason that some FPCG producers chose to acquire other FPCG producers.

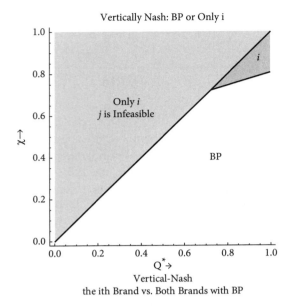

**FIGURE 11.2**  Optimal Channel Breadth with Brand Pricing: A Vertical-Nash, Decentralized Channel (Two Manufacturers)

## 11.5.2 One Manufacturer with Two Brands

Now consider a retailer that obtains both brands from one manufacturer; in this case we are concerned with the BP *versus* CP decision at both channel levels. A two-brand, bilateral-monopoly channel is more characteristic of a world in which large corporations control multiple brands, while the model of two manufacturers selling to a common retailer depicted an earlier time when many manufacturers sold a single brand in a product category. Manufacturer control of multiple brands may be due to the *i*th manufacturer having acquired the *j*th manufacturer, or because it has developed a second brand in-house. In the case of FPCGs, there is evidence that both strategies have been followed.

Should a decentralized, vertical-Nash channel distribute one brand, both brands priced with BP, or both brands priced with CP when the manufacturer offers two brands? There are two possible channel organizations: a bilateral monopoly, or a monopoly manufacturer that sells through two independent retailers (each carrying a different brand). The latter case is formally the same as a bilateral monopoly in which the retailer uses BP; because only the identities are reversed, we do not pursue this case any further.

We start by considering the manufacturer and retailer in a bilateral-monopoly channel when they *both* use BP. Should both brands be sold? The profit difference replicates expression (11.13) since both channel members earn the same profit: $\left(\pi^{VN,BP^*} - \pi^{VN,One^*}\right) = \left(\Pi^{VN,BP^*} - \Pi^{VN,One^*}\right)$. Whether one brand or two brands are sold pivots on the relative base demands of the two brands (i.e., $Q^*$) and the degree of brand differentiation ($\chi$)—as shown in Figure 11.2.

If the manufacturer clings to a BP policy when the bilateral-monopoly retailer uses CP, we have expression (11.14) for the retailer, so both brands are distributed; but the manufacturer is just as disadvantaged as were two independent manufacturers in the preceding subsection. Within the context of our model, it makes no difference whether the $i$th and $j$th brands are controlled by two decision makers or only one (BP-using) decision maker at manufacture. But matters are different when the manufacturer uses CP.

Suppose the manufacturer uses CP while the bilateral-monopoly retailer uses BP (or, equivalently, suppose the manufacturer sells a different brand to each of two retailers). This merely requires that CP had been discovered by manufacturers before retailers implemented it. Roles are now reversed; expression (11.14) holds—but with the LHS representing the difference in manufacturer profits, so it is the retail level that is disadvantaged.

Finally, let both manufacturer and retailer employ CP. The consequence is that channel members reap more profit by selling both brands than they would if they were to produce/sell a single brand—whatever the degree of brand differentiation. This conclusion again replicates a vertically integrated channel. In short, no matter the channel structure, the introduction of CP in place of BP leads to more brands being made available over that portion of parameter space in which only one brand would be offered with BP.

Is joint use of CP a stable equilibrium in a bilateral-monopoly channel? Suppose the manufacturer uses CP and the retailer employs BP (or vice versa). As the proof is somewhat laborious, it is omitted, but the results are unambiguous: as we noted at (11.14), whichever channel member uses CP gains profit at the expense of the BP-using channel member. Use of CP by both members of the channel is the unique, stable equilibrium.

Whether the channel is integrated or decentralized, when firms become aware of CP as an alternative to BP, they will adopt it. If the manufacturer "discovers" CP before the retailer, the manufacturer's profit will rise by switching to CP while the retailer's profit declines. And, if the retailer discovers CP first, the manufacturer's profit will decline while the retailer's profit increases. Either way, the "late discoverer" must adopt CP as a defensive maneuver. Consequently, within the context of our model, when a new brand is proposed in a world of category pricing, it will be introduced.

In practice there are other important issues that are outside our model: fixed costs of developing and promoting a product require a new brand to meet a minimum sales level; limited shelf space and inventory holding costs impose the same constraint on slow-moving items. In short, CP encourages retailers to distribute more brands, just as it stimulates manufacturers to develop (or acquire) more brands. Nonetheless, we stress that CP is not the sole factor that has caused this real-world outcome.

Observation: Joint use of CP, which is the unique, stable equilibrium, encourages product categories with more brands than does BP. This holds no matter how similar the brands are; even minor brand variants are introduced with CP; in contrast, with BP greater brand differentiation is required for a new brand to be worth introducing.

## 11.5.3 Consumers' Surplus

Natural questions to ask are whether consumers benefit more from one brand or two brands, more from BP or CP, more from a vertically integrated or from a vertical-Nash channel? Answers to two—not three—of these questions are intuitive. First, consumers always prefer a broader product category that is optimally priced, whether BP or CP is used. Second, for a fixed number of brands, consumers prefer BP to CP; that is to say, they prefer the lower prices that are caused by price competition. This means that consumers prefer a broader range of brands in the portion of parameter space where one brand is sold under BP, but both brands when CP is used.

The third question is subtler. When CP is used, consumers prefer vertical integration, since it eliminates double marginalization, a point made by Spengler (1950). However, when the pricing policy is BP, as it arguably was prior to the 1970s, an absolute statement cannot be made, for the answer depends on parametric values. In Figure 11.3 we provide visual insight into this issue. The left-hand graph (Figure 11.3A) simply combines Figures 11.1 and 11.2. In the triangle labeled {1,1} only one brand is sold with either channel structure; and, in the triangle labeled {2,2}, both brands are offered with either channel structure. (The first number is the number of brands in a vertically integrated channel; the second number provides the same information in a vertical-Nash channel.) In both the {1,1} and {2,2} cases, consumers' surplus is higher with vertical integration because prices are lower. But, in the tetragon labeled {1,2}, the vertically integrated channel sells only one brand, while the decentralized channel distributes both brands, so there is a trade-off between the benefit of breadth with a vertical-Nash channel and the benefit of a lower price for the $i$th brand with vertical integration.

Figure 11.3B adjudicates breadth versus prices; which is preferred pivots on the sign of:

$$\left(CS^{VI,One^*} - CS^{VN,NPLP^*}\right) = B\left(Q_i^{One^*}\right)^2 \left(\frac{\left(45 - 88\,c^2 + 16\,c^4\right) - 96\,cQ^*}{\phantom{x}} - \frac{4\left(9 + 4c^2\right)\left(Q^*\right)^2}{8\left(9 - 4c^2\right)^2}\right). \tag{11.15}$$

The numerator of (11.15) is positive in the pentagonal area labeled VI{1,2} in Figure 11.3B: price dominates breadth. But when the numerator is negative, breadth dominates price; this is shown in the triangle labeled VN{1,2}.

Observation: Parametric values exist for which a decentralized, vertical-Nash channel creates more consumers' surplus than a vertically integrated channel by offering more brands in a product category. However, this can occur only if the $j$th brand's base level of demand is less than about three-fifths of the $i$th brand's base demand level.

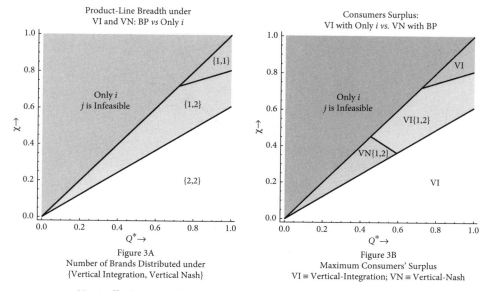

Figure 3A
Number of Brands Distributed under
{Vertical Integration, Vertical Nash}

Figure 3B
Maximum Consumers' Surplus
VI ≡ Vertical-Integration; VN ≡ Vertical-Nash

**FIGURES 11.3** Vertically Integrated and Vertical-Nash Channels One Brand or Two Brands with Brand Pricing

## 11.5.4 A Prisoners' Dilemma

CP is the equilibrium pricing policy in a vertically integrated channel and it is also the optimal pricing policy. But in a decentralized, vertical-Nash channel, it is *only* the equilibrium policy. Over much of parameter space, decentralized channel members earn *less* than they would if both of them used BP! However, neither manufacturer nor retailer individually can afford to revert to BP, for whoever first returns to BP would be worse off than it would be by staying with CP. If they both returned to BP, both of them would be tempted to defect to CP. In short, for a substantial range of parametric values, decentralized-channel members are trapped in a prisoners' dilemma: they are worse off than they would be if they were both to use BP, but each of them is better off than they would be if they were independently to switch to BP.

Figure 11.4 visually presents the values at which it is profit maximizing for both channel members to use category pricing (denoted as CP) or brand pricing (denoted as BP). The prisoners' dilemma boundary is given by:

$$\Delta\Pi_C^{PD} = 2\chi B \left( Q_i^{One\star} \right)^2 f^{PD}\left( \chi, Q^* \right) = 0,$$

$$\text{where } \Delta\Pi_C^{PD} \equiv \left( \Pi_C^{VN,CP} - \Pi_C^{VN,BP} \right)$$

$$\text{and } f^{PD}\left( \chi, Q^* \right) \equiv \left( \frac{\chi\left( 27 - 20\chi^2 \right)\left[ 1 + \left( Q^* \right)^2 \right] - 2Q^*\left( 27 - 36\chi^2 + 16\chi^4 \right)}{9\left( 1 - \chi^2 \right)\left( 9 - 4\chi^2 \right)^2} \right). \quad (11.16)$$

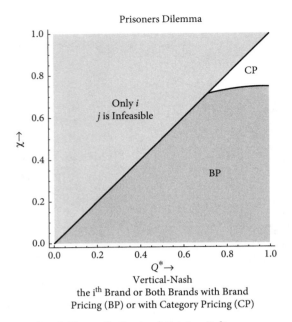

**FIGURE 11.4**  A Decentralized Channel's Optimal Pricing Policy

Expression (11.16) is the difference in *channel* profits between joint use of CP and joint use of BP. As the channel is organized as vertical-Nash, with linear demand channel members share the profit difference (11.16) equally. Numerical analysis of (11.16) reveals that category pricing is optimal if and only if brands are not too differentiated: $\chi > 0.75$ at $Q^* = 1$ ($\chi > 0.72$ as $Q^* \to \chi$). While all profits are increased by a joint CP–policy in the CP–zone of Figure 11.4, the BP–zone represents a prisoner's dilemma—both channel members would be better off with the unstable brand-pricing policy. When two brands can be marketed with BP or CP, a decentralized channel is caught in a prisoner's dilemma over most of parameter space. Unless brands are not very differentiated, the unique, stable equilibrium (joint use of CP) lowers profits for manufacturer, retailer, and the channel relative to the profit that would be attained with joint use of BP.

# 11.6 PROMOTION

Whenever two brands are distributed, total channel profit is maximized when the brands have the same base demand ($Q^* = 1$) and are maximally differentiated (i.e., $\chi = 0$). This is true whether category pricing or brand pricing is used. So far we have assumed that $Q^*$ and $\chi$ are exogenous on the (simplistic) grounds that it is impossible to *compel* customers to regard two brands as equally desirable, or to treat them as totally distinct. But it is possible to use promotion (e.g., advertising) to persuade customers that a brand is more desirable than they had originally thought; similarly, perceived brand differentiation can be raised (or lowered) with promotion.

First, a brand may be promoted without reference to other brands. Doing so for the $k$th brand will impact $Q^*$ directly through the $A_k$ parameter in the representative consumer's utility function, affecting demand for rival brands as well (see (11.3)). Advertising such as "Suave makes you look as if you spent a fortune on your hair" should have had this type of an impact.[6] Budweiser's "For all you do, this Bud's for you" is another example. Second, advertising may promote the notion that "our brand is different," thereby lowering the $T$ parameter in the representative consumer's utility function;[7] this will diminish the value of $\chi$. One example is Apple Computer's "Think different" campaign (1998) that was meant to lower $\chi$ by increasing brand differentiation. Third, an advertising campaign may increase $Q^*$ and simultaneously lower $\chi$.[8] An early example was "there's always room for J-E-L-L-O"; a more recent one is Taco Bell's "Think outside the bun." The flipside is also possible; in the 1970s (when BP was the pricing norm) Suave shampoo ran television ads saying "Suave does what theirs does for less than half the price," presumably raising $A_{Suave}$ and lowering $\chi$.

From the viewpoint of a manager, the decision to promote a brand, or to differentiate two brands, would seem to be straightforward: set the marginal net revenue from an increase in $Q^*$ (or from a decrease in $\chi$) equal to the marginal cost of achieving this effect. While managers may not know the specifics of the demand that they face, they can readily assess whether additional promotional dollars augment net revenue. Analysis reveals that under both brand pricing and category pricing, the marginal net revenue from an increase in $Q^*$ raises marginal net revenue at an increasing rate, so a category manager should be able to move, step-by-step, to the optimal level of promotion. Provided that the cost of increasing $Q^*$ also rises at an increasing rate (as seems reasonable), there will be an interior optimum.

In contrast, the net revenue impact of a decrease in $\chi$ differs by pricing policy. Under category pricing, marginal net revenue increases at an increasing rate (as with $Q^*$). But with brand pricing, lowering $\chi$ leads to marginal net revenue that increases at a decreasing rate (in the zone labeled BP⁻ in Figure 11.5) down to a critical value (call it $\tilde{\chi}^{BP}(Q^*)$); thereafter it rises at an increasing rate (the zone labeled BP⁺). $\tilde{\chi}^{BP}(Q^*)$ is the boundary between BP⁺ and BP⁻.

The key point of Figure 11.5 is that a brand manager whose brand is located in the BP⁻ region will see a declining marginal impact of promotion on $\chi$; therefore, the manager may deduce that extra spending is unwarranted. This can limit resources devoted to promoting brand differentiation, leading a brand-pricing firm to engaging in a nonoptimal level of promotion.

## 11.7  Discussion and Extensions

Here we briefly overview a few managerial implications, discuss some related research within and beyond the framework of our model, and offer suggestions for future research.

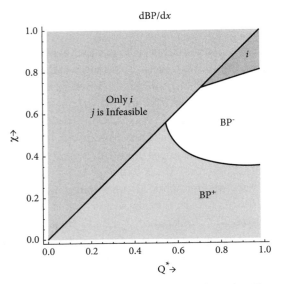

**FIGURE 11.5**  Brand Pricing in a Vertical-Nash Channel Effect of a Change in $\chi$ on Channel Profit

## 11.7.1 Managerial Implications and Observations

We make three points. First, unlike price—which a retailer can control to the penny—establishing a base level of demand, or a degree of brand differentiation, is inherently imprecise. For this reason, knowledge of the specific rate of change of profit in response to promotion is of practical importance. Second, as is well-known, whichever channel member pays for promotion provides a suboptimal amount for the channel. The reason is that whoever pays the full cost garners only a fraction of the extra profit. This shortfall can be corrected with a two-part tariff that shares promotional costs that affects one brand (Jeuland and Shugan 1983) or both brands (Ingene et al. 2012). Co-op advertising is a practical example of cost sharing.

Third, the prisoners' dilemma zone in Figure 11.4 (labeled BP) may be meaningless if it is in both channel members' interest to use brand pricing rather than category pricing in this area. We believe that, to some extent, this occurs in practice. Consider PepsiCo, which sells multiple brands of soft drinks, energy drinks, juices, tea and coffee, and water. These examples clearly are gross substitutes, but are they all priced by one category manager? Supermarkets obviously stock juices in the dairy department, and tea and coffee in an aisle that is typically *not* the aisle(s) that carry soft drinks, energy drinks, and water. This hints that there may be at least three category managers at retail and (possibly) at manufacture. We suggest that there may be a positive $\chi$ value (call it $\underline{\chi}$) below which brands are treated as members of different categories: brands for which $\chi \in \left(0, \underline{\chi}\right)$ are priced with BP, while brands for which $\chi \in \left(\underline{\chi}, 1\right)$ are priced according to a CP policy. If PepsiCo (more generally, the manufacturer) uses the same criterion as the retailer, and if $\chi$ is in the vicinity of 0.75, the prisoners' dilemma would be nothing more than a theoretical curiosity. Our intuition, which has developed over years of interaction with retailers, is that they have an implicit $\chi$, but that it is below 0.75. Our sense is that there is a real-world prisoners' dilemma for many (perhaps most) FPCGs, but that it is not as severe as indicated by Figure 11.4.

## 11.7.2 Related Research in a Distribution-Channel Context

In this section we summarize briefly a handful of papers that have addressed new product decisions in a channel context.

### 11.7.2.1 New Products Introduced by Manufacturers

Marketers have traditionally studied product lines from the manufacturer's point of view (e.g., Moorthy 1988). One justification for a firm to develop a product line is to segment the market so as to price discriminate across heterogeneous consumers. Moorthy (1984) showed that consumer self-selection has significant implications for how products are designed and how prices are chosen by a monopolist. Villas-Boas (1998) analyzed a manufacturer who distributes through an independent retailer. Two market segments with distinct (high and low) quality preferences were modeled. Villas-Boas found that a manufacturer-Stackelberg leader will obtain distribution of both products only if wholesale prices ($W_1$ and $W_2$) are not "too high" and ($W_1 - W_2$) is not "too great." The key issue entailed balancing manufacturer and retailer interests.

Large retailers, who account for most sales, often act as gatekeepers that can make, or break, a new product variant, a new brand, or even a new product category; so retail distribution should not be ignored when planning a product line. Urban and Hauser (1993) emphasized that the manufacturers should include the retailer's preferences in their decisions to introduce new products. Corstjens and Corstjens (1995) suggested that consumer companies might be more successful if they put more effort into creating value for retailers as well as for consumers.

A more recent paper analyzed the potential of various new product designs[9] to generate profit for the manufacturer and for a dominant retailer who must be induced to stock the product (Luo et al. 2007). The authors used a hierarchical Bayesian conjoint experiment to assess consumer preferences for the possible designs; they also modeled rival manufacturers' expected reactions. This led to a decision support system for use "as a category management tool to educate the retailers regarding how to make price adjustments in its product line in response to the introduction of a new product" (Luo et al. 2007, 160). In our terms, they estimated demand $E[A_j]$[10] as a precursor to estimating profit potential across product variants, given that rival manufacturers adjust their wholesale prices in response to the focal firm's actions.

A recent game-theoretic paper (Dong et al. 2009), which built on an earlier paper by one of the present authors (Ingene and Coughlan 2007), showed that a prisoners' dilemma can exist over a broad range of demand curves, including ones in which brands are vertical strategic substitutes (VSS), complements (VSC), or both VSC and VSS (depending on prices).[11] Unlike this chapter, Dong et al. (2009) assumed that two products are always sold and that the products have symmetric demands. They did not derive their demand from an underlying utility function, they did not report consumer's surplus, and they did not query the impact of promotion.

Since retailers only carry products that they anticipate as profit generating, it is important to determine if retailers use category or brand pricing. Kök et al. (2009) found that category pricing is common, at least for larger retailers. But what else drives a retailer's decision to stock a new product? Everdingen et al. (2011) examined antecedents of a Dutch supermarket chain's product-adoption decisions. They found adoption probability to be positively related to (i) expected gross margin relative to the average gross margin in the category; (ii) expected trade support (e.g., slotting fees); (iii) anticipated category growth; and (iv) perceived product uniqueness. In our terms, (i) and (ii) relate to the retailer's expected margin (slotting fees raise the margin); (iii) reflects anticipated growth in $A_i$ and $A_j$; and (iv) is a measure of expected $\chi$.

### 11.7.2.2 New Products Introduced by Retailers

As store brands have become increasingly popular, marketers have begun asking "How should a retailer position its store brand when it also sells established national brands?" Choi and Coughlan (2006) used an analytical model to examine optimal positioning of a private label brand relative to two national brands that are differentiated on the basis of quality and features, where the former is treated as "more is better" and the latter is regarded as having a finite ideal point; for example, flavor of tea. With feature differentiation between the national brands, they found that a high- (low-)quality private label should be positioned closer to the national brand with greater (lesser) demand; but if national brands have identical features, a private label should offer different features, with differentiation proportional to the private label's relative quality. Like our model, Choi and Coughlan (2006) use a representative consumer to derive demand. In our terminology, features are "product variants"; since we did not examine this wrinkle, the Choi-Coughlan paper should be regarded as complementary to ours. However, their national brand manufacturers sell only a single brand, while their retailer sells three brands using category pricing, so they do not find a prisoners' dilemma, nor do they ask if the retailer *should* introduce a private label, or if it should drop one of the national brands.

Chung and Lee (2009) examined a retailer's product quality decision for store brand(s). The retailer seeks to maximize its profit from the product category: the national brand(s) and the store brand. Manufacturers' quality decisions are driven by balancing product cannibalization against product differentiation, while the retailer is also concerned with its share of category profits. As the relative magnitudes of these factors vary with the distribution of consumer quality consciousness, optimal store brand quality should vary by product category. Unlike our work, they model consumers as heterogeneous in quality. What is uninvestigated is the prospect of manufacturers redesigning their brand quality in response to store brand entry.

### 11.7.2.3  Network Externalities

The success of new products ultimately depends on consumers' acceptance of them. Thus, successful innovation must understand customer needs and then develop products that meet those needs. Direct or indirect network externalities may influence consumers' acceptance of new products. Direct network externalities increase a product's value as the number of users of the product rises. A classic example is the telephone; a more recent example is an online social network. In both cases, the more users there are, the more useful the network is.

Indirect network externalities raise the value of a product due to the availability of related products. One example is computer software and hardware; they form a system, so the supply of software and the demand for hardware affect each other's demands. An indirect network effect entails a specific temporal pattern, giving rise to the "chicken-and-egg" paradox: consumers wait to adopt hardware until enough software is available; software-creators delay designing software until enough consumers have adopted the hardware (Caillaud and Jullien 2003).

How do network externalities affect the diffusion rate and the consequent economic value of a new product? Conventional wisdom suggests that it should drive faster market growth due to a bandwagon effect (Rohlfs 2001). For example, the adoption of Microsoft Word by a small fraction of the population may have enhanced its utility and triggered diffusion. Conversely, network externalities may also create initially slow growth because potential customers wait for early adopters, who are needed for later adopters to obtain sufficient utility to themselves be willing to adopt (Goldenberg et al. 2010). Using an agent-based model, an aggregate-level model, and separating network effects from word of mouth, Goldenberg et al. (2010) found that network externalities have a substantial chilling effect on the net present value of new products.

### 11.7.2.4  Potential Avenues for Future Research

There are several potential avenues for future research. First, one might follow the lead of Choi and Coughlan (2006) by investigating the decisions at manufacture and retail with two versus three brands. A key question would be whether there is a stable equilibrium at two brands, or if three brands are inevitable. Importantly, with three or more brands, the degree of differentiation between the $i$th and $j$th brands need not equal that between the $j$th and $k$th, or the $i$th and $k$th. Second, one might endogenize the $\chi$ − value that separates categories. Doing so may ameliorate, and might eliminate, the prisoners' dilemma that we find. Third, one might explore other channel structures, such as one manufacturer offering two brands to two retailers.

Fourth, marketing analyses tend to treat the Internet as an alternative distribution channel that competes with bricks-and-mortar retailers. While there is this aspect to the Internet, it does not tap into the Internet's unique aspects; we highlight five aspects:

(1) The Internet effectively aggregates demand across geographic areas, so product demands that were too small to be served by a local merchant may be satisfied by an online retailer. This may lead to some products that previously were available only in the largest cities to be available everywhere; it may even enable products that could not economically be sold anywhere to become available everywhere. In either case, some monies that would have been spent locally will shift to the Internet, potentially diminishing the number of products that can be offered by local merchants.

(2) Online distribution can also reduce the trial cost of marketing new products, thus allowing for more new products into a market.

(3) The Internet provides online information, as well as information exchange among consumers, so it may alter consumers' product-adoption decisions. This raises the question of how firms can leverage social network effects when they introduce new products. It also offers an interactive platform that may be employed to allow consumers to cocreate new products.

(4) The Internet allows manufacturers to disintermediate by marketing their products directly to consumers.

(5) A multichannel retailer's online "store" may affect its adoption of new products. Because inventory holding costs are lower, and stock-turns are apt to be faster online than offline, a new product that is nonviable for a bricks-and-mortar store may be acceptable online, so a multichannel retailer may sell the item online only— or, if the manufacturer offers quantity discounts, it may also offer the product in its stores when it would not have done so without having multiple channels.

## 11.8 ACKNOWLEDGEMENT

This chapter builds on a mathematical foundation laid by Ingene and Coughlan (2007). That paper did not address promotion. The most recent version (Coughlan and Ingene 2011), which is under review, focuses on a decentralized channel with a manufacturer-Stackelberg leader; it does not cover the optimal number of brands in a category, nor most of the issues that follow from the stylized facts that set the stage for this chapter (although Figure 11.4 appears in the 2011 version).

## NOTES

1. Marketers use the term *coordinated* to denote a decentralized channel that sets the same prices and sells the same quantities as a vertically integrated channel. An uncoordinated channel is generally believed to underperform a vertically integrated/coordinated channel.

2. The marketing literature uses the language "product-line pricing" (we call this CP) and non-product-line pricing (we call this BP). Conventional language fails to draw a distinction

between product categories, brands, and variants within a brand. Note that within FPCG categories, each brand typically has product variants that are highly substitutable (as with Powerade). In some cases they also carry complementary products (as with shampoos and conditioners). Brand management (with its associated BP) was developed at Procter & Gamble (P&G) in the early 1930s (McCraw 2000); P&G shifted to category management (with its associated CP) in the mid-1980s (Freeman 1987).

3. All square footage figures (except King Kullen) are directly from, or are calculated from, corporate 10-K reports.

4. A simplified version of demand system (11.3) is used widely in marketing channels research (e.g., McGuire and Staelin 1983; Choi 1991; Ingene and Parry 1995; Lee and Staelin 1997); in particular, it is not unusual to see $A_i = A_j$ and $B = 1$.

5. As it operates solely as a shift factor, we standardize $B\left(Q_i^{One^*}\right)^2$ to unity in Figure 11.1 and all subsequent Figures.

6. Suave shampoo references are from Albion (1994); later ones are from http://taglineguru.com/survey05.html.

7. Promotion might also impact the rate of change of marginal utility, $B$. In the interests of parsimony, we set aside this complication.

8. One might argue that the Wendy's and Apple campaigns affected base demand as well as brand substitutability.

9. Their focal product was a handheld power tool.

10. Throughout this section we label the current product the $i$th product and the potential entrant the $j$th product.

11. VSS demand gives a unique, finite price; VSC demand means that quantity demanded is positive as price goes to infinity; this seems implausible, at least for frequently purchased consumer goods.

## References

Albion, M. 1994. "Suave (C)." Case Number 585019-PDF-ENG, revised October 19, 1994. Cambridge, MA: Harvard Business School Publishing.

Caillaud, Bernard, and Bruno Jullien. 2003. "Chicken & Egg: Competition among Intermediation Service Providers." *The RAND Journal of Economics* 34 (2): 309–28.

Choi, S. C. 1991. "Price Competition in a Channel Structure with a Common Retailer." *Marketing Science* 10:271–96.

Choi, S. C., and A. Coughlan. 2006. "Private Label Positioning: Quality versus Feature Differentiation from the National Brand." *Journal of Retailing* 82:79–93.

Chung, H., and E. Lee. 2009. *"Store Brand Quality and Retailer's Product Line Design."* Mimeo, Whitman School of Business, Syracuse University, Syracuse, NY.

Corstjens, J., and M. Corstjens. 1995. *Store Wars: The Battle for Mindspace and Shelfspace.* Wiley: Chichester.

Coughlan, A., and C. Ingene. 2011. "Product-Line Pricing: Its Impact on Horizontal and Vertical Externalities in Distribution Channels." Working paper, University of Mississippi, Oxford, MS.

Dong, L., C. Narasimhan, and K. Zhu. 2009. "Product Line Pricing in a Supply Chain." *Management Science* 55 (10): 1704–17.

Everdingen, Y., L. Sloot, E. van Nierop, and P. B. Verhoef. 2011. "Towards a Further Understanding of the Antecedents of Retailer New Product Adoption." *Journal of Retailing* 87:579–97.

Freeman, L. 1987. "P&G Widens Power Base; Adds Category Managers." *Advertising Age* 58, October 12.

Goldenberg, Jacob, Barak Libai, and Eitan Muller. 2010. "The Chilling Effects of Network Externalities." *International Journal of Research in Marketing* 27:4–15.

Ingene, C. A., and A. Coughlan. 2007. "Product-Line Pricing: Optimum or Pessimum." Working paper, University of Mississippi, Oxford, MS.

Ingene, C. A., and M. Parry. 1995. "Channel Coordination When Retailers Compete." *Marketing Science* 14 (Fall): 360–77.

Ingene, C. A., S. Taboubi, and G. Zaccour. 2012. "Game-Theoretic Coordination Mechanisms in Distribution Channels: Integration and Extensions for Models without Competition." *Journal of Retailing 88 (4): 476–96.*

Jeuland, A., and S. Shugan. 1983. "Managing Channel Profits." *Marketing Science* 2 (Summer): 239–72.

Kök, G., L. F. Marshall, and R. Vaidyanathan. 2009. "Assortment Planning: Review of Literature and Industry Practice." In *Retail Supply Chain Management*, edited by N. Agrawal and S. Smith, 99–153. Amsterdam: Kluwer Academic Publishers.

Lee, E., and R. Staelin. 1997. "Vertical Strategic Interaction: Implications for Channel Pricing Strategy." *Marketing Science* 16 (Fall): 185–207.

Luo, L., P. K. Kannan, and B. Ratchford. 2007. "New Product Development under Channel Acceptance." *Marketing Science* 26 (March–April): 149–63.

McCraw, T. 2000. *American Business, 1920–2000: How It Worked.* Wheeling, IL, and Lancaster, UK: Harlan Davidson.

McGuire, T., and R. Staelin. 1983. "An Industry Equilibrium Analysis of Downstream Vertical Integration." *Marketing Science* 2 (Spring): 161–92.

Moorthy, K. S. 1984. "Market Segmentation, Self-Selection, and Product Line Design." *Marketing Science* 3 (Fall): 288–307.

——. 1988. "Product and Price Competition in a Duopoly." *Marketing Science* 7 (Spring): 141–68.

Rohlfs, J. 2001. *Bandwagon Effects in High-Technology Industries.* Cambridge, MA: MIT Press.

Spengler, J. 1950. "Vertical Integration and Antitrust Policy." *Journal of Political Economy* 58 (August): 347–52.

Subramanian, U., J. Raju, S. Dhor, and Y. Wong. 2010. "Competitive Consequences of Using a Category Captain." *Management Science* 56 (October): 1739–65.

Urban, G. L., and J. R. Hauser. 1993. *Design and Marketing of New Products.* Upper Saddle River, NJ: Prentice-Hall.

Villas-Boas, M. 1998. "Product Line Design for a Distribution Channel." *Marketing Science* 17 (2): 156–69.

Zenor, M. 1994. "The Profit Benefits of Category Management." *Journal of Marketing Research* 31 (May): 202–13.

# PART V

## STRATEGY AND BUSINESS COMPETITION

# CHAPTER 12

# MARKET IMPERFECTIONS AND SUSTAINABLE COMPETITIVE ADVANTAGE

FELIX OBERHOLZER-GEE
AND DENNIS A. YAO[1]

## 12.1 INTRODUCTION

IN many social sciences, scholars share a common frame of reference that helps orient their field. In economics, the model of perfect competition in which companies earn zero economic profits constitutes one such frame. By contrast, the shared framework in strategic management differs radically from that in economics. A fundamental premise within the strategy field is that companies' financial performances vary widely with some organizations earning supranormal profits even in the long run. Strategy scholars seek to identify the sources of these profits and to develop advice on how to attain and sustain them.

Broadly speaking, the strategy literature can be divided into three schools of thought regarding the key sources of supranormal profits. The first school emphasizes the structure of markets and firms' positions in this structure (Porter 1980), while the second and third schools focus on firm-internal resources over which companies exercise control (Wernerfelt 1984) and the bounded rationality of actors (Cyert and March 1963), respectively. Each school emphasizes a different primary locus of profitability. One locus is external to the firm, one is internal to companies, and one is rooted in cognition and organizational learning.

In this essay, we argue that a theory of market imperfections constitutes a useful complement to these three views of strategic management. Each of the strategy schools ultimately describes instances in which markets remain less than perfectly competitive and have, to varying degrees, implicitly addressed market imperfections. An explicit market-imperfection lens, we contend, sharpens our insights regarding the mechanisms that promote superior profitability.[2] This approach also highlights connections between the strategy literature and work in industrial organization, contract theory, and economics more broadly. Finally, the analysis of market imperfections suggests a practical way for managers to assess their business environment and identify sources of competitive advantage.

The next Section describes the field of strategic management and its generally accepted principles. Section 12.3 then introduces the market imperfections framework and discusses how it can illuminate the sources of competitive advantage. In section 12.4, we discuss a general process that allows both scholars and managers to identify potential sources of competitive advantage. Section 12.5 briefly addresses the primary differences in perspectives taken by strategy and industrial organization and is followed by a section that illustrates some recent research that crosses the boundaries between the two fields. Section 12.7 concludes.

## 12.2  WHAT IS STRATEGY?

A company's strategy is an integrated set of choices that specifies the industries in which a firm will operate and how it will compete (Porter 1980, 1996). Strategists seek to formulate and implement plans that enable their organizations to outperform companies in the same industry over the longer term. A strategic plan is considered successful if it allows the company to earn a sustainable price premium or to occupy a favorable cost position.

The academic strategy field combines insights from business policy, organizational behavior, and general management. Early strategy work liberally applied ideas from economics, and industrial organization in particular, to questions of strategy (Ghemawat 2002). More recently, strategy has drawn upon sociology. Along with the changes in disciplinary focus, strategy scholars explored more varied sources of sustainable competitive advantage. While early work emphasized market structure as the main driver of differences in financial performance across companies, more recent theories emphasize the resources that are internal to the firm and the cognitive abilities and limitations of senior managers.

While there are many approaches to strategic management, practitioners and academics agree on several underlying principles.[3]

First, in almost every segment of the economy, significant and persistent differences in profitability between companies exist. Moreover, as Figure 12.1 illustrates, the most profitable companies consistently earn returns that exceed their cost of capital. As the returns on invested capital in Figure 12.1 are five-year averages, these supranormal profits reflect more than fleeting competitive advantages. They mirror firms' strategic choices.

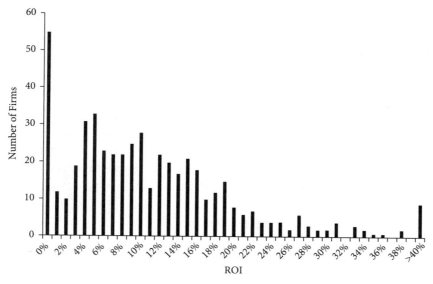

**FIGURE 12.1** Frequency Distribution of Average ROI for S & P 500 Companies 2007–2011

Second, companies that outperform their rivals create more value, whether by raising customer willingness-to-pay or by lowering supplier willingness-to-sell. "Added
value" of some sort is a necessary condition for value capture and superior performance
(Brandenburger and Stuart 1996, 2007).

Third, strategic management is distinct from operational excellence (Porter 1996).
The latter moves the firm to the efficiency frontier which allows it to produce a given set
of products or services at minimum cost. Strategic decisions, by contrast, are broader.
They specify how the firm will add value for its customers, suppliers, and companies
producing complements.

Fourth, managers and strategy scholars agree on the importance of aligning a
firm's organization and activities with its strategy. Building on the pioneering work of
Lawrence and Lorsch (1967), there is substantial evidence that high-performing organizations distinguish themselves by closely aligning activities and strategic choices (Porter
1980). According to this view, no one right way to organize exists. Rather, a company's
organization and system of activities need to match its strategic position. Consider, for
example, Industria de Diseño Textil (Inditex), the fashion house that owns the Zara
brand. Inditex makes a series of organizational and operational choices that defy conventional industry practices (Ghemawat and Nueno 2006). For instance, the company is
vertically integrated into production; it owns manufacturing and distribution facilities
in high-cost Spain; and it advertises little. Each of these choices is grounded in Inditex's
strategy for Zara. Zara is a fast follower of forward fashion trends. It pursues a strategy
of limited production runs that reduce the need for sales and that generate a substantial price premium. Zara achieves the operational flexibility that is required to quickly
produce fashionable clothes and accessories by vertically integrating into production in

close proximity to its major European markets. The chain advertises comparatively little because its stores, located in premier locations, attract curious shoppers who are eager to snap up the limited production volumes. As the example illustrates, Inditex's choices create added value in the context of its strategy for Zara, but its practices are not a general blueprint for success in the fashion industry.

Fifth, many strategists agree that there are three main sources of competitive advantage: market structure and the firm's position in this structure, resources and capabilities, as well as limits to rationality. There is an ongoing debate as to the relative importance of these sources, but the available empirical evidence suggests that each of them can help illuminate persistent differences in financial performance (Hoopes et al. 2003; McGahan and Porter 2002; Rumelt 1991). We briefly describe each of the approaches and identify key aspects of these schools of thought.

## 12.2.1  Market Structure and Competitive Positions

Building on insights from industrial organization, Michael Porter's (1980) work is foundational for understanding the effects of market structure on strategy and variation in financial performance. His five-forces framework—the idea that companies compete for rents with buyers, suppliers, current and future rivals, as well as substitute products—promotes a broad view of competition. Under this approach, companies are in contention not only with rival firms but also with suppliers and buyers. A superior bargaining position vis-à-vis these players is one source of competitive advantage. Porter (1980, 1996) emphasizes industry structure and firm positioning as reasons why rents associated with superior competitive positions are not competed away. Barriers to entry, for example, may be high in industries characterized by large fixed costs. In addition, many competitively superior positions are protected by trade-offs. As such, imitating a rival, while technically feasible, may not be attractive to companies if imitation forces them to serve their current customers less effectively. Consider the example of Commerce Bank (Frei 2006). Commerce entered retail banking with a value proposition that emphasized friendly customer service. It funded its investment in service by offering low deposit rates and by keeping its product portfolio very simple. As a result, it attracted a specific set of customers who valued service highly but were not sensitive to rates. Rival banks found it difficult to imitate Commerce. Their customers valued friendliness, of course, but many of them were unwilling to forgo superior rates or a broader range of products. Trade-offs such as these help protect accrued rents.

## 12.2.2  Resources and Capabilities

According to the resource-based view of strategic management (Wernerfelt 1984; Peteraf 1993), superior competitive positions are built on valuable resources and the capabilities that are developed around them. The Walt Disney Company's control of its cartoon characters, for example, allows the organization to successfully compete in movies, theme parks, hotels, and cruise ships. Resources such as Mickey Mouse are valuable because they are scarce and difficult to imitate. Building on its cartoon characters, Disney developed a distinctive set of capabilities such as its ability to cross-sell products across many industries and markets (Rukstad et al. 2009). To confer a true competitive advantage, the cost of creating resources and building associated capabilities must not exceed their market value (Barney 1986).

### 12.2.3  Cognitive Limitations

A third research tradition in strategic management explores the implications of bounded rationality. For example, evolutionary economics emphasized organizational routines and the difficulties associated with acquiring and transmitting knowledge within and across companies (Nelson and Winter 1982). More recent work focuses on patterns of cognition that make identifying distant business opportunities challenging (Gavetti 2012). Because it is difficult to spot new business opportunities, the prices of some resources in the economy will not accurately reflect their market values. Companies that appreciate possible future uses of these resources can acquire them below market value and generate supranormal profits. For example, Southwest Airlines recognized early on the value of offering point-to-point service between underutilized secondary airports. By the time Southwest's rivals and new entrants recognized the value of service from a secondary airport, Southwest's competitive position was secured by long-term contracts and network effects (Oberholzer-Gee et al. 2007).

## 12.3  MARKET IMPERFECTIONS

Each proposed source of competitive advantage, as represented in the various schools of strategy thought, must explain why created value is not competed away. The value of the market imperfections framework that is developed in this Section is that it directly addresses the competition problem by focusing on a small set of underlying conditions under which competition is impaired.

Before discussing how market imperfections link to competitive advantage, it is useful to introduce Brandenburger and Stuart's (1996) notion of value-based strategy. Figure 12.2 represents a "value stick," which is a simple graph indicating a company's competitive position. The difference between customer willingness-to-pay (WTP) and supplier willingness-to-sell (WTS), both of which represent the opportunity cost of these parties, is the total value created by the firm. The difference between WTP and price reflects consumer rent. Analogously, the difference between cost and WTS represents supplier margins. Note that the value stick depicts a representative customer and supplier, suppressing heterogeneity (and its strategic consequences) within these

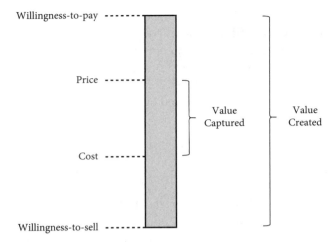

**FIGURE 12.2** The Value Stick Representation

groups. The fraction of value that companies capture is the difference between price and cost.

This simple representation highlights two sources of competitive advantage: a superior ability to create value and a favorable bargaining position vis-à-vis customers or suppliers. The conditions assumed in the benchmark economic model (complete markets and complete information; see, e.g., Arrow and Hahn 1971) imply that supranormal profits or supplier rents would attract entry and drive prices down to the level associated with efficient markets. Persistent competitive advantages, therefore, reflect some sort of market imperfection.

Three types of imperfections tend to be particularly important in creating opportunities for superior financial performance: market power, information imperfections, and transaction costs. Each of these imperfections is the result of market characteristics that deviate from the standard efficient market model. For instance, market power exists in the presence of production economies and demand-side network externalities. Information imperfections characterize many real-world situations, including, for example, instances in which customers have difficulty assessing the quality of products and services. Transaction costs associated with verifying various types of contingencies may interfere with contracting between parties. Whenever such market imperfections are present, firms can take strategic actions that may result in supranormal profits. For instance, first-mover advantages may accrue to companies that compete in environments with significant network externalities. Similarly, brand building is particularly valuable when the quality of products is difficult to ascertain. Table 12.1 provides an overview of the structural characteristics of markets and technologies that produce imperfections along with some implications of these imperfections for strategy.[4]

Market imperfections, we argue, are the primary reasons why industry leaders can sustain superior financial performance. In fact, it is possible to interpret the history of research in strategic management as the identification and exploration of important

### Table 12.1  Market Imperfections and Strategic Opportunities

| Category of Market Imperfection | Sources | Implications for Strategy |
|---|---|---|
| Market Power | Production economies Scale Scope Learning Network externalities Intellectual property protection Access to undervalued scarce resources | Reduces number of viable competitors Supports differentiation and exploitation of switching costs Sustains value to innovation Increases value to early mover or pre-emptive actions or investments Increases value of related product lines (scope) Increases value to control of standard (network) |
| Information Imperfections | Buyer inability to assess quality Buyer or seller inability to observe relevant actions of other party Rival inability to imitate | Supports value of brand, reputation, informative advertising, or other signaling-related actions Increases value of long-term relationships and relational contracts Sustains advantages due to tacit knowledge (e.g.,organizational culture) or innovation |
| Transaction Costs | Costs associated with market exchange inability to specify or verify contingencies inability to prevent unauthorized use | Interferes with contracting solutions May increase local market power May interfere with markets to provide information Factors into make versus buy choice |

reasons why market imperfections arise and persist. Porter's framework, for instance, describes circumstances under which firms have market power vis-à-vis suppliers and customers. The resource-based view of strategy emphasizes the difficulty of trading scarce resources in markets. These difficulties are often rooted in information asymmetries and transaction costs.

We believe that there are substantial advantages to analyzing strategic opportunities through the lens of market imperfections as opposed to the traditional strategy frameworks. This is more than a question of language and analytic convenience. Many of the commonly used strategy frameworks are analytically imprecise and may lead managers and scholars to suspect strategic opportunities where none exist and to ignore real business prospects (Yao 1988). We illustrate the advantages of the market imperfections lens by comparing the analysis of two potential sources of competitive advantage, high fixed costs and a reputation for quality, with and without the imperfections framework.

The presence of high fixed costs can act as a barrier to entry that supports supranormal profits (Porter 1980). But not every instance of fixed costs leads to such profits. Wal-Mart Stores, Inc., offers an illustrative example. The company invests significant sums in its IT systems. These systems provide suppliers with superior information about the local demand for products (Oberholzer-Gee 2008). Because it is less expensive to supply Wal-Mart compared to other companies, supplier WTS declines (see Figure 12.2) and Wal-Mart can lower its cost without hurting supplier margins. However, if investments in IT generate excess returns, an efficiency-based view of markets would lead us to expect that competing companies will quickly introduce similar systems. Importantly, the fixed cost of IT can be spread across the entire US market, making it likely that several competitors can reach minimum efficient scale. This analysis suggests that investments in IT can produce short-term rents. But it is more difficult to understand how IT alone might result in a lasting competitive advantage. By contrast, a second type of fixed costs, Wal-Mart's investments in logistics, are much more difficult to replicate. These investments generate significant economies of density (Holmes 2011). Because these fixed costs are local in nature—they can only be spread across the local volume of sales—rural markets, Wal-Mart's home base, are often not large enough to justify a rival's investment in superior logistics. As a consequence, Wal-Mart can raise prices in smaller markets where it faces rivals with a cost disadvantage or no rivals at all (Bradley et al. 2002). The comparison of these two types of fixed costs suggests that it is the combination of economies of scale and limited market size that generates sustainable excess returns. This example illustrates why a focus on market imperfections yields a more precise and nuanced analysis. It highlights the circumstances under which fixed costs do in fact constitute a market imperfection. A particular entry barrier, fixed cost in the forgoing example, constitutes a source of superior returns only if it represents a true market imperfection.

Now consider a reputation for quality as a potential source of supranormal profits. Such a reputation is seen by the resource-based view of the firm as a valuable resource in part because it cannot easily be traded in existing markets (Dierickx and Cool 1989; Peteraf 1993). Reputation can generate sustainable supranormal returns particularly in markets characterized by imperfect information. Consider the example of a bank that compensates a star trader at less than her full market value. Ordinarily, the trader would leave the organization to join a better-paying rival. However, if it is difficult for the rival bank to know if the trader's reputation rests on her unique trading skills or on superior research provided to her by the bank's analysts, the rival may hesitate to make a better offer. In this example, the reason that reputation cannot easily be traded does not reflect the properties of reputation. Rather it is the information asymmetry that allows the employer to pay less than the trader's marginal product. Remove the asymmetry such that the rival bank knows that the trader has superior skills and the current employer loses its competitive advantage.

As these examples demonstrate, popular strategic advice—e.g., hide behind barriers to entry or build a superior reputation—is often imprecise in that such strategic actions will be successful only if a specific set of conditions holds. These conditions characterize true market imperfections. Typically, two or more imperfections work together to sustain competitive advantage. Efforts to develop a valuable brand provide a good example. Branding appears to contribute unequally to the profitability of firms. Coca-Cola's brand, valued at $71 billion (Interbrand 2011), has greatly contributed to the company's financial performance. By contrast, the brands of many automakers do not seem to translate into comparable financial performance. The reason is not that the companies lack marketing skills or valuable brands. Ford's brand, for example, was valued at $7 billion in 2011 which places it in the top fifty worldwide. But Coke's brand is of much greater strategic value than is Ford's. Coke's (and Pepsi's) marketing expenditures increase industry fixed costs to a level that makes entry into the branded cola market unattractive. This, in turn, results in a market that is less than perfectly competitive and protects high prices for colored sugar water (Yoffie and Kim 2010). By contrast, the high fixed costs associated with marketing automobiles are not as effective in deterring entry (e.g., Hyundai), primarily because the relative size of the fixed costs as a fraction of sales is not as large. Thus, one of the rationales for building a brand, deterring entry, applies better to the cola industry than to the automobile industry. Marketing expenditures constitute a much more significant imperfection in the former market than in the latter.

## 12.4  A Process to Identify Competitive Advantage

The foregoing discussion underscores the overall need for, and the specific characteristics of, a simple inquiry that will help identify competitive advantage and assess strategic opportunities. The inquiry is two-fold: the first step involves the identification of the distinctive value the firm delivers to buyers and suppliers. The second step assesses how that distinctiveness can be sustained. We begin by isolating the firm's relative distinctiveness to its customers and its suppliers. In essence, we ask how a specific company's value stick in Figure 12.2 differs from the typical value stick in the industry. Firms might have an advantage in creating value (higher WTP and lower WTS), or they might capture a greater fraction of the value they create.

Generally, strategy scholars believe that a firm's distinctiveness, and hence competitive advantage, will fall largely into the WTP/price *or* the WTS/cost categories. Achieving distinctiveness in both categories is difficult because raising WTP/price involves an activity system within the firm that usually cannot also optimally support lower WTS/costs. Porter (1980), for example, suggests three generic strategies: an industry-wide differentiation strategy (corresponding to emphasizing increased relative WTP/price), an industry-wide low-cost strategy (corresponding to a WTS/cost advantage), and a focus strategy that caters to particular customer segments (corresponding to offering superior value to a segment of buyers relative to the offerings made by industry-wide competitors).[5] Firms that try to achieve both differentiation and low costs while serving the entire market are seen as "stuck in the middle" and are typically outcompeted by those pursuing more specialized strategies.

Step two in the suggested analysis addresses the sustainability of the isolated advantage. The market imperfections identified in Table 12.1 provide a useful way to analyze the sustainability question. Basically, one examines whether the distinctive features of a firm's offerings depend on market imperfections. If this is not the case, the competitive advantage is likely to be transitory. An examination of the returns on investment over time reveals a strong reversion to the mean which suggests that the category of sustainable excess returns is relatively limited (Figure 12.3).

One can assess a strategic opportunity using a variant of the two-step analysis. First, the strategic opportunity is analyzed in terms of the value that it creates. In Figure 12.4,

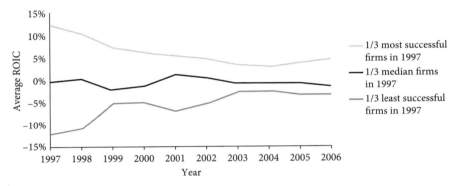

**FIGURE 12.3** Mean Reversion in Returns - Return on Invested Capital of S&P 500 Firms

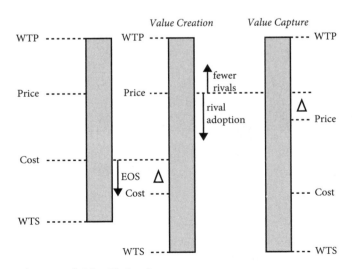

**FIGURE 12.4** Adoption of a New Technology

for example, we consider the adoption of a new technology. This new technology reduces costs, thereby adding value to the market. We ask next whether the added value can be captured and sustained. This step links advantage to specific market imperfections and inquires whether the advantages identified in step one are sustainable or are likely to be undermined by imitation. In the example of a new cost-reducing technology, key questions include whether the new technology is an opportunity for new entry and whether current rivals can profitably adopt the technology. The answers to these questions address whether a market imperfection prevents competition from undermining value. With respect to entry, suppose the new technology exhibited strong economies of scale relative to previous technologies and these economies were not exhausted until production volumes equivalent to a substantial fraction of the market demand were reached. Market power, as augmented by this technology, would make some value capture sustainable. In contrast, if the new generation of technology exhibited less economies of scale than the previous generation, competition would increase and incremental value capture would decrease. Figure 12.4 depicts circumstances in which the new technology increases economies of scale. In the value capture part of the figure, the new technology reduces costs through both the underlying cost reduction innovation and through larger economies of scale. The middle bar shows the effect of this technology before accounting for rival reactions (and possible own price changes). The value capture part of the figure shows the market effect of the new technology: greater economies of scale reduce the number of rivals, which is shown as a force leading to higher price. At the same time, existing rivals are able to adopt a variant of the technology—full adoption is assumed here to be impeded by an information imperfection—which creates more competition and pushes price lower.

Having explored the ability of rival firms to replicate the focal firm's competitive advantage, a third step is to assess whether government regulators (or other third parties) might act to limit the market imperfection (see Oberholzer-Gee and Yao (2012a, 2012b) for a fuller discussion of this point). If this is not the case, the focal firm is likely to enjoy a sustainable competitive advantage and supranormal profits.

## 12.5 Strategic Management and Industrial Organization

The market imperfections framework we develop in this essay is, of course, part of a long tradition of applying the models and methods of microeconomics and industrial organization to the theory and practice of strategic management. Michael Porter's work is perhaps the best-known example of economics' influence on strategy. The close connections between economics and strategy notwithstanding, there are important differences between the two fields, three of which warrant particular consideration.

### 12.5.1 Frame of Reference

In economics, the model of perfect competition in which companies earn zero economic profits constitutes the standard frame of reference. Observing superior performance, economists are trained to expect that market forces will eventually erode profit differences across firms. By contrast, in strategic management, the starting point is that many organizations earn supranormal profits even in the long run. Markets are typically seen as imperfect, which makes the imitation of successful firms more challenging.

### 12.5.2 Relevant Decision Maker

Research in industrial organization typically adopts the perspective of the benevolent social planner who is interested in the welfare implications of company decisions and market interventions. The focus in strategic management is narrower, and it emphasizes the generation of rents by companies. As a result, the integration of government actions into strategy frameworks has been quite difficult. Although government can have a decisive influence on industry and firm profitability, in practice as well as in scholarly strategy work, governments and nongovernmental organizations typically remain an afterthought (Oberholzer-Gee and Yao 2012b).

### 12.5.3 Heterogeneity

Strategists are concerned with differences across companies. By contrast, the mean effects of strategic decisions and policy interventions are the main concern in industrial organization. Economic studies that consider heterogeneity across companies often consider broad categories such as incumbents and entrants or first-movers and laggards.

## 12.6 CONNECTIONS BETWEEN ECONOMICS RESEARCH AND STRATEGY RESEARCH

The differences in perspective Section 12.5 identified pose both opportunities and challenges to cross-pollination between the two fields. Four examples of such cross-pollination will be explored. The first two examples, relational contracts and the market for ideas, illustrate how recent ideas developed in economics have resonance in strategy. We then discuss two formal economic analyses that are closely related to and inspired by strategy and management work on disruptive technologies and the resource-based view of the firm, respectively. Notwithstanding the nature of these four examples (two in each direction), to date the vast majority of the direct influence has taken the form of economics informing strategy rather than vice-versa, though the latter (strategy informing economics) has also begun to occur.

Research on relational contracts illustrates how economic theory continues to inform questions of strategy. Relational contracts are informal agreements and unwritten codes of conduct that influence the behavior of managers and firms (Bull 1987; for a survey, see Malcomson 2012). In a recent contribution, Gibbons and Henderson (2012) argue that relational contracting helps explain why competitively valuable practices can be well understood and yet diffuse slowly. For example, science-driven drug discovery has diffused slowly even though managers clearly understood the benefits of this approach. According to Gibbons and Henderson, this practice requires the formulation and enforcement of a relational contract between companies and their employees. These contracts are difficult to establish because companies have to solve the twin problems of clarity and credibility. Senior managers need to communicate clearly the nature of the relational contract—what does it mean for Merck's researchers to behave "almost as if" they were academics? The managers also need to make the company's promises credible—what are the consequences if Merck's researchers do in fact behave "almost as if" they were academics? In our approach, clarity refers to an information asymmetry; the desired behavior is difficult to articulate. Credibility, on the other hand, is an issue of transaction costs in the sense that all relevant contingencies are impossible to predict, much less verify. Gibbons and Henderson argue that the dual problems of clarity and credibility, and in particular their interaction, help explain why managers often face great difficulty imitating practices that would yield a competitive advantage. Due to these market imperfections, Merck's science-based drug discovery remained the source of superior financial performance over long periods of time.

Economics research regarding the market for ideas provides another example of how insights from microeconomics can be applied to strategy. The basic problem this area addresses is how an idea, which must be revealed to be valued, can be sold when potential buyers are able to freely expropriate it (Arrow 1962). The market for ideas suffers from an information imperfection and a transaction costs imperfection. The information imperfection is that the value of the idea is the private knowledge of the seller. The transaction costs imperfection is that the seller cannot prevent those who learn the idea from using it. Anton and Yao (1994) suggest that this conundrum can partially be solved if the seller fully reveals the idea to one potential buyer (thereby solving the information imperfection) and then "blackmails" the potential buyer into paying the seller not to reveal the idea to another buyer (partially solving the expropriation problem posed by the transaction costs imperfection). The potential buyer will succumb to this credible blackmail threat to preserve its monopoly use of the idea, which would otherwise be undermined if the idea were also known to a competitor. In turn, the seller should receive at least the difference between profits associated with monopoly use and profits associated with duopoly use.

The pure market for ideas problem is a polar case as the legal system affords intellectual property owners varying degrees of protection from expropriation, yet the underlying problem remains first order in a significant fraction of intellectual property settings. Hence, the insights from the market-for-ideas research have numerous implications for the strategy literature, especially regarding the flow of knowledge across firms. As an example, consider the question posed in the entrepreneurial strategy literature regarding the conditions under which an employee-inventor with a valuable, but not yet revealed, idea would exploit her idea through the firm or through a less-efficient start-up.[6] An extension of the blackmail analysis suggests that some start-ups may arise because there are not enough profits generated through the commercialization of the invention by the firm to pay the employee as much as she would obtain through a start-up, while still compensating the firm for its outside option threat of expropriating the invention and competing in a duopoly against the ensuing start-up (Anton and Yao 1995). The firm has the option of expropriation because (under the blackmail approach to solving the Arrow paradox) the invention is revealed to the firm before a contract is negotiated between the inventor and the firm. This economic incentive explanation for start-ups is, of course, nonexclusive to other explanations such as disagreement between the inventing employee and the firm management regarding the idea's value (Klepper and Sleeper 1995).

Ideas in the strategy and management field have also inspired some closely related economic analyses.[7] Adner and Zemsky (2005), for example, build an analytical model based on Christensen's (1997) informal theory of disruptive technologies, which explains why established firms may ignore promising new technologies in favor of established technologies that initially better meet the needs of the mainstream market segment. Adner and Zemsky's model allows for the emergence of competition between two differentiated technologies with characteristics and associated market segments that mirror those animating Christensen's theory. Their analysis establishes conditions under which disruption will occur and, thereby, adds precision to our understanding of Christensen's ideas. In addition, Adner and Zemsky's analysis of the effects of potentially disrupting technologies focuses attention on the boundaries of competition among old and new technologies and may, in turn, prompt a revisiting of received wisdom in other areas, such as the merger literature, which had found that efficiencies were necessary conditions for mergers to be profitable to the merging parties when market concentration postmerger was not high (see, e.g., Salant et al. 1983).

As a second example, consider work on time compression diseconomies. Such diseconomies have been identified in the conceptual literature on the resource-based view of the firm as a critical determinant of the degree to which an asset can be imitated (Dierickx and Cool 1989). Pacheco-de-Almeida and Zemsky (2007) formally develop this idea in a model that trades off the higher marginal cost associated with developing a resource more quickly (a variant of market imperfections deriving from production economies) against the value of having the resource available sooner. Pacheco-de-Almeida and Zemsky's analysis of this trade-off provides a deeper understanding of the dynamic nature of time compression diseconomies and the degree to which resources with such features are difficult to replicate. Their model also allows the authors to examine the implications of time compression diseconomies for the decision of a firm to license and the competitive effects of different levels of absorptive capacity.

# 12.7  CONCLUSION

The dominant schools in current strategy scholarship characterize the sources of competitive advantage by emphasizing market structure, resources, and the bounded rationality of managers. Because competitive advantage depends ultimately on some limit on competition, a direct focus on the forces that constrain competition is valuable. In this chapter, we argued that the lens of market imperfections provides this direct focus and, thereby, offers additional precision and reliability to existing methods of assessing competitive advantage. Furthermore, because the market imperfections approach naturally links economic theory and strategic management concepts, its use may also facilitate cross-pollination across the fields.

## NOTES

1. Harvard Business School, Boston, MA 02163; foberholzer@hbs.edu and dyao@hbs.edu. This article substantially builds on the ideas described in Oberholzer-Gee and Yao (2012a). The authors thank Hillary Greene and the editors for helpful comments and suggestions.
2. Our market imperfection framework builds on Yao (1988) which explores why a market failures perspective adds value to a barriers-to-entry approach to competitive advantage.
3. See our earlier discussion in Oberholzer-Gee and Yao (2010).
4. See, Baumol et al. (1982), Scitovsky (1950), Williamson (1975) for discussions regarding market power imperfections, information imperfections, and transaction costs, respectively, and Shapiro and Varian (1998) for the application of these ideas to the information economy.
5. Ghemawat and Rivkin (2006) suggest using the firm's activities to identify competitive advantage (e.g., purchasing). This approach highlights areas in which a firm can improve its internal alignment so that activity level choices deliver better value to the target customer.
6. Here we consider an example where if the idea is exploited through a start-up, it would be difficult for a third party to determine if the idea was discovered while the inventor was an employee of the firm or after the inventor left the firm.
7. Some papers that bridge the strategy and economics literatures are inspired by case studies (see, e.g., Casadesus-Masanell and Ghemawat (2006) and Casadesus-Masanell and Yoffie (2007)).

## REFERENCES

Adner, Ron, and Peter Zemsky. 2005. "Disruptive Technologies and the Emergence of Competition." *RAND Journal of Economics* 36:229–54.

Anton, James, and Dennis Yao. 1994. "Expropriation and Invention: Appropriable Rents in the Absence of Property Rights." *American Economic Review* 84:190–209.

——. 1995. "Start-ups, Spin-offs, and Internal Projects." *Journal of Law, Economics & Organization* 11:362–78.

Arrow, Kenneth. 1962. "Economic Welfare and the Allocation of Resources for Inventions." In *The Rate and Direction of Inventive Activity: Economic and Social Factors*, edited by R. Nelson, 609–25. Princeton, NJ: Princeton University Press.

Arrow, Kenneth, and Frank Hahn. 1971. *General Competitive Analysis*. San Francisco: Holden-Day.

Barney, Jay. 1986. "Strategic Factor Markets: Expectations, Luck, and Business Strategy." *Management Science* 32:1231–41.

Baumol, William, John Panzar, and Robert Willig. 1982. *Contestable Markets and the Theory of Industry Structure*. New York: Harcourt Brace Jovanovich.

Bradley, Stephen P., Pankaj Ghemawat, and Sharon Foley. 2002. "Wal-Mart Stores, Inc." Harvard Business School, case 794024.

Brandenburger, Adam M., and Harborne W. Stuart. 1996. "Value-Based Business Strategy." *Journal of Economics & Management Strategy* 5:5–24.

——. 2007. "Biform Games." *Management Science* 53:537–49.

Bull, C. 1987. "The Existence of Self-enforcing Implicit Contracts." *Quarterly Journal of Economics* 102:147–59.

Casadesus-Masanell, Ramon, and Pankaj Ghemawat. 2006. "Dynamic Mixed Duopoly: A Model Motivated by Linux vs. Windows." *Management Science* 52:1072–84.

Casadesus-Masanell, Ramon, and David Yoffie. 2007. "Wintel: Cooperation and Conflict." *Management Science* 53:584–98.

Christensen, Clayton. 1997. *The Innovator's Dilemma*. Boston: Harvard Business School Press.

Cyert, Richard, and James March. 1963. *A Behavioral Theory of the Firm*. Englewood Cliffs, NJ: Prentice Hall.

Dierickx, Ingemar, and Karel Cool. 1989. "Asset Stock Accumulation and Sustainability of Competitive Advantage." *Management Science* 35:1504–11.

Frei, Frances, and Corey Hajim. 2006. "Commerce Bank." Harvard Business School, case 603080.

Gavetti, Giovanni. 2012. "Toward a Behavioral Theory of Strategy." *Organization Science* 23:267–85.

Ghemawat, Pankaj. 2002. "Competition and Business Strategy in Historical Perspective." *Business History Review* 76 (Spring): 37–74.

Ghemawat, Pankaj, and Jose Luis Nueno. 2006. "ZARA: Fast Fashion." Harvard Business School, case 703497.

Ghemawat, Pankaj, and Jan Rivkin. 2006. "Creating Competitive Advantage." Harvard Business School, note 798062.

Gibbons, Robert, and Rebecca Henderson. 2012. "Relational Contracts and Organizational Capabilities." *Organization Science* 23:1350–64.

Holmes, Thomas J. 2011. "The Diffusion of Wal-Mart and Economies of Density." *Econometrica* 79:253–302.

Hoopes, David G., Tammy L. Madsen, and Gordon Walker. 2003. "Why Is There a Resource-based View? Toward a Theory of Competitive Heterogeneity." Special Issue, *Strategic Management Journal* 24:889–902.

Klepper, Steven, and Sally Sleeper. 1995. "Entry by Spinoffs." *Management Science* 51:1291–1306.

Lawrence, Paul, and Jay W. Lorsch. 1967. *Organization and Environment*. Boston: Harvard Business School Press.

Malcomson, J. M. 2012. "Relational Incentive Contracts." In *The Handbook of Organizational Economics*, edited by R. Gibbons and J. Roberts. Princeton, NJ: Princeton University Press.

McGahan, Anita M., and Michael E. Porter. 2002. "What Do We Know about Variance in Accounting Profitability?" *Management Science* 48 (7): 834–51.

Nelson, Richard, and Sidney Winter. 1982. *An Evolutionary Theory of Economic Change.* Cambridge, MA: Belknap Press.

Oberholzer-Gee, Felix. 2008. "Wal-Mart: In Search of Renewed Growth." Columbia CaseWorks, case 080408.

Oberholzer-Gee, Felix, and Dennis A. Yao. 2010. "Antitrust—What Role for Strategic Management Expertise?" *Boston University Law Review* 90:1457–77.

———. 2012a. "Strategies Beyond the Market." Harvard Business School, note 707469.

———. 2012b. "Integrated Strategies." Working Paper, Harvard Business School, Boston, MA.

Oberholzer-Gee, Felix, Dennis Yao, Libby Cantrill, and Patricia Wu. 2007. "Lobbying for Love? Southwest Airlines and the Wright Amendment." Harvard Business School, case 707470.

Pacheco-de-Almeida, Goncalo, and Peter Zemsky. 2007. "The Timing of Resource Development and Sustainable Competitive Advantage." *Management Science* 53:651–66.

Peteraf, Margaret. 1993. "The Cornerstones of Competitive Advantage: A Resource-Based View." *Strategic Management Journal* 14:179–91.

Porter, Michael E. 1980. *Competitive Strategy.* New York: Free Press.

———. 1996. "What Is Strategy?" *Harvard Business Review* November/December: 61–78.

Rukstad, Michael G., David J. Collis, and Tyrrell Levine. 2009. "Walt Disney Co.: The Entertainment King." Harvard Business School, case 701035.

Rumelt, Richard P. 1991. "How Much Does Industry Matter?" *Strategic Management Journal* 12:167–85.

Salant, Steven W., S. Switzer, and R. Reynolds. 1983. "Losses from Horizontal Merger: The Effects of an Exogenous Change in Industry Structure on Cournot-Nash Equilibrium." *Quarterly Journal of Economics* 98:185–99.

Scitovsky, Tibor. 1950. "Ignorance as a Source of Oligopoly Power." *American Economic Review* 40:48–53.

Shapiro, Carl, and Hal Varian. 1998. *Information Rules: A Strategic Guide to the Network Economy.* Boston: Harvard Business Review Press.

Wernerfelt, Birger. 1984. "A Resource-Based View of the Firm." *Strategic Management Journal* 5:171–80.

Williamson, Oliver. 1975. *Markets and Hierarchies: Analysis and Antitrust Implications.* New York: Free Press.

Yao, Dennis A. 1988. "Beyond the Reach of the Invisible Hand: Impediments to Economic Activity, Market Failures, and Profitability." *Strategic Management Journal* 9:59–70.

Yoffie, David, and Renee Kim. 2010. "Cola Wars Continue: Coke and Pepsi in 2010." Harvard Business School, case 711462.

# CHAPTER 13

# THE NEW MANAGERIAL ECONOMICS OF FIRM GROWTH: THE ROLE OF INTANGIBLE ASSETS AND CAPABILITIES

## DAVID J. TEECE[1]

## 13.1 INTRODUCTION

GROWTH in an innovation-driven company requires managers to solve two related problems. In the short term, operations must be perfected and costs minimized. In the medium-to-long term, management must direct innovative activity toward addressing new technological, market, and business model opportunities, which frequently requires transforming the organization's structure and strategy. Put differently, in the short run it's about doing things right; in the longer run it's about doing the right things. Traditional managerial economics helps a lot with the first challenge but obfuscates the second. Developing capabilities to innovate can help with the longer-run challenge without jeopardizing the first.

The long-run challenge is about much more than just investing in R&D. However large the company's R&D budget, and however talented the company's engineers and scientists, the presence of talent on the payroll won't by itself guarantee that an organization will generate or capture much of the value from innovation. Witness Nokia outspending Apple on R&D but losing to Apple in the smartphone wars. Without entrepreneurial managers,[2] the right business model, good intellectual property protection, some control over complementary assets, and of course an appealing value proposition to the customer, innovation efforts will, in terms of profits, be in vain. Good strategic management and what I call "dynamic capabilities" are important for long-run viability and financial success. An understanding of dynamic capabilities has only recently emerged as an area of interest and investigation in managerial economics.

The premise behind this chapter is that, if managerial economics is going to address innovation and growth, it must come to grips with intangible assets and capabilities. These are critical to building and maintaining competitive advantage; and, without competitive advantage, a firm is unlikely to grow. Hence, a (managerial) theory of the growth of the firm must account for the sources of competitive advantage. Many textbooks in managerial economics are silent on this.[3] Textbooks in strategic management are more likely to discuss the requirements for competitive advantage. This chapter tries to meld managerial economics and strategic management by implicitly suggesting that the two cannot be divorced.

The chapter begins by discussing intangible assets, cospecialized complements, and increasing returns, followed by an introduction to the Dynamic Capabilities framework. With these elements understood, the limited applicability of a great deal of "textbook" managerial economics can be appreciated. Subsequent sections discuss the management of key intangible assets: business models, organizational design, and intellectual property. These are largely neglected or at best poorly understood in much of the managerial economics literature. The chapter concludes with some reflections on the role of the entrepreneurial manager, a crucial agent who is nonetheless poorly represented in the mainstream economics literature.

## 13.2 HYPERCOMPETITION AND THE GROWING IMPORTANCE OF INTANGIBLE ASSETS

In the nineteenth and twentieth centuries, the assets that economists saw as sources of value were the traditional factors of production: land, labor, and capital. These still matter for national economies, but their ownership by firms does not guarantee financial success. In today's global economy, access to intermediate goods, (most) information, and investment resources is so widely available that some say the world is "flat" (Friedman 2005). In particular, intermediate goods and services that might once have been hard to access are now available "off the shelf," thus enabling a system of global specialization. But with a flatter landscape, leveled by hypercompetition (D'Aveni 1994), the capabilities required for business enterprises to orchestrate (control and coordinate) global resources remain scarce and often geographically isolated.

It is well recognized that markets in most advanced and advancing economies are more competitive than they were half a century ago—or even a generation ago.[4] Trade and investment barriers have been lowered, which has opened up markets to international commerce and ratcheted up the speed at which short-term advantages are competed away. Perhaps of even greater importance has been the global transfer of technological know-how and capabilities, not through foreign aid, but through the investment and trading activities of multinational firms, many of them initially headquartered in the United States. The end of the Cold War brought the elimination of many regulatory barriers to technology transfer. Accompanying this has been the vertical disintegration of business organizations, which led to a complementary increase in purchasing and partnering arrangements with offshore enterprises.

As a result, the relative positioning of enterprises located in developing countries with respect to technological and organizational skills has improved steadily. Changes in these countries, such as the relaxation of government ownership and central planning in China and India, has further stimulated growth in these economies, often with support from the activities of multinationals based in the United States, Europe, and elsewhere. These developments have worked together with trade liberalization championed by the United States to dramatically sharpen competition in the global economy.

As a consequence of these powerful, long-term trends, the former sources of competitive advantage encompassed in traditional managerial economics—like scale and scope economies and privileged access to raw materials—have faded in importance. If your market is too small to capture scale economies for an input—or even a whole product— you can often outsource on competitive terms with manufacturers that aggregate the demands of large and small buyers to fully take advantage of scale economies. In light of these developments, the focus of managerial economics needs to be modified.

Management was never just about achieving scale efficiency and minimizing cost. It is even less so today. Of increasing importance are the innovation and change required to achieve firm growth and survival. The most important sources of differentiation and profit now flow from the knowledge and creativity of talented individuals working cooperatively, and from the hard-to-imitate practices of successful organizations. These factors undergird the generation, ownership, and management of intangible assets. The capabilities of building and astutely managing these intangibles and their related complements have come to overshadow production-related economies of scale and scope as determinants of competitive outcomes in many contexts.

Perhaps the most identifiable class of intangible assets not commonly available, nor easily traded, is technological know-how. Know-how and other intangibles are "sticky assets" that are often semipermanently tied to other assets, which often become the "bottleneck" (least replicable/imitable) links in a product's value chain. Thus Dell's direct sales and build-to-order business model was embodied in manufacturing, distribution, and IT systems that competitors found difficult to imitate, at least for many years (Kraemer et al. 2000). Ownership (or control) of such intangibles and their complements allows innovating firms to differentiate and establish some degree of competitive advantage. They cause "hills"—and sometimes high "mountains"—to appear on otherwise flat competitive landscapes. Intangible assets are the new "natural resources" of the global economy; they underpin enterprise (and national) wealth generation capacities.

Intangible assets provide a basis for profitability because they are hard to "build" and difficult to manage. They are also unlikely to be traded (i.e., markets, if they exist, will be "thin") because their underlying value often derives from the presence of complementary assets, which reduces the number of buyers who will be willing and able to pay for the knowledge asset's full potential strategic value (i.e., without buying the entire company). Furthermore, some knowledge assets can be costly to transfer (Teece 1981).

Given these characteristics, intangible assets are harder to access than many other asset classes and must therefore usually be "built," or created, by the firm that wants them. Investment in R&D and other learning activities are the most common ways of doing so. Their creation depends on managerial action (such as resource allocation and/or contracting), on private investment, and on public investment associated with national systems of innovation (Nelson 1993).

Ironically, even in natural resource industries, profits (for the business enterprise, but not necessarily for the nation state) flow fundamentally from the ownership and use of intangibles, and much less from ownership of the (natural) resource. The highest profits flow to those firms that develop extraction technologies, deploy them effectively and safely, and build privileged relationships with nation states and other constituencies. For example, in the petroleum industry, it can be said that oil is "found" in the mind, not in the ground; locating new reserves in deep water requires both (organizationally embedded) know-how and, in many jurisdictions, relationships with nation-states to secure exploitation and production rights. Put differently, oil reserves are found using the knowledge empires of the major petroleum companies and their specialist suppliers.

In short, intangible assets are a very economically significant asset class, with powerful implications for building and maintaining competitive advantage at the enterprise and at the national levels. Table 13.1 summarizes the differences between intangible and physical assets along selected dimensions.

Another intangible asset of central importance (besides know-how) is the firm's business model—i.e., the structure of a firm's value proposition to its customers (Chesbrough and Rosenbloom 2002; Teece 2010)—and the design of an organization that will deliver a (superior) solution to the customer. Business model innovations, discussed below, are critical to success in unsettled markets where traditional revenue and pricing models no

## Table 13.1: Intangible Assets Compared With Physical Assets

|  | Intangible Assets | Physical Assets |
| --- | --- | --- |
| Variety | Heterogeneous | Homogeneous |
| Property rights | Often fuzzy | Usually clear |
| Market transactions | Infrequent | Frequent |
| General awareness of transaction opportunity | Low | High |
| Recognized on balance sheets | No | Yes |
| Possible strategic value | High | Low |

longer are applicable. The growth of the Internet is both allowing and requiring business model innovation in many industries ranging from music to insurance. In particular, the Internet requires new pricing structures because users are accustomed to getting information for free. Digital rights owners and information providers are challenged to think of ways of charging for ancillary or premium services (so-called "freemium" approaches) while not running afoul of Internet users' expectations of receiving large amounts of information or other digital commodities for free.

The other main classes of intangible assets, apart from formally identified intellectual property such as patents, are business process know-how, customer and business relationships, reputations, organizational culture, and values. These types of assets define the firm's operational capabilities, the activities that its employees are collectively able to carry out with sufficiency.

Intangible assets are rarely recorded on corporate balance sheets. As a consequence, existing accounting-based approaches have a hard time coming to grips with them. Alan Greenspan, former Chairman of the US Federal Reserve System, once noted the challenge of "developing a framework capable of analyzing the growth of an economy increasingly dominated by conceptual products" (Greenspan 2004). Conceptual products are built using intangible assets.

## 13.3  THE SALIENCE OF COSPECIALIZED COMPLEMENTS

In general, intangible assets by themselves will not yield value; they must almost always be combined with other intangible and physical complements, then bundled as a product to yield value for a customer. Ownership and/or control of noncommodity complementary assets is therefore also necessary for competitive success (Teece 1986, 2006).

Complementarity is not a new phenomenon. The development of high-octane fuels in the 1940s by oil refiners enabled the creation and optimization of high-compression engines by auto manufacturers. When complements are cospecialized (worth much more together than apart), and/or need to be created/developed to enable the evolution of the market for one's product, managerial "control" of the complements becomes critical. Whether that control is achieved through ownership or simply through setting the rules for a supporting ecosystem depends on the facts and circumstances.

Cospecialization is becoming ubiquitous for devices and services that span multiple industries, such as smartphones that combine functions of computing, communication, and consumer entertainment products. As Nokia CEO Stephen Elop said in his February 2011 (internal) "burning platform" memo, "The battle of devices has now become a war of ecosystems, where ecosystems include not only the hardware and software of the device, but developers, applications, ecommerce, advertising, search, social applications, location-based services, unified communications and many other things.

Our competitors aren't taking our market share with devices; they are taking our market share with an entire ecosystem."[5]

High-interdependency business environments require managers to select an appropriate organizational design and business model and to develop an ecosystem strategy. Failure to recognize the importance of cospecialized complements in fixed supply can drain away profits, or worse. The existence of technological complementarities, the external presence of intellectual property rights, and the importance of standards change the nature of the required technology management approaches and business strategies. Innovation in one product or service often increases the value of its complement(s) and may require the in-licensing of patent portfolios to facilitate design and operating freedom. Much more will be said about this in a subsequent section.

As new bases of competitive advantage have gained in significance and the critical roles of intangibles and complements have become more fully appreciated, old ways of looking at competition have had to be abandoned. Porter's Five Forces framework (Porter 1980) applied the structure-conduct-performance paradigm of industrial organization economics to strategy, focusing on evaluating suppliers, customers, and the threat of new entrants and/or substitute products. This framework is not without insight, but it's not up to the task of revealing the dominant logic of value creation and value capture in most new industries, and even in many of the old.

## 13.4 MANAGERIAL ECONOMICS IN THE AGE OF INCREASING RETURNS

The application of microeconomic models to managerial decision making may continue to have a role to play in optimizing the performance of firms at a given point in time. However, the traditional forms of economic analysis fail to inform market entry strategies, investment allocations, and technology choices.

Economic theory has not entirely ignored the importance of innovation. Enlightened economic historians (e.g., Kuznets 1966) have long emphasized the role of technology and organization in economic development. A small cadre of economists—including the late Edwin Mansfield, Richard Nelson, Chris Freeman, Sidney Winter, Paul David, Nathan Rosenberg, Giovanni Dosi, and David Mowery—have specialized in analyzing the role of technological change in firms and industries. But the stylized treatment of innovation in the mainstream economics literature is of little use to managers or policy makers. For example, the patent race (e.g., Reinganum 1981), a common innovation model, assumes that rivals are all pursuing a known technological objective, not the uncertain and fluid goals that generally characterize industrial research.

Textbook understandings of how markets operate and how firms compete have been derived from the work of economists such as Marshall, Cournot, and Chamberlin. The workhorse neoclassical economics framework assumes smooth cost curves and diminishing returns; and it assigns to all industry participants an identical production function, implying the use of identical technologies by all competitors. An industry equilibrium with numerous participants arises because marginal-cost curves slope upwards, thereby exhausting scale advantages at the level of the firm and making room for multiple industry participants. This approach was useful for understanding nineteenth-century factories and even many twentieth-century activities. However, major deficiencies in this view of the world have been apparent for some time.

Over the past hundred years, developed economies have undergone a transition from the manufacturing of goods to the processing of information, with the share of manufacturing in GDP declining steadily. Today, even many companies classified by national statistics agencies as manufacturers, such as Apple, do not fabricate anything themselves. Apple's in-house activities are limited to design, brand-building, retail services, and ecosystem oversight, with the processing of physical inputs and finished products outsourced to third parties (Dedrick et al. 2009). In the Internet era, online activities are rapidly disintermediating transactions and steadily displacing brick-and-mortar operations. Examples include the undermining of the US Postal Service by e-mail and the gradual elimination of book and video stores in favor of online portals that fill the same function.

As a consequence of the shift to knowledge activities, an ever larger share of the economy is characterized by increasing returns, of a type that Brian Arthur (1988) calls "increasing returns to adoption."[6] With increasing returns, mechanisms of positive feedback reinforce the winners. For whatever reason a firm emerges as a leader—acumen, chance, technology—increasing returns amplify the advantage. A leading firm need not be the pioneer and need not have the best product, but, once it has achieved a certain critical mass, it will retain an advantage at least until changes in the business environment shift the bases of competition.

The increasing returns phenomenon is itself driven by several factors. First, consider large up-front costs. Once a high-tech industry is established, large up-front research, development, and design engineering costs are typical as firms compete on time-to-market. This is most amplified with software products where the first copy costs hundreds of millions of dollars, and the marginal cost of the second copy is zero, or very nearly so. But it also applies to, for example, Internet portals, which make large up-front investments in their interface, branding, and infrastructure, after which they can provide a platform for a growing number of external merchants at a relatively small incremental cost.

Expanding opportunities to monetize intellectual property via licensing also enhance returns. Consider standards. To establish networks and interoperability, compatibility standards are usually critical. If such standards are proprietary, ownership of key patents that are essential to the standard can yield significant returns, despite requirements for "fair, reasonable, and nondiscriminatory" licensing terms. This is because the development cost of the technology is sunk and the marginal cost of each licensing agreement is small.

Increasing returns also occur in the presence of network externalities, in which the value of a good or service rises for all users as their numbers expand. This was true of wired telephone networks and PC software, but the effect has become ubiquitous in the era of the wireless Internet, with new services like Facebook and Twitter growing "virally" to reach millions of users.

Customer learning and investment in high-technology products (e.g., applications on a smartphone) amplify switching costs (e.g., to a phone using a different operating system). Successful products and platforms will also attract investments in specialized complements that enhance the value of the core product/platform and increase the pool of those with an incentive to support it. This pulls competition "forward" in the sense that providers must compete especially hard for the original sale, knowing that sales of follow-along equipment and other services will be easier. While such "lock-in" is rarely permanent, it may nonetheless be decisive.

Producer learning also plays a role. In certain cases, producers become more efficient as experience is gained, placing competitors with less experience at a disadvantage. In the case of Internet companies, vast quantities of proprietary data about user behavior can drive a wedge between the market leader and its rivals. Producer learning is also important in chemical and other manufacturing industries where complex processes are involved.

The economics of increasing returns requires corporate strategies different from those of the previous century. In winner-take-all (or winner-take-the-lion's-share) contexts, the payoff associated with getting the timing right (not being too early or too late) and with organizing sufficient resources once an opportunity opens up is magnified. Very often, competition is like a high-stakes game of musical chairs. Being well positioned when a dominant design emerges is essential. Strategy involves choosing what games to play, as well as playing with skill. Multimedia, web services, mobile software, and electronic commerce are all markets where the rules are unstable, the identity of the players subject to sudden change, and the payoff matrix uncertain. Rewards go to those good at sensing and seizing opportunities.

In an increasing returns environment, there is little return to pinching pennies, and high returns to rapidly seizing opportunities. Cost minimization within an obsolete business plan is a strategic dead-end. Constant scanning for emerging threats and opportunities is essential, as is the ability to reorient the organization with alacrity.

The world of atomistic competition portrayed in neoclassical economic models and assumed in many managerial economics textbooks is giving way to a world of winner-take-all markets where the competition that matters is based on platform design and promotion. A new theoretical framework is needed to guide the growth of firms involved in creating and marketing conceptual, rather than physical, products. The Dynamic Capabilities framework (Teece et al. 1990, 1997; Teece 2007, 2009) has been developed to respond to that need.

## 13.5 DYNAMIC CAPABILITIES: AN INTRODUCTION

The Dynamic Capabilities framework provides substance to what some scholars and practitioners have in mind when they refer to "corporate agility." Dynamic capabilities reflect an important element of creative managerial and entrepreneurial activity (e.g., pioneering new markets) by the top management team and other expert talent. They are also, however, rooted to some degree in organizational routines (e.g., product development along a known trajectory) and analysis (e.g., of investment choices).

It is perhaps easiest to understand what dynamic capabilities are by juxtaposing them against ordinary capabilities. Ordinary capabilities, which are more firmly rooted in routines than are dynamic capabilities, enable defined economic tasks to be performed collectively and efficiently. The essence of both ordinary and dynamic capabilities is that they cannot generally be bought (apart from acquiring the entire organization); instead, they must be built. This characteristic makes dynamic capabilities in particular a difficult-to-imitate asset of a type that can contribute to competitive advantage.

Dynamic capabilities are rooted in three clusters of competence: (1) identification and assessment of an opportunity (*sensing*); (2) mobilization of resources to address an opportunity and to capture value from doing so (*seizing*); and (3) continued renewal (*transforming*). Sensing, seizing, and transforming are essential if the firm is to sustain itself as markets and technologies change.

Sensing is an inherently entrepreneurial set of capabilities that involves exploring technological opportunities, probing markets, and listening to customers, along with scanning the other elements of the business ecosystem. It requires management to build and "test" hypotheses about market and technological evolution, including the recognition of latent demand. The world wasn't clamoring for a coffeehouse on every corner, but Starbucks, under the guidance of Howard Schultz, recognized and successfully exploited the potential market. As this example implies, sensing requires managerial insight and vision—or an analytical process that can serve as a proxy for it.

Seizing entails the design and implementation of business models to satisfy customers and capture value. Such models identify and combine the relevant complementary assets in ways that are consistent with business viability. Seizing also involves securing access to capital and the necessary human resources. Employee motivation is also vital. Good incentive design is a necessary but not sufficient condition for superior performance in this area; management techniques for fostering creative activity such as new product development must be more flexible than the control systems that might be suitable for repetitive activities (Teece 2011). Strong relationships must also be forged externally with suppliers, complementors, and customers.

Transforming, or realigning the enterprise's resources, is needed most obviously when radical new opportunities are to be addressed. Recognizing strategic errors and adjusting accordingly is a critical part of becoming and remaining successful. But transformations are also needed periodically to soften the rigidities that develop over time from asset accumulation, standard operating procedures, and insider misappropriation of rent streams. A firm's assets must also be kept in alignment to achieve the best strategic "fit" between firm and ecosystem, between structure and strategy, and among assets. Complementarities need to be managed continuously (reconfigured as necessary) to achieve evolutionary fitness, avoiding loss of value should market leverage shift to favor external complements.

# 13.6  Capturing Value

## 13.6.1  General

Sensing and transforming are well-known phenomena discussed by this author and others elsewhere (e.g., Teece 2007; Tushman and O'Reilly 1997). Hence, in this contribution, the focus will be on perhaps what is the least understood dynamic capability—what I call "seizing," or capturing value. Companies that are narrowly focused on invention and sensing on a technological level (creating value) will generally not perform well commercially. Inventive activity without a commercialization strategy and access on competitive terms to complementary assets is unlikely to be successful.

Businesses can run into trouble from failing to clearly understand their relationship to their customers. Developments in the global economy have changed the traditional balance between customer and enterprise. New communications and computing technology, and the establishment of reasonably open global trading regimes, mean that customers have more choices, their likes and dislikes are finding expression more directly, and the time available for fixing problems before business is lost has shrunk considerably. Businesses therefore need to be more customer-centric than ever before.

A business must also be able to prevent the imitation of its key intangibles. As explained above, many intangibles are inherently difficult to imitate, but that does not mean it's impossible. Legal barriers to imitation protect some knowledge assets, but these are of limited importance in some industries, either due to the pace of change or to weak rights enforcement (e.g., digital music). Other intangibles are "protected" by overall causal ambiguity about the sources of the firm's advantages (Lippman and Rumelt 1982).

Successful strategies to capture value require choosing an appropriate mechanism for the protection of intellectual property (e.g., trade secrets versus patents) and deciding which activities must be performed by the firm or procured in the market. Capturing value also requires crafting a business model.

## 13.6.2  Business Models

A business model (Chesbrough and Rosenbloom 2002; Teece 2010) defines a product's value proposition for customers and how the firm will convert that to profit. A business model defines an organizational and financial architecture which embraces and integrates in a consistent fashion (1) the feature set of the product or service; (2) the benefit (value proposition) from consuming/using the product or service; (3) the market segments to be targeted; (4) the "design" of revenue streams and cost structure; (5) the way products/services are to be combined and offered to the customer; and (6) the mechanisms by which value is to be captured.

In mainstream economics textbooks, where demand curves are typically portrayed as being well specified, there is simply no need to worry about the value proposition to the customer, or about mechanisms to capture value. In the real world, however, the ability to sense and seize a previously untapped consumer want/need can lead to breakthrough success, as with the Apple iPhone, which created its own market for a phone fused with intuitively designed computing capabilities.

A business model is distinct from a business plan. It is a conceptual, rather than a financial, representation of a business. A business model is more generic than a business strategy. Selecting a business strategy is also a more granular exercise than designing a business model. Coupling competitive strategy analysis to business model design requires segmenting the market, creating a value proposition for each segment, setting up the apparatus to deliver that value, and then devising methods to prevent the business model from being undermined through imitation by competitors or disintermediation by customers.

Strategy analysis is thus an essential step in designing a sustainable business model. Unless the business model survives the filters which strategy analysis imposes, it is unlikely to be viable.

When a business model is difficult to imitate—and if it is used to pioneer a winner-take-all market—it can be a source of sustained profitability. But in today's high-velocity markets, the period of time before which major new challenges necessitate adjustments to a model can be relatively short. Consider Apple's iPhone, introduced in 2007, featuring tight integration of hardware and software and supported by an exclusive deal with a major wireless carrier. Apple's entry supercharged the nascent smartphone market. While the iPhone has continued not only to be popular but also profitable, Google's search ad-"subsidized" Android ecosystem, which launched its first phones in 2008, grew to be the largest category of smartphones by 2010. While this did not imitate Apple's business model, it challenged it because Android-based smartphones came from a variety of companies at a range of different price points. Apple responded in 2011 by leaving older iPhone models on the market at prices that made some units free to the consumer after a carrier subsidy.

Once established, business models, like many organizational elements, can be difficult to change. For example, American Express and Discover have been trying to adjust their respective models so that they will continue to issue cards themselves while simultaneously looking to persuade banks to act as card issuers for them. Their main competitors, Visa and MasterCard, provide network services. Because they don't compete with banks in issuing cards, they are well positioned to be the bank's preferred partners. Thus American Express and Discover are unlikely to have (and indeed have not had) much success trying to replicate the Visa/MasterCard business model while still maintaining their own internal issuing and acquiring functions.[7]

To summarize, a business model must be something more than just a good or logical way of doing business. It must also be inimitable in certain respects, either by virtue of being hard to replicate, or by being unpalatable for competitors to replicate because it would disturb their existing relationships in some way. And when business conditions shift, management must be ready to revise the model—and perhaps the company—to profit from the new reality.

## 13.6.3  Organizational Design

A business model must be supported by an organization's design, including the boundaries of the firm as determined by the necessary make-or-buy decisions and horizontal product market scope. The goal is to determine how best to accomplish the development, manufacturing, and distribution of end products and services.

In theory, an inventor/innovator could simply license its patent(s) to others, then sit back to reap the profits. This may be possible in the rare cases of extremely important, pioneering patents but for most inventions it is not realistic. Most technology requires training to be put into use, and any technology, even one that is relatively modular, is difficult and costly to transfer between organizations (Teece 1981). Patented inventions require complementary assets to be valuable, and these must often be provided by the inventor. Consider the example of ARM, Ltd., a very successful company whose intellectual property is included in the processor chips inside the vast majority of cell phones on the market, among numerous other electronics products. ARM does not just provide a "blueprint" that its licensees turn around and use; it provides the associated software and, in many cases, extensive technical support for using its intellectual property (IP).

The point is that naively investing in the development of technological devices without understanding the broader panoply of factors involved in creating and capturing value is unlikely to pay off. Building and deploying intangible assets and shaping ecosystems require access to—and, often, ownership of—complements. Absent the ability to orchestrate complements effectively, management will be hard-pressed to deliver financial success.

The organizational conundrum that managers confront has at least two dimensions. First, the delivery of product/process innovation to the market in some usable form requires combining inputs/components up and down the vertical chain of production. The profitability of the inventor/innovator can be compromised significantly when economic muscle (i.e., scarcity, inimitability, or other isolating mechanisms) is possessed by owners of required inputs/components. One of the prime examples of this is the success of Microsoft and Intel in retaining a substantial share of the profits in the personal computer industry (Dedrick et al. 2009).

Second, most innovations require complementary products and services to produce value in consumption. Hardware requires software (and vice versa); operating systems require applications (and vice versa); digital music players require digital music and ways of distributing digital music (and vice versa); mobile phones need mobile phone networks (and vice versa); web browsers and web search engines require web content (and vice versa); airlines require airports (and vice versa). In short, technology must be embedded in a system to yield value to the user/consumer. Appropriability is at risk if other entities control required elements of the system.

From this perspective, organizational design is a matter of ensuring access to required components and complements at preferential or competitive prices. In some instances, this will require the firm to build or buy the necessary capabilities to avoid a loss of profits to the owner of a bottleneck asset. The firm must also be prepared to change its assessment over time because the identity of bottleneck assets may shift due to innovation elsewhere in the system.

Over the past two decades, our understanding of capturing value by carefully choosing the architecture of the enterprise (especially the boundaries of its ownership and its control of complementary assets) has expanded greatly. This body of work has come to be known as the Profiting From Innovation (PFI) framework.[8]

PFI addressed a puzzle that had not been well explained in the previous literature; namely, why do highly creative, pioneering firms often fail to capture the economic returns from innovation? The original framework (Teece 1986) cites several examples (e.g., EMI in CAT scanners, Bowmar in calculators), and the phenomenon does indeed endure. The first-generation PC manufacturers all but disappeared from the scene (and even IBM, a pioneer of the Microsoft-Intel PC industry, exited the business by selling its PC business to a Chinese company, Lenovo, in 2005). Xerox (PARC) and Apple invented the graphical user interface, but Microsoft Windows dominates the PC market with its follow-on version of the same product. Netscape invented the browser, but Microsoft captured more of the market. Apple's iPod was not the first MP3 player, but it has a commanding position in the category today. Merck was a pioneer in cholesterol-lowering drugs (Zocor), but Pfizer, a late entrant, secured a superior market position with Lipitor.

At first glance, it is tempting to say that these examples reflect the result of Schumpeterian gales of creative destruction where winners are continually challenged and overturned by entrants.[9] Indeed, entrants with potentially disruptive innovations are almost always waiting in the wings, but many of the cited cases involved mostly incremental/imitative entrants rather than the radical breakthroughs typically invoked in accounts of Schumpeterian competition.

More importantly, there is ample variance in the outcomes from entry, with many cases where first or early movers captured and sustained significant competitive advantage over time. Genentech was a pioneer in using biotechnology to discover and develop drugs, and thirty years later was the second largest biotechnology firm (and also the most productive in its use of research and development dollars) right up to its acquisition by Hoffmann-La Roche in 2009. Intel invented the microprocessor and still has a leading market position forty years later. Dell pioneered a new distribution system for personal computers and, despite recent challenges and many would-be imitators, remained the leader until it was bypassed by Hewlett-Packard in 2007. Toyota's much studied "Toyota Production System" has provided the automaker a source of competitive advantage for decades despite numerous and sustained attempts at imitation, with the company finally becoming the world's biggest car manufacturer in 2008. It took the crippling of nuclear power plants by the massive earthquake and tsunami that struck Northeast Japan in March 2011 to dislodge the company from first place.

The Profiting From Innovation framework points to the appropriability regime, along with the business model and organizational design, as the leading factors behind why some innovators profit from innovation while others lose out—often to imitators—and why it is not inevitable that the pioneers will lose. Teece (2006, 1140) summarizes PFI's rules by saying that firms should rely on markets unless there are compelling reasons to internalize. Such reasons could be grounded in one of two major circumstances: (a) cospecialization, which would lead to transaction costs if heavy reliance was made externally (i.e., on externally provisioned assets/services); (b) shoring up the appropriability situation by building or buying complementary assets that the innovation would likely drive up in value, or that were otherwise important to getting the job done.

The Dynamic Capabilities framework embeds PFI in a broader context and identifies some additional factors, most notably whether the firm's competences/complementary assets are sufficiently advanced to enable it to competitively self-supply the required inputs or services. But in some cases, the component or complement may not exist anywhere in the economy, leaving the firm no alternative. This is most often the case when industries are new, and potential suppliers and distributors do not have the capabilities in place to meet the needs of innovators. In such cases, it is often most expedient for the developer/manufacturer to integrate upstream and/or downstream, particularly when strategic or time-to-market considerations make it counterproductive to spend time convincing a potential supplier of the value of making the necessary investments.

This is not a new phenomenon. Alfred Chandler (1992, 87) noted that during the Second Industrial Revolution that began in the late nineteenth century, the reason for the "initial move forward into distribution and marketing by entrepreneurs … was that often suppliers and distributors had neither sufficient knowledge of the novel complex products nor the facilities required to handle them efficiently. This is why so many of the new companies met their needs by building almost immediately a national marketing and distribution network staffed by their managers and workers."

There are also dynamic technology considerations that affect decisions about organizational design (de Figueiredo and Teece 1996). An innovator's ability to pace, direct, control, and guard the development of new products and technologies poses risks to competitors (Chesbrough and Teece 1996). If this innovation is left to a nonintegrated supplier, the downstream firm may then have no choice but to purchase critical components from a supplier who also emerges as a competitor. This occurred with Samsung, a supplier of displays and microchips to Apple, and now a serious rival in smartphones and tablet computers.

The outsourcing of components used in new products also raises hazards of technology leakage to competitors who are not part of the contract. Arrow (1962) first brought to light the disclosure problem in the market for know-how and others have since elaborated on this and related technology transfer problems (Goldberg 1977; Teece 1981, 1985, and 1986). The leakage can occur vertically (upstream and downstream) as well as horizontally (Silverman 1996).

A subtler hazard in such a relationship is the inability to pace or direct the evolution of new products that depend on a supplier's proprietary technology. The software industry provides an illustration of how an integrated firm can pace technological development downstream of its operating system. Microsoft develops its operating systems in-house. It also develops certain applications while relying for additional applications on independent software vendors who in turn rely on Windows for their development environment. Windows acts as a constraint on some of the technological features of the downstream application (e.g., protocols for data exchange). Microsoft's ability to pace its upstream operating system technology and its ability to use its intimate knowledge of that technology in its applications software helped it to become one of the dominant players in applications.

If a firm has no input into a supplier's development process, the supplier might be able to independently shape the trajectory of the technology. This can be mitigated to some extent by close collaboration with the supplier or the requirement that it regularly provide a "roadmap" of its future technology plans. But the downstream firm will remain unable to control the pace of technology deployment unless competing suppliers can be played off each other.

Another reason that a firm faces hazards when relying on an external supplier for complementary innovation is the difficulty associated with accomplishing the coordination of complementary assets and activities. This is related to what Richardson (1960) and Williamson (1975) have called "convergence of expectations." Investment (in research and development) must be coordinated between upstream and downstream entities, and this is difficult to effectuate using contractual mechanisms.

Coordination is of greatest concern when innovation is systemic (Teece 1988).[10] Systemic innovation requires harmonized action by all parties (e.g., the development of new cameras and film that instant photography required). When there is asymmetry in capabilities between firms, achieving harmonization is difficult. Boeing discovered this to its cost when it decided to rely on a global array of suppliers to develop parts for its new 787 Dreamliner as a cost-sharing measure; some suppliers lacked the capabilities to develop parts of the necessary quality, and Boeing had cut back its monitoring capability. Deficits in the capabilities of suppliers resulted in years of delay (Michaels and Sanders 2009). The Boeing experience echoes that of Lockheed three decades earlier when the L1011 wide-bodied plane was delayed by the failure of Rolls Royce to develop and deliver on time the RB211 jet engine for the L1011, effectively putting Lockheed out of the civilian aircraft industry. This was not an exercise of opportunism by Rolls Royce; rather it reflected Rolls Royce's inability to achieve ambitious technological goals, its lack of the (ordinary) capabilities needed to develop and deliver on time.

Teece (1996, 2000) and Chesbrough and Teece (1996) have analyzed the difficulties in coordinating the development of complementary technologies when pursued independently and governed by contract. Delays are frequent and need not result from strategic manipulation; they may simply flow from uncertainty, limited capabilities, and divergent goals amongst the parties. In the presence of these hazards, maintaining technological control of the innovation trajectory sometimes requires vertical integration (including heavy investment in R&D). When this is not possible because of time-to-market or other considerations, other strategies for (re)shaping the industry's architecture must be pursued, for example, through corporate venture investments in the supply base to build a competitive market for key complements (Pisano and Teece 2007).

Once the firm's architecture of supply and distribution had been crafted, its managers must provide the orchestration, or "system integration" function. The prevalence of outsourcing has made this integration function a strategic competence of the first order (Pisano and Teece 2007; Prencipe et al. 2003).

## 13.6.4 Appropriability and Intellectual Property Strategies

The fundamental imperative for profiting from an innovation is that unless the inventor/innovator enjoys strong natural protection against imitation and/or strong intellectual property protection, then the potential future stream of income is at risk. The relevant appropriability regime is thus critical to shaping possible outcomes. Appropriability regimes can be "weak" (innovations are difficult to protect because they can be easily copied and legal protection of intellectual property is ineffective) or "strong" (innovations are easy to protect because knowledge about them is tacit and/or they are well protected legally). Regimes differ across fields of endeavor, not just across industries and countries.

Appropriability regimes change over time, and the regime applicable to a given innovation can be influenced by firms (Pisano and Teece 2007). For example, a firm with strong downstream complementary asset positions might decide that it is in its interest to weaken the upstream appropriability regime, as in the case of IBM making its server operating system available as a nonproprietary product to gain advantage in the sale of related hardware, applications, and services (Merges 2004). More commonly, firms work to strengthen appropriability regimes by lobbying for stronger intellectual property rights enforcement. An individual firm can improve the appropriability of its patents under some circumstances, such as by having them adopted as a formal industry standard, which may make competitors less likely to work around the patent. Control of key patents in a successful standard has numerous potential benefits, including licensing revenue, privileged access to new technologies, and influence over the technology trajectory.

In some industries, particularly where the innovation is embedded in processes, trade secrets are a viable alternative to patents. Trade secret protection is possible, however, only if a firm can put its product before the public and still keep the underlying technology secret. Many industrial processes, including semiconductor fabrication, are of this kind.

Patents can in some cases be used to slow rivals and generate profits. However, patents rarely, if ever, confer strong appropriability, outside of special cases such as new drugs, chemical products, and rather simple mechanical inventions (Levin et al. 1987). Many patents can be "invented around" at modest cost (Mansfield et al. 1981; Mansfield 1985). They are especially ineffective at protecting process innovation. Often patents provide little protection because the legal and financial requirements for upholding their validity or for proving their infringement are high, or because, in many countries, law enforcement for intellectual property is weak or nonexistent.

While a patent is presumed to be valid in many jurisdictions, validity is never firmly established until a patent has been upheld in court. A patent is merely a passport to another journey down the road to enforcement and possible licensing fees. The best patents are those that are broad in scope, have already been upheld in court, and cover a technology essential to the manufacture and sale of products in high demand.

Despite the shortcomings of patents as a means of protecting a firm's profits, they have gained salience for value capture because firms in a number of industries are looking to their patent portfolios as a direct source of income. Patents have long been valuable in some industries, such as pharmaceuticals, and they have become a critical competitive tool/weapon in electronics.

In many instances, patent strategies are not just a matter of protecting a particular invention. Developing new commercially viable products increasingly requires the combination of a very large number of inventions, leading to an innovation environment that has been called "multi-invention" (Somaya et al. 2011). In some industries (notably biotechnology), one needs to use earlier patented innovations simply in order to conduct new research.

Multi-invention contexts are not a recent phenomenon. New technologies in the early twentieth century—cars, airplanes, telephones, radios—also combined components, protected by IP rights, from multiple parties. What is different now is the depth and complexity of the IP landscape. At the peak of automobile innovation in the early 1920s, about 400 motor vehicle patents (US patent class 180) were being issued each year by the US Patent and Trademark Office (USPTO). By contrast, in the last few years, in an active area like semiconductor manufacturing (US patent class 438), the USPTO issued approximately 7000 patents annually. Many of these inventions were aimed at building up a large defensive portfolio that overlaps with rivals' sphere of knowledge (Grindley and Teece 1997; Hall and Ziedonis 2001). In other words, the greater emphasis placed by companies on the protection and monetization of knowledge assets has amplified the requirement for protecting and extending one's own assets.

Innovators in these multi-invention settings must craft a patent strategy that covers how they access proprietary (and patented) technology held by others and manage patent rights on their own inventions. That is, an innovator must (a) identify strategies for in-licensing patented technology held by others that it wishes to use in its own products and (b) identify strategies for either out-licensing its own technology to others or choosing not to license use-rights to others (and, if necessary, to take legal action to protect its IP against infringers). In many contexts, parties agree to a cross-license, whereby each party receives a license to use the other's technology to make its own products.

Somaya et al. (2011) identify three generic patent strategies: proprietary strategies, defensive strategies, and leveraging strategies. In practice, of course, it may make sense to pursue a mixture of different strategies, depending on the nature of the innovation in question. In turn, as summarized in Table 13.2, these strategies have implications for the firm's activities in each of three broad domains: patenting, licensing, and enforcement.

Table 13.2: Generic Patent Strategies in Different Domains of Patent Activity

| | Patenting Domain | Licensing Domain | Enforcement Domain |
|---|---|---|---|
| Extended Proprietary Strategy | Expend resources to obtain tight protection; Patent "invent-arounds" | Licensing unlikely; Seek substantial royalties | Aggressive enforcement; Settlement of suits less likely (seek injunctions?) |
| Leveraging strategy | Patent technologies likely useful to others | Willing to license; Develop licensing program to identify licensees | Litigation used to induce licensing; Willing to settle litigation |
| Defensive Strategy | Patent preemptively; Build defensive portfolios; Invalidate and invent around others' patents | Cross-licensing; Patent in-licensing | Avoid litigation where possible; Seek licenses and settlement of litigation. |

Source: Table 2 from Somaya et al. (2011)

### 13.6.4.1 Proprietary Strategy

The ability to "stake out and defend a proprietary market advantage" is often cited as the primary benefit of patents (Rivette and Kline 2000, 56). However, as noted above, patent protection generally tends to be imperfect and porous. Therefore, to obtain any tangible protection for a key technology, a firm usually must work to fill in the gaps in its patent portfolio.

When pursuing this proprietary strategy, the firm ideally shores up the quality and breadth of its patent rights by obtaining well-researched and well-written pioneering patents. The company can also foreclose the strategic paths of competitors by patenting potential "invent arounds" as well as follow-on and complementary inventions.

Firms need to weigh the benefits of patent protection against its costs. Successfully obtaining a patent through the "patent prosecution" process before the US Patent and Trade Office is not cheap, and broad geographic protection requires seeking protection in at least certain key countries. Pursuing an expensive proprietary patent strategy may be justified for technologies that underlie a core competency, entail high strategic stakes, or are otherwise critical for the company's competitive advantage (Somaya 2003).

### 13.6.4.2 Defensive Strategy

Rather than seeking to dominate a technology area, an enterprise may simply desire the freedom to design and innovate without being constrained by the patents owned—or likely to be owned in the future—by others. Patents held by others can pose a significant challenge to commercializing an innovation, especially in multi-invention settings.

To protect against unwitting infringement, companies need an effective "defensive" patent strategy. One common defensive strategy is to develop a portfolio of patents to offer in cross-licensing settlements.[11] In essence, this means that the company should aim to patent not only inventions important to itself, but also those important to others. Patenting into a rival's domain of weakness is sometimes possible, and may be effective (Merges 2004). There are data to show that having a patent portfolio that "reads on" a competitor's technologies increases the likelihood and speed of settlement in a patent suit brought by that competitor (Lanjouw and Schankerman 2002; Somaya 2002). However, defensive patent portfolios may be ineffective against patent owners that do not practice their invention, such as individual inventors or universities.

A defensive strategy succeeds by leading to workable agreements with other patent holders. One option is to cross-license with each patent holder individually, but an alternative is to license through a patent pool, in which the holders share the relevant patents with each other on a nondiscriminatory basis. When there are multiple parties with interrelated blocking positions, patent pools can reduce the transaction costs for each party to obtain the freedom to operate.

### 13.6.4.3  Leveraging Strategy

In many situations, patents hold value for the firm without the added time and expense of a proprietary or defensive strategy. The "leveraging" strategy relies on using the patent holder's power to exclude as a way to achieve other goals.

A leveraging strategy takes advantage of patents obtained in the course of the company's inventive efforts to generate revenue and cement alliances. Firms like IBM and Texas Instruments (TI) have earned substantial licensing revenues and other considerations by leveraging their patent rights into business deals.

Typically, these patent-only transactions involve no know-how transfer because the licensees are already using (i.e., infringing) the patents in question. Such patent leveraging strategies work best when patent rights are strong and cover valuable inventions that provide significant utility to other firms. In pursuing a leveraging strategy, it is not the aim of the patent-holding firm to stop third parties from using its technology, but rather to obtain reasonable compensation for that use; thus its enforcement actions are typically calibrated to force a license and to settle any ongoing litigation.

In addition to royalty revenues, leveraging strategies can generate other benefits. For example, there are often more applications for the underlying technology than the innovator can effectively exploit, creating opportunities for other firms to develop the technology and take it in new directions. By granting licenses to firms pursuing non-rivalrous applications, the innovator can reduce their incentive to invent around its invention and thus establish its technology as the de facto standard in the field. In other contexts, a firm can leverage its control over a patent to encourage incorporation of the firm's technology in a de jure standard in exchange for a commitment to license the technology on reasonable terms (Shapiro and Varian 1999). In both cases, leveraging patent rights into licensing arrangements not only increases expected future revenues but may also encourage external development of the original technology, which in turn will help to maintain the firm's technological advantage over rivals in the longer term.

# 13.7 CONCLUSION: ENTREPRENEURIAL MANAGERIAL ECONOMICS

To correct one lacuna in managerial economics, this chapter has emphasized the management of intangible assets. But the long-term health of the enterprise requires entrepreneurial managerial skills which are also underrepresented in mainstream approaches to guiding the economic choices of firms.

Entrepreneurial managers are an essential element of the profitable enterprise—and vital to the sensing, seizing, and transforming of dynamic capabilities. The responsibilities of entrepreneurial managers transcend the tool kit of optimization and forecasting that drives much of managerial economics.

Kirzner (1979) and Shane (2003) analyze entrepreneurship as a process of discovering opportunities. But entrepreneurship also encompasses the proactive creation of opportunities (through research and development), the accurate assessment of them, and the mobilization of resources to address them.

Top management's entrepreneurial and leadership skills assist (but do not guarantee) the firm's long-run viability. The entrepreneur must understand how the various inputs in a creative exercise are likely to interact with one another, and then respond flexibly as they coevolve. Periodic, if not continuous, asset orchestration—involving achieving asset alignment, coalignment, and redeployment—is necessary to minimize internal conflict and to maximize complementarities inside the enterprise.

The wellspring of the requisite capabilities remains enigmatic and difficult for many firms to harness. Some firms, usually inspired by an individual, can successfully embed the capabilities throughout the organization, while others remain overly reliant on a single individual, or simply fail to respond to opportunities and threats. Yet most economic models implicitly assume that adequate strategy and coordination skills are readily available to all firms.

The standard tools of managerial economics must be balanced carefully with an understanding of the more creative function of entrepreneurial managers. Short-run optimization must not blind the company's stewards to the need for medium-term revamps and long-term reallocations. The Dynamic Capabilities framework encompasses these broader perspectives without ignoring the short-run pressures facing modern management.

## NOTES

1. I would like to thank Dr. Greg Linden for assistance in preparing this chapter. I am also grateful to the editors of the Handbook for helpful comments.

2. The economics and management literatures sometimes distinguish between managers, defined as those who "run" or "manage" a firm's operations, and entrepreneurs, who establish new enterprises and strike out in new directions. The entrepreneurial manager is a hybrid: still a manager but capable of thinking and acting entrepreneurially. The late Steve Jobs at Apple was such a person.

3. Many managerial economics textbooks are based on optimization (and cost minimization) and use Marshallian cost curves, implicitly ignoring capabilities and innovation.

4. Perhaps the best characterization is that of semiglobalization (Ghemawat 2003; Ghemawat and Ghadar 2006). Semiglobalization recognizes that, while there has been a significant opening up of once-protected markets to competition, the process isn't complete. Because of persistent market heterogeneity, business strategies must be local and global at the same time.

5. The leaked Nokia memo was widely reproduced online. See, for example, http://www.engadget.com/2011/02/08/nokia-ceo-stephen-elop-rallies-troops-in-brutally-honest-burnin/ (accessed February 12, 2010).

6. A number of economists have worked on developing the concepts discussed in this section. These include network externalities (Katz and Shapiro 1986), switching costs (Klemperer 1987), and learning economies (Krugman 1987), to name a few. See Shy (2001) for an overview of network economics and its applicability to a number of different industries.

7. See de Figueiredo and Teece (1996) for an analysis of some ways to mitigate the hazards of competing with one's suppliers.

8. The core papers in the Profiting From Innovation (PFI) framework are Teece (1986, 2006). The intellectual origins of the framework can be traced to Williamson (for his work on contracting), Abernathy and Utterback (for their work on the innovation life cycle), to economic historians like Nathan Rosenberg and Alfred Chandler (for their work on complementary technologies), to Nelson and Winter (for their work on the nature of knowledge), and to Schumpeter (for his focus on the need for value capture). See Winter (2006) for a review of PFI's intellectual origins.

9. There is a long literature on the role of new entrants in dislodging established firms. See, for instance, Anderson and Tushman (1990), Clark (1985), Henderson and Clark (1990), and Christensen (1997).

10. Autonomous innovations, which do not require coordinated activities between parties, are the opposite of a systemic innovation. An autonomous innovation can be "plugged in" to a bigger project. This is possible when standards define modular interfaces. The open architecture of the IBM personal computer, for instance, allowed innovation in hard disk drives to advance more or less independently from that of other components.

11. In the electronics and semiconductor industries, where overlapping developments and mutually blocking patents are inevitable, enterprises regularly cross-license patents with each other to ensure that they have the freedom to innovate and manufacture without inadvertent infringement. In patent cross licenses, technology is not usually transferred, because the parties are generally capable of (and often already are) using the technology in question without assistance. A license in this instance simply confers the right to use the intellectual property without being sued for infringement (Grindley and Teece 1997).

# References

Anderson, Philip, and Michael L. Tushman. 1990. "Technological Discontinuities and Dominant Design: A Cyclical Model of Technological Change." *Administrative Science Quarterly* 35:604–33.

Arrow, Kenneth J. 1962. "Economic Welfare and the Allocation of Resources of Invention." In *The Rate and Direction of Inventive Activity: Economic and Social Factors*, edited by National Bureau of Economic Research, 609–25. Princeton, NJ: Princeton University Press.

Arthur, W. Brian. 1988. "Competing Technologies: An Overview." In *Technical Change and Economic Theory*, edited by Giovanni Dosi, Christopher Freeman, Richard Nelson, Gerald Silverberg, and Luc Soete, 590–607. London: Pinter Publishers.

Chandler, Alfred D. 1992. "Organizational Capabilities and the Economic History of the Industrial Enterprise." *Journal of Economic Perspectives* 6:79–100.

Chesbrough, Henry, and Richard S. Rosenbloom. 2002. "The Role of the Business Model in Capturing Value from Innovation: Evidence from Xerox Corporation's Technology Spin-Off Companies." *Industrial and Corporate Change* 11:529–55.

Chesbrough, Henry, and David J. Teece. 1996. "When is Virtual Virtuous: Organizing for Innovation." *Harvard Business Review* 74:65–73.

Christensen, Clayton M. 1997. *The Innovator's Dilemma: When New Technologies Cause Great Firms to Fail*. Boston, MA: Harvard Business School Press.

Clark, Kim B. 1985. "The Interaction of Design Hierarchies and Market Concepts in Technological Evolution." *Research Policy* 14:235–51.

D'Aveni, Richard A., with Robert Gunther. 1994. *Hypercompetition: Managing the Dynamics of Strategic Maneuvering*. New York: Free Press.

Dedrick, Jason, Kenneth L. Kraemer, and Greg Linden. 2009. "Who Profits from Innovation in Global Value Chains?: a Study of the iPod and Notebook PCs." *Industrial and Corporate Change* 19:81–116.

de Figueiredo, John M., and David J. Teece. 1996. "Mitigating Procurement Hazards in the Context of Innovation." *Industrial and Corporate Change* 5:537–59.

Friedman, Thomas L. 2005. *The World Is Flat: A Brief History of the Twenty-first Century*. New York: Farrar, Straus and Giroux.

Ghemawat, Pankaj 2003. "Semiglobalization and International Business Strategy." *Journal of International Business Studies* 34:138–52.

Ghemawat, Pankaj, and Fariborz Ghadar. 2006. "Global Integration ≠ Global Concentration." *Industrial and Corporate Change* 15:595–623.

Goldberg, Victor P. 1977. "Competitive Bidding and the Production of Precontract Information." *Bell Journal of Economics* 8:250–61.

Greenspan, Alan. 2004. "Remarks on Intellectual Property Rights." Paper presented at the Stanford Institute for Economic Policy Research Economic Summit, Stanford, CA, February 27. Available at Federal Reserve Board, accessed April 28, 2010, http://www.federalreserve.gov/boarddocs/speeches/2004/200402272/default.htm.

Grindley, Peter C., and David J. Teece. 1997. "Managing Intellectual Capital: Licensing and Cross-Licensing in Electronics." *California Management Review* 39:8–41.

Hall, Bronwyn H., and Rosemarie H. Ziedonis. 2001. "The Patent Paradox Revisited: An Empirical Study of Patenting in the U.S. Semiconductor Industry, 1979–1995." *RAND Journal of Economics* 32:101–28.

Henderson, Rebecca M., and Kim B. Clark. 1990. "Architectural Innovation: The Reconfiguration of Existing Product Technologies and the Failure of Established Firms." *Administrative Science Quarterly* 35:9–30.

Katz, Michael L., and Carl Shapiro. 1986. "Technology Adoption in the Presence of Network Externalities." *Journal of Political Economy* 94:822–41.

Kirzner, Israel M. 1979. *Perception, Opportunity and Profit: Studies in the Theory of Entrepreneurship.* Chicago: University of Chicago Press.

Klemperer, Paul. 1987. "Markets with Consumer Switching Costs." *Quarterly Journal of Economics* 102:375–94.

Kraemer, Kenneth L., Jason Dedrick, and Sandra Yamashiro. 2000. "Refining and Extending the Business Model with Information Technology: Dell Computer Corporation." *Information Society* 16:5–21.

Krugman, Paul. 1987. "The Narrow Moving Band, the Dutch Disease, and the Consequences of Mrs. Thatcher: Notes on Trade in the Presence of Scale Economies." *Journal of Development Economics* 27:41–55.

Kuznets, Simon. 1966. *Modern Economic Growth: Rate, Structure, Spread.* New Haven, CT: Yale University Press.

Lanjouw, Jean, and Mark Schankerman. 2002. "Enforcing Intellectual Property Rights: Suits, Settlements and the Explosion of Patent Litigation." Unpublished manuscript, London School of Economics, June.

Levin, Richard C., Alvin K. Klevorick, Richard R. Nelson, and Sidney G. Winter. 1987. "Appropriating the Returns from Industrial Research and Development." *Brookings Papers on Economic Activity* 1987:783–831.

Lippman, S. A., and R. P. Rumelt. 1982. "Uncertain Imitability: An Analysis of Interfirm Differences in Efficiency under Competition." *Bell Journal of Economics* 13:418–38.

Mansfield, Edwin, Mark Schwartz, and Samuel Wagner. 1981. "Imitation Costs and Patents: An Empirical Study." *Economic Journal* 91:907–18.

Mansfield, Edwin. 1985. "How Rapidly Does New Industrial Technology Leak Out?" *Journal of Industrial Economics* 34:217–23.

Merges, Robert P. 2004. "A New Dynamism in the Public Domain." *University of Chicago Law Review* 71:183–203.

Michaels, Daniel, and Peter Sanders. 2009. "Dreamliner Production Gets Closer Monitoring." *Wall Street Journal*, October 8. http://online.wsj.com.

Nelson, Richard R., ed. 1993. *National Systems of Innovation.* New York: Oxford University Press.

Pisano, Gary P., and David J. Teece. 2007. "How to Capture Value from Innovation: Shaping Intellectual Property and Industry Architecture." *California Management Review* 50:278–96.

Porter, Michael. 1980. *Competitive Strategy: Techniques for Analyzing Industries and Competitors.* New York: Free Press.

Prencipe, Andrea, Andrew Davies, and Michael Hobday, eds. 2003. *The Business of Systems Integration.* Oxford: Oxford University Press.

Reinganum, Jennifer F. 1981. "Dynamic Games of Innovation." *Journal of Economic Theory* 25:21–41.

Richardson, G. B. 1960. *Information and Investment: A Study in the Working of the Competitive Economy.* London: Oxford University Press.

Rivette, Kevin G., and David Kline. 2000. "Discovering New Value in Intellectual Property." *Harvard Business Review* 78:2–12.

Shane, Scott Andrew. 2003. *A General Theory of Entrepreneurship: The Individual-Opportunity Nexus*. Northampton, MA: Edward Elgar.

Shapiro, Carl, and Hal R. Varian. 1999. *Information Rules: A Strategic Guide to the Network Economy*. Boston, MA: Harvard Business School Press.

Shy, Oz. 2001. *The Economics of Network Industries*. Cambridge, UK: Cambridge University Press.

Silverman, Brian S. 1996. "Technical Assets and the Logic of Corporate Diversification." PhD diss., University of California, Berkeley.

Somaya, Deepak. 2002. "Patent Strategy Viewed through the Lens of Patent Litigation." PhD diss., Haas School of Business, University of California, Berkeley.

——. 2003. "Strategic Determinants of Decisions Not to Settle Patent Litigation." *Strategic Management Journal* 24:17–38.

Somaya, Deepak, David J. Teece, and Simon Wakeman. 2011. "Innovation in Multi-Invention Contexts: Mapping Solutions to Technological and Intellectual Property Complexity." *California Management Review* 53:47–79.

Teece, David J. 1981. "The Market for Know-how and the Efficient International Transfer of Technology." *Annals of the Academy of Political and Social Science* 458:81–96.

——. 1985. "Multinational Enterprise, Internal Governance, and Industrial Organization." *American Economic Review* 75:233–38.

——. 1986. "Profiting from Technological Innovation." *Research Policy* 15:285–305.

——. 1988. "Technological Change and the Nature of the Firm." In *Technical Change and Economic Theory*, edited by Giovanni Dosi, Christopher Freeman, Richard Nelson, Gerald Silverberg, and Luc Soete, 256–81. London: Pinter Publishers.

——. 1996. "Firm Organization, Industrial Structure, and Technological Innovation." *Journal of Economic Behavior and Organization* 31:193–224.

——. 2000. *Managing Intellectual Capital: Organizational, Strategic, and Policy Dimensions*. Oxford: Oxford University Press.

——. 2006. "Reflections on Profiting from Innovation." *Research Policy* 35:1131–46.

——. 2007. "Explicating Dynamic Capabilities: The Nature and Microfoundations of (Sustainable) Enterprise Performance." *Strategic Management Journal* 28:1319–50.

——. 2009. *Dynamic Capabilities and Strategic Management: Organizing for Innovation and Growth*. New York: Oxford University Press.

——. 2010. "Business Models, Business Strategy and Innovation." *Long Range Planning* 43:172–94.

——. 2011. "Human Capital, Capabilities and the Firm: Literati, Numerati, and Entrepreneurs in the 21st-Century Enterprise." In *The Oxford Handbook of Human Capital*, edited by Alan Burton-Jones and J.-C. Spender, 527–62. Oxford: Oxford University Press.

Teece, David J., Gary Pisano, and Amy Shuen. 1990. "Firm Capabilities, Resources, and the Concept of Strategy." CCC Working Paper 90-8, Center for Research in Management, University of California, Berkeley.

——. 1997. "Dynamic Capabilities and Strategic Management." *Strategic Management Journal* 18:509–33.

Tushman, Michael L., and Charles A. O'Reilly. 1997. *Winning through Innovation: A Practical Guide to Leading Organizational Change and Renewal*. Boston, MA: Harvard University Press.

Williamson, Oliver E. 1975. *Markets and Hierarchies*. New York: Free Press.

Winter, Sidney G. 2006. "The Logic of Appropriability: From Schumpeter to Arrow to Teece." *Research Policy* 35:1100–1106.

# CHAPTER 14

## STRATEGIES FOR NETWORK INDUSTRIES*

### OZ SHY

## 14.1 INTRODUCTION

ON the demand side, network industries are characterized by buyers and technology users whose utility and benefits from a product or service are determined, to a large degree, by the number of other consumers using the same or a compatible brand. On the supply side, in network industries profit is heavily influenced by the number of other producers or suppliers who use the same or a compatible technology. Loosely speaking, a brand's adoption rate and its popularity significantly influence consumers' willingness to pay for the brand, which then influences the firms' profits.[1]

Firms' strategic behavior and managerial decision making in network industries may differ from those in other industries. This happens because an increase in the demand for one brand need not reduce the demand for competing brands. For example, at the time of writing this article, new tablet computers are being introduced to a market that is dominated by iPads pioneered by Apple Computers. Should Apple be concerned about increased competition in the tablet computers market? Not according to a recent report which argues that Apple is not overly concerned about the impact on iPad sales of the Kindle Fire, which is sold by Amazon, the largest online retailer. Instead, Amazon's tablet might actually help iPad sales in the long run.[2] This example shows that competition in network markets, which increases sales in the aggregate, may actually enhance the demand facing incumbent firms by making the product more popular.

The analysis in this chapter makes use of the following terminology. Consider an industry with firms (service providers) producing (supplying) differentiated goods, which we call *brands*. Brands are said to be *compatible* if they are capable of working together. "Working together" may imply many things, depending on the particular type of product or service. Compatibility usually refers to the ability of brands to communicate with one another, to operate the same software, to link up with the same components, and so on. Consequently, brands based on the same technical *standards* are compatible. In situations where products are incompatible, *converters* can sometimes be employed to create compatibility.

To illustrate how the choice of standards affects the dynamic allocation of market shares among firms adopting different technical standards, Figure 14.1 shows the dynamic battle for market-share dominance in the market for word processing software over the eleven years 1986 to 1996.[3]

Figure 14.1 indicates that WordPerfect dominated the market for word processors from 1986 until 1991, reaching a peak of 47% in 1990, at which time Word for DOS held the second highest share of 16%. In 1991 WordPerfect accounted for 39% while Word for Windows had 26%. In 1992 the shares changed to 23% and 39%, respectively. In 1996 WordPerfect's share fell below 1% while Word for Windows increased to 88%.

The dynamic pattern of market shares displayed in Figure 14.1 raises the question of what could be the causes for the fast replacement of WordPerfect by Microsoft Word for Windows as the dominant product? To investigate this question, it is necessary to look also at the market share of Word for DOS, shown in Figure 14.1, which resembles very much the market share of WordPerfect: both peaked around the same time, between 1989 and 1990. As it turned out, the decline of both of these word processors corresponded with the fast adoption of the Windows operating system and the decline in direct use of DOS, the disk operating system that dominated the PC market during the 1980s. When the Windows version of WordPerfect was introduced during 1991 and 1992, Word for Windows had already become the dominant software, so it was too late for WordPerfect to be able to reverse its fast downward trajectory. This example demonstrates the importance of standard compatibility. On machines running DOS only, users preferred WordPerfect over Microsoft Word. However, when the Windows operating system was introduced, users then began preferring Word for Windows over all

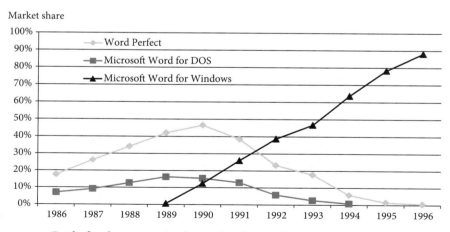

**FIGURE 14.1** Battle for dominance in the market for word processors (1986–96)

*Note:* Market shares are measured in dollar revenue

DOS-based word processors since Word for Windows supported the easier-to-use mouse-supported graphical interface.

What can managers learn from this case study? First, the mangers of WordPerfect almost certainly failed to predict how quickly consumers would switch from DOS to Windows operating system. Second, Word for Windows inherited a technical advantage over WordPerfect because Word was developed by Microsoft, which also developed and sold the Windows operating system.[4]

The dynamic patterns involving the rise and fall of technical standards, such as the word processor case analyzed above, highlights several of the strategic issues and dilemmas facing managers of firms that operate in network industries. More specifically, managers should be able to answer the following questions:

(i) **Early or late introduction?** Should the firm develop the first standard in the market, or wait until competitors "try" the market first? In other words, is there a first- or a second-mover advantage in this market?

(ii) **Leader versus follower?** Should the firm attempt to capture and force its standard over the entire market and become the leading brand, or should the brand be confined to a small niche market and sold mainly to consumers with a greater willingness to pay for the specific brand?

(iii) **Which standard?** For products with late introductions, should the firm's new brand be compatible with existing brands, or operate on a different incompatible standard?

(iv) **Backward compatibility of new technology?** Should a newly introduced technology be backward compatible in the sense of being compatible with older versions, or should it be introduced as a totally new product, new service, or new design?

(v) **License new technology?** Should the firm license its technology or standard to other firms, or risk having competing firms developing competing standards?

This essay will selectively survey the literature that develops tools for addressing these questions, focusing on the methodologies that offer the greatest promise in applied managerial applications. This presentation will rely heavily on numerical examples, and, in so doing, the reader should be able to identify the parameters that influence the profitability and define the trade-offs associated with the strategic choices in network industries.

## 14.2  OPERATING AND SELLING IN NETWORK INDUSTRIES

To operate profitably in any market requires a comprehensive study of the market. Generally, this involves learning how consumers react to prices, promotions, and advertising by all firms within the market. However, operating in network industries is more complicated because of the need to fully understand existing technical standards and to predict the future technical standards that may be introduced by existing or newly entering firms. In particular, it is necessary that the firm estimate buyers' demand behavior in the presence of network (adoption) externalities. As shown in the following subsection, failing to identify how network effects alter the price-quantity relationship may bias the entire prediction of consumer demand and therefore has the potential for causing faulty and costly strategic decisions.

## 14.2.1  Network Effects and Market Demand

Network goods and network connections are generally classified as "stock" goods because consumers' buying decisions are confined to two alternatives: buying exactly one unit or not buying at all. For example, in the markets for telephone and Internet service, most consumers either connect to one network or choose to avoid the service altogether. In contrast, "flow" goods are nonnetwork, perishable goods, such as supplies, for which consumers continually repurchase the goods. The examples analyzed in this chapter focus on network goods in which each individual faces an all (i.e., one unit) or nothing decision.

Consider first a simple demand structure with no network effects, as illustrated in the left panel of Figure 14.2. There are assumed to be $n_1 = 100$ consumers who are willing to pay no more than \$10 for the product/service, $n_2 = 100$ consumers unwilling to pay more than \$20, and $n_3 = 100$ consumers unwilling to pay more than \$30.

Formally, we will denote consumers' valuations or, equivalently, their maximum willingness to pay, by $V_1 = \$10$, $V_2 = \$20$, and $V_3 = \$30$. To find the revenue maximizing price, given that each consumer buys at most one unit, the left panel in Figure 14.2 shows the firm sells $q = n_3$ units when the price is \$30 and earns revenue of \$3,000 (= \$30 × 100). If the price is reduced to \$20, the firm sells $n_2 + n_3$ units and collects \$4,000 [= \$20(100 + 100)]. If the price is further reduced to \$10, the firm sells $n_1 + n_2 + n_3$

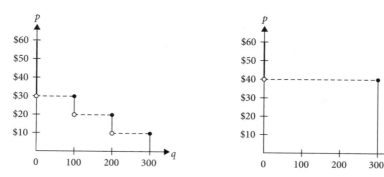

**FIGURE 14.2** *Left*: Demand function with no network effects. *Right*: Demand with network effects

units and collects \$3,000 [= \$10(100 + 100 + 100)]. Hence, in the absence of demand network effects, also called adoption externalities, the revenue maximizing price is \$20.

Suppose now that consumers' preferences exhibit network externalities. The second column in Table 14.1 ($q = 0$) displays the original preferences corresponding to Figure 14.2 (left panel). The third ($q = 100$), fourth ($q = 200$), and fifth ($q = 300$) columns show how the utility of each consumer type is enhanced with an increase in the total number of consumers buying the same product (or subscribing to the same service).

More "technically oriented" readers should note that the entries in Table 14.1 were computed from the consumer utility (willingness to pay) function given by $V_i = v_i + 0.1q$, for each buyer type $i = 1,2,3$. For example, a type 3 buyer's maximum willingness to pay for the brand is $V_3 = v_3 + 0.1q = 30 + 0.1 \times 200 = \$50$ when 200 consumers buy the same brand. Thus, moving to the right on each row shows how buyers' willingness to pay increases when more people buy this brand. Type 3's basic valuation for this brand is \$30. It increases by \$10 to \$40 when 100 consumers buy this brand, and to \$60 when all 300 buy this brand.[5]

The aggregate (across types) market demand function corresponding to Table 14.1 is depicted in Figure 14.2 (right panel), which shows that quantity demanded is zero for all prices above \$40. To see why this is true, suppose price is \$50. At this price, type 2 consumers buy only if the network size reaches 300 consumers. Since type 1 consumers will not buy at a price of \$50 even if the network size is 300, the network size at this price cannot be 300. Also, if the network size reaches only 200 buyers, type 2 will not pay more than \$40. This in turn further reduces the network size to 100 buyers, in which case even type 3 consumers will not pay this price. Therefore, as Figure 14.2 (right panel) shows, quantity demanded is zero for all prices greater than \$40. For all prices less than or equal to \$40, the network size is maximized, reaching 300 buyers.

In Figure 14.2, comparing the shape of demand with no network effects (left panel) to demand under network effects (right panel) reveals that the former demand has four price segments (or kinks) whereas the latter has only two price segments. This happens because network effects tend to generate "herd" behavior leading to situations where either all consumers buy the product/service or all do not buy it. In the absence of network effects, the demand displayed in Figure 14.2 (left panel) shows that any one buyer's willingness to pay is totally independent of other consumers' purchase decisions.

To compute the revenue maximizing price under network effects, Figure 14.2 (right panel) shows sales volume is zero at any price above \$40. If the price is reduced to \$40,

### Table 14.1  Buyers' willingness to pay under network effects

| Buyer type | $q = 0$ | $q = 100$ | $q = 200$ | $q = 300$ |
|---|---|---|---|---|
| 1 | \$10 | \$20 | \$30 | \$40 |
| 2 | \$20 | \$30 | \$40 | \$50 |
| 3 | \$30 | \$40 | \$50 | \$60 |

the firm sells $n_1 + n_2 + n_3$ units and collects \$12,000 [= \$40(100 + 100 + 100)]. Hence, the revenue maximizing price is \$40 when network effects are present.

Comparing the revenue maximizing prices without and with network effects reveals that in the first case it is profitable to serve only 200 customers, whereas in the second case it is profitable to serve all 300 of them. This happens because network effects enhance consumers' willingness to pay and, hence, increasing the number of buyers increases total surplus that the firm can extract from its customers.

## 14.2.2 Crossing the Chasm: The Critical Mass

The previous section has illustrated the sensitivity of consumers' willingness to pay to the total number of buyers in the market. It follows that the introduction of new products or services in network industries may require the establishment of a minimum customer base. That is, a small customer base may be insufficient to generate an aggregate willingness to pay that would cover unit production cost. The minimum customer base needed for generating a sufficient level of willingness to pay is often referred to as the *critical mass*. Intuitively, this is just like going to a social party. There is a minimum number of people below which no one would bother to attend. This is why party organizers tend to inform all invitees of the number of others who plan to come. Formally, for every given price, the critical mass is defined as the minimum number of buyers (subscribers) below which no consumer would find it beneficial to buy (subscribe to) this product (service).

It must emphasized that the critical mass varies with price, and thus the critical mass must be expressed as a function of price, $m(p)$. Since an increase in price will require a larger network of users to convince buyers/subscribers that this purchase is beneficial to them, $\Delta m(p)/\Delta p > 0$.

In Table 14.1, the critical mass at price of \$60 is $m(60) = 300$ buyers; however, this critical mass cannot be achieved because, as shown in Table 14.1, type 1 and type 2 buyers' willingness to pay is less than \$60. Note that the computation of the critical mass should start at the customers with the greatest willingness to pay (type 3 in this example) because they are likely to be the first to purchase this product (or connect to the service). This method corresponds to a view in the marketing literature (see Moore 1991), which argues that marketers should focus on one group of customers at a time, using each group as a base for marketing to the next group. The most difficult step is crossing the chasm between visionaries (the early adopters) and pragmatists (the early majority). The demand structure described in Table 14.1 translates "visionaries" into type 3 buyers.

The critical mass corresponding to the market demand shown in Table 14.1 is illustrated by the starred line in Figure 14.3. For sufficiently low prices ($p < \$30$), the critical mass is zero because the stand-alone value of this product/service for type 3 buyers is \$30 even if there are no other consumers who use this good. Next, Table 14.1 shows that type 3 buyers are willing to pay up to \$40 only if the network of users is greater than or equal to 100 users. In this case, the critical mass is 100 buyers. When the price rises to \$50, the

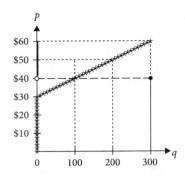

**FIGURE 14.3** Critical mass and market demand under network effects

critical mass becomes 200 users. And the critical mass becomes 300 when the price is further increased to $60.

Finally, Figure 14.3 can be used to derive the relationship between the critical mass and aggregate market demand. If the firm sets the price below $40, the market demand ($q = 300$) exceeds the critical mass ($0 \leq m \leq 100$), in which case the good will be adopted by all potential buyers. In contrast, setting high prices ($p > \$40$) would generate demand below the critical mass. Since the critical mass cannot be achieved in equilibrium, the product introduction is likely to fail in this price range.

## 14.2.3 Three Different Approaches to Analyzing Compatibility

The literature on compatibility can be classified into three groups:

> **Network externalities approach.** The utility of each user varies directly with the number of consumers using or connecting to the same or a compatible brand. Examples include the telephone, email, and social networks, although computer standards are also often analyzed under this paradigm. (See Katz and Shapiro 1985; and Farrell and Saloner 1986.)
>
> **Components approach.** Utility is derived from a *system* of components. Examples include computer keyboards and monitors, or stereo audio receivers and speakers. Each component by itself does not deliver any benefit. A user must assemble an entire system to derive utility from it. Compatibility refers to the technical ability to combine components produced by different manufacturers into a single system. (See Matutes and Regibeau 1988; and Economides 1989.)
>
> **Supporting services approach.** Users do not derive utility from hardware alone. Users' utility is enhanced as the number of software packages written for the specific hardware brand they buy rises. Examples include hardware and software designed for specific operating systems, such as Windows, Unix, and Mac; in the

case of video standards, compatibility refers to the ability of a hardware brand to run software written specifically for a competing brand. (See Chou and Shy 1990, 1996; Church and Gandal 1992a, 1992b; and Markovich and Moenius 2009.)

## 14.2.4  Two- versus One-Way Compatibility

The distinction between two- and one-way compatibility can easily be explained using the software approach described in Section 14.2.3. Consider two competing hardware brands, labeled $A$ (Artichoke) and $B$ (Banana). Examples of hardware we have in mind include computers, audio players, and video players, all of which run standard-specific software. Let $\sigma_A$ denote the number of software packages (or movie titles) written or produced specifically for Artichoke hardware; $\sigma_B$ is similarly defined. Let $s_A$ and $s_B$ denote the number of software packages that can effectively run on Artichoke and Banana machines. The second column in Table 14.2 shows that $s_A = \sigma_A$ and $s_B = \sigma_B$ when the two hardware brands are incompatible. When both machines are compatible, all users have access to all software, hence $s_A = s_B = \sigma_A + \sigma_B$. If the Artichoke hardware producer makes its machine compatible with software written specifically for Banana machines, but Banana machines remain incompatible with Artichoke's software, then $s_A = \sigma_A + \sigma_B > \sigma_B = s_B$.

Suppose that Banana machines are incompatible with the software written specifically for Artichoke machines. The strategic dilemma facing the managers of Artichoke is to identify the conditions under which it is profitable to make the Artichoke machine compatible with the software written specifically for Banana machines. Computer hardware producers, such as Sun and Apple, faced this dilemma in the late 1980s and early 1990s, namely, whether to let their machines' floppy disk drives be compatible with the 1.44 megabyte diskettes that were popular on DOS machines.

Looking at Table 14.2, the reader may be tempted to conclude that the producer of Artichoke hardware can gain only by making Artichoke machines compatible with Banana software, because compatibility increases the value of Artichoke hardware by enlarging the variety of software applications that can be run on Artichoke machines from $s_A = \sigma_A$ to $s_A = \sigma_A + \sigma_B$. As it turns out, this conclusion may be incorrect if we take into consideration the long-term response of the software industry. To see this we analyze the case displayed on the bottom row of Table 14.2 in which Artichoke is compatible

**Table 14.2  Comparing incompatibility, two-way, and one-way compatibility under the software approach**

|  | SA | SB |
|---|---|---|
| Incompatible | $\sigma_A$ | $\sigma_B$ |
| Two-way compatible | $\sigma_A + \sigma_B$ | $\sigma_A + \sigma_B$ |
| One-way compatible | $\sigma_A + \sigma_B$ | $\sigma_B$ |

with Banana software, but not the other way around. Consider the problem faced by a software-developing firm which debates whether to write software supporting the Artichoke hardware or the Banana hardware (assuming that supporting both machines is not feasible). Writing Artichoke software implies that only Artichoke users would buy this software. However, writing software specifically for Banana machines implies that Artichoke and Banana users both would buy this software. Thus, software sales are higher when the software firm develops Banana software than when it is developing software for Artichoke machines. Therefore, in the long run, software writers would support Banana machines only, which eventually would diminish the value of Artichoke machines.

Finally, although one-way compatibility was analyzed using the software approach to compatibility, it is also possible to interpret one-way compatibility using the network externalities approach. Consider, for example, automatic teller machines (ATMs). Commercial banks can make ATMs one-way compatible so that customers of bank *A* are able withdraw money from ATMs located at branches of bank *B*, but not the other way around. In the airline industry we observe alliances that give passengers full credit for miles flown on their own flights, but lower credit for flights taken on other carriers. All of these arrangements are generally negotiated among the competing companies in the industry.

## 14.3 SWITCHING COSTS AND LOCK-IN

Consumers are said to be *locked-in* if they bear a substantial cost of switching to competing brands. Switching costs could be generated by contractual provisions. For example, wireless phone carriers tend to give "free" cell phones to customers who are willing to lock themselves in for two years, with heavy penalties for breaking the contract. Sellers of photocopying machines provide large discounts to customers who sign exclusive service agreements that prohibit customers from obtaining maintenance services from independent third parties. Not all switching costs are generated by contracts. Consumers may get locked in if they acquire a large variety of software supporting only the particular hardware they have already purchased, but will not run on competing machines. Learning curve effects also generate switching costs. For example, users may incur significant costs in becoming familiar with a new operating system when they switch between UNIX, Windows, and the Mac OS. The literature on lock-in and switching costs is surveyed in Farrell and Klemperer (2007).

The above discussion highlights the profit motivation for locking consumers into long-term contracts, propriety software, or postpurchase services. However, managers should bear in mind that, over time, consumers may learn to avoid lock-ins by searching for hardware and aftermarket services that do not bind them to a particular seller or require the payment of fees if they decide to switch. For example, a significant number of wireless phone users have learned over the years to avoid long-term contracts and instead to look for prepaid phone services despite the fact that prepaid services charge higher per-minute prices.

To demonstrate the effect of switching costs on prices, consider a consumer who has purchased brand $A$ before and now debates whether to repurchase brand $A$ or to switch to brand $B$. The consumer's utility function can be written as

$$U = \begin{cases} v_A - p_A & \text{if continues to purchase brand } A \\ v_B - p_B - S & \text{if switches to buying brand } B, \end{cases}$$

where $v_A$ and $v_B$ are the basic willingness to pay for the brands, $p_A$ and $p_B$ are brand prices, and $S$ is the cost of switching from brand $A$ to brand $B$.

For the sake if illustration, suppose that consumers equally value the brands such that $v = v_A = v_B$. Then, the consumer will continue purchasing brand $A$ if $p_A \leq p_B + S$, that is, if the price of $A$ is lower than the price of $B$ plus the switching cost. The consumer will switch to brand $B$ if $p_B < p_A - S$, that is, if firm $B$ subsidizes the consumer's switching cost. Now consider the problem of seller $A$. If $p_B$ is given, firm $A$'s profit maximizing price is $p_A = p_B + S$. Thus, the price seller $A$ can charge is proportional to the magnitude of the switching costs, $S$. This implies that firm $A$ should attempt to make switching more costly to its consumers because switching costs enhance its monopoly power over locked-in customers.

But, there is another way of looking at this situation. Consumers who have already "learned their lesson" will try to avoid lock-ins by considering "open systems" especially if several competing brands are available. Some consumers will be willing to pay a premium (up to $S$) for brands to which being locked in is less probable. Therefore, locking-in consumers is a profitable strategy for loyal customers, but may be unprofitable if it deters new customers from buying the brand.

## 14.4  STANDARDIZATION AND COMPATIBILITY DECISIONS

Section 14.2.3 defined and interpreted the concept of machine compatibility. This section analyzes firms' incentives to make their machines compatible with rival brands. Compatibility decisions can be made noncooperatively or cooperatively among the firms in the industry. A noncooperative decision requires a firm to evaluate whether making a machine compatible with rival brands is profit enhancing, taking into consideration the compatibility decisions of competing firms. A cooperative decision requires firms jointly to agree to adhere to a certain standard; the standard may be developed by one of the firms or by a joint venture of firms in the industry.

## 14.4.1 Noncooperative Choice of Compatibility

Section 14.2.4 analyzed a decision made by one firm to make its machine compatible with the rival's machine. We now analyze whether all firms in a given industry could benefit by agreeing on technical standards that would make their machines compatible with other brands.

There are many examples of industries in which competing firms produce compatible products. The compact cassette, a standard developed in the 1960s, was probably the most popular analog audio standard in the sense that it was adopted by virtually all producers of tape recorders (hardware) and music publishers (software). The Dutch electronics-maker Philips, which developed this standard, ensured worldwide adoption of it by agreeing to license the format free of charge to rival manufacturers. The compact disc replaced the compact cassette as a uniform standard during the 1980s and 1990s. This standard was later adopted by computer manufacturers as a content storage device. Another example of industry-wide compatibility is the way commercial banks in many countries have negotiated agreements that allow customers to withdraw cash at any ATM, including ATMs located at branches of competing brands.

However, examples also exist of industries in which firms produce incompatible products. Operating systems for computers (Unix, Windows, Mac OS) and operating systems for mobile phones (Android, Apple, Windows Mobile) serve as cases in point. We also observe industries in which firms form groups where each of them conforms to a single standard that is incompatible with the standards of other groups. Airline alliances also provide some good examples: Star Alliance, which is composed of twenty-seven airlines including Air Canada, Lufthansa, Scandinavian, Thai Airways, United; Sky Team which is composed of fifteen airlines, including Air France, KLM, Alitalia, China Airlines, and Delta; and Oneworld which is composed of twelve airlines, including American, British, Cathay, and JAL. Airlines within each alliance share a common reservation system through code-sharing agreements, and alliances also allow passengers to obtain some frequent flier miles on all flights made via carriers within the same group.

The solid lines in Figure 14.4 are the price best-response functions of firm $A$ and firm $B$, when brands $A$ and $B$ are incompatible with each other.

As with any Bertrand price competition game, the best-response-functions, $p_A = R_A(p_B)$ and $p_B = R_B(p_A)$, are upward sloping, implying that each firm raises its price in response to an increase in the price of the rival brand. However, to simplify our analysis here, we will assume that buyers set a maximum price that they are willing to pay for each brand. Therefore, the best-response functions in prices are upward-sloping up to given threshold levels denoted by $\bar{p}_A$ and $\bar{p}_B$ in Figure 14.4.

In all panels of Figure 14.4, the equilibrium prices for the incompatible brands are denoted by ∎. In Figure 14.4 (left panel), if each producer designs its machine to be compatible with the other machine, $A$-buyers and $B$-buyers both increase their willingness to pay, thereby shifting upward each firm's price best-response function, as shown by the dashed lines. Figure 14.4 (left panel) demonstrates a case with sufficiently low

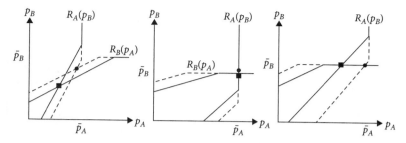

**FIGURE 14.4** Price best-response functions: The effect of compatibility decisions on equilibrium brand prices (▪ under incompatibility, • under compatibility). *Solid line*: Machine is incompatible. *Dashed line*: Machine is made to be compatible with the rival's brand. *Left*: Compatible brands equilibrium. *Middle*: Incompatible brands equilibrium. *Right*: One-way compatibility

equilibrium prices under incompatibility, so that the rise in the equilibrium prices due to the added compatibility features (marked by •) are still below buyers' maximum willingness to pay price levels, $\bar{p}_A$ and $\bar{p}_B$.

Figure 14.4 (middle panel) illustrates the opposite case. Added compatibility features by each brand-producing firm cannot raise equilibrium prices because buyers will refuse to pay beyond their preset budgets, $\bar{p}_A$ and $\bar{p}_B$ In this case, neither firm will invest in making its machines compatible with the rival brand. Figure 14.4 (right panel) illustrates a one-way compatibility equilibrium in which firm $A$ can increase its price by making its brand compatible with brand $B$. However, because firm $B$ cannot increase its price beyond $\bar{p}_B$, it cannot gain from making its machine compatible with brand $A$.

## 14.4.2  Standard Committees and Semicollusion

Consider a service in which consumers value and benefit from having all brands operate on a single standard. However, brand producing firms may not be able to coordinate and agree on a single technical standard that would guarantee compatibility among them. Following Farrell and Saloner (1988), assume that coordination on a uniform standard can be accomplished noncooperatively (firms just choose to adhere to the same technical standards without explicit negotiations), or via a jointly formed committee which discourages incompatibility among brands.

Suppose that firm $A$ and firm $B$ have two time periods in which to agree or disagree on a uniform technical standard. Firm $A$ develops standard $\alpha$ and firm $B$ develops standard $\beta$. The main diagonal in Table 14.3 (left panel) reflects the profit gains from agreeing on a uniform standard (compatibility) relative to not achieving compatibility (off-diagonal). Next, comparing the lower-left with the upper-right quadrants (firms select incompatible standards) shows that firm $A$ and firm $B$ earn higher profits when each adopts its own standard rather than the competitor's standard. Formally, $\pi_A^\ell(\alpha,\beta)=\pi_B^\ell(\alpha,\beta)=2>0=\pi_A^\ell(\beta,\alpha)=\pi_B^\ell(\beta,\alpha)$.

**Table 14.3 Standard coordination: Noncooperation versus joint committee**

|  |  | Firm B | | | | Firm B | | | | Firm B | |
|---|---|---|---|---|---|---|---|---|---|---|---|
|  |  | $\alpha$ | $\beta$ | | | $\alpha$ | $\beta$ | | | $\alpha$ | $\beta$ |
| Firm A | $\alpha$ | 6, 4 | 2, 2 | | $\alpha$ | 6, 4 | 2, 2 | | $\alpha$ | 6, 4 | 3, 3 |
|  | $\beta$ | 0, 0 | 4, 6 | | $\beta$ | 3, 3 | 4, 6 | | $\beta$ | 3, 3 | 4, 6 |
|  |  | Final game | | | | Pregame: No committee | | | | Pregame: Committee | |

Let $\delta_A$ and $\delta_B$ denote the probabilities that firm $A$ and firm $B$ choose standard $\alpha$, respectively. The mixed strategy equilibrium of the final game, Table 14.3 (left panel), is $\delta_A^\ell = 0.75 = 1 - \delta_B^\ell$. Thus, each firm chooses its preferred standard with probability 0.75 and the competing standard with probability 0.25. Hence, the expected profit for each firm from the final game is $E\pi_A^f = E\pi_B^f = 0.75 \cdot 0.25 \cdot 6 + 0.75^2 \cdot 2 + 0.25^2 \cdot 0 + 0.25 \cdot 0.75 \cdot 4 = 3$.

Table 14.3 (middle panel) illustrates a noncooperative pregame. The only difference between this pregame and the final game are the profits of outcome $(\beta, \alpha)$ in the lower-left quadrants (each firm earns a profit of 3 compared to 0). The interpretation of this result is that firms do not accept zero profits during the middle pregame and choose to have a final round which has an expected profit of 3 for each firm. All three other outcomes end the game without proceeding to the final game. The mixed strategy equilibrium of the middle game is $\delta_A^m = 0.6 = 1 - \delta_B^m$. Thus, each firm chooses its own standard with probability 0.6 and the competing standard with probability 0.4.

Table 14.3 (right panel) shows the profit levels in a pregame in which the firms establish a joint committee with a mandate to reject offers $(\alpha, \beta)$ and $(\beta, \alpha)$ that lead to multiple standards, and to force the parties to postpone decision making to the final game which has an expected profit of 3 for each firm. The mixed strategy equilibrium of the right game is $\delta_A^r = 0.75 = 1 - \delta_B^r$. Thus, each firm chooses its own standard with probability 0.75 and the competing standard with probability 0.25.

This model yields two predictions:

(a) Not forming a committee increases the probability of achieving a uniform standard *sooner* (at the pregame stage) relative to when a committee is formed.

(b) Over the two negotiation periods, the probability of achieving a uniform standard is greater when a committee is formed at the pregame stage.

To prove (a), the probability of achieving a uniform standard without a committee (the main diagonal of Table 14.3 (middle panel)) is $0.6 \cdot 0.4 + 0.4 \cdot 0.6 = 0.48$. The probability of achieving a uniform standard with a committee (the main diagonal of Table 14.3 (right panel)) is $0.75 \cdot 0.25 + 0.25 \cdot 0.75 = 0.375 < 0.48$. Intuitively, in the absence of a committee, firms lower the probability of selecting their own standards in order to avoid the outcome $(\alpha, \beta)$ in which each earns a profit of 2 without having a final game. In contrast, a committee ensures that the outcome $(\alpha, \beta)$ will be rejected and the firms will have a second chance to achieve compatibility during the final-period game.

To prove (b), the probability of achieving a uniform standard over the two periods without a committee at the pregame stage is $0.48 + 0.25^2 \cdot 0.375 \approx 0.5$. Note that $0.25^2$ is the probability of reaching the disagreement displayed in the lower-left corner of Table 14.3 (middle panel), which is the only outcome leading to a final game. The probability of achieving a uniform standard with a committee over the two periods of negotiation is $0.375 + (1 - 0.375)0.375 \approx 0.61 > 0.5$. Note that $1 - 0.375$ is the probability of disagreement displayed in the lower-left and the upper-right quadrants of Table 14.3 (right panel), both leading to a final game. This happens because a committee increases the probability of having a final game relative to a pregame without a committee.

# 14.5  DIGITAL CONVERGENCE AND BUNDLING

Not long ago, newspapers were printed only on paper, music was distributed on vinyl records and magnetic tapes, photos were printed on special paper treated with chemical solutions, TV was transmitted via aerial signals and copper cables, and movies were distributed on rolled films. The Internet did not exist and telephone lines were earthbound and each strand of the copper-wire cables could carry only one signal at a time. The digital revolution that intensified during the late 1980s unified the distribution of these diverse media. New technologies were introduced to enable the recording of all types of media in electronic digital formats (zeros and ones).

Today, Internet service providers (ISPs) can use a single copper or fiber optic line to transmit a large volume and variety of content simultaneously. Telephone, TV, and Internet connections are tied (bundled) into services sold as comprehensive packages. Selling packages of voice, video, and data transmission services instead of selling each separately has proven to be a highly profitable strategy that can generate sufficient amounts of revenue to cover the quasi-fixed costs associated with the heavy investments in infrastructure.

Consider a local monopoly ISP facing two consumers with willingness to pay as displayed in Table 14.4. Consumer 1 is willing to pay no more than $9 for a TV subscription and $3 for an Internet subscription. The second consumer's maximum willingness

| Table 14.4  Tying of digital services | | |
| --- | --- | --- |
| Consumer | Television ($T$) | Internet ($I$) |
| 1 | $9 | $3 |
| 2 | $2 | $8 |
| ISP's connecting cost | $1 | $1 |

to pay are $2 and $8, respectively. The ISP incurs a cost of $1 to connect a subscriber to each service.

### 14.5.1  Pricing Content Separately (S)

Inspecting the second column in Table 14.4 reveals that only one consumer will subscribe to TV if $p_T = \$9$, whereas two consumers will subscribe if $p_T = \$2$. The profit made from TV subscriptions when setting $p_T = \$9$ is $\pi_T = 9 - 1 = \$8$. The profit made when setting $p_T = \$2$ is $\pi_T = 2(2 - 1) = \$2$. Hence, $p_T = \$9$ is the profit-maximizing TV subscription fee.

Inspecting the third column in Table 14.4 reveals that only one consumer will subscribe to the Internet if $p_I = \$8$, whereas two consumers will subscribe if $p_I = \$3$. The profit from setting $p_I = \$8$ is $\pi_I = 8 - 1 = \$7$. The profit from setting $p_I = \$3$ is $\pi_I = 2(3 - 1) = \$4$. Hence, $p_I = \$8$ is the profit-maximizing Internet subscription fee. Summing up, when the ISP does not bundle services it earns a profit given by $\pi^S = \pi_T + \pi_I = \$7 + \$8 = \$15$.

### 14.5.2  Pricing Bundled Packages (B)

Suppose that the ISP offers customers a single package containing a subscription both to TV and Internet for a single price denoted by $p_B$. Inspecting each row in Table 14.4 reveals that consumer 1 will not pay more than $p_B = 9 + 3 = \$12$ for this package, whereas consumer 2 will not pay more than $p_B = 2 + 8 = \$10$. Therefore, the ISP earns a profit $\pi^B(12) = 12 - 2 \cdot 1 = \$10$ if $p_B = \$12$, whereas the profit becomes $\pi^B(10) = 2(10 - 2 \cdot 1) = \$16$ if $p_B = \$10$. Thus, the ISP's profit-maximizing price for the packaged services is $p_B = 2 + 8 = \$10$ and the profit is $\pi^B(10) = 2(10 - 2 \cdot 1) = \$16 > \$15 = \pi^S$. Therefore, bundling can enhance the ISP's profit beyond the level made when TV and Internet services are sold separately. Shy (2008, sec. 4.2) analyzes more general bundling pricing strategies, such as mixed bundling in which the seller offers packages and individual services simultaneously.

## 14.6  SOFTWARE PIRACY AND MARKET SEGMENTATION

Without copy protection, digital information and software are easy to copy and transfer. Developers of digital information have the following (not mutually exclusive) options:

(a) To build protection mechanisms into the product in order to make copying more difficult.

(b) Take legal actions against copyright violators.
(c) To bundle the product or service with additional features and extra services that would be accessible only to buyers but not to unregistered users.

Option (a) was commonly used during the 1980s in the early days of personal computers. However, software developers started removing protection during the 1990s mostly because protective devices caused severe technical failures, which buyers did not like. Option (b) imposes significant litigation costs that do not contribute to the improvement of the product itself. Therefore, litigation has been found to be a failing strategy because it did not increase sales. In fact, in 2008 the Recording Industry Association of America (RIAA) decided to stop mass ligation against individuals.[6] The RIAA concluded that litigation had little effect in generating sales. The initial claim that the downloading of music contributed to the decline of CD sales may have been wrong because this decline may have been caused by a technology change from bulky CD players to light memory-based players, such as the iPod.

The major flaw in the reasoning behind copyright litigation is the assumption that each free or illegal download is equivalent to a sales loss of one unit. Zentner (2006), Liebowitz (2006), Rob and Waldfogel (2006, 2007), De Vany and Walls (2007), Oberholzer-Gee and Strumpf (2007), and Waldfogel (2009) demonstrate empirically that this is not necessarily the case. To see this result, let $n^b$ denote the number of buyers and $n^d$ the number of downloads without paying. Then, ideally, we want to estimate the coefficients $\beta$ and $\gamma$ in the equation

$$n^b = \alpha - \beta n^d + \gamma \left( n^b + n^d \right), \tag{1}$$

and determine whether $\beta \geq 0$ and $\gamma \geq 0$. The magnitude of $\beta$ determines the degree of substitution between downloads and sales. $\beta = 1$ implies that each download results in exactly one unit fewer sales, whereas $0 \leq \beta < 1$ implies a smaller sales loss. In the extreme case, $\beta = 0$ implies that downloads have no effects on sales. The parameter $\gamma \geq 0$ measures the intensity of network effects and how willingness to buy increases with the number of other consumers who use the same brand. Notice that $n^b$ appears on both sides of (1) because buyers are influenced by the total number of users regardless of how users acquire digital content. Assuming that $0 \leq \gamma < 1$, equation (1) implies that the marginal effect of downloading on sales can be estimated by $\partial n^b / \partial n^d = (\gamma - \beta)/(1 - \gamma)$. Note that downloading increases sales if $\gamma > \beta$ and reduces them if $\gamma < \beta$; see Conner and Rumelt (1991) for a more complete model. Peitz and Waelbroeck (2006) find that publishers can enhance their profits by allowing free downloading and sampling of digital products, because consumers are willing to pay more if the match between a product's characteristics and their tastes is improved.

Option (c) on the above list is a strategy intended for segmenting the market by providing additional services to paying customers. Extra services include telephone support, free or discounted upgrades, and additional features. To demonstrate how this can be done, consider a market with one consumer who is support-oriented and a second consumer who is support-independent. The support-oriented consumer's willingness to pay is $100 if no one else buys it, and $200 if both buy it. Similarly, the support-independent consumer valuations are $20 and $40, respectively. These valuations reflect strong network effects in which consumers double their willingness to pay if other consumers also use the same product or service. Now suppose that the seller invests $I$ to provide additional services to consumers who actually buy the software and assume that the support-oriented consumer prefers buying over downloading at the given market prices.

The seller has two options. To protect the software so that only paying customers can use it, or not to protect it so that it can be downloaded freely (without the support component which is available only to buyers). Table 14.5 computes the profit levels as a function of prices under the protection and no protection options.

When the seller protects the software, the number of users equals exactly the number of buyers because there is no free downloading and piracy is not possible. In contrast, when software is unprotected, the number of users may exceed the number of buyers.

When software is protected, setting price less than or equal to $40 ($p \leq \$40$) would induce both consumers to buy, yielding a maximum profit of $80 (= 2 × $40). Raising the price to $100 would eliminate the support-independent buyer, yielding a profit of $100. Observe that the support-dependent buyer will not pay more than $100 as long as no one else is buying it (no network effects).

When software is unprotected, the support-independent consumer downloads and uses it without paying. Therefore, with network effects, the support-dependent consumer's willingness to pay rises to $200, yielding a $200 profit. Thus, this example demonstrates that no protection could be a profitable strategy in industries where consumer preferences exhibit strong network effects.

It is important to emphasize that a no-protection policy can be profitable only if the seller can provide buyers with additional services that would convince the support-oriented consumer to pay for the software rather than using the free download version. In the above model, unprotecting increases profit by $100 compared with protecting, which means that nonprotection is a profitable strategy as long as the seller's cost of providing additional features to buyers is less than $I = \$100$.

### Table 14.5 Comparing profits under free downloads and with copy protection.

|  | Protected Software | | | | Unprotected Software | | | |
|---|---|---|---|---|---|---|---|---|
| Price ($p$) | $20 | $40 | $100 | $200 | $20 | $40 | $100 | $200 |
| # buyers | 2 | 2 | 1 | 0 | 1 | 1 | 1 | 1 |
| # users | 2 | 2 | 1 | 0 | 2 | 2 | 2 | 2 |
| Profit | $40 | $80 | $100 | $0 | $20 | $40 | $100 | $200 |

Note: # users includes buyers plus those who download without paying

Finally, note that litigation is not profitable in this scenario not only because of legal fees, but also because the elimination of the service-independent consumer from the market will reduce the service-dependent customer's willingness to pay from $200 down to $100. Gayer and Shy (2006) identify additional complications with litigation stemming from conflicts of interest among artists, publishers, and their lawyers.

# 14.7  Innovation and New Technology Adoption

Innovation facilitated by investments in research and development is necessary for maintaining a firm's position in the market. Developing new technologies often requires a complete redesign of the product or service, its features, or even its functionality. If a newly improved technology is incompatible with an old technology, new consumers (or firms) may face a trade-off between reaping the benefits associated with the higher-quality technology and continuing to enjoy connectivity with "old" consumers who may not be able to switch. Apple provides a good example of this trade-off. In 2001 it introduced its first portable digital music player, the iPod, which required special software making it incompatible with existing digital music players. A few analysts predicted failure based on this partial compatibility, but history showed that consumers were willing to sacrifice some compatibility to gain a higher-quality product. Following Shy (1996), Figure 14.5 illustrates the trade-off between network size and quality using ordinary consumer indifference curves.

Figure 14.5 (left panel) illustrates a significant difference in quality between technology 1 and technology 2 (i.e., $Q_2 - Q_1$ is large). Although technology 2 is incompatible with the older technology, new users are still better off purchasing it. Figure 14.5 (right panel) illustrates the opposite case in which the utility loss from being incompatible with the old technology outweighs the gain in quality between technology 2 and technology 1. In this case, technology 2 will not be adopted by new buyers.

FIGURE 14.5 Trade-off between quality and network size. ▪ utility from lower quality compatible with old technology. • utility from higher quality incompatible technology

## 14.8 ANTITRUST CONSIDERATIONS

Network industries often present additional dilemmas for competition authorities and for antitrust jurisprudence. This is because network effects tend to attract a large number of consumers around the same platforms and standards, which may lead to an industry dominated by a few or even one firm.

It should be mentioned that being a single seller does not by itself constitute a violation of the law. What count as violations are the actions firms with large market shares take to deter entry or to prevent expansion of market shares of competing firms. In the United States, Section 2 of the Sherman Act (1890) refers to these actions as "attempting to monopolize." In Europe, Article 86 of the EC Treaty calls such actions an "abuse of dominant position." Thus, although competition laws do not prevent firms from reaching dominant positions, managers should exercise more caution in making sure that consumers' preferences for large networks are not used to prevent the emergence of competing networks.

Lawsuits filed in the United States and Europe against Microsoft, which had 90% to 95% of the global PC operating systems market, provide good examples. Microsoft was sued for its anticompetitive actions, not for its dominance. In a 1998 lawsuit, the US Department of Justice accused Microsoft of using its dominant position in the market for operating systems to gain a dominant position in the market for Internet browsers by bundling its Internet Explorer with its Windows operating system. This strategy is commonly referred to as *leverage*. In 2004, the European Commission fined Microsoft 497 million Euros and ordered the company to provide a version of Windows without Windows Media Player, claiming that Microsoft "broke European Union competition law by leveraging its near monopoly in the market for PC operating systems onto the markets for work group server operating systems and for media players."[7]

Leveraging generally relies on bundling (see Section 14.5) and lock-in (see Section 14.3). The seller exploits consumers' preferences for purchasing complementary products and services to gain dominance in new markets; see Carbajo et al. (1990) and Seidmann (1991) for formal analyses. Finally, Section 14.4.2 discussed coordination of standards among competing firms. Negotiators of interfirm agreements must exercise extreme care not to mix coordination of technical standards with marketing strategies in general, and pricing in particular. Exchanging price information among competitors constitutes a violation of Section 1 of the Sherman Act and is viewed as a criminal offense, thus subjecting firms found guilty of such violations to large fines and company executives to prison sentences.

## 14.9 CONCLUDING REMARKS

The purpose of this chapter is to identify some important strategic considerations for firms operating in network industries which might be of interest to researchers in managerial economics. Network economics is a relatively new field in economics, which is often regarded as a subfield of the study of Industrial Organization. However, more than twenty years of research, much of which is summarized in this chapter, has paved the way for understanding the main strategic issues facing firms and the central policy issues associated with network industries that create unique challenges for regulatory authorities.

For business decision making, network economics does not change fundamental managerial principles but rather adds some additional complications. Companies must formulate business models regardless of the type of industry in which they operate. Proper pricing techniques must be carefully designed as in any other type of industry. The main difference is that, in network industries, pricing decisions must be integrated into the firm's general strategy with the aim to lock-in potential customers into a specific standard. In order to accomplish this objective, the service may need to be split into two components: one which is provided for free (or at low cost) and the other which is sold at a premium. This pricing strategy is often referred to as *market segmentation*, meaning the service is redesigned to be sold at different prices targeted to consumer groups with different demand elasticities.

The reader may be familiar with Skype, a provider of telephony services transmitted via VoIP (voice-over-Internet-protocol) technology. What some readers may not know is that Skype was not the first to offer such services. Other companies, such as VocalTec, developed and sold VoIP technologies long before Skype existed. The key to Skype's success was the decomposition of the service into a computer-to-computer service and a computer-to-phone network service. To lure consumers into using VoIP in order to create the necessary network size at or beyond the critical mass, Skype did not charge for phone calls made between two personal computers linked to the Internet. A similar tactic was used by Adobe which introduced its Portable Document Format (PDF) as a totally new product in the early 1990s. For the sake of building a new network of users, Adobe distributed its Acrobat Reader version free of charge, allowing users to read PDF documents but not to create or edit them. Adobe's business model was based on profits made from publishers that did produce and distribute these PDF files. These business models are in place up to this very day (see skype.com, VocalTec.com, and adobe.com).

To conclude our discussion of business models, a properly designed pricing strategy becomes even more important in network industries because it adds a dynamic dimension, both *before* and *after* the minimum network size is established. Strangely enough, conventional business school curricula do not emphasize teaching students "how to price." Thus, typical MBAs are not trained well enough to manage firms seeking strategically to introduce new standards; and in particular they lack the knowledge of how a firm's pricing structure can be integrated into the dynamic evolution of a new network of users.

As for antitrust policy, the core principles have not changed. Actions taken by firms for the purpose of lessening competition and impeding the entry of new firms will continue to be challenged by competition authorities. However, promoting competition in network industries will involve an additional challenge to antitrust authorities because they must ensure that new entrants can interconnect with established firms. In some instances, the authorities will need to determine the access price entrants must pay to use the infrastructure built and maintained by dominant operators. Virtual cell phone operators provide a good example of such a policy. Some retail stores and pharmacy chains offer cell phone services under less-familiar brand names sold at lower prices than the three or four dominant service providers. These operators are called *virtual* because they do not operate their own antennas. Instead, virtual operators access the networks owned by the large operators. Such networks are often referred to as *essential facilities*. The role of the competition authorities is therefore to ensure that dominant operators provide access to small operators and do not charge prohibitively high access prices, while allowing the dominant providers to recover their costs. How competition authorities determine access prices is beyond the scope of this chapter, but the reader should bear in mind that other industries, such as public utilities, adhere to similar principles. Maintaining competition in these industries often involves a separation of production from transmission services (see chap. 20 for analyses of vertical structures).

## Notes

* I thank Stan Liebowitz for his help in preparing Figure 14.1. The views and opinions expressed in this paper are those of the author and do not necessarily represent the views of the Federal Reserve Bank of Boston or the Federal Reserve System.

1. For some references and discussions of network economics see Katz and Shapiro (1994), Economides (1996), Shy (2001, 2011), Liebowitz (2002), Church and Gandal (2005), and Birke (2009). This essay does not provide a complete list of references. Readers who seek to enhance their reading on topics discussed in this essay are encouraged to consult these surveys which contain more comprehensive reference lists.

2. *PC Magazine*, December 5, 2010, http://www.pcmag.com/article2/0,2817,2397227,00.asp.

3. Market shares in Figure 14.1 do not sum to 100% because smaller market shares (WordStar, DisplayWrite, Samna Word, and Multimate) are not displayed for the sake of clarity.

4. Replacement of dominant standards is common in most network industries. Besen and Johnson (1986) and Besen (1992) describe the evolutions and dominance of color TV and radio standards in the United States. The adoption patterns of other technical standards are discussed in Shapiro and Varian (1998). See Liebowitz and Margolis (2001) for a comprehensive analysis of the Microsoft case.

5. The first analytical formulation of demand under network effects is attributed to Rohlfs (1974), who constructed a continuous demand function for a telecommunications service. The analysis here introduces a discrete version of his model.

6. Sarah McBride and Ethan Smith, 2008, "Music Industry to Abandon Mass Suits," *Wall Street Journal*, December 19, http://online.wsj.com/article/SB122966038836021137.html.

7. European Competition Commission, press release IP/04/382, Brussels, March 24, 2004.

## References

Besen, S. 1992. "AM versus FM: The Battle of the Bands." *Industrial and Corporate Change* 1 (2): 375–96.

Besen, S., and L. Johnson. 1986. "Compatibility Standards, Competition, and Innovation in the Broadcasting Industry." *Rand Corporation*, Report no. R-3453-NSF.

Birke, D. 2009. "The Economics of Networks: A Survey of the Empirical Literature." *Journal of Economic Surveys* 23 (4): 762–93.

Carbajo, J., D. De Meza, and D. Seidmann. 1990. "A Strategic Motivation for Commodity Bundling." *The Journal of Industrial Economics* 38 (3): 283–98.

Chou, C., and O. Shy. 1990. "Network Effects without Network Externalities." *International Journal of Industrial Organization* 8 (2): 259–70.

———. 1996. "Do Consumers Gain or Lose When More People Buy the Same Brand?" *European Journal of Political Economy* 12 (2): 309–30.

Church, J., and N. Gandal. 1992a. "Integration, Complementary Products, and Variety." *Journal of Economics & Management Strategy* 1 (4): 651–75.

———. 1992b. "Network Effects, Software Provision, and Standardization." *Journal of Industrial Economics* 40 (1): 85–103.

———. 2005. "Platform Competition in Telecommunications." In *Handbook of Telecommunications Economics*, edited by M. Cave, S. Majumdar, and I. Vogelsang, 2:119–55. Amsterdam and Boston: Elsevier.

Conner, K., and R. Rumelt. 1991. "Software Piracy: An Analysis of Protection Strategies." *Management Science* 37 (2): 125–39.

De Vany, A., and W. Walls. 2007. "Estimating the Effects of Movie Piracy on Box-Office Revenue." *Review of Industrial Organization* 30 (4): 291–301.

Economides, N. 1989. "Desirability of Compatibility in the Absence of Network Externalities." *American Economic Review* 79 (5): 1165–81.

———. 1996. "The Economics of Networks." *International Journal of Industrial Organization* 14 (6): 673–99.

Farrell, J., and P. Klemperer. 2007. "Coordination and Lock-In: Competition with Switching Costs and Network Effects." In *Handbook of Industrial Organization*, edited by M. Armstrong and R. Porter, 3:1967–2072. Amsterdam: Elsevier.

Farrell, J., and G. Saloner. 1986. "Standardization and Variety." *Economics Letters* 20 (1): 71–74.

———. 1988. "Coordination through Committees and Markets." *Rand Journal of Economics* 19 (2): 235–52.

Gayer, A., and O. Shy. 2006. "Publishers, Artists, and Copyright Enforcement." *Information Economics and Policy* 18 (4): 374–84.

Katz, M., and C. Shapiro. 1985. "Network Externalities, Competition, and Compatibility." *American Economic Review* 75 (3): 424–40.

———. 1994. "Systems Competition and Network Effects." *Journal of Economic Perspectives* 8 (2): 93–115.

Liebowitz, S. 2002. *Rethinking the Network Economy: The True Forces that Drive the Digital Marketplace.* New York: Amacom Books.

———. 2006. "File Sharing: Creative Destruction or Just Plain Destruction?" *Journal of Law and Economics* 49 (1): 1–28.

Liebowitz, S., and S. Margolis. 2001. *Winners, Losers & Microsoft; Competition and Antitrust in High Technology.* Oakland, CA: Independent Institute.

Markovich, S., and J. Moenius. 2009. "Winning while Losing: Competition Dynamics in the Presence of Indirect Network Effects." *International Journal of Industrial Organization* 27 (3): 346–57.

Matutes, C., and P. Regibeau. 1988. "'Mix and Match': Product Compatibility without Network Externalities." *Rand Journal of Economics* 19 (2): 221–34.

Moore, G. 1991. *Crossing the Chasm.* New York: Harper Business Essentials.

Oberholzer-Gee, F., and K. Strumpf. 2007. "The Effect of File Sharing on Record Sales: An Empirical Analysis." *Journal of Political Economy* 115 (1): 1–42.

Peitz, M., and P. Waelbroeck. 2006. "Why the Music Industry May Gain from Free Downloading— The Role of Sampling." *International Journal of Industrial Organization* 24 (5): 907–13.

Rob, R., and J. Waldfogel. 2006. "Piracy on the High C's: Music Downloading, Sales Displacement, and Social Welfare in a Sample of College Students." *Journal of Law and Economics* 49 (1): 29–62.

———. 2007. "Piracy on the Silver Screen." *Journal of Industrial Economics* 55 (3): 379–95.

Rohlfs, J. 1974. "A Theory of Interdependent Demand for a Communications Service." *Bell Journal of Economics and Management Science* 5 (1): 16–37.

Seidmann, D. J. 1991. "Bundling as a Facilitating Device: A Reinterpretation of Leverage Theory." *Economica* 58 (232): 491–99.

Shapiro, C., and H. Varian. 1998. *Information Rules*. Boston: Harvard Business School Press.

Shy, O. 1996. "Technology Revolutions in the Presence of Network Externalities." *International Journal of Industrial Organization* 14 (6): 785–800.

———. 2001. *The Economics of Network Industries*. Cambridge and New York: Cambridge University Press.

———. 2008. *How to Price: A Guide to Pricing Techniques and Yield Management*. Cambridge and New York: Cambridge University Press.

———. 2011. "A Short Survey of Network Economics." *Review of Industrial Organization* 38 (2): 119–49.

Waldfogel, J. 2009. "Lost on the Web: Does Web Distribution Stimulate or Depress Television Viewing?" *Information Economics and Policy* 21 (2): 158–68.

Zentner, A. 2006. "Measuring the Effect of Music Downloads on Music Purchases." *Journal of Law and Economics* 49 (1): 63–90.

# CHAPTER 15

# INTERNALIZATION THEORY AS THE GENERAL THEORY OF INTERNATIONAL STRATEGIC MANAGEMENT: PAST, PRESENT AND FUTURE

ALAIN VERBEKE* *WITH* LIENA KANO**

## 15.1 INTRODUCTION

INTERNALIZATION theory, as the general economic theory of the multinational enterprise (MNE), has contributed enormously to explaining the existence and functioning of MNEs during the past four decades (Buckley and Strange 2011). Internalization theory's key point, as a positive theory of the firm, is that exploiting and augmenting the firm's knowledge-based assets across national boundaries can be performed through a variety of operating modes, whereby a limited number of parameters determine the "optimal" mode to be selected and retained. International activities are sometimes most efficiently undertaken "internally"—that is, within the MNE's hierarchical structure. Built largely on Coasean (1937) transaction cost economics foundations, and first formulated in Buckley and Casson's (1976) classic work, the internalization approach has strongly influenced the international business (IB) literature since its inception (Safarian 2003). The theory has been the subject of substantial scholarly dialogue, and various refinements and extensions have made it the analytical tool *par excellence* for the study of international strategic management decisions, more specifically in the context of three types of governance choices: (1) the choice of the firm's boundaries; (2) the structuring of the interfaces with the external environment; and (3) the firm's internal organization (see Casson 1979, 1986, 1987; Rugman 1981; Buckley 1998a, 1998b; Buckley 1983; Hennart, 1982; Teece 1983).

As the IB research field has matured, so has internalization theory. Conventional internalization theory, exemplified by the work of Buckley and Casson (1976), Hennart (1982) and Rugman (1981), focused primarily on the parameters stimulating firms to expand across borders and on MNE entry mode choices. It largely ignored internal governance issues and the selection of organizational structures within the MNE. Subsequent internalization theory developments, brought *inter alia* by Rugman and Verbeke's work (1992, 2003, 2004), constitute what can be called the "new" internalization theory, with the focus shifting to the MNE's internal organization and network capabilities. This expanded focus was achieved by infusing a "dynamic capabilities"-like perspective into transaction cost economics thinking, with an emphasis on generating, exploiting, and rejuvenating firm-specific advantages (FSAs), especially those related to knowledge-based assets (Rugman and Verbeke 2008). This integration of complementary conceptual perspectives has made internalization theory particularly powerful as a general theory of the firm. The new internalization theory can explain the choice of MNE boundaries, as well as the firm's internal governance and its interactions with external environmental forces. Parsimonious, in addition to being relevant to managerial decision making, internalization theory covers a variety of aspects of the MNE's functioning while building upon a limited number of foundational principles (Rugman and Verbeke 2008).

In this chapter, we analyze internalization theory's impact on IB research. We review its intellectual foundations and key applications, and conclude with a projection of internalization theory's future contributions to IB research. We show how an internalization perspective can enrich analysis of various contemporary IB phenomena.

## 15.2 INTERNALIZATION THEORY: ESSENTIAL ARGUMENT, ANTECEDENTS AND HISTORY

Internalization theory was first conceptualized by Buckley and Casson (1976) and has its origins in a number of studies, including the work of Coase (1937), Hymer (1968, 1976) and McManus (1972). Coase (1937), who sought to explain the existence of hierarchies as opposed to markets by analyzing transaction costs involved in effecting exchanges, provides perhaps the most critical antecedent to internalization theory. In Coase's view, a hierarchy supersedes the market if the costs of organizing exchanges within a firm are lower than the market transaction costs; internalization theory extends these arguments developed for the domestic context to the MNE. To "internalize" means to perform a transaction within the firm, and internalization theory essentially describes the MNE as an internal market that operates across national boundaries (Verbeke and Greidanus 2009). The theory focuses on the relative costs and benefits of coordinating cross-border economic activities internally, through managerial fiat, rather than externally through the market (Buckley and Strange 2011). The core argument is that profit-maximizing firms internalize markets for intermediate goods (especially various types of knowledge and experience embodied in intangible assets such as technology, production know-how, patents, brand reputation, etc.) across national borders in the face of various market imperfections. These imperfections can take the form of information asymmetries between buyers and sellers, government-imposed trade barriers, unenforceable national patent systems, the lack of futures markets for knowledge generation, imperfect knowledge pricing, etc. (DeGennaro 2005; Rugman et al. 2011). Market imperfections can be bypassed by bringing economic activities under common ownership and control; if these activities are located in different countries, then an MNE will result (Buckley and Strange 2011). Further, the MNE will organize bundles of activities internally so as to enable development and exploitation of FSAs in intermediate products: The proprietary ownership and internal deployment of these FSAs serves to overcome the sometimes formidable challenges of assessing the value of knowledge and pricing it in external markets, with the pricing outcome being influenced by expected future value creation and value capture by the parties involved. Internalization becomes a governance mechanism for managing the FSA development and exploitation process in its entirety (Rugman and Verbeke 2008).

Developed by Hymer ([1960] 1976, 1968), the concept of FSAs is deeply embedded in Buckley and Casson's (1976) work and is often viewed as the starting point for internalization decisions (Safarian 2003). Hymer's insight was that foreign direct investment (FDI) only takes place when the benefits of exploiting FSAs through internalization are higher than the additional costs of conducting business across borders. These additional costs may include, *inter alia*, information costs facing MNEs *vis-à-vis* host country rivals, discriminatory treatment by governments and foreign exchange risks. Zaheer (1995) later coined the phrase "liability of foreignness" to describe these costs of doing business abroad. Hymer focused primarily on institutional differences among nations and the resulting hazards facing foreign MNEs (Eden and Miller 2004). However, Hymer did not really develop a complete theory of optimal operating mode choice. Internalization theory, in contrast, explicitly addresses this issue. Assuming that the MNE commands FSAs sufficient to compensate for the additional costs of doing business abroad, internalization theory seeks to explain *how* the MNE overcomes market imperfections (Buckley and Casson 1976; Casson 1979). Here, Hymer's concept of FSAs and his focus on market imperfections in final product markets is extended: internalization of intermediate product markets becomes the core of a theory to explain FDI and the MNE's existence (Rugman 1981; Rugman et al. 2011).

Hymer correctly viewed FDI as a firm-level strategy decision driven by FSAs rather than as a mere financial investment decision determined by interest rate differentials across nations (Dunning and Rugman 1985). The latter perspective represented the prevailing orthodoxy in international economics research at that time. Hymer essentially pioneered a firm-level industrial organization approach, as opposed to a financial portfolio investment approach, to explain FDI. Hymer's approach was popularized by Kindleberger (1969), and later through Dunning's (1981) eclectic paradigm, termed "eclectic" for its comprehensive melding of several theory streams on FDI (Rugman 1986). Also known as the Ownership-Location-Internalization (OLI) paradigm, Dunning's model combines ownership, internalization, and location advantages to explain foreign entry mode choices and their economic efficiency implications. Location advantages capture differences among countries and regions, whereas ownership and internalization advantages reflect prior firm-level strategy decisions and their outcomes. While representing a comprehensive framework to explain foreign entry mode choices and the economic efficiency implications thereof, the eclectic paradigm suffers from a relative lack of parsimony when compared with internalization theory (Rugman et al. 2011). As explained above, a critical challenge for MNEs is to select the governance structure (e.g., internalization versus usage of the external market) that will be the most effective one among feasible, real world alternatives to exploit and further develop FSAs. Here, the (O) advantage is closely intertwined with the (I) advantage, because to "internalize" means to perform a transaction *within* the firm, which is often a necessary condition for profitable FSA exploitation to occur. (O) is also inseparable from the (L) advantage, as costs and benefits derived from FSA ownership are unavoidably influenced by location factors (Itaki 1991).

Rugman (1981) emphasized that each MNE commands an idiosyncratic set of FSAs, which gives it a competitive advantage over rivals. These FSAs relate to special knowledge or capabilities unavailable to or inimitable by competitors, except at a high cost and in the long run. This line of reasoning invites a comparison with the contemporary resource-based view (RBV) of the firm pioneered by Barney (1991). While the FSA concept predates the RBV by a full decade, it does have its origins in the pioneering work of Edith Penrose (1959), whose view of the firm as an evolving collection of resources was incorporated in modern RBV thinking (Rugman and Verbeke 2002). Similar to Penrose's view that economic value creation stems from effective and innovative management of resources, internalization theory posits that the MNE's international success is determined by effective FSA utilization. Internalization theory's departure from its Penrosean roots, however, is manifested in its view of the environment: while Penrose believed that constraints to the firm's growth resided with the entrepreneur (or entrepreneurial management team), internalization theory ascribes a more active role to the environment and sees it as a constraining or enabling force, as embodied in the notion of country-specific advantages (CSAs) (Rugman 1981). CSAs (e.g., natural resources, low-cost labor available in a particular location, etc.) reflect the attractiveness of particular expansion targets distributed across geographic space to the MNE and essentially determine, along with the firm's FSAs, whether or not internal organization of the MNE's international activities is the most effective governance mode.

As mentioned above, internalization theory is deeply rooted in the transaction cost economizing logic—and could therefore be referred to as "transaction cost internalization," or TCI. Internalization theory, however, goes beyond Oliver Williamson's (1975) TCE focus on the possibility of redeploying assets involved in a transaction without the loss of economic value (i.e., managing "the transaction in its entirety"; see below), toward a broader interest in dynamic processes of efficiently developing and exploiting FSAs across borders (i.e., managing the "innovation process in its entirety"). From an internalization theory perspective, the MNE as an institution becomes itself a governance mechanism specialized in resource recombination: The TCE foundations are thus augmented with a dynamic capabilities-like perspective (Teece et al. 1997). Fittingly, the unit of analysis shifts from TCE's focus on the individual transaction to internalization theory's focus on the firm.[1] Interestingly, the core idea that the MNE is an internal market operating across national boundaries, was developed by so-called "Reading School" scholars (Buckley and Casson 1976; Rugman 1981) independently of the foundational TCE work of Oliver Williamson (1975, 1981a). The two streams developed in parallel (Rugman 1986), and the obvious link between both only became apparent as a result of two influential publications. First, Williamson's former student David Teece crafted an extension of Williamson's conceptual framework (largely based on a mainly domestic American institutional context) to include an international dimension (Teece 1981, 1983). Second, Jean-Francois Hennart published his 1977 doctoral dissertation on internalization theory and the MNE (Hennart 1982; Rugman and Verbeke 2008).

Beyond its role in marrying the two transatlantic streams of thought on MNE theory (Rugman 1986), Hennart's work can be seen as the beginning of a shift toward the "new" internalization theory, as he was the first scholar to address internal organizational issues involved in internalization. Specifically, Hennart focused on managing interdependencies between economic actors located in different countries, which involves accessing, recombining, and orchestrating the productive usage of various sets of geographically dispersed resources within the MNE (Hennart 1982). Hennart's significant contribution is his drawing attention to the role of complementary resources of foreign actors that the MNE may require for exploiting its own FSAs. MNEs' foreign expansion decisions thus depend on the availability of such complementary resources. This line of thinking was further developed in Hennart's most recent work, where he argues that boundaries between FSAs and CSAs are blurrier than commonly assumed, and that host country CSAs are not necessarily readily accessible to the expanding MNE. In this context, the MNE's international expansion is seen as an equilibrium outcome of strategic decisions made by MNE managers, and by the economic actors who own or control host nation CSAs (Hennart 2009).

## 15.3 EVOLUTION OF INTERNALIZATION THEORY

The central concerns of early internalization theory (Buckley and Casson 1976; Rugman 1981) included economic efficiency, identification of parameters that stimulate international expansion, and entry mode choice. While respecting the above concerns, the focus of more recent extensions of internalization theory (Hennart 1982, 2009; Rugman and Verbeke 1992, 2003) has shifted to internal organization, alternative governance choices within the MNE, and MNE network analysis. Broadly speaking, new internalization theory aims to establish linkages with the strategic management perspective on the MNE (Rugman and Verbeke 2008); see below.

## 15.3.1  Entry Mode Choice

The term "foreign operation mode" is generally accepted to mean the MNE's way of operating in foreign markets; more specifically, it has been defined as "the organizational arrangements that a company uses to conduct international business activities" (Benito et al. 2009, 1458). The mode of entry into a foreign market has long been a frontier issue in international management research (Madhok 1997), and has predominantly been conducted from the internalization viewpoint (Buckley and Casson 1976; Rugman 1980). According to this perspective, FDI will result when internalizing transactions within the MNE is more efficient than performing transactions with an external market partner (Madhok 1997). Hennart's (1992) treatment of entry mode choice postulates that the FDI decision depends on the nature of the transaction beyond its costs in a narrow sense—for example, on such characteristics of the transaction as the risk of proprietary knowledge dissipation, the risk of adverse effects on brand name reputation, the relative ease (or lack thereof) of accessing requisite complementary knowledge held by third parties, and the possibility (or lack thereof) of pricing and protecting knowledge in the foreign market.

Rugman (1980, 1981) expanded the analysis of entry mode choice by contrasting FDI with alternative entry mode choices such as licensing, franchising, and joint venture formation. Further, Rugman offered a dynamic extension by showing that the mode of entry may change over time as the relative costs and benefits associated with each entry mode strategy change, and by constructing potential switchover points for each possible entry mode over time. Specifically, switchover points depend on the relative costs of servicing foreign markets and the potential to avoid dissipation of the rents derived from FSAs: Typically, exporting to foreign markets with the FSAs embodied in final products is the first step, followed by engaging in FDI and, finally, licensing a foreign producer when the technology licensed reaches the point of no longer determining the firm's survival (Rugman 1980; Fina and Rugman 1996).

Interestingly, this model of foreign operation mode stages contradicts a theory of the *internationalization process*, developed by a group of Scandinavian researchers and frequently referred to as the Uppsala model. Internationalization theory draws upon the behavioral theory of the firm (Cyert and March 1963) and proposes that international expansion is a function of the MNE's past international experience and knowledge base (Johanson and Wiedersheim 1975; Johanson and Vahlne 1977, 1990; Luostarinen 1979). The model postulates that firms undertake international expansion in an incremental and path-dependent manner, typically entering a foreign market by exporting and progressing to establish a sales subsidiary, to invest in local assembly and packaging, to form a joint venture, and finally to move to full scale local production and marketing by a wholly owned subsidiary once enough experiential market knowledge is gained (Aharoni 1966). From the internalization theory perspective, this model neglects two critical elements: first, it is the nature of the MNE's FSAs that determines potential internalization benefits, and second, the presence or absence of market imperfections affects the possibility of external market transactions (Rugman et al. 2011). Further, the Uppsala model has been criticized for its lack of serious conceptual grounding and generalizability, as well as its vague treatment of key concepts such as geographic proximity and experiential learning (Rugman 2005).

Contemporary research on entry mode choice continues the dynamic extension of internalization theory. Benito et al. (2009) propose a dynamic model of the choice and evolution of foreign operation modes, whereby firms do not necessarily choose among well-specified discrete alternatives, but rather select mode packages, and engage in frequent within-mode adjustments and mode role changes. The model allows for the simultaneous presence of multiple modes in various types of combinations, and recognizes that the choice of mode is as likely to be an emergent response to environmental circumstances as a deliberate strategic decision. Similar to the Uppsala model, the mode choice and change framework draws on the behavioral theory of the firm and acknowledges path dependency of entry mode decisions, but here experiences with an operation mode can in themselves be seen as the firm's FSAs to be drawn upon for international operations. Further, CSAs are recognized as influencing entry mode choices, as well as their combination or recombination. This creative extension of entry mode theorizing introduces a history, context, and process-oriented dimension to internalization theory, and offers a richer, more dynamic, and, importantly, more realistic conceptualization of international expansion.

Chen (2005) extends internalization theory's treatment of entry mode choice to include alternative market institutions such as arm's length comarketing, contractual comarketing, and original equipment manufacturing (OEM). The core argument is that the choice of an optimal entry mode depends on the relative costs and benefits of both the market for technology and the market for manufacture; while technology transfer across borders, and the related choice between inter alia licensing and FDI, has been addressed by internalization theory, other value chain activities have been largely neglected. Chen's model positions technology transfer in the broader context of the entire value chain, including the manufacturing/marketing linkages with the final products market. The model specifically recognizes the role of strategic assets controlled by host country-based economic actors in the MNE's final choice of an operating mode.

Another recent state-of-the-art extension of internalization theory's treatment of entry mode choice can be found in Hennart (2009), who, as mentioned above, focuses on transactional characteristics of complementary local assets and models foreign market entry as the assignment of equity between MNEs and owners of complementary local FSAs. At the core of Hennart's argument is the recognition that CSAs have owners, and that the optimal mode of entry will maximize the welfare of those owners as well as that of the MNE (Chen 2005; Hennart 1988, 1989, 2000; Yeung and Mirus 1988). Traditional internalization theory, while acknowledging the role of CSAs in internalization, does not explicitly recognize their transactional characteristics. In contrast, Hennart builds on Teece's (1986) insight that owners of specialized complementary assets play a greater role than generally understood. He argues that entry mode choice is essentially a choice of an assignment of residual rights between the MNE and host country CSA owners, and that the selected configuration will typically maximize total potential rents by assigning residual rights to the party whose behavior is the most difficult to constrain—that is, equity will be held by the MNE or by local firms or shared between them. This will determine whether the MNE will enter a foreign market through greenfields, brownfields, licensing, partial acquisitions, or acquisitions. If both parties' behaviors are equally difficult to constrain, an equity joint venture (EJV) will result. Hennart uses his *bundling model* to predict how entry modes will evolve over time, showing that the deepening of the MNE's commitment in a host country (e.g., from licensing to FDI) depends largely on the efficiency of the markets for complementary local assets and for the MNE's own FSAs. Hennart's bundling approach makes a significant contribution to internalization theory by drawing attention to the inappropriateness of the conventional MNE-centric approach, and by explaining the evolution of the MNEs' entry modes in foreign countries.

## 15.3.2  MNE's International Expansion Strategy: The Four Dimensions of Distance

Critical to understanding CSAs is the notion of distance between the home and host country. Ghemawat describes four dimension of distance—cultural, administrative (or institutional), geographic (or spatial), and economic—and argues that distance still matters in assessing host country advantages despite advances in information and communications technologies that are supposed to make the world a smaller place. From the internalization theory perspective, distance is a critical phenomenon that affects transferability, deployability, recombination, and exploitation of FSAs across borders.

As distance—whether economic, cultural, institutional, or merely geographic—increases, so do the costs of doing business abroad, as well as challenges in effectively deploying FSAs in a host environment. Distance exacerbates both bounded rationality challenges (Simon 1959) by making it more difficult for head office managers to understand the subsidiary environment, and bounded reliability problems (Verbeke and Greidanus 2009) by limiting the extent to which the head office can engage in proper monitoring, correction and goal alignment with the subsidiary.

To add to the complexity of the notion of distance, various distance dimensions are not independent of each other, but rather intertwined and mutually influencing each other—for example, regional economic integration fosters institutional coordination, which in turn may contribute to decreasing cultural and economic distance through improved mobility of labor and managerial best practices. It is then the compounded distance, defined as the need to manage various distance dimensions simultaneously, that has the most substantial effect on the firm's ability to deploy successfully and efficiently its FSAs abroad (Rugman et al. 2011). The internalization perspective suggests that the level of the MNE's multinationality and its geographic scope will be determined by the extent to which the MNE is able to deploy and recombine its FSAs to cope with compounded distance between the home and host countries.

## 15.3.3  MNE Internal Governance: Differentiated Network MNEs

Rugman and Verbeke (1992) have provided what is perhaps the most important substantive extension of internalization theory, namely the distinction between location-bound and non-location-bound (LB and NLB) FSAs. NLB FSAs are those FSAs that are easily transferable across borders and are available to the entire MNE network. Typically, such FSAs are developed at headquarters (HQ) and include technological, marketing, or administrative knowledge. LB FSAs, on the other hand, are available only to certain affiliates within the MNE, whether the headquarters or subsidiaries.

LB FSAs may also include capabilities in local responsiveness (in order to overcome various dimensions of distance) developed at the subsidiary level in host countries. One of the most interesting strategic aspects of LB FSAs is that some of them can become "best practices," and can be transformed into NLB FSAs and transferred to the MNE network.

The above distinction has led to a fundamental evolution in internalization theory thinking: from the view of the MNE as a monolithic organization fully controlled through hierarchical decisions about FDI from the head office (Rugman and Verbeke 2001) toward an analysis of the MNE as a differentiated network. The point here is that each MNE affiliate commands idiosyncratic FSA bundles. The content, development, and exploitation trajectory of these FSA bundles over time determine each affiliate's role in the MNE and drive interactions with other affiliates (Rugman and Verbeke 2003, 2008).

What follows is recognition that the MNE can have multiple patterns of FSA development and deployment. Verbeke (2009) identifies ten patterns of FSA development depending on their place of origin, transferability, upgradeability, deployability across the MNE network, and the level of head office control. The MNE's key role is then to master this variety of FSA development patterns through recombining resources and establishing linkages with CSAs and complementary resources of external actors. The recombination capability in itself becomes the MNE's highest-order FSA (Verbeke, 2009)—akin to the dynamic capabilities school's high-order capability to maintain competitiveness through enhancing, combining, protecting, and reconfiguring the enterprise's intangible and tangible assets (Teece 2007).

This notion of multiple potential patterns of FSA development gave rise to the concept of subsidiary-specific advantages (SSAs)—i.e., strengths developed at the subsidiary level (Rugman and Verbeke 2001)—which are embedded in subsidiaries and cannot be simply transferred to the rest of the MNE work, although they do have international exploitation potential. The SSA concept recognizes the subsidiary's potentially complex roles in FSA generation and exploitation: if a particular subsidiary has this kind of special expertise, it may be wisest to let that subsidiary expand beyond its initially assigned charter, and to stimulate the exploitation of its SSAs internationally (Bartlett and Ghoshal 1986). Further, each subsidiary can be simultaneously associated with multiple roles and FSA development patterns within the MNE.

A similar logic applies to the concept of alliance-specific advantages (ASA), or advantages that are embedded in alliances and cannot be simply transferred to the individual partner firms (Verbeke 2009). Like SSAs, ASAs have international exploitation potential, but cannot be simply diffused across the partner firms because of alliance-specific isolating mechanisms (McGee and Thomas 1986), which exist predominantly due to tacitness, context-specificity, and embeddedness of knowledge within the alliance. The introduction of the concept of ASA represents an important extension of internalization thinking to MNE alliance networks.

## 15.3.4 MNE's Internal Governance: M-Form versus Metanational Solution

With its greater focus on internal MNE governance, the new internalization theory has been instrumental in analyzing the efficacy of specific organizational forms, such as the multidivisional, or M-form (Chandler 1962), versus the metanational form (Doz et al. 2001). In their highly influential book, Doz et al. proposed a new set of governance principles reflecting, in their minds, a "metanational" model of the MNE, whereby the company is organized around three distinct activity levels: sensing, mobilizing, and operationalizing innovations. To perform and coordinate these activities, the MNE utilizes sensing and magnet units, which work outside the realm of the MNE's operating divisions. Sensors identify and seek out geographically dispersed, unique bodies of valuable knowledge, while magnets recombine the various unique pieces of knowledge identified by the sensors into commercially viable products. Operating divisions then implement the new solutions put forward by the sensors and magnets.

Internalization theory, however, suggests different governance principles likely to improve the efficiency and effectiveness of the MNE's functioning. From an internalization theory perspective, the sensor, magnet, and operating division units should be assessed in terms of their capacity to recombine novel resources and to turn them into actual NLB FSAs (Verbeke and Kenworthy 2008). Internalization theory looks at innovation—represented in the MNE by resource recombination—in its entirety; consistent with Buckley's (2009) concept of the global factory, this means that R&D and other efforts to develop and access new knowledge cannot be structurally divorced from production, marketing, and sales. To achieve innovation, the MNE must engage in integrative resource recombination practices throughout its value chain. It follows, then, that structural separation of innovation activities in sensor and magnet units, from the rest of the organization—i.e., the operating divisions—is unlikely to help the MNE innovate, and the metanational form of governance is therefore unlikely to displace the conventional M-form organizational structure (Verbeke and Kenworthy 2008; Rugman et al. 2011). Empirical evidence will, of course, be the ultimate judge of the metanational governance form's validity; current reality, however, suggests that most MNEs still fit under the M-form umbrella.

## 15.3.5  Theory of Regional Strategy and Structure

Globalization or the increased economic interdependence among nations has been the subject of much debate in the IB literature. Proponents of a "globalization" framework argue that consumer needs are becoming increasingly homogenized, largely due to technological advances, and correspondingly, markets are becoming globalized, which means that the MNE must design "global strategies" (Levitt 1983; Yip 2002). Specifically, the MNE should standardize its products and services worldwide in order to achieve economies of scale, and should implement uniform strategies throughout the value chain and across all markets.

Yet, very few MNEs are truly global. A global company can be defined as having less than 50% of sales (or assets) in its home region, and at least 20% of sales (or assets) in each of the triad regions, the triad being defined as consisting of NAFTA, the expanded European Union, and Asia, with these three regions representing the bulk of worldwide technological innovations and demand for products embodying these innovations (Rugman and Verbeke 2004). Empirical evidence suggests that increases in international sales occur predominantly within the MNE's home region of the triad, and that substantial barriers to trade and FDI among regions of the triad still exist (Rugman 2000). In a study of intraregional sales of the world's 500 largest companies, 380 firms had available geographic segment data; these firms accounted for 79.2% of the total revenue of the 500 largest firms and had an average sales volume of $29.2 billion in 2001. The study showed that the average intraregional sales across these 380 firms represented 71.9%; further, only 9 of the 380 firms (2.4%) were in fact global (Rugman and Verbeke 2004). There is no trend toward globalization, and the world's largest MNEs remain highly intraregional in their sales and assets (Oh and Rugman 2007; Rugman and Verbeke 2008).

From an internalization theory perspective, the false assumption made by global strategy advocates is that NLB FSAs, embodied in standardized products, production processes, and marketing routines, can easily overcome distance. In reality, the non-location-boundedness of FSAs is often overstated. Distance and a strong liability of foreignness, which remain at both regional and national levels, lead to challenges in transferring, deploying, and profitably exploiting FSAs across borders (Rugman and Verbeke 2008). Location-bound FSAs must still be developed in host environments to achieve national responsiveness. Development of such LB FSAs is associated with a cost of doing business abroad, which rises with the increase of cultural, economic, geographic, and institutional distance across regional boundaries. In the end, adaptation costs may turn out to be so high that home region expansion is preferred over global expansion. It follows, then, that it may be appropriate for the MNE to tailor its strategy to fit a specific role in each triad region, rather than to impose an integrated strategy throughout its network (Rugman and Verbeke 2004, 2007). The key strategic challenge is to achieve the right balance between NLB and LB FSAs in each region where the MNE has a presence (Rugman and Verbeke 2003).

In terms of striking such balance, the internalization theory lens can also be applied to the so-called "transnational solution" to MNE management proposed by Bartlett and

Ghoshal (1989). These authors' integration/responsiveness framework assumes that the focus on socialization ("normative integration") inside the MNE is sufficient to make the differentiated network MNE function effectively, and to achieve both national responsiveness and global integration. In reality, however, internal MNE governance requires a mix of socialization, price-based coordination, and hierarchical control to function effectively. The transnational solution, requiring classification and coordination of affiliates based on their FSA bundles, and the subsequent coordination of these affiliates in a network through normative integration, may become too complex, and may therefore be replaced by a regional solution (Rugman and Verbeke 1992).

## 15.3.6 Internalization Theory and Evolutionary View of the MNE

In their milestone *JIBS* article, Kogut and Zander (1993) develop a new view of the MNE, informed by the behavioral (Cyert and March 1963) and evolutionary (Nelson and Winter 1982) theories of the firm. They suggest that the MNE represents a superior governance mechanism for transferring tacit knowledge across borders because it possesses combinative capabilities. MNEs exist not because of external market imperfections, but because they act as repositories of embedded knowledge, whereby internal routines allow for effective knowledge transfer. The knowledge transfer process itself is a platform for future knowledge generation and transfer, grounded in a social context. Kogut and Zander argue that internalization theory focuses on the minimization of transaction costs rather than on potential value generation, that it overemphasizes opportunism ("self-interest seeking with guile": Williamson 1981b, 1545), and that it focuses on individual transactions, in terms of transfer of proprietary knowledge bundles across borders, without considering the broader context that should include the MNE's past and future, as well as its social nature.

While the above criticisms usefully suggest that it is beneficial to adopt a more eclectic approach to studying international expansion than focusing merely on narrow transaction cost parameters (Verbeke 2003), their validity is questionable, especially if assessed from the "new" internalization theory perspective. *First*, while conventional internalization theory indeed focused mainly (though not exclusively) on TCE-based parameters to explain MNE expansion patterns and technology transfer choices, new internalization theory focuses on managing innovation in its entirety—it is therefore concerned not merely with single-transaction economizing, but also with strategizing for value creation purposes. *Second*, Kogut and Zander's questioning of the opportunism assumption is useful, as the concept of opportunism has indeed been the subject of much academic debate. Opportunism has been criticized for its narrow conceptual focus, inaccurate portrayal of human nature and the lack of sufficient empirical support (Tsang 2006), and it has even been argued that concerns surrounding the behavioral assumption of opportunism reduce the legitimacy of TCE as a general theory of the firm (Verbeke and Greidanus 2009). Yet, in this particular case, the criticism is perhaps misdirected. While the assumption of opportunism is indeed central to Williamson's version of TCE, it is not a focus of internalization theory, which is much more concerned with the behavioral assumption of bounded rationality. In addition, bounded reliability (Verbeke and Greidanus 2009)—which represents a broader envelop-concept to explain failure of economic actors to make good on open-ended promises irrespective of intent—is more relevant than opportunism and has had a larger role in internalization theory (Rugman and Verbeke 2008). *Third*, internalization theory does not divorce specific transactions from prior or future transactions—rather, every transaction is considered in the broad context of managing the MNE's network, whereby it is prior investments that permit the development of organizational routines to allow know-how to be transferred abroad (Verbeke 2003). In other words, it is rather naive to assume that combinative capabilities held by a firm simply appear and make the firm superior to external markets: investments are required to create the combinative capability, and these investments are driven by internalization theory considerations on the firm's boundaries. *Fourth*, an MNE possessing combinative capabilities to perform tacit knowledge transfers is not a sufficient condition for internalization: the benefits and costs of alternative governance forms must be assessed simultaneously. For example, external actors such as key distributors, suppliers, or industry partners may command complementary FSAs, so that cooperative governance may be more efficient. In addition, if bundles of tacit knowledge do not fit with the MNE's core businesses, de-internalization may still be comparatively more efficient (Rugman and D'Cruz 2001).

## 15.3.7 Multinationality-Performance Relationship

Over the past fifty years, the IB literature has suggested various linkages between multinationality and performance, and a number of authors have tried to find a systematic relationship between the increase in the degree of the firm's multinationality and its bottom line. These studies have been published in credible outlets, yet their results are largely inconsistent (Verbeke and Brugman 2009). Most recently, multinationality-performance research has identified an S-curve relationship between multinationality and performance, allegedly the outcome of three distinct stages during the MNE's internationalization process: in the first stage, an increase in multinationality induces a decline in performance as the firm learns how to operate in foreign markets and overcome the liability of foreignness and newness; in the second stage, performance starts to rise with the increase in multinationality; in the third stage, large foreign operations become too difficult to manage, and the firm's performance again declines as the firm overextends itself. On the surface, this research has important normative implications for managers, suggesting that higher multinationality is likely to yield higher performance until an overextension threshold is reached.

The above S-curve multinationality-performance reasoning, however, contradicts the most basic principles of internalization theory—as, in fact, does the mere notion that a fixed, systematic multinationality-performance relationship should exist in the MNE (Hennart 2007; Verbeke and Brugman 2009). From an internalization theory perspective, the MNE will select entry modes and geographic configurations to best match its FSAs, with the environment acting as a constraining or facilitating force. Domestic and international success will therefore be determined by the firm's ability to develop, transfer, deploy, and exploit its FSAs rather than by its geographic scope per se. To illustrate this point, Verbeke and Brugman (2009) conducted a quality test of extant empirical research on the multinationality-performance relationship by examining the twenty most influential multinationality-performance publications. This exercise uncovered serious conceptual and measurement challenges that essentially invalidate the results of most past studies. Kirca et al. (2011) conducted a meta-analysis of 120 independent samples reported in 111 studies to test the predictions of internalization theory in the context of the multinationality-performance relationship, and found that the multinationality-performance relationship is moderated by FSAs, and that the impact of FSAs on the multinationality-performance relationship is influenced by a number of elements, including the type of FSA, industry characteristics, and the firm's R&D and advertising intensity. Essentially, the meta-analysis' results confirm the key point that no generalizable recommendation can be formulated on an optimal degree of multinationality without an in-depth knowledge of individual firms' FSAs and environments (Verbeke and Brugman, 2009)—an insight particularly relevant for practitioners, who might otherwise engage in a misguided quest for optimal multinationality instead of focusing on FSA development.

## 15.3.8  A Note on the Changing Nature of FSAs

Conventional empirical studies adopting an internalization theory lens have traditionally focused on two types of FSAs: technology-based ones and marketing-related ones (e.g., brand names), with the strength of these FSAs approximated by the MNE's R&D and advertising spending, respectively. These imperfect proxies may have represented an acceptable approximation for the MNE's FSAs in the past, but certainly did not capture the MNE's uniqueness in qualitative terms. For example, such uniqueness could reside in the MNE's absorptive capacity to digest different cultures and to employ productively managers of many nationalities. Contemporary internalization theory, which embodies a dynamic capabilities-like view of the firm, recognizes the role of higher-order FSAs beyond those associated with branding and technology—for example, FSAs in managerial expertise, which are often at the heart of achieving superior performance, yet are not easily measured in quantitative terms. In his plea to rethink IB research methodology, Yair Aharoni (1993) argued it is very difficult, if not impossible, to capture MNE success stories by using industry averages and statistical tests. Outlier stories typically get buried in statistical databases, so that the uniqueness of MNEs is not truly captured. Aharoni suggests that IB scholars would understand much more about companies' FSAs if they relied more on the tools of the business historian than those of the mainstream economist. He also argues that statistical analysis of performance differentials among firms should be complemented with historical, case-based analysis and longitudinal research in order to understand the underlying FSAs of *outlier* successful MNEs, as well as the absence of needed FSAs in failed firms.

The warning against overgeneralization when studying FSAs is particularly poignant in the context of emerging economy MNEs (EMNEs), whose key competitive strengths are often not measurable by traditional proxies. EMNEs may have dramatically different FSAs as compared to developed economy MNEs, and their trajectory of FSA development may also be different—for example, many large EMNEs typically build technological capacity by purchasing technology or entering into alliances to gain access to existing technology instead of investing in R&D. The point here is that with the growing awareness of the complexity, uniqueness, and intangibility of MNEs' FSAs comes an added challenge of capturing these FSAs empirically. Here, the RBV literature may be useful: RBV scholars have been instrumental in developing a multitude of proxies for empirically measuring a firm's resource base (see Newbert 2007, for a comprehensive overview of RBV-grounded empirical articles). New proxies will undoubtedly aid in evaluating the *unique* FSAs of a range of *unique* MNEs (including EMNEs).

## 15.3.9   Operationalizing Internalization Theory in Four Types of International Strategic Management Research

In his classification of IB research, Sjoerd Beugelsdijk (2011) suggests that most research questions in international strategic management fall within one of four general categories, based on 1) their focus on the firm versus the environmental context; and 2) their "comparative" versus "interactive" approach. What results is a two-by-two matrix, with the following types of research questions relevant to each quadrant:

1. In quadrant 1, the focus is on the comparative analysis of firms, holding contextual variation constant. For example, how do firms from one particular domestic context organize their activities in one specific foreign context (e.g., Japanese MNEs' entry into the United States)?
2. Quadrant 2 includes the interactive analysis of firms, with contextual variation held stable. In other words, how do relationships unfold between firms from context A and firms from context B (e.g., how do joint ventures evolve between European and American firms in the high technology sector in California)?

| Analytical approach | Source of variation | |
| --- | --- | --- |
| | Firm-level | Location |
| Comparative | 1. Differences in FSAs matter most (*international application of RBV*) | 3. Differential location characteristics matter most (*competitive advantage of nations*) |
| Interactive | 2. Interactions between MNEs' FSAs from different countries matter most | 4. Interactions between location characteristics of country pairs matter most |

FIGURE 15.1.  Generic types of international strategic management studies *(adapted from Beugelsdijk, 2011)*

3. In quadrant 3, the central research issue is the international comparative analysis of contexts, with no variation in firm characteristics. In other words, how do contextual differences affect supposedly "identical" firms (e.g., what is the impact of country-level institutional quality on the choice of MNE head office location)?

4. Finally in quadrant 4, an interactive analysis is performed of different contexts, with no variation in firm characteristics. How do the characteristics of pairs of locations, or changes in these characteristics affect supposedly "identical firms"? (E.g., what is the managerial impact of particular scores on a Kogut and Singh (1988) index of cultural distance? What is the impact of trade agreements on FDI: does increased trade complement or substitute for FDI?)

In the first type of studies, differences in FSAs among companies matter the most, suggesting that these studies can be categorized as international RBV applications, but with internalization considerations featuring prominently in predicting MNE strategic choices. In the second type of studies, interactions between FSAs from firms with different nationalities matter the most. Each company's FSAs are believed to embody home country CSAs. Here, higher distance typically leads to higher transaction costs and higher complexity in making strategy choices. In the third type of IB research, only differences in CSAs matter: the message is often that particular CSAs (such as a properly enforced patent protection regime or high institutional quality) will reduce transaction costs for MNEs at the macrolevel, thereby attracting and fostering the growth of particular types of economic activities. The fourth type of studies deals with interactions between CSAs of different countries, and the changes therein over time. This can be a key input for the second type of studies.

Contemporary internalization theory-based work can be largely positioned in quadrants 2 and 4 in Figure 15.1. Internalization theory's analytical approach is interactive in nature, with its key concern being the *recombination* of the MNE's LB and NLB FSAs with home and host countries' CSAs, whereby access to the latter may actually be controlled by host country actors. In one of the newest iterations of internalization theory, namely Hennart's (2009) bundling approach discussed above, quadrant 4 is collapsed into quadrant 2: Here, CSAs are not exogenous macro parameters, but are controlled by resource owners in a host country and not necessarily readily accessible by the MNE. Accessing CSAs requires further recombination capabilities and FSA development on the MNE's part.

# 15.4 THE FUTURE OF INTERNALIZATION THEORY: A FEW EXTENSIONS

As an efficiency-based, positive theory of MNE functioning and organization (Rugman and Verbeke 2008), internalization theory can be readily augmented to explain a wide range of emerging issues in IB. In this section, we consider a few potential application areas.

## 15.4.1  International Entrepreneurship and "Born Globals"

International entrepreneurship involves the identification and exploitation of opportunities for international exchange (Ellis 2011). International entrepreneurship research, which has been argued to be a critical emerging area in IB (Dimitratos and Jones 2005; Styles and Seymour 2006; Young et al. 2003; Zahra 2005; Ellis 2011), distinguishes itself from other IB theories by its emphasis on the process of recognition and exploitation of business opportunities. International entrepreneurship researchers argue that internalization theory focuses on large, well-established MNEs, and neglects the pursuit of entrepreneurial opportunities (Autio 2005); further, internalization theory is believed to tend toward one-sided, firm-centric explanations of IB activity (Toyne 1989), to the neglect of a variety of governance options available to the entrepreneur. International entrepreneurship research, in contrast, began as a response to the globalization of markets, and encompasses so-called "born-globals": These are firms that internationalize while still young and small (Knight and Cavusgil 1996; McDougall and Oviatt 2000), and whose expansion is rapid and opportunity-driven (Zahra et al. 2005) as opposed to incremental and inhibited by risk aversion. Born-globals' rapid and dedicated internationalization from inception is believed to be driven by entrepreneurs' ideas and knowledge which may have potential global application; while small ideas may incubate local firms, big ideas will incubate MNEs (Buckley and Casson 2009). Born-globals are most frequently "market seekers" in their internationalization motives (Verbeke 2009): this kind of international expansion pattern is particularly prevalent among firms operating in small open economies (e.g., New Zealand, Israel, Denmark, etc.) where domestic demand is limited (Knight et al. 2001).

However, closer scrutiny of the born-global phenomenon reveals that born-globals' international sales are achieved largely within their home regions. Research found that Danish born-globals generated the vast majority of their international sales in Europe (predominantly in Germany, which accounted for 50% of their sales), while American born-globals generated 53% of their total sales domestically (Knight et al. 2004). Despite a vast amount of literature on born-globals, there is a paucity of robust empirical evidence of any true born-global firms, in the sense of having an equal presence in all regions of the triad, other than a few technology firms from India and some small firms from Israel (Rugman and Almodovar 2011). This suggests that born-globalism may be no more than an illusion (Rugman et al. 2011), and that born-globals can often be more accurately described as born-regionals (Rugman 2000; Fisch and Oesterle 2003; Lee 2010; Lopez et al. 2009).

Similar to its treatment of the regionalization phenomenon, internalization theory explains born-globals' lack of "globalness" by difficulties in overcoming interregional economic, cultural, geographic, and institutional distance and liability of foreignness and newness. Shortage of sufficiently developed FSAs to support FDI likely explains the fact that born-globals' opportunistic foreign sales usually take the form of exporting. It should also be noted that the so-called globalization of markets that supposedly gave rise to the born-global phenomenon is not supported by internalization theory thinking—distance, as convincingly shown by Ghemawat (2001), still matters. While it is certainly conceivable that a big idea will breed global demand (e.g., imagine a pharmaceutical firm that develops a cure for cancer), global implementation requires an *expert recombination* of the company's FSAs with multiple CSAs in diverse locations, which is extremely challenging. Global governance will likely prove difficult for a young firm, presenting multiple challenges throughout the firm's value chain (i.e., finding reliable distribution systems and local partners throughout the world), and leading to consequent bounded reliability and bounded rationality challenges.

In response to criticism from international entrepreneurship scholars cited above, it should be noted the new internalization theory has long moved away from its MNE-centric focus (see Hennart 2009). Internalization theory recognizes the complex and multilateral nature of international exchange, is no longer restrictive in its treatment of expansion options available to the MNE, and is presently well equipped to explain the born-global phenomenon—including the relative scarcity of born-globals and their prevailing regional rather than truly global nature.

## 15.4.2 Emerging Economy MNEs

Emerging economies, comprised of countries with a rapid pace of development and government policies that favor economic liberalization, are assuming an increasingly prominent position in the world economy (Wright et al. 2005), as well as in MNE strategic activity (Verbeke 2009). Hoskisson et al. (2000) identified sixty-four emerging economies, of which fifty-one were rapidly growing developing countries, and thirteen were in transition from centrally planned to market economies. The growth of emerging economies is reflected in an upsurge of IB research on the topic over the past decade. The emerging economies phenomenon offers three broad areas for consideration by IB scholars: situations where firms from developed economies enter emerging economies, situations where firms from emerging economies enter developed economies, and situations where firms from emerging economies enter other emerging economies.

The last two areas of research have spurred a vivid debate among IB scholars regarding the relevance of extant IB frameworks to explain EMNE behavior. As many MNEs from the BRIC (Brazil, Russia, India, and China) and VISTA (Vietnam, Indonesia, South Africa, Turkey, and Argentina) countries, as well as from Mexico and Thailand, achieved success in their international expansion, the question arose as to whether existing IB theories can accommodate the new phenomenon, or whether a significant adjustment to extant theory, or even an entirely new theory is required to study EMNEs. To date, no consensus has emerged on the topic (Ramamurti 2009). A sizeable group of researchers (see Child and Rodrigues 2005; Filatotchev et al. 2007; Luo and Tung 2007; Mathews 2002a, 2002b, 2006a, and 2006b; Peng et al. 2001) believe that EMNEs represent a new class of firms that pursues internationalization patterns drastically different from developed country MNEs, and therefore call for new theory development. Others (see Buckley et al. 2007; Dunning 2006; Hennart 2011; Narula 2006; Rugman

2009) suggest that EMNEs' internationalization patterns and internal organization can be easily addressed within existing IB paradigms. Yet, a third group of authors (see Cuervo-Cazurra and Genc 2008; Guillen and Garcia-Canal 2009; Ramamurti 2009) posit that extant IB theories can be applied to EMNEs, but only if substantially adapted and augmented.

Unfortunately, the rejection of existing IB theories, and especially internalization theory as the general theory of the MNE (including the EMNE) appears to be associated with an incomplete understanding thereof. Proponents of a new or a significantly augmented theory have voiced three main charges against the internalization paradigm:

The *first* one relates to the fact that EMNEs operate in an institutional environment significantly different from that prevailing in developed economies (Peng et al. 2001), and therefore require a new institution-based theory. However, internalization theory has been successful in dealing with institutional distance, including institutional distance between developed and emerging economies, which is reflected in differential transaction costs. Transaction costs are likely to rise due to economizing challenges presented by institutional differences (Wright et al. 2005). For example, MNEs from developed economies competing in emerging economies face such consequences of increased institutional distance as a lack of transparency, lax intellectual property rights protection, weak legal and financial systems, etc. This is likely to create bounded rationality and bounded reliability challenges (Verbeke and Greidanus 2009), potentially increasing transaction costs. In contrast, local competitors and EMNEs from other emerging economies will have a competitive advantage over their rivals from developed countries due to the lower institutional distance (or a complete lack thereof) and will, consequently, face lower transaction costs. In other words, from the internalization theory perspective, institutions matter due to their potential to affect the additional costs of doing business abroad.

The *second* charge against the use of internalization theory for EMNE research relates to internalization theory's focus on development and exploitation of FSAs. Proponents of a new theory suggest that emerging economy multinationals do not in fact possess FSAs and thus internalize to acquire new FSAs rather than to exploit existing ones. For example, Mathews (2002a, 2002b, 2006a, 2006b) suggests that Asian EMNEs, which he terms *Dragon* multinationals, are essentially resource-poor, yet have successfully expanded abroad without FSAs. This is argued to make EMNEs unsuitable for theoretical analysis driven by the notion of FSAs—the very feature that EMNEs supposedly lack. We believe that this misconception stems from the confusion surrounding the notion of FSAs, and from the failure to differentiate between conventional internalization theory and its contemporary form. As discussed in the previous section, conventional proxies for empirical measurement of FSAs—R&D and advertising spending—are meaningless in the emerging economy context: first, EMNEs' key competitive strengths are not necessarily related to technology and branding, and second, even if EMNEs do cultivate technological and branding FSAs, these FSAs may not be measurable by traditional proxies, as their development path may not be associated with R&D and advertising spending. The point here is that EMNEs' FSAs are different from those of developed economies' MNEs, rather than absent altogether. Examples of nontraditional FSAs found in EMNEs include entrepreneurial quality of management (as seen in India's Tata Group's innovative Nano product), expertise in managing international mergers and acquisitions (as demonstrated by Mexico's Cemex), etc.

Many IB scholars have recognized the differential nature of EMNEs' FSAs and acknowledge that those FSAs can be exploited through FDI (see Cuervo-Cazzura and Genc 2008; Guillen and Garcia-Canal 2009; Ramamurti 2009; Zeng and Williamson 2007). Some EMNE-related FSAs mentioned in the literature include a better understanding of emerging market customers and ability to adapt technology to develop products suited for special needs customers (relevant when expanding to other emerging economies and competing with developed country MNEs), cost innovations and operational excellence forced by sparse resources, privileged access to home countries' CSAs, adversity advantage (ability to effectively function in difficult conditions), networking skills, political know-how, etc. Still, we argue that internalization theory predictions stand despite the idiosyncratic nature of EMNEs' FSAs, which essentially represent recombination capabilities (Verbeke 2009). The nature of an MNE's FSAs (higher-order ones versus technology-based ones) does not affect internalization theory's main prediction that the firm's international success will depend on its ability to successfully match its set of FSAs with host country CSAs. It is the generic characteristics of these FSAs (e.g., transferability across borders and inimitability) and CSAs (easily transacted in open markets or not), rather than the FSAs' particular characteristics (branding, technology or management capability) that will determine optimal entry mode choice and subsequent governance of developed country MNEs and EMNEs alike.

Related to the above point, the *third* proposed rationale for a new EMNE-based theory is the EMNEs' alleged, unique motivation to internationalize, which is to mitigate/eliminate relative competitive disadvantages as opposed to exploiting advantages as developed country MNEs do (Child and Rodrigues 2005). Noneconomic objectives for expansion are argued to produce different internationalization patterns. Guillen and Garcia-Canal (2009) identify nine motivations for EMNEs' FDI documented in the literature: backward linkage into raw materials, forward linkage into foreign markets, home-country government curbs, spreading of risk, movement of personal capital abroad, following a home-country customer to foreign markets, investment in new markets in response to economic reforms in the home country, acquisition of intangible FSAs, and exploitation of intangible FSAs. A closer look at the motivations listed above will reveal that many could be found in developed country MNE expansions, as well. In fact, all of those strategic goals fit neatly into an existing typology of internationalization motivations: natural resource seeking, market seeking, strategic resource seeking, and efficiency seeking (Dunning and Lundan 2008; Verbeke 2009), and as such hardly necessitate a new theory (see Table 15.1).

All of this is not to say that the emerging economy context does not warrant a unique approach—it does indeed, but internalization theory's emphasis on matching FSAs and CSAs (Rugman 1981, 1996) is particularly relevant to address this uniqueness. Let us

Table 15.1. EMNE internalization motivations versus existing motivation framework

| Four motivations for international expansion in existing IB framework (Dunning and Lundan 2008; Verbeke 2009) | EMNE's motivations for international expansion identified in extant literature (Guillen and Garcia-Canal 2009) |
| --- | --- |
| Natural resource seeking | Backward linkage into raw materials |
| Market seeking | Home-country government curbs |
| | Investment in new markets in response to economic reforms in the home country |
| | Following a home-country customer to foreign markets |
| | Forward linkage into foreign markets |
| Strategic resource seeking | Movement of personal capital abroad |
| | Acquisition of intangible FSAs |
| | Exploitation of intangible FSAs (i.e. recombining intangible FSAs with borrowed technology) |
| Efficiency seeking | Spreading of risk |

look, for example, at developed country MNEs entering emerging economies. MNEs are required to engage in novel activities for new business creation in a foreign country, rather than simply seek to sell a product or service (Yiu et al. 2007). FSA development patterns for an MNE entering an emerging economy will be unique, with extant NLB FSAs necessarily combined with substantial bundles of LB FSAs developed in the host country (Verbeke 2009). Developing LB FSAs in national responsiveness and higher order FSAs in resource recombination becomes particularly critical, as does enlisting complementary FSAs of external actors. Such enlisting may be critical given comparative deficiencies in the rule of law, as well as entrenched networks among government agencies, various local organizations, and local and foreign firms that typically characterize emerging economies (Zhou and Poppo 2010).

To conclude, the new internalization theory, with its blend of TCE and RBV components, its dynamic view on FSAs and its focus on finding an optimal combination of FSAs and CSAs, is well equipped to handle additional complexities presented by the emerging economy context. Unfortunately, it is currently underutilized in the study of emerging economies; to date, four conceptual perspectives—TCE, agency theory, RBV, and institutional theory—have been identified as leading theories in the field (Hoskisson et al. 2000; Peng et al. 2001; Meyer and Peng 2004). Internalization theory, which effectively blends the transaction costs and RBV/dynamic capabilities perspectives, and systematically takes into account institutional context, can significantly enhance our understanding of both EMNEs and developed country MNEs' expansion into emerging economies.

# 15.5 CONCLUSION

Internalization theory is a powerful and comprehensive IB research tool that "represents a quantum leap in our understanding of the MNE" (Hennart 1986, 801). Standing on the shoulders of giants such as Coase and Penrose, internalization theory has evolved considerably since its inception over forty years ago, from a relatively static, narrow economic efficiency-based model to a dynamic theory focusing on developing, deploying, exploiting, and augmenting complex FSA bundles in equally complex location-specific contexts. The range of internalization theory's applications has also widened from the early focus on entry mode choices to explaining such contemporary phenomena as MNE strategy-structure choices, regionalization strategies, and emerging economy MNEs.

Internalization theory provides a simultaneous focus on the firm, commanding FSAs and attempting to economize on transaction costs so as to effect value creation and capture, and on the environment as an influencing force. Internalization theory thereby offers a comprehensive view of the interactions between the firm and its environment, much needed in strategic management theory (Hoskisson et al. 1999). Internalization theory can assist in the efforts to blend TCE and RBV-thinking that mainstream strategic management scholars have been undertaking during the past two decades.

One of internalization theory's great strengths is its managerial relevance and significant normative agenda. At the microlevel, internalization theory is concerned with identifying and correcting short- and medium-term inefficiencies, such as wrong entry mode choices, excessive internalization, nonadaptation of governance structures to new environmental conditions, etc. At the macrolevel, internalization theory has far-reaching public policy implications: only if public policy makers and regulators understood correctly the drivers of MNE behavior could the positive societal spillover effects of MNE activities be optimized through appropriate macrolevel governance (Rugman 1981). In line with Teece's (1984) thinking on the benefits of blending theories and managerial best practices, we conclude by suggesting that internalization theorists should work with practitioners and regulators so as to combine research findings with best practices in business and public policy. Such blending will further increase internalization theory's substantive contribution to IB scholarship and to the broader field of strategic management.

# LIST OF ABBREVIATIONS

| | |
|---|---|
| ASA | Alliance-specific advantage |
| BRIC | Brazil, Russia, India, and China |
| CSA | Country-specific advantage |
| EMNE | Multinational enterprise from an emerging economy |
| FDI | Foreign direct investment |
| FSA | Firm-specific advantage |
| IB | International business |
| LB FSA | Location bound firm-specific advantage |
| M-form | Multidivisional form of governance |
| MNE | Multinational enterprise |
| NLB FSA | Non-location-bound firm-specific advantage |
| OLI | Ownership, Location, Internalization |
| RBV | Resource-based view of the firm |
| R&D | Research and development |
| TCE | Transaction cost economics |
| TCI | Transaction cost internalization (alternative description of internalization theory) |
| VISTA | Vietnam, Indonesia, South Africa, Turkey, and Argentina |

## NOTES

1. In their review of the past fifty years of international business history, Rugman et al. (2011) demonstrate that the core unit of analysis continues to shift with the international business field's ongoing development, which includes the recognition of the network nature of the MNE and the evolving role of the subsidiary. The unit of analysis in much contemporary internalization theory work has shifted from the *firm* to the *subsidiary* and the *subsidiary manager*.

## REFERENCES

Aharoni, Y. 1966. *The Foreign Investment Decision Process*. Boston: Division of Research, Graduate School of Business Administration, Harvard University.

——. 1993. "In Search for the Unique: Can Firm-Specific Advantages Be Evaluated?" *Journal of Management Studies* 30:31–49.

Autio, E. 2005. "Creative Tension: The Significance of Ben Oviatt's & Patricia McDougall's article 'Toward a Theory of International New Ventures.'" *Journal of International Business Studies* 36 (1): 9–19.

Bartlett, C., and S. Ghoshal. 1986. "Tap Your Subsidiaries for Global Reach." *Harvard Business Review* 64:87–94.

——. 1989. *Managing Across Borders—The Transnational Solution.* Boston, MA: Harvard Business School Press.

Barney, J. B. 1991. "Firm Resources and Sustained Competitive Advantage." *Journal of Management* 17 (1): 99–120.

Benito, G. R., G. B. Petersen, and L. Welch. 2009. "Towards More Realistic Conceptualisations of Foreign Operation Modes." *Journal of International Business Studies* 40:1455–70.

Beugelsdijk, S. 2011. "Dynamics of Globalization: Location Specific Advantages or Liabilities of Foreignness?" *Advances in International Management* 24:181–210.

Buckley, P. J. 1983. "New Theories of International Business: Some Unresolved Issues." In *The Growth of International Business,* edited by M. Casson, 34–50. London: George Allen and Unwin.

——. 1998a. "Analyzing Foreign Market Entry Strategies: Extending the Internalization Approach." *Journal of International Business Studies* 29 (3): 539–62.

——. 1998b. "Models of the Multinational Enterprise." *Journal of International Business Studies* 29 (1): 21–44.

——. 2009. "The Internalisation Theory of the Multinational Enterprise: A Review of the Progress of a Research Agenda after 30 Years." *Journal of International Business Studies* 40 (9): 1563–80.

——. 2009. "Internalization Thinking—from the Multinational Enterprise to the Global Factory." *International Business Review* 18 (3): 224–35.

Buckley, P. J., and M. Casson. 1976. *The Future of the Multinational Enterprise.* Basingstoke and London: Macmillan.

——. 2009. "The Internalisation Theory of the Multinational Enterprise: A Review of the Progress of a Research Agenda after 30 Years." *Journal of International Business Studies* 40: 1563–1580.

Buckley, P. J., J. Clegg, A. R. Cross, X. Liu, H. Voss, and P. Zheng. 2007. "The Determinants of Chinese Outward Foreign Direct Investment." *Journal of International Business Studies* 38:499–518.

Buckley, P. J., and R. Strange. 2011. "The Governance of the Multinational Enterprise: Insights from Internalization Theory." *Journal of Management Studies* 48(2): 460–70.

Casson, M. 1979. *Alternatives to the Multinational Enterprise.* New York: Holmes & Meier.

——. 1986. "General Theories of Multinational Enterprise: Their Relevance to Business History." In *Multinationals: Theory and History,* edited by P. Hertner and G. Jones, 42–63. Aldershot: Gower.

——. 1987. *The Firm and the Market.* Oxford: Basil Blackwell.

Chandler, A. D. 1962. *Strategy & Structure.* Cambridge, MA: MIT Press.

Chen, S.-F. 2005. "Extending Internalization Theory: A New Perspective on International Technology Transfer and Its Generalization." *Journal of International Business Studies* 36:231–45.

Child, J., and S. B. Rodrigues. 2005. "The Internationalization of Chinese Firms: A Case for Theoretical Extension." *Management and Organization Review* 1:381–410.

Coase, R. H. 1937. "The Nature of the Firm." *Economica,* n.s., 4 (16):386–405.

Cuervo-Cazurra, A., and M. Genc. 2008. "Transforming Disadvantages into Advantages: Developing-Country MNEs in the Least Developed Countries." *Journal of International Business Studies* 39:957–79.

Cyert, R. M., and J. G. March. 1963. *A Behavioral Theory of the Firm.* Englewood Cliffs, NJ: Prentice Hall.

DeGennaro, R. P. 2005. "Market Imperfections." Working Paper, Federal Reserve Bank of Atlanta, 2005–12.

Dimitratos, P., and M. V. Jones. 2005. "Future Directions for International Entrepreneurship Research." *International Business Review* 14 (2): 119–28.

Doz, Y., J. Santos, and P. Williamson. 2001. *From Global to Metanational: How Companies Win in The Knowledge Economy.* Boston: Harvard Business School Press.

Dunning, J. H. 1981. *International Production and the Multinational Enterprise.* London: George Allen and Unwin.

——. 1988. "The Eclectic Paradigm of International Production: A Restatement and Some Possible Extensions." *Journal of International Business Studies* 19 (1): 1–31.

——. 2006. "Comment on Dragon Multinationals: New Players in the 21st Century Globalization." *Asia-Pacific Journal of Management* 23:139–41.

Dunning, J. H., and S. M. Lundan. 2008. *Multinational Enterprises and the Global Economy.* Cheltenham, UK, and Northampton, MA: Edward Elgar Publishing.

Dunning, J. H., and A. M. Rugman. 1985. "The Influence of Hymer's Dissertation on the Theory of Foreign Direct Investment." *American Economic Review: Papers and Proceedings* 75 (2): 228–60.

Eden, L., and S. R Miller. 2004. "Distance Matters: Liability of Foreignness, Institutional Distance and Ownership Strategy." *Volume Advances in International Management* 16: 187–221.

Ellis, P. D. 2011. "Social Ties and International Entrepreneurship: Opportunities and Constraints Affecting Firm Internalization." *Journal of International Business Studies* 42:99–127.

Filatotchev, I., R. Strange, J. Piesse, and Y.-C. Lien. 2007. "FDI by Firms from Newly Industrialised Economies in Emerging Markets: Corporate Governance, Entry Mode and Location." *Journal of International Business Studies* 38:556–72.

Fina, E., and A. M. Rugman. 1996. "A Test of Internalization Theory and Internationalization Theory: The Upjohn Company." *Management International Review* 36 (3): 199–213.

Fisch, J. H., and M.-J. Oesterle. 2003. "Exploring the Globalization of German MNCs with the Complex Spread and Diversity Measure." *Schmalenbach Business Review* 55 (1): 2–21.

Ghemawat, P. 2001. "Distance Still Matters: The Hard Reality of Global Expansion." *Harvard Business Review* 79 (8): 137–47.

Guillen, M., and E. Garcia-Canal. 2009. "The American Model of the Multinational Firm and the 'New' Multinationals from Emerging Economies." *Academy of Management Perspectives* 23:23–35.

Hennart, J. F. 1982. *A Theory of Multinational Enterprise.* Ann Arbor: University of Michigan Press.

——. 1986. "What Is Internalization?" *Review of World Economics* 122:791–804.

——. 1988. "A Transaction Cost Theory of Equity Joint Ventures." *Strategic Management Journal* 9 (4): 361–74.

——. 1989. "Can the 'New Forms of Investment' Substitute for the 'Old Forms'? A Transaction Costs Perspective." *Journal of International Business Studies* 20 (2): 211–33.

——. 2000. "Transaction Costs Theory and the Multinational Enterprise." In *The Nature of the Transnational,* 2nd ed., edited by C. Pitelis and R. Sugden, 72–118. London: Routledge.

——. 2007. "The Theoretical Rationale for a Multinationality/Performance Relationship." *Management International Review* 47:423–52.

——. 2009. "Down with MNE Centric Theories! Market Entry and Expansion as the Bundling of MNE and Local Assets." *Journal of International Business Studies* 40:1432–54.

——. 2011. "Don't Cry for Argentina! Emerging Market Multinationals and the Theory of the Multinational Enterprise." Paper presented at the European International Business Academy (EIBA) Conference, Bucharest, Romania.

Hoskisson, R. E., L. Eden, C.-M. Lau, and M. Wright. 2000. "Strategy in Emerging Economies." *Academy of Management Journal* 43:249–67.

Hoskisson, R. E., M. A. Hitt, W. P. Wan, and D. Yiu. 1999. "Theory and Research in Strategic Management: Swings of a Pendulum." *Journal of Management* 25 (3): 417–55.

Hymer, S. H. 1968. "La Grande Corporation Multinationale." *Revue Economique* 19 (6): 949–73.

———. 1976. *The International Operations of National Firms: A Study of Direct Foreign Investment.* Cambridge: MA: MIT Press.

Itaki, M. 1991. "A Critical Assessment of the Eclectic Theory of the Multinational Enterprise." *Journal of International Business Studies* 22:445–60.

Johanson, J., and J.-E. Vahlne. 1977. "The Internationalization Process of the Firm: A Model of Knowledge Development and Increasing Foreign Market Commitments." *Journal of International Business Studies* 8 (1): 23–32.

———. 1990. "The Mechanism of Internationalization." *International Marketing Review* 7 (4): 11–24.

Johanson, J., and P. F. Wiedersheim. 1975. "The Internationalization of the Firm—the Four Swedish Cases." *Journal of Management Studies* 12 (3): 305–22.

Kindleberger, C. P. 1969. *American Business Abroad: Six Lectures on Direct Investment.* London: Yale University Press.

Kirca, A. H., G. T. Hult, K. Roth, S. T. Cavusgil, M. Z. Perryy, M. B. Akdeniz, S. Z. Deligonul, J. Mena, W. A. Pollitte, J. J. Hoppner, J. C. Miller, and R. C. White. 2011. "Firm-Specific Assets, Multinationality, and Financial Performance: A Meta-Analytic Review and Theoretical Integration." *Academy of Management Journal* 54 (1): 47–72.

Knight, J., J. Bell, and R. McNaughton. 2001. "Born Globals: Old Wine in New Bottles?" Paper read at the ANZMAC Conference, Auckland, New Zealand.

Knight, G. A., and S. T. Cavusgil. 1996. "The Born Global Firms: A Challenge to the Traditional International Theory." In *Advances in International Marketing*, edited by S. Cavusgil, S. Madsen, and T. Madsen, 8:11–26. Greenwich, CT: JAI Press.

Knight, G. A, T. K. Madsen, and P. Servais. 2004. "An Inquiry into Born Global Firms in Europe and the USA." *International Marketing Review* 21 (6): 645–65.

Kogut, B., and H. Singh. 1988. "The Effect of National Culture on the Choice of Entry Mode." *Journal of International Business Studies* 19 (3): 411–32.

Kogut, B., and U. Zander. 1993. "Knowledge of the Firm and the Evolutionary Theory of the Multinational Corporation." *Journal of International Business Studies* 19 (3): 411–32.

Lee, I. H. 2010. "The M Curve: The Performance of Born-Regional Firms from Korea." *The Multinational Business Review* 18 (4): 1–22.

Levitt, T. 1983. "The Globalization of Markets." *Harvard Business Review* 61 (3): 92–102.

Lopez, L. E., S. K. Kundu, and L. Ciravegna. 2009. "Born Global vs. Born Regional: Evidence from an Exploratory Study on the Costa Rican Software Industry." *Journal of International Business Studies* 40 (7): 1228–38.

Luo, Y., and R. Tung. 2007. "International Expansion of Emerging Market Enterprises: A Springboard Perspective." *Journal of International Business Studies* 38:481–98.

Luostarinen, R. 1979. *Internationalization of the Firm.* Helsinki: Academie Economicae, Helsinki School of Economics.

Madhok, A. 1997. "Cost, Value and Foreign Market Entry Mode: The Transaction and the Firm." *Strategic Maagement Journal* 18: 39–61.

Mathews, J. 2002a. *Dragon Multinationals.* Oxford: Oxford University Press.

———. 2002b. "Competitive Advantages of Latecomer Firms: A Resource-Based Account of Industrial Catch-Up Strategies." *Asia-Pacific Journal of Management* 19:467–88.

———. 2006a. "Dragon Multinationals: New Players in 21st Century Globalization." *Asia-Pacific Journal of Management* 23:5–27.

———. 2006b. "Response to Professors Dunning and Narula." *Asia-Pacific Journal of Management* 23:153–55.

McDougall, P. P., and B. M. Oviatt. 2000. "International Entrepreneurship: The Intersection of Two Research Paths." *Academy of Management Journal* 43 (5): 902–6.

McGee, J., and H. Thomas. 1986. "Strategic Groups: Theory, Research, and Taxonomy." *Strategic Management Journal* 18:15–30.

McManus, J. C. 1972. "The Theory of the International Firm." In *The Multinational Firm and the Nation State,* edited by G. Paquet, 66–93. Toronto: Collier-Macmillan.

Meyer, K. E., and M. W. Peng. 2004. "Identifying Leading Theories for Research on Central and Eastern Europe: Transactions, Resources, and Institutions." Working paper, Copenhagen Business School and The Ohio State University.

Narula, R. 2006. "Globalization, New Ecologies, New Zoologies, and the Purported Death of the Eclectic Paradigm." *Asia-Pacific Journal of Management* 23:143–51.

Nelson, R. R., and S. G. Winter. 1982. *An Evolutionary Theory of Economic Change.* Cambridge, MA: Harvard University Press.

Newbert, S. L. 2007. "Empirical Research on the Resource-Based View of the Firm: An Assessment and Suggestions for Future Research." *Strategic Management Journal* 28: 121–46.

Oh, C. H., and A. M. Rugman. 2007. "Multinationality and Regional Performance, 2001–2005." In *Regional Aspects of Multinationality and Performance,* edited by A. M. Rugman, 31–43. Research in Global Strategic Management 13. Oxford: Elsevier.

Peng, M. W., Y. Lu, O. Shenkar, and D. Wang. 2001. "Treasures in the China Shop: A Review of Management and Organizational Research on Greater China." *Journal of Business Research* 52:95–110.

Penrose, E. 1959. *The Theory of the Growth of the Firm.* New York: Wiley.

Ramamurti, R. 2009. "What Have We Learned about EMNEs." In *Emerging Multinationals from Emerging Markets,* edited by R. Ramamurti and J. Singh, 399–426. Cambridge, UK: Cambridge University Press.

Rugman, A. M. 1980. "A Test of Internalization Theory." *Managerial and Decision Economics* 2 (4): 211–19.

———. (1981) 2006. *Inside the Multinationals: The Economics of Internal Markets.* New York: Columbia Press. Reissue, Basingstoke, UK, and New York: Palgrave Macmillan.

———. 1986. "New Theories of the Multinational Enterprise: An Assessment of Internalization Theory." *Bulletin of Economic Research* 38:101–18.

———. 1996. *The Theory of Multinational Enterprises.* Cheltenham, UK: Edward Elgar.

———. 2000. *The End of Globalization.* London: Random House Business Books.

———. 2005. *The Regional Multinationals: MNEs and "Global" Strategic Management.* Cambridge and New York: Cambridge University Press.

———. 2009. "Theoretical Aspects of MNEs from Emerging Economies." In *Emerging Multinationals in Emerging Markets,* edited by R. Ramamurti and J.V. Singh, 42–63. Cambridge, UK: Cambridge University Press.

Rugman, A. M., and P. Almodovar. 2011. "The Born Global Illusion and the Regional Nature of International Business." In *The Future of Foreign Direct Investment and the Multinational*

*Enterprise,* edited by R. Ramamurti and N. Hashai, 265–83. Research in Global Strategic Management 15. Bingley, UK: Emerald.

Rugman, A. M., and J. D'Cruz. 2001. *Multinationals as Flagship Firm: Regional Business Networks.* Oxford and New York: Oxford University Press.

Rugman, A. M. and A. Verbeke. 1992. "A Note on the Transnational Solution and the Transaction Cost Theory of Multinational Strategic Management." *Journal of International Business Studies* 23 (4): 761–71.

——. 2001. "Subsidiary—Specific Advantages in Multinational Enterprises." *Strategic Management Journal* 22 (3): 237–50.

——. 2002. "Edith Penrose's Contribution to the Resource-Based View of Strategic Management." *Strategic Management Journal* 23 (8): 769–80.

——. 2003. "Extending the Theory of the Multinational Enterprises: Internalization Theory and Strategic Management Perspectives." *Journal of International Business Studies* 34 (2): 125–37.

——. 2004. "A Perspective on Regional and Global Strategies of Multinational Enterprises." *Journal of International Business Studies* 35 (1): 3–18.

——. 2007. "Liabilities of Regional Foreignness and the Use of Firm-Level versus Country-Level data: A Response to Dunning et al. (2007)." *Journal of International Business Studies* 38:200–205.

——. 2008. "Internalization Theory and Its Impact on the Field of International Business." In *International Business Scholarship: AIB Fellows on the First 50 Years and Beyond,* edited by Jean J. Boddewyn, 155–74. Research in Global Strategic Management 14. Bingley, UK: Emerald Group Publishing Limited.

Rugman, A. M., A. Verbeke, and Q. T. K. Nguyen. 2011. "Fifty Years of International Business Theory and Beyond." *Management International Review* 51 (6): 755–86.

Safarian, A. E. 2003. "Internalization and the MNE: A Note on the Spread of Ideas." *Journal of International Business Studies* 34:116–24.

Simon, H. A. 1959. "Theories of Decision Making in Economics and Behavioral Science." *American Economic Review* 49:253–83.

Styles, C., and R. G. Seymour. 2006. "Opportunities for Marketing Researchers in International Entrepreneurship." *International Marketing Review* 23 (2): 126–45.

Teece, D. 1981. "The Multinational Enterprise: Market Failure and Market Power Considerations." *Sloan Management Review* 22 (3): 3–17.

——. 1983. "Technological and Organizational Factors in the Theory of the Multinational Enterprise." In *The Growth of International Business,* edited by M. Casson, 51–62. London: George Allen & Unwin.

——. 1984. "Economic Analysis and Strategic Management." *California Management Review* 16 (3): 87–110.

——. 1986. "Profiting from Technological Innovation: Implications for Integration, Collaboration, and Public Policy." *Research Policy* 15 (6): 285–305.

——. 2007. "Explicating Dynamic Capabilities: The Nature and Microfoundations of (Sustainable) Enterprise Performance." *Strategic Management Journal* 28 (13): 1319–50.

Teece, D., G. Pisano, and A. Shuen. 1997. "Dynamic Capabilities and Strategic Management." *Strategic Management Journal* 18 (8): 537–56.

Toyne, B. 1989. "International Exchange: A Foundation for Theory Building in International Business." *Journal of International Business Studies* 20 (1): 1–17.

Tsang, E. 2006. "Behavioral Assumptions and Theory Development: The Case of Transaction Cost Economics." *Strategic Management Journal* 27:999–1001.

Verbeke, A. 2003. "The Evolutionary View of the MNE and the Future of Internalization Theory." *Journal of International Business Studies* 34:498–504.

———. 2009. *International Business Strategy*. Cambridge, UK: Cambridge University Press.

Verbeke, A., and P. Brugman. 2009. "Triple Testing the Quality of Multinationality—Performance Research: An Internalization Theory Perspective." *International Business Review* 18:265–75.

Verbeke, A., and N. S. Greidanus. 2009. "The End of the Opportunism vs. Trust Debate: Bounded Reliability as a New Envelope Concept in Research on MNE Governance." *Journal of International Business Studies* 40:1471–95.

Verbeke, A., and T. Kenworthy. 2008. "Multidivisional vs. Metanational Governance of the Multinational Enterprise." *Journal of International Business Studies* 39:940–56.

Verbeke, A., L. Li, and A. Goerzen. 2009. "Toward More Effective Research on the Multinationality and Performance Relationship." *Management International Review* 49:149–62.

Williamson, O. E. 1975. *Markets and Hierarchies: Analysis and Antitrust Implications: A Study in the Economics of Internal Organizations*. New York: Free Press, Macmillan.

———. 1981a. "The Economics of Organization: The Transaction Cost Approach." *The American Journal of Sociology* 87 (3): 548–77

———. 1981b. "The Modern Corporation: Origins, Evolution, Attributes." *Journal of Economic Literature* 19:1537–68.

Wright, M., I. Filatotchev, R. E. Hoskisson, and M. W. Peng. 2005. "Guest Editors' Introduction: Strategy Research in Emerging Economies: Challenging The Conventional Wisdom." *Journal of Management Studies* 42:1–33.

Yeung, B., and R. Mirus. 1988. "On the Mode of International Expansion: The Role of Agency Costs in an Expanded Framework." Paper read at the Academy of International Business conference, San Diego, CA.

Yip, G. 2002. *Total Global Strategy II*. Upper Saddle River, NJ: Prentice Hall.

Yiu, D. W., C. Lau, and G. D. Bruton. 2007. "International Venturing by Emerging Economy Firms: The Effects of Firm Capabilities, Home Country Networks, and Corporate Entrepreneurship." *Journal of International Business Studies* 38:519–40.

Young, S., P. Dimitratos, and L. P. Dana. 2003. "International Entrepreneurship Research: What Scope for International Business Theories?" *Journal of International Entrepreneurship* 1 (1): 31–42.

Zaheer, S. 1995. "Overcoming the Liability of Foreignness." *Academy of Management Journal* 38 (2): 341–63.

Zahra, S. A. 2005. "A Theory of International New Ventures: A Decade of Research." *Journal of International Business Studies* 36 (1): 20–28.

Zahra, S. A., J. S. Korri, and J. F. Yu. 2005. "Cognition and International Entrepreneurship: Implications for Research on International Opportunity Recognition and Exploitation." *International Business Review* 14 (2): 129–46.

Zeng, M., and P. J. Williamson. 2007. *Dragons at Your Door: How Chinese Cost Innovation Is Disrupting Global Competition*. Boston: Harvard Business School Press.

Zhou, K. Z., and L. Poppo. 2010. "Exchange Hazards, Relational Reliability, and Contracts in China: The Contingent Role of Legal Enforceability." *Journal of International Business Studies* 41:861–81.

# CHAPTER 16

········································································

# COMPETITIVE STRATEGY IN THE NONPROFIT SECTOR

········································································

SHARON M. OSTER

## 16.1 INTRODUCTION

········································································

THE nonprofit sector employs 8% of US workers, including most academic economists, and generates approximately 5% of the US GDP. And yet, while there is a lot written concerning public policy for the sector, we see much less literature on how we might apply our economics tools of strategy and industrial organization to better understand how the sector works or to better manage operations. In this chapter I provide a somewhat idiosyncratic scan of the field of nonprofit strategy.

When applied in the for-profit sector, research and teaching in the field of competitive strategy involves one of two broad questions: (1) What accounts for differences in the profitability of different industries?, and (2) Given a particular industry structure, are there ways an individual firm can outperform its rivals? For many years, Michael's Porter's Five Forces analysis has been the workhorse framework for the study of the first of these questions, with its emphasis on the key entry barriers well-known to the industrial organization community (Porter, 1980). The second question has often involved the use of game theory to analyze a firm's position relative to its rivals and how strategic behavior influences current and potential rivals. Tools like Porter's cost versus differentiation advantage and added value (Pankash and Ghemawat 1991; Brandenburger and Stuart 1996) have been staples in this area.

Notice, however, that there is a key assumption about organizational behavior that undergirds these two defining questions: Both in deciding whether to enter an industry and in making strategic choices after entry, firms are assumed to strive to maximize profits. Indeed, the subfield is called Competitive Strategy for a reason! Even when for-profit firms engage in "co-opetition," as Brandenburger and Nalebuff have termed the mix of cooperation and competition, the goal is firm well-being, not industry welfare (Brandenburger and Nalebuff 1996). In the case of nonprofits, the study of competitive strategy begins with a recognition that this key assumption does not typically hold. Nonprofits are generally not modeled as profit-seeking entities, and there are many occasions in which the individual nonprofit organization sacrifices individual well-being for the benefit of a larger mission. This chapter begins by reviewing the literature on the objective function of the typical nonprofit. I will argue that issues of entry and exit, and pricing in particular, will look somewhat different in the nonprofit sector as a consequence of these differences in organizational objectives.

Once we finish our review of the role of objectives in strategy development in the nonprofit sector, we will turn to a review of the connection between nonprofit production and strategy. The goods and services produced in the nonprofit sector have some special features, features that privilege the nonprofit form. The most prominent theory of why we have nonprofits is the hidden quality theory developed by Arrow (1963), and Hansmann (1980), and formalized by Glaeser and Shleifer (2001). As we will describe later in this chapter, theory tells us that nonprofits have a comparative advantage in the production of quality in complex, hard to evaluate goods and services. Nonprofits are further distinguished by their economic support. Most typically, revenue is collected to support nonprofit goods and services not simply from direct users or consumers but from donors and often governments.[1] The output of many nonprofits has features of the classic public good, in which a single unit of output is simultaneously consumed by multiple parties and the benefits from this output is valued by summing up these multiple benefits (Oster 2010). The multiple stream of benefits simultaneously generated by the typical nonprofit to several different constituents complicates the development of strategy. Again, we will find the tools of Competitive Strategy useful but they will need some reconfiguring.

## 16.2  STRATEGY TO WHAT END?

### 16.2.1  The Objective Function of the Nonprofit

For organizational economists, ownership forms emerge as a response to underlying fundamentals of demand and costs in markets. When ownership incentives are economically important and scale economies small, we often find partnerships. When economies of scale and scope are large, we find large conglomerates. For the nonprofit, since the work of Arrow (1963) and later Hansmann (1980), economists have argued that nonprofit firms emerge when goods and services are hard to evaluate, and trust replaces, at least to some extent, direct knowledge in determining quality. In Arrow's early articulation of institutions in the hard-to-evaluate medical care area, trust emerged as a consequence of a set of professional canons that softened the profit motive for the doctors manning offices and hospitals, in favor of quality and output levels. Later work by Philipson and others similarly argued for modeling nonprofits as output-maximizers subject to break-even constraints, reflecting both preferences of workers for output and altruistic concern by those workers for consumer welfare (Lakdwalla and Philipson 2006; Weisbrod 1998; Philipson and Posner 2011). Much of the work on health care organizations adopts this approach predicting lower prices and higher output for nonprofits.

For Hansmann (1980), the central fact of the nonprofit is the legal requirement that nonprofits not redistribute any surplus to a class of owner entrepreneurs. The inability of these entrepreneurs to extract profits directly softens their profit incentives. These softer incentives in turn create trust on the part of consumers for goods and services whose quality is hard to measure. Notice that we have the same conclusion as the Arrow model, but the source of profit softening is the law rather than medical ethics. In a formalization of the Hansmann theory, Glaeser and Shleifer (2001) model entrepreneurs as choosing the nonprofit form when the gains to that entrepreneur from high-quality production enabled by the nonprofit form exceed the costs of not being able to take any residual earnings in cash. In this model we also find worker sorting as entrepreneurs who, for altruistic or personal reasons, prefer quality and thus choose the nonprofit form.

Another perspective on the objective function of the nonprofit is that what nonprofits maximize (or, as it sometimes posited, *should* maximize) is not one's own individual organizational value, but the organization's contribution to the industry value as a whole. Consider Mark Moore's observation on what nonprofits should be doing (note the normative perspective here): "Their goal should be to strengthen the industry as a whole by widely sharing their ideas about what works and by encouraging as many other firms to enter the industry as possible." (Moore 2003, 9).

From our perspective, the key question is how differences in objectives affect our use of competitive strategy? How much difference does it make in applying the tools of strategy if firms maximize output or quality instead of profits, or if they adopt an industry value-added approach?

## 16.2.2  Exit and Entry Strategies in the Sector

An interesting place to examine differences in strategy is in the area of entry and exit, a key focus of strategy. In the for-profit world, we teach our students that new firms enter an industry whenever profits are supernormal. For this reason, long-term existence of excess profits tells us that barriers to entry exist, though of course it remains to us to figure out their nature. In the absence of profit maximization, our conclusions about when to expect entry and exit and how they operate are less clear.

To illustrate my point, consider a simple, Hotelling-like model of entry into a differentiated industry. As we will see, for a range of reasons, most nonprofits produce differentiated products; indeed, monopolistic competition is the modal nonprofit industry structure. Assume we have a market for orchestral performances in an isolated area with one hundred customers. Customers are divided in their preferences as the chart below indicates, with the majority of people preferring Mozart, and equal minorities preferring Telemann and Schoenberg. For simplicity, I have imposed symmetry in the customer valuations or willingness-to-pay numbers.

**Table 16.1  Author's Example Entry Example in the Nonprofit Orchestral Business**

| Customer/Type/Number | Willingness to pay for Mozart Performance | Willingness to pay for Telemann Performance | Willingness to pay for Schoenberg Performance |
|---|---|---|---|
| Mozart/60 | $100 | $20 | $20 |
| Telemann/20 | $20 | $100 | $20 |
| Schoenberg/20 | $20 | $20 | $100 |

Further assume a company can specialize in only one type of music, that it has capacity to serve all one hundred customers, that customers go to only one performance, and that all costs are fixed (here I will assume costs are zero for simplicity). A profit-maximizing monopoly producer, unable to price discriminate, in this situation produces Mozart, sells it at $100, earning $6000 and filling 60% of the house. A quantity-maximizing nonprofit, unable to price discriminate, also produces Mozart but sells it at a price of $0, the marginal cost, filling the house but earning nothing (Thank goodness for donations!). Notice that a perfect price discriminating profit-maximizer would offer two tiers of tickets, and sell out the house, looking on the output side just like the nonprofit. (And like the perfect competitor as we well know).

The story gets more interesting as we look at the entry of a second firm. In this setting, given that one firm can serve the entire market, the social optimum is for a second entrant to produce either Telemann or Schoenberg. A for-profit second entrant will compare the potential of earning $2000 by performing either Telemann or Schoenberg or competing for the larger $6000 market. With no competitive advantage to either firm, we might expect market sharing by two firms both producing Mozart and each making a maximum of $3000, assuming no price competition. Alternatively, the two firms might compete Bertrand-style until price is driven down and the Telemann $2000 earnings appear attractive. Note, however, the deleterious effect that the second entrant has on the first entrant would not typically be taken into account by that entrant. What about the nonprofit interested in social value maximization? Before a new entry, the monopoly nonprofit was charging $0, selling 100 tickets and creating social value of $100(60) + $20 (40) = $6800. A new entrant producing Telemann or Schoenberg changes the industry valuation to: $100(60) + $100(20) + $20(20) = $8400, for an increment to the music lovers in this town of $1600. By contrast, if the nonprofit had followed the for-profit strategy and produced a second Mozart-focused company, no value increment would have been created. For a social-value-maximizing nonprofit firm, the entry form will look very different from the for-profit entry we are accustomed to.

The example here is simple and contrived, but the point comports well with the empirics of the nonprofit sector: copycat entry is much less likely among nonprofits than among for-profits and differences in their objective functions are at least one reason.

Notice too that the entry story also tells us that nonprofit industries will *ceteris paribus* have more horizontal differentiation than the for-profit industry counterpart would, and thus pricing competition will generally be softer. Again, we will see reinforcing reasons for both of these features of the industry as we pursue our story.

Of course, in many ways, the intuitions we have about entry from the for-profit setting hold as we shift sectors. In a classic paper on entry in the for-profit sector, Bresnahan and Reiss (1987) examine patterns of entry in a set of service industries in cities of varying size as a way to measure the fixed costs of those industries and to examine strategic effects of new entry. Cities have to be "big enough" in terms of population to produce revenues sufficient to warrant the investment of site-specific fixed costs by firms. We can apply that same logic to analyze entry in the nonprofit arts community. How big a city do we need to support an opera company? A symphony? A ballet company? How much bigger does a city need to be to support a second company in each art form?

In order to look at this question, I collected data on the city location of all of the professional opera, symphony, and dance companies in the US and matched those data with the census of cities. Virtually every city with a population over one million has a symphony, an opera company, and a ballet company. At what city size does the modal city have each of these art forms? For opera and ballet, the answer is about 300,000 people; for the symphony, which is both more popular and likely has lower fixed costs, cities of 150,000 people provide enough support. To attract a second company, symphonies need a population of 500,000 or more, while opera and ballet need a population over a million to support second companies.[2] Notice that one needs well more than twice as many people to attract a second company than a first, which is also true when one looks at for-profit industries.

Why might we expect that it would take more than a doubling of city size to support a second entrant in an industry? Among for-profits, where entry is a response to profit-seeking, the standard answer is that increased competition from a second entrant reduces the per capita profitability in the industry, typically as a result of price competition. Among nonprofit arts organizations, the same effect will hold, though the greater level of product type differentiation in the sector would be expected to reduce the competitive effect somewhat. But there are other forces at work that likely contribute to the large city size needed to induce second entry in the arts. In our discussion of nonprofit manager/entrepreneurs we noted the tendency of some to take into account the value created in the industry as a whole; in some ways any negative profit effect caused by a second entrant on the initial entrant may be partially internalized by that new entrant. This would, of course, increase the necessary city size for a second entrant. In the arts, donor preferences also play an enormous role. In the aggregate, 40% of the revenue of performing arts organizations comes from donors. Donors may well differentially value supporting the first opera or dance company in a city over the second company. In this case, donor support may well mean that smaller cities than warranted by audience demand will support a first performing arts company, but that generating donor support for a second entrant will be considerably harder. In this respect, it is interesting to note that we do find in the data evidence of opera, dance, and symphonies in rather small cities; the distribution of city sizes of companies has fatter tails than one might expect in the for-profit sector. Glimmerglass Opera located in the small town of Cooperstown, NY, is a good example; not surprisingly, it earns 65% of its revenues from private donations, much higher than the average opera company more dependent on audience support. Notice from this example, that as we consider standard strategy issues of entry, we need to take into account both the special objectives of the sector and its dependence on donor funding as well as customers.

Turn now to the issue of exit. Recent work by Harrison and Laincez (2008), using exhaustive Form 990 data on nonprofits collected by the Urban Institute, indicates that exit rates from the nonprofit sector are well below what we see in the for-profit sector, even correcting to the best we can for product line. Why might we see this? Return again to our basic economics models. Exit occurs from industries because firms can no longer earn the opportunity cost of the capital invested in that venture. Stated another way, for-profit entrepreneurs abandon ventures when they think their capital can be more profitably used elsewhere. But, as Harrison and Laincez point out, one of the defining constraints of the nonprofit sector is that the founding entrepreneur cannot take his or her capital and begin a new venture; the law requires that when a nonprofit exits, any remaining capital must go into another state-approved charitable pot. For the social entrepreneur, the opportunity cost of his or her capital may well be seen as zero. The legal rules about the capital structure of the nonprofit thus affect not only their product choice when operating, but their incentives to exit. As we will see in the next section of this paper, the fact that nonprofits are fed by multiple revenue streams further reduces exit rates.

## 16.3 Pricing Strategies in the Nonprofit

Pricing strategies are one of the mainstays of competitive analysis. When do we see price wars versus coordinated pricing in an industry? When might firms use pricing to deter entry or "punish" rivals? When do we see bundled prices or price discrimination? How do we think about these questions in the nonprofit sector?[3]

In contrast to most of the for-profit sector, the nonprofit's access to alternative funding mechanisms means that for some organizations, for some periods, actually not charging for services may be viable. While most health care organizations rely on earned income for the bulk of their revenues, religious organizations earn less than 10% of their revenues from fees. Few churches charge formal admission prices for Sunday services. Why not? The rationing function of prices, so fundamental to microeconomic thinking, is problematic for nonprofits that are focused on outputs as we described earlier. For nonprofits who maximize output subject to a survival constraint that takes into account costs of production and other sources of revenue like donations, prices are a necessary fact of life rather than a profit-making tool. Indeed, for many nonprofits the key pricing issue is figuring out how to use prices to raise revenue without reducing output. Price discrimination is clearly an attractive strategy in this respect. And, as it happens, some of the features of the sector not only increase the attractiveness of price discrimination, but also enhance an organization's ability to make discrimination stick.

An organization using price discrimination charges different prices to individuals or groups of individuals for identical goods or services. In the earlier example, a discriminating profit maximizing firm would charge $100 for a performance to a Mozart-lover, but only $20 to attendees who prefer Telemann or Schoenberg. Discrimination allows a firm to expand its market to consumers with a lower willingness to pay, without sacrificing revenue on high willingness to pay consumers. Notice, as in the earlier example, that perfect price discrimination allows a monopolist to mimic a competitive firm in output levels, albeit with a considerably higher profit. For a nonprofit, discrimination similarly allows for revenue generation from an activity in a way that has minimal effect on the marginal consumer and thus output levels.

Of course, much stands in the way of a firm discriminating across customers. In some cases, it may be impossible or prohibitively expensive for a firm to stratify customers based on willingness to pay. Competition from firms selling similar products will naturally compress prices as firms compete for the high-margin customer on the top end of the industry demand curve. Some degree of market power is required to sustain price discrimination. In still other cases, arbitrage across customers prevents discrimination. In solving these problems, nonprofits have some natural advantages. As we just argued, most nonprofits are differentiated, so that products are not perfect substitutes. Competition across firms for the high-margin customer will thus be muted, perhaps considerably. Many nonprofits provide services (a college education, health care, or day care, for example) for which arbitrage on the consumer side is not possible. Finally, many nonprofits are aided by their own consumers in identifying high willingness to pay. The canonical example here is the financial statement provided by applicant seeking college aid. Indeed, some have argued that paying donations is a form of voluntary price discrimination in the sector (Hansmann 1981; Kushner and Brooks 2000).

An added wrinkle in the price discrimination story in the nonprofit world comes because many nonprofits care not only about how many people they serve, but *who* they serve. A price-discriminating for-profit firm focuses on extracting rents from its inelastic consumers, without making any moral judgments about the worthiness of the more-elastic consumers to receive better deals. For many nonprofit firms charging higher prices to a low-income customer with few choices than to a high-income consumer located in a broader marketplace may be anathema though the elasticities work in that direction. Several models of nonprofit health care provision incorporate the idea that the value of a customer in the nonprofit's objective function may vary with patient demographics, giving rise to a particular form of price discrimination (Dranove 1988; Schlesinger 1998; Deneffe and Masson 2002).

The nonprofit sector is also characterized by a greater degree of subsidization across product lines. Just as some nonprofit managers favor some customers over others, so too some favor some product lines over others, for reasons beyond their contribution to profits. There is some evidence that some nonprofits use monopoly positions in part of their market to subsidize product lines that exhibit public good features (Eckeland and Steinberg 1993).

Thus far, I have focused on differences in using pricing strategies in the nonprofit world. But, of course, many nonprofits rely heavily on earned income and use many of the same principles we see in the for-profit world. This is particularly the case in the performing arts sector (e.g., Touchstone 1980; McCain 1987; Prieto-Rodriguez and Fernandez-Blanco 2006). Nonprofits running commercial ventures often look very similar to for-profits in their pricing (Weisbrod 1998). Indeed an interesting recent article by Nelson and Zeckhauser (2003) describes the pricing strategies of the Renaissance church in selling private chapels in Florentine churches. Interesting from a modern perspective is the fact that chapel naming rights were *bundled* with perpetual masses and burial rights in these sales. Notice that the church has bundled some services for which it arguably has monopoly power (masses and burial rights) with naming rights for which there is presumably more competition.

We have looked so far at a few of the ways in which backing away from profit maximization in the nonprofit world affects our use of the tools of competitive strategy. We turn now to examine the way in which the nature of nonprofit production influences our use of strategy.

# 16.4 Nonprofit Production and Strategy

## 16.4.1 Value Creation in Multiple Revenue Source Nonprofits

Nonprofits typically rely on four main sources of revenues. Private payments for service on average comprise 49% of revenues. Government grants are another 29%, with 12% coming from private contributions or donations and 7% from investment income. While the importance of each of these revenue sources varies across sectors, the only sector among the nonprofits deriving more than 60% of its revenues from one of the four sources is the relatively small international services sector, which derives 70% of its revenue from private donations. For the rest of the sector, the sources of revenue are relatively unconcentrated as organizations depend on multiple sources for their survival.

In some cases, the nonprofit generates different forms of revenue by producing and marketing different products. A social service agency provides foster care under a government grant, but also generates revenue by renting space to another nonprofit. In this case, the social service agency would look a lot like a multiproduct firm. In analyzing the industry dynamics of this organization, we would need to recognize that it occupies several industries—foster care and the local rental business—and if we were going to use, say, Porter's Five Forces to analyze the profitability of the social service agency, we would need to look separately at these two industries. For each separate product line, one would look at existing competitors, substitutes, potential entrant, the power of suppliers, and the power of buyers, as a way of categorizing the supply and demand forces giving rise to profitability in each industry. This would be quite similar to work we would do with PepsiCo, for example, in analyzing its beverage business versus its snack food division. Of course, this analysis would tell us only potential profits from the foster care industry, or from rentals, and the agency might well choose to operate within that industry in a way to not maximize those profits. But the analysis of profit potential would look on the face of it quite similar. And, indeed, nonprofit organizations—especially those contemplating entry into new, more commercial businesses—are using tools like Porter's forces more than they once did.

For most nonprofits, however, revenue sources vary not because they are selling multiple products to different buyers but because they are in effect selling the same output to multiple buyers, each of whom values the output at different rates and for different reasons. Consider the 2011 exhibit of the contemporary Korean artist, Lee Ufan, at the Guggenheim museum in New York. Part of the funds for this exhibit comes from museumgoers who pay an admissions fee. Presumably we would analyze their demand for the show in much the same way we analyze demand for other goods and services. Samsung Corporation is another funder of the exhibit. The basis for their funding is quite different; perhaps the leadership of Samsung believes that support for Korean artists will help their profitability. The Korea Foundation also supported the show as part of its mission of promoting Korean art. Individual donors also contribute, in part in search of the "warm glow" benefit of philanthropy described by Andreoni (1990). Some support, in the form of tax relief, comes from New York City, perhaps on the grounds of stimulating tourism and thus city economic development. If the Guggenheim was interested in examining the potential profitability of this show via a Porter Five Forces analysis, it would need to apply the framework multiple ways. From the perspective of the museumgoer, we would typically take a relatively local perspective, with rivals, entrants, and substitute products likely in the New York metropolitan area. Substitutes might include movies, for example. Buyers would have little power, though we would likely want to think about members versus day visitors separately. The same show from a donor perspective looks quite different. Samsung has many possible philanthropic possibilities, most of them not in New York. Substitutes from its perspective may include relief and development organizations as well as other arts organizations. Donors in general are less atomistic than are museumgoers. An analysis of profitability might well teach the museum a good deal, but each revenue stream will have its own story to tell and determining the profit potential in the museum industry will involve adding up the potential associated with the range of possible revenue providers.

Another feature of the multiple streams of benefits generated by much nonprofit production of their goods and services is that many of these benefits will be nonrival in consumption, much like many public goods. Having one more museumgoer attend the Ufan show does not reduce benefits from the show to any other of its supporters. Indeed, Samsung's value from the exhibit is likely enhanced by the knowledge that there are people going to the museum, admiring Lee Ufan's work. Thus, calculating the value created by the exhibit—the first step in an Added Value exercise for example—requires one to vertically sum the willingness to pay of all affected parties, rather than look at the highest willingness-to-pay recipient. For the Guggenheim, the value of a day's worth of the Lee Ufan exhibit consists of the sum of value of all attendees, plus the value to Samsung, plus the value to the Korea Foundation, plus the value to the city, plus the value to future art historians excited about the record created of Ufan's work and so on.

For some categories of benefits from the Guggenheim's exhibit, the process of extracting value created is not unlike what we observe in the for-profit sector. Museumgoers pay admissions prices; big sponsors like Samsung provide donations that in some cases look a lot like advertising contracts. Some of the benefits from the Guggenheim show, however, maybe not only nonrival but nonexcludable and these benefits will be hard to monetize. The Guggenheim can prevent a nonpaying customer from seeing the Ufan show, but there is no way to prevent a Korean immigrant from being proud of the spillover from the show to public image of Korean art. When nonexcludability is a large part of the value story, we normally expect the public sector to play a role. The tax deductibility of donations given by the public sector to the nonprofit sector is one way to reduce the free rider problem normally seen with nonexcludable goods. Indeed, early work by Weisbrod characterized nonprofits as the "third sector," supplementing the public sector (Weisbrod 1977).

Moreover, in extracting value from donors in general, the nonprofit has a natural advantage. The nondistribution constraint that promotes trust among consumers of nonprofit goods and services also creates trust in the donor market. Indeed the fact that these benefit recipients are often less close to the point of production of the nonprofit good than is the direct service user likely increases the need for trust.

While the streams of benefits produced by a nonprofit to its various constituents may be nonrival in consumption, they are typically not independent. In many cases, donor values increase with client use. A donor to Save the Children, for example, typically cares a good deal about how many children are being served by the charity. Samsung may well care about how many people attend the Ufan exhibit, particularly if they see their contribution as a marketing device. In this case, any increased revenue from raising prices to users will be offset by declines in contributions from donors. In a number of areas, economists have found some crowding out of donations by increases in earned income (Segal and Weisbrod 1998), from public funding,[4] and from endowment growth (Oster 2003). The product design that maximizes flows from one revenue source may well not be the same as that from a second. The museumgoer may well respond to an exhibit structure seen as a little lowbrow from the perspective of a sophisticated, donating art patron. Interesting work by Pierce on US opera companies suggests that as the percent of revenue coming to an opera company from the National Endowment of the Arts increases, the number of unusual and controversial operas produced also increases. The greater the federal funding, the less overlap we see in opera repertoires—for example, less *Madame Butterfly*, more *Faust* (Pierce 2000). Similar results were found for theatre in England (O'Hagan and Neligan 2005). Both pricing and product design are made more complicated by the collective nature of some nonprofit goods.

The multiple revenue sources of the nonprofit also complicate the dynamics of the competitive process that underlies the field of strategy. In industries in which donor revenues are substantial, there is no necessary reason to suppose that competition among nonprofits will weed out inefficient service producers. Founder-donors may well be willing to subsidize over long periods of time an operation that is quite inefficient at delivering client services relative to its rivals. Thus, one might well find a class of vanity-nonprofits in which philanthropists—aided by the taxing authorities—support operations that effectively drive out of business much more well-run rivals.

We noted earlier in this review the relatively low exit rate of nonprofits. The multiple revenue sources of the sector play a role here too. In contrast to the for-profit sector, there are very few single product firms. Even those firms producing only one service are in some metaphysical sense generating multiple services by virtue of the different benefit streams coming to various payers/donors. Since government grants, private philanthropy, and client fees are not perfectly correlated, this feature of the nonprofit creates a level of diversification that reduces failure risk. Interesting work by Hansmann et al. (2003), looking at the hospital industry, finds strong evidence that nonprofit hospitals adjust their capacity within specialty units much slower than their for-profit rivals in response to demand shifts. Indeed, Hansmann et al. suggest that a conversion of non-profit hospitals to for-profit may enhance efficiency in the sector by speeding the elimination of unneeded capacity, referring to the "trapped capital" in the sector.

## 16.4.2  Usual Sources of Competitive Advantage in the Sector

Competitive advantage occurs when firms outcompete their rivals, earning supernormal profits in otherwise average-profit industries. Broadly speaking, competitive advantage comes in one of two flavors: a cost advantage allowing a firm to earn higher-than-average profits while charging a common market price, and a differentiation advantage allowing a firm to earn higher-than-normal profits by charging a higher price without offsetting cost increases. The for-profit strategy literature spends considerable time trying to understand the basis for an individual firm's competitive advantage.

In the nonprofit sector, almost all competition is of the differentiation variety. As we saw in the entry example, belief in an overriding social mission can reduce incentives to imitative entry and focus nonprofits on differentiation. But the fact that donations form an important revenue source for the nonprofit plays a role as well. In the fundraising world, the promise that one is delivering something different or better seems to be much more attractive than a promise to lower costs. Donor taste for differentiation will drive the structure of a nonprofit industry to the monopolistically competitive equilibrium in which firms operate at too small a scale from a cost perspective. In some sense, donors—especially donor-founders—subsidize production inefficiency on the client side to support demand side gains on the philanthropic side. Early in the history of a nonprofit, when the founder-social entrepreneur is still active, a focus on differentiation seems especially strong.

Other features of the nonprofit sector also favor a differentiation strategy. Most nonprofit goods and services are experience goods, rather than search goods, thus accenting the role of trust in assuring quality. In these markets, reputation and image are very important, even in distinguishing among nonprofits, and imitation will be more difficult, making an organization's competitive advantage more sustainable. Because the nondistribution constraint prevents nonprofits from raising funds via equity markets, nonprofits also tend to arise in industries in which the minimum efficient scale is not over-large, again favoring a differentiation strategy. Interestingly, in the health care market where technology and regulatory forces have tended to increase scale economies, we have seen a number of for-profit conversions. In the absence of scale economies in production, a natural basis for a cost advantage—large size—disappears. Finally, the differentiation strategy fits well with the less-formal, less-hierarchical management style that typifies the worker-focused nonprofit structure.

What are the standard bases of differentiation in the sector? With complex products, product design is obviously important. In a world in which it is difficult to determine quality and efficacy perfectly, and scale economies are modest, horizontal differentiation is favored. Reputation also plays a substantial role even among nonprofits. One of the reasons we see so many franchise operations in the nonprofit sector is that this form allows for service delivery by local operations while still benefitting from a national reputation (Oster 1996; Young and Faulk 2010).

Especially interesting is the nature of differentiation in markets in which nonprofits and for-profits coexist. Coexistence is common in the health care where almost 20% of the hospitals are for-profit, and conversion to the for-profit form is increasing across the sector, including within the Blue Cross-Blue Shield family. Nursing homes, day care, and increasingly higher education are all mixed markets. What can we say about the differentiation strategy of nonprofits in the context of mixed markets?

Of course the first question one might ask is why we have markets with both nonprofit and for-profit firms. Nonprofits have clear advantages from a tax perspective, potentially reducing their production costs for a given quality. They further have a trust advantage for consumers without undertaking marketing or other reputation-building expenditures. One might thus have expected that nonprofits would have squeezed out for-profits in these fields. Susan Rose-Ackerman was one of the first economists to try to understand the forces that sustain coexistence, using the example of the day care industry (Rose-Ackerman 1986). In her model, nonprofit providers ration their supply in response to their pursuit of quality service and for-profits serve as marginal producers entering when it is profitable to do so, and providing generally lower-quality care. Work in the health care area often assumes that nonprofits and for-profits specialize in different parts of the product space. For-profits focus on products and services for which scale economies are more important, given their access to equity capital, and subsectors in which demonstrating quality is easier. Nonprofits specialize in segments of the health care space in which quality is very hard to demonstrate and/or the provision of care has large externalities for which public or private subsidy is required. For example, Lindrooth and Weisbrod (2007) find that for-profit hospices respond more strongly than do nonprofits to incentives built in to the Medicare system by selecting patients with longer expected stays who are more profitable to serve. Interestingly, in the hospital market there is work suggesting that in markets in which nonprofits compete more intensively with for-profits, nonprofit behavior tends to mimic the for-profit, holding other market conditions constant (Cutler and Horwitz 1999; Duggan 2002).

One of the direct implications of the hidden quality theory of nonprofits is that their quality is higher than would be produced by a for-profit. How much evidence is there that this is in fact the case? Most of the empirical work examining nonprofit and for-profit performance outcome differences has been done in the health care area (Schlesinger and Gray 2006 provide a comprehensive review). In the end, the evidence linking ownership form and quality of output in the sector has been mixed. The same problems in measuring quality that encourage the nonprofit form make it hard to evaluate quality performance. We can see that costs are higher in the nonprofit firms: Staff-client ratios have been found to be lower at for-profit nursing homes (Weisbrod 1988) and day-care centers (Mauser 1998), but outcomes evidence has been mixed and difficult to sort out given ubiquitous selection issues. Here, too, there is ample room for new research.

## 16.5  CONCLUSIONS

Twenty years ago, the nonprofit sector was more or less a tabula rasa for an industrial organization economist. Organizational economists and sociologists had done considerable, excellent work, as had economists working on public policy, taxation, and the like, but the use of some of the standard models of entry, differentiation, and the like were little applied to the sector. As this review has, I hope, indicated, much has now changed. Even behavioral economists have begun to explore the sector. Still, much remains to be done. Increasingly we see nonprofits and for-profits competing in the same space. Education and health care are two prominent examples, but even in the arts, for-profit competition is increasing. Why and what difference does it make to strategies or outcomes? Is there a way to take better advantage of scale economies in the nonprofit area, given the donor-drive for novelty and institutional barriers to mergers in the field? Will we continue to see convergence in managerial practice of for-profits and nonprofits? Given the importance of the sector in areas like education and health that are so key to productivity growth in developed economies, the payoff to research in these areas can only grow.

## NOTES

1. For two excellent reviews of multiple financing sources for nonprofits, see Weisbrod (1998); and Chang and Tuckman (2010).
2. Given how few US cities have populations over one million, it is hard to be precise about the second-entry numbers.
3. Seaman (2010) provides an excellent review of the empirical pricing literature in the nonprofit sector.

4.  See Steinberg (1985) for a classic treatment of this question and Tinkelman (2010) for a recent review of this literature.

## References

Andreoni, James. 1990. "Impure Altruism and Donations to Public Goods: A Theory of Warm Glow Giving." *Economic Journal* 100:1447–58.

Arrow, Kenneth. 1963. "Uncertainty and the Welfare Economics of Medical Care." *American Economics Review* 53 (5): 941–73.

Brandenburger, Adam, and Harborne Stuart. 1996. "Value-based Business Strategy." *Journal of Economics and Management Strategy* 5 (1): 5–24.

Brandenburger, Adam, and Barry Nalebuff. 1996. *Co-opetition.* New York: Doubleday.

Bresnahan, Timothy, and Peter Reiss. 1987. "Do Entry Conditions Vary across Markets?" *Brookings Papers on Economic Activity* 3:833–81.

Chang, Cyril, and Howard Tuckman. 2010. "Income Diversification." In *Handbook of Research on Nonprofit Economics and Management*, edited by Bruce Seaman and Dennis Young, 5–17. Cheltenham, UK: Elgar Press.

Cutler, David, and J. R. Horwitz. 1999. "Converting Hospitals from Not for Profit to For-Profit Status." In *The Changing Hospital Industry: Comparing Not for Profit and For Profit Institutions*, edited by David Cutler, 45–90. Chicago: University of Chicago Press.

Deneffe, Daniel, and Robert Masson. 2002. "What do Not-for-Profit Hospitals Maximize?" *International Journal of Industrial Organization* 20:461–92.

Dranove, David. 1988. "Pricing by Nonprofit Organizations." *Journal of Health Economics* 7:47–57.

Duggan, Mark. 2002. "Hospital Market Structure and the Behavior of Not-for-Profit Hospitals." *Rand Journal* 33:433–46.

Eckel, Catherine, and Richard Steinberg. 1993. "Competition, Performance and Public Policy Towards Nonprofits." In *Nonprofit Organizations in a Market Economy*, edited by D. Hammack and Dennis Young, 57–81. San Francisco: Jossey-Bass.

Ghemawat, Pankash. 1991. *Commitment: The Dynamic of Strategy.* New York: Free Press.

Glaeser, Edward, and Andrei Shleifer. 2001. "Not for Profit Entrepreneurs." *Journal of Public Economics* 81:99–115.

Hansmann, Henry. 1980. "The Role of Nonprofit Enterprise." *Yale Law Journal* 89:835–901.

———. 1981. "Nonprofit Enterprise in the Performing Arts." *Bell Journal of Economics* 2:835–901.

Hansmann, Henry, Daniel Kessler, and Mark McClellan. 2003. "Ownership Form and Trapped Capital in the Hospital Industry." In *The Governance of Not-for-profit Organizations*, edited by Edward Glaeser, 45–69. Chicago: University of Chicago Press.

Harrison, Teresa, and Christopher Laincez. 2008. "Entry and Exit in the Nonprofit Sector." *B.E. Journal of Economic Analysis and Policy* 8:1–42.

Kushner, Ronald, and Arthur Brooks. 2000. "The One Man Band by the Quick Lunch Stand: Modeling Audience Response to Street Performances." *Journal of Cultural Economics* 24:65–77.

Lakdwalla, Darius, and Tomas Philipson. 2006. "The Nonprofit Sector and Industry Performance." *Journal of Public Economics* 90:1681–98.

Lindrooth, Richard, and Burton Weisbrod. 2006. "Do Religious Nonprofit and For-Profit Organizations Respond Differently to Financial Incentives? The Hospice Industry." *Journal of Health Economics* 26:342–57.

Mauser, Elizabeth. 1998. "The Importance of Organizational Form: Parent Perceptions versus Reality in the Daycare Industry." In *Private Action and Public Good*, edited by Walter Powell, 124–136. New Haven, CT: Yale University Press.

McCain, Roger. 1987. "Scalping: Optimal Contingent Pricing of Performances in the Arts and Sports." *Journal of Cultural Economics* 11:1–21.

Moore, Mark. 2003. "The Public Value Scorecard: A Rejoinder and an Alternative to Strategic Performance Measurement and Management in Nonprofit Organizations by Robert Kaplan." Working Paper, Hauser Center.

Nelson, Jonathan, and Richard Zeckhauser. 2003. "A Renaissance Instrument to Support Nonprofits: The Sale of Private Chapels in Florentine Churches." In *The Governance of Nonprofit Organizations*, 143–81. Chicago: University of Chicago Press.

O'Hagan, John, and Adriana Neligan. 2005. "State Subsidies and Repertoire Conventionality in the Nonprofit English Theatre Sector: An Econometric Analysis." *Journal of Cultural Economics* 29:35–57.

Oster, Sharon. 1996. "Nonprofit Organizations and Their Local Affiliates." *Journal of Economic Behavior and Organizations* 30:83–95.

———. 2003. "Is There a Dark Side to Endowment Growth?" In *Maximizing Revenue in Higher Education*, edited by F. King Alexander and Ronald Ehrenberg, 81–93. San Francisco: Jossey Bass.

———. 2010. "Product Diversification and Social Enterprise." In *Handbook of Research on Nonprofit Economics and Management*, edited by Bruce Seaman and Dennis Young, 195–207. Cheltenham, UK: Elgar.

Philipson, Tomas, and Richard Posner. 2011. "Antitrust in the Not For Profit Sector." *Journal of Law and Economics* 52:1–18.

Pierce, J. Lamar. 2000. "Programmatic Risk Taking by American Opera Companies." *Journal of Cultural Economics* 24:45–63.

Porter, Michael. 1980. *Competitive Strategy*. New York: Free Press.

Prieto-Rodriguez, Juan, and Victor Fernandez-Blanco. 2006. "Optimal Pricing and Grant Policies for Museums." *Journal of Cultural Economics* 30:169–81.

Rose-Ackerman, Susan. 1986. "Altruistic Nonprofit Firms in Competitive Markets: The Case of Day-Care Centers in the United States." *Journal of Consumer Policy* 9:291–310.

Schlesinger, Mark. 1998. "Mismeasuring the Consequences of Ownerships." In *Private Action and the Public Good*, edited by Walter Powll and Elisabeth Clemens, 85–113. New Haven, CT: Yale University Press.

Schlesinger, Mark, and Bradford Gray. 2006. "Nonprofit Organizations and Health Care: Some Paradoxes of Persistent Scrutiny." In *The Nonprofit Sector: A Research Handbook*, 2nd ed., edited by Walter Powell and Richard Steinberg, 378–431. New Haven, CT: Yale University Press.

Seaman, Bruce. 2010. "Pricing Strategies." In *Handbook of Research on Nonprofit Economics and Management*, edited by Bruce Seaman and Dennis Young, 142–56. Cheltenham, UK: Elgar.

Segal, Lewis, and Burton Weisbrod. 1998. "Interdependence of Commercial and Donative Revenues." In *To Profit or Not to Profit*, edited by Burton Weisbrod, 105–28. Cambridge: Cambridge University Press.

Tinkelman, Daniel. 2010. "Revenue Interactions: Crowding Out, Crowding In or Neither?" In *Handbook of Research on Nonprofit Economics and Management*, edited by Seaman and Young, 18–41. Cheltenham: Elgar.

Touchstone, Susan. 1980. "The Effects of Contributions on Price and Attendance in the Lively Arts." *Journal of Cultural Economics* 4:33–46.

Weisbrod, Burton. 1977. *The Voluntary Sector: An Economic Analysis*. Boston: Lexington Books.

——. 1988. *The Nonprofit Economy*. Cambridge: Harvard University Press.

——. 1998. "Modeling the Nonprofit Organization as a Multiproduct Firm: A Framework for Choice." In *To Profit or Not to Profit*, edited by Burton Weisbrod, 47–64. Cambridge: Cambridge University Press.

Young, Dennis, and Lewis Faulk. 2010. "Franchises and Federations." In *Handbook of Research on Nonprofit Economics and Management*, edited by Bruce Seaman and Dennis Young, 220–37. Cheltenham, UK: Elgar.

# PART VI

ORGANIZATION
AND MOTIVATION
IN THE
MODERN FIRM

......

# CHAPTER 17

# ORGANIZATIONAL DESIGN AND FIRM PERFORMANCE

......

## MASSIMO G. COLOMBO, MARCO DELMASTRO, AND LARISSA RABBIOSI

## 17.1 INTRODUCTION

SINCE the seminal work of Chandler (1962), business economics and management scholars have emphasized that the organization of firms' activities crucially influences their performance.[1] Accordingly, since the early 1960s the theoretical economic literature has been particularly interested in the design of the firm's internal organization, and studies in management, organization science, and business history have produced a large body of qualitative evidence on this issue. Large scale econometric studies that examine the performance impact of firms' organizational design, and changes made to it, are more recent. This chapter provides a critical survey of this stream of studies in order to highlight "stylized facts" supported by robust quantitative empirical findings, and to link them to insights provided by theoretical work. We also offer some suggestions about future research on these topics.

A view that is popular with scholars in organizational design and practitioners is that, since the 1980s, a new "flexible" organizational design paradigm has gained ground in the industrialized countries (Womack et al. 1990; Roberts 2004). Adoption of this new paradigm has involved a delayering and corresponding increase in the span of control (Wang 2009; Guadalupe and Wulf 2010), a decentralization of decision power down the corporate hierarchy (Colombo and Delmastro 2004), and the adoption of practices that have been labelled variously as "high performance," "flexible," "high commitment," "innovative," and "alternative" (e.g., Huselid 1995; Michie and Sheehan 1999). In this chapter we assess whether and when the presumption that adoption of this new paradigm results in superior performance, is supported by robust empirical evidence.

First, we show that the new paradigm is based on a series of superadditive effects between different elements of firm organization (Milgrom and Roberts 1995), and that the adoption of individual elements in isolation has negligible, and sometimes even negative, effects on firm performance. Second, we suggest that, in this domain, there is no "one size fits all" solution. In line with the evidence provided by the pioneering studies conducted at Aston University in the 1960s (e.g., Pugh et al. 1969b), and the insights offered by theoretical work on organizational design, we might expect the impact of organizational design on firm performance to be contingent on firm-, industry-, and country-specific factors. These moderating factors have received limited although growing attention in the quantitative empirical literature. In reviewing this emergent and still quite fragmented empirical literature, we take the opportunity to present both empirical regularities and open issues, and to indicate avenues for future research.

A final preliminary remark on measurement issues is in order. The organizational design of firms covers a wide range of dimensions. Here we focus on selected dimensions that can be measured using quantitative indicators (Colombo and Delmastro 1999, 2008). Specifically, we consider i) *organizational configuration*, ii) *allocation of decision-making authority*, and iii) *adoption of formal organizational practices*.[2] The first two dimensions reflect the structural characteristics of firm organization. We will refer to the variables included in these categories as "structural organizational variables" (SOVs). The organizational configuration is reflected in the organizational depth—i.e., the number of layers between the bottom and the top of the pyramidal hierarchy—and shape—i.e., the span of control, defined as the number of subordinates reporting directly to a superior. The allocation of decision-making authority refers to the level in the organization responsible for taking a selected number of strategic and/ or operating decisions. Accordingly, decision-making authority is centralized when decision-making power is concentrated in the upper levels of the hierarchy, and decentralized when responsibility is delegated to the lower hierarchical levels. In relation to organizational practices, we focus on "innovative work practices" (IWPs) and "human resource management practices" (HRMPs). The former refer to how employees perform their tasks (e.g., in groups or in isolation), the latter are aimed at eliciting effort and collaborative behavior from workers and aligning their objectives with those of the firm.[3]

By firm performance we mean labor (and/or capital) productivity and economic and financial performance. Other related streams of literature, which for reasons of space are not examined here, include studies that analyze the effects of adoption of organizational practices and other changes in organizational design, on workers' salaries (e.g., Bailey et al. 2001; Forth and Millward 2004; Handel and Gittleman 2004; Osterman 2006), and job satisfaction (e.g., Appelbaum et al. 2000; Freeman and Kleiner 2000; Godard 2001). We also do not consider work on the organizational design-innovation link (e.g., Michie and Sheehan 1999, 2003; Laursen and Foss 2003; Beugelsdijk 2008; Zhou et al. 2011).

The chapter is organized as follows. Section 17.2 surveys the indications in different streams of the theoretical economic literature on the link between organizational design and firm performance. In Section 17.3, after highlighting the methodological problems associated with measures of firm organization, we review a selection of large-scale quantitative empirical work on the performance impact of different dimensions of firm organizational design, in isolation and in combination. Section 17.4 reviews work on the role of firm heterogeneity at country, industry, and firm level, in shaping the organizational design-firm performance relationship. We provide some suggestions for future research in this field. Section 17.5 concludes the chapter.

## 17.2 THEORETICAL FRAMEWORK

Before looking at the econometric evidence on the relationship between organizational design and firm performance, we propose some brief theoretical perspectives on *why* we should expect organizational design dimensions to impact on firm performance. In a nutshell, the organizational design-firm performance link can be explained by the effects of the organizational variables on (i) information and communication costs, (ii) agency costs engendered by the opportunism of individual employees, and iii) the motivations of individual employees to exploit their knowledge and skills to the benefit of their employers.

The "information processing" perspective suggests that the firm's organization must be designed so as to minimize distortions and failures in the transmission of information (Keren and Levhari 1979, 1983, 1989) and delays in the implementation of decisions (Radner 1993; Van Zandt 1999a). In general, the larger the number of information items to be gathered, processed, and transmitted, the greater the benefits that will be engendered by the adoption of a deeper organizational structure which allows for reductions to planning and implementation times (Radner 1993). This argument presumes the contextual adoption of a decentralized decision system. Indeed, while allowing tasks to be performed concurrently by an informed decision maker, decentralization of decision authority reduces delays and information leaks (Radner 1993; Van Zandt 1999b). Conversely, if decision making processes are centralized, loss of information problems increase with, and performance is adversely affected by greater organizational depth. Centralized organizations suffer from information overload, which slows decision making (Sah and Stiglitz 1986).

In accordance with this view, the "knowledge hierarchy" literature (e.g., Garicano 2000) has shown that the selective delegation of decisions (i.e. notably, the delegation of operating decisions) down the pyramidal hierarchy "protects" the valuable time of top managers who then can focus their attention and effort on crucial (i.e., strategic) decisions (see also Harris and Raviv 2002). More generally, decentralized decision making allows firms to benefit from the specialization of tasks, even when it increases communication costs and coordination needs (Bolton and Dewatripont 1994).

Williamson (1975, 1985) argued that the inefficiencies of a centralized organization in handling large flows of information are clearly illustrated by the defects of large U(unitary)-form enterprises organized along functional lines (i.e., R&D, production, sales, and finance). As the size of the operations of U-form enterprises increases, the information load on top managers similarly increases to the extent that decision-making processes become inefficient. Oliver Williamson (1975, 134; see also Chandler 1962) describes it thus:

> The ability of the management to handle the volume and complexity of the demands placed upon it became strained and even collapsed. . . . Bounds of rationality give rise to finite spans of control, which in turn requires that additional hierarchical levels be introduced as the U-form enterprise expands. . . . Adding hierarchical levels can, if only for serial reproduction reasons, lead to an effective loss of control through incomplete or inaccurate transmittal of data moving up and instructions moving down the organisational hierarchy.

The information processing inefficiencies of the U-form organization paved the way to the emergence in the 1920s of the M(multidivisional)-form. By replacing functional operating units with semiautonomous profit centres (i.e., divisions organized mostly by product line or geographical market), the M-form organization reduced the volume of information that top management had to work with, allowing a greater focus on strategic decision making, including control of the operating decisions made by divisional managers. In other words, the valuable time of the chief executive officer (CEO) and other top managers was protected by divisional managers being assigned responsibility for operating decisions.[4]

The "decentralization of incentive" stream of literature views the pyramidal hierarchy as a series of principal-agent relations, in which, as might be expected, the objectives of agents and principals generally are not aligned (e.g., Mookherjee 2006). Hence, the design of the firm's organization is aimed at alleviating "loss of control" problems generated by these agency relations. In particular, if the unique contribution of each employee to value creation cannot be demonstrated, employees will have a strong incentive to shirk and free-ride. Studies in this stream show that if the span of control increases, the probability of subordinates being checked decreases, leading to higher agency costs and poorer firm performance (Calvo and Wellisz 1978, 1979; Rosen 1982; Qian 1994). However, this negative effect on firm performance can be mitigated by the adoption of organizational practices that make the nature of work more observable, allow the measurement of the unique contributions of individual employees, and provide adequate rewards for individual performance, thereby realigning employees' behavior with the strategic goals of the firm (Wright and McMahan 1992). Thus, decentralization of decision authority, if coupled with the adoption of these practices, can lead to superior firm performance (Snell 1992).

A recent stream of work on the delegation of decision authority takes its inspiration from Hayek's (1945) seminal work on the use of knowledge in society[5] and emphasizes that individual employees often possess specific knowledge (Jensen and Meckling 1992) that is relevant to the firm's operations and provides the employee with an information advantage over his or her superior. Delegation of decision authority to these individuals allows their knowledge to contribute to decision making (Aghion and Tirole 1997). Colocation of knowledge and decision authority occurs also when employees are instructed to inform corporate superiors about relevant information in their possession and decision authority is centralized in the superior. However, in this latter case, if the transferred information cannot be verified by a third party (i.e., it is "soft" information, Stein 2002), employees may communicate it strategically to superiors in order to influence decisions that will be in their (employees') favor (Dessein 2002; Alonso and Matouschek 2008). The ensuing loss of information can lead to poor-quality decisions. Problems related to the loss of information that occurs when decisions are centralized and the loss of control problems engendered by delegating decisions to individuals whose interests diverge from those of the firm because of the existence of private nonmonetary benefits of decision making, can be alleviated through the adoption of incentive-based compensation schemes that link agents' rewards to their performance. It has been shown that such compensation schemes are relatively more effective for reducing loss of control problems than for limiting loss of information problems (Dessein 2002; Alonso et al. 2008; Rantakari 2008). This argument provides further support for the view that the joint adoption of a decentralized decision system and suitable organizational practices leads to better firm performance.

The studies referred to above focus on the link between the organizational structure variables and firm performance, with organizational practices playing an accessory role. Other researchers have concentrated on the direct impact of organizational practices on firm performance. In the resource-based view of the firm, interest has intensified around understanding how organizational practices can become a source of sustained competitive advantage (e.g., Schuler and Jackson 1987; Wright and McMahan 1992; Koch and McGrath 1996). The adoption of suitable organizational practices allows firms to build firm-specific human capital which ultimately influences firm performance. Specifically, these practices can affect organizational performance both through improved performance from individual employees and through a reduction in the costs generated by employee turnover (Batt 2002). For instance, firm practices such as selecting, hiring, training, and teamwork result in more skilled and better motivated employees who are more capable of seizing opportunities and making effective decisions. At the same time, high-powered compensation schemes, profit-sharing arrangements, and ongoing investments in training and empowerment create trust and enhance motivation and attachment among employees, all of which positively affects firm performance by inducing lower quit rates.

# 17.3 ECONOMETRIC EVIDENCE ON THE EFFECT OF ORGANIZATIONAL DESIGN ON FIRM PERFORMANCE

In this section, we review large scale econometric work on the link between the firm's organizational design and labor (and/or capital) productivity and financial performance.[6] This is summarized below before detailed discussion of the empirical evidence.

First, relatively few individual specific dimensions of firm organizational design show a significant and positive effect on firm performance. The results seem not to be consistent across countries, industries or firm characteristics (e.g., size). In light of the theoretical contributions surveyed in Section 17.2, which emphasize the superadditive effects among various dimensions of firms' organizational design, these findings are hardly surprising. Second, in line with the theoretical predictions, there are complementarities between individual organizational design dimensions: the adoption in combination of different organizational design dimensions (e.g., decentralized decision system and high-powered compensation schemes) generally shows a positive and significant effect on firm performance. This evidence is especially robust as regards IWPs and HRMPs adopted as a system. An indication of superadditive effects on firm performance can be found also in the complementarities between organizational practices and the structural aspects of organizational design. However, only a few studies focus on these issues and existing work has examined only a partial set of possible interactions.

Note also that, in this section, we do not discuss methodological issues concerning econometric procedures, causality, and measurement of performance outcomes, although these are fundamental issues. We would refer the reader to the works by Bloom and Van Reenen (2011), Boselie et al. (2005), Colombo and Delmastro (2008), Huselid and Becker (1996), Wright et al. (2005). However, before we examine the empirical studies, we offer some methodological hints on how to measure firms' organizational design variables, an issue that is often overlooked by the empirical literature.

## 17.3.1  On Measuring Firms' Organizational Design

The pioneering work on organizations developed in the 1960s at Aston University (see Pugh et al. 1963; Pugh et al. 1968, 1969b; Pugh et al. 1969a) provides a stylized but thorough description of the organization based on several dimensions. While there are many interesting aspects to firm organization—the Aston group's analyses developed a total of more than two hundred variables—large-scale quantitative studies require the identification of a limited number of key aspects of organizational design, which can be measured using objective, quantitative indicators (on this issue, see also Colombo and Delmastro 1999, 2008).

A serious weakness in the econometric literature is the lack of consensus on a uniform definition of these indicators, which makes comparison across studies and generalizations quite hazardous. This weakness is pervasive in the study of the effect of IWPs and HRMPs on firm performance. On the one hand, there are considerable ambiguities as to the exact meaning of these practices. On the other hand, there is no clear distinction between these two types of practices (Becker and Gerhart 1996). For instance, some authors use the term IWP to refer also to supporting HRMPs related to incentive-based compensation schemes, training, promotion, recruitment, and dismissal practices (e.g., Huselid 1995; Ichniowski and Shaw 1995; Ichniowski et al. 1997; Cully et al. 1998).

Another limitation is the recourse to perceptual measures gathered through surveys. Since these measures are subjective, they are liable to response bias and are hardly comparable across surveys (for indications on how these problems can be alleviated, see Bloom and Van Reenen 2010b). This latter problem could be alleviated by the use of qualitative variables defined in previous studies. However, objective indicators are preferable although more difficult to secure. Indeed, the structural characteristics of firm organization, such as organizational configuration and allocation of decision-making authority, could be measured using objective indicators. One way to operationalize these variables is to draw on secondary sources of information—e.g., public or internal reports, personnel records (Rajan and Wulf 2006; Smeets and Warzynski 2008)—or specific ad hoc field analyses (Delmastro 2002), to obtain data on the number of hierarchical levels and the span of control at each level of the pyramidal hierarchy. Measures of the allocation of decision authority can be derived following Acemoglu et al. (2007) among others, who proxy delegation of decision authority by firm's organization into profit centres. Managers responsible for both revenues and costs are more likely to have considerable autonomy compared to a cost (revenue) centre manager who is responsible only for costs (revenues). Also, measures of the allocation of decision authority among agents can be derived through analysis of contractual agreements for the top businesses functions (e.g., CEO, president) or well-designed questionnaires and industrial relations surveys (Colombo and Delmastro 2004; Meagher and Wait 2008).

A third serious problem in this field is related to the widespread use (and abuse) of dummy variables. Dummy variables that take account of changes in SOVs (e.g., "decentralization," "delayering") are misleading because they do not provide information on the exact (initial and final) organizational design configuration. Delayering may increase the efficiency of a very bureaucratic firm, but may be inappropriate for an already flat organization. Therefore, analysis of the effect of delayering on firm performance will be inadequate if the initial configuration of the pyramidal hierarchy (and the eventual extent of its shrinkage) is not considered.

In addition, the adoption of individual (or systems of) organizational practices is generally captured through simple dummy variables. This method has some serious limitations since dummy variables do not do justice to the *extent* of use of the practices under consideration. The extent of their use can be expressed either as the proportion of the workforce involved in a particular practice (i.e., coverage), or the degree to which an employee experiences or uses the practice (i.e., intensity) (Boselie et al. 2005). The extent of use is an important aspect that is neglected in much of the empirical literature (for exceptions, see Huselid 1995; Guest et al. 2003). Two related issues concern the precise identification of the job groups to which the practice refers—an operationalization that is limited in the empirical literature (for an exception, see Lepak and Snell 2002)—and measurement of the effective use of the practices that control for inadequate implementations (for an exception, see Huselid et al. 1997).

## 17.3.2  The Effect of Individual Organizational Variables in Isolation

Most studies that try to assess the effects on firm performance of individual organizational variables consider specific IWPs or HRMPs. Results are mixed. For instance, Black and Lynch (1996) failed to detect any statistically significant relationship between individual IWPs (i.e., use of TQM and benchmarking) and productivity. However, they found that two specific HRMPs—proportion of time spent in formal training outside working hours, and use of grades as a priority in recruiting, respectively—were positively correlated with the productivity of manufacturing and nonmanufacturing establishments (see also Black and Lynch 2001). Huselid (1995) found no link between individual HRMPs (i.e., teamwork, empowerment, recruitment, and training) and productivity. In a similar vein, other work, primarily based on British cross-sectional data (Wood and de Menezes 1998; Perotin and Robinson 2000; Addison and Belfield 2001; Guest et al. 2003) found mixed results concerning the relationships between labor productivity and organizational practices, such as training, practices aimed at improving employee participation in control (e.g., quality circles), returns (e.g., profit-related pay) and communication, or practices related to employee representation and equal opportunities.

The findings regarding the link between individual IWPs and HRMPs and productivity are ambiguous also in studies that use panel data estimation techniques. For instance, no statistically significant evidence of a positive effect on labor productivity of the adoption of IWPs, such as job rotation, TQM, and benchmarking, was detected for US firms (Cappelli and Neumark 2001; Black and Lynch 2004). On the other hand, quality circles (Caroli and Van Reenen 2001) and IWPs capturing reengineering (Black and Lynch 2004) respectively exhibited a significant positive effect on productivity in French and US establishments. Practices related to self-managed teams showed either no effect (Caroli and Van Reenen 2001) or a negative statistically significant effect (Black and Lynch 2004). In relation to HRMPs, training, pay for quality and skills, and profit sharing compensation schemes had no impact on firm performance (Cappelli and Neumark 2001; Black and Lynch 2004).

Empirical work analyzing the relationship between the structural dimensions of firms' organization and firm performance are limited (Arvanitis, 2005; Bloom et al. 2012. For a review of older contributions, see Dalton et al. 1980; Capon et al. 1990). Baum and Wally (2003) found centralization of strategic decisions, and decentralization of operating decisions to be positively related to firm performance while the study by Bloom et al. (2012) suggests a weak association between decentralization and higher productivity. With regard to vertical depth, estimates based on US data show no effect of this variable on changes in labor productivity (Black and Lynch 2004), while delayering (i.e., decrease in vertical depth) is shown to have a positive effect on productivity in the case of French plants (Caroli and Van Reenen 2001). However, these findings are not replicated in a large study of Swiss firms (Arvanitis 2005), which found that neither decrease in the number of hierarchical layers nor delegation of decision making from managers to employees were positively associated with firm performance.

### 17.3.3  The Effect of Bundles of Organizational Practices

Several studies have examined the effect generated by the adoption of *bundles* of IWPs and HRMPs. The work by Ichniowski and colleagues on production lines in the steel industry is an influential example of this literature. Ichniowski et al. (1997) examine the impact on productivity, measured by the percentage of scheduled time that a line actually runs, of the adoption by these lines of IWPs, such as teamwork and flexible job assignment, and several complementary HRMPs relating to incentive pay schemes, recruiting, employment security, skills training, and communication between management and labor. They show that the highest productivity levels are associated with the adoption of all the innovative practices under examination and the lowest level corresponds to a very traditional work organization: underperforming lines did not adopt any new practices (see also Ichniowski 1990; Gant et al. 2002).

Different systems of practices have been found to have a positive effect on firm performance. Huselid's (1995) "employee skills and organization" and "employee motivation" systems are positively and significantly related to different indicators of firm performance (productivity, profitability, Tobin's Q). Kato and Morishima (2002), based on a twenty-year panel data set relating to 126 Japanese-listed manufacturing firms, found that the joint adoption of employee participation practices, incentive compensation schemes, joint labor-management committees, and shop floor committees had a positive impact on productivity, but only after seven or more years after their adoption. Cappelli and Neumark (2001) found evidence of synergistic effects between pay for skills and profit sharing. Pendleton and Robinson (2010) show that, to be effective, stock plans need to be used in combination with other forms of employee involvement and voice (i.e., amount of time devoted to employees' questions and views in workplace meetings and team briefings), even when the latter have an independent positive effect on productivity. Huselid et al. (1997) showed that teamwork and empowerment are positively related to a subsequent gross rate of return on capital, although they detected no relation with Tobin's Q. Finally, Guest et al. (2003) found a positive significant association between heavy use of HRMPs and profit per employee. However, when they controlled for previous performance the effect disappeared.[7]

### 17.3.4  The Joint Effect of Organizational Practices and the Dimensions of Organizational Structure

Empirical work that considers IWPs and/or HRMPs and SOVs together is scant. Black and Lynch (2001) examine the use of TQM and benchmarking, the extent of training of workers and use of profit sharing compensation schemes, and—as SOVs—number of managerial levels in plants (i.e., vertical depth) and average number of workers per supervisor (i.e., span of control). They find no evidence of synergistic gains from combinations of different IWP/HRMPS and SOVs (Black and Lynch 2001, 440). However, Arvanitis's (2005) study of the productivity effects from the reorganization of firms in Switzerland find a positive effect on productivity when SOVs are bundled together in a single indicator with a set of HRMPs.

Other studies document that when changes in SOVs coincide with the adoption of IWPs and/or HRMPs, there are positive effects on firm performance. Focusing on business services, Bertschek and Kaiser (2004) consider both the enhancement of team work, an IWP, and the flattening of the firm hierarchy (i.e., delayering). Labor productivity is measured as the ratio of total sales to total employment. The authors conclude, based on their estimates, that firms that adopt teamwork practices and reduce the number of hierarchical layers in the firm are clearly better off compared to the hypothetical case of no work reorganization. Bauer (2003) examines the joint occurrence of delayering with decentralization of decision authority to subordinates and teamwork (i.e., an "organizational change" index) and shows a positive and statistically significant effect on the productivity of German establishments in the period 1993–95. Janod and Saint-Martin (2004), applied nonparametric estimates to 2404 French manufacturing firms and show that work reorganization—measured by a dummy variable for firms involved in two or more organizational changes related to self-directed work teams, quality circles, and other organizational design adaptations such as delayering and greater versatility of the work force—has a substantial, positive, and statistically significant effect on both labor and capital productivity. In other words, labor and capital were used more efficiently by reorganized firms. These effects are stronger for firms that introduced a larger number of organizational changes. Colombo et al. (2007) use a sample of 109 Italian firms observed in the period 1991–97 to study the effects on firm profitability (i.e., earnings from continuing operations before interest expenses and taxes) of the adoption of both IWPs and HRMPs and of changes in SOVs. The IWPs included self-managed teams, job rotation, and TQM practices; the HRMPs included pay for quality and skills and profit sharing compensation schemes, and SOVs were measured by vertical depth and a quantitative measure of the allocation of the plant's selected strategic decisions among plant manager, his superior, and his subordinates. In line with the view that there are synergies among organizational practices, an index capturing the adoption of the bundle of IWPs and HRMPs under consideration exhibited a positive significant effect on firm profitability. Even more interestingly, the positive impact of these practices increased dramatically with the extent of delegation of decision authority down the pyramidal hierarchy. With all variable set at their mean value, a standard deviation increase of both the organizational practice index and the delegation variable resulted in a 64% increase in profitability. In contrast, they found no evidence of complementarities between delayering and decentralization of decision authority, or between delayering and adoption of IWPs and HRMPs.

# 17.4   The Role of Contingency Factors

As emphasized in Section 17.2, an "optimal" firm organizational design depends on the extent of information processing, communication, and agency costs, and the distribution of relevant knowledge among organization members. Therefore, country-, industry- and firm-specific contingencies that influence the above factors are likely also to influence the organizational design-firm performance link. Econometric studies that explicitly consider these moderating effects applying a contingency perspective are rare. Most existing work examines how the above-mentioned contingencies shape firms' organizational design, thereby providing indirect evidence on the issue under consideration here.[8]

This section provides a review of these studies, and links the results obtained to the theoretical discussion. We highlight issues that, in our view, offer promising avenues for future research.

## 17.4.1   The Socioeconomic Environment

From an institutional theory perspective, *regulatory* (e.g., existing laws and rules), *cognitive* (e.g., representations, schemas, inferential sets) and *normative* (e.g., individuals' norms and values) dimensions can be used to characterize the institutional environments in which firms operate (Scott 1995). These characteristics differ across countries. Kostova (1999, p. 314) studies transnational transfers of organizational practices and claims that "(1) countries differ in their institutional characteristics; [and] (2) organizational practices reflect the institutional environment of the country where they have been developed and established."

First, the regulatory component of the institutional environment can make certain dimensions of a firm's organization more or less efficient. Consider, for instance, systems of rewards based on individual incentives, which are aimed at reducing the agency costs within organizations. In some Western European countries labor market regulations restrict or oppose these types of compensation schemes (e.g., unionized firms). Second, if the dimensions of the firm's organizational design are in conflict with the cognitive environment of the country in which the firm is located, firm employees might have a negative attitude toward implementing such an organizational design (Kostova 1999). Third, the values and norms of different national cultures affect the efficiency of the organizational design dimensions (for a more general approach to corporate culture see Kreps 1990; for institutional-based differences between the decision-making practices in Japanese firms and those in Western companies, see, e.g., Adler 1995). For instance, the United States scores higher for individualism (Hofstede 1984) and, compared to their US counterparts, European workers tend to place a higher value on leisure

and family time. Therefore, although productivity-based incentives have proven beneficial to firm performance in the United States (Milgrom and Roberts 1995), the costs
of implementing and using them in different—and very distant—institutional environments may outweigh their benefits.

Environments with unreliable legal systems and high levels of paternalistic justification of authority are likely to encourage strong centralized control and be associated
with lower levels of trust, which discourage reliance on employees' skills and commitment to the organization. Under these institutional conditions, delegation of authority
is likely to involve problems related to greater loss of control arising from coordination
and agency costs, compared to the costs of delegation faced by firms in countries (such
as the Scandinavian countries) where a shared understanding of priorities, levels of
mutual trust and commitment, relevance of quality and expertise of subordinates, are
higher (for a review of the relationship between institutional features and firm characteristics, see Whitley 2010).

In line with the above arguments, there are some large-scale empirical analyses
aimed at systematically examining how firms' organizational design dimensions vary
with the socioeconomic environments in different countries. The work by Bloom and
Van Reenen (2007, 2010a) provides preliminary evidence on firms specialized in different styles of management, across countries. The authors collected comprehensive,
qualitative information on 18 management practices related to four areas: shop-floor
operations; monitoring; target setting management; and incentives. Firms in the US,
India, and China scored highest for management practices including reward and promotion and systems to hire and retain the most productive employees. US firms scored
highest for incentives while Japanese, Swedish and German firms achieved the highest relative scores for monitoring and target setting management practices. Degree of
decentralization also varied across countries with firms in Asia being more centralized than Scandinavian and Anglo-Saxon firms. Also, in regions where high percent-
ages of the population adhered to hierarchical religions (e.g., Roman Catholic, Islamic,
Eastern Orthodox), plants were less decentralized than in regions with a relatively lower
shares of hierarchical religions (Bloom et al. 2012). This evidence conforms to the view
that in countries where agents have confidence in the rules of society and trust each
other, agency costs are low, which renders decentralization of decision authority more
efficient.

To our knowledge, no large-scale econometric study has tested whether the performance impact of different dimensions of firms' organizational design depends on
country-specific institutional characteristics such as those referred to above.

## 17.4.2  Industry- and Firm-Specific Effects

Several industry- and firm-specific factors are likely to influence firms' information
processing, communication, and agency costs, and the value of the specific knowledge
possessed by individual firm members, and to moderate the organizational design-firm

performance relation. While systematic coverage of these factors is beyond the scope of this chapter, here we focus selectively on those factors that have attracted the widespread interest of scholars. We consider: i) product market competition; ii) human capital and knowledge intensity of firms; and iii) firms' innovation and technology strategies.[9]

### 17.4.2.1  Product Market Competition

Several studies examine the effects of product market competition on firms' organizational design. Bloom and Van Reenen (2007) document a significant positive association between an aggregate score reflecting adoption of the best management practices and product market competition, proxied alternatively by degree of import penetration (i.e., share of total imports in domestic production), the Lerner competition index (i.e., 1-profits/sales), and a qualitative variable capturing the number of the firm's competitors. Although these are simple correlations, the authors note that any endogeneity bias is likely to generate underestimation of the effect of competition on management practices. These findings are consistent with evidence of the greater diffusion of these management practices in the United States, where competition supposedly is stronger than in other countries (see also Bloom and Van Reenen 2010a). Acemoglu et al. (2007) analyze the antecedents of the decentralization of decision making, proxied by organization by profit centres, in French and British firms. They find that firms operating in more competitive industries, where level of competition is proxied by the Lerner competition index, are more decentralized. These findings are confirmed in Bloom et al. (2010), which investigates the relation between product market competition and decentralization of decision making from CEOs to plant managers, in medium-sized (100- to 5000-employee) manufacturing firms located in several different countries. They consider decisions relating to capital investments, recruitment of new employees, new product introduction, and sales and marketing, and calculate an aggregate decentralization of decision authority index. They found a robust positive association between the three above-mentioned measures of competition and the decentralization index (for similar evidence using plant level data from the 1995 Australian Workplace Industrial Relations Survey, see Meagher and Wait 2008). Guadalupe and Wulf (2010) study the causal effect of competition from trade liberalization on various characteristics of firms' organizational design. The authors exploit a unique panel dataset on the firm hierarchies in large US firms (1986–99) and the Canadian-US Free Trade Agreement 1989 "policy experiment," which constitutes an exogenous increase in competition for US firms due to the removal of tariffs. They show that increasing competition leads firms to i) become flatter (i.e., reduce the number of positions between the CEO and division managers), and ii) increase the number of positions reporting directly to the CEO (i.e., CEO's span of control). These changes allegedly imply greater decentralization of decision making. Moreover, they detect an increase of division managers' total and performance-based pay. Finally, Colombo and Grilli (2013), for a sample of Italian owner-managed high-tech start-ups, show that the likelihood of appointing a salaried manager, another move associated with more decentralized decision making, is greater for firms that operate in industries where pressure from competitors is strong.

Overall, the evidence is consistent with the argument that among firms that face strong product market competition, delegation of decisions down the pyramidal hierarchy and adoption of complementary IWPs and HRMPs—including reward systems aimed at limiting divergence of agents' objectives from those of their employer—have a positive effect on firm performance. In highly competitive environments, timely decision making is fundamental for firm performance. Decentralization of (operating) decisions preserves the time of top managers, who can focus on crucial strategic decisions, and avoids delays in implementing decisions. The reduction in agency problems engendered by greater competition reinforces this effect. Again, to our knowledge, no study has provided evidence that the link between these organizational design characteristics and firm performance is stronger in the presence of stronger product market competition.

### 17.4.2.2 *The Human Capital and Knowledge Intensity of Firms*

In human capital intensive firms, specific knowledge relevant to firms' operations is likely to be dispersed among employees, rather than being concentrated in the CEO function. Under these circumstances, the decentralization of decision authority downward in the pyramidal hierarchy, combined with the adoption of suitable IWPs and HRMPs, should have a more positive effect on firm performance than in low human capital intensive firms.

In line with this view, Bloom and Van Reenen (2007) show that firms with more skilled employees have better overall management practices and, in particular, are more likely to adopt practices relating to promotion, rewards, hiring, and firing (i.e., better "people management") relative to monitoring and target setting management practices (i.e., "fixed capital management practices"). Acemoglu et al. (2007) show that firms that operate in more heterogeneous industries, are more innovative because they are closer to the technological frontier of the industry, and are younger are more decentralized. These effects are stronger in high-tech industries. These findings can be interpreted as indirect evidence that adoption of a decentralized decision system is more beneficial when the specific knowledge possessed by firms' employees is crucial to firms' operations.

Human capital is especially important for high-tech start-ups. Moreover, these firms are usually resource constrained, and the opportunity cost of senior management time is greater than in more established firms. Therefore, it can be expected that the adoption of a more structured organizational design and a more decentralized decision system will be especially beneficial for these firms. The fact that agency costs generally are small due to the small size and limited diversity of firms' operations should strengthen this effect. The (rather limited) available empirical evidence supports this view. Sine et al. (2006) examine the organizational design of a sample of Internet service ventures founded in 1996, and operating in the United States during the period 1996–2001. They found that the firms exhibiting the best performance in terms of sales growth, a typical indicator of business success for this type of firm, were those with greater specialization of decisions among members of the top management team and a relatively larger number of managerial positions given the size of the firm's operations (i.e., greater administrative intensity given by the ratio of managers to total employment). Bertoni et al. (2011) document that the creation of a middle management layer in Italian, high-tech, owner-managed start-ups, leading to an increase in firms' vertical depth (i.e., a switch from a two-layer to a three-layer pyramidal hierarchy), and the associated decentralization of (some) decision authority, have a large positive effect on firms' sales growth rates.[10]

### 17.4.2.3 *The Innovation and Technology Strategies Adopted by Firms*

Several studies analyze the joint impact of organizational design variables and indicators capturing use of information and communication technologies (ICTs) on firm performance, and find evidence of superadditive effects between these two sets of variables (for a review, see Colombo and Delmastro 2008; Bloom and Van Reenen 2011). Also, several scholars have suggested that the *type* of technology matters, making a distinction between information technologies (such as Enterprise Resource Planning software) and communication technologies (such as the Internet). The latter technologies, in addition to reducing communication costs, should make centralization of decisions more effective, while adoption of information technologies could be expected to have the opposite effect, since these technologies increase the ability of firms' personnel to acquire and process information autonomously. The results in Bloom et al. (2009a) support these predictions (of the effects of communication technologies on delegation of decision authority, see also Colombo and Delmastro 2004).

A more general perspective, which is gaining ground, considers the role of the type of innovation strategy adopted by firms and, notably, firms' reliance on technological collaborations with third parties.[11] There is a vast literature addressing how firms' technological collaborations with external actors, including lead customers, other firms, universities, and communities of practice, generate competitive advantage, thus improving firm performance (Richardson 1972). The general theoretical framework supporting the association between these collaborative relationships and firm performance shows that these external links allow firms to access and share the distributed knowledge possessed by their partners. When this knowledge is absorbed by the firm, this enhances the range and quality of its information and capabilities, leading to better performance. Also, external relationships increase the firm's exposure to the opportunities and potential benefits embedded in the dynamic network(s) of its partners (e.g., Kogut 2000). In searching for innovation opportunities firms increasingly are being forced to open their boundaries (Laursen and Salter 2006), and the use of external knowledge in their innovation activities has been shown to improve their general performance (DeCarolis and Deeds 1999).

The design of suitable organizational structures and practices can facilitate the acquisition, assimilation, transfer, and exploitation of the knowledge firms obtain from external sources (Colombo et al. 2011). In general, it can be assumed that the partner firm's specific knowledge possessed by individual organization members is fundamental to take full advantage of these collaborative relationships. Hence, collaborative relationships should have a more positive effect on firm performance if firms adopt a decentralized decision system and support IWPs and HRMPs. However, the knowledge insourced from partners must be combined with internal knowledge in order for the firm to exploit it commercially. This combination is not straightforward and leads to higher coordination costs when decision authority is widely decentralized. Lastly, this trade-off is likely to be influenced by the type of partner, which makes the specific knowledge possessed by individual organization members more or less valuable to the firm (see, e.g., the emergent work on the organization of firms that do business with the open-source software community, especially Alexy and Leitner 2011; Colombo et al. 2012). Analysis of the performance impact of the interaction between the firm's internal organization and external knowledge insourcing strategies, is a promising avenue for future research.

## 17.5 CONCLUSIONS

This chapter shows that economists and management scholars interested in the organizational design-firm performance relationship have moved from a focus on the effect of individual elements of the firm's organization to a systemic view, in which it is the overall configuration, interdependencies, and synergies (i.e., "the horizontal fit," Wright and Snell 1998) in the different dimensions of the firm's organization that matter (e.g., Ichniowski 1990; Arthur 1994; Ichniowski and Shaw 1999; Bloom and Van Reenen 2007; Colombo et al. 2007). This view is supported by robust evidence of superadditive effects between the different elements of firms' organizational design.

We also examined country-, industry- and firm-specific contingencies that influence the organizational design-firm performance link. Although this literature is relatively undeveloped, evidence on the role of these contingent factors supports the view that there is no unique optimal organizational design configuration, or "new lean type" or any other type of organizational configuration. Although some general historical trends can be identified regarding, for example, the flattening of the hierarchy in large established firms, the decentralization of decision authority, and the growing international diffusion of "best" management practices (on this, see also Bloom and Van Reenen 2011), the optimal organization is deeply shaped by factors such as the extent of product market competition, the human capital intensity of firms' operations, the innovation strategies adopted by firms, and the institutional characteristics of the countries in which firms are located.

Future econometric work should provide a more comprehensive examination of the *mechanisms* through which the different factors that determine firm heterogeneity affect the link between organizational design and firm performance. An additional beneficial effect of this type of research would be to provide a robust test of the predictions developed by the theoretical discussion of firms' organizational design. A better understanding of these issues would help to explain *why* the "optimal" organizational design is contingent on the firms' environment and strategies, and would highlight which (if any) organizational design dimensions are likely to be the best for the majority of firms, on average.

## NOTES

1. This idea goes back to Adam Smith ([1776] 1969), who illustrated how in the pin factory, adoption of a suitable organization of production resulted in dramatic productivity gains.
2. See Colombo and Delmastro (2008) for extensive documentation from business history of the fundamental importance of these organizational dimensions.
3. In this work, if not otherwise specified, we use IWPs to refer to one or more of the following practices: self directed teams, quality circles, job rotation, and total quality management. HRMPs will refer to use of individual and team incentive schemes, recruiting, skills training, and communication practices. Other practices will be mentioned and described individually (e.g., motivation, learning, job satisfaction) (e.g., Wagner 1994). We acknowledge that formal procedures and practices include other aspects of the organization ranging from the accounting system to hiring and dismissal policies. Accordingly, the literature on the adoption of innovative practices comprises other important aspects that are not covered in this chapter.
4. As explained below, this organization also attenuated the agency costs arising from opportunistic behavior by managers.
5. "If we … agree that the economic problem of society is mainly one of rapid adaptation to changes in particular circumstances of time and place, … decisions must be left to the people who are familiar with these circumstances, who know directly of the relevant changes and of the resources immediately available to meet them.… We must solve it by some form of decentralisation" (Hayek 1945, 524).
6. The studies reviewed here are only part of the extant empirical literature on this issue. In particular, we do not consider qualitative evidence provided by case studies, such as the well-known study of the NUMMI automobile assembly plant, jointly owned by General Motors and Toyota (see Krafcik 1988; Wilms 1995). For a review of this literature see, for example, Huselid (1995), Cappelli and Neumark (2001), Ichniowski and Shaw (2003). See Appelbaum et al. (2000) for a thorough analysis based on qualitative data on the performance effects of IWPs and HRMPs in the medical electronic instruments and imaging, steel, and apparel industries. On these last two industries see also Arthur (1994), and Bailey (1993), and Berg et al. (1996), respectively.
7. For studies investigating the effect on firm performance of different combinations of organizational practices in specific industries, see, among others, Appleyard and Brown (2001), Bartel (2004), Batt (1999), Jones et al. (2010a, 2010b), Macduffie (1995), Youndt et al. (1996), and Richard and Johnson (2001).
8. We could argue that a firm designs its organization so as to maximize profits. Therefore, observing the heterogeneity in organizational design across firms, reflecting the different environments firms face and the different strategies they adopt, provides useful, but indirect insights into the impact of organizational design on firm performance.
9. Also important are the firm's ownership and corporate governance. In a series of studies, Bloom and colleagues consider the peculiarities of the organizational design of firms as diverse as multinational enterprises, family firms, and private equity owned firms. For a review of these studies, see Bloom and Van Reenen (2011).

10. For a more comprehensive discussion of these issues see Colombo and Rossi Lamastra (Forthcoming).

11. This body of studies is part of a larger management literature that focuses on the alignment of HRMPs and the strategic management process of the firm—i.e., vertical fit (Wright and Snell 1998)—as a source of value (e.g., Schuler and Jackson 1987; Huselid 1995; Delery and Doty 1996; Youndt et al. 1996). In this perspective, other typical contingent factors related to firms' strategy include the competitive positioning of firms (Porter 1985) and their strategic business processes (Becker and Huselid 2006).

## REFERENCES

Acemoglu, D., P. Aghion, C. Lelarge, J. Van Reenen, and F. Zilibotti. 2007. "Technology, Information and the Decentralization of the Firm." *Quarterly Journal of Economics* 122:1759–99.

Addison, J. T., and C. R. Belfield. 2001. "Updating the Determinants of Firm Performance: Estimation Using the 1998 UK Workplace Employee Relations Survey." *British Journal of Industrial Relations* 39:341–66.

Adler, N. 1995. *International Dimensions of Organizational Behavior.* Boston: PWS-Kent.

Aghion, P., and J. Tirole. 1997. "Formal and Real Authority in Organizations." *Journal of Political Economy* 105:1–29.

Alexy, O., and M. Leitner. 2011. "A Fistful of Dollars: Are Financial Rewards a Suitable Management Practice for Distributed Models of Innovation?" *European Management Review* 8:165–85.

Alonso, R., W. Dessein, and N. Matouschek. 2008. "When Does Coordination Require Centralization?" *American Economic Review* 98:145–79.

Alonso, R., and N. Matouschek. 2008. "Optimal Delegation." *Review of Economic Studies* 75:259–93.

Appelbaum, E., T. Bailey, P. Berg, and A. Kalleberg. 2000. *Manufacturing Advantage: Why High Performance Work Systems Pay Off.* Ithaca, NY: Cornell University Press.

Appleyard, M. M., and C. Brown. 2001. "Employment Practices and Semiconductor Manufacturing Performance." *Industrial Relations* 40:436–71.

Arthur, J. B. 1994. "Effects of Human Resource Systems on Manufacturing Performance and Turnover." *Academy of Management Journal* 37:670–87.

Arvanitis, S. 2005. "Modes of Labor Flexibility at Firm Level: Are There Any Implications for Performance and Innovation? Evidence for the Swiss Economy." *Industrial and Corporate Change* 14:993–1016.

Bailey, T. 1993. "Organizational Innovation in the Apparel Industry." *Industrial Relations* 32:30–48.

Bailey, T., P. Berg, and C. Sandy. 2001. "The Effect of High-Performance Work Practices on Employee Earnings in the Steel, Apparel, and Medical Electronics and Imaging Industries." *Industrial and Labor Relations Review* 54:525–43.

Bartel, A. P. 2004. "Human Resource Management and Organizational Performance: Evidence from Retail Banking." *Industrial and Labor Relations Review* 57:181–203.

Batt, R. 1999. "Work Organization, Technology, and Performance in Customer Service and Sales." *Industrial and Labor Relations Review* 52:539–64.

———. 2002. "Managing Customer Services: Human Resource Practices, Quit Rates, and Sales Growth." *Academy of Management Journal* 45:587–97.

Bauer, T. K. 2003. "Flexible Workplace Practices and Labor Productivity." Discussion paper, Institute for the Study of Labor (IZA), No. 700. Accessed January 17, 2013. http://hdl.handle.net/10419/20637.

Baum, J. R., and S. Wally. 2003. "Strategic Decision Speed and Firm Performance." *Strategic Management Journal* 24:1107–29.

Becker, B. E., and B. Gerhart. 1996. "The Impact of Human Resource Management on Organizational Performance: Progress and Prospects." *Academy of Management Journal* 39:779–801.

Becker, B., and M. A. Huselid. 2006. "Strategic Human Resources Management: Where Do We Go from Here?" *Journal of Management* 32:898–925.

Berg, P., E. Appelbaum, T. Bailey, and A. L. Kalleberg. 1996. "The Performance Effects of Modular Production in the Apparel Industry." *Industrial Relations* 35:356–73.

Bertoni, F., M. G. Colombo, and L. Grilli. 2011. "Venture Capital Financing and the Growth of High-Tech Start-Ups: Disentangling Treatment from Selection Effects." *Research Policy* 40:1028–43.

Bertschek, I., and U. Kaiser. 2004. "Productivity Effects of Organizational Change: Microeconometric Evidence." *Management Science* 50:394–404.

Beugelsdijk, S. 2008. "Strategic Human Resource Practices and Product Innovation." *Organization Studies* 29:821–47.

Black, S. E., and L. M. Lynch. 1996. "Human-Capital Investments and Productivity." *American Economic Review* 86:263–67.

———. 2001. "How to Compete: The Impact of Workplace Practices and Information Technology on Productivity." *Review of Economics and Statistics* 83:434–45.

———. 2004. "What's Driving the New Economy?: The Benefits of Workplace Innovation." *Economic Journal* 114:97–116.

Bloom, N., L. Garicano, R. Sadun, and J. Van Reenen. 2009a. "The Distinct Effect of Information Technology and Communication Technology on Firm Organization." Discussion paper, CEP, 927.

Bloom, N., R. Sadun, and J. Van Reenen. 2012. "The Organization of Firms across Countries." *Quarterly Journal of Economics* 127: 1663–1705.

———. 2010. "Does Product Market Competition Lead Firms to Decentralize?" *American Economic Review Papers and Proceedings* 100:434–38.

Bloom, N., and J. Van Reenen. 2007. "Measuring and Explaining Management Practices across Firms and Countries." *Quarterly Journal of Economics* 122:1351–1408.

———. 2010a. "Why Do Management Practices Differ across Firms and Countries?" *Journal of Economic Perspectives* 24:203–24.

———. 2010b. "New Approaches to Surveying Organizations." *American Economic Review: Papers and Proceedings* 100:105–9.

———. 2011. "Human Resource Management and Productivity." In *Handbook of Labor Economics*, edited by O. Ashenfelter and D. Card, 4b:1697–1767. San Diego and Amsterdam: Elsevier.

Bolton, P., and M. Dewatripont. 1994. "The Firm as a Communication Network." *Quarterly Journal of Economics* 109:809–39.

Boselie, P., G. Dietz, and C. Boon. 2005. "Commonalities and Contradictions in HRM and Performance Research." *Human Resource Management Journal* 15:67–94.

Calvo, G. A., and S. Wellisz. 1978. "Supervision, Loss of Control, and the Optimum Size of the Firm." *Journal of Political Economy* 86:943–52.

——. 1979. "Hierarchy, Ability, and Income Distribution." *Journal of Political Economy* 87: 991–1010.

Capon, N., J. U. Farley, and S. Hoenig, S. 1990. "Determinants of Financial Performance: A Meta-Analysis," *Management Science* 36:1143–59.

Cappelli, P., and D. Neumark. 2001. "Do 'High-Performance' Work Practices Improve Establishment-Level Outcomes?" *Industrial and Labor Relations Review* 54:737–75.

Caroli, E., and J. Van Reenen. 2001. "Skill-Biased Organizational Change? Evidence from a Panel of British and French Establishments," *Quarterly Journal of Economics* 116:1449–92.

Chandler, A. D. 1962. *Strategy and Structure: Chapters in the History of the Industrial Enterprise.* Cambridge, MA: MIT Press.

Colombo, M. G., and M. Delmastro. 1999. "Some Stylized Facts on Organization and Its Evolution." *Journal of Economic Behavior and Organization* 40:255–74.

——. 2004. "Delegation of Authority in Business Organizations: An Empirical Test." *Journal of Industrial Economics* 52:53–80.

——. 2008. *The Economics of Organizational Design.* New York: Palgrave MacMillan.

Colombo, M. G., M. Delmastro, and L. Rabbiosi. 2007. "'High Performance' Work Practices, Decentralization, and Profitability: Evidence from Panel Data." *Industrial and Corporate Change* 16:1037–67.

Colombo, M. G., and L. Grilli. 2013. "The Creation of a Middle-Management Level by Entrepreneurial Ventures: Testing Economic Theories of Organisational Design." *Journal of Economics and Management Strategy* 22: forthcoming.

Colombo, M. G., and C. Rossi Lamastra. Forthcoming. "The Organizational Design of High-Tech Start-Ups: State of the Art and Directions for Future Research." In *Handbook of Economic Organization,* edited by A. Grandori. Cheltenham, UK: Edward Elgar.

Colombo, M. G., E. Piva, and C. Rossi Lamastra. 2012. Authorizing employees to collaborate with communities during working hours: When is it valuable for firms?." *Long Range Planning,* forthcoming.

Colombo, M. G., L. Rabbiosi, and T. Reichstein. 2011. "Organizing for External Knowledge Sourcing." *European Management Review* 8:111–16.

Cully, M., S. Woodland, A. O'Reilly, G. Dix, N. Millward, A. Bryson, and J. Forth. 1998. *The 1998 Workplace Employee Relations Survey: First Findings.* London: DTI.

Dalton, D. R., W. D. Todor, M. J. Spendolini, G. J. Fielding, and L. W. Porter. 1980. "Organization Structure and Performance: A Critical Review." *Academy of Management Review* 5:49–64.

DeCarolis, D. M., and D. L. Deeds. 1999. "The Impact of Stocks and Flows of Organizational Knowledge on Firm Performance: An Empirical Investigation of the Biotechnology Industry." *Strategic Management Journal* 20:953–68.

Delery, J. E., and D. H. Doty. 1996. "Modes of Theorizing in Strategic Human Resource Management: Tests of Universalistic, Contingency, and Configurational Performance Predictions." *Academy of Management Journal* 39:802–35.

Delmastro, M. 2002. "The Determinants of the Management Hierarchy: Evidence from Italian Plants." *International Journal of Industrial Organization* 20:119–37.

Dessein, W. 2002. "Authority and Communication in Organizations." *Review of Economic Studies* 69:811–38.

Forth, J., and N. Millward. 2004. "High-Involvement Management and Pay in Britain." *Industrial Relations* 43:98–119.

Freeman, R. B., and M. M. Kleiner. 2000. "Who Benefits Most from Employee Involvement: Firms or Workers?" *American Economic Review* 90:219–23.

Gant, J., C. Ichniowski, and K. Shaw. 2002. "Social Capital and Organizational Change in High Involvement and Traditional Work Organizations." *Journal of Economics & Management Strategy* 11:289–328.

Garicano, L. 2000. "Hierarchies and the Organization of Knowledge in Production." *Journal of Political Economy* 108:874–904.

Godard, J. 2001. "High Performance and the Transformation of Work? The Implications of Alternative Work Practices for the Experience and Outcomes of Work." *Industrial and Labor Relations Review* 54:776–805.

Guadalupe, M., and J. Wulf. 2010. "The Flattening Firm and Product Market Competition: The Effect of Trade Liberalization on Corporate Hierarchies." *American Economic Journal: Applied Economics* 2:105–27.

Guest, D. E., J. Michie, N. Conway, and M. Sheehan. 2003. "Human Resource Management and Corporate Performance in the UK." *British Journal of Industrial Relations* 41:291–314.

Handel, M. J., and M. Gittleman. 2004. "Is There a Wage Payoff to Innovative Work Practices?" *Industrial Relations* 43:67–97.

Harris, M., and A. Raviv. 2002. "Organization Design." *Management Science* 48:852–65.

Hayek, F. A. 1945. "The Use of Knowledge in Society." *American Economic Review* 35:519–30.

Hofstede, G. H. 1984. *Culture's Consequences: International Differences in Work-Related Values.* Beverly Hills, CA: Sage Publications.

Huselid, M. A. 1995. "The Impact of Human-Resource Management-Practices on Turnover, Productivity, and Corporate Financial Performance." *Academy of Management Journal* 38:635–72.

Huselid, M. A., and B. E. Becker. 1996. "Methodological Issues in Cross-Sectional and Panel Estimates of the Human Resource-Firm Performance Link." *Industrial Relations* 35:400–22.

Huselid, M. A., S. E. Jackson, and R. S. Schuler. 1997. "Technical and Strategic Human Resource Management Effectiveness as a Determinant of Firm Performance." *Academy of Management Journal* 40:171–88.

Ichniowski, C. 1990. "Human Resource Management Systems and the Performance of U.S. Manufacturing Businesses." Working Paper, National Bureau of Economic Research, 3449, Cambridge, MA.

Ichniowski, C., and K. Shaw. 1995. "Old Dogs and New Tricks: Determinants of the Adoption of Productivity-Enhancing Work Practices." *Brookings Papers on Economic Activity* 1995:1–65.

——. 1999. "The Effects of Human Resource Management Systems on Economic Performance: An International Comparison of U.S. and Japanese Plants." *Management Science* 45:704–21.

——. 2003. "Beyond Incentive Pay: Insiders' Estimates of the Value of Complementary Human Resource Management Practices." *Journal of Economic Perspectives* 17:155–80.

Ichniowski, C., K. Shaw, and G. Prennushi. 1997. "The Effects of Human Resource Management Practices on Productivity: A Study of Steel Finishing Lines." *American Economic Review* 87:291–313.

Janod, V., and A. Saint-Martin. 2004. "Measuring the Impact of Work Reorganization on Firm Performance: Evidence from French Manufacturing, 1995–1999." *Labour Economics* 11:785–98.

Jensen, M., and C. Meckling. 1992. "Specific and General Knowledge, and Organizational Structure." In *Contract Economics,* edited by W. H. Werin and L. H. Wijkander, 251–74. Cambridge, MA, and Oxford: Blackwell.

Jones, D. C., P. Kalmi, and A. Kauhanen. 2010a. "Teams, Incentive Pay, and Productive Efficiency: Evidence from a Food-Processing Plant." *Industrial and Labor Relations Review* 63:606–26.

——. 2010b. "How Does Employee Involvement Stack Up? The Effects of Human Resource Management Policies on Performance in a Retail Firm." *Industrial Relations* 49:1–21.

Kato, T., and M. Morishima. 2002. "The Productivity Effects of Participatory Employment Practices: Evidence from New Japanese Panel Data." *Industrial Relations* 41:487–520.

Keren, M., and D. Levhari. 1979. "The Optimum Span of Control in a Pure Hierarchy." *Management Science* 25:1162–72.

——. 1983. "The Internal Organization of the Firm and the Shape of Average Costs." *Bell Journal of Economics* 14:474–86.

——. 1989. "Decentralization, Aggregation, Control Loss and Costs in a Hierarchical Model of the Firm." *Journal of Economic Behavior and Organization* 11:213–36.

Koch, M. J., and R. G. McGrath. 1996. "Improving Labor Productivity: Human Resource Management Policies Do Matter." *Strategic Management Journal* 17:335–54.

Kogut, B. 2000. "The Network as Knowledge: Generative Rules and the Emergence of Structure." *Strategic Management Journal* 21:405–25.

Kostova, T. 1999. "Transnational Transfer of Strategic Organizational Practices: A Contextual Perspective." *Academy of Management Review* 24:308–24.

Krafcik, J. F. 1988. "Triumph of the Lean Production System." *Sloan Management Review* 30:41–52.

Kreps, D. M. 1990. "Corporate Culture and Economic Theory." In *Perspectives on Positive Political Economy,* edited by J. Alt and K. Shepsle, 90–143. Cambridge and Melbourne: Cambridge University Press.

Laursen, K., and N. J. Foss. 2003. "New Human Resource Management Practices, Complementarities and the Impact on Innovation Performance." *Cambridge Journal of Economics* 27:243–63.

Laursen, K., and A. Salter. 2006. "Open for Innovation: The Role of Openness in Explaining Innovation Performance among U.K. Manufacturing Firms." *Strategic Management Journal* 27:131–50.

Lepak, D. P., and S. A. Snell. 2002. "Examining the Human Resource Architecture: The Relationships among Human Capital, Employment, and Human Resource Configurations." *Journal of Management* 28:517–43.

Macduffie, J. P. 1995. "Human-Resource Bundles and Manufacturing Performance— Organizational Logic and Flexible Production Systems in the World Auto Industry." *Industrial and Labor Relations Review* 48:197–221.

Meagher, K., and A. Wait. 2008. "Who Decides About Change and Restructuring in Organizations?" CEPR Discussion Papers 587, Research School of Economics, Australian National University.

Michie, J., and M. Sheehan. 1999. "HRM Practices, R&D Expenditure and Innovative Investment: Evidence from the UK's 1990 Workplace Industrial Relations Survey (Wirs)." *Industrial and Corporate Change* 8:211.

——. 2003. "Labour Market Deregulation, 'Flexibility' and Innovation." *Cambridge Journal of Economics* 27:123–43.

Milgrom, P., and J. Roberts. 1995. "Complementarities and Fit: Strategy, Structure, and Organizational Change in Manufacturing." *Journal of Accounting and Economics* 19:179–208.

Mookherjee, D. 2006. "Decentralization, Hierarchies, and Incentives: A Mechanism Design Perspective." *Journal of Economic Literature* 44:367–90.

Osterman, P. 2006. "The Wage Effects of High Performance Work Organization in Manufacturing." *Industrial and Labor Relations Review* 59:187–204.

Pendleton, A., and A. Robinson. 2010. "Employee Stock Ownership, Involvement, and Productivity: An Interaction-Based Approach." *Industrial and Labor Relations Review* 64:3–29.

Perotin, V., and A. Robinson. 2000. "Employee Participation and Equal Opportunities Practices: Productivity Effect and Potential Complementarities." *British Journal of Industrial Relations* 38:557–83.

Porter, M. E. 1985. *Competitive Advantage: Creating and Sustaining Competitive Performance.* New York: Free Press.

Pugh, D. S., D. J. Hickson, and C. R. Hinings. 1969a. "An Empirical Taxonomy of Structures of Work Organizations." *Administrative Science Quarterly* 14:115–26.

Pugh, D. S., D. J. Hickson, C. R. Hinings, K. M. Macdonald, C. Turner, and T. Lupton. 1963. "A Conceptual Scheme for Organizational Analysis." *Administrative Science Quarterly* 8:289–315.

Pugh, D. S., D. J. Hickson, C. R. Hinings, and C. Turner. 1968. "Dimensions of Organization Structure." *Administrative Science Quarterly* 13:65–105.

Pugh, D. S., D. J. Hickson, C. R. Hinings, and C. Turner. 1969b. "The Context of Organization Structures." *Administrative Science Quarterly* 14:91–114.

Qian, Y. 1994. "Incentives and Loss of Control in an Optimal Hierarchy." *Review of Economic Studies* 61:527–44.

Radner, R. 1993. "The Organization of Decentralized Information Processing." *Econometrica* 61:1109–46.

Rajan, R., and J. Wulf. 2006. "The Flattening Firm: Evidence from Panel Data on the Changing Nature of Corporate Hierarchies." *Review of Economics and Statistics* 88:759–73.

Rantakari, H. 2008. "Governing Adaptation." *Review of Economic Studies* 75:1257–85.

Richard, O. C., and N. B. Johnson. 2001. "Strategic Human Resource Management Effectiveness and Firm Performance." *International Journal of Human Resource Management* 12:299–310.

Richardson, G. 1972. "The Organization of Industry." *Economic Journal* 82:883–96.

Roberts, J. 2004. *The Modern Firm. Organizational Design for Performance and Growth.* New York and Oxford: Oxford University Press.

Rosen, S. 1982. "Authority, Control, and the Distribution of Earnings." *Bell Journal of Economics* 13:311–23.

Sah, R. K., and J. E. Stiglitz. 1986. "The Architecture of Economic Systems: Hierarchies and Polyarchies." *American Economic Review* 76:716–27.

Schuler, R. S., and S. E. Jackson. 1987. "Linking Competitive Strategies with Human Resource Management Practices." *Academy of Management Executive* 1:207–19.

Scott, W. R. 1995. *Institutions and Organizations.* Thousand Oaks, CA: Sage.

Sine, W. D., H. Mitsuhashi, and D. A. Kirsch. 2006. "Revisiting Burns and Stalker: Formal Structure and New Venture Performance in Emerging Economic Sectors." *Academy of Management Journal* 49:121–32.

Smeets, V., and F. Warzynski. 2008. "Too Many Theories, Too Few Facts? What the Data Tell Us about the Link between Span of Control, Compensation and Career Dynamics." *Labour Economics* 15:687–703.

Smith, A. [1776] 1969. *The Wealth of Nations.* London: Penguin Books.

Snell, S. A. 1992. "Control Theory in Strategic Human Resource Management: The Mediating Effect of Administrative Information." *Academy of Management Journal* 35:292–327.

Stein, J. C. 2002. "Information Production and Capital Allocation: Decentralized Versus Hierarchical Firms." *Journal of Finance* 57:1891–1921.

Van Zandt, T. 1999a. "Decentralized Information Processing in the Theory of Organizations." In *Contemporary Economic Issues,* vol. 4, *Economic Design and Behavior,* edited by M. Sertel, 125–60. London: MacMillan Press Ltd.

———. 1999b. "Real-Time Decentralized Information Processing as a Model of Organizations with Boundedly Rational Agents." *Review of Economic Studies* 66:633–58.

Wagner, J. A. 1994. "Participation's Effects on Performance and Satisfaction—A Reconsideration of Research Evidence." *Academy of Management Review* 19:312–30.

Wang, L. 2009. "Ownership, Size, and the Formal Structure of Organizations: Evidence from US Public and Private Firms, 1992–2002." *Industrial and Corporate Change* 18:595–636.

Whitley, R. 2010. "The Institutional Construction of Firms." In *The Oxford Handbook of Comparative Institutional Analysis,* edited by: G. Morgan, J. Campbell, C. Crouch, O. K. Pedersen, and R. Whitley, 453–95. Oxford: Oxford University Press.

Williamson, O. E. 1975. *Markets and Hierarchies: Analysis and Antitrust Implications.* New York: Free Press.

———. 1985. *The Economic Institutions of Capitalism.* New York: Free Press.

Wilms, W. 1995. *Nummi: An Ethnographic Study.* New York: Free Press.

Womack, J., D. Jones, and D. Roos. 1990. *The Machine That Changed the World.* New York: Rawson Associates.

Wood, S., and L. de Menezes. 1998. "High Commitment Management in the UK: Evidence from the Workplace Industrial Relations Survey, and Employers' Manpower and Skills Practices Survey." *Human Relations* 51:485–515.

Wright, P. M., T. M. Gardner, L. M. Moynihan, and M. R. Allen. 2005. "The Relationship between HR Practices and Firm Performance: Examining Causal Order." *Personnel Psychology* 58:409–46.

Wright, P. M., and G. C. McMahan. 1992. "Theoretical Perspectives for Strategic Human Resource Management." *Journal of Management* 18:295–320.

Wright, P. M., and S. A. Snell. 1998. "Toward a Unifying Framework for Exploring Fit and Flexibility in Strategic Human Resource Management." *Academy of Management Journal* 23:756–72.

Youndt, M. A., S. A. Snell, J. W. Dean, and D. P. Lepak. 1996. "Human Resource Management, Manufacturing Strategy, and Firm Performance." *Academy of Management Journal* 39:836–66.

Zhou, H. B., R. Dekker, and A. Kleinknecht. 2011. "Flexible Labor and Innovation Performance: Evidence from Longitudinal Firm-Level Data." *Industrial and Corporate Change* 20:941–68.

........................................................................

# CHAPTER 18

# DESIGN AND IMPLEMENTATION OF PAY FOR PERFORMANCE

........................................................................

## MICHAEL GIBBS[*]

## 18.1 INTRODUCTION

........................................................................

INCENTIVE compensation is an important tool for a firm trying to improve employee performance. If designed well, an incentive plan motivates the employee to work harder, smarter, and in better alignment with the firm's objectives. It can also improve recruitment and retention. If designed poorly, it can undermine these objectives. The design and implementation of pay for performance involves complex trade-offs and has several interacting components. Fortunately, incentive compensation has been one of the most actively studied topics in economics in the last two decades, with related work in accounting and management. A large, mature, and robust literature now provides a useful framework for designing and implementing pay for performance. Several excellent surveys of this research are available (e.g., Gibbons 1998; Murphy 1999; Prendergast 1999; Bushman and Smith 2001). The purpose of this chapter is not to provide yet another survey, but to use the lessons of the economic literature on incentives to discuss how to design and implement pay for performance in practice.

Compensation systems have several roles beyond creating incentives (e.g., Waggoner et al. 1999; Ittner and Larcker 2002). This fact is most evident in performance evaluation. Firms may use an evaluation to monitor and reward effort. However, performance also depends on factors other than effort, such as the employee's abilities, training, information, and working relationship with colleagues. Firms may therefore use an evaluation for job assignments,

[*] I am grateful to many colleagues from whom I have learned about this topic, including George Baker, Gary Becker, Michael Beer, Jed DeVaro, Bengt Holmstrom, Kathryn Ierulli, Michael Jensen, Edward Lazear, Alec Levenson, Kenneth Merchant, Kevin J. Murphy, Canice Prendergast, Sherwin Rosen, Mark Vargus, Wim Van der Stede, and Cindy Zoghi.

promotions, to diagnose weaknesses in job design or personnel policies, and to provide feedback and coaching. I focus on incentives, but it is important to keep in mind that an incentive plan interacts with, and may undermine or reinforce, other personnel objectives.

The approach used in economics is called Agency Theory. Many situations involve agency relationships, such as a real-estate agent working on behalf of a home buyer, or a politician working on behalf of voters. Although the intuition of agency theory applies quite broadly, I focus on an employee working as an agent on behalf of the principal, his employer.

## 18.1.1 Three Components of an Incentive Plan

I will argue that a useful approach to designing an incentive plan is to consider three components, and two types of evaluation, in a particular sequence. I follow that sequence in this chapter; thus we walk through the logical steps of designing an incentive plan.

To illustrate the major points, I use a simple model of pay for performance that is similar to most of the literature.[1] The employee's effect on the employer's objective, "output" Q, depends on efforts $e_i$ in multiple tasks performed on the job, $i = 1, \ldots, n$. The employee is risk and effort averse, with utility $U = E[\text{Pay}] - \frac{1}{2}R\sigma^2_{Pay} - \frac{1}{2}C\sum_i e_i^2$. The second term adjusts the first term for risk aversion; combined they are the certainty equivalent value of risky income to the employee. R is the coefficient of absolute risk aversion. With our assumptions below, from the employee's perspective $\sigma^2_{Pay}$ does not depend on $e_i$, so the risk premium is independent of effort choice. C is the marginal disutility of effort. The employee chooses efforts $e_i$ to maximize U, subject to a participation constraint that $U \geq 0$, with the employee's reservation utility (from leisure or alternative employment) normalized to zero.

The firm maximizes expected profit from the employee = $E[Q - \text{Pay}]$ by using an incentive plan with three components, as in Figure 18.1. It chooses a *Performance Measure* P and ties that to pay. P must depend on efforts for any incentive to exist. Pay equals *Base Salary* S plus *Pay for Performance Relationship* I(P), Pay = S + I(P). The employee's optimal efforts on each task are found by solving:

$$\max_{e_i} S + E[I(P)] - \frac{1}{2}R\sigma^2_{Pay} - \frac{1}{2}C\sum_i e_i^2$$

$$\Rightarrow e_i^* = \frac{\frac{dI}{dP}E\left[\frac{\partial P}{\partial e_i}\right]}{C}, \nabla i \tag{18.1}$$

Equation (18.1) immediately provides useful insights about incentive-plan design. Base salary S does not appear—it is not a key driver of incentives because it does not vary with performance.[2] The role of base salary is to adjust overall compensation to labor market rates, so that the firm can maximize profits while attracting and retaining

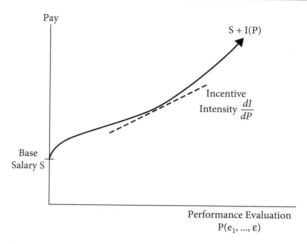

**FIGURE 18.1.** Pay-for-Performance Plan
A pay plan has 3 components: Performance Evaluation P; Pay for Performance I(P), and Base Salary S.

employees with appropriate skills. Thinking about base salary first when considering a pay plan is common, as it is a key issue in employment negotiations. However, it is the least important component of pay for incentives.

Equation (18.1) reveals the two components to emphasize in designing an incentive plan. The first is the *Incentive Intensity*, dI/dP, which is sometimes called the *shape* of the pay-performance relationship, because it is the slope in Figure 18.1. The second is how sensitive the performance evaluation is to effort, $\partial P/\partial e_i$. I will show that the effectiveness of the performance evaluation is the major determinant of the incentive intensity. Therefore, the first step in designing an incentive plan is performance evaluation, our next topic. Once the firm has chosen the performance evaluation method, and understands the properties of the evaluation, it can set how pay varies with performance.

## 18.1.2  Two Methods of Performance Evaluation

There are two general methods of performance evaluation: numeric and subjective. Examples of numeric performance measures include unit sales for a salesperson, stock price for a CEO, or a customer satisfaction index for a service representative. *Subjective Evaluation* uses supervisor discretion and judgment to gauge performance. An example is an annual merit rating (on a numeric scale or using verbal categories such as "Meets Expectations").

The distinction between numeric and subjective evaluation is not cut-and-dried, because subjectivity can arise in the evaluation P, pay for performance I(P), or both. Consider a salesperson whose performance is measured as unit sales $X$. However, suppose the bonus is not calculated by formula (such as *Bonus* = $b \cdot X$, where $b$ is the commission), but instead the supervisor uses her discretion to award a bonus. As a second example, consider an executive whose performance is quantified using two measures: profits and percentage growth in sales. His bonus is based solely on those two measures, but the weights on each are at the discretion of the supervisor. In both cases, the measures are numeric, but how they are used to calculate rewards is subjective. A third example arises when the reward's value cannot be quantified and so a formula cannot be stated. The value of a promotion is the discounted present value of uncertain increased compensation over an unknown future period.

With that caveat, let us first focus on the narrow question of whether a firm should use one or more numeric measures to quantify the employee's contributions, or instead use subjective evaluation. All else equal, a numeric evaluation is preferable. The employee knows exactly how his performance will be measured, and numeric measures usually can be tracked easily, so he will know where he stands at any point in time. By contrast, subjective evaluations raise issues of fairness, bias, and trust (see below). Furthermore, I will argue that firms often use subjective evaluation to complement numeric measures. For those reasons, the proper starting place is to quantify the employee's performance as well as possible, yielding one or more numeric measures, and analyze the properties of those measures to decide what weight should be placed on them for determining rewards. As a second step, the firm should then decide whether it might use subjective evaluation in addition to, or instead of, numeric performance measures.

## 18.2  NUMERIC PERFORMANCE MEASURES: BASIC PROPERTIES

Because this section focuses on the term $E[\partial P/\partial e_i]$ in equation (18.1), assume incentive pay in its simplest form, a linear bonus with commission rate b: $I(P) = b \cdot P$; in fact, this form is extremely common in practice. I now show the incentive intensity b depends on several important properties of the performance measure.

Let output and the performance measure have the simple forms $Q = \sum_i q_i e_i + \mu$ and $P = \sum_i p_i e_i + \varepsilon$, where $q_i$ and $p_i$ are the marginal products of effort on Q and P, and $\mu$ and $\varepsilon$ denote the influence of random factors on each (uncontrollable by the employee or firm; both with mean = 0). Both sets of marginal products $q_i$ and $p_i$ may be random from the firm's perspective. However, I assume the employee knows the values of $p_i$ before choosing effort levels. Finally, a performance measure may be scaled in many different units, with I(P) rescaling into dollars. As an example, a firm might use a customer satisfaction index as a measure, and pay a commission on the level of the index. To abstract from such scaling details, assume the vectors |q| and |p| are of equal length 1:

$$\sqrt{\sum q_i^2} = \sqrt{\sum p_i^2} = 1.$$

With these further assumptions, (18.1) becomes

$$e_i^* = \frac{bp_i}{C}$$

$$\Rightarrow \frac{de_i^*}{db} = \frac{p_i}{C} \tag{18.2}$$

The latter part of (18.2) describes how efforts respond to changes in incentive intensity. The firm chooses b to maximize expected profits E[Q – Pay], given (18.2) and the employee's participation constraint. This is equivalent to maximizing total surplus:

$$\max_b E\left[\sum q_i e_i\right] - \frac{1}{2}Rb^2\sigma_\varepsilon^2 - E\left[\frac{1}{2}C\sum e_i^2\right] \Rightarrow E\left[\sum_i q_i p_i / C\right] - Rb\sigma_\varepsilon^2 - E\left[b\sum_i p_i^2 / C\right] = 0$$

$$\Rightarrow b^* = \frac{E\sum q_i p_i}{E\sum p_i^2 + RC\sigma_\varepsilon^2}. \tag{18.3}$$

Equation (18.3) describes the optimal incentive intensity as a function of properties of the performance measure. Several cases illustrate those properties.

## 18.2.1  Uncontrollable Risk and Distortion

Risk in the employee's work environment has two important effects on incentives. Consider a single-task job so that $P = p{\cdot}e + \varepsilon$. By (18.2), $P = \left(bp^2/C\right) + \varepsilon$, so the variance of performance is $\sigma_P^2 = \left(b/C\right)^2\sigma_p^2 + \sigma_\varepsilon^2$. Because I assume the employee observes his marginal products p before choosing effort, the first term is not risk from the employee's perspective. It corresponds to what I call controllable risk below. Consider the effect of the second, $\sigma_\varepsilon^2$, which I call uncontrollable risk.

*Case 1:* $P = Q$, $\sigma_\varepsilon^2 = 0$. The firm measures output without error, and uses it as the performance measure. The optimal incentive intensity is $b^* = 1$. This is the benchmark case providing first-best effort, $e_i^* = p_i/C$. All cases below are second best because of imperfections in the performance measure.

*Case 2:* $P = Q$ (so that $\mu = \varepsilon$), $\sigma_\varepsilon^2 > 0$. The firm measures output, but with error. The optimal incentive intensity is $b^* = \dfrac{1}{1 + RC\sigma_\varepsilon^2} < 1$. This illustrates a key theme in the early theoretical literature on incentives: the trade-off between uncontrollable risk and incentives (Holmstrom 1979; Banker and Datar 1989). Because $b^* < 1$, $e^*$ is lower than in Case

1, as is expected output. Our first property of a performance measure is the extent of *Uncontrollable Risk* or measurement error. The greater the measurement error $\sigma_\varepsilon^2$, the weaker the strength of the incentive. Measurement error imposes risk on the employee to the extent that pay varies with the measure. Stronger incentives punish more for bad luck, and reward more for good luck ($\varepsilon \lesseqgtr 0$). A firm may be able to reduce measurement error by spending resources to measure performance more accurately. Doing so would allow it to provide stronger incentives, though at additional measurement costs. To the extent that the measure has error, the firm must compensate the employee via a risk premium in the base salary. Therefore, the firm lowers b*, even though doing so reduces incentives, trading off incentives with salary and measurement costs. Empirical evidence on whether the incentive intensity tends to be lower in more risky environments is mixed. I discuss why that mixed evidence makes sense below, after introducing the concept of controllable risk.

*Case 3:* $P \neq Q$, $\sigma_\varepsilon^2 > 0$, $q_i$ and $p_i$ are not random. The optimal incentive intensity is

$$\Rightarrow b^* = \frac{\sum q_i p_i}{\sum p_i^2 + RC\sigma_\varepsilon^2} = \frac{\cos(\theta)}{1 + RC\sigma_\varepsilon^2}. \tag{18.4}$$

$\cos(\theta)$ is the cosine of the angle between the vectors $|p|$ and $|q|$, a measure of the extent to which the marginal products of effort on the performance measure match those on output (Datar, Kulp & Lambert 2001; Baker 2002; Feltham & Xie 1994). Our second important performance measure property is *Distortion*. Note that $\cos(\theta) < 1$ if any $p_i \neq q_i$, so b* is lower than in Case 2. If P is distorted compared to Q, the employee has incentives to provide too much or too little of some types of effort. The more distorted the performance measure is, the lower the optimal incentive intensity.

To see the effect of distortion, suppose a worker has two tasks: producing high-quality parts, and producing as many as possible per hour. Output is $Q = q_1 e_1 + q_2 e_2$, where the first term represents quantity and the second quality. $q_i$ represents the relative weight of each task in creating firm value. Similarly, $P = p_1 e_1 + p_2 e_2$, and $p_i$ represents the weight of each task in the performance measure. If P gives relatively more weight to task 1, compared to Q, the employee has too strong an incentive to perform task 1 compared to task 2. This is an important intuition about performance measurement and incentive-plan design. An incentive plan's goal is not merely to motivate an employee to work harder, but also to balance motivation across different tasks (Holmstrom and Milgrom 1991). A good measure rewards relatively more for more highly valued tasks, and relatively less for less-valued tasks.[3] Many observed problems with incentive systems can be attributed to imbalanced multitask incentives (Kerr 1975).

Virtually all performance measures distort incentives, because they are only proxies for the firm's objective. For example, revenue ignores costs. Profit includes revenue and costs but is distorted because it is measured over one period. A manager evaluated based on this year's profits has an incentive to avoid maintenance or investments in R&D, which involve costs today to generate future benefits. The one common performance measure that arguably might *not* distort incentives is a publicly traded firm's stock price (rescaled by multiplying by the number of shares outstanding). One important benefit of a well-functioning stock market is that it provides a free performance measure for executives. A stock market is a prediction market providing an estimate of the discounted present value of future cash flows accruing to stockholders. To the extent that the Efficient Markets Hypothesis (Fama 1991) holds, stock prices weight present and future profits correctly and produce an undistorted performance measure. Of course, stock price also has a great deal of uncontrollable risk, for example, macroeconomic conditions, so it is also a volatile performance measure.

Distortion of a performance measure creates the first of three types of "gaming" of an incentive system described in this chapter. The second is manipulation, which arises in Case 4.

## 18.2.2 Controllable Risk

*Case 4*: $P \neq Q$; $\sigma_\varepsilon^2 > 0$; $q_i$ and $p_i$ are random; the employee observes $p_i$ before he chooses effort, but the firm does not. Here I add two important new issues: the employee's marginal products of effort may be stochastic, and the employee often has better information than the supervisor about how to focus efforts at any point in time, because he is doing the job. The optimal incentive intensity is as in (18.3), which is hard to interpret, but the single-task case provides useful intuition. If $Q = q \cdot e$ and $P = p \cdot e$, our scaling assumption implies $E(q) = E(p) = 1$, and

$$\Rightarrow b^* = \frac{Eqp}{Ep^2 + RC\sigma_\varepsilon^2} = \frac{1 + \rho\sigma_q\sigma_p}{1 + \sigma_p^2 + RC\sigma_\varepsilon^2}, \tag{18.5}$$

where $\rho$ is the correlation between $q$ and $p$, $\rho \leq 1$, and $b^* < 1$. As in Case 3, distortion affects incentives: the smaller is $\rho$, the smaller is $b^*$.

Equation (18.5) illustrates a new property of performance measures: *Controllable Risk*, $\sigma_p^2$. Because the employee observes the marginal product of effort on the performance measure before choosing effort, he can use that information to work harder when p is larger, and to work less when p is smaller. That reaction is the efficient response to variation in marginal products of effort, as long as P is reasonably correlated with actual output Q. This effect can raise or lower the optimal incentive intensity, depending on $\rho$, $\sigma_p^2$, and $\sigma_p^2$. For example, if the firm can use output as the performance measure as in

Case 2, $b^* = \dfrac{1+\sigma_q^2}{1+\sigma_q^2 + RC\sigma_\mu^2}$, which is larger than $b^*$ in Case 2. The difference is that now

the employee has valuable information about varying marginal products of effort. The firm increases the incentive intensity to motivate the employee to use that information to allocate effort efficiently. More generally, define $\alpha = \dfrac{\sigma_q}{\sigma_p}$ as a measure of the relative precision of the employee's information about how to do his job, and rewrite (18.5) as

$b^* = \dfrac{1+\alpha\rho\sigma_p^2}{1+\sigma_p^2 + RC\sigma_\varepsilon^2}$. The more precise the employee's information about how his effort

affects the performance measure, the stronger the incentive should be, all else equal. The effect is, of course, reinforced by less distortion or larger ρ.

This is important new intuition about incentive-plan design. A good evaluation motivates the employee to use his information, expertise, experience of events as they unfold at work, and so forth to allocate effort and make decisions in ways that promote the firm's objective. When the employee knows things the firm does not about how to do the job, the firm cannot provide proper guidance. However, a well-chosen performance measure can, rewarding more for high-value tasks and less for low-value tasks. In fact, this insight helps explain why firms use incentives and performance evaluation at all. If no environmental uncertainty were present, the firm might simply tell the worker what to do and how to allocate time to different tasks. It would then *monitor* the worker for compliance. However, that approach is effective only if the supervisor knows more than the employee about how to allocate effort optimally. If the employee knows more, the firm needs to motivate him to use his information on the firm's behalf, by choosing a measure that captures the effects of the employee's controllable risk.

Controllable risk is a relatively new idea in the principal-agent literature (Baker 1992; Prendergast 2002a, 2002b). The role of risk is not as simple as the early literature suggested (Case 2). If the employee cannot control environmental uncertainty affecting performance, the firm lowers the incentive intensity. However, to the extent that the employee can control environmental uncertainty, raising the incentive intensity to motivate good decision making may be optimal (to the extent that the measure is not too distorted). This distinction explains why the empirical literature attempting to test whether greater risk leads to weaker incentives yielded mixed results: it failed to recognize the distinction between controllable and uncontrollable risk. More recent empirical work (DeVaro and Kurtulus 2010; Barrenechea-Méndez et al. 2011) does find incentives tend to be stronger when the employee has more controllable risk, and weaker when he has more uncontrollable risk.

Controllability is a term the managerial accounting literature has used, but not rigorously defined, for many years. It does not necessarily mean an employee can control whether an event occurs. Rather, it means the employee has some ability to control a random event's impact on firm value. Consider a factory roof that collapses under accumulated snow. The storm is a random event, but the plant manager can partially control the effect of the storm on firm value. The manager can take precautions against foreseeable risks, such as proper maintenance. He can react to events when they occur, such as sending employees to the roof with shovels. Finally, he may be able to act after the event to mitigate damage, such as finding a roofing company that can make immediate emergency repairs so that production can resume quickly. Along similar lines, employees can take preparations and react profitably to exploit unexpected positive events.

As the collapsing-roof example illustrates, whether variability in the performance measure is controllable or uncontrollable is a subtle issue. Economic theory can help explain the distinction, but ultimately a firm must use some judgment to decide the extent to which risks are controllable or uncontrollable. In fact, I will argue this is a primary reason for the use of subjective evaluation.

## 18.2.3  Manipulability

Earlier I stated that distortion in a measure causes the first of three types of gaming of an incentive system. I refer to the second type as manipulation, a special case of controllable risk. Return to (18.5) but assume $\rho < 0$. This can occur if an employee can take actions that improve the measure but at the same time reduce firm value.[4] Consider Prendergast's (2002a) example of a surgeon whose performance measure is mortality rates. The surgeon has an incentive to use his expertise and examination of patients—information he possesses that his employer does not—to avoid operating on patients with the most complex and risky medical problems. Those may be the patients the hospital most hopes to serve. This example illustrates an additional property of a performance measure, *Manipulability*. Manipulation is a special case of controllable risk, but distinguishing it is useful to highlight that an employee may be able to use his information not to increase firm value, but strategically to game the incentive system to increase rewards.

The literature has not consistently used the terms "gaming," "distortion," and "manipulation." In an attempt to clarify, I distinguish three ways an employee can game an incentive system (distortion and manipulation are the first two), and distinguish between distortion and manipulation. Courty and Marschke (2008) and Sloop and van Praag (2011) use "distortion" to refer to both distortion and manipulation (they do recognize the theoretical distinction). I define manipulation as different from distortion because the distinction is useful in designing and implementing an incentive plan. The firm takes both into account in ex ante incentive-plan design by reducing the incentive intensity, choosing additional measures, or using subjective evaluation. It may also address manipulation ex post through subjective evaluation or implicit rewards as described below.

# 18.3  Numeric Performance Measures: Other Considerations

## 18.3.1  Degrading of Performance Measures

An interesting implication of distortion and manipulability is that numeric performance measures may degrade over time (Courty and Marschke 2004, 2008). Suppose a firm finds that historically P has been a good proxy for Q (marginal products of effort on P are highly correlated with those on Q). It implements a bonus based on this measure. However, the performance measure is distorted, giving too much weight to Task 1 and too little to Task 2. The employee's behavior would not have been distorted if no incentive had been in place beforehand. Placing an incentive on the measure, though, will change the employee's behavior, resulting in greater emphasis on Task 1, which means the measure will be less effective than anticipated. Such an effect is inevitable, because virtually all performance measures distort incentives in some way.

Manipulation causes additional degradation of a measure in a more subtle way. Incentives spawn creativity. Once rewards are based on a measure, the employee has an incentive not just to increase output, but also to learn how to better manipulate the measure. For example, a more experienced CFO may be better able to "manage earnings" (a familiar example of manipulation in accounting) than an inexperienced CFO.

Finally, one should expect a measure's effectiveness to degrade because the environment changes. If Q evolves over time, a P chosen because it matches the initial $Q_0$ becomes more distorted when it does not evolve alongside Q. For all of these reasons, a firm should expect a performance measure to be somewhat less useful in practice than initially expected and to degrade gradually over time. A good incentive system needs regular updating of performance measures.

## 18.3.2  Scope of the Performance Measure

I described four performance measure properties: controllable and uncontrollable risk, distortion, and manipulation. In choosing a measure, a firm may face a trade-off between these measures. Some argue a trade-off is likely between uncontrollable risk and distortion, so that measures with low distortion tend to have high uncontrollable risk, and measures with high distortion tend to have low uncontrollable risk (Datar et al. 2001; Van Praag and Cools 2001; Baker 1992). The intuition is that if only two relevant properties are present (uncontrollable risk and distortion), and measurement cost is concave in $\rho$ and $\sigma_p^2$, a firm would never choose a measure if an alternative is no worse on either dimension, and better on at least one. This logic implies a negatively sloped "performance measurement frontier" in which the firm trades off uncontrollable risk and distortion.

We can generalize this idea with the concept of performance measurement, *Scope*: the extent to which the measure is more narrowly focused or broadly defined. A measure's scope may vary on several dimensions. For example, profit is broader than revenue or cost, because it incorporates both of those measures. In a sense, profit includes more tasks in the performance measure than the other two. The scope of a profit measure could also be expanded along the dimension of time, say, three years instead of one, or a discounted present value style measure such as economic value added (EVA). Similarly, a measure's scope can vary from narrow to broad on the group of employees that are included, from individual to group, business unit, or firm-wide performance.

Measurement scope illustrates nicely the argument that a trade-off exists between a measure's uncontrollable risk and distortion. Consider the performance measure with the broadest scope, stock price. It is the most common measure for CEOs of publicly traded companies, but most firms also use other measures such as earnings in CEO incentive contracts (Murphy 1999). This measure includes the effects of all possible actions the employee can take that affect firm value, and therefore has little or no distortion. At the same time, it has a large amount of uncontrollable risk because it includes the effects of all coworkers, plus many other random variables. Because of this high risk, most firms also use other measures for CEO incentives and rarely use stock price as incentives for employees below the executive level.[5] A firm can filter out much of the uncontrollable risk by choosing a measure that is narrower in scope. Accounting earnings is such an example. Revenue and cost are far more controllable than stock price. However, the narrower focus generates greater distortion, because some employee actions are left out of the measure.

As a firm varies a performance measure's scope, it is also likely to face similar trade-offs with controllable risk and manipulation. The possibility that controllable and uncontrollable risks are positively correlated across measures seems likely. Random events tend to be partly controllable and partly uncontrollable. In the roof-collapse example, the storm was an act of nature, but to some extent, the manager could control its effects on firm value. Even macroeconomic conditions may be partially controllable by a firm, through actions such as currency or interest-rate hedging, or varying production over the business cycle. If uncontrollable and controllable risks are positively correlated, broader measures will tend to have more of both, and narrower measures less. We have a second trade-off, between the two types of risk. Narrower measures are also likely to be more manipulable. Manipulating a single line item is much easier than manipulating the overall size of a budget. When a measure is affected by a smaller number of variables, the effects of each tend to be larger, so manipulating one is more likely to be effective. In addition, because narrow measures tend to have less uncontrollable risk, random noise is less likely to overwhelm attempted manipulation.

Putting these arguments together, we see that in choosing a performance measure, a useful concept is the measure's scope. Once the firm decides which aspects of performance it wishes to incorporate in the evaluation, it may have latitude in how broadly or narrowly to implement the measure along several dimensions. Broader measures tend to have less distortion, include more controllable risk, and be less manipulable. However, they also tend to have more uncontrollable risk. To reduce uncontrollable risk, almost all measures narrow their focus at the cost of more distortion, less controllable risk, and more potential for manipulation.

## 18.3.3  Combining Multiple Performance Measures

We saw that weaknesses in performance measures imply lower optimal incentive intensities. A firm can also address these weaknesses by using additional performance measures or subjective evaluation. Here I consider the use of additional measures. These can be combined into a single measure, with weights the firm chooses (e.g., profit combines revenue and cost). Managers can also use them separately by awarding multiple bonuses for different measures. Firms use both methods (Murphy 1992; Gibbs et al. 2009). If we assume linear pay for performance, the two methods are equivalent. Banker and Datar (1989) showed that for a wide class of joint density functions for uncontrollable risk, measures can be aggregated linearly (pay may then be a nonlinear function of the aggregate measure).

Holmstrom (1979) initially developed the "Informativeness Principle": an additional measure firms should use in an incentive plan if it provides marginal information about employee effort. Research has discussed the question of relative weights, primarily in the context of uncontrollable risk and distortion. Adding measures can reduce distortion, because measures usually emphasize different aspects of the job. A common example is the Balanced Scorecard, in which a firm collects a variety of measures including qualitative factors such as customer satisfaction (Kaplan and Norton 1996). Balanced Scorecards were developed to incorporate dimensions of performance that traditional measures tend to ignore. A problem with combining measures to reduce distortion is that they often vary substantially in uncontrollable risk. Measures with more uncontrollable risk should receive lower incentive intensities, and measures with more controllable risk should receive high incentive intensities. This implies an incentive system combining performance measures with different levels of risk will have imbalanced multitask incentives, or weak overall incentives in order to preserve balanced motivation (Holmstrom and Milgrom 1991).

Firms may also combine performance measures to reduce uncontrollable risk, if measurement errors are negatively correlated. Consider $P_3 = b_1 P_1 + b_2 P_2$, where $b_i$ is the weight on measure $P_i$, which has measurement error $\varepsilon_i$. Measurement error of $P_3$ is

$$\sigma_3^2 = b_1^2 \sigma_1^2 + b_2^2 \sigma_2^2 + 2b_1 b_2 \sigma_{12}.$$ If $\sigma_{12} < 0$, lowering overall risk by combining measures

may be possible. One important example is relative performance evaluation (Lazear and Rosen 1981; Gibbons and Murphy 1990), in which supervisors evaluate an employee relative to colleagues or some other reference group. This evaluation may be effective if measurement error is common to employees in the group, which relative comparison filters out. Once more, however, trade-offs can exist. Relative evaluation may also distort incentives if the employee can take actions to affect the group against which he is compared or if he can cooperate with or sabotage colleagues (Lazear 1989).

Virtually no analysis exists regarding how controllable risk affects the optimal combination of performance measures in an incentive system, reflecting the relatively new nature of that concept. Speculatively, a positive correlation between the extent of controllable risk and the use of multiple measures seems likely. See the discussion of how incentives are related to job design below.

## 18.4 SUBJECTIVE PERFORMANCE EVALUATION

An important method to address shortcomings in performance measures is subjective performance evaluation. Thinking of *any* job in which subjective evaluation or supervisor discretion does not play some role in incentives is difficult. Managers implicitly reward or punish employees through job assignments, office location, threat of termination, promotion, and so forth. Formal bonus plans must occasionally be reset (e.g., measures degrade over time, or targets must be reset each year), which involves discretion. Finally, many plans make explicit use of discretion: firms determine evaluations subjectively, or use measures as inputs into discretionary raises and bonuses. In this section, I consider the important role of discretion in incentive systems, focusing on the costs and benefits of subjective performance evaluation. The discussion of subjectivity is much shorter than the discussion above about numeric evaluation, but that difference does not reflect the relative (un)importance of subjectivity. This section is shorter because it builds easily on the prior discussion, and because research on this topic is much more sparse.

A substantial literature discusses potential problems arising from subjective evaluation (Murphy 1992; Prendergast and Topel 1993; Murphy and Cleveland 1995; Prendergast 1999). Because the evaluation is at the supervisor's discretion, supervisor preferences and incentives may play a role in the evaluation. A supervisor might engage in favoritism toward some employees, or manipulate the evaluation process to reduce compensation costs. Such behavior might expose the firm to legal liabilities from lawsuits alleging discrimination or wrongful termination. Subjective evaluation can also distort incentives. The employee might act as a "Yes Man," behaving in ways the supervisor prefers and that correlate imperfectly with firm value (Prendergast 1993). That employee may try to manipulate the evaluation by making negative evaluations personally costly for the supervisor (Milgrom 1988; Milgrom and Roberts 1988). As a response to such influence costs, the supervisor might be too lenient or reduce the variance of evaluations (leniency and centrality biases). Supervisors might also have hindsight bias, holding the employee responsible for factors that are known by the supervisor ex post, but that the employee did not know at the time he performed the work. Finally, subjective evaluations have their own form of uncontrollable risk for the employee: they are difficult to verify and enforce contractually, so they require relational contracting and adequate trust of the supervisor (Baker et al. 1994).

Because virtually all jobs use subjectivity, it must have some benefits. A smaller literature considers these (e.g., Murphy and Oyer 2003; Gibbs et al. 2004). Subjective evaluations are an alternative means by which a firm can address limitations of numeric measures. Subjective evaluation allows the supervisor to incorporate her own observations about employee performance that are not reflected in a numeric measure, and allows her to do so dynamically and to incorporate ex post settling up.

The supervisor can reduce distortions by incorporating other dimensions of performance (quality, customer satisfaction) into the overall evaluation. In principle, such factors might be quantified as in a Balanced Scorecard, but as noted earlier, such an approach often suffers from significant measurement error. A supervisor's judgment may be more accurate. If so, she can give such dimensions of the job relatively more weight in the overall evaluation, balancing multitask incentives with stronger overall incentive intensity.

Subjective evaluation may allow for a more subtle treatment than the simple trade-offs of uncontrollable risk with controllable risk, distortion, and manipulation in selecting numeric measures. A supervisor can reduce uncontrollable risk by "backing out" effects of adverse uncontrollable events from the evaluation, while holding the employee responsible for controllable risks by punishing poor decisions and rewarding good ones. Consider again the collapsed-roof example. The supervisor can evaluate the extent to which the storm was predictable, whether the manager adequately planned and prepared, how he reacted as the event unfolded, and so on. The supervisor can weigh the evidence and decide the factors for which to hold the manager responsible, and which to ignore. No measure chosen ex ante will be able to incorporate all of these considerations and adjust to the unique circumstances of a given situation. Subjective evaluations seem almost inevitable in such situations.

Discretion in an incentive system provides a way to reduce manipulation, because it allows for ex post settling up. If a measure indicates high performance but the supervisor has other information or personal observations suggesting the performance was due in part to manipulation, she can reduce the evaluation or punish the employee. The threat of such punishment can deter manipulation. One way firms might implement this is through a discretionary cap on the total level of a bonus.

Discretion in incentive systems has additional benefits beyond mitigating weaknesses in numeric measures. One such benefit is flexibility. Changing a performance measure or bonus formula in the middle of the year is possible, but at some renegotiation cost. Subjective evaluations and discretionary rewards are, by definition, changeable over time, thereby allowing the supervisor to adapt the incentive system to changing economic conditions, or adjust it if errors in design are discovered.

Another benefit of subjectivity is that the evaluation can promote other goals. Consider again the manager of the factory with the collapsed roof. When the supervisor evaluates performance, she can identify ways to improve job design, resources, information, or training. She can coach the manager on what he should have done differently, what to learn from the experience, and how he should change his behavior on the job. A firm should keep such multiple roles in mind when using subjective evaluations. For example, many firms schedule evaluations for employee coaching at different times of the year than evaluations for determining compensation and incentives, in order to try to minimize conflicts between the two goals (Murphy and Cleveland 1995).

Only a small empirical literature exists on the use of subjective evaluation or discretion in incentive systems (e.g., Hayes and Schaefer 2000; Ittner et al. 2003; Murphy and Oyer 2003; Gibbs et al. 2004, 2009), presumably because quantifying the concepts is difficult. The evidence is consistent with the uses of discretion described above. For example, firms employ subjective evaluations to reduce short-term incentives implied by numeric measures, and to motivate employees to cooperate more with other organizational units. They use implicit rewards such as threat of termination to punish detected manipulation. Gibbs et al. (2004) found supervisors were more likely to award subjective bonuses if achieving a bonus target was difficult and had significant consequences if not met, and if the manager's department had an operating loss for the year. These findings indicate the use of subjectivity to filter out uncontrollable risk. A department's loss may be due to poor performance, but it may also be due to bad luck. Subjectivity allows the firm to punish the former but reward the latter in ways that may be impossible with numeric measures.

# 18.5  Pay-Performance Relationship

The second step in designing an incentive plan is to set the pay-for-performance relationship I(P). In (18.1), incentives are driven by dI/dP, how pay varies with performance. Little systematic evidence exists on how firms set pay-performance shapes. Gibbs et al. (2009) summarize primary bonus contracts for auto dealership department managers. Two percent of them involve lump-sum bonuses, 6% have a floor, 2% have a cap, and 98% are simple linear functions. Interestingly, if an employee receives a second or third bonus, those are much more likely to have complex shapes such as lump sums or caps. Murphy (2000) finds executive incentive contracts make greater use of pay caps (80%) and lump-sum rewards at performance thresholds (20%). Both find all contracts are linear or piecewise linear. In general, pay-for-performance shapes tend to be quite simple, perhaps because they are easier for employees to understand, which improves trust in the incentive system. Banker and Datar (1989) and Holmstrom and Milgrom (1991) provide theoretical justifications for linearity.

I discuss properties of two common pay-performance shapes. Figure 18.2a illustrates an incentive plan in which the employee receives a lump-sum bonus if performance exceeds a *threshold* T, so dI/dP = 0 to the left and right of T, and dI/dP = ∞ when the employee's performance puts him right at the margin between winning and losing the reward. Figure 18.2b illustrates a plan in which the employee earns a linear bonus for performance beyond a threshold ("floor"), but pay is capped for performance above a second threshold.

Consider Figure 18.2a. A couple of problems may arise. First, if the firm sets the threshold either too high or too low, the employee may have little incentive (Roy (1952) famously called such behavior "goldbricking"). Second, if the employee is near the threshold T, he has a strong incentive to engage in the third method of gaming an incentive system—shifting output between periods in order to increase compensation (Healy 1985; Courty and Marschke 2004). Managers and salespeople with this type of incentive plan often "sandbag" their performance, delaying sales until next year if they have already met the threshold, or trying to push customers to accelerate purchasing if they have not yet met the threshold (Oyer 1998). Both of these types of behaviors can have negative effects on firm value. In addition, if the performance measure is manipulable, the temptation to manipulate is strong when performance is close to T. Similar effects can arise if the incentive intensity (slope) changes less dramatically at a certain level of performance. The general lesson is that smoother pay-performance shapes, particularly simple linear relationships, are less likely to cause problems.

Promotion-based incentives have a similar pay-performance shape, because the reward is all or nothing if the employee does or does not meet the promotion criteria T. That form of incentive can have surprising effects on performance evaluation. If a supervisor provides accurate feedback, employees have strong incentives if they are near T, but may slack off if they are below or above it. This effect would be most severe for employees performing below T, because reducing effort would push them further from T, whereas the opposite would occur for those above T. For these reasons, supervisors may give *less informative* evaluations, and particularly avoid giving negative feedback (Hansen 2010). These observations may help explain the observation that performance-rating distributions almost always exhibit leniency and centrality bias, especially when promotion stakes are high.

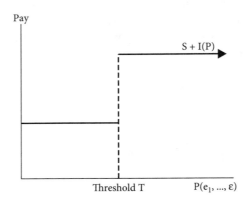

**FIGURE 18.2A.** Lump-Sum Bonus
Lump-sum bonus for performance above threshold T. Promotion-based incentives have the same shape.

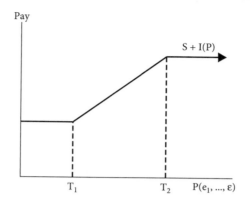

**FIGURE 18.2B** Bonus with Floor & Cap
Base salary is paid for performance below $T_1$; a bonus is paid for performance above $T_1$, up to $T_2$.

Given the negative effects of thresholds, why are they used? One reason is that they may allow the firm to use a stronger incentive intensity while keeping expected compensation at competitive rates or avoiding risks of high turnover in years when uncontrollable risk yields low performance (Oyer 2000; Murphy 2001). An additional benefit may be that paying a base salary for low performance reduces the employee's risk aversion—employees are most averse to large downside risks—which may motivate them to take more chances on the job. A subtle agency problem that has received almost no attention is conflicts between the firm and employee over risk taking. Firms are generally less risk-averse than employees, so employees may be more cautious than is efficient. CEOs, for example, might pursue diversification strategies in order to reduce uncertainty in their compensation, even though shareholders prefer focused strategies. By limiting downside compensation risk as in Figure 18.2b, a firm may be better able to motivate employees to experiment and take risks on the job. Conversely, if a firm wishes to motivate employees to be conservative (e.g., risk management in a bank), it might use a pay-performance shape that limits upside compensation potential and reduces pay when performance is low.

Some firms use caps on incentives as illustrated in Figure 18.2b. To understand the trade-offs in using a cap, remember two things about a performance measure. First, the measure is a function of the employee's effort, but also his ability and human capital. Second, a performance measure may be affected by manipulation and by measurement error/uncontrollable risk. A problem with a cap is that it is more likely to affect employees with high levels of skills and talent; therefore, it might adversely affect employee selection. A benefit of a cap, however, is that in many cases, high levels of a performance measure are more likely to reflect measurement error or manipulation than high levels of talent or effort. If an employee's performance is unusually good, he may simply have gotten lucky—or he may have cheated in some way. If odds are low that unusually high performance is due to effort and talent, a cap may be useful to deter manipulation and avoid rewarding good luck. Finally, a firm might also use a subjective cap, reserving the right to limit a bonus payout if the firm deems high performance to be due to luck or manipulation. However, although such a practice makes sense in theory, it runs the risk of a ratchet effect (see next section).

## 18.6  IMPLEMENTATION

In this section, I briefly discuss implementation of pay for performance. The first issue arises in implementing nearly all incentive plans. The last three involve ways in which pay for performance interacts with other personnel policies and objectives.

### 18.6.1  The Ratchet Effect

Every incentive plan needs to be changed from time to time. Measures and targets degrade. Errors in design need correcting. Strategy and structure change, requiring focus on different activities. Changing an existing plan risks a *ratchet effect*. This effect occurs when an employee's expectations about future changes in the incentive system reduce incentives today, and it can occur for several reasons.

Suppose a firm sets commission rates for salespeople by determining expected sales and then dividing expected sales into the going rate for workers with similar skills. The firm uses current sales as one factor in setting expected sales for next year. This practice implies a ratchet effect because if the employee increases sales this year, he receives a lower commission next year. Similarly, growth-based targets or performance measures would seem to cause ratchet effects automatically. An additional cause may be a desire to lower labor costs. In our example, if the firm decides employees earn "too much," it lowers the commission. However, an employee may have high income because he has high performance due to strong talent or effort. The desire to reduce labor costs may end up punishing both.

Ratchet effects have received surprisingly little empirical study beyond Roy's (1952) famous description (Levenson et al. 2012). Some theoretical analysis exists (Lazear 1986; Gibbons 1987). Given the many parameters of an incentive system that may need to be changed, ratchet effects are likely a common concern in implementing incentive systems. The famous Lincoln Electric case (Milgrom and Roberts 1995) provides insights into how a firm might reduce ratchet effects. The company has an explicit policy of not changing piece rates unless a change occurs in methods of production. Piece rates are set by a special department with great expertise at setting accurate rates (they set approximately 10,000 piece rates per year, according to a company executive I know). Employees are allowed to challenge piece rates, and their complaints are taken seriously. Expected compensation is pegged to wage data from the Bureau of Labor Statistics, eliminating discretion over one determinant of piece rates. Top managers have strong pay for performance, which reduces their temptation to lower compensation for employees in ways that reduce firm performance.

Perhaps most importantly, the firm makes effective use of relational contracting. Founder James Lincoln had a passionate belief in individual effort and reward—he even wrote pamphlets about the topic. His strong beliefs imprinted on the company's culture, which emphasizes hard work and high rewards based on individual output. This culture is preserved partly by a policy of promotion from within, so that most executives started in entry-level jobs. The firm has not varied incentive policies significantly in over 75 years. This history gives the firm a strong reputation with employees, who are thereby unlikely to worry high performance will be punished by ratcheting of the incentive system.

## 18.6.2  Matching Incentives and Job Design

Pay for performance does not operate in a vacuum, but interacts with other personnel policies and goals. One important example is job design. Holmstrom and Milgrom (1991) note that one way to deal with the problem of imbalanced multitask incentives arising from tasks with large differences in uncontrollable risk is to split the job, bundling easy-to-measure tasks in one job and hard-to-measure tasks in another. Prendergast (2002a) argues that delegation and multitasking are likely to have important effects on optimal performance evaluation. The degree of controllable risk in a job is, to some extent, within the firm's choosing. Consider two different work environments. In the first, work is largely the same from one day to another, so there is little controllable risk. In the second, unexpected situations arise, and the optimal allocation of effort changes daily, so there is high controllable risk. In the first case, the firm has a good idea of what the employee should do, and delegates few decisions. It tells the employee what to do and monitors compliance, so little or no pay for performance is needed. In the second case, the worker possesses information about how to best perform the job, as in Case 5. To exploit that information, the firm delegates decisions, and uses pay for performance to motivate good decision making. Thus jobs with greater delegation are likely to have stronger pay-for-performance links.

Evaluation methods should also vary with the degree of delegation. I argued above that broader measures or use of multiple measures may be required if controllable risk is important. In such situations, a firm may also emphasize outputs instead of inputs in evaluation. Input-based measurement makes sense when the firm has a good idea about how the employee should do the job. Output-based measurement is better when the firm does not know how to guide employee efforts. Finally, subjective evaluation is likely to be more important for jobs with more delegation and controllable risk. It allows the firm to better incorporate controllable risk in the evaluation while filtering out controllable risk. It allows for ex post consideration of new information in evaluating the employee, whereas the firm must choose a numeric measure in advance. Finally, jobs with high controllable risk and delegation are more likely in changing environments, and subjective evaluation provides greater flexibility.

Finally, Prendergast (2002a) argues the degree of multitasking in a job is also likely to be positively related to the use of pay for performance. The earlier literature on multitasking suggested the opposite might be true, because of the difficulty of balancing incentives across tasks with different uncontrollable risk. His counterargument is that jobs with more tasks are more costly to monitor, which might tip the balance toward incentives. An additional argument is suggested by Gibbs et al. (2010), who also provide evidence of a strong positive correlation between delegation and multitasking (but do not have data on incentives). A more complex job with multiple tasks may create greater worker knowledge that can drive continuous improvement. Continuous improvement in turn may require delegation so that the worker can use his information to test and implement new methods. Delegation would then be complementary with incentive pay.

Because this area of study is new, the empirical literature is small but growing (e.g., Brown 1990; MacLeod and Parent 1999; Ortega 2009; DeVaro and Kurtulus 2010; Barrenechea-Méndez et al. 2011) and is generally consistent with the arguments made here.

## 18.6.3 Motivating Creativity

A special aspect of how incentives match job design is motivation of creativity. Psychologists argue that pay for performance undermines creativity (Kerr 1975). To an economist, such a claim seems odd, given the enormous innovation the profit motive generates in markets. This topic is too broad to cover fully, but I provide brief remarks. When used properly, incentives do not necessarily undermine creativity.

A distorted performance measure, however, can easily undermine creativity. Rewarding a professor for the quantity of published articles distorts incentives toward publication in low-quality journals. In extreme cases, the professor might even manipulate the system by setting up his own journal. Most examples of incentives undermining creativity stem from distorted numeric measures. Quantifying creative activities is often hard; therefore they are likely to receive relatively low weight in numeric measures. Where creativity is important, a firm should consider broader, output-based measures and subjective evaluation, much as discussed in the prior subsection.

The pay-for-performance relation also matters. Creativity requires experimentation with new methods, which implies mistakes. Reducing the employee's downside risk from mistakes will counteract employee risk aversion, leading to more willingness to experiment. A firm might reduce downside risk for the employee in several ways, including job-security provisions, a relatively high base salary for performance below some target level of performance, or discretionary bonuses to "back out" the effects of mistakes on formal bonuses. All incentives amount to ways to make the pay-performance shape similar to that of a call option. This may be one reason why stock options are a common form of compensation in small startup firms, where innovation is particularly important.

## 18.6.4  Pay for Performance and Employee Selection

Performance depends on effort, but also on innate talent and accumulated human capital. Generally speaking, stronger pay for performance is likely to improve employee selection, because it provides stronger rewards to those whose ability and skills better match the job. Lazear (2000) studied the effects of a new pay-for-performance plan on the productivity of windshield installers. Productivity rose dramatically, and he estimated that approximately half of this increase was a result of selection (the other half to motivation). More research is required to gauge whether this strong selection effect of pay for performance occurs more broadly. Nevertheless, it does suggest a firm should consider potential selection benefits when designing a pay-for-performance plan.

Employee selection is affected not just by incentive intensity, but also by performance evaluation. Bouwens and van Lent (2006) find that selection improves when a firm uses performance measures that are less distorted and have less uncontrollable risk. This finding makes sense, as stronger incentives increase the links between the employee's performance, pay, and firm objectives. Helliwell and Huang (2010) find employees place a large value (compensating differential) on the extent to which they trust management. Together these findings suggest that how subjective evaluation and discretion in incentive systems are implemented is likely to have important effects on recruitment, turnover, and labor costs, in addition to motivation.

# 18.7  FUTURE RESEARCH

In this section, I sketch some areas for future research briefly, due to limited space. Some questions build on prior research in straightforward ways. Others involve collecting new data. Finally, many interesting questions involve thinking about incentives as a *system*. Most research focuses on a specific piece of an incentive plan, such as a single performance measure or bonus. However, we have seen that an incentive plan is complex, involving several instruments, with formal and informal components. Complementarities or trade-offs exist between most of these pieces. Incentives also arise implicitly, through promotions, career concerns, and so forth, all of which will interact with formal incentives. Finally, compensation and evaluation interact with other personal policies and objectives, notably job design and employee selection. A great deal of interesting research is yet to be done on how the various pieces of an incentive system fit together, and with other parts of organizational design.

## 18.7.1  Worker Preferences

Researchers rarely give much thought to the utility assumptions behind agency models, but doing so might be interesting. Many models are of the form employed here, with a risk-aversion adjustment for income variance. However, controllable risk implies effort variance. Even if an employee observes his marginal products before choosing effort, effort is still uncertain at the stage where the incentive contract is established, and so in principle should affect base salary. I am unaware of any evidence on whether effort variance affects compensation. For employees, being effort risk averse creates a cost of controllable risk.

Also of interest is whether diminishing marginal utility of income affects effort. If employees enjoy high payoffs on exercise, this issue may be relevant for companies that use employee stock options. It may be especially relevant for CEOs and executives with extremely high remuneration. The growing use of such compensation instruments, and of income levels for highly skilled workers in advanced economies, suggests this issue might be worth study.

## 18.7.2 Performance Evaluation

A great deal of research has been devoted to evaluation (especially numeric measures), but many important questions are not fully understood. How prevalent is manipulation (as distinguished from distortion)? How can a firm evaluate whether an employee is more likely to use controllable risk to increase firm value, or to manipulate the measure? How do firms address manipulation in practice? Finally, is manipulation by the firm in reporting performance also a concern?

Another interesting question is whether improved performance evaluation alone, without explicit incentives, might improve employee performance. Employees may have intrinsic motivation and also some extrinsic motivation from implicit incentives such as promotions. Performance evaluation can provide the employee with training and with feedback about the effects of his actions and decisions. Training and feedback could drive continuous improvement and human capital acquisition, even if no explicit incentives were applied by the firm.

Limited empirical research exists about how firms address flaws in performance measures, beyond reducing the incentive intensity. Presumably firms also use multiple measures, including subjectivity and implicit incentives, and may alter the shape of the pay-performance relationship. Linking such practices to properties of performance measures would be quite interesting.

The performance measurement frontier—trade-offs faced when choosing performance measures—is an interesting question, though studying it may be difficult because inferring much about measures that firms do not choose is difficult. A good starting place for research would be to focus on a specific type of job where evaluation is simple, such as CEOs or sales. Studying measures that vary in scope along several dimensions may also be a useful approach.

I emphasized that subjectivity and discretion are almost inevitable and necessary in the design and implementation of incentives. Observation suggests they are in fact ubiquitous. Despite this fact, most research focuses on formulaic bonuses and numeric measures, likely because such compensation schemes are more amenable to formal modeling and data collection. However, widespread use of subjectivity suggests economists devote more effort to understanding this topic in theory and practice. Many issues are not fully understood. How prevalent are subjective evaluations? In what types of jobs? How are they conducted? What is the relative importance for incentives of subjectivity, discretion, and implicit rewards compared to explicit, numeric approaches?

An interesting issue discretion raises is incentives for the supervisor. Instead of a simple principal-agent problem, incentives for the evaluator matter (Murphy 1992). Several papers cited in this chapter consider this issue theoretically, but I am unaware of empirical research on how supervisor incentives affect incentives for subordinates. Investigating the effects of supervisor incentives on the subordinate's evaluation method, distribution of performance ratings, incentive intensity, and effectiveness of relational contracting between the firm and the employee would be interesting.

### 18.7.3  Group Incentives

Group incentives appear prevalent (including gain sharing, profit sharing, options, and stock ownership plans), yet explaining them with standard agency theory is hard. Recall from (18.1) that $e_i^* = \dfrac{dI}{dP} E\left[\dfrac{\partial P}{\partial e_i}\right]$. Incentives require that efforts have tangible effects on the performance measure and that income varies reasonably with the measure. Group-based pay seems to yield low values for each. Performance is based on the actions of all employees, so the evaluation has a great deal of uncontrollable risk and a low signal-to-noise ratio. The tie of income to the evaluation is also usually small. For example, imagine an employee participates in profit sharing in a company with 5000 employees, and by his own efforts increases profits by $1 million. On average, his share of his contribution is $200, or b = 0.0002. Putting these together, we see that it is implausible that such schemes might actually generate much incentive. A few studies have analyzed profit-sharing plans, but systematic evidence on how productivity varies with incentives in such systems would be revealing. Firms may adopt these policies for other purposes (e.g., implicit risk sharing, or to reduce variability in cash flows through a business cycle).

### 18.7.4  Methodology

Two recent advances in economics seem interesting for the study of pay for performance: behavioral economics and field experiments. Incentives involve individual worker behavior, supervisor judgment, and relational contracting. These topics may all benefit from study by behavioral economists. In addition, economists are making greater use of field experiments. Firms sometimes experiment with changes in pay-for-performance plans, and studying such examples to gain a more precise understanding of the effects of incentive-plan design would be of great interest. Lazear's Safelite study (2000) is an early example of such.

# 18.8  CONCLUSIONS

I briefly conclude by summarizing the implications of research on incentives for designing and implementing pay for performance in practice. Incentive compensation is one of the most successful areas in economic research. An enormous body of research exists, from highly abstract and technical to empirical and descriptive. A healthy interplay between theory and empirics results in an advanced understanding of key issues and trade-offs, and provides a structured way of thinking through the design and implementation of incentives.

A useful way to think about incentives is to use the structure of this chapter. Firms can design an incentive plan in three stages. First, choose the performance evaluation method, including one or more numeric performance measures and subjective evaluation. This issue is by far the most important and complex to address in designing incentives. Most problems derive from the method of evaluation. When considering measures, a firm should account for uncontrollable and controllable risk, distortion, manipulability, and scope. The evaluation should, fundamentally, be matched to the job design. Second, establish the pay-for-performance relationship. This process involves setting weights or incentive intensities for bonus plans, choosing any performance targets, and deciding whether the incentive plan should have floors or caps. Third, set base salary to adjust for risk, effort, and prevailing labor market rates.

Importantly, an incentive plan is a *system* of interrelated parts. Understanding the individual pieces, such as the properties of a specific performance measure, is easy. Understanding how the pieces relate to each other is also necessary. One performance measure may help reduce distortion or uncontrollable risk in one dimension and raise them in another. Subjective evaluation will probably be necessary to detect and deter manipulation, encourage greater risk taking, or encourage the employee to take more initiative in using his knowledge to promote firm objectives. A measure may have a great deal of uncontrollable risk, implying the firm may want to put in a floor on incentive compensation to reduce risk. The measure might be manipulable, so that an explicit or discretionary cap may be useful.

Finally, an incentive plan has both formal and informal elements. The formal elements are the natural starting point, but thinking carefully about the informal elements is important. Subjective evaluation plays a critical role in improving the evaluation by filtering out certain risks while including others, reducing distortions, and deterring manipulation. This requires effort by the firm to avoid favoritism and other biases, training and incentives for supervisors so that evaluations are effective, and development of reasonable trust of the firm by employees. Effective relationship contracting can also reduce concerns about ratchet effects. For these reasons, careful implementation is important for an incentive plan to realize maximum potential.

## NOTES

1. By "pay" and "rewards" throughout, I mean anything the employee values that the firm can give more or less of, as a function of performance. Monetary compensation is most important, but other examples include benefits, a nicer office, promotions, preferred job assignments, or access to training.

2. This is a slight simplification, as base salary may be higher than in alternative jobs. In such a case, an employee who is terminated for poor performance suffers a loss. That differential is an additional way in which total compensation varies with performance. Including such effects (sometimes called efficiency wages) is a simple intuitive extension of our discussion. Base salary might also imply income effects on the marginal utility of income and marginal disutility of effort.

3. I assume the marginal disutility of effort is the same for all tasks. If not, a measure should give more weight to tasks that are less costly to the worker, because the firm has to compensate for the disutility of effort.

4. If $\rho < 0$, $b^*$ might be negative, in which case the firm uses the measure to punish undesirable outcomes. However, it might still be that $b^* > 0$ when $\rho < 0$ (Baker 1992). Incentive pay motivates total effort as well as allocation across tasks. When $\rho < 0$, the measure gives the wrong signals about how to allocate effort, but might be used anyway to motivate greater average effort.

5. This statement holds except in employee stock or option plans. These plans are a puzzle from the perspective of this chapter, because for lower-level employees, the performance measure has extreme uncontrollable risk, and the share of increased stock value accruing to an employee due to his actions is essentially zero. See Oyer and Schaefer (2005).

## REFERENCES

Baker, George P. 1992. "Incentive Contracts and Performance Measurement." *Journal of Political Economy* 100:598–614.

——. 2002. "Distortion and Risk in Optimal Incentive Contracts." *Journal of Human Resources* 37 (4): 729–51.

Baker, George P., Robert Gibbons, and Kevin J. Murphy. 1994. "Subjective Performance Measures in Optimal Incentive Contracts." *Quarterly Journal of Economics* 109:1125–56.

Banker, Rajiv, and Srikant Datar. 1989. "Sensitivity, Precision, and Linear Aggregation of Signals for Performance Evaluation." *Journal of Accounting Research* 27:21–39.

Barrenechea-Méndez, Marco A., Pedro Ortin-Ángel, and Eduardo Rodes-Mayor. 2011. "Uncertainty, Job Complexity and Incentives: An Empirical Analysis of Spanish Industrial Firms." Working paper, Universitat Autònoma de Barcelona.

Bouwens, Jan, and Laurence van Lent. 2006. "Performance Measure Properties and the Effect of Incentive Contracts." *Journal of Management Accounting Research* 18:55–75.

Brown, Charles. 1990. "Firms Choice of Method of Pay." *Industrial and Labor Relations Review* 43 (3): 165–82.

Bushman, Robert M., and Abbie J. Smith. 2001. "Financial Accounting Information and Corporate Governance." *Journal of Accounting and Economics* 32:237–333.

Courty, Pascal, and Gerald Marschke. 2004. "An Empirical Investigation of Gaming Responses to Explicit Performance Incentives." *Journal of Labor Economics* 22 (1): 23–56.

——. 2008. "A General Test for Distortions in Performance Measures." *Review of Economics and Statistics* 90 (3): 428–41.

Datar, Srikant, Susan Cohen Kulp, and Richard Lambert. 2001. "Balancing Performance Measures." *Journal of Accounting Research* 39 (1): 75–92.

DeVaro, Jed, and Fidan Ana Kurtulus. 2010. "An Empirical Analysis of Risk, Incentives and the Delegation of Worker Authority." *Industrial and Labor Relations Review* 63 (4): 637–57.

Fama, Eugene. 1991. "Efficient Capital Markets: II." *Journal of Finance* 46 (5): 1575–1617.

Feltham, Gerald, and Jim Xie. 1994. "Performance Measure Congruity and Diversity in Multi-Task Principal-Agent Relations." *The Accounting Review* 69:429–453.

Gibbons, Robert 1987. "Piece-Rate Incentive Schemes." *Journal of Labor Economics* 5:413–29.

——. 1998. "Incentives in Organizations." *Journal of Economic Perspectives* 12 (4): 115–32.

Gibbons, Robert, and Kevin J. Murphy. 1990. "Relative Performance Evaluation for Chief Executive Officers." *Industrial and Labor Relations Review* 43:30–52.

Gibbs, Michael, Alec Levenson, and Cindy Zoghi. 2010. "Why Are Jobs Designed the Way They Are?" *Research in Labor Economics* 30:107–54.

Gibbs, Michael, Kenneth Merchant, Mark Vargus, and Wim Van der Stede. 2004. "Determinants and Effects of Subjectivity in Incentives." *The Accounting Review* 79 (2): 409–36.

——. 2009. "Performance Measure Properties and Incentive System Design." *Industrial Relations* 48 (2): 237–64.

Hansen, Stephen. 2010. "The Benefits of Limited Feedback in Organizations." Working paper, Universitat Pompeu Fabra.

Hayes, Rachel M., and Scott Schaefer. 2000. "Implicit Contracts and the Explanatory Power of Top Executive Compensation." *Rand Journal of Economics* 31:273–93.

Healy, Paul. 1985. "The Effect of Bonus Schemes on Accounting Decisions." *Journal of Accounting and Economics* 7:85–107.

Helliwell, John F., and Haifang Huang. 2010. "How's the Job? Well-Being and Social Capital in the Workplace." *Industrial and Labor Relations Review* 63 (2): 205–27.

Holmstrom, Bengt. 1979. Moral Hazard and Observability. *Bell Journal of Economics* 10:74–91.

Holmstrom, Bengt, and Paul Milgrom. 1991. "Multitask Principal-Agent Analyses: Incentive Contracts, Asset Ownership, and Job Design." *Journal of Law, Economics and Organization* 7:24–52.

Ittner, Christopher D., and David F. Larcker. 2002. "Determinants of Performance Measure Choices in Worker Incentive Plans." *Journal of Labor Economics* 20 (S2): S58–90.

Ittner, Christopher D., David F. Larcker, and Marshall W. Meyer. 2003. "Subjectivity and the Weighting of Performance Measures: Evidence from a Balanced Scorecard." *The Accounting Review* 78 (3): 725–58.

Kaplan, Robert S., and D. P. Norton. 1996. *The Balanced Scorecard: Translating Strategy into Action.* Boston, MA: Harvard Business School Press.

Kerr, Steven. 1975. "On the Folly of Rewarding A, While Hoping For B." *Academy of Management Journal* 18:769–83.

Lazear, Edward P. 1986. "Salaries and Piece Rates." *Journal of Business* 59 (3): 405–31.

——. 1989. "Pay Equality and Industrial Politics." *Journal of Political Economy* 97 (3): 561–80.

——. 2000. "Performance Pay and Productivity." *American Economic Review* 90 (5): 1346–61.

Lazear, Edward P., and Sherwin Rosen. 1981. "Rank Order Tournaments as Optimal Labor Contracts." *Journal of Political Economy* 89 (5): 841–64.

Levenson, Alec, Cindy Zoghi, Michael Gibbs, and George Benson. 2012. "Optimizing Incentive Plan Design: A Case Study." Working paper, USC.

MacLeod, W. Bentley, and Daniel Parent. 1999. "Job Characteristics and the Form of Compensation." *Research in Labor Economics* 18:177–242.

Milgrom, Paul. 1988. "Employment Contracts, Influence Activities, and Efficient Organization Design." *Journal of Political Economy* 96:42–60.

Milgrom, Paul, and John Roberts. 1995. "Complementarities and Fit: Strategy Structure, and Organizational Change in Manufacturing." *Journal of Accounting and Economics* 19:179–208.

Murphy, Kevin J. 1992. "Performance Measurement and Appraisal: Motivating Managers to Identify and Reward Performance." In *Performance Measurement, Evaluation, and Incentives*, edited by William J. Bruns, 37–62. Boston: Harvard Business School Press.

——. 1999. "Executive Compensation." In *Handbook of Labor Economics*, edited by Orley Ashenfelter and David Card, 3:2485–2563. New York: North Holland.

——. 2000. "Performance Standards in Incentive Contracts." *Journal of Accounting and Economics* 30:245–78.

Murphy, Kevin R., and J. N. Cleveland. 1995. *Understanding Performance Appraisal: Social, Organizational, and Goal-Based Perspectives*. Thousand Oaks, CA: Sage Publications.

Murphy, Kevin J., and Paul Oyer. 2003. "Discretion in Executive Incentive Contracts: Theory and Evidence." Working paper, USC.

Ortega, Jaime. 2009. "Employee Discretion and Performance Pay." *The Accounting Review* 84 (2): 589–612.

Oyer, Paul. 1998. "The Effect of Sales Incentives on Business Seasonality," *Quarterly Journal of Economics* 113 (1): 149–86.

——. 2000. "A Theory of Sales Quotas with Limited Liability and Rent Sharing." *Journal of Labor Economics* 18 (3): 405–26.

Oyer, Paul, and Scott Schaefer. 2005. "Why Do Some Firms Give Stock Options to All Employees? An Empirical Examination of Alternative Theories." *Journal of Financial Economics* 76:99–133.

Prendergast, Canice. 1993. "A Theory of 'Yes Men.'" *American Economic Review* 83:757–70.

——. 1999. "The Provision of Incentives in Firms." *Journal of Economic Literature* 37:7–63.

——. 2002a. "The Tenuous Trade-off between Risk and Incentives." *Journal of Political Economy* 110 (5): 1071–1102.

——. 2002b. "Uncertainty and Incentives." *Journal of Labor Economics* 20 (S2): S115–37.

Prendergast, Canice, and Robert Topel. 1993. "Discretion and Bias in Performance Evaluation." *European Economic Review* 37:355–65.

Roy, Donald. 1952. "Quota Restriction and Goldbricking in a Machine Shop," *American Journal of Sociology* 57 (5): 427–42.

Sloof, Randolph, and Mirjam van Praag. 2011. "Testing for Distortions in Performance Measures: An Application to Residual Income Based Measures Like Economic Value Added." Working paper, University of Amsterdam.

Van Praag, Mirjam, and Kees Cools. 2001. "Performance Measure Selection: Aligning the Principal's Objective and the Agent's Effort." Working paper, University of Amsterdam.

Waggoner, Daniel B., Andy D. Neely, and Mike P. Kennerly. 1999. "The Forces That Shape Organisational Performance Measurement Systems: An Interdisciplinary Review." *International Journal of Production Economics* 60–61:53–60.

# CHAPTER 19

·······················································

# VERTICAL MERGER

·······················································

## RICHARD S. HIGGINS AND MARK PERELMAN

## 19.1 INTRODUCTION[1]

·······················································

RESOURCE use is organized either within a business firm or between firms through market transactions. Stated most simply, management can "make or buy" (Rubin 1990).[2] When assets and resources are used internally to make products, there is "integration," and, when these goods and services are traded between separate firms there is "no integration." Integration can be "vertical," "horizontal," or "conglomerate." This chapter addresses several theories of integration through merger of activities at successive stages of production and distribution under different market conditions—namely, vertical merger.

Vertical merger is variously motivated by gains from: (1) achieving better coordination of activities while avoiding costly negotiations with other firms; (2) realizing potential market power or from enhancing extant market power; (3) creating market power or protecting existing market power; (4) promoting technological development; and (5) removing uncertainty of supply.[3]

In almost all theories of vertical merger, contractual imperfections are the source of the advantages of integration. In many theories, imperfect contracting is the result of incomplete information, including uncertainty and impacted information and, according to some theories, investments are not contractible either ex post or ex ante. Presumably, with full (or "perfect") information, complete contracts could be devised and if also enforceable at minimal cost, there would be no value in vertical integration. For example, a contract between bilateral monopolists to transfer an intermediate product at marginal cost and to share downstream monopoly rent is efficient.[4] In the present paper, most of the pricing externalities addressed occur in the context of complete and perfect information but arise from prohibitive transaction costs—for example, the familiar case of "double marginalization." In those few instances in which imperfect information is the critical cause of the pricing externality, this is acknowledged explicitly.

But for vertical integration, imperfect contracting prevents surplus-maximizing actions, except when competition is perfect. With imperfect competition, firms have market power. Thus, potential efficiencies attend vertical integration when a firm or firms have market power at one or more stages of production. To complicate matters, the presence of market power before merger implies the possibility of enhanced market power after merger, which, in theory, makes for ambiguous welfare effects.

Antitrust economics attempts to identify market conditions that are predictive of the net competitive effects of vertical merger. At present, the world's major antitrust agencies seem to agree in principle on the most appropriate model of vertical merger to apply; however, based on accounts of recent cases, the EU authorities appear to exert greater efforts to inform this model with econometrics than do the US authorities which, by inference, abhor foreclosure even when procompetitive.[5] This chapter provides a basis for evaluating their success in this regard.

## 19.2 Vertical Merger with Constant Marginal Cost

### 19.2.1 Double Marginalization

The welfare effects of vertical merger were originally analyzed in the context of constant marginal cost (Spengler 1950 and, for a modern treatment, see Carlton and Perloff 2005, 420). In the simplest case, an upstream input monopolist sells to downstream firms that compete imperfectly with constant marginal cost. When the monopolist must use linear pricing because of contracting imperfections, the downstream buyers take the input price to be parametric and they interact according to a specific oligopoly equilibrium model. Because downstream producers thus ignore the impact of their pricing decisions on the volume demanded from the monopolist, equilibrium exhibits *double marginalization*. Here, the joint-profit maximum actually lowers price because the pricing externality is thereby eliminated. In this instance, vertical merger is one way that the input monopolist can control both stages of production, thus preventing deadweight loss. Also, in this simple case, consumer welfare is enhanced notwithstanding vertical foreclosure. Moreover, if there were downstream Cournot competition with fixed, sunk costs of entry, vertical merger would eliminate the wasteful duplication of capital as well as double marginalization.

The next analytical wrinkle along these lines is due to Salinger (1988). In his model there is imperfect competition both up- *and* downstream. He investigates the likelihood of "foreclosure," which he defines as an increase in the merchant-market input price. When one upstream firm vertically integrates and, by assumption, refuses to deal with its unaffiliated downstream rivals, the market power of the nonintegrated input suppliers is enhanced. A priori, the postmerger level of the merchant-market input price appears indeterminate; however, since the integrated firm competes downstream at a lower marginal cost, which diverts output away from the nonintegrated downstream firms and which reduces merchant-market input demand, the ability of the noninte-grated upstream firms to raise price profitably is dampened, notwithstanding their enhanced market power. In Salinger's general case, with $N$ up- and $M$ downstream pro-ducers, and with vertical merger of some arbitrary extent, final output may rise or fall, and the wholesale price may rise or fall. In the event that wholesale price increases, it is still possible in his model for final output to expand; thus, Salinger finds that final output may increase even in the face of input foreclosure, as he defines it.

Salinger was criticized (Gaudet and Long 1993; Higgins 1999) for his fundamental foreclosure assumption—that is, the assumption that vertically integrated firms do not supply output to nonintegrated buyers. On the contrary, unless exogenously barred, the vertically integrated firms operate in the merchant input market. Partial integration is profitable, and follow-on integration may be as well. When follow-on integration is prof-itable, full vertical integration occurs, all double marginalization is avoided, and final output rises. Most importantly, the integrated firms participate in the merchant input market, either as net buyers or net sellers, and additional partial integration unambigu-ously raises consumer welfare. Thus, in the context of fixed coefficients and quantity setting among up- and downstream producers of a homogeneous product, no empirical analysis of vertical merger is necessary; a priori, vertical integration raises consumer welfare.

## 19.2.2  Variable Proportions

Historically, a more important theoretical advance addressed the *neutrality* result attributed to Professors Director and Levi (1957). When input proportions are fixed, an upstream monopolist selling into a perfectly competitive downstream market is indif-ferent between integrating downstream and charging the nonintegrated monopoly input price. This "neutrality" of vertical integration is an illustration of the famous, if not notorious, "single monopoly profit theorem."

Vernon and Graham (1971) demonstrated that the generality of this neutrality prop-osition does not hold under conditions of variable proportions. Without vertical inte-gration, downstream firms will shift away from using an input that is made relatively expensive through monopoly pricing, provided their production technologies are con-sistent with input substitution. However, inputs are used most efficiently when their rel-ative marginal value products are proportional to their relative prices; thus, just as there are deadweight losses associated with monopoly pricing of a final good, there are gains to be achieved by controlling input substitution when the input price is raised above mar-ginal cost. Warren-Boulton (1974) simulated market outcomes subject to assumptions about ranges of parameters for market demand and for CES and Cobb-Douglas produc-tion functions. He found that the total welfare effects of vertical merger are ambiguous.

Finally, Westfield (1981) proved analytically that the effects of vertical merger on consumer welfare are ambiguous as well. To the surprise of many, subject to variable proportions, vertical merger may cause final output price to fall.[6]

The theory of vertical integration under variable proportions indicates that vertical merger alters the combined incentives of the successive stages under vertical separation. That is, vertical merger does nothing to prohibit input substitution; instead, it removes the incentives to substitute the cheaper input as the monopolized input's price increases.

The models of fixed and variable input proportions analyzed in these historical exchanges ignore the presence of sunk cost—that is, they are essentially long-run analyses, which is surprising since antitrust enforcement concentrates on the short run. Some interesting particular findings flow from specific short-run models of competition when the cost of entry or of capacity is sunk.

## 19.3  VERTICAL MERGER WITH INCREASING MARGINAL COST

### 19.3.1 Theory

In the short run, capacity is committed to the market and, as capacity utilization increases by expanding the usage of variable inputs, marginal cost rises. In general, there are variable proportions in the short run by definition. Thus, one expects that Westfield's long-run results will a fortiori obtain in the short run and, in general, they do. "Raising rivals' costs" (RRC) is introduced here as an important illustration of the ambiguous welfare effects of vertical merger.

The RRC literature, initiated by Salop and Scheffman (1983), demonstrates that there may be instances in which a firm—typically, a dominant firm but, also perhaps, a group of firms that jointly achieve dominance through coordination—may raise the marginal costs of its rivals without a corresponding increase in its own marginal cost. The higher marginal costs of its rivals enable the dominant firm to exploit its market power along a higher residual demand curve. RRC analysis is most applicable to an antitrust analysis of exclusionary practices; however, since a persistent concern of antitrust practitioners is vertical foreclosure, its role in the economics of vertical merger is prominent.[7] While the RRC literature has provided antitrust practitioners with a framework for describing the potential anticompetitive use of exclusionary practices, it has generally failed to map structural parameters to competitive harm—in contrast to "harm to competitors"—at least in the context of market transactions alone. In contrast, RRC's anticompetitive implications clearly apply when the conduct complained of is illegal independent of antitrust law; for example, US Tobacco's upsetting of its rival's smokeless tobacco displays surely raised Conwood's marginal cost.[8] But, whether the treble-damage carrot should be used to motivate civil enforcement against theft is, at least, controversial.

Higgins (2009) has addressed the possible effects of RRC through vertical merger in the context of short-run equilibrium with price competition and fixed, sunk cost of capacity. Perfect competition downstream is assumed in order to avoid endowing vertical merger with known efficiencies associated with preventing double marginalization. However, because of the presence of downstream quasi rents, the latter assumption does not eliminate altogether the efficiencies of vertical integration. Two categories of variable proportions are analyzed: in one, a specific variable input is used in fixed proportion to output, though not in fixed proportion to the sunk-cost input and, in the other, both input proportions and the input/output ratio vary with output.

When the input/output ratio is fixed, partial vertical merger limited to a share of downstream capacity short of dominant-firm status reduces the marginal cost of the integrated firm *without* raising the marginal cost of the rival nonintegrated competitors. Rivals' costs are not raised; instead, the integrated firm's costs are reduced, which harms competitors just the same. In this case, vertical merger is always procompetitive.[9] In contrast, with full-blown variable proportions the familiar welfare ambiguities return; however, even here almost all of the parameter space yields procompetitive merger, at least in the context of the linear-quadratic model.[10] Remarkably, integration may completely foreclose downstream rivals from access to the monopolized input while, at the same time, lowering final output price.

Figure 19.1 provides some insight into why vertical merger is often procompetitive under the conditions posited. The following simple example is used to illustrate the principal effects of vertical merger in the short run. Marginal cost is $(c/s_j)q_j + kp_x$ for each downstream firm with capacity share $s_j$. (Here, $p_x$ is the input price, and k is the input/output ratio.) The implied supply curve is depicted in Figure 19.1. Absent integration, conditional

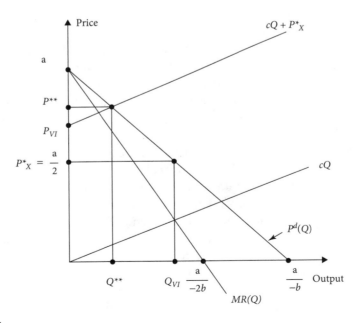

**FIGURE 19.1**

on $p_x$, the short-run final-product equilibrium is described by $cQ^s + kp_x = a + bQ^D$, $Q^S = Q^D$. Thus, in stage two, market equilibrium output is $Q^* = (a - kp_x)/(c - b)$. In stage one, the monopolist chooses $p_x$ to maximize $(p_x - mc_0)kQ^*$. With $mc_0 = 0$ and k = 1, $p_x = a/2$. Thus, $Q^{**} = a/2(c - b), P^{**} = a(2c - b)/2(c - b)$, and monopoly profit, $\pi_m$, is $a^2/4(c - b)$. Total quasi-rent is $P^{**}Q^{**}/2 - \pi_m = ca^2/4(c - b)^2$, and total producer surplus is equal to $a^2(3c - 2b)/8(c - b)^2$. Alternatively, in the case of full integration, the input monopolist maximizes $(a + bQ)Q - cQ^2/2$. The equilibrium output and final price are $a/(c - 2b)$ and $a(c - b)/(c - 2b)$, and total surplus is $a^2/(c - 2b)$.

A comparison of the two cases is depicted in Figure 19.1: output is greater under integration, and total surplus is also larger by $(ac)^2/4(c - b)^2(c - 2b)$. Without integration, simple pricing by the input monopolist creates externalities because the adverse impact of higher input price on quasi-rents downstream does not enter the monopolist's profit function. That is, vertical merger puts the critical decision maker in a position to appreciate its pricing decisions' effects on the value of sunk cost assets. As in prior illustrations, antitrust horizontal merger enforcement is likely to prevent the input monopolist from acquiring all of the downstream producers and, thus, potential social gains would not be realized fully. Note, however, that if the input/output ratio were not constant, the general Westfield model would apply, which suggests that final output price may increase even if the downstream market remains perfectly competitive.

## 19.3.2 Applications

The US antitrust agencies have analyzed theories of complete or partial foreclosure in several cases such as: *Pacific/Enova* (1998); *Barnes & Noble/Ingram* (1999); *AOL/ Time Warner* (2000); *Premdor/Masonite* (2001); *Cytyc/Digene* (2002); *Synopsys/Avant!* (2002); *Google/DoubleClick*; and—as the result of these theories—they have blocked two mergers and requested remedies and divestitures in the other cases.[11] Except for *Google/ DoubleClick*, the outcomes are consistent with the familiar analyses of vertical mergers, which are predicated either on input foreclosure or enhanced likelihood of coordination.[12] For example, in *Pacific/Enova*, the RRC mantra is reprised in the Competitive Impact Statement:[13] Enova is shown to have a monopoly over gas transmission and storage in Southern California which it supplies to Pacific and its two competitors. Absent merger, *Enova* charges a nondiscriminatory monopoly price; however, post merger, it allegedly would have the ability and incentive to raise price to Pacific's rivals, thereby raising their marginal costs and, in turn, shifting electricity demand to Pacific from its rivals, with the alleged effect of raising the price of electricity throughout Southern California. Further by way of example, in *Cytyc/Digene*, the Commission discounted the consumer benefits from combining complementary products independently supplied by companies with market power for the sake of introducing some degree of competition in one market notwithstanding persistent monopoly in the other. The foregoing analysis in this chapter suggests that evidence of foreclosure is not sufficient reason to challenge a vertical merger and that, moreover, the requisite competitive analysis is quite involved.[14]

Apparently, the same RRC vertical foreclosure model has been dispositive in guiding recent EC nonhorizontal merger investigations as well. Based on the Commission's description of the in-depth economic analysis consulted, the EU is taking seriously the possible coincidence of foreclosure and consumer surplus gain. In *TomTom/Teleatlas*, the Commission considered evidence of up- and downstream demand elasticities, pass-through rates, and input/output cost ratios in its evaluation of the likelihood of full and partial vertical foreclosure.[15] Shortly after notification of the *TomTom/Teleatlas* combination, a parallel combination between Nokia and NAVTEQ was announced. After a tortuous analysis of the likelihood of anticompetitive vertical foreclosure, given the combination of TomTom and Teleatlas, the Commission concluded that the Nokia acquisition would not significantly impede competition. In both cases, the Commission appears not to have relied on a priori predictions of competitive effects based on theory and fundamental empirics (see note 10, supra) but, instead, to have undertaken a simulation of market equilibrium before and after merger based on alternative assumptions about foreclosure. In contrast to its treatment of potential vertical foreclosure, the Commission appears to have given the potential for anticompetitive coordinated effects short shrift.[16]

## 19.4 DIAGONAL MERGER

Vertical integration, in contrast to integration in general, refers of course to firms related as buyers and sellers. When contracting is imperfect, vertical integration alters firms' incentives to achieve more closely the joint value maximum of the related operations and, in many instances, this reduces waste and increases total welfare; it sometimes increases consumer welfare as well. Integration closely related to vertical integration, which has come to be called "diagonal merger" (Higgins 1997), also alters incentives, thus increasing profitability.

The quintessential example is one in which an input monopolist (or, at least, a single firm with significant market power) sells to downstream buyers who compete significantly with firms in a related market that do not use the monopolized input. The related downstream market need not be part of the same relevant market as defined by the pre-2010 Horizontal Merger Guidelines.[17] In this case, the upstream monopolist is constrained in its pricing to a degree by downstream buyers' substitution away from the good that is produced with the aid of the monopolized input. In short, when the price of the input is raised, the price of the downstream product that uses it increases, which causes demand to shift to substitute products. Of course, there is diversion of this sort in general in response to a final price increase because of household budget constraints, but the loss of sales is felt only diffusely except when the diversion is to significant, direct substitutes.

With or without control, if the upstream monopolist possessed an ownership interest in the substitute product market, its incentive to raise the input price would be greater.

As a result, a higher input price is profit-maximizing as a product of diagonal merger. Diagonal ownership enables the input monopolist to capture some of the runoff that results when it raises price in the vertically related market, just as in the analysis of unilateral effects in the context of interbrand competition with and without joint ownership.

Diagonal merger raises the value of the input monopoly and reduces consumer welfare, as wasteful substitution is thereby encouraged. Moreover, vertical control is unnecessary; the effect can be achieved through stock-market investments which are unlikely to entail significant costs. This apparent anticompetitive effect is entirely the result of a change in the monopolist's incentives. This incentive effect contrasts with that described above in which some means of unifying control through vertical integration is necessary to increase profit.[18] "Apparent" because some practitioners may contend that the input monopolist should be able to exploit its market power to the fullest; however, in contrast, most would likely maintain that the monopolist should not be allowed to engage a separate market in its efforts to exploit more fully its customers. We feel uncomfortable endorsing this latter view wholeheartedly for reasons that will be more evident when reading Section 19.5.3 below.

## 19.5  Leverage Theory

The monopoly leveraging hypothesis maintains that an input monopolist may be able to leverage its market power into another market. Allegedly, this leveraging is accomplished either by denying "downstream" rivals access to the monopolized input or by conditioning access to the input on sales of a related product. In the first instance, denial of access is unprofitable unless predicated on integration, perhaps through contract and, in the second instance, integration is necessary for tying the two products effectively. In either case, the presumed goal of the input monopolist is to leverage its market power by inducing exit and preventing reentry or by preventing entry in the first instance. That is, the conduct is designed to extend monopoly to a second market or to protect market power in the original monopoly input market.[19]

### 19.5.1  Access Denial through Pricing

This situation has been illustrated above in Section 19.2.1. An input monopolist selling to several downstream firms with constant marginal cost and fixed proportions is unable to exploit its market power fully if the downstream firms compete imperfectly. By integrating downstream or, for that matter, creating an additional downstream firm, the other downstream producers can be eliminated through a price squeeze. There is no need expressly to deny downstream rivals access to the monopolized input because the downstream rivals are unable to cover marginal cost given the input and the output prices of the integrated firm. Thus, monopoly upstream is leveraged into monopoly downstream, which is more valuable than the single monopoly profit subject to double marginalization. In this instance, however, consumer welfare is increased since the final price is lower with foreclosure than without and, as indicated above, duplicative sunk-cost investments may be avoided.

## 19.5.2  Discriminatory Access[20]

When the upstream firm is an integrated natural monopolist, price regulation has commonly been imposed. For example, consider a bottleneck monopoly with large fixed, sunk costs of capacity and insignificant constant marginal cost. And, initially, suppose that there are constant returns to scale in the downstream or complementary market. These conditions are consistent with so-called potentially competitive ancillary markets, the most famous alleged example of which is long-distance, land-line telephone service in the United States. Although price regulation may take various forms, here, by assumption, average cost is public knowledge, and final price is set equal to overall LRAC. Simple Ramsey pricing of this sort is second best.

In the instant illustration, full information is presumed to be available to the hypothetical regulator; more realistically, information is costly, and even benign regulation uses resources. One response to costly regulation has been an attempt to reduce the burden of regulation by setting only the access price, allowing the downstream price to be set through competition. Two versions have been tried: in one, the natural monopolist is prohibited altogether from owning downstream assets and, in the other, vertical integration is permitted with price regulation at the upstream stage.

In the first instance, without integration—including integration through contract— the natural monopolist has no incentive to deny access to any of the downstream producers. Of course, it does have incentives to exploit its upstream monopoly to the fullest. Thus, vertical separation has usually been accompanied by access price regulation. In this instance, the regulator allegedly focuses on the average cost of the bottleneck operation, leaving final price regulation to competition.

Less burdensome regulation with vertical separation is an illusion, however (Higgins and Mukherjee 2010). This is because the average-cost access price depends on the downstream net demand price function. In other words, the regulator must have information about costs at both stages of production as well downstream demand in order to set the access price properly. Thus, even when there is near-perfect competition in the downstream market absent integration, there is no essential difference between regulation of the integrated firm and regulation of the essential upstream facility.[21]

## 19.5.3  Leveraging Market Power through Tying[22]

Closely related to vertical integration is common ownership of firms that produce complementary products, for example, cameras and film. Although unnecessary, most examples of such complementarity seem to involve a durable good and ancillary disposables. Often the producer of the primary product (the "camera") is integrated into production and sale of the complementary product (the "film"). The coproduction of these complementary activities is equivalent to vertical integration, though the actual integration may be performed by the final customer. Classic examples of such tie-in sales are described in *International Salt* and in *IBM*.[23] In both instances, the *disposable* is allegedly used to meter the use of the durable for the purpose of engaging in first degree price discrimination.

In a similar but different vein, Nalebuff (2005) elaborates on models of Burstein (1960) and Blair and Kaserman (1978) in which integration, together with tying, is used to exploit more fully the surplus under the demand curve for the tying good.[24] In the simplest treatment, a monopolist in one product integrates into production of a secondary product, whose demand is independent of that for the primary good. By assumption, here, the primary-good monopolist offers buyers of the tying product a full-requirements contract for the tied good.[25] The monopolist may offer the tying contract and nothing at all besides—a naked tie—or, alternatively, it may offer to sell the products separately at prices that satisfy one or the other of two possible conditions. In one case, the stand-alone price of the tying good is above the no-tying monopoly price so that without expressly denying customers access to the tying good separately, no customer finds it economical to purchase it on this stand-alone basis. In the other alternative, the a la carte price equals the no-tying monopoly price for the tying good (see Higgins 2013).

In the case of the naked tie, the overall offer consisting of the tying contract or nothing is credible for the very reasons that Rasmusen et al. (1991) are able to justify an exclusive agreement requiring no compensation, when lots of customers are unable to coordinate their responses. In this instance, the tying agreement entails a tying-good price lower than the no-tying monopoly price along with a tied-good price that exceeds marginal cost, provided that these prices are set to preserve for buyers the surplus they would receive buying only the tied good in the competitive market. Provided that most of the tied-good customers also would purchase the tied good at its competitive price, these buyers will elect the tying agreement.

At first glance, it appears that integration here results in monopolization of the tied-good market provided that most of the tied-good customers also demand the tying good. Certainly the price of the tied good is increased above marginal cost. However, under the circumstances, the supercompetitive price in the tied-good market is offset by a price less than the simple monopoly price in the tying-good market. In other words, the effect on consumer surplus in both markets must be considered in assessing whether integration and tying is anticompetitive.

As described, the tying contract raises total welfare: consumer welfare is unchanged while the tying good monopolist's profits are increased. The surplus derives from second-best Ramsey pricing, which the monopolist finds optimal. In other words, the deadweight loss associated with its simple monopoly price for the tying good is mitigated by expanding sales of the monopolized product in exchange for a higher price in the otherwise perfectly competitive market. There is a social gain from balancing the deadweight losses across markets, the lesson of the theory of the second best.[26]

What is certain is that the value of the tying-good monopoly is increased by virtue of the tying contract. Here, integration and tying enable the monopolist to exploit more fully its market power in the primary market and, in so doing, to raise total welfare without reducing consumer welfare. However, tying may also provide a means for the tying-good monopolist to leverage market power into the tied-good market—that is, to monopolize it, but see Higgins (2012).

# 19.6  Exclusive Dealing

In the section above, integration with associated tying was analyzed. Tying establishes exclusive dealing for the tied good by conditioning access to the monopolized tying good on purchasing all tied-good requirements from the tying-good monopolist. In general, exclusive dealing does not require tying and, normally, exclusive dealing has been analyzed outside the context of vertical integration. But, intuitively, an upstream monopolist can replicate an exclusive deal with a downstream producer through vertical integration. For that reason, exclusive dealing contracts (EDCs) are analyzed briefly in this section.

## 19.6.1  Entry Deterrence

In this regard it is ideal to start with the Aghion-Bolton model (see Aghion and Bolton 1987). Non–Chicago School economists were forced to admit the cogency of analysis like Bork's (1978) and Posner's (1976), which maintained that with full information, buyers would not agree to avoid purchasing from a lower-price supplier now or in the future unless he or she were compensated for foregoing the option.[27] Aghion and Bolton demonstrated how potential newcomers could be forestalled from entering a noncoincident market through exclusive agreements between an incumbent and consumers, provided the entrant were not party to the agreement.

The Aghion-Bolton model depends critically on the following assumptions: (1) asymmetric information; (2) commitment in the form of a liquidated damages contract enforced by a third party; and (3) lack of contracting between the potential entrant and consumers.

There are two periods; thus, the noncoincident market is next period's market for a homogeneous product available in two periods. The input is transformed into the output on a one-to-one basis subject to constant marginal cost. Consumers buy one unit whenever the sales price is below their reservation price, equal to 1. There is one incumbent seller with marginal cost, 1/2. Consumers and the incumbent producer are uncertain about the potential entrant's marginal cost but they know that the range is [0, 1].

The potential entrant knows its own costs before deciding to enter or not to enter. The a priori pdf is uniform. There is no cost of entry per se. Entry occurs or does not occur in period 2, depending on market conditions and the presence or absence of an exclusive contract between the incumbent and consumers. There is no risk aversion.

Without an exclusive agreement, in period 1, the incumbent monopolist charges price = 1 and exploits consumer surplus fully, earning profit, 1/2. In period 2, if the entrant's cost is less than 1/2 it enters and charges price just a tad below the incumbent's marginal cost, 1/2. If the entrant's marginal cost exceeds 1/2, there is no entry and the incumbent charges 1, with profit equal to 1/2. Thus, half the time there is entry and the expected second-period surpluses for consumers, incumbent and entrant are, respectively, 1/2×1/2, 1/2×1/2 and 1/2×1/4, or 8/32, 8/32 and 4/32.

The equilibrium contract of exclusion (see Aghion and Bolton 1987 for proof) calls for consumers either to buy from the incumbent or, instead, to buy from the entrant and pay the incumbent what the incumbent would have gained had it sold the product in the absence of entry, 1/2. To induce consumers to agree to the exclusive contract the incumbent contracts to sell at 3/4 in the second period. Thus, a consumer who buys from the entrant gives up surplus 1/4 because it could have bought from the incumbent at price 3/4 and, thus, the entrant must charge the consumer a price at most equal to 1/4 because the consumer must also pay 1/2 to the incumbent according to the contract when it buys from the entrant. In order for the entrant to make any money selling at 1/4, its cost must be less than 1/4. The probability of entry then is 1/4 and, on average, given entry, it makes 1/4−1/8=1/8.

Consumers receive expected value 1/4: this is required since, otherwise, they would be worse off with than without the exclusive deal and would reject it.[28] The incumbent receives 1/4 without entry and 1/2 with entry. The entrant receives 0 without entry and 1/8 with entry. The probability of entry is 1/4. Thus, consumers' expected surplus is 8/32, the incumbent's is 10/32, and the entrant's is 1/32.

Comparing these payoffs to those without exclusive dealing, it is clear that consumers are no worse off and the incumbent is better off with the exclusive dealing contract, earning an additional 2/32. The entrant is worse off by 3/32. Losses exceed gains; thus exclusive dealing here is anticompetitive based on the total-welfare standard but competitively neutral based on the consumer-welfare standard.

The authors observe that entry is less likely—i.e., deterred—and total welfare is lower when exclusive contracts are allowed.[29] In effect, the incumbent has used the contract with the liquidation clause as a commitment device, based on presumed costless, third-party enforcement.[30] A simple exchange of promises—for consumers to pay the incumbent if they buy from the entrant and for the incumbent to charge price 3/32 when entry does not occur—would not be credible.

What if there were full vertical integration instead of the contract just described? Though integration is unrealistic in this case in the first instance, even, if possible, the incumbent and consumers combined would be unable to commit credibly. When integrated, the liquidated damages contract would be equivalent to mutual promises within the same person. Thus, here is an example in which vertical integration gives the monopolist incentives to act against self-interest by eliminating a commitment mechanism.

It is not uncommon for actors to gain ex ante from agreeing to restrict their conduct ex post and, in the absence of renegotiation, such agreements may credibly deter rivals' conduct by rendering it unprofitable given the commitment. The role of commitment is discussed briefly in Section 19.6.3 below.

## 19.6.2  Contracting Externalities and Leveraging Market Power

Bernheim and Whinston (B-W) (1986, 1998) define a simple model of exclusive versus common agency involving two upstream manufacturers selling differentiated products to a single downstream retailer. They demonstrate that when the manufacturers are able to use nonlinear contracts the competitive equilibrium yields the fully integrated joint profit and, while some solutions entail exclusive supply, no exclusive dealing contract (EDC) is needed to reach this outcome.[31] In their model there are no contracting externalities—at least, initially.

The authors then introduce contracting externalities: in the one case, there is a noncoincident retail market to be developed in the future in which that market's retailer is not party to the contracting in period 1; and, in the other case, retail prices are unobservable, thus introducing moral hazard, which cannot be disciplined without cost because the retailer is assumed to be risk averse. That is, a high-powered contract is necessary for proper incentives, which contract in turn has an adverse effect on expected utility for risk-averse individuals. The resulting pricing externalities make exclusive contracts, which require enforcement, second best under some conditions. In the moral-hazard case, for example, vertical integration would remove the contracting externality caused by nonverifiable retail prices.[32]

# 19.7  VARIOUS ROLES OF COMMITMENT IN VERTICAL MERGER

## 19.7.1  Digression on Commitment

Commitment is a means of assuring specific conditional future conduct when the decision maker at present anticipates that at a future time or in the event of a cognizable contingency, different actions will be preferred. Thus, in the case of intertemporal optimization, with special discounting functions, a decision maker may find himself chronically choosing new control paths that are inconsistent with the paths chosen earlier. Alternatively, in leadership games, when followers have rational expectations about the controls chosen by the leader, time inconsistency may also arise (Kydland and Prescott

1977; Petit 1990; Dockner et al. 2000; and Maskin and Tirole 1987, 1988a, 1988b). In these situations, rational decision makers will either seek different, more flexible, and farsighted strategies, or avail themselves of commitment mechanisms. A commitment device may bind the decision maker in the event of time inconsistency.

Commitment is necessary when conduct threatened in response to specific irreversible actions of a rival or rivals would not maximize expected long-run profit were the rival(s) to ignore the threat. The general principle is that it can be in a firm's interest to reduce its own freedom of choice in the future. Thus, for example, individuals may remove their own temptations to renege on a promise or to forgive others' transgressions. As in the Aghion-Bolton discussion above, one means of committing to future conduct that is not in the decision maker's self-interest at the future date is to sign a contract to be enforced by a third party, which would require the incumbent to pay a fine to the contracting party if it reneged on its promise.

## 19.7.2  Raising Rivals' Costs (II)

Ordover, Saloner, and Salop (OSS) (1990) purport to demonstrate that even with marginal cost pricing in the input market, vertical merger may be used successfully to raise rivals' costs through foreclosure, to the detriment of final consumers and downstream competitors. In their model, before merger, differentiated-product duopolists compete downstream, and upstream duopolists compete a la Bertrand to supply a homogeneous input. Marginal costs up- and downstream are constant. Absent integration, the downstream firms take as given the wholesale price equal to marginal cost, and they choose prices to maximize profit, given the observed price charged by the other. A Nash equilibrium in prices is thus defined.

The authors then explore the effects of vertical merger by one pair of up- and downstream firms. They demonstrate that if the integrated firm successfully commits not to supply the nonintegrated downstream firm, its upstream rival is able to exercise monopoly power in the merchant input market. At a higher price of the input to the nonintegrated firm, this firm's reaction function shifts to higher nonintegrated-firm prices. Both of the new equilibrium final prices rise. The integrated firm is better off, and the nonintegrated input supplier is better off, while the downstream nonintegrated firm suffers losses.

If these were the general implications of vertical merger, the results of the OSS paper would not be in question. However, the foregoing analysis is incomplete. At the post-merger merchant market input price, the sum of up- and downstream profits for the nonintegrated firms may be less than the profit of each pair of firms when both pairs are vertically integrated, which, notably, is equal to each firm's share of industry profit when neither pair is integrated. Under such conditions, the only way for the single merged entity to avoid follow-on integration is to stand ready to satisfy merchant market input demand fully at a threshold price. This latter input price is the critical price that separates profitable follow-on integration from unprofitable follow-on integration.

The assumptions in the OSS model are controversial. In this regard, Reiffen (1992) is credited with demonstrating that the OSS result is unrelated to vertical integration but, instead, is the implication of the authors' assumption about price commitment.[33] Reiffen assumes for illustrative purposes that before vertical integration, with each downstream rival obtaining the input at marginal cost, one downstream firm commits to a higher downstream price. In other words, one of the downstream firms acts like a Stackelberg leader. Thus, one downstream firm sets price in stage one, anticipating its rival's reaction to this price in stage two. In the context of this model (with so-called strategic complements), both prices rise above their no-leadership levels, and both downstream firms' profits increase as well.

Unless the price commitment necessary to achieve the Stackelberg outcome were more feasible in the input market than in the output market, vertical merger is unnecessary to achieve the OSS result. The authors provide no basis for this possibility and, as such, their model is irrelevant as an analysis of vertical integration. That is, the price commitment necessary for the OSS outcome could just as easily be achieved if at all without vertical merger.

## 19.7.3  Impacted Price Information

Hart and Tirole (1990) focus on an input monopolist's inability to exploit fully its potential monopoly profit because wholesale profit flows are not contractible. Specifically, because the terms of contracts with downstream retailers are unobservable and non-verifiable (by assumption), the upstream monopolist is unable to commit to contracts that would maximize joint value. In this context, vertical merger facilitates the required commitment.[34]

In the simplest version of their model, a monopolist supplies one of two or both retailers. There is constant marginal cost at each stage. The retailers contract for a quantity and a transfer to the monopolist, and the downstream market clears: that is, $Q_1 + Q_2 = p^d(Q)$. Ideally, the monopolist would offer one retailer a contract that would entail input supply equal to the integrated monopoly output (assuming an input-output ratio of unity) sold at marginal cost in return for all of the downstream rent, and zero supply to the second retailer. Alternatively, the monopolist might supply both retailers half the monopoly output in return for half the monopoly rent from each. As the authors observe, these contracts are not credible, because once a retailer has accepted the monopolist's offer, the monopolist could earn more profit by agreeing to sell the other retailer a quantity that would lower industry profits below the monopoly level.

Under these circumstances, the equilibrium contracts are those that the retailer would fully anticipate. For example, if the monopolist were to offer the first retailer $Q_0$ at marginal cost the retailer would correctly anticipate that the second retailer would be offered the quantity that would maximize the monopolist's profit and that the rent it could afford to pay would be $\left(Q_0/Q^*\right)\left[p^d(Q_0+Q^*)-c\right](Q_0+Q^*)$, where $Q^*$ maximizes

$\left[ p^d(Q_0 + Q) - c \right] Q$. Subject to these expectations the monopolist would maximize profit by choosing the Cournot equilibrium market output.[35]

Thus, in order to realize monopoly profit the input monopolist needs a way of committing to supply the monopoly output, $Q_M$. One way for the monopolist to do this is to integrate. Whatever its internal supply, $Q_I$, it will not impose losses on itself by selling more than $Q_M - Q_I$ to the other retailer. Of course, with the cost conditions presumed, the monopolist can fully exploit its market power by integrating with only one retailer and producing and selling everything through the one outlet.[36]

## 19.7.4 Intertemporal Opportunism

The inability to make commitments is present in the famous durable goods monopoly problem introduced by Coase (1972). In his model there is a rental demand for a durable good, which is produced by a monopolist. The value of the durable is the present value of its service rentals, given a stock of durables and a stationary rental demand. (It is easiest for illustrative purposes to imagine the durable good being infinitely durable.) But, the magnitude of the outstanding stock of durables is under the control of the monopolist, subject to the demand for additions to this stock. As a consequence, a buyer will value the durable or durables it has purchased on the basis of the discounted future demand prices, which depend on the predicted path of the stock of the durable.

If a buyer paid the present value of $p^d(Q_0)$ for the durable he would be harmed were the stock subsequently increased to $Q_1$. At the same time, the monopolist would profit ex ante from selling the monopoly stock (marginal rental revenue equals marginal period cost), but would profit even more if once this level of stock were sold to buyers, the monopolist could sell additional units of the durable. In fact, if consumers did not correctly anticipate this opportunistic conduct, the monopolist would practice so-called "intertemporal price discrimination," walking buyers down their demand price functions selling incrementally more and more until the stock outstanding made $p^d(Q^*)$ = $mc$. With this practice, the inframarginal buyers will have paid more than the final marginal-cost price. In this way it appears that the monopolist would capture most of the consumer surplus under the demand curve and above marginal cost.

Of course, to describe intertemporal price discrimination in this way is to prove that consumers would refuse to purchase at any price above marginal cost. Thus, unless the monopolist were able to commit to his initial buyers that only the initial period monopoly output would be sold, his monopoly would be worth zero. Doubtless the reader will think of several alternative means of effecting this commitment—for example, leasing the durable. The one of interest here is vertical integration. The monopolist as owner of the outstanding stock would be expected to protect the value of his capital. That is, the vertically integrated durable goods monopolist would not cheat itself (see Comanor and Rey 2004).

# 19.8 CONCLUSION

In this chapter we address the principal issues associated with vertical merger from an antitrust perspective—that of evaluating its competitive effects. In this regard, we concern ourselves with the profitability and the welfare effects of vertical merger between one or more firms in an input market and one or more firms in an output market. In most instances, competitive effects are addressed in the context of market power and, in many of these instances, there is a single input supplier with market power—a "monopolist." Two principal bases for vertical merger are recognized: (1) resolving pricing externalities resulting from contracting costs—i.e., transaction costs—and (2) engaging in monopolization to extend market power or to protect extant market power.

Our principal conclusion is that vertical merger rarely is anticompetitive, but it often harms competitors. Virtually all economists acknowledge that distinguishing anticompetitive conduct from aggressive competitive behavior is difficult. But as Reiffen and Vita (1995) observe so astutely, procompetitive effects of vertical merger are most likely when premerger market power is significant. In fact, there is very little economic theory that does not conclude by noting that a priori vertical merger is more likely to promote than harm competition. These difficulties notwithstanding, antitrust enforcers are suspicious of single-firm conduct by dominant firms, and evidence of foreclosure has often been cited to justify agency or judicial sanction. These views have widespread currency even though simple economic theory demonstrates that foreclosure of competitors often increases consumer welfare. Most recently, however, the EU has applied merger simulation analyses of some vertical mergers that only a decade ago would have been condemned a priori based on concerns about vertical foreclosure. By insisting on pre- and postmerger simulations, the expected cost of types I and II errors may thus be minimized subject to a reasonable evidentiary burden.

## NOTES

1. In preparing the present economic analysis of vertical merger, we have benefitted immensely from Jeffrey Church's survey for the European Commission (2004).
2. The limits of internal organization are explicitly recognized in several theories of the firm (for an overview see Gibbons 2005). According to the "property rights" theory of the firm (Grossman and Hart 1986), contracts are incomplete and specific investments are noncontractible ex ante. Asset ownership affects each party's share of surplus which, in turn, influences ex ante investment incentives. Under such circumstances, joint profit maximization may require that one party own all of the assets—that is, the activities would be organized within the firm with one party, the residual claimant, directing efforts. In the "incentive system" theory of the firm (Holmstrom and Tirole 1989), the focus is on the incentive problems of principal and agent, which are ignored by the property rights theory. Optimal contracts reflect the realities of asset ownership and agent incentives. "If

the incentives from asset ownership hurt the principal's efforts to create incentives via contract, then the principal should own the asset (i.e., integration is efficient)" (Gibbons 2005, 10). Third, in the so-called "adaptation" theory of the firm (Simon 1951; Williamson 1971, 1975; Klein and Murphy 1988, 1997; and Klein 1996, 2000), decisions affecting the joint value of assets must be made after uncertainty is resolved, assuming the infeasibility of ex ante contracting and efficient ex post negotiation. Under these circumstances it is sometimes second best to endow one party with control ("within firm" decisions) who, as "boss," will make self-interested decisions when uncertainty is resolved instead of decentralizing authority ("between firm" decisions). This adaptation theory has been expanded by Klein (interfirm relational adaptation) to include self-enforcing agreements or implicit contracts (Klein and Murphy 1988; and Klein 1996). In the "rent-seeking" theory of the firm, asset specificity causes hold-up problems after investments are made, which can be avoided by bringing the transactions inside the firm. The rent-seeking theory originates with Tullock (see chap. 6 in Congleton et al. 2008) and has been studied thoroughly by many authors since (please see Congleton et al. 2008). The rent-seeking theory of the firm specifically is attributed to Williamson (1971, 1979, 1985) and Klein et al. (1978). Firm transactions are more likely than market transactions when asset specificity and accompanying "appropriable quasi-rents" are present.

3. For an expanded coverage of these motivations, see Carlton (1978).

4. Problems of monitoring contracted conduct remain: the upstream firm may gain ex post from the contract if it cheats and transfers output at somewhat more than marginal cost. According to some economists the incompatibility of divisional incentives may remain even after vertical integration. For example, Alchian and Demsetz (1972, 777) observe that: "It is common to see the firm characterized by the power to settle disputes by fiat, by authority, or by disciplinary actions superior to that available in the conventional market. This is a delusion. The firm does not own all its inputs. It has no power of fiat, no authority, no disciplinary action any different in the slightest degree from ordinary market contracting between any two people."

5. This discrepancy may only be apparent. The EU provides substantially more information about its decision making than do the US agencies. Below, several recent cases from both sides of the Atlantic are reviewed.

6. This result in counterintuitive; one expects that if downstream producers shift away from the monopolized input as its price without vertical integration is raised above marginal cost, the monopolist would see a more elastic demand than in the case of fixed proportions and thus arrest the price increase at a level lower than that with fixed proportions. Thus, intuitively, the constant marginal cost function of the downstream producers should rise less as well, which would result in a lower final output price. And, indeed, Westfield proves that when familiar production functions apply, vertical merger usually reduces consumer welfare which, by the way, was not the standard welfare criterion for merger at the time. A reprise of the results of vertical merger with variable proportions subject to today's consumer welfare standard might revivify vertical merger enforcement.

7. Also see Scheffman and Higgins (2003, 2004).

8. See *Conwood Co. v. U.S. Tobacco Co.*, 290 F.3d 768, 778 (6th Cir. 1990) and discussion in Scheffman and Higgins (2003).

9. Obviously, if the input monopolist were able to purchase substantial downstream capacity it would thereby acquire market power in the downstream market whether or not the acquisition raised its market power beyond that possessed already in the input market.

10. It is demonstrated, in the context of the linear-quadratic model, that information about the magnitude of final demand elasticity at the competitive price without merger along with the share of downstream capacity to be acquired is sufficient to predict the competitive effects of merger. Thus, simulation of the market effects of vertical merger is unnecessary. Also, remarkably, integration may completely foreclose downstream rivals from access to the monopolized input while, at the same time, lowering final output price.

11. Details on the cases mentioned above can be found at: *United States v. Enova Corp.*, 107 F. Supp 2d 10 (DDC 2000); Patrick M. Reilly and John R. Wilke, FTC Staff to Fight Barnes & Noble Bid for Wholesaler, Wall Street Journal, June 1, 1999, at B16; Press Release: Federal Trade Commission Approves AOL/Time Warner Merger with Conditions (December 14, 2000); United States v. Premdor, Competitive Impact Statement, Civ. Action No. 1:01CV01696 (D.D.C. filed August 3, 2001); Press Release, Federal Trade Commission Seeks to Block Cytyc Corporation's acquisition of Digene Corporation, FTC File No. 021–0098 (June 24, 2002); Press Release, Federal Trade Commission Votes to Close Investigation of Acquisition of Avant! Corporation by Synopsys, Inc, FTC File No. 021–0049 (July 26, 2002). Also, see News Release, December 20, 2007: Federal Trade Commission Closes Google/DoubleClick Investigation; Proposed Acquisition "Unlikely to Substantially Lessen Competition."

12. Were it not for the Commission's recent infatuation with conduct remedies the Google/DoubleClick deal would surely have been challenged.

13. *U.S. v. Enova Corporation*, "Competitive Impact Statement," U.S. District Court of the District of Columbia, 1998. http://www.justice.gov/atr/cases/indx47.htm.

14. In *Google/DoubleClick*, the Antitrust Division challenged the merger on the basis of concerns about vertical foreclosure and, unlike in the EU investigations described below, there was no apparent thorough RRC analysis (however, see note 5 supra). See News Release, December 20, 2007: Federal Trade Commission Closes *Google/DoubleClick* Investigation; Proposed Acquisition "Unlikely to Substantially Lessen Competition." Novel conduct remedies imposing nondiscriminatory behavior and quotas on R&D spending may have substituted for econometric analysis.

15. The Commission applied a model of downstream differentiated products and, most likely, one with homogeneous products upstream. Assuming differentiated downstream products is analogous in effect to assuming capacity limitations and rising marginal cost with homogeneous products. In each instance, there is a cost of foreclosure: that is, in both cases there is extant sunk-cost capital available that yields income when utilized. Thus, as in the two instances described, in general the theoretical effects of vertical merger are ambiguous. See TomTom/Teleatlas-Case COMP/M.4854 (2008) at http://ec.europa.eu/competition/mergers/cases/decisions/m4854_20080514_20682_en.pdf, and see Frot (2011).

16. While substantially less extensively and intensively reported, the Commission concluded that the acquisition would not increase price transparency beyond that which was present when both NAVTEQ and Teleatlas were vertically separated.

17. Prior to the most recent round of horizontal merger guidelines the "smallest market principle" applied (Werden 2003). The hypothetical monopolist test was first applied, and if a related market were not necessary to include in order to generate a "small yet significant nontransitory increase in price" (a "SSNIP"), it was considered to be in a separate, though related antitrust market. The proposed new guidelines have abandoned the smallest market principle. Prior to that, such related markets were included in antitrust analysis as "semi-horizontal" markets (see Werden 1982).

18. Readers are probably more familiar with incentive effects in antitrust cases involving joint ventures. Often, in the case of joint ventures, control is granted to one of the parties to the joint venture or, alternatively, the control is invested in the JV itself. When one or more of the JV partners continue to compete with the joint venture, the JV does not necessarily increase the partners' control over output but, instead, presents the partners with a different profit objective. Specifically, the profit function of each partner combines the partner's separate profit function and some share of the JV's profit function. Since the latter is affected by the output chosen by the non–JV firm, the JV partner with separate competing assets will consider how its output decision affects its own profit as well as its share of the profit created by diverting sales to the JV. As in the case of diagonal merger or diagonal ownership, the incentives of the joint venture partner to restrict output is enhanced, at least, directionally (Bresnahan and Salop 1986).

19. Carlton's and Waldman's (2002) dynamic model of tying is proffered as an explanation for monopolization in the second sense; tying to protect market power in the tying-good market is not addressed here.

20. See Kaserman and Mayo (1993).

21. In contrast, if vertical integration were permitted, the upstream monopolist would have incentives to deny downstream rivals access to the bottleneck facilities even if downstream competition potentially were perfect. Raising the cost of its downstream rivals enables the integrated natural monopolist to exploit the upstream market power it would enjoy absent access regulation through pricing in the unregulated downstream market. That is, vertical integration may provide a means for the natural monopolist to avoid price regulation. Also, when access price regulation is constraining, the natural monopolist has incentives to discriminate against its downstream rivals using nonprice instruments to prevent equal access. There is a long history of economic analysis of such situations (e.g., see discussion of the Efficient Components Pricing Rule; Baumol 1983; and Willig et al. 1997).

22. The strategic use of tying described by Whinston (1990) and by Carlton and Waldman (2002) is not addressed in this paper.

23. *International Business Machines Corporation v. United States*, 298 U.S. 131 (1936) or *International Salt Company v. United States*, 332 U.S. 392 (1947). Also see Peterman (1979) and Cummings and Ruhter (1979) for discussions of the cases.

24. When products are related the concept of the surplus under a single product demand is ambiguous since each demand curve depends on the price of the other related product. Line integrals are required to express consumer surplus accurately.

25. An offer of the tying good at less than the stand-alone monopoly price along with the tied good requirements at a price above marginal cost is equivalent to an offer of a discounted bundle. For example, if the stand-alone monopoly price of the tying good is 50 with demand $Q^d = 100 - P$ and the perfectly competitive price of the tied good is 20, with demand $q^d = 1000 - p$, a bundle in which the tying good is sold for 15 and the tied good for 22 will cause consumers to elect the tie because their gain in tying good consumer surplus, 2362.5, outweighs their loss of tied good surplus, 1958. The monopolist loses 1750 of tying-good profit and gains 1956 of tied-good profit. The price of the tied good has been effectively reduced by 2362.5/978 = 2.4, not increased by 2. See Nalebuff (2003).

26. In their paper on "quantity forcing," Schwartz and Vincent (2008) maintain that full requirements contracts or "tie outs" are likely to be less effective than use of nonlinear pricing. They further maintain that a special form of nonlinear pricing in which the monopolist demands a fixed fee for a very small purchase from it of the tied good—a

"minimal tie-in"—is more efficient (i.e., is accompanied by less deadweight loss) than a tie-out. Generally, they are skeptical that tying agreements are used for so-called rent extraction, but see Higgins (2012).

27. Farrell (2005) insightfully explains that whether or not a consumer who accepts an exclusive dealing contract is better off depends on the value of his alternative—that is, on the relevant welfare benchmark.

28. Thus, Bork's (1978) and Posner's (1976) contention that consumers will not accept an exclusive dealing contract unless they are compensated is satisfied and, still, exclusive dealing is profitable and anticompetitive. Moreover, Rasmusen et al. (1991) demonstrate that when consumers are unable to coordinate their responses to the input monopolist's exclusive dealing contract, the monopolist will often be able to avoid even this cost of exclusive dealing.

29. One might take issue with this outcome, since there is nothing to prevent the incumbent from buying from the entrant whenever the entrant can supply it at less than marginal cost, 1/2. Thus, the entrant would come in whenever its marginal cost is less than ½, just as in the case without an exclusive contract. In this case, the expected total surplus is the same with or without an exclusive contract.

30. Critical to the foreclosure outcome is the presumption that the entrant cannot contract with the customers (see Innes and Sexton 1994). When all players are party to the contract ex ante, only inefficient entry is deterred.

31. That is, the sum of profit for the retailer and the two manufacturers combined is maximized, even when one of the manufacturers earns zero profit. A similar model is analyzed by O'Brien and Shaffer (1997). They demonstrate that nonlinear pricing can be used to support two-product and one-product equilibrium outcomes, without exclusive dealing contracts. These competitive equilibrium outcomes maximize vertically integrated profit (for the two upstream manufacturers and the single downstream retailer).

32. The original analysis of exclusive dealing by Mathewson and Winter (1987) differs from that of B-W. In the M-W model the upstream firms facing downward-sloping demands do not contract with the downstream retailer efficiently; instead, only linear pricing is addressed, which creates pricing externalities that, in turn, create a demand for exclusive dealing even absent noncoincident markets. Similarly, Salinger (1991) presents a model of vertical merger in which before merger two differentiated product manufacturers produce upstream for sale to a single downstream monopolist. He shows that when the monopolist merges with one of the upstream manufacturers, "The net impact on prices depends in a complicated manner on the demand system, i.e., all own and cross price elasticities of demand, marginal costs, and the level of double marginalization pre-merger for the integrated good" (Church 2004, 104). In both the M-W and the Salinger models, the downstream, integrated monopolist carries both upstream products.

33. Reiffen also notes up front that the OSS model applies to a very special case in which upstream marginal cost pricing is abandoned with just a single firm foreclosing input supply to the nonintegrated downstream firm, which would be impossible with more than two upstream Bertrand rivals prior to merger.

34. These same results are demonstrated in O'Brien and Shaffer (1992). They demonstrate that nonlinear pricing alone will not support the full vertically integrated outcome when rival retailers are unable to observe the wholesale contracts offered them by a single manufacturer. Vertical restraints, such as minimum resale price maintenance, together with nonlinear pricing will support the fully integrated equilibrium at higher prices than

possible without the vertical restraints. Vertical merger provides another means by which the manufacturer can credibly commit not to supply more than the vertically integrated output. Thus, vertical merger reduces consumer welfare under these circumstances and, presumably, would be enjoined by public antitrust enforcement.

35. Even with $N$ retailers, each retailer would anticipate $Q_T = \left[ N/(N+1) \right](a-c)/-b$, when demand price is $p^d = a + b\,Q$.

36. When there are $N$ retailers downstream, vertical integration with only one retailer is not sufficient to guarantee that the integrated firm would not exercise ex post opportunistic behavior towards the others when selling to multiple retailers. Of course, as indicated, the monopolist need not sell through any but its internal downstream affiliate.

# REFERENCES

Aghion, P., and P. Bolton. 1987. "Contracts as a Barrier to Entry." *American Economic Review* 77:388–401.

Alchian, A. A., and H. Demsetz. 1972. "Production, Information Costs, and Economic Organization." *American Economic Review* 62:777–95.

Baumol, W. 1983. "Some Subtle Pricing Issues in Railroad Regulation." *International Journal of Transport Economics* 10:341–55.

Bernheim, D., and M. Whinston. 1986. "Common Agency." *Econometrica* 54:923–42.

——. 1998. "Exclusive Dealing." *Journal of Political Economy* 106:64–103.

Blair, R. and D. L. Kaserman. 1978. "Vertical Integration, Tying, and Antitrust Policy." *American Economic Review* 68:397–402.

Bork, R. 1978. *The Antitrust Paradox*. New York: Basic Books.

Bresnahan, Timothy F. and Stephen C. Salop. 1986. "Quantifying the Competitive Effects of Production Join Ventures." *International Journal of Industrial Organization* 4:155–75.

Burstein, M. L. 1960. "The Economics of Tie-In Sales." *The Review of Economics and Statistics* 42:68–73.

Carlton, Dennis. 1978. "Vertical Integration: An Overview." Prepared for Communications Subcommittee of the Committee on Interstate and Foreign Commerce, US House of Representatives Hearings on H.R. 13015, August 3. http://faculty.chicagobooth.edu/dennis.carlton/more/Vertical%20Integration%20an%20Overview.pdf.

Carlton, Dennis, and Jeffrey M. Perloff. 2005. *Modern Industrial Organization,* 4th ed. Boston: Pearson/Addison Wesley.

Carlton, Dennis, and Michael Waldman. 2002. "The Strategic Use of Tying to Preserve and Create Market Power in Evolving Industries." *Rand Journal of Economics* 33:194–220.

Church, Jeffrey R. 2004. *The Impact of Vertical and Conglomerate Mergers on Competition*. Brussels: European Commission. Accessed on December 22, 2012. http://ec.europa.eu/competition/mergers/studies_reports/merger_impact.pdf.

Coase, R. 1972. "Durable Goods Monopolists." *Journal of Law and Economics* 15:143–50.

Comanor, W., and P. Rey. 2004. "Vertical Mergers and Market Foreclosure." *Research in Law and Economics* 21:445–58.

Congleton, R. D., A. L. Hillman, and K.A. Konrad, eds. 2008. *40 Years of Research on Rent Seeking*. Berlin: Springer-Verlag.

Cummings, F. Jay, and Wayne E. Ruhter. 1979. "The Northern Pacific Case." *Journal of Law and Economics* 22:329–50.

Director, A. and E. Levi. 1957. "Law and the Future: Trade Regulation." *Northwestern University Law Review* 51:281–90.

Dockner, E., S. Jorgensen, N. van Long, and G. Sorger. 2000. *Differential Games in Economics and Management Science.* Cambridge, UK: Cambridge University Press.

Farrell, Joseph. 2005. "Deconstructing Chicago on Exclusive Dealing." *Antitrust Bulletin* 50:465–76.

Frot, E. 2011. "The Empirics of Vertical Integration and Foreclosure." *Concurrences* 2:33–39.

Gaudet, O., and N. Y. Long. 1993. "Vertical Integration, Foreclosure and Profits in the Presence of Double Marginalization." Working Paper, Departement de Sciences Economiques de l'Université du Québec a Montréal.

Gibbons, R. 2005. "Four Formal(izable) Theories of the Firm?" *Journal of Economic Behavior and Organization* 58:200–245.

Grossman, S., and O. Hart. 1986. "The Costs and Benefits of Ownership: A Theory of Vertical and Lateral Integration." *Journal of Political Economy* 94:691–719.

Hart, O., and J. Tirole. 1990. "Vertical Integration and Market Foreclosure." *Brookings Papers on Economic Activity* 1990:205–86.

Higgins, Richard S. 1997. "Diagonal Merger." *Review of Industrial Organization* 12:607–23.

——. 1999. "Competitive Vertical Foreclosure." *Managerial and Decision Economics* 20:229–37.

——. 2009. "Vertical Merger: Monopolization for Downstream Quasi-rents." *Managerial and Decision Economics* 30:183–91.

——. 2013 (Forthcoming). "Tying to Mitigate Deadweight Loss." In *The FTC at Thirty*, Volume in Honor of James C. Miller III. Oxford, UK: Oxford University Press.

Higgins, Richard S., and Arijit Mukherjee. 2010. "Deregulation Redux: Does Mandating Access to Bottleneck Facilities Necessarily Improve Welfare?" *Public Choice* 142:363–77.

Holmstrom, B. R, and J. Tirole. 1989. "The Theory of the Firm." In *Handbook of Industrial Organization,* edited by R. Schmalensee and R. Willig, 61–133. Amsterdam: North-Holland.

Innes, Robert, and Richard J. Sexton. 1994. "Strategic Buyers and Exclusionary Contracts." *American Economic Review* 84:566–84.

Kaserman, D., and J. Mayo. 1993. "Monopoly Leveraging Theory: Implications for Post-Divestiture Telecommunications Policy." Center for Business and Economic Research, The University of Tennessee.

Klein, Benjamin. 1996. "Why Hold-ups Occur: The Self-Enforcing Range of Contractual Relationships." *Economic Inquiry* 34:444–63.

——. 2000. "The Role of Incomplete Contracts in Self-Enforcing Relationships." *Revue D'Economie Industrielle* 92:67–80.

Klein, Benjamin, Robert A. Crawford, and Armen A. Alchian. 1978. "Vertical Integration, Appropriable Rents and the Competitive Contracting Process." *Journal of Law and Economics* 21:297–326.

Klein, Benjamin, and Kevin M. Murphy. 1988. "Vertical Restraints as Contract Enforcement Mechanisms." *Journal of Law and Economics* 31:265–97.

——. 1997. "Vertical Integration as a Self-Enforcing Contractual Arrangement." *American Economic Review* 87:415–20.

Kydland, F. E., and E. C. Prescott. 1977. "Rules Rather Than Discretion: The Inconsistency of Optimal Paths." *Journal of the Political Economy* 85:473–91.

Maskin, E., and J. Tirole. 1987. "A Theory of Dynamic Oligopoly, III." *European Economic Review* 31:947–68.

——. 1988a. "A Theory of Dynamic Oligopoly, I." *Econometrica* 56:549–69.

——. 1988b. "A Theory of Dynamic Oligopoly, II." *Econometrica* 56:571–99.

Mathewson, F., and R. Winter. 1987. "The Competitive Effects of Vertical Agreements: Comment." *American Economic Review* 77:1057–62.

Nalebuff, B. J. 2003. "Bundling, Tying, and Portfolio Effects, Part 1: Conceptual Issues." Department of Trade and Industry, UK, Economics Paper 1.

——. 2005. "Exclusionary Bundling." *The Antitrust Bulletin* 50:321–70.

O'Brien, Daniel P. and Greg Shaffer. 1992. "Vertical Control with Bilateral Contracts." *Rand Journal of Economics* 23:299–308.

——. 1997. "Nonlinear Supply Contracts, Exclusive Dealing, and Equilibrium Market Foreclosure." *Journal of Economics and Management Strategy* 6:755–85.

Ordover, J. A., G. Saloner, and S. C. Salop. 1990. "Equilibrium Vertical Foreclosure." *American Economic Review* 80:127–42.

Peterman, J. L. 1979. "The International Salt Case." *Journal of Law and Economic* 22:351–64.

Petit, M. L. 1990. *Control Theory and Dynamic Games in Economic Policy Analysis.* Cambridge, UK: Cambridge University Press.

Posner, R. 1976. *Antitrust Law: An Economic Perspective.* Chicago: University of Chicago Press.

Rasmusen, Eric B., J. Mark Ramseyer, and John Shepherd Wiley, Jr. 1991. "Naked Exclusion." *American Economic Review* 81:1137–45.

Reiffen, D. 1992. "Equilibrium Vertical Foreclosure: Comment." *American Economic Review* 82:694–97.

Reiffen, D., and M. Vita. 1995. "Comment: Is There New Thinking on Vertical Mergers?" *Antitrust Law Journal* 63:917–41.

Rubin, Paul H. 1990. *Managing Business Transactions.* New York: Free Press.

Salinger, M. 1988. "Vertical Mergers and Market Foreclosure." *Quarterly Journal of Economics* 103:345–56.

——. 1991. "Vertical Mergers in Multi-product Industries and Edgeworth's Paradox of Taxation." *Journal of Industrial Economics* 39:545–56.

Salop, S. and D. Scheffman. 1983. "Raising Rivals' Costs." *American Economic Review* 73:267–71.

Scheffman, David T., and Richard S. Higgins. 2003. "Twenty Years of Raising Rivals' Costs: History, Assessment, and Future." *George Mason Law Review* 12 (2): 371–87.

——. 2004. "Vertical Mergers: Theory and Policy." *George Mason Law Review* 12 (4): 967–77.

Schwartz, Marius, and Daniel R. Vincent. 2008. "Quantity 'Forcing' and Exclusion: Bundled Discounts and Non-Linear Pricing." In *Issues in Competition Law and Policy,* edited by Wayne D. Collins and Joseph Angland, 2:939–76. Chicago: American Bar Association.

Simon, Herbert. 1951. "A Formal Theory of the Employment Relationship." *Econometrica* 19:293–305.

Spengler, J. J. 1950. "Vertical Integration and Antitrust Policy." *Journal of Political Economy* 58:347–52.

Vernon, John M., and Daniel A. Graham. 1971. "Profitability of Monopolization by Vertical Integration." *Journal of Political Economy* 79:924–25.

Warren-Boulton, Frederick R. 1974. "Vertical Control with Variable Proportions." *Journal of Political Economy* 82:783–802.

Werden, Gregory J. 1982. "Section 7 of the Clayton Act and the Analysis of 'Semihorizontal' Mergers." *Antitrust Bulletin* 27:135–60.

——. 2003. "The 1982 Merger Guidelines and the Ascent of the Hypothetical Monopolist Paradigm." *Antitrust Law Review* 71:253–69.

Westfield, Fred M. 1981. "Vertical Integration: Does Product Price Rise of Fall?" *American Economic Review* 7:334–46.

Whinston, M. 1990. "Tying, Foreclosure, and Exclusion." *American Economic Review* 80:837–59.

Williamson, O. 1971. "The Vertical Integration of Production: Market Failure Considerations." *American Economic Review* 61:112–23.

——. 1975. *Markets and Hierarchies: Analysis and Antitrust Implications*. New York: Free Press.

Willig, R., W. J. Baumol, and J. A. Ordover. 1997. "Parity Pricing and its Critics: A Necessary Condition for Efficiency in Provision of Bottleneck Services to Competitors." *Yale Journal on Regulation* 14:145–64.

# CHAPTER 20

# THE EVOLVING MODERN THEORY OF THE FIRM[1]

## ROBERT MANESS AND STEVEN N. WIGGINS

## 20.1 INTRODUCTION

BUSINESS firms are used widely to allocate resources in market economies. The allocation methods used within firms, moreover, differ substantially from those used in markets. These differences include the fact that allocation within firms is not governed by arm's-length market prices, there is common ownership of assets, the incentive structures within firms differ substantially from those in markets, authority is often used to make and implement decisions, and there is long-term trade between the firm and its workers.[2] The reliance on firm allocation is puzzling given the view that markets are powerful, efficient tools of allocation. The modern theory of the firm addresses the reasons why agents use firms, providing insights into both the costs and benefits of firm allocation as compared to market allocation.

The issue of market versus firm allocation is quite important. Evidence indicates that the total value of allocation decisions made within firms is approximately of the same magnitude as those made in markets (see, e.g., LaFontaine and Slade 2007). Managers also spend enormous sums acquiring and merging with other firms, thereby bringing certain transactions within the boundaries of a single firm. The worldwide volume of such transactions exceeded $1.6 trillion in 1997 (Holmstrom and Roberts 1998). A typical employee works in a firm of substantial size, and those employees repeatedly show up at the same workplace each day over long periods of time. Hart (2011) points out that Wal-Mart had 1.8 million employees in 2007, and that in 2001 a randomly selected employee in the United Kingdom worked in a firm with 935 employees. These employment transactions are clearly influenced by a larger labor market, but there is a substantial long-term commitment, and workers are assigned tasks and evaluated within a hierarchy, and their wages are set bureaucratically. These varied statistics show that the decision to use firm allocation is important, and not captured well in the simple, standard neoclassical model of the firm.

The modern theory of the firm traces its roots to Coase (1937). Coase argued that firms exist because there are circumstances where the transaction costs of using market allocation are high. He posited that in these situations firms are a more efficient way to allocate resources because they reduce transaction costs. The field largely lay fallow until Williamson (1971, 1975) and Klein et al. (1978) began to address the costs of using markets. According to these authors firm allocation is superior to market allocation when there exist substantial transaction-specific sunk investments; that is, investments whose value is rooted in continued trade between two specific parties. Classic examples include a coal mine located next to an electric power plant and the General Motors/Fisher Body joint investments in the construction of automobiles. The quasi-rent streams created by these investments generate the potential for "holdup" as parties haggle over the associated quasi-rent stream. Joint ownership of the assets under firm allocation reduces haggling costs and creates a setting where a single owner will maximize overall value. This "transaction cost theory of the firm" continues to represent a major thread of modern research on the theory of the firm.

Scholars subsequently have built on the foundation laid by these early investigators. The later contributions include both theoretical and empirical research, and have led to a deeper understanding of why firms exist and when firm allocation will be chosen over market allocation.

This essay provides a highly selective evaluation of the evolving modern theory of the firm, focusing on the most prominent theories and empirical work. The essay also focuses primarily on the make-or-buy decision, which considers vertical integration in manufacturing, leaving aside issues of internal organization. We also consider more briefly forward integration into retailing and franchising.

Section 20.2 begins with some key methodological points. Section 20.3 then examines the major theories and discusses their similarities and differences. Section 20.4 reviews and critiques the major empirical work, and Section 20.5 offers some concluding remarks.

## 20.2 THE ANALYTICAL METHODS OF THE THEORY OF THE FIRM

Modern work on the theory of the firm presupposes that transactions, information, coordination and incentives do not change per se because a transaction is brought within a firm (see, also, Grossman and Hart 1986; Hart 1995; Gibbons 2005; and Van den Steen 2010). This methodological starting point appears deceptively to be modest, but in fact is a central feature separating this modern literature from other approaches described below. According to this method, one should conceptualize a set of tasks, the individuals who carry out those tasks, and the information they possess. Integration does not per se change their behavior, the information each has available, or the efficiency of the coordination of their activities. Instead, integration can affect only the efficiency of allocation by influencing the incentives of agents to invest and to share information. Thus, theoretical models of the firm require a detailed specification of exactly how incentives differ in market versus firm organization.

By way of illustration, compare the modern theory of the firm approach with the standard microeconomics textbook model of a firm. That model postulates a "firm" simply as a production function and assumes implicitly that all incentives within the firm are aligned with the residual claimant. Integration changes incentives only with respect to the objective function. Under separate ownership the price effects of output decisions each enter independently into the individual firm's objective function. Under joint ownership, the single firm internalizes the price effects of output decisions on overall profits.

More telling, there is no meaningful distinction between transactions that occur within a firm as compared to a market. If one carefully considers the standard neoclassical theory of the firm, transactions occur as if they were in a market. The example of physical capital perhaps best illustrates this distinction. In the standard theory of the firm profitability is not affected by whether capital is rented or owned. Similarly, workers are indistinguishable from one another, and the theory would be consistent with workers randomly showing up at different firms across various days, weeks, or months.

In fact, however, transactions within firms are quite different from those in markets. The capital used in firms is often highly specialized and firms often own this capital. Williamson (1971, 1975, 1979, 1985) and Klein et al. (1978) pointed out that as capital becomes more specialized its allocation will not be governed by a rental market but instead capital will be owned by the firm. Even labor markets can be influenced by the presence of specialized investments. Workers are often long-term employees presumably because they have firm-specific human capital. These workers and the firm jointly invest in learning, which may be as simple as the economies generated by repetition and experience in performing the same specialized tasks. The implication is that firm allocation differs from market allocation because of the incentive for repeated dealing and long-term trade.

The modern theory of the firm addresses the choice between firm and market allocation by specifying a group of related tasks and evaluating the comparative efficiency of firm and market allocation. A common setup is to specify these tasks as requiring both proper incentives for investment (or effort) and the need for coordination, but where "the market" cannot be used to solve both problems simultaneously. For example, consider separate tasks involving two agents who must invest and then trade with one another. The underlying market imperfection is that after the initial investment, the value the agents can achieve in inside trade with one another exceeds the value that can be achieved in trade with outsiders, creating an incentive for repeated dealing. The value differential associated with inside trade creates a quasi-rent flow that leads to possible misappropriation. The models also typically assume a limitation on the ability to write complete contracts by highlighting that some investment decisions (or effort) are not contractible. Limitations on contractibility can occur either because outsiders cannot observe uncertain outcomes or because of limited court enforcement.

In such an arrangement, market allocation will be inefficient because parties will realize less than the full marginal value of their investments due to possible misappropriation and because they may or may not reveal their private information. The "costs and benefits of integration" then turn on the micro level incentives the agents face that determine both the level of investment and the efficiency of exchange. Closing the model depends on the exact specification of how integration differs from nonintegration. In some theories, firms differ from markets because of differences in incentives for rent seeking over appropriable quasi-rents from specialized assets, in others the differences turn on the right to control specialized assets, and so forth.

This methodology places a premium on identifying the differences in incentives between markets and firms and contrasts sharply with other approaches that do not focus on the specific incentive differences created by firm versus market allocation. The models below focus on specific limitations on incentives and contracting using a setup similar to that described above. Each model builds in a particular imperfection that effectively uses a particular limitation to provide insight into the make-or-buy decision. Before turning attention to that decision, we begin with a brief discussion regarding the unresolved issue of what defines a firm.

## 20.3  THEORIES OF THE FIRM

### 20.3.1  What is a Firm?

The standard definition of a firm used in the modern theory of the firm begins with an underpinning similar to the neoclassical theory of the firm. That is, the defining characteristics of a firm are (1) ownership or control of the physical assets used in production (manufacturing equipment), (2) workers are employees of the firm, and (3) a claim on the residual (revenue net of costs) generated from the sale of output. These theories also build on the neoclassical assumption that the objective of the firm is to combine inputs in a cost-minimizing way and produce the output that maximizes profits.

While the modern theory of the firm shares these numerous underpinnings with the neoclassical model, there are also substantial differences. A key difference regards economies of scale. Demsetz (1997, 2008) has argued that the traditional neoclassical approach based on economies of scale explains why firms exist, and that the more modern approaches are not needed to explain the variety of organizational forms observed in the economy.

He also argues that the basic definition of a firm used in transaction cost models is needlessly arbitrary and that erroneous conclusions have been drawn about the role and nature of firms by focusing on Coase's insight regarding the costs of using the market system (Demsetz 1997, 2008). He states that the operating definition of the firm in modern theory of the firm models is that "the firm is an institution in which the management of some people by others displaces the 'management' of people by the price system" (Demsetz 2008, 127). He argues that the neoclassical definition is simpler and more informative—the firm is an economic institution that specializes in production. Within this framework, economies of scale and the scope of the market define the limits to firm size, not opportunistic behavior or other factors highlighted in the modern theory of the firm.

Demsetz's argument, and the neoclassical model, is simply incomplete. Economies of scale are a technological phenomenon regarding production, not one of governance, and thus technology alone cannot explain why a firm exists. Without the types of arguments advanced above and below, there is no reason a "firm" could not rent extensive capital from third parties, thereby establishing a large plant with extensive capital, realizing all available economies of scale but without owning that capital. Workers, moreover, hypothetically could be combined with the capital not as employees but as contract labor. The transactions involving the rented capital and contract workers would not be a part of a "firm" as we normally think of it.

This hypothetical approach, however, ignores a substantial component of specialized production. Intuition suggests that it would be impractical to rent the specialized capital in a large manufacturing plant and that firms typically buy such assets because rental markets are imperfect. Employees also get better at assigned tasks as they gain experience, and repeatedly work at the same firm. These long-term arrangements are based on the premise that both capital and workers in a firm are specialized and that their value to the firm exceeds their value in the "market." Hence economies of scale may play a role, but they can only be used to explain the existence of a firm only in conjunction with an incentive for repeated dealing. This incentive creates market imperfections, and these imperfections must be specified for economies of scale to translate into an incentive for firm governance.

In contrast to the neoclassical approach, the theories described below carefully specify the market imperfections that both lead to and limit firm allocation. Investigators generally have been quite precise regarding the economic structure of transactions and how production and transactions within a firm differ from those found in the prototypical economic market.

Where the modern theory of the firm differs from the neoclassical approach is to go further and determine how specific features of transactions and the limitations of contract determine whether a given transaction takes place within a single firm or is carried out in two separate firms. For instance, how do informational or other restrictions on the ability to contract affect whether a transaction occurs within the firm or across markets? How does the structure of a transaction alter incentives, and what is the subsequent impact on the surplus generated from a transaction? How is decision-making authority allocated within the firm? These are issues on which neoclassical theory largely is silent and for which economies of scale largely are irrelevant, but which the modern theory of the firm seeks to address.

This silence of the neoclassical model covers a wide range of economic behavior that should be brought within the scope of economic analysis. Examples include such wide-ranging phenomena as all upstream and downstream integration decisions, the well-known phenomenon of entrepreneurial enterprises being separate, and different organizational forms that are used for production and distribution, some of which involve integration and some of which do not. More telling, the standard neoclassical model predicts that workers will randomly move across firms and that there are no economies of repeated dealing, which do not fit the data.

Demsetz's view and the neoclassical model of the firm also ignore observed variation in governance that is observed in modern market economies. Governance within firms differs substantially from the spontaneous order found in markets. Modern theories of the firm recognize that the make-or-buy decision is driven by more than mere technology, and instead that the costliness of information, the inherent incompleteness of contracts, and the need to provide proper incentives and coordination can at times be better carried out within a firm, and at other times through a market. These governance issues are central to understanding why particular institutions are used and these issues are distinct from technological concerns. The various models presented below share the methodology of focusing on the limitations of markets to provide incentives and efficiently carry out exchange.

These methods do not, however, share a common definition of a firm, a goal that remains elusive. Each of the models and approaches described below posits a particular limitation by defining a firm and the limitations of contract and bargaining in a particular way. In transaction cost theory, there is costly bargaining after investment, while in property rights theory, such bargaining is costless. In Van den Steen (2010) a firm incorporates an equilibrium delegation of authority, while in Wiggins (1995) a firm can more credibly commit to extraordinary compensation. There are also numerous other approaches described below and in the literature. Each approach provides insight into the larger problem, but at present one simply cannot nest these models. Still, work continues in this direction and the hope is that a more general model will be developed.

## 20.3.2  Transaction Cost Theories

Our analysis begins by briefly elaborating on the approach of Williamson and Klein et al. regarding transaction costs economics. Williamson (1971, 1975) developed the concept of "relationship specific sunk investments" as assets whose value depends substantially on continued trade between two specific parties (Williamson 1979, 1985; see also Holmstrom and Roberts 1998). The value of these investments deteriorates substantially if trade does not continue between two specific parties, creating appropriable quasi-rents. This deterioration in value creates the possibility of holdup where either party can engage in rent-seeking by threatening to terminate trade. Such rent-seeking is called "holdup." Williamson postulates that joint ownership of these specific investments avoids haggling costs. At its heart this transactions-cost theory is a rent-seeking model where integration is designed to reduce inefficient haggling over appropriable quasi-rents.

Klein et al. (1978) further developed the rent-seeking model. They present the now well-known case of the integration of General Motors and Fisher Body in the 1920s (see also Klein 1988, 2000, 2004). They argue that the desire to avoid costly haggling over appropriable quasi-rents drove General Motors to acquire Fisher Body. More specifically, General Motors bought Fisher Body to curtail costly and inefficient strategic behavior by the Fisher brothers that increased their profits at the expense of General Motors.

The description of the relationship between GM and Fisher Body contained in Klein et al. (1978) has been highly influential as an example of how the potential for holdup problems in the presence of transaction specific assets can lead to vertical integration. By one count, between 1978 and 2000 at least twenty-two papers and many textbooks repeated all or part of the Klein et al. version of the GM-Fisher Body story (Coase 2006). While the story of GM and Fisher Body has frequently been cited as the paradigmatic example of vertical integration to avoid the holdup problems associated with transaction specific assets, the actual facts surrounding GM's relationship with Fisher Body in the 1920s are disputed. The original description of the holdup problem was that Fisher Body, which made auto bodies for GM cars, refused to locate its production facility close to GM's assembly plants to retain the flexibility to sell auto bodies to other manufacturers, and thus avoid potential ex post opportunistic behavior by GM.

Ronald Coase argues that the original description contained in Klein et al. is incorrect, and that even prior to its full acquisition, GM owned a controlling stake (60%) of Fisher Body (Coase 2000, 2006). Coase argues further that the dispute surrounding Fisher Body's refusal to locate its production facility close to GM's assembly plant was resolved amicably and would have been regardless of whether GM acquired the remaining 40% interest in Fisher Body. In a 2007 paper, Klein disputes Coase's reading of history and states that the evidence, including a copy of the original contract between GM and Fisher Body prior to GM's acquisition, supports the original conclusion from his 1978 work with Crawford and Alchian. Regardless of the resolution of a particular dispute, the highly specialized nature of the working relationship between GM and Fisher Body, which involved both physical and human capital, created an incentive for internal organization and that outcome occurred as predicted by transaction cost theory.

The transaction cost/rent-seeking model predicts that when transactions involve substantial transaction specific sunk investments, parties are inclined to organize the associated transactions within a single firm. Integrated asset ownership reduces haggling costs because a single residual claimant has an incentive to maximize overall firm value. A firm's owners can make decisions by fiat, which can be a more efficient way to make decisions than the haggling that would take place in a market.

Williamson (1985) offers an important elaboration of the basic model, citing three elements of transactions that influence organizational form: the level of asset specificity, transaction frequency, and uncertainty. Williamson posits that each of these leads to greater incentives for integration. Asset specificity influences integration because it is associated with increases in appropriable quasi-rents, raising the incentive to haggle. Williamson also argues that frequent transactions increase the incentives to integrate, but that this effect can be ambiguous because frequent transactions increase a future quasi-rent flow, providing greater reputational discipline (Klein and Leffler 1981; Taylor and Wiggins 1997; and Wiggins 1995). Uncertainty increases the incentive to integrate because uncertainty increases contracting costs and the room for haggling.

The theories of integration laid out by Williamson and Klein et al. are key building blocks of the modern theory of the firm. "Transaction costs theory" is limited, however, because it is informal. Despite this limitation, successful empirical tests of transaction cost theory rapidly followed its development (see Monteverde and Teece 1982; Anderson and Schmittlein 1984; Masten 1984; and Joskow 1985, 1988). This empirical work is discussed further below.

A key limitation of transaction cost theory is that it is silent regarding the costs of integration. Subsequent theoretical work following transaction cost theory has focused attention on these costs. The earliest formal model to specifically identify the costs of integration was Grossman and Hart (1986). Following Gibbons (2005) theories of the firm can be usefully divided into four general categories: (1) transaction cost theory (or "rent-seeking") described above; (2) a "property-rights" theory of the firm as originally developed by Grossman and Hart (1986); (3) an "adaptation" theory, as discussed by Simon (1951), Williamson (1975), Wiggins (1990), and Klein and Murphy (1988, 1997); and (4) an "incentive system" theory, as described in Holmstrom and Milgrom (1991), Holmstrom and Tirole (1991), and Wiggins (1995).

## 20.3.3  Property Rights and the Theory of the Firm

The largest branch of work following the transaction cost approach is the property rights theory developed by Grossman and Hart (1986), Hart and Moore (1990) and others.[3] The key contribution of Grossman and Hart was to provide the first model containing a unified treatment of the costs and benefits of integration. The trade-off that Grossman and Hart envision is built into the model by having two tasks, each carried out by a distinct agent who invests in physical capital. The level of investment is noncontractible.

Grossman and Hart use a model where there is costless ex post bargaining and bargained shares are affected by each party's asset ownership share. If one party can make substantial investments to raise value while the other party's efforts have little impact, then ownership should be assigned to the first party. In contrast, when both parties' investments are important, then independent ownership will result in significant investments by both agents, enhancing overall efficiency. This trade-off in the efficiency of investment defines both the costs and benefits of ownership. In the various models cited above by Hart, Grossman, and Moore, asset ownership is the defining influence regarding bargaining outcomes and incentives.

Equally important, and distinct from the transaction cost model, greater asset specificity does not lead to stronger incentives to integrate. The reason is that the benefits of ownership described by Grossman and Hart are driven by marginal incentives to invest ex ante and the returns to those investments rather than ex post haggling. In contrast, the transaction cost literature focuses on ex post haggling over the quasi-rents of sunk investments, which leads to inefficient allocation as the key cost of using market organization. Some have described Grossman and Hart as "formalizing" Williamson and Klein et al. Such is not the case because the empirical implications of the Grossman and Hart approach are quite different from the implications of the transaction cost literature (see, e.g., Whinston 2003).

There are two key contributions of Grossman and Hart, and several distinct limitations. The first contribution is that Grossman and Hart provide the first unified treatment of the costs and benefits of integration. This unified treatment filled a major gap. The second key contribution is the general theoretical approach to such trade-offs. Grossman and Hart posit a model with two investment problems, conceptually "upstream" and "downstream." Ownership is assigned in such a way as to minimize the losses from underinvestment. Subsequent models have built on this type of trade-off and the Grossman and Hart argument that contracts are incomplete. Such incompleteness is very much in the spirit of transaction cost theory, but it takes a different form in Grossman and Hart and other models that followed.

The key limitation of the Grossman and Hart approach is the specific way in which property rights are defined and the incompleteness of contracts that they suppose. Another key limitation is that their model can be difficult to test. We deal with their basic modeling here, and discuss empirical testing below.

According to Grossman and Hart the ownership of physical assets determines incentives to invest. They also substantially distinguish between an upstream firm buying a downstream firm and the reverse. In our view, Holmstrom (1999) correctly has criticized the property rights model in this regard. The property rights theory of the firm is not a theory of the firm at all, but merely a theory of the allocation of ownership rights between individuals. In modern economies, what separates the firm from other organizational forms is that the firm generally owns all nonhuman assets used in internal production. A literal view of the property rights theory would predict that property rights should be distributed widely among individuals involved in production, but that is not observed. Holmstrom (1999, 88) observes: "When firms own assets, these assets are tied together in a fashion that makes it impossible for a person to own 30% of one of the firm's assets and 50% of another of the firm's assets. If I own 10% of firm A, I own 10% of all its assets. But in a model where assets provide the only incentives, it is clear that this is generally inefficient."

The property rights view also stands in contrast to widely held ownership of the shares of the modern corporation. The empirical regularity regarding the ownership of shares also poses problems for Demsetz' criticism of the modern theory of the firm. Demsetz has argued that the neoclassical model provides a more coherent explanation for why firms exist—that there are gains to specialization in production and that firms are those economic entities that specialize in production (see Demsetz 1997, 2008). Partial ownership of assets and ownership by outsiders present a problem for Demsetz' interpretation of firms since they should effectively be owned completely by single entities. Uniform partial shares of ownership of all the assets used in production by a firm presents another issue because Demsetz argues that higher transaction costs will counterintuitively lead to more and smaller firms. Partial ownership share across all assets complicates the process of breaking up one firm into smaller pieces.

In a related vein, Grossman and Hart emphasize that their theory of property rights applies to assets, but does not involve differences in the compensation arrangements. Wiggins (1995), discussed in more detail below, observes that extraordinary compensation in small firms (e.g., Facebook) is tied directly to ownership. He uses this argument to analyze the substantial differences in compensation arrangements for small independent enterprises as compared to those found in large firms. Such observations are not consistent with property rights theory.

Although the property rights model presented a complete theory of the firm in the sense that it discussed both benefits and costs of vertical integration and it allowed a balancing of those benefits and costs to determine optimal organizational form, it nonetheless contained other weaknesses. Not surprisingly, these weaknesses and shortcomings in the Grossman and Hart approach have led to refinements and modifications of the property rights model, as well as attempts to overcome these weaknesses through refinements and modifications of the general transaction cost model. We now turn to two such approaches—the first an elaboration of the basic transaction cost approach contained in adaptation theories, and the second the incentive system approach that flows from weaknesses in the property rights model.

## 20.3.4  Adaptation Theories

Adaptation theories represent a third major line of research in the theory of the firm. These theories of the firm differ from other types of theories by considering the efficiency of adaptation over time as uncertainty is resolved. Adaptation theories focus on whether a firm's internal decisions will result in more efficient resource allocation than decisions made through the market.

The adaptation literature traces its roots to Knight (1921) and Simon (1947, 1951). Simon in particular developed models of authority within an organization. Authority occurs when one party can give instructions to the second party, a second party generally follows those instructions, and he often does so even when he believes another decision would be better. The latter distinguishes authority from advice and Simon points to it as a central distinction of the employment relationship. Simon then uses his model to describe settings where it is efficient for parties to allocate resources using such an authority arrangement rather than locking in decisions in advance. Simon's results turn on whether the negotiated decisions made ex ante would be better than the decision made ex post using authority.

Williamson (1975) picks this idea up and argues that firms can be superior to markets in terms of their ability to adapt to different circumstances (see also Coase 1937; Arrow 1974; and Gibbons 2005). Williamson calls this "relational adaptation" a key advantage of firm allocation.

Wiggins (1990) addresses formally the adaptability of long-term contracts versus firms. He posits upstream and downstream production where the upstream manager (or owner) must invest and has private information about cost shocks. The downstream manager (or owner) also must invest and has private information about demand shocks. Hence efficiency turns on both investment incentives and the adjustment to two types of shocks. This model is a special case of the transaction cost model because transaction specific investments prevent use of a market to create appropriate incentives. Under a long-term contract, individual owners have appropriate incentives to invest efficiently, but will strategically reveal private information. Under integrated ownership one manager owns the enterprise and the other is paid a fixed wage. The owner will invest efficiently but the manager paid a fixed wage will underinvest. The benefit is that this manager will not strategically reveal private information, permitting the firm to adjust to both types of shocks. The trade-off is that a contract will result in efficient investment both upstream and downstream, but less flexible adjustment to shocks, while a firm results in inefficient investment at one stage, but more flexible adjustment to shocks. The limitation of this approach is that it uses a single period model and does not consider the incentives for repeated dealing.

In a series of papers, Klein argues that arrangements between firms in markets can also provide for efficient adaptation (see, e.g., Klein and Murphy 1988, 1997; and Klein 1996, 2000) and emphasizes that even market transactions are often buttressed by long-term relationships. These long-term relationships can foster superior adaptation because the reputational incentives of repeated dealing create powerful incentives. These types of reputational arguments have been further elaborated in Taylor and Wiggins (1997). That paper shows how long-term trading contractual relationships based on reputation can be highly efficient and flexible instruments.

Other key contributions in this area include Aghion et al. (2003) and Hart and Holmstrom (2010). These authors extend the basic analysis to consider the microtheoretic details of information and decision making, developing the important theoretical distinction between contracting over decisions and contracting over decision rights. They argue that while parties can individually decide their own actions and may not be able to contract ex ante over a specific joint decision, they can contract over who has the right to make a decision (see also Baker et al. 2008, 2011). This distinction is quite valuable because it raises the issue regarding how decisions are actually made within a firm.

Van den Steen (2010) takes up this issue and provides a very nice formal treatment of the structure of authority within a firm that impacts the firm's adaptability. In his model a firm is structured so that even if decision rights are not directly contractible, parties can still yield to the authority of others. His basic argument is that an employee within a firm does not own its physical assets, which limits the employee's outside options so that the nonowner will yield authority to the owner. Under this approach, authority will be assigned and followed even if the right to make a decision is not directly contractible.

These contributions regarding adaptation have advanced substantially our understanding of firm versus market organization. The results show that repeated dealing in markets and in firms can lead to efficient adaptation and strong incentives. The results have also begun to deepen our understanding of how authority can develop within firms and how that authority can influence the adaptability of the firm to economic change.

The limitation of these papers is that each model is highly specialized, focusing on one issue but omitting other important components of the adaptation problem. As a result, the models cast a bright light on their individual issues, but leave out other important issues. It is likely that the make-or-buy decision more often than not involves a complicated interplay of factors discussed separately in the literature, including economies of scale, transaction costs, incompleteness of contracts, opportunism, marginal investment incentives, and the costs of ex post adaptation, among others. At present we lack an integrated model of adaptation. Still, there is a growing, insightful set of analyses, each generating a better understanding of particular elements of the problem. The hope is for the development of a more comprehensive understanding of the comparative adaptability of firms and markets, as well as a better understanding of the interplay between the many factors that affect the choice of which transactions take place within firms and which take place within markets.

## 20.3.5  Incentive System Models of the Firm

Holmstrom and Milgrom (1991, 1994) and Holmstrom (1999) have developed an alternative theory of the firm tied to incentives and multitasking. This approach is rooted in the idea that most jobs involve multiple tasks and each task affects total surplus. When agent performance is measurable, compensation can be tied to performance and agents can allocate effort efficiently among tasks. When an agent must accomplish multiple tasks that vary with respect to how well performance can be measured, strong incentives tied to particular tasks can reduce the effort agents expend on other tasks, reducing overall efficiency (see Andersen 1985; and Anderson and Schmittlein 1984). Integration is used in this setting when difficult-to-measure tasks are important. The more general problem of organizational choice is to balance these competing incentives for the agent in a way that maximizes achievable surplus.

The optimal incentive contract model developed by Holmstrom and Milgrom rationalizes these observations, providing a model of second-best alternatives. If one offers low-powered incentives to an independent contractor then that contractor can divert effort to other activities of value to the independent firm, including, for example, diverting effort to tasks on behalf of another firm that offers high-powered incentives. Organizing tasks within firms, on the other hand, permits greater control because the firm can assign tasks to the worker and monitor overall performance. Hence integration will be used when "low-powered" incentives are appropriate. On the other hand, outside procurement will be used when "high-powered," focused incentives are required since the incentives themselves result in an appropriate level of effort for the task at issue.

This approach explains why low-powered incentives are common in firms and high-powered incentives are common in arm's-length exchange. Holmstrom (1999) goes on to argue that the low-powered incentives of firm organization result in higher levels of cooperation.

## 20.3.6  Incentives and Entrepreneurial Theories

Wiggins (1995) approaches entrepreneurship from an incentive perspective. He looks at entrepreneurial activities and attempts to explain why such activities are commonly carried out in small firms where the entrepreneur is the principal owner. He identifies entrepreneurial activities as ones where there is substantial uncertainty regarding the outcome of an economic activity and he develops an incomplete contracting model where the credibility of commitment to high-powered incentives limits entrepreneurial activities in large firms. Such incentives are preferred because they obviate the need for costly monitoring of entrepreneurial activities within the firm. The underlying problem is that in entrepreneurial settings, such as the development of new technologies or other highly uncertain activities, there is a low probability of success. Wiggins shows that when there is a low probability of success, reputation cannot be used within a firm to enforce high-powered incentives, which leads to contractual failure. This contractual failure leads to a second-best outcome in which costly monitoring is required.

Small, independent enterprises offer an organizational alternative featuring high-powered incentives. In such enterprises there is a credible commitment to high levels of compensation associated with ownership of the residual income stream. The entrepreneur owns the income stream enabling a more credible commitment to high-powered incentives. Innovative activities are limited, however, in settings where the exploitation of the entrepreneurial output requires the resources of a large firm. Vertical integration into "entrepreneurial activities" can enhance the exploitation of entrepreneurial output, but such integration inherently weakens incentives due to commitment problems. This argument explains the bureaucratization of research efforts found when large firms buy out entrepreneurial enterprises, often dampening the "entrepreneurial spirit."

Incentive system models have also been used successfully to explain entrepreneurial activity in the distribution of ownership of retail outlets. Firms with extensive distribution networks often vest ownership of such outlets in local hands through franchising and similar arrangements. A rich theoretical literature has developed to explain why companies with dispersed retail outlets sometimes use local ownership of those outlets.

A primary component of this literature regards the choice between franchising and corporate ownership for those companies that choose to franchise. In these models of franchising, one party (the franchisor) makes investments in brand names, advertising, and business methods, while the local manager (the franchisee) makes investments and focuses effort on operating the local outlet. The franchisor, as in the make-or-buy decision described above, must choose whether to integrate and own the local outlet or contract with a local owner (the franchisee).

The predictions of models of franchising versus retail integration are similar to the models above: When the marginal returns to one party's efforts become larger, that party should face higher powered incentives through ownership (LaFontaine and Slade 2007, 2010). Many of these models also incorporate risk-sharing provisions and moral hazard to explain the typical franchise contract where franchisee payments consist of two parts: (1) an up-front payment for the right to own the outlet, and (2) a continuing payment as a percentage of the revenues the outlet generates. These models generally predict that integration is less likely when the local retailer's effort is more important, and that integration is more likely when the upstream firm's effort is more important. These models also predict that the greater risk found in more uncertain settings is also associated with higher levels of integration.

Maness (1996) expands this line of research to explain why supermarkets and department stores, which would appear to share many of the characteristics of franchise chains, rarely franchise. Maness uses a variant of an incentive system model that also builds on the credibility of commitment. The analysis begins by noting that ongoing franchise payments are nearly always based on revenues rather than profits or costs. This arrangement suggests that costs are noncontractible. With noncontractible costs, the choice between vertical integration and franchising depends on the marginal productivity of efforts regarding cost management. Franchising will be efficient when there is a large return to effort in reducing downstream costs, while integrated ownership will be efficient when high returns to controlling costs are found upstream. Maness (1996) concludes that supermarkets and department stores rarely franchise because control over inventory costs and other centralized costs matters more to joint surplus than local costs so that low-powered incentives for local cost control are sufficient.

# 20.4  EMPIRICAL TESTS OF THE COMPETING MODELS

We now turn to the empirical work on the theory of the firm and begin with an examination of the major tests of the transaction cost theory of the firm. The empirical literature often treats the transaction cost theory and what we have described as the adaptation models above in a similar vein. We adopt this convention by not attempting to distinguish between tests that directly involve the level of transaction specific investment and the other properties that Williamson identifies as affecting the magnitude of the holdup problem, namely the frequency of transactions and the overall level of uncertainty. We then turn our attention to whether or not these tests apply to the property rights theory as often has been claimed. We leave aside tests of franchising both because that literature is distinct from the make-or-buy theory presented above, and because there are good reviews of that literature.[4]

## 20.4.1  Empirical Tests of Transaction Cost Theories

Perhaps the strongest and most consistent empirical result in the literature on the theory of the firm is that higher levels of transaction specific assets increase the likelihood of internal procurement. There have been a wide range of successful tests of the empirical predictions of transactions-cost theory in such disparate industries as auto manufacturing (Monteverde and Teece 1982), defense manufacturing (Masten 1984), electricity generation (Joskow 1985), shipping (Pirrong 1993), and others. These empirical papers have focused on the effect of transaction specific assets on the choice of organizational form, and the influence of other factors that potentially affect the likelihood of holdup, such as complexity or uncertainty.

Monteverde and Teece (1982) developed the first empirical test of the hypotheses contained in Williamson and Klein et al. Indeed, the empirical test they undertake follows naturally from the GM-Fisher Body example first described by Klein et al. (1978). Monteverde and Teece attempted to test whether transaction cost theories can explain the actual procurement practices of GM and Ford. In particular, the authors hypothesize that there can be specific investments in human capital (know-how) in the development of automobile components, and that high levels of these transaction specific assets lead to lock-in and the potential for larger ex post haggling costs. They measure the degree of asset specificity using an ordinal measure of the amount of engineering effort required to design a given component. The authors found that the decision to use internal procurement was statistically significant and positively correlated with the level of engineering effort required for design. They also found that when a component is specific to a given type of car, as opposed to being used in multiple types, procurement was more likely to be internal. These results are consistent with the rent-seeking hypothesis.

Joskow (1985) focuses on whether coal procurement decisions by electricity generation companies are consistent with transaction cost models. Joskow's analysis contains more descriptive detail than the regression model of Monteverde and Teece (1982). His analysis focuses on location specificity by considering procurement decisions for electricity generators that site their production facilities near the mouth of a coal mine. After building these facilities, electricity generators are locked-in to the coal mine, since the costs of switching to alternative suppliers is likely higher due to transportation costs. Joskow finds that it is much more likely that there will be common ownership for the mine and the electricity plant for "mine mouth" plants than for others. He also finds that when contracts are used to procure coal in mine mouth plants they tend to be of longer duration.[5] Both results provide strong support that relationship-specific investments and haggling costs affect organizational choice.

Masten (1984) presents a detailed empirical analysis of procurement decisions for missile systems. Masten directly tests Williamson's three-part characterization of the factors that affect organizational choice by examining the general contractor's decision to use internal or external procurement for various missile components. For each component,

Masten measures uncertainty by assessing component complexity, which he links to the cost of contracting. He also measures the specialization of a component for a particular use and the degree to which collocation between manufacturing and assembly is important. Masten uses a limited dependent variable framework to assess whether these factors affect the likelihood of internal procurement. He finds that complexity and component specificity significantly increase statistically the probability of internal procurement. He also finds a positive but statistically insignificant effect from collocation. Once again, these results are consistent with the empirical predictions of the transaction cost model.

Later studies have also attempted to assess versions of the transaction cost model, using various different measures of asset specificity. Pirrong (1993) assessed contracting choices in the bulk shipping industry and their relationship to "temporal specificity," which he defines by time and space factors in the shipping industry that increase haggling costs. He finds that higher levels of temporal specificity lead to longer contracts as the parties attempt to minimize haggling costs and holdup problems.

Gonzales-Diaz et al. (2000) examine specificity and subcontracting decisions in the construction industry. To measure asset specificity, the authors create an index of the number of other firms offering similar services. They find that subcontracting is less prevalent when asset specificity grows.

Ciliberto (2006) assesses how changes in healthcare financing associated with the rise of health maintenance organizations affect the integration decision between hospitals and physicians. He hypothesizes that hospitals make specific investments for the benefit of patients of managed care entities. The rise of managed care in the 1990s increased the gains to investments in specific assets, provided a hospital could increase the likelihood that managed care patients would choose it over rival hospitals. One way that hospitals can increase this likelihood is by vertically integrating with physicians who can strongly influence the hospitals their patients choose. Ciliberto's empirical tests find that hospitals vertically integrated into physician services or involved in joint ventures with physicians invest more than hospitals that negotiate managed care contracts independently of physicians. He further finds, consistent with transaction cost predictions, that the likelihood of vertical integration is positively correlated with managed care penetration in the county where the hospital is located.

There are numerous other empirical tests of transaction cost models covering issues such as the type of specific assets, including physical assets, human capital, site specificity, temporal specificity, complexity, and uncertainty (see, e.g., LaFontaine and Slade 2007). These varied empirical tests of the predictions of transaction cost models provide virtually uniform support transaction cost theory. The next issue regards the applicability of these results to other theories, and in particular to property rights theory.

## 20.4.2  Empirical Tests of Property Rights Models

There has been substantial discussion and confusion regarding the similarity of the predictions of transaction cost theory and property rights theory. This confusion seems rooted in the fact that both theories share a foundation built on contractual incompleteness and quasi-rents. However, closer inspection of the two theories shows that in fact they are empirically distinct (see, e.g., Whinston 2003; Holmstrom and Roberts 1998; and Gibbons 2005). The key distinction relates to the particular bargaining imperfections in the two theories and how those imperfections lead to inefficiency. In transaction cost theory, the imperfection involves ex post haggling over the appropriable quasi-rents of transaction specific investments. Such haggling, which is tied directly to the *level of transaction specific investments*, raises costs and dissipates value. Accordingly, any increase in quasi-rents will increase the probability of integration in the transaction cost theory of the firm. In contrast, property rights theory presupposes that ex post bargaining is efficient but that ex ante investment will be inefficient to the extent that it benefits the other party. As a result, the property rights model's predictions turn on the *marginal returns to investment*. The property rights model also emphasizes that the ex ante level of investment is noncontractible, since otherwise parties could simply contract and achieve an efficient level of investment.

The empirical tests described above generally measure only the level of transaction specific investment, and do not focus on either the marginal returns to investment or on the contractibility of ex ante investment. Thus, these tests do not apply directly to property rights theory.

For example, Monteverde and Teece (1982) do not describe whether the transaction specific investments that are important to driving the results are noncontractible.[6] In the absence of noncontractible investments, the standard property rights theory makes no predictions about organizational form. An evaluation of Masten (1984) and Joskow (1985) leads to similar conclusions.

This general problem, along with the issue that predictions of property rights models depend on difficult-to-observe marginal incentives to invest, has resulted in fewer empirical tests of those models than of transaction cost theory. At least some tests, however, have been developed. These tests have focused on natural experiments created by changing technology or other factors that allow researchers to identify changes in the marginal returns to investment by one or both parties to a transaction.

One such test has been developed around the impact of the widespread adoption of onboard computer systems in the trucking industry that allow trucking companies to more closely monitor driving patterns. Baker and Hubbard (2003, 2004) test the impact of the adoption of onboard computer systems on ownership patterns for tractor-trailers. Baker and Hubbard argue that onboard computer systems provide sufficiently detailed data to allow parties to contract directly over driving behavior, affecting the marginal returns to investment for both parties. Baker and Hubbard find that driver ownership of tractor-trailers fell following the adoption of these computers, particularly on long-haul routes. They assert that this pattern is consistent with the property rights model. In particular, they assert that while the allocation of ownership to drivers increases incentives to maintain truck value, it reduces efficiencies regarding truck usage because the dispatcher does not have the right to control driver-owned trucks, which can lead to inefficient scheduling. Since onboard computers facilitate detailed monitoring of driver behavior, they improve the returns to integration relative to owner-operator arrangements. These systems reduce the costs associated with driver moral hazard when the company owns the trucks while allowing the more efficient allocation of trucking resources since the dispatcher can more tightly control scheduling of company-owned trucks. Thus, onboard computer systems increased the likelihood of integration through company ownership of trucks.

Baker and Hubbard (2003) also provide an empirical test of elements of the incentive model of the firm. As noted above, the incentive model developed by Holmstrom and Milgrom is rooted in job design and incentives when jobs involve multiple tasks. Baker and Hubbard studied the tasks undertaken by truck drivers and conducted empirical testing which demonstrates that elements of job design (whether truckers simply drove the truck, or provided other services) also affected the allocation of ownership rights, a result that is consistent with both the standard property rights theory of Grossman and Hart, and the later variations of the property rights models of Holmstrom and Milgrom (1991, 1994).

## 20.4.3  Empirical Tests That Attempt to Distinguish Transaction Cost Explanations and Property Rights Explanations

Most of the empirical work in the literature attempts to test one theory at a time. For instance, Monteverde and Teece test transaction costs models while Baker and Hubbard test the property rights models. A nested approach encompassing a simultaneous test of multiple theories would allow answering the question of which theory provides the explanation that better fits the data. Such an approach would be especially useful if one could identify an industry with variation across firms and/or across time in the levels of transaction specific assets (the key element of the predictions of the transaction costs approach) and in the marginal returns to investments or effort of the parties (a key element of the predictions of the property rights approach). Identifying settings with sufficient data to perform such tests is daunting. One reason goes back to the difficulty inherent in identifying and measuring the marginal returns to effort—the key variable in the property rights approach.

Despite the daunting obstacles to such comparative tests, at least a few investigators have risen to this challenge. Woodruff (2002) provides a comparative test of the transaction cost model and the property rights model using measures of noncontractibility and transaction specific assets in the Mexican footwear industry. Woodruff notes that the transaction cost framework focuses only on the benefits to integration while the property rights framework includes both the benefits and costs of integration. Woodruff identifies three aspects of shoe manufacturing that can affect transaction specific assets and marginal incentives to invest: (1) the heterogeneity of the goods produced, (2) the quality of the materials used in production, and (3) the rate at which fashions change.

He then shows that property rights models and transaction cost models make similar predictions regarding the likelihood of integration from the first two factors. For the third factor, however, he argues that the two models make opposite predictions. The property rights model predicts less forward integration by manufacturers into retailing when fashions change rapidly because retailers need high-powered incentives to stock shoes desirable to customers. On the other hand, the transaction cost model predicts more forward integration when fashions change rapidly to protect specific investments in shoe design and manufacturing. His empirical test shows, consistent with the prediction of the property rights model, that integration by shoe manufacturers into retailing is less likely when fashions change rapidly.

Acemoglu et al. (2010) also provide a comparative test of the transaction cost framework and the property rights framework using plant level data across manufacturing industries in the United Kingdom. Their empirical approach uses measures of technological intensity rather than of transaction specific investments. They argue that investments in technology, especially in R&D, are particularly susceptible to holdup problems and haggling costs. They then develop a set of industry pairs, where each industry pair consists of one that supplies a given input and another that purchases or uses that input in production. They show that property rights theory predicts a positive correlation between the technological intensity of the downstream firms and vertical integration, but a negative correlation between the technological intensity of the upstream firms and vertical integration. Investment incentives of upstream and downstream firms should display the opposite correlation. These patterns are confirmed in the data: downstream technological intensity (as measured by the ratio of R&D expenditures to value added) leads to more integration while greater technological intensity upstream leads to less integration.

## 20.4.4 Empirical Tests of Other Theory of the Firm Models

The empirical work on the remaining theories is quite limited. One interesting study is provided by Azoulay (2004). He investigates the outsourcing decision of pharmaceutical companies regarding clinical trials. Azoulay finds that when clinical trials are data intensive they are more likely to be outsourced, while knowledge intensive trials involving novel drugs or hypotheses tend to be carried out internally. Azoulay argues that knowledge production is harder to measure than data production and that internal procurement ensures that agents have incentives to put forth effort in both tasks. This finding is consistent with the multitasking model of Holmstrom and Milgrom.

Another broad source of empirical literature on theory of the firm is in franchising. The empirical literature on franchising provides at least indirect evidence on the incentive system framework. One relevant area of franchising research involves the decision by gasoline refiners to own or franchise retail outlets. Papers by Shepard (1993) and Slade (1996) focus on the decision that gasoline refiners face in choosing whether to own retail gasoline outlets. Both studies present findings that are consistent with the incentive system framework of Holmstrom and Milgrom where the decision on whether to own a station or franchise it is based on the problem of inducing effort and allocating effort among multiple tasks.

# 20.5  CONCLUDING REMARKS

Since Coase's original observation about the costs of using markets, economists have made great strides in understanding the reasons why firms exist and the factors that limit their size. However, as the discussion above makes clear, a single unified approach that captures the many theoretical aspects of the decision to integrate vertically remains elusive. For now, the theoretical models tend to focus on individual aspects of the decision concerning whether to use markets or to vertically integrate.

If anything, the theoretical models have moved further from synthesis. While the property rights approach of Grossman and Hart and others was initially viewed as a formalization of the earlier work of Williamson and Klein et al., subsequent research showed that the models were quite distinct both theoretically and empirically. Later amplifications and modifications, such as the incentive system and the adaptation approaches, only served to generate additional factors affecting the make-or-buy decision and to make new predictions.

Normally, empirical work would serve to distinguish among various theoretical approaches based on their ability to predict actual integration patterns. Under that standard, the resounding winner is the transaction cost approach, which has generated the largest body of empirical testing and results that almost uniformly confirm its explanatory power. However, this is somewhat misleading since the transaction cost approach is more readily testable due to the nature of its predictions relating the presence and size of specific investments. In contrast, the property rights and incentive system approaches depend on harder to measure marginal incentives. Where natural experiments have allowed tests of these approaches, they have fared well.

Thus, it appears likely that the choice of organizational form is complex and involves many dimensions, where the strength of any one factor depends on the circumstances. Integrating these factors into a full explanation of the integration decision will require more research and further empirical testing. This is especially true since most researchers acknowledge that a single explanation for how firms make the decision to use internal or market procurement is unlikely to hold in all circumstances. Indeed, it will often be true that multiple factors will interact simultaneously in driving the integration decision.

Given this reality more nested empirical approaches that permit simultaneous tests of various theories of the firm are needed to distinguish between theories and determine the role of various forces affecting the choice between market and firm organization. Developing such empirical models is likely to be exceedingly difficult given data limitations and the difficulty of measuring key variables. Still, some tests have been developed and more are likely on the way.

## Notes

1. We would like to thank William Shughart and Christopher Thomas for their helpful suggestions in various stages of our drafting process.
2. Note in contrast that the "theory of the firm" found in most microeconomics textbooks focuses attention on production functions, essentially postulating a firm as a subset of markets that typically allocate resources in essentially the same way as a market. This approach, however, leaves unresolved the issue of why firms exist, and yields unreasonable predictions, such as the absence of long-term employment contracts or common asset ownership.
3. Hart (1995) provides a more detailed overview of this literature.
4. See, e.g., LaFontaine and Slade (2007) who provide a detailed review of the empirical literature on franchising. See also Holmstrom and Roberts (1998).
5. Others have studied the influence of transaction specific investments on the length of contracts, including Crocker and Masten (1988) and Pirrong (1993).
6. See also Whinston (2003) for a further discussion of these issues.

## References

Acemoglu, Daron, Phillippe Aghion, Rachel Griffith, and Fabrizio Zilibotti. 2010. "Vertical Integration and Technology: Theory and Evidence," *Journal of the European Economic Association* 8 (5): 989–1033.

Aghion, Patrick, Matthias Dewatripont, and Patrick Rey. 2004. "Transferable Control." *Journal of the European Economic Association* 2:115–38.

Anderson, Erin. 1985. "The Salesperson as Outside Agent or Employee: A Transaction Cost Analysis." *Management Science* 4:234–54.

Anderson, Erin, and David C. Schmittlein. 1984. "Integration of the Sales Force: An Empirical Examination." *Rand Journal of Economics* 15:385–95.

Arrow, Kenneth. 1974. *The Limits of Organization.* New York: W. W. Norton & Co.

Azoulay, Pierre. 2004. "Capturing Knowledge Within and Across Firm Boundaries: Evidence from Clinical Development." *American Economic Review* 94:1591–1612.

Baker, George P., and Thomas N. Hubbard. 2003. "Make Versus Buy in Trucking: Asset Ownership, Job Design, and Information." *American Economic Review* 93:551–72.

———. 2004. "Contractibility and Asset Ownership: On-Board Computers and Governance in U.S. Trucking." *Quarterly Journal of Economics* 119:1443–79.

Baker, George, Robert Gibbons, and Kevin J. Murphy. 2008. "Strategic Alliances: Bridges Between 'Islands of Conscious Power.'" *Journal of the Japanese and International Economies* 22:146–63.

———. 2011. "Relational Adaptation." Unpublished manuscript, MIT, Cambridge, MA.

Ciliberto, Federico. 2006. "Does Organizational Form Affect Investment Decisions?" *Journal of Industrial Economics* 54:63–93.

Coase, Ronald H. 1937. "The Nature of the Firm." *Economica* 4:386–405.

———. 2000. "The Acquisition of Fisher Body by General Motors." *Journal of Law and Economics* 43:15–31.

———. 2006. "The Conduct of Economics: The Example of Fisher Body and General Motors." *Journal of Economics and Management Strategy* 15:255–78.

Crocker, Keith, and Scott Masten. 1988. "Mitigating Contractual Hazards: Unilateral Options and Contract Length." *RAND Journal of Economics* 19:327–43.

Demsetz, Harold. 1997. *The Economics of the Business Firm*. New York: Cambridge University Press.

——. 2008. *From Economic Man to Economic System*. New York: Cambridge University Press.

Gibbons, Robert. 2005. "Four Formal(izable) Theories of the Firm?" *Journal of Economic Behavior and Organization* 58:200–245.

Gonzáález-Diaz, M., Benito Arruñada, and A. Fernandez. 2000. "Causes of Subcontracting: Evidence from Panel Data on Construction Firms." *Journal of Economic Behavior and Organization* 42:167–87.

Grossman, Sanford J., and Oliver D. Hart. 1986. "The Costs and Benefits of Ownership: A Theory of Vertical Integration." *Journal of Political Economy* 94:691–719.

Hart, Oliver, and John Moore. 1990. "Property Rights and the Nature of the Firm." *Journal of Political Economy* 98:1119–58.

Hart, Oliver. 1995. *Firms, Contracts and Financial Structure*. Oxford: Oxford University Press.

——. 2011. "Thinking about the Firm: A Review of Daniel Spulber's *The Theory of the Firm*." *Journal of Economic Literature* 49 (1): 101–13.

Hart, Oliver, and Bengt Holmstrom. 2010. "A Theory of Firm Scope." *Quarterly Journal of Economics* 125 (2): 483–513.

Holmstrom, Bengt. 1999. "The Firm as a Subeconomy." *Journal of Law, Economics, and Organization* 15:74–102.

Holmstrom, Bengt, and Paul Milgrom. 1991. "Multi-Task Principal-Agent Analyses: Incentive Contracts, Asset Ownership, and Job Design." *Journal of Law, Economics, and Organization* 7:24–51.

——. 1994. "The Firm as an Incentive System." *American Economic Review* 84:972–91.

Holmstrom, B., and J. Roberts. 1998. "The Boundaries of the Firm Revisited." *Journal of Economic Perspectives* 12:73–94.

Holmstrom, B., and J. Tirole. 1991. "Transfer Pricing and Organizational Form." *Journal of Law, Economics, and Organization* 7:201–28.

Joskow, Paul L. 1985. "Vertical Integration, and Long-Term Contracts: The Case of Coal-Burning Electric Generation Plants." *Journal of Law, Economics, & Organization* 1:33–80.

——. 1988. "Asset Specificity and the Structure of Vertical Relationships: Empirical Evidence." *Journal of Law, Economics, & Organization* 4:95–117.

Klein, Benjamin. 1988. "Vertical Integration as Organizational Ownership: The Fisher Body-General Motors Relationship Revisited." *Journal of Law, Economics, and Organization* 4:199–213.

——. 1996. "Why Hold-ups Occur: The Self-Enforcing Range of Contractual Relationships." *Economic Inquiry* 34:444–63.

——. 2000. "Fisher-General Motors and the Nature of the Firm." *Journal of Law and Economics* 43:105–41.

——. 2004. "Fisher Body-General Motors Once Again: What Is a Holdup?" Unpublished manuscript, MIT, Cambridge, MA.

——. 2007. "The Economic Lessons of Fisher Body-General Motors." *International Journal of the Economics of Business* 14:1–36.

Klein, Benjamin, R. Crawford, and A. Alchian. 1978. "Vertical Integration, Appropriable Rents, and the Competitive Contracting Process," *Journal of Law and Economics* 21:297–326.

Klein, Benjamin, and Keith B. Leffler. 1981. "The Role of Market Forces in Assuring Contractual Performance." *Journal of Political Economy* 89:615–41.

Klein, Benjamin, and Kevin M. Murphy. 1988. "Vertical Restraints as Contract Enforcement Mechanisms." *Journal of Law and Economics* 31:265–97.

——. 1997. "Vertical Integration as a Self-Enforcing Contractual Arrangement." *American Economic Review* 87:415–20.

Knight, F. (1921) 1965. *Risk, Uncertainty, and Profit.* New York: Hart, Schaffner, and Marx. Reprint, New York: Harper and Row.

LaFontaine, Francine, and Margaret Slade. 2007. "Vertical Integration and Firm Boundaries: The Evidence." *Journal of Economic Literature* 45:629–85.

——. 2010. "Transaction Cost Economics and Vertical Market Restrictions—Evidence." *Antitrust Bulletin* 55 (3): 587–612.

Maness, Robert. 1996. "Incomplete Contracts and the Choice between Vertical Integration and Franchising." *Journal of Economic Behavior and Organization* 31:101–15.

Masten, Scott E. 1984. "The Organization of Production: Evidence from the Aerospace Industry." *Journal of Law and Economics* 27:403–17.

Monteverde, K., and David J. Teece. 1982. "Supplier Switching Costs and Vertical Integration in the Automobile Industry." *Bell Journal of Economics* 13:206–13.

Pirrong, S. Craig. 1993. "Contracting Practices in Bulk Shipping Markets: A Transaction Cost Explanation." *Journal of Law and Economics* 36:937–76.

Shepard, Andrea. 1993. "Contractual Form, Retail Price, and Asset Characteristics in Gasoline Retailing." *RAND Journal of Economics* 24:58–77.

Simon, Herbert. 1947. *Administrative Behavior.* New York: Free Press.

——. 1951. "A Formal Theory of the Employment Relationship." *Econometrica* 19:293–305.

Slade, Margaret E. 1996. "Multitask Agency and Organizational Form: An Empirical Exploration." *International Economic Review* 37:465–86.

Taylor, Curtis, and Steven Wiggins. 1997. "Competition or Compensation: Supplier Incentives under the American and Japanese Subcontracting System." *American Economic Review* 87:598–618.

Van den Steen, Eric. 2010. "Interpersonal Authority in a Theory of the Firm." *American Economic Review* 100 (1): 466–90.

Whinston, Michael D. 2003. "On the Transaction Cost Determinants of Vertical Integration." *Journal of Law, Economics, and Organization* 19:1–23.

Wiggins, Steven N. (1990) 1997. "The Comparative Advantage of Long Term Contracts and Firms." *Journal of Law, Economics, and Organization* 6 (1): 155–170. Reprint, *The Theory of the Firm*, edited by Mark Casson. Cheltenham, UK: Edward Elgar Publishing Limited.

——. 1995. "Entrepreneurial Enterprises, Endogenous Ownership, and the Limits to Firm Size." *Economic Inquiry* 33 (1): 54–69.

Williamson, Oliver E. 1971. "The Vertical Integration of Production: Market Failure Considerations." *American Economic Review* 61:112–23.

——. 1975. *Markets and Hierarchies: Analysis and Antitrust Implications.* New York: Free Press.

——. 1979. "Transaction Cost Economics: The Governance of Contractual Relations." *Journal of Law and Economics* 22:233–61.

——. 1985. *The Economic Institutions of Capitalism.* New York: Free Press.

Woodruff, C. 2002. "Non-Contractible Investment and Vertical Integration in the Mexican Footwear Industry." *International Journal of Industrial Organization* 20:1197–1224.

# PART VI

FINANCIAL STRUCTURE AND CORPORATE GOVERNANCE

# CHAPTER 21

....................................................................................

# FINANCING THE
# BUSINESS FIRM

....................................................................................

## LEONCE BARGERON AND KENNETH LEHN

ONE of the most widely studied topics in financial economics during the past fifty years has been the causes and consequences of firms' financing decisions. Firms face a large menu of financing choices, including "plain vanilla" debt, common equity, and various hybrid forms of financing that share features of both debt and common equity, such as convertible debt and preferred stock. The factors that govern these choices and the effects of these choices on the values of firms have been the focus of a large theoretical and empirical literature for the past several decades.

Since Modigliani and Miller's seminal paper on capital structure and the cost of capital in 1958, three alternative, but not mutually exclusive, theories have emerged to explain the pattern of business financing: (i) the "trade-off" theory, (ii) the "pecking order" theory, and (iii) the "market timing" theory. An abundant literature has attempted to test the three theories and many papers have found empirical evidence consistent with the predictions of the three theories. However, the extant evidence also reveals some puzzling results suggesting that our theories of corporate financing policies are far from complete. In particular, some of the results in the literature are anomalous and others are not robust with respect to time periods or subsamples of firms stratified by size. Furthermore, the variables that are consistently found to be associated with the financing of firms explain a small percentage of the variation in observed capital structures.

This chapter begins by documenting the wide variation in the financing activities of firms. It then describes Modigliani and Miller's propositions, which serve as the cornerstone for modern theories of corporate finance. We follow this discussion with a description of the three major theories of capital structure, along with a brief review of the evidence corresponding to each theory. Finally, we offer some commentary on possible avenues of future research.

## 21.1  THE FINANCING OF FIRMS VARIES WIDELY

It is useful to begin by documenting that there is wide variation in the financing decisions made by firms. For example, Barclay and Smith (2005) find that the average debt-to-value ratio (measured as the book value of debt divided by the sum of the book value of debt, the book value of preferred stock and the market value of common equity) for a sample of 8,800 firms during 1950–2003 is approximately 0.21. They find considerable variation around the average—25% of the sample had debt-to-value ratios in excess of 0.33 and another 25% had debt-to-value ratios of less than 0.05. More recently, Graham and Leary (2011) also document wide variation in the capital structures of firms. They further report that there is more cross-sectional than "within firm" variation in leverage and that the cross-sectional variation in leverage increased substantially from 1974 to 2009.

To illustrate the continuing variation that exists in the financing decisions of firms, we computed the debt-to-value ratios as of December 30, 2011, for the thirty companies that comprise the Dow Jones Industrial Average. These data are reported in Table 21.1.

The table shows that the average and median debt-to-value ratios for the thirty companies are 0.322 and 0.227, respectively. The ratios range widely from 0.068 (Chevron) to 0.848 (JP Morgan Chase). Given that debt financing is an inherent part of the operations of financial firms, we replicated the analysis for the twenty-five companies in the Dow Jones Industrial Average that are not financial institutions. For these firms, the average and median debt-to-value ratios are 0.250 and 0.194, respectively, and they also range widely from 0.068 (Chevron) to 0.638 (Alcoa). This wide variation in capital structure leads to a natural question that has been the focus of much of the literature in financial economics—why do some firms, such as Chevron, Intel, and Microsoft, have relatively low debt-to-value ratios, while other firms, such as Alcoa, Hewlett-Packard, and Caterpillar, have relatively high debt-to-value ratios?

## 21.2  MODIGLIANI AND MILLER

The starting point for understanding the financing behavior of firms is the seminal paper by Modigliani and Miller (1958). Before Modigliani and Miller's paper, there was no scientific theory of corporate finance in general or capital structure in particular. Firms made capital structure decisions based on rules of thumb and academic economists largely ignored the topic. In one of the few academic papers that probed the financial policies of firms before Modigliani and Miller,[1] Weston (1954, 126) wrote that "the traditional rules-of-thumb set forth in investment and corporate finance books ... are often criticized as arbitrary, since their empirical or logical basis is not usually established with clarity or persuasiveness. Given uncertainty, it is not possible to develop definitive rules of action as a rational basis for decision-making." Modigliani and Miller,

## Table 21.1  Debt–to–Value Ratios for the thirty companies in the Dow Jones Industrial Average, December 31, 2011

| Company | Debt (D) | Pfd. Stock | Common Equity | Value (V) | D/V |
|---|---|---|---|---|---|
| Alcoa | $16.3 | $0.1 | $9.2 | $25.6 | 0.638 |
| American Express | 20.0 | 0.0 | 54.8 | 74.8 | 0.219 |
| AT&T | 112.2 | 0.0 | 179.2 | 291.4 | 0.385 |
| Bank of America | 409.3 | 19.5 | 56.4 | 485.2 | 0.844 |
| Boeing | 32.1 | 0.0 | 54.5 | 86.6 | 0.371 |
| Caterpillar | 45.4 | 0.0 | 58.6 | 103.9 | 0.436 |
| Chevron | 15.4 | 0.0 | 211.9 | 227.3 | 0.068 |
| Cisco Systems | 18.9 | 0.0 | 97.2 | 116.1 | 0.163 |
| Coca-Cola | 33.6 | 0.0 | 158.9 | 192.5 | 0.174 |
| Disney | 20.8 | 0.0 | 67.4 | 88.1 | 0.236 |
| E.I. du Pont | 26.6 | 0.2 | 42.3 | 69.1 | 0.384 |
| Exxon Mobil | 56.6 | 0.0 | 406.3 | 462.9 | 0.122 |
| General Electric | 518.1 | 0.0 | 189.1 | 707.1 | 0.733 |
| Home Depot | 13.0 | 0.0 | 64.8 | 77.8 | 0.167 |
| Hewlett-Packard | 48.2 | 0.0 | 51.1 | 99.3 | 0.485 |
| IBM | 52.8 | 0.0 | 216.7 | 269.5 | 0.196 |
| Intel | 9.8 | 0.0 | 123.5 | 133.3 | 0.074 |
| Johnson & Johnson | 32.0 | 0.0 | 179.2 | 211.2 | 0.152 |
| J.P. Morgan Chase | 748.5 | 7.8 | 126.3 | 882.6 | 0.848 |
| Kraft Foods | 36.9 | 0.0 | 66.0 | 102.9 | 0.359 |
| McDonald's | 14.1 | 0.0 | 102.7 | 116.7 | 0.120 |
| Merck | 18.1 | 0.0 | 114.9 | 133.1 | 0.136 |
| Microsoft | 20.1 | 0.0 | 218.4 | 238.5 | 0.084 |
| Pfizer | 63.0 | 0.0 | 166.4 | 229.4 | 0.275 |
| Procter & Gamble | 43.4 | 1.2 | 183.5 | 228.2 | 0.190 |
| 3M | 9.7 | 0.0 | 57.3 | 67.0 | 0.145 |
| Travelers | 81.6 | 0.0 | 24.4 | 106.0 | 0.770 |
| United Technologies | 19.8 | 0.0 | 66.2 | 86.1 | 0.230 |
| Verizon | 88.1 | 0.0 | 113.6 | 201.7 | 0.437 |
| Wal-Mart | 59.2 | 0.0 | 204.7 | 263.9 | 0.224 |
| | | | Mean | | 0.322 |
| | | | Median | | 0.227 |
| | | | Mean (exc. financials) | | 0.250 |
| | | | Median (exc. financials) | | 0.196 |

who won Nobel prizes in large part because of their work in this area, revolutionized the way that both academics and the business community think about the financing decisions of firms. More generally, the scientific framework developed by Modigliani and Miller marked the beginning of the modern theory of corporate finance.

Modigliani and Miller showed that in a world of no taxes and "perfect" capital markets—i.e., markets in which there are no transaction costs (i.e., no market frictions)—then capital structure decisions do not affect firm value. The intuition behind this result, referred to as Modigliani and Miller's Proposition I, or the "irrelevance proposition," is as follows.

A firm's value is determined by the present value of its expected cash flows, which are generated by the firm's assets. A firm's asset structure, depicted on the left-hand side of its balance sheet, represents the use of capital that it raised from investors. For simplicity's sake, let us assume two types of investors—debtholders and stockholders. Both debtholders and stockholders provide the firm with capital and they differ with respect to the nature of the claim they receive in exchange for their capital. Debtholders receive a fixed claim—i.e., a claim in which they are to receive a fixed amount of cash at specified points in time—whereas stockholders receive a residual claim—that is, a claim on whatever cash flows exist after all other claimants have been paid. By their nature, debt represents a claim that is senior to equity in the event of bankruptcy. Hence, debt can be thought of as owning a claim on the "safer" part of a firm's cash flows, which makes it less risky than an equity claim in the corresponding firm.

Within Modigliani and Miller's framework, the capital structure decision is, in effect, a decision as to how to slice the firm's cash flows and value between two different types of claims, debt and equity. But, in the Modigliani and Miller world, the way in which the cash flows and value is sliced has no effect on the level of the cash flows and hence, no effect on value. Under Modigliani and Miller's Proposition I, capital structure is irrelevant in the sense that it has no effect on firm value.

Furthermore, Modigliani and Miller showed that, holding a firm's assets constant, the risk of a firm's equity increases as the firm issues more debt, a result referred to as Modigliani and Miller's Proposition II.[2] The intuition behind this result is as follows. In the same way that all of a firm's cash flows and value are partitioned between debt and equity, all of the risk associated with the firm's assets, its so called "business risk," is borne in some combination by debt and equity. Holding its assets, and hence its business risk, constant, as a firm issues more debt it apportions a larger amount of the "safer" part of its expected cash flows to debt, thereby increasing the risk of the remaining equity claims and the required return on equity. Although the issuance of debt increases the expected equity cash flows per share, these equity cash flows are discounted at a higher rate, reflecting the increased risk of equity. Mathematically, the increase in equity cash flows per share is offset by the higher discount rate on equity, thereby leaving the company's stock price unaffected.[3]

Although Modigliani and Miller's research can be interpreted as suggesting that capital structure is irrelevant for firm value, in our view, the import of their paper is that it provides a framework for understanding the conditions under which capital structure decisions can have an effect on firm value. By showing that capital structure is irrelevant in a world of no taxes and no market frictions, Modigliani and Miller, in effect, identify the set of conditions for which the violation of at least one is necessary, but not sufficient, in order for capital structure to be relevant for firm value. Specifically, if the assumption of no taxes or no market frictions is relaxed, then it is possible that the values of firms are affected by their capital structure decisions.

Most of the large literature on capital structure since Modigliani and Miller has attempted to flesh out (i) how taxes and market frictions affect the capital structures of firms and, relatedly, (ii) how capital structure decisions affect the values of firms.[4] Three theories, which are not mutually exclusive, have evolved to explain the financing decisions of firms: (i) the trade-off theory, (ii) the pecking order theory, and (iii) the market timing theory. Each of these is discussed in turn.

# 21.3  THE TRADE-OFF THEORY

The trade-off theory of capital structure posits that managers establish target debt-to-value ratios that maximize the value of their firms, based on a consideration of the marginal benefits and marginal costs of additional debt. In the initial depictions of the trade-off theory, the benefits of debt are its associated tax savings and the costs of debt are the expected costs of financial distress (e.g., DeAngelo and Masulis 1980; Bradley et al. 1984). Subsequently, the benefits of debt have been expanded to include the mitigation of agency costs and information asymmetries. As the benefits and costs of debt are likely to vary from firm to firm, the trade-off theory leads to testable predictions about the determinants of capital structure. A discussion of these benefits and costs follows.

## 21.3.1  The Benefits of Debt

The US corporate tax code and those of most developed countries allows companies to treat interest expense, but not retained earnings and dividends, as a tax deductible item. As a result, the corporate tax code encourages companies to use debt, rather than equity, financing. Ignoring personal taxes and other market frictions for the moment, the value of a firm is equal to its value as an all-equity firm plus the present value of its interest tax shields, which suggests that if only corporate taxes are considered, firms should be financed entirely with debt.

However, as Miller (1977) points out, in order to assess the effect of capital structure on firm value, one has to consider how corporate debt affects both the corporate taxes paid by the firm and the personal taxes paid by the firm's debtholders and stockholders. Personal taxes are relevant to the capital structure decision because investors require companies to compensate them for the personal taxes they incur on income they receive from their holdings of the firm's debt and equity. Accordingly, companies have an incentive to minimize all taxes on corporate income, including taxes paid by both the corporation and its investors.

In the United States, debtholders pay the personal income tax rate on interest income they receive, while stockholders pay the personal income tax rate on their dividend income and the capital gains rate on any gains they realize from the sale of their stock. In effect, the personal tax rate paid by stockholders on their equity income is a blended rate based on the personal income tax rate, the capital gains rate, and the percentage of their equity income that takes the form of dividends versus capital gains. Given that the capital gains rate is typically less than the personal income tax rate and stockholders can elect to defer the capital gains rate until they sell their shares, the effective personal tax rate on equity income is typically less than the personal rate on interest income. In short, whereas the corporate tax rate confers an advantage on debt financing, the personal tax rate typically favors equity financing. Hence, the net effect of both the corporate and the personal tax code on the financing decisions of firms depends on the corporate tax rate, the personal income tax rate, and the capital gains tax rate.[5]

In addition to potential tax savings, another advantage of debt financing is that, for some firms, debt can mitigate the agency costs associated with the stockholder-manager relationship. Jensen (1986) argues that these agency costs are most pronounced in firms that generate large amounts of free cash flow—that is, cash flow in excess of what is necessary to fund positive net present value (NPV) projects. Whereas stockholders prefer that managers distribute the free cash flow to them in the form of dividends or stock repurchases, managers often prefer to retain the cash to fund new investments, including acquisitions, even though, by definition, these projects are not value-creating. The firm can mitigate this conflict by issuing debt and using the proceeds to repurchase an equivalent amount of equity. By raising the debt-to-value ratio, the firm has committed the free cash flows to debt payments, which restricts management from investing in value-destroying projects. There is considerable evidence from studies of leveraged recapitalizations (Denis and Denis 1993) and private equity transactions (Kaplan 1989; Wruck 1989) that debt strengthens managerial incentives in ways consistent with Jensen's theory.

Another advantage of debt that has been proffered in the literature is that debt issues can mitigate potential asymmetries in the information possessed by managers and investors (Blazenko 1987; Ross 1977). According to this theory, it is assumed that managers generally have more information about the future fortunes of their firms than do outside investors. Given this information asymmetry, managers who believe their companies' stock prices are undervalued may wish to signal this information to the market in an attempt to increase their companies' stock prices. Because the disclosure of private information may reduce its value, managers often seek credible ways of signaling that the firms' expected cash flows are higher than the market believes without disclosing the reason for the managers' optimism. However, in order for the signal to be credible, there must be adverse consequences for the managers if it turns out the companies' stock prices were not actually undervalued. One way that managers can credibly signal positive information to the market is through the issuance of debt. Outside investors are likely to infer that the managers believe that the companies' future cash flows will be sufficient to service the additional debt. If not, then the managers suffer the consequences of being unable to make the additional debt payments. Hence, in a world of costly information, the issuance of debt can serve as a credible signal that the companies' future cash flows are likely to be higher than outside investors expect.

## 21.3.2 The Cost of Debt

The primary disadvantage of debt financing is the expected costs associated with financial distress,[6] which is a function of the probability of financial distress and the costs the company incurs if it is in financial distress. These costs include direct costs (e.g., bankruptcy court fees, legal fees, and so forth), which generally are thought to be relatively small,[7] as well as various indirect costs, which potentially can be quite large.

Perhaps the most important indirect cost of financial distress is the underinvestment problem initially identified by Myers (1977). According to this theory, firms in financial distress have an incentive to underinvest in positive NPV projects because of a conflict between the stockholders and debtholders in such firms. By definition, if a firm is in financial distress, its debt obligations have market values that are less than their corresponding face values. The stockholders, who still control the firm as it approaches bankruptcy, are reluctant to finance positive NPV investment projects because the value created by the projects would accrue, in part or in whole, to the debtholders. An empirical prediction, which generally has been validated by the evidence, is that firms with significant growth opportunities should rely less on debt financing, as the potential costs of the underinvestment problem are especially large for these firms (Barclay et al. 2003; Rajan and Zingales 1995).

Another indirect cost associated with financial distress is that stockholders in distressed firms have incentives to overinvest in highly risky, negative NPV projects. This incentive also reflects a conflict that exists between stockholders and debtholders in distressed firms. Because the equity value of distressed firms is small in comparison with the value of its debt, stockholders face an asymmetric payoff from investing in risky negative NPV projects—they face relatively little downside if the project fails and they capture a disproportionate amount of the upside if the project succeeds. Because these projects are negative NPV on an ex ante basis, they represent an additional cost of financial distress. Furthermore, because debtholders are aware of these potential conflicts as of the time the debt is issued, they will require covenant protection, higher interest payments, or both, to compensate them for this risk.

A third indirect cost of financial distress is that the operating cash flows of distressed companies might suffer because vendors and customers become reluctant to enter into contracts with the companies, given the high likelihood of bankruptcy. Altman (1984) and Opler and Titman (1994), among others, find evidence that the sales and market shares of companies decline when they are in financial distress, which is consistent with the view that distress raises contracting costs with vendors and customers. The reduction in firm value associated with these contracting costs represents another indirect and potentially large cost of financial distress, especially for firms in certain industries. For example, manufacturers of durable goods may face especially large expected costs of financial distress. When customers purchase durable goods, they generally expect the manufacturer to provide a stream of services over the expected life of the product. All else equal, the expected value of this stream of services is lower for financially distressed firms than it is for other firms. Consequently, customers are less likely to buy durable goods from financially distressed manufacturers than they are from other manufacturers, causing additional declines in the operating cash flows of the financially distressed firms. The incremental decline in operating cash flows associated with the firm's leverage is another indirect cost of financial distress and, hence, a cost of issuing debt.

## 21.3.3  Empirical Evidence on the Trade-Off Theory

The trade-off theory has been tested extensively over the past few decades and much of the evidence is consistent with its predictions. Regarding the benefits of debt, Mackie-Mason (1990) and Graham (1996) find a direct relation between a firm's marginal tax rate and its leverage, which is consistent with the prediction that tax savings represent a benefit of debt. Also, studies find an inverse relation between market-to-book ratios and leverage ratios (Smith and Watts 1992), which is consistent with several hypotheses, including the hypothesis that leverage mitigates the agency costs of free cash flow, which are most pronounced in low-growth firms.

Much of the evidence is also consistent with the hypothesis that an inverse relation exists between the expected costs of financial distress and leverage. An inverse relation exists between the volatility of a firm's earnings, which affects the probability of financial distress, and its leverage (Titman and Wessels 1988). The inverse relation between market-to-book ratios and leverage, cited above, also is consistent with the hypothesis that high-growth firms avoid debt because of the underinvestment problem identified by Myers (1984). In addition, numerous studies document that leverage is directly related to the tangibility of a firm's assets, which in turn are presumed to be inversely related to the costs of financial distress (Long and Malitz 1985).

In addition to the evidence consistent with the static trade-off model, the literature finds that firms act as if they adjust to target debt ratios (Jalilvand and Harris 1984). A recent paper by Fama and French (2011) finds that firms issue new debt and equity in ways consistent with the hypothesis that firms gravitate to target debt-to-value ratios. However, the paper notes that this effect is generally small, suggesting that new securities issues are not driven primarily by a desire to move to a target capital structure.

Although some of the extant evidence is consistent with the trade-off theory, the literature also finds results contrary to the trade-off theory. For example, prior to MacKie-Mason (1990) and Graham (1996), there was little evidence establishing a relation between taxes and leverage ratios, prompting Myers (1984, 588) to write that "I know of no study clearly demonstrating that a firm's tax status has predictable, material effects on its debt policy." Furthermore, US firms, especially railroads and utilities, relied heavily on debt financing during the 1800s, prior to the enactment of a federal corporate income tax in 1909,[8] which suggests that the financing decisions of firms during this period were driven by factors other than taxes. Similarly, Baskin and Miranti (1997) note that UK firms relied on debt financing before that nation adopted a company tax in 1947 and that they continued to use debt after the United Kingdom reduced the effective corporate income tax rate substantially in 1973.[9]

The result that is perhaps most inconsistent with the static trade-off theory is the evidence on the relation between firm profitability and leverage. The trade-off theory predicts that a direct relation should exist between a firm's profitability and its leverage, since corporate income taxes increase as a firm's profit increases, all else equal. However, studies consistently find exactly the opposite—a significant inverse relation exists between profitability and leverage (Titman and Wessels 1988; Rajan and Zingales 1995).[10] Scholars have attempted to develop dynamic trade-off models that might explain this result (e.g., Fischer et al. 1989), but, in our view, the inverse relation between leverage and profitability suggests that taxes may be a second-order consideration in financing decisions. Frank and Goyal (2009, 4) state that "we suspect that agency costs of debt are likely quite important relative to taxes. Our findings reproduce the well-known fact that tax effects are relatively hard to identify in the data."

## 21.4 THE PECKING ORDER THEORY

The pecking order theory, developed by Myers (1984) and Myers and Majluf (1984), posits that a financing hierarchy exists in which firms prefer to finance their financing deficits (i.e., the difference between operating cash flows and the sum of short-term debt payments, the current portion of long-term debt, dividend payments, investments in working capital, and capital expenditures) with retained earnings as opposed to external financing, and that among the sources of external financing, firms prefer external debt to external equity. Hence, under the pecking order theory, external equity is the first-best financing choice when all other sources have been exhausted.

The pecking order theory is premised on the assumption that information is asymmetrically distributed between managers and investors. Because managers have more information about their firms than do investors, firms incur adverse selection costs when they issue securities. Furthermore, it is assumed that the severity of the information asymmetries and, hence, the magnitude of the adverse selection costs, increase in the risk of a firm's securities. Consistent with this view, it is well documented in the literature that the stock prices of companies decline significantly on average when they announce equity issues but not when they announce debt issues (Asquith and Mullins 1986; Eckbo 1986). According to the pecking order theory, these adverse selection costs cause managers to prefer the pecking order as described above.[11]

In contrast to the trade-off theory, the pecking order theory does not assume that firms establish target leverage ratios. Shyam-Sunder and Myers (1999, 220) write that "in the pecking order theory, there is no well-defined optimal debt ratio. The attraction of interest tax shields and the threat of financial distress are assumed second-order." Instead, a firm's capital structure at any point in time reflects the cumulative effect of its past financing decisions, each of which was made on the basis of the status of the firm's financing deficit and the availability of the three types of financing at the time.

## 21.4.1  Empirical evidence on the pecking order theory

Some of the early tests of the pecking order theory found results that are consistent with the theory. For example, Shyam-Sunder and Myers (1999) tested the predictions of the pecking order theory by examining the relation between net debt issues and the financing deficits of firms, which are calculated as the difference between operating cash flows and the sum of dividend payments, capital expenditures, investments in working capital, and the current portion of long-term debt. Under the pecking order theory, one would expect that firms generally finance these deficits with net debt, as opposed to net equity, issues. For a sample of 157 firms during 1971–89, Shyam-Sunder and Myers (1999) find that net debt issues are directly related to the financing deficit and that the coefficient on the financing deficit is approximately one, indicating that the deficits generally are financed entirely with net debt issues, a result that is consistent with the predictions of the pecking order theory.

However, more recent papers find evidence contrary to the pecking order theory. Using a sample of several thousand US firms over the period of 1971 to 1998, Frank and Goyal (2003) find that (i) external finance is used extensively by firms and often exceeds the investment requirements of firms, (ii) external equity constitutes a substantial proportion of external finance, and (iii) the financing deficit is more closely associated with net equity issues than it is with net debt issues. Using a similar method, Fama and French (2011) find that the pecking order theory predicts net debt issues well during 1963–82, but not thereafter. The results in Frank and Goyal (2003) and Fama and French (2011) appear to be explained, at least in part, by the changing composition of public companies over time. In particular, both sets of results indicate that small, young, high-growth firms, which account for a larger proportion of public companies over time, are as likely to finance their deficits with external equity rather than external debt, contrary to the predictions of the pecking order theory.

# 21.5  THE MARKET TIMING THEORY

An alternative theory, the market timing theory, posits that the asymmetry of information between managers and outside investors can affect the financing decisions of firms in another way. If managers believe that their companies' securities are mispriced, they will attempt to exploit the mispricing in a way that allows them to raise capital in the least-cost way. For example, if they believe their companies' stock prices are overvalued, then they can create value for their existing shareholders by issuing shares (Asquith and Mullins 1986; Myers and Majluf 1984). Alternatively, if they believe their companies' stock is undervalued, they have incentives to repurchase shares and/or to issue debt (Ditmar 2000; Vermaelen 1981). As they issue or repurchase shares, the capital structures of their firms change, not because they are gravitating towards an optimal capital structure, but instead because of the mispricing of their companies' shares. Hence, under this theory, a firm's capital structure at any point in time is a function of the past mispricing of its securities.

One version of the market timing theory assumes that securities (especially equity securities) are frequently mispriced and that the mispricing can persist over time (Baker and Wurgler 2002). According to this version, the mispricing can occur either because the market is not efficiently processing public information or because the managers have private information that is not yet reflected in the securities' prices. An alternative version of the market timing theory is that the securities are not in reality mispriced but that managers mistakenly believe they are (Fama and French 2011). For example, there may be rational reasons why a company might have an unusually high price-to-earnings (PE) ratio, yet, according to this version of the theory, managers might issue shares because they mistakenly believe the stock is overvalued. Regardless of whether securities are in fact mispriced, the market timing theory holds that financing decisions are the outcomes of attempts to time the market.

### 21.5.1  Empirical Evidence on the Market Timing Theory

It is difficult to test the market timing theory directly given the challenge of identifying securities that are either mispriced or believed by managers to be mispriced. The variable that is most frequently used as a proxy for mispriced equity securities is the ratio of the market value of a firm's equity to the book value of its equity. Studies generally find a direct relation between market-to-book ratios and equity issues, which is consistent with the market timing theory (Fama and French 2011). However, the result also is consistent with the trade-off theory, which, combined with the difficulty of measuring securities that are mispriced or thought by managers to be mispriced, makes it a rather weak result.

## 21.6  Concluding Comments

A rich theoretical and empirical literature on the financing decisions of firms has developed since the pioneering work of Modigliani and Miller (1958) more than fifty years ago. The literature has documented some empirical regularities that square well with parts of the three major theories, yet the evidence as a whole doesn't provide compelling support for any of them. DeAngelo and DeAngelo (2007) provide a rather bleak assessment of the evidence, stating that "the empirical corporate finance literature ... is now left with no empirically viable theory of capital structure."

Most of the empirical research on capital structure to date has focused on relatively large panel databases that include firms from various industries, a methodology that we frequently use and generally favor. However, other experimental designs may complement the existing literature and potentially provide new insights that can enrich existing theories of capital structure. We suggest three possibilities.

First, historical studies of the financing activities of firms are likely to yield insights that are perhaps masked by the large databases we typically use. For example, as discussed above, US firms relied heavily on debt financing during the 1800s, before the enactment of the federal corporate income tax. This suggests that, at least for these firms, tax savings were not a consideration in the decision to issue debt. More recent versions of the trade-off theory might suggest that firms in the 1800s issued debt to mitigate agency problems between managers and shareholders. However, this also seems unlikely, as firms that relied heavily on debt financing, such as railroads, generally had fairly concentrated equity ownership and significant growth opportunities, not the characteristics associated with the agency costs of free cash flow. If neither taxes nor agency costs explain the use of debt by railroads and other firms in the 1800s, what does explain it? A careful empirical study of business finance in the 1800s might identify additional determinants of business financing that apply today.

A second approach that may enrich the existing literature is to focus on firms that become targets of activist shareholders because of their capital structures. In the extreme, firms that are acquired in private equity transactions typically experience radical changes in their capital structures that generally are thought to be transitory. There is, of course, a large literature on these transactions and studies generally find evidence consistent with Jensen's (1986) theory related to the agency costs of free cash flow. However, it seems to us that other corporate control transactions that are motivated by a desire to change capital structures less radically have been understudied in the literature. For example, a hedge fund, Taconic Capital, recently filed a SEC Form 13D in which it stated it had acquired a 5.1% equity stake in CA, Inc., a software company. Taconic stated that it believes the company "could immediately implement actions that would result in a significant increase in the value of its common stock," including the installation of "an efficient capital structure."[12] Studies of 13D filings made by activist shareholders who want to change the target firms' capital structures could address several issues, including (i) why were these firms and not others targeted, (ii) does the activism move firms closer to what might be predicted by the trade-off theory, and (iii) how are the stock prices of these target firms affected?

Third, clinical studies of industries that undergo major changes in capital structure seem to us to be a promising area of research. Goyal et al. (2002) studied how the capital structure of defense firms and various attributes of the firms' debt contracts changed as the growth opportunities of defense firms initially increased substantially with the election of Ronald Reagan as president in 1980 and then declined substantially after the Berlin Wall fell in 1989. The evidence supported the view that growth opportunities are a significant determinant of both the level and structure of debt issued by firms. Similar experiments presumably can be conducted on firms in industries subject to other shocks, such as changes in regulation, taxes, information asymmetries, and so forth.

In addition to employing other research approaches that are complementary to the large sample studies, in our view, it is desirable to focus on improving our measurement of some key variables, including, perhaps most importantly, leverage. Two recent papers, Graham and Leary (2011) and Fama and French (2011) allude to this. In particular they cite recent work by Cornaggia et al. (2009), Rampini and Viswanathan (2010), Rauh and Sufi (2010), and Welch (2011), all of whom point out that leverage for many firms is understated if one looks only at balance sheet data. In particular, they argue that operating leases, which are an off-balance sheet item, can constitute a large amount of debt for many firms, yet this component of debt is often ignored in the literature.

For example, as of December 31, 2010, United Continental Holdings, the holding company for the merged United Airlines and Continental Airlines, reported long-term debt of $11,434 million and capital leases of $1,036 million on its balance sheet, for a total of $12,480 in total balance sheet debt. However, the footnotes to its financial statements indicate total aircraft operating lease payments from 2011 through beyond 2015 of $10,877 million and other operating lease payments of $10,577 million over the same period. Using a 10% discount rate, the present value of the operating leases exceeds the amount of debt on United Continental's balance sheet.[13] Hence, for many companies, especially in industries such as airlines or retail, the balance sheet debt may comprise a relatively small proportion of the company's debt.[14] The use of more accurate measures of leverage and other key variables in studies of capital structure is an important step forward for the literature.

## NOTES

1. We reviewed the table of contents for the *Journal of Finance* from its inception in August 1946 through December 1957, the year before the publication of Modigliani and Miller's paper. Of the 471 papers published in the journal over this period, only two examined the decisions of firms to use debt versus equity financing. See Weston (1954, 1955).
2. By holding assets constant, it follows that a firm uses the proceeds from the issuance of debt to repurchase an equivalent amount of equity.
3. The prevailing wisdom, before Modigliani and Miller, was that an advantage of debt financing was that it increased net income. For example, Weston (1954, 125) wrote that "a firm incurs debt in order to increase net income." Modigliani and Miller's Proposition II showed that although the incurrence of debt might increase a firm's net income, it would not affect the company's stock price.
4. As an interesting historical note, Ronald Coase (1960) was writing the "The Problem of Social Cost," which showed that resource allocation is invariant with respect to the initial assignment of property rights in a world of zero transaction costs, at roughly the same time that Modigliani and Miller were developing their "invariance proposition." In effect, Modigliani and Miller's invariance proposition is a special case of Coase's result.

Apparently, Modigliani/Miller and Coase were unaware of each other's work at the time their papers were published.

5. Brealey and Myers (2003, 494) present the formula that shows the relative advantage of debt as a function of the corporate tax rate and the personal tax rates paid by debtholders and stockholders.

6. Financial distress includes both bankruptcy and situations, short of bankruptcy, in which investors believe there is a relatively high probability that a company will default on its debt obligations.

7. In the first published study of the direct costs of bankruptcy, Warner (1977) found that these costs ranged from less than 1% to approximately 5% for eleven railroads that filed for bankruptcy during the period of 1930–55. When weighted by the probability of bankruptcy as of the time the debt is issued, these direct costs appear small and perhaps inconsequential for the financing decisions of firms.

8. Baskin and Miranti (1997) point out that although the federal corporate income tax was formally established in 1913, the Corporation Excise Tax Law, which effectively taxed corporate net income, was passed in 1909.

9. The United Kingdom adopted liberal depreciation deductions and an imputation system in which firms could deduct personal taxes on dividends from their income tax liabilities, which reduced the effective corporate income tax rate. See Baskin and Miranti (1997).

10. This result holds for the twenty-five nonfinancial firms listed in Table 21.1. The average and median profit margins during 2011 for the firms with above-median leverage are 7.9% and 7.2%, respectively, as compared with 16.8% and 14.5%, respectively, for the firms with below-median leverage.

11. In addition to the adverse selection costs, the direct costs of issuing securities can give rise to a pecking order in which managers prefer internal to external financing and the use of external debt to external equity.

12. CA's stock price increased 4.4% on the day of the announcement. We have not conducted an event study to determine whether the residual return is statistically significant.

13. Ignoring a firm's operating leases also can distort a firm's reported profits. Under US accounting rules, a firm includes the entire amount of an operating lease payment in either cost of goods or selling general administrative expense, even though a large proportion of the payment represents interest expense on the lease. This causes the operating profits on a firm's income statement to be understated. In the case of United Continental, it reported an operating profit of $976 million for fiscal year 2010. With more than $12 billion in operating leases, the implicit interest expense on the operating leases might well be $1,000 million or more, which means that United Continental's "true" operating profit might well be more than twice the amount reported on its income statement.

14. Post-retirement related liabilities (i.e., unfunded pension and health care benefits) are another component of debt that often is overlooked in empirical studies of capital structure.

## References

Altman, Edward I. 1984. "A Further Empirical Investigation of the Bankruptcy Cost Question." *Journal of Finance* 39:1067–89.

Asquith, Paul, and David W. Mullins, Jr. 1986. "Equity Issues and Offering Dilution." *Journal of Financial Economics* 15:61–89.

Baker, Malcolm, and Jeffrey Wurgler. 2002. "Market Timing and Capital Structure." *Journal of Finance* 57:1–32.

Barclay, Michael J., Leslie M. Marx, and Clifford W. Smith, Jr. 2003. "The Joint Determination of Leverage and Maturity." *Journal of Corporate Finance* 9:149–67.

Barclay, Michael J., and Clifford W. Smith, Jr. 2005. "The Capital Structure Puzzle: The Evidence Revisited." *Journal of Applied Corporate Finance* 17:8–17.

Baskin, Jonathan Barron, and Paul J. Miranti. 1997. *A History of Corporate Finance.* Cambridge: University of Cambridge Press.

Blazenko, George W. 1987. "Managerial Preference, Asymmetric Information, and Financial Structure." *Journal of Finance* 42:839–62.

Bradley, Michael, Gregg A. Jarrell, and E. Han Kim. 1984. "On the Existence of an Optimal Capital Structure: Theory and Evidence." *Journal of Finance* 39:857–78.

Brealey, Richard A., and Stewart C. Myers. 2003. *Principles of Corporate Finance.* New York: McGraw-Hill/Irwin.

Coase, R. H. 1960. "The Problem of Social Cost." *Journal of Law and Economics* 3:1–44.

Cornaggia, Kimberly Rodgers, Laurel Franzen, and Timothy T. Simin. 2009. "Capital Structure and the Changing Role of Off-Balance Sheet Lease Financing." Working Paper, American University, Washington, DC.

DeAngelo, Harry, and Linda DeAngelo. 2007. "Capital Structure, Payout Policy, and Financial Flexibility." Working Paper, University of Southern California, Los Angeles, CA.

DeAngelo, Harry, and Ronald Masulis. 1980. "Optimal Capital Structure under Corporate and Personal Taxation." *Journal of Financial Economics* 8:3–29.

Denis, David J., and Diane K. Denis. 1993. "Managerial Discretion, Organizational Structure, and Corporate Performance: A Study of Leveraged Recapitalizations." *Journal of Accounting and Economics* 16:209–36.

Ditmar, Amy K. 2000. "Why Do Firms Repurchase Stock?" *Journal of Business* 73:331–55.

Eckbo, B. Espen. 1986. "Valuation Effects of Corporate Debt Offerings." *Journal of Financial Economics* 15:119–51.

Fama, Eugene F., and Kenneth R. French. 2011. "Capital Structure Choices." Working Paper, University of Chicago, Chicago, IL.

Fischer, Edwin O., Josef Zechner, and Robert Heinkel. 1989. "Dynamic Capital Structure Choice: Theory and Tests." *Journal of Finance* 44:19–40.

Frank, Murray Z., and Vidhan K. Goyal. 2003. "Testing the Pecking Order Theory of Capital Structure." *Journal of Financial Economics* 67:217–48.

———. 2009. "Capital Structure Decisions: Which Factors are Reliably Important?" *Financial Management* 38:1–37.

Goyal, Vidhan K., Kenneth Lehn, and Stanko Racic. 2002. "Growth Opportunities and Corporate Debt Policy: The Case of the U.S. Defense Industry." *Journal of Financial Economics* 64:35–59.

Graham, John R. 1996. "Debt and the Marginal Tax Rate." *Journal of Financial Economics* 41:41–73.

Graham, John R., and Mark T. Leary. 2011. "A Review of Empirical Capital Structure Research and Directions for the Future." *Annual Review of Financial Economics* 3:309–45.

Jalilvand, Abolhassan, and Robert S. Harris. 1984. "Corporate Behavior in Adjusting to Capital Structure and Dividend Targets: An Econometric Study." *Journal of Finance* 39:127–45.

Jensen, Michael C. 1986. "Agency Costs of Free Cash Flow, Takeovers, and Corporate Finance." *American Economic Review* 76:323–29.

Kaplan, Steven N. 1989. "The Effects of Management Buyouts on Operating Performance and Value." *Journal of Financial Economics* 24:217–54.

Long, Michael S., and Ileen B. Malitz. 1985. "Investment Patterns and Financial Leverage." In *Corporate Structure in the United States*, edited by Benjamin M. Friedman, 325–52. Chicago: University of Chicago Press.

MacKie-Mason, Jeffrey K. 1990. "Do Taxes Affect Corporate Financing Decisions?" *Journal of Finance* 45:1471–93.

Miller, Merton H. 1977. "Debt and Taxes." *Journal of Finance* 32:261–75.

Modigliani, Franco, and Merton H. Miller. 1958. "The Cost of Capital, Corporation Finance and the Theory of Investment." *American Economic Review* 48:261–97.

Myers, Stewart C. 1977. "Determinants of Corporate Borrowing." *Journal of Financial Economics* 5:147–75.

——1984. "The Capital Structure Puzzle." *Journal of Finance* 39:575–92.

Myers, Stewart C., and Nicholas S. Majluf. 1984. "Corporate Financing and Investment Decisions When Firms Have Information the Investors Do Not Have." *Journal of Financial Economics* 13:187–221.

Opler, Tim C., and Sheridan Titman. 1994. "Financial Distress and Corporate Performance." *Journal of Finance* 49:1015–40.

Rajan, Raghuram G., and Luigi Zingales. 1995. "What Do We Know About Capital Structure? Some Evidence from International Data." *Journal of Finance* 50:1421–60.

Rampini, Adriano S., and S. Viswanathan. "Collateral, Risk Management, and the Distribution of Debt Capacity." *Journal of Finance* 65:2293–2322.

Rauh, Joshua D., and Amir Sufi. 2010. "Capital Structure and Debt Structure." *Review of Financial Studies* 23:4242–80.

Ross, Stephen. 1977. "The Determination of Capital Structure: The Incentive Signalling Approach." *Bell Journal of Economics* 8:23–40.

Shyam-Sunder, Lakshmi, and Stewart C. Myers. 1999. "Testing Static Tradeoff against Pecking Order Models of Capital Structure." *Journal of Financial Economics* 51:219–44.

Smith, Clifford W., and Ross L. Watts. 1992. "The Investment Opportunity Set and Corporate Financing, Dividend and Compensation Policies." *Journal of Financial Economics* 32:263–92.

Titman, Sheridan, and Roberto Wessels. 1988. "The Determinants of Capital Structure Choice." *Journal of Finance* 43:1–19.

Vermaelen, Theo. 1981. "Common Stock Repurchases and Market Signaling: An Empirical Study." *Journal of Financial Economics* 9:139–83.

Warner, Jerold B. 1977. "Bankruptcy Costs: Some Evidence." *Journal of Finance* 32:337–47.

Welch, Ivo. 2011. "Two Common Problems in Capital Structure Research: The Financial Debt-to-Asset Ratio and Issuing Activity Versus Leverage Changes." *International Review of Finance* 11:1–17.

Weston, J. Fred. 1954. "Norms for Debt Levels." *Journal of Finance* 9:124–35.

——. 1955. "Toward Theories of Financial Policies." *Journal of Finance* 10:130–43.

Wruck, Karen H. 1989. "Organizational Changes and Value Creation in Leveraged Buyouts: The Case of O. M. Scott & Sons Company." *Journal of Financial Economics* 25:163–90.

.....................................................................................................................................

# CHAPTER 22

# CORPORATE GOVERNANCE
# AND FIRM PERFORMANCE

.....................................................................................................................................

## ANUP AGRAWAL AND CHARLES R. KNOEBER

THIS chapter reviews the sizeable literature on corporate governance and firm performance in economies with relatively dispersed stock ownership and an active market for corporate control, such as the United States and the United Kingdom. This review is not intended to be exhaustive and we apologize to authors whose work is not cited. Instead, we provide a conceptual overview, suggest important issues, and offer a pathway to the larger literature. We start in section 22.1 by outlining a framework of the basic agency problem between managers and shareholders and the corporate governance mechanisms that have evolved to address this problem. Section 22.2 deals with the relation between firm performance and inside ownership. Section 22.3 pertains to the relation between firm performance and monitoring by large shareholders, monitoring by boards, and shareholder rights regarding takeover of the firm. Section 22.4 considers the relation between governance regulation and firm performance. Section 22.5 deals with the relation between governance and firm performance in family firms. Finally, section 22.6 provides a summary and identifies some remaining puzzles and unresolved issues for future research.

## 22.1 THE AGENCY PROBLEM

.....................................................................................................................................

Owners (i.e., shareholders) of a firm have a claim on the firm's net income. As a consequence, their interest is in greater net income and its multiperiod, present value analog—a higher stock price. Call this profit, and label it $\pi$. Larger $\pi$ means better performance. However, owners do not operate their firm; they employ managers to do this for them. Hired managers have no inherent interest in firm profit since this belongs to the owners, but their behavior affects profit. To capture this, think of a manager choosing what Demsetz (1983) calls on-the-job consumption or what is often referred to as private benefits. Call this $a$. On-the-job consumption may be in the form of perks, such as airplane use, but it is much broader. Not working hard, not taking chances, or indulging one's political tastes with company resources are all forms of $a$. Importantly, profit depends inversely on $a$, or $\pi(a)$ where $\pi' < 0$. Since the benefits of $a$ are enjoyed by managers while the costs are borne by owners (lower profit), managers will choose an $a$ that is too large from the owners' point of view.[1] This is the agency problem. Managers' incentives are not aligned with those of the owners. The result is lower profit or worse performance. Solving or ameliorating the agency problem provides better incentives to managers and results in better firm performance.

There are two fundamental ways for owners to address the agency problem. The first way is to make the managers part owners—that is, inside ownership. As part owners, managers will still enjoy the benefits of on-the-job consumption but will now also incur some of the costs. The greater is inside ownership, the more aligned are the interests of owners and managers. The advantage of inside ownership as a way to address the agency problem is that owners do not have to monitor managers. Profit (or stock price), $\pi$, is the *outcome* of manager behavior, and it is publicly observed. When owners are enriched, managers (as owners) are automatically enriched as well. The disadvantage of inside ownership is that profit depends on many things in addition to manager behavior, $a$. This makes profit a noisy signal of what managers have done. There are two undesirable consequences of this noise. First, by diffusing the link between better manager behavior (less $a$) and manager reward, it dilutes the incentive for managers to behave better. Second, it imposes risk on managers because their reward is partly determined by things beyond their control. Since managers are risk averse, they must be paid more to bear this risk.

The second way is for owners to monitor managers in order to try to measure *input* $a$ directly and then to reward or penalize managers based upon their measured behavior. The advantage of rewarding managers based on owner monitoring is that it makes the link between manager behavior and reward less noisy. So, incentives can be made stronger and managers need bear less risk. The disadvantage is that it is costly for owners to monitor. This is a particular problem because owners face a free-rider problem. Each owner benefits from better manager behavior when another owner incurs the cost of monitoring. Each, then, would like to free-ride on the monitoring effort of others. Motivating owner monitoring becomes a problem.

Neither way of addressing the agency problem is perfect. Moreover, both ways allow for differences in firm mechanisms that in turn determine the effectiveness of owner response to the agency problem. Sometimes firms adopt these mechanisms; sometimes they are imposed on them. The set of such mechanisms employed by a firm is what we call corporate governance.

## 22.2  INSIDE OWNERSHIP

Greater inside ownership raises the cost to managers of on-the-job consumption, $a$, and so should lead to less $a$ and, in turn, larger firm profits. The empirical literature assessing the relationship between inside ownership and firm performance largely began with a 1988 paper by Morck et al. For large US firms in 1980, they regress Tobin's q (measured as the market value of a firm divided by the book value of its total assets) on the fraction of the firm owned by its board of directors. Using a piecewise linear model, they find a surprising relation. For inside ownership less than 5%, increasing ownership results in improved firm performance (larger Tobin's q); but for inside ownership between 5% and 25%, increasing ownership results in poorer firm performance (and there is little effect for inside ownership greater than 25%). McConnell and Servaes (1990) extend this analysis to the years 1976 and 1986 and to a broader set of firms. Instead of a piecewise linear model, they estimate a quadratic model, including both the fraction of inside ownership and its square. And they find a similar result. Increasing inside ownership results in improved firm performance up to about 50% inside ownership in 1976 and up to about 38% inside ownership in 1986, but beyond that increased inside ownership worsens firm performance.

Morck et al. suggest a rationale for the non-monotonic relation between inside ownership and firm performance. In addition to inside ownership giving managers a claim on firm profits, it also gives managers voting power. As this power becomes greater, managers will be harder to displace and so become more entrenched. Increased inside ownership, then, has two opposing effects on managerial incentives. Managers behave better because they have a stake in firm profits, but they behave worse because they are less afraid of dismissal. The latter implies that owners are monitoring the managers and linking manager tenure to manager behavior (the second way to address the agency problem). Importantly, this means that there are multiple mechanisms at work and that these act together to provide incentives to managers.

Two issues bedevil the interpretation of the non-monotonic relation between inside ownership and firm performance. One is multiple mechanisms. A regression that looks at inside ownership alone is likely mis-specified and so the inside ownership effect may be spurious. The second is the endogeneity of inside ownership and firm performance. Since inside ownership is chosen by the firm, treating it as arising exogenously may lead to misleading estimates of the effect of inside ownership on firm performance. Starting with the second issue, Demsetz (1983) and later Demsetz and Lehn (1985) consider the relation between ownership concentration (their focus is not exclusively on inside ownership) and firm performance. If firms choose inside ownership optimally, then it will differ across firms depending on a firm's costs and benefits of greater insider ownership. Where cost is high or benefit is low, inside ownership will be small; where cost is low or benefit is high, insider ownership will be large. So, inside ownership will vary among firms, but if each firm has chosen it optimally then all are maximizing profits. There should be no cross-sectional relation between inside ownership and firm performance. That such a relation exists suggests either that firms do not choose optimally (the implicit assumption in Morck et al. 1988; and McConnell and Servaes 1990) or that something else (such as the cost or benefit of inside ownership) is driving both firm performance and inside ownership. If this endogeneity is accounted for empirically, the relation between inside ownership and firm performance should evaporate.

With these two issues in mind, Agrawal and Knoeber (1996) examine the relation between inside ownership and firm performance (again, using Tobin's q) for large US firms in 1987. Using a quadratic model like McConnell and Servaes (1990), they find a similar nonlinear relation between inside ownership and firm performance. And, when they introduce six other mechanisms that also provide incentives to managers (tied to the concentration of ownership by outsiders, board composition, and the markets for managers, capital and corporate control) into the estimation, the relation between inside ownership and firm performance largely disappears. When they estimate a simultaneous equation system consisting of one equation for each of the six governance mechanisms and an equation for Tobin's q to account for the simultaneity and endogeneity of these governance mechanisms and firm performance, this relationship evaporates.

Himmelberg et al. (1999) provide a similar finding. Using panel data for 1982–92, they find strong evidence that unobserved heterogeneity among firms is an important determinant of inside ownership. Controlling for this heterogeneity with firm fixed effects, the relation between inside ownership and firm performance disappears. Both the simultaneous equations and the firm fixed effects approaches are subject to several criticisms. First, it is very difficult to find appropriate instrumental variables for each equation and poor instruments may disguise an underlying relationship. Second, the simultaneous equations approach is quite sensitive to model specification. A mis-specification of any equation affects the entire system and inflates the standard errors (i.e., reduces t-statistics) of the coefficient estimates. Finally, firm fixed effects require within-firm variation in inside ownership to drive changes in firm performance. Zhou (2001) argues that within-firm variation in inside ownership is small and unlikely to motivate changes in long-term decision making by managers and so ultimately in firm performance. So even if inside ownership does affect firm performance, evidence of this relation is unlikely to survive the use of firm fixed effects.

Gompers et al. (2010) return to the rationale that Morck et al. (1988) provide for the non-monotonic relation they find between inside ownership and firm performance. Greater inside ownership engenders two opposing incentive effects. As owners, managers' claim on profits means that they pay more for their on-the-job consumption but as owners with votes, managers are more secure in their jobs. Looking at firms with dual-class stock which divide cash-flow rights differently from voting rights, they are able to estimate the two incentive effects separately. They find that, holding voting rights constant, an increase in cash-flow rights improves firm performance (at least until inside ownership is quite large). And holding cash-flow rights constant, an increase in voting rights reduces firm performance. Combined, greater inside ownership has a non-monotonic effect on firm performance (industry-adjusted Tobin's q), similar to that in McConnell and Servaes (1990). Moreover, these results persist after using instrumental variables to account for endogeneity.

Although primarily concerned with the endogeneity of inside ownership, Cho (1998) considers the path by which inside ownership may affect firm performance. He posits that inside ownership affects the level of firm investment (measured either by capital expenditures or R&D expenditures), which in turn affects firm performance. Using a piecewise linear model and data for large US firms in 1991, he finds an empirical relation between inside ownership and investment level that is similar to that found by Morck et al. (1988), suggesting that this may be the path along which inside ownership affects firm performance. But when 2SLS is used to account for the endogeneity of these variables, the relation disappears.

Coles et al. (2012) push this approach further. They develop a parsimonious structural model in which optimal inside ownership and firm performance are jointly determined in equilibrium. They then use data for firms during the 1993–2000 period to calibrate this model, solving for the implied unobservable parameters that would make observed choices optimal. They then use this model to simulate data and use it to estimate a regression model like that in McConnell and Servaes (1990). And they find a very similar result. As inside ownership increases, Tobin's q at first rises and then falls. This suggests that the empirical non-monotonic relation between inside ownership and firm performance may indeed be spurious. More interestingly, employing the standard instrumental variables and fixed effects treatments to the simulated data does not eliminate this spurious relation. The endogeneity problem appears particularly difficult to solve here.

## 22.3  MONITORING

Section 22.3.1 deals with monitoring by large shareholders, section 22.3.2 deals with monitoring by boards, and section 22.3.3 deals with shareholder rights regarding takeover of the firm.

### 22.3.1  Large Shareholders

Because they receive a large proportion of firm profits, large shareholders, such as blockholders and institutional investors, have stronger incentives to monitor and contract with managers to reduce agency problems (see, e.g., Demsetz and Lehn 1985; Shleifer and Vishny 1986; and Holderness 2003). However, blockholders can also use their power to extract private benefits. Analyzing block sales, Barclay and Holderness (1989, 1992) argue that in the absence of private benefits, blocks should trade at the exchange price. They find that on average, blocks command a substantial premium over the exchange price, suggesting that blocks confer private benefits. Moreover when blocks are sold at a premium, stock prices typically increase (though not to the block price), suggesting both shared and private benefits of block ownership. But Atanasov et al. (2010) find that publicly traded firms with corporate blockholders who own substantial minority stakes are valued at substantial discounts to peers, which suggests that such blockholders extract private benefits that exceed any shared benefits from their ownership.

McConnell and Servaes (1990) find no significant relation between firm valuations (i.e., Tobin's q) and the existence or holdings of an outside blockholder. They examine a large sample of NYSE and AMEX firms for two years, 1976 and 1986. Mehran (1995) also finds no significant relationship between firm performance (both Tobin's q and return on assets) and outside blockholdings. In a similar vein, Holderness and Sheehan (1988) find no significant differences between the accounting rates of return or Tobin's q of paired majority-owned and diffusely held corporations. But these early studies do not take into account the endogeneity of blockholdings.

Becker, Cronqvist and Fahlenbrach (2011) separate the selection and treatment effects of individual outside blockholder existence on firm (operating) performance. Using the number of wealthy individuals per public firm in the state of a firm's headquarters as an instrument for blockholder presence in a firm, they find that blockholder presence significantly improves firm performance. Their sample consists of about 6000 firm-years of data on S&P 1500 firms from 1996 to 2001.

Agrawal and Nasser (2011) argue that neither board independence nor outside blockholder presence alone may be a match for CEO power in most firms. Nominally independent directors with negligible shareholdings may have neither sufficient incentive nor the ability to confront a powerful CEO, especially if they have been handpicked by the CEO. While an outside blockholder has an incentive to monitor the CEO, without a board seat, he may lack sufficient information and a regular forum for monitoring the CEO. Thus, independent directors who are blockholders (IDBs) enjoy a unique position and power in a firm. IDBs can use this power to increase firm valuation, which would benefit all shareholders, but can also extract private benefits. Using a panel containing about 11,500 firm-years for S&P 1500 firms over the 1998–2006 period, Agrawal and Nasser find that firms with IDBs have higher valuations, as measured by Tobin's q. They explicitly account for the endogeneity of IDB presence and control for board independence and outside blockholder presence, neither of which has a significant effect on q. About three-fourths of the IDBs in their sample are individual investors, who drive most of their results.

Another stream of the literature examines the relation between stockholdings of other large investors, such as institutions and activist hedge funds, and firm performance. These investors have incentives to monitor and they can pressure managers to adopt better corporate governance. Black (1998), Karpoff (2001) and Gillan and Starks (2007) provide excellent reviews of the large literature on institutional activism. These reviews show that activism by institutional investors, such as mutual funds and pension funds, does not improve firm performance. This ineffectiveness is often attributed to regulatory and institutional constraints. On the other hand, as Brav et al. (2009) discuss in their review of the literature on hedge fund activism, activist hedge funds are more successful in influencing corporate boards and managers, leading to better stock returns and operating performance.

## 22.3.2  Boards

The board of directors is the locus for monitoring and rewarding (penalizing) managers. However, this is not the only role that boards play. They also act as advisors providing input into strategic decision making. Our focus is monitoring, but nothing comes free. Better monitoring likely means poorer advising.

Boards are typically measured by two characteristics—their size (number of members) and their composition (fraction of members who are outsiders or independent of management). With either characteristic, there is a trade-off between more information and more effective decision making. Bigger boards bring more (sources of) information but make coming to a collective decision more difficult. Similarly more outsider-oriented boards sacrifice information that insiders bring, but may be more unified in what to do given the available information. An optimal board is one with the size and composition that adjusts this trade-off to maximize firm value. If boards are constituted optimally, they likely will differ across firms, reflecting the relative value of better information and better execution. However, following Demsetz (1983), looking across firms, there should be no relation between board structure and firm performance. The evidence is mixed.

Yermack (1996) examines large US firms from 1984 to 1991 and finds a strong negative effect of board size on Tobin's q. Boards seem systematically to be too big. Moreover, this is very costly. For a firm with eight board members (the average is about twelve), an extra member reduces firm value by $100 million; for a firm with fifteen board members, an extra member reduces firm value by $50 million. This is a puzzling finding. Why should essentially all firms appear unwilling, despite the substantial rewards, to reduce board size? One possibility is that the trade-off between information and execution changed for all firms (say because globalization made all markets more competitive) due to an increase in the relative value of execution. So, boards that once were optimal no longer are. All firms will adjust, but those with higher adjustment costs will do so more slowly. During this process there will be a negative relation between board size and firm performance. But in addition, we should see board size falling on average. This is exactly what has happened, with board sizes falling by about two members since Yermack's study.

Hermalin and Weisbach (1991) investigate the relation between the fraction of board members who are outsiders and Tobin's q for firms during five different years (mostly in the 1970s). They estimate a piecewise linear model using instrumental variables to account for endogeneity. They find no relation between board composition and firm performance, consistent with firms choosing board composition optimally.

Duchin et al. (2010) take advantage of the natural experiment provided by the implementation of Sarbanes-Oxley Act (SOX) rules requiring minimum proportions of outside directors. They first predict firm changes in the proportion of outside (independent) directors during 2000–2005 (SOX passed in 2002). They then regress changes in firm performance over the same period on the (predicted) change in board composition. If board composition was optimal and SOX-induced changes are suboptimal, then firm performance should fall. And where those induced changes are greatest, firm performance should fall the most. Increases in the proportion of outsiders should be negatively related to firm performance. For firms where insiders are an important source of information (where analysts' predictions show great dispersion), this is indeed the case. But for firms where insiders are not an important source of information (dispersion among analysts' predictions is small), the induced increase in the proportion of outsiders increases firm performance. This suggests that for this set of firms, board composition was not chosen optimally.

Boards structure themselves into smaller committees for certain tasks. The number of such committees varies across boards, but their purposes comport with the two roles that boards play—monitoring and advising. Audit, nominating, and compensation committees focus on monitoring. Others such as the finance and investment committees focus on advising. Klein (1998), like Hermalin and Weisbach (1991), finds no relation between the proportion of outside directors and firm performance among large US firms in the early 1990s. Similarly, she finds no relation between firm performance and the proportion of outsiders on committees focused on monitoring, but she finds a negative relation between firm performance and the proportion of outsiders on committees focused on advising. The latter result suggests that insiders play an important informational role and that boards may not take sufficient advantage of this.

Faleye et al. (2011) characterize outside board members as intensively engaged in monitoring if a majority are on at least two committees devoted to monitoring. Based on a sample of S&P 1500 firms over the 1986–2006 period, they find evidence that this effort is successful. Firms with outsiders intensively engaged in monitoring provide smaller excess CEO compensation and are more likely to dismiss a CEO for poor performance. But these gains come at a cost—less intensive advising—and this cost is exhibited in poorer acquisition returns and poorer innovation. Moreover, the net effect of intensive outsider monitoring is to reduce firm performance (lower Tobin's q). This result survives controls for the endogeneity of board structure, including a test on firms that were forced to change committee structure by SOX. Adams and Ferreira (2009) focus on women directors (mostly outsiders) and find a similar result. Women directors serve disproportionately on monitoring committees and the greater is the fraction of women board members, the more likely it is that a poorly performing CEO will be fired. But firm performance declines with the fraction of women directors, even accounting for endogeneity.

## 22.3.3 Shareholder Rights

Gompers et al. (GIM 2003) use the incidence of twenty-four governance rules to construct a Governance Index (G) to measure the level of shareholder rights at S&P 1500 firms during the 1990s. Most of these rules are antitakeover provisions (ATPs) in the corporate charter or bylaws, such as classified boards, fair price provisions, or poison pills; others are state antitakeover laws that apply to firms incorporated in the state. GIM find that firms with stronger shareholder rights (i.e., fewer ATPs) had higher valuations (Tobin's q), higher profits and higher stock returns. The results on q and profits are puzzling: Why don't shareholders of all firms demand more rights to increase the profitability and value of their investments? And the results on stock returns are inconsistent with weak-form market efficiency.

GIM argue that weak shareholder rights may cause additional agency costs and so compromise operating performance. If investors underestimate these additional costs, stock returns would be lower than expected, leading to lower valuations. GIM find some support for this explanation in the form of more capital spending and takeover activity, suggesting greater agency costs, in firms with weak shareholder rights. Alternatively, since governance provisions are not adopted randomly, they may not cause higher agency costs, but their presence may be correlated with other characteristics that produced abnormal returns in the 1990s. In support of this omitted variables explanation, the authors find that industry effects explain some of their results. They conclude that the remaining performance differences, which are economically large, were either directly caused by governance provisions or were related to unobservable or hard-to-measure characteristics correlated with them.

Bebchuk et al. (BCF 2009) provide a more parsimonious specification of GIM's main results. They construct an entrenchment index based on just six of the twenty-four provisions in the G-index that essentially replicates GIM's results on firm valuation and abnormal stock returns. These six provisions are staggered board terms, limits to shareholder bylaw amendments, poison pills, golden parachutes, and supermajority requirements for mergers and amending charters. The other eighteen provisions in the G-index are unrelated to valuation and abnormal returns.

Cremers and Nair (2005) show that GIM's results hold only if stronger shareholder rights are accompanied by large institutional ownership. They find that a long-short portfolio, formed from the group of firms with high ownership by institutional blockholders or public pension funds, that holds stocks of firms with weak ATPs and shorts stocks of firms with strong ATPs has large positive abnormal returns; the corresponding portfolio formed from the group of firms with low ownership by institutional blockholders or public pension funds has insignificant abnormal returns. Their results also imply that takeovers and large shareholders are complementary governance mechanisms. This relation is stronger in firms with low leverage, consistent with theories in which higher debt reduces the probability of takeover (see, e.g., Stulz 1988; and Harris and Raviv 1988).

Masulis, Wang and Xie (2007) identify one channel through which ATPs can reduce firm value. They find that firms with more ATPs make worse acquisitions, as evidenced by lower abnormal returns upon announcement. This result continues to hold in a subsample of firms that (likely) adopted ATPs several years before acquisitions, reducing the likelihood of reverse causality from firms adopting ATPs just before making bad acquisitions. Their results continue to hold after controlling for CEO quality, reducing the possibility of spurious correlation caused by bad CEOs adopting takeover defenses for entrenchment purposes *and* making poor acquisitions. And these results are robust to controlling for a variety of other governance mechanisms, including product market competition, leverage, CEO equity incentives, institutional ownership, and board characteristics.

Giroud and Mueller (2011) argue that managers of firms in noncompetitive industries do not have strong incentives to reduce slack and maximize profits, so the benefits of good governance (i.e., strong shareholder rights) should be larger for such firms. They find that firms with weak governance have lower equity returns, worse operating performance, and lower firm value, but only in noncompetitive industries. Firms with weak governance also have lower labor productivity and higher input costs, and make more value-destroying acquisitions, but only in noncompetitive industries. Finally, they find that firms with weak governance in noncompetitive industries are more likely to be targeted by activist hedge funds, suggesting that investors take actions to mitigate the inefficiency.

Lehn et al. (2007) reexamine the GIM and BCF findings of a negative relation between valuation multiples and governance indices during the 1990s to test whether causation runs from governance to valuation or vice versa. They find that valuation multiples during the early 1980s, a period preceding the adoption of the antitakeover provisions comprising the governance indices, are highly correlated with valuation multiples during the 1990s. After controlling for valuation multiples during 1980–85, they find no significant relation between contemporaneous valuation multiples and governance indices during the 1990s. Their findings suggest that firms with low valuations were more likely to adopt provisions comprising the governance indices, not that the adoption of these provisions depresses valuations.

Core et al. (2006) reexamine GIM's puzzling finding that firms with weak shareholder rights exhibit significant stock market underperformance. If poor governance *causes* poor stock returns, it must be that investors are surprised by the poor operating performance of weak governance firms. To assess this, Core et al. examine the relations between G and either analyst forecast errors or earnings announcement returns. They find that while firms with weak shareholder rights exhibit significant operating underperformance, neither analysts' forecast errors nor abnormal returns upon earnings announcements show evidence that this underperformance surprises the market. Alternatively, weak governance may cause lower stock returns if the stock returns of firms with more ATPs (i.e., weak governance) drop when investors are surprised by the diminished probability of receiving a takeover bid. But here the authors find that weak governance firms are taken over at about the same rate as strong governance firms, and the return differences related to G are not sensitive to excluding firms that were taken over. Those results do not support the idea that weak governance causes poor stock returns. Core et al. suggest that GIM's result that firms with poor governance experience low stock returns may be specific to the 1990s time-period of their study or to the tech stock bubble of the late 1990s because the result is sensitive to the exclusion of technology firms and does not hold in the four years (2000–2003) following GIM's sample period.

Johnson et al. (2009) return to the GIM and BCF findings of large positive long-term abnormal returns on a zero-cost investment portfolio that is long in stocks of firms with strong shareholder rights and short in stocks of firms with weak shareholder rights. They find that these two groups of firms differ from the population of firms and from each other in how they cluster across industries. GIM adjust for industry-clustering in their portfolio using the Fama and French (1997) forty-eight-industry classification and find statistically significant abnormal returns of approximately 5.8% per year during the

1990s. Johnson et al. argue that the Fama-French forty-eight-industry classification is too coarse to measure industry returns accurately. With tests that adjust for industry returns using narrower, more precise three-digit SIC industries, they find statistically zero long-term abnormal returns for GIM's long-short governance portfolio.

Lewellen and Metrick (2010) dispute Johnson et al.'s result. Using an alternative industry adjustment, they confirm a large positive abnormal return during the 1990s on GIM's zero-cost long-short governance portfolio. Moreover, they argue that since a narrowly defined industry classification includes fewer firms in an industry than a broadly defined classification, industry returns computed using the former may contain high levels of idiosyncratic noise. They conclude that narrowly defined industry classifications are not necessarily better than broader classifications. Finally, using the Johnson et al. empirical specification, they find that a majority of the industry-adjusted asset pricing tests with the strongest empirical properties also yield statistically and economically significant industry-adjusted returns on the GIM governance portfolio.

Bebchuk et al. (2012) present evidence to suggest that the positive long-run returns on the GIM and BCF long-short governance portfolios were specific to their 1990s sample period. With the same methodology, they find statistically zero abnormal return on this portfolio during the subsequent 2000–2008 period. They find that the existence and subsequent disappearance of the abnormal return on this portfolio cannot be fully explained either by additional common risk factors suggested in the literature for augmenting the Fama-French-Carhart four-factor model (such as the liquidity risk factor of Pastor and Stambaugh 2003; the downside risk factor of Ang et al. 2006; and the takeover risk factor of Cremers et al. 2009) or by the Lewellen and Metrick (2010) industry-adjustment. They suggest that the positive return disappeared in the 2000s as investors learned about the abnormal return on this portfolio and invested in it.

## 22.4 GOVERNANCE REGULATION

La Porta et al. (2002) find that international variation in legal rules on investor protection affects firm value. Investor protection in US firms varies according to the firm's state of incorporation. Each state has its own corporate laws and court system. States differ in the resources they devote to resolving corporate disputes and sometimes customize legal rules to suit local firms or interest groups. Delaware corporate law is the nation's most important as more than half of all public firms are incorporated there. Legal scholars have long debated Delaware law's effect on agency costs and firm value. Based on a sample of about 4500 US public companies during 1981–96, Daines (2001) finds that Delaware corporate law improves firm valuation (i.e., Tobin's q) and facilitates the sale of public firms. He finds that Delaware firms are worth significantly more than similar firms incorporated elsewhere, after controlling for other factors and accounting for endogeneity. Delaware firms are also more likely to receive takeover bids and subsequently be acquired.

Dahya and McConnell (2007) examine the relation between changes in board composition and corporate performance in the United Kingdom over 1989–96, a period that surrounds the 1992 publication of the Cadbury Report, which recommends at least three outside directors for public companies. While the recommendation was not enacted into UK law, legislation was to follow if companies failed to comply with it voluntarily. In addition, the London Stock Exchange requires a statement from its listed companies indicating whether the company is compliant with the Cadbury recommendations and, if not, to explain why not. Contrary to their expectation, the authors find that this "quasi-mandated" board structure is associated with an improvement in the performance of UK companies. They find that companies that add directors to comply with this standard exhibit a significant improvement in operating performance both in absolute terms and relative to various peer group benchmarks. They also find a statistically significant increase in stock prices around announcements that outside directors were added in conformance with this recommendation.

High-profile corporate scandals in the United States in the early 2000s led to the adoption of tough, new governance rules as part of SOX and the listing requirements of major US stock markets. Chhaochharia and Grinstein (2007) find that the announcement of these rules had a significant effect on firm value. They focus on five main provisions of the new rules, dealing with insider trading, financial reporting, related party transactions, internal controls, and board and committee independence. For each provision, they construct portfolios of more compliant and less compliant firms. In general, they find that firms that were less compliant with the rules earn larger, positive abnormal returns in the announcement year compared to more compliant firms. They argue that the provisions on internal controls and director independence can affect small firms and large firms differently. For these provisions, they find that within the group of less compliant firms, large firms earn positive abnormal returns, while small firms earn negative abnormal returns, suggesting that some provisions are detrimental to small firms.

Zhang (2007) examines the effects of SOX by examining market reactions to related legislative events. Using an international asset pricing model to estimate normal US returns, she finds that US firms experienced significantly negative cumulative abnormal returns around key SOX events. She then examines the cross-sectional variation of US firms' returns around these events and finds that the nonaudit services and governance provisions appear to impose net costs on firms. Deferring the compliance of section 404 internal control provisions appears to result in significant cost savings for small firms.

An important purpose of SOX was to improve the accuracy and reliability of accounting information reported to investors. As such, it is the most important legislation affecting corporate financial reporting enacted in the United States since the 1930s. Li et al. (2008) argue that the WorldCom fraud announcement changed the political landscape for substantive financial accounting reform. They find significantly positive returns for the US stock market associated with eight SOX events following the WorldCom revelations. Instead of trying to adjust for a normal US stock market return, the authors consider other contemporaneous news (focusing on macroeconomic events, accounting scandals, and related accounting issues) when analyzing the market return on SOX event days. They also find a positive relation between individual firms' stock returns on SOX event days and the extent of earnings management (i.e., "manipulation") across firms. Their results are consistent with investors anticipating that the more extensively firms had managed earnings in the past, the more SOX would constrain earnings management in the future and so improve the quality of financial statement information.

One of the most controversial provisions of SOX is section 404. This section, implemented by the US Securities and Exchange Commission (SEC) in 2003, requires a company to introduce and periodically test procedures that monitor its internal control systems ensuring accurate financial reports. The rule requires managers to report their findings annually in the 10K report to shareholders and outside auditors to attest to management's assessment of the company's controls. The SEC intended these procedures to help companies deter financial fraud by detecting fraudulent reporting early, improving the reliability of financial statements. Critics argue that this requirement is quite onerous and costly, particularly for small companies.

Iliev (2010) investigates the effect of SOX section 404 on firm values, using a natural quasi-experiment to isolate the effects of this provision. US firms with a public float[2] under $75 million could delay section 404 compliance (to fiscal year 2007 for the management report and to June 2010 for auditor's attestation), and foreign firms under $700 million could delay the auditor's attestation requirement to fiscal year 2006. Iliev uses a regression discontinuity design that compares the companies that were just above the rule's cutoff and had to file the report to companies that were just below the cutoff and did not have to file the report. He finds that section 404 compliance leads to higher audit costs and less earnings management, measured by discretionary accruals. Management report filers have higher returns around SOX-related announcements of delays in section 404 implementation. Overall, section 404 compliance led to conservative reported earnings, but also imposed real costs. On net, it reduced the market values of small firms.

## 22.5 FAMILY FIRMS

Family firms where managers are related to (substantial) shareholders introduce social considerations into the agency problem. This may help or hurt. An advantage is that the manager may have nonmonetary reasons to reduce on-the-job consumption. He may care about the welfare of the other shareholders or he may take pleasure in the success of the firm either of which naturally aligns his interest with that of the owners. A disadvantage is that the (family) owners may care about the manager. This may deter them from monitoring and punishing the manager for bad behavior, allowing her to pursue her interest at their expense. Incentives may be better or worse in a family firm. A second effect is that family firms draw managers mostly from close kin, and this pool likely yields a less able manager than the broader pool of managers.

A focus of research on family firms has been CEO successions. When a family firm chooses a new CEO, often replacing the founding family member, what is the effect of choosing the new CEO from among the family? Anderson and Reeb (2003) examine large US firms during 1993–99 and compare the performance of firms choosing a family CEO with those choosing an outsider. Accounting measures of performance seem better with family succession, but Tobin's q shows no difference. Villalonga and Amit (2006) look at a similar set of firms but find that choosing a succeeding CEO from within the family reduces Tobin's q. However, this seems to be true only for the first successor to a founder. For third and later generations, family succession has no differential effect. Cucculelli and Micucci (2008) examine a large sample of Italian firms in the late 1990s. Using a difference-in-difference method, they find a decline in accounting performance with family successions, but only for those firms that had previously performed well.

Bennedsen et al. (2007) look at Danish firms using similar methods and also find a decline in accounting returns with family succession. Moreover, controlling for endogeneity with instrumental variables they find an even larger effect. Perez-Gonzalez (2006) investigates the source of this performance decline. Using data for US firms during 1980–2000, he finds that accounting performance declines with family succession, but only for new CEOs who did not attend selective undergraduate schools. To the extent that attendance at these schools indicates greater ability, this finding implies that the incentive effects of family firms are a wash (the good balances the bad), but when drawing from the family pool results in a low ability CEO, performance at the family firm suffers.

## 22.6  SUMMARY AND SUGGESTIONS FOR FUTURE WORK

Characterizing the mechanisms of corporate governance and their empirical relation to firm performance has generated a huge literature. We have organized our survey of this literature with no intention of being exhaustive. Instead, we have been quite selective. Our intent is to provide a conceptual overview, to suggest important issues, and to offer a portal to the larger literature. The extent of this larger literature is a reflection of the importance of the topic and of the difficulties in analysis. We provide here a bird's-eye view of the literature that we have discussed, note some important contributions, and identify some remaining puzzles and unresolved issues for future research.

The persistent finding of a non-monotonic relation between the extent of inside ownership and firm performance is a puzzle that has motivated a large literature, but no resolution. One rationale is that inside ownership creates offsetting incentives for managers by simultaneously providing automatic reward for better firm performance and insulation from penalty for poor performance. The strongest evidence for this rationale derives from work on dual-class stock which allows these two effects to work separately. Another rationale is that the puzzling relation is spurious. The fragility of the relation to several techniques to control for mis-specification and endogeneity problems supports this rationale, as does recent structural work showing that this relation can arise spuriously with no fundamental underpinning.

Similar to the first rationale for the insider shareholding puzzle, more concentrated shareholding by outsiders provides both an incentive for better monitoring which should improve firm performance and power to extract private benefits which should impede firm performance. Here, again, any empirical relation between blockholding and firm performance will be confounded by endogeneity problems. Controlling for endogeneity, it appears that the better monitoring effect dominates, at least in the United States, where blockholdings tend to be relatively small compared to the controlling shareholders that characterize firms in much of the world. The likely pathway for this better monitoring is blockholder presence on the board of directors, and recent evidence suggests that it is the combination of blockholding and board membership that improves firm performance.

But it is not just monitoring that boards do; they also provide strategic advice. The literature on boards examines the adjustments to board size, composition, and internal board structure that firms make and whether these adjustments optimally balance the two roles and so maximize firm value. There is some evidence that boards are typically too large and that, where strategic advice is important, they are too outsider-oriented. And there is evidence that boards structure themselves (with committees) to focus too much on monitoring. Why this is the case is a puzzle.

The market for corporate control imposes discipline on managers from outside the firm, but it may also upset internal arrangements that firms make to address the agency problem. Firms sometimes adopt antitakeover provisions that impede the market for corporate control (the label given is "weak shareholder rights") and so relax this outside discipline. Indexes measuring the extent of these antitakeover provisions appear negatively related to firm performance, suggesting that the external market for corporate control is more effective (at least at the margin) than internal mechanisms to address the agency problem. Further results suggest that this result may be limited to firms with large blockholders (who perhaps facilitate the market for corporate control) or to firms in noncompetitive industries (which lack product market discipline). Moreover, some evidence suggests that the relation between antitakeover provisions and firm performance is time-period specific or perhaps the spurious result of the endogeneity of antitakeover provisions. This issue is not yet settled.

Like the market for corporate control, legal rules and regulations can impose discipline from outside the firm that helps address the agency problem, but these rules can also impede internal mechanisms. The positive relation between firm value and Delaware incorporation (making a firm subject to Delaware corporate law) suggests that regulation of corporate governance can improve firm performance. Some additional evidence on the effect of federal governance regulation in the United States, specifically rules that followed the corporate scandals of the early 2000s, supports this. Those firms less compliant with the new regulations fared better than more compliant firms (as did firms with a history of managing earnings), which suggests that where the new rules had greater impact, they did more good. Quasi-regulation in the United Kingdom focusing on mandated board structures appears to have had a similar effect. But other evidence suggests that the new US rules, especially those that most directly impacted internal monitoring by mandating strong internal controls, made matters worse and reduced firm value. The longer term effects of such governance regulation remain an open question for future research.

Following the adoption of recent governance regulations in the United States and the United Kingdom, many other countries have also either adopted, or are considering, similar regulations. This trend provides a fertile ground for future research. One open research question is the conditions under which governance regulation is beneficial. How does the regulation (and enforcement) of firm-level governance interact with country-level rules on investor protection and the quality of the judicial environment and of other institutions within which firms operate? And what effects do they have on firms and investors?

Finally, in a similar way, kinship ties can provide incentives to managers of family firms in addition to the incentives in nonfamily firms. But these same ties can inhibit discipline from family shareholders. Evidence suggests that these two effects offset each other, providing no net advantage to family firms. But evidence also suggests that family firms are disadvantaged by their overreliance on managers from the smaller family pool. An interesting but as yet unexamined question is the effect of nepotism on the incentives and compensation of outside hires.

## NOTES

1. Owners will tolerate *a* to the extent that managers "pay" for this with lower monetary compensation, since that will not lower profit.
2. A company's public float is the part of its outstanding equity that is not held by management or large shareholders.

## REFERENCES

Adams, Renee B., and Daniel Ferreira. 2009. "Women in the Boardroom and Their Impact on Governance and Performance." *Journal of Financial Economics* 94:291–309.

Agrawal, Anup, and Charles R. Knoeber. 1996. "Firm Performance and Mechanisms to Control Agency Problems between Managers and Shareholders." *Journal of Financial and Quantitative Analysis* 31:377–97.

Agrawal, Anup, and Tareque Nasser. 2011. "Blockholders on Boards and CEO Compensation, Turnover and Firm Valuation." Working Paper, Social Science Research Network. http://papers.ssrn.com/sol3/papers.cfm?abstract_id=1443431.

Anderson, Ronald C., and David Reeb. 2003. "Founding-Family Ownership and Firm Performance: Evidence from the S&P 500." *Journal of Finance* 58:1301–27.

Ang, Andrew, Joseph Chen, and Yuhang Xing. 2006. "Downside Risk." *Review of Financial Studies* 19:1191–1239.

Atanasov, Vladimir, Audra Boone, and David Haushalter. 2010. "Is There Shareholder Expropriation in the United States? An Analysis of Publicly Traded Subsidiaries." *Journal of Financial and Quantitative Analysis* 45:1–26.

Barclay, Michael J., and Clifford G. Holderness. 1989. "Private Benefits from Control of Public Corporations." *Journal of Financial Economics* 25:371–96.

———. 1992. "The Law and Large Block Trades." *Journal of Law and Economics* 35:265–94.

Bebchuk, Lucian A., Alma Cohen, and Allen Ferrell. 2009. "What Matters in Corporate Governance?" *Review of Financial Studies* 22:783–827.

Bebchuk, Lucian A., Alma Cohen, and Charles C. Y. Wang. 2012. "Learning and the Disappearing Association between Governance and Returns." *Journal of Financial Economics* (forthcoming).

Becker, Bo, Henrik Cronqvist, and Rüdiger Fahlenbrach. 2011. "Estimating the Effects of Large Shareholders Using a Geographic Instrument." *Journal of Financial and Quantitative Analysis* 46:907–42.

Bennedsen, Morten, Kasper M. Nielsen, Francisco Perez-Gonzalez, and Daniel Wolfenzon. 2007. "Inside the Family Firm: The Role of Families in Succession Decisions and Performance." *Quarterly Journal of Economics* 122:647–91.

Black, Bernard S. 1998. "Shareholder Activism and Corporate Governance in the United States." In *The New Palgrave Dictionary of Economics and the Law*, edited by Peter Newman, 459–65. Houndmills, UK: Palgrave Macmillan.

Brav, Alon, Wei Jiang, and Hyunseob Kim. 2009. "Hedge Fund Activism: A Review." *Foundations and Trends in Finance* 4:185–246.

Chhaochharia, V., and Y. Grinstein. 2007. "Corporate Governance and Firm Value: The Impact of the 2002 Governance Rules." *Journal of Finance* 62:1789–1825.

Cho, Myeong-Hyeon. 1998. "Ownership Structure, Investment, and the Corporate Value: An Empirical Analysis." *Journal of Financial Economics* 47:103–21.

Coles, Jeffrey L., Michael L. Lemmon, and J. Felix Meschke. 2012. "Structural Models and Endogeneity in Corporate Finance: The Link between Managerial Ownership and Corporate Performance." *Journal of Financial Economics* 103:149–68.

Core, John E., Wayne R. Guay, and Tjomme O. Rusticus. 2006. "Does Weak Governance Cause Weak Stock Returns? An Examination of Firm Operating Performance and Analysts' Expectations." *Journal of Finance* 61:655–87.

Cremers, K., J. Martijn, and Vinay B. Nair. 2005. "Governance Mechanisms and Equity Prices." *Journal of Finance* 60:2859–94.

Cremers, K., J. Martijn, Vinay B. Nair, and Kose John. 2009. "Takeovers and the Cross-Section of Returns." *Review of Financial Studies* 22:1409–45.

Cucculelli, Marco, and Giacinto Micucci. 2008. "Family Succession and Firm Performance: Evidence from Italian Family Firms." *Journal of Corporate Finance* 14:17–31.

Dahya, Jay, and John J. McConnell. 2007. "Board Composition, Corporate Performance, and the Cadbury Committee Recommendation." *Journal of Financial and Quantitative Analysis* 42:535–64.

Daines, Robert M. 2001. "Does Delaware Law Improve Firm Value?" *Journal of Financial Economics* 62:525–58.

Demsetz, Harold. 1983. "The Structure of Ownership and the Theory of the Firm." *Journal of Law and Economics* 26:375–90.

Demsetz, Harold, and Kenneth Lehn. 1985. "The Structure of Corporate Ownership: Causes and Consequences." *Journal of Political Economy* 93:1155–77.

Duchin, Ran, John G. Matsusaka, and Oguzhan Ozbas. 2010. "When Are Outside Directors Effective?" *Journal of Financial Economics* 96:195–214.

Faleye, Olubunmi, Rani Hoitash, and Udi Hoitash. 2011. "The Costs of Intense Board Monitoring." *Journal of Financial Economics* 101:160–81.

Fama, Eugene F., and Kenneth R. French. 1997. "Industry Costs of Equity." *Journal of Financial Economics* 43:153–93.

Gillan, Stuart L., and Laura T. Starks. 2007. "The Evolution of Shareholder Activism in the United States." *Journal of Applied Corporate Finance* 19:55–73.

Giroud, Xavier, and Holger M. Mueller. 2011. "Corporate Governance, Product Market Competition, and Equity Prices." *Journal of Finance* 66:563–600.

Gompers, Paul A., Joy L. Ishii, and Andrew Metrick. 2003. "Corporate Governance and Equity Prices." *Quarterly Journal of Economics* 118:107–55.

———. 2010. "Extreme Governance: An Analysis of Dual-Class Firms in the United States." *Review of Financial Studies* 23:1051–88.

Harris, Milton, and Arthur Raviv. 1988. "Corporate Control Contests and Capital Structure." *Journal of Financial Economics* 20:55–86.

Hermalin, Benjamin E., and Michael S. Weisbach. 1991. "The Effects of Board Composition and Direct Incentives on Firm Performance." *Financial Management* 20:101–12.

Himmelberg, Charles, Glenn Hubbard, and Darius Palia. 1999. "Understanding the Determinants of Managerial Ownership and the Link between Ownership and Performance." *Journal of Financial Economics* 53:353–84.

Holderness, Clifford G. 2003. "A Survey of Blockholders and Corporate Control." *Federal Reserve Bank of New York Economic Policy Review* 9:51–64.

Holderness, Clifford G., and Dennis P. Sheehan. 1988. "The Role of Majority Shareholders in Publicly Held Corporations: An Exploratory Analysis." *Journal of Financial Economics* 20:317–46.

Iliev, Peter. 2010. "The Effect of SOX Section 404: Costs, Earnings Quality, and Stock Prices." *Journal of Finance* 65:1163–96.

Johnson, Shane, Theodore Moorman, and Sorin M. Sorescu. 2009. "A Reexamination of Corporate Governance and Equity Prices." *Review of Financial Studies* 22:4753–86.

Karpoff, Jonathan, M. 2001. "The Impact of Shareholder Activism on Target Companies: A Survey of Empirical Findings." Working Paper, University of Washington.

Kenneth Lehn, Sukesh Patro, and Mengxin Zhao. 2007. "Governance Indexes and Valuation: Which Causes Which?" *Journal of Corporate Finance* 13:907–28.

Klein, April. 1998. "Firm Performance and Board Committee Structure." *Journal of Law and Economics* 41:275–303.

La Porta, Rafael, Florencio Lopez-de-Silanes, Andrei Shleifer, and Robert Vishny. 2002. "Investor Protection and Corporate Valuation." *Journal of Finance* 57:1147–70.

Lewellen, Stefan, and Andrew Metrick. 2010. "Corporate Governance and Equity Prices: Are Results Robust to Industry Adjustments?" Working Paper, Yale University.

Li, Haidan, Morton Pincus, and Sonja O. Rego. 2008. "Market Reaction to Events Surrounding the Sarbanes-Oxley Act of 2002 and Earnings Management." *Journal of Law and Economics* 51:111–34.

Masulis, Ronald, Cong Wang, and Fei Xie. 2007. "Corporate Governance and Acquirer Returns." *Journal of Finance* 62:1851–89.

McConnell, John L., and Henri Servaes. 1990. "Additional Evidence on Equity Ownership and Corporate Value." *Journal of Financial Economics* 27:595–612.

Mehran, Hamid. 1995. "Executive Compensation Structure, Ownership, and Firm Performance." *Journal of Financial Economics* 38:163–84.

Morck, Randall, Andrei Shleifer, and Robert Vishny. 1988. "Management Ownership and Market Valuation: An Empirical Analysis." *Journal of Financial Economics* 20:293–316.

Pastor, Lubos, and Robert F. Stambaugh. 2003. "Liquidity Risk and Expected Stock Returns." *Journal of Political Economy* 111:642–85.

Perez-Gonzalez, Francisco. 2006. "Inherited Control and Firm Performance." *American Economic Review* 96:1559–88.

Shleifer, Andrei, and Robert W. Vishny. 1986. "Large Shareholders and Corporate Control." *Journal of Political Economy* 94:461–88.

Stulz, Rene M. 1988. "Managerial Control of Voting Rights: Financing Policies and the Market for Corporate Control." *Journal of Financial Economics* 20:25–54.

Villalonga, Belen, and Raphael Amit. 2006. "How Do Family Ownership, Control, and Management Affect Firm Value?" *Journal of Financial Economics* 80:385–417.

Yermack, David. 1996. "Higher Market Valuation of Companies with a Small Board of Directors." *Journal of Financial Economics* 40:185–213.

Zhang, Ivy Xiying. 2007. "Economic Consequences of the Sarbanes-Oxley Act of 2002." *Journal of Accounting and Economics* 44:74–115.

Zhou, Xianming. 2001. "Understanding the Determinants of Managerial Ownership and the Link between Ownership and Performance: Comment." *Journal of Financial Economics* 62:559–71.

# PART VIII

# PUBLIC POLICY
# FOR MANAGERS

# CHAPTER 23

........................................................................................................

# MANAGING WORKPLACE SAFETY AND HEALTH

........................................................................................................

## THOMAS J. KNIESNER AND JOHN D. LEETH

## 23.1 INTRODUCTION

........................................................................................................

MANAGERIAL incentives to improve workplace safety come in many forms, including the moral aspect of a concern for the well-being of other human beings. Financially, market forces encourage managers to worry about occupational safety and health. Workers will not accept employment in work sites they know are hazardous unless they are compensated for doing so. The positive relationship between wages and risk means that the market rewards managers with improving safety records with lower labor costs and punishes managers with deteriorating safety records with higher labor costs. Eliminating hazards may be expensive but the wage reduction may more than pay for the costs of additional safety efforts. Here we examine the market forces encouraging managers to provide safe working environments and government actions augmenting the market forces.

Public policies aimed at improving occupational safety and health include state laws requiring firms to provide insurance coverage for their workers for industrial injuries and illnesses and to comply with federal workplace safety and health standards. State workers' compensation laws hold firms strictly liable for industrial injuries. Regardless of fault, employers must pay all of an injured worker's medical bills and a portion of lost income. In return for no-fault insurance coverage, workers cannot sue employers for damages due to work-related injuries. The federal Occupational Safety and Health Administration (OSHA) establishes safety and health standards and then enforces the standards by inspecting and fining firms for noncompliance. Both workers' compensation and OSHA rely on financial incentives to encourage managers to improve safety. Managers can lower the cost of purchasing workers' compensation insurance by reducing injuries and claims for benefits, and they can reduce expected OSHA penalties by complying with OSHA safety and health standards.

Although less direct, government research into the causes and consequences of workplace hazards can have a significant impact on occupational safety and health. If workers and managers are unaware of a potential danger, then workers cannot take actions to protect themselves and managers cannot attempt to minimize or eliminate the danger. The National Institute for Occupational Safety and Health (NIOSH), a government agency created at the same time as OSHA, gathers information and conducts scientific research about workplace injuries and illnesses and disseminates the information to the public.

The legal system is the final pillar in the US safety policy system. The exclusive remedy clause of workers' compensation prevents workers from suing their employers for damages from industrial accidents and diseases, but workers may bypass the limitation by suing other parties under product liability law. The ability of workers to prevail in product liability suits skyrocketed beginning in the 1960s when the courts moved to a strict liability standard wherein manufacturers are legally responsible for damages if the products they produce are unreasonably dangerous or if they fail to warn their customers of the potential hazards. The success of product liability suits spills over into occupational safety by expanding the incentives of manufacturers to produce safe equipment and products for industrial use and to warn workers of possible dangers.

In what follows, we first develop the general economic model of production and the workplace when there are inevitable risks to health and safety. We then add seriatim the components that condition the managerial decisions that firms make considering workplace health and safety, which include the workers' willingness to expose themselves to jobs that could harm their health, government regulations, mandatory no-fault compensation insurance, information issues, and tort liability court decisions. In all cases we attempt to provide evidence on the relative economic importance of the factor conditioning management decisions. A major conclusion is that the private market for labor, as reflected in the compensation workers demand for exposure to health risks, gives the largest economic incentive to managers for workplace health and safety altering decisions. We conclude with what are likely to be the most important issues on the horizon, including issues of fairness and equity concerning workplace health and safety.

## 23.2  RISK CHOICES AND HEDONIC EQUILIBRIUM

Before we can discuss the role of government in altering managerial incentives to improve workplace safety and health, we need to examine how workers and firms make decisions regarding risk. One might believe that no one willingly gambles with their health, but people take risks every day. They drive in small cars; they smoke; they eat too much red meat; they exercise too little; and they drink too much. The key is that for people to be willing to take risks they must get something in return to compensate. In the area of workplace health and safety, for a worker to choose to work in a more hazardous workplace he or she must get a higher wage (inclusive of fringe benefits) to offset the greater chance of an injury or illness. Improving workplace safety is expensive and firms may be willing to pay higher wages to their workers to avoid the added costs.

One way to model a firm's provision of safety is to view safety as an input into the production process, similar to capital and labor. To ease the analysis that follows, we will assume employers offer identical hours of work, and workers accept employment in one firm only. Further, we will focus on a single job characteristic, $\pi$, the probability of a standard workplace injury or illness, which is known to both workers and firms. Finally, we will assume that both labor and product markets are competitive.

With the basic economic assumptions in mind, expected profit can be represented algebraically as

$$\bar{g} = R(p_0, S(\pi), n, k; \mu) - W(\pi)(1-\pi)n - p_s s(\pi) - p_k k - P_b(\pi)bn - V(\pi, e) - d\pi, \quad (23.1)$$

where $\bar{g} \equiv$ expected profit,

$R(\cdot) \equiv$ the expected revenue function,

$p_O \equiv$ the per-unit price of output,

$s \equiv$ the quantity of safety measures with $s = S(\pi)$; $S(\cdot)$ is the safety production function and $S' < 0$,

$n \equiv$ the number of workers,

$k \equiv$ the quantity of capital,

$\mu \equiv$ a parameter representing the efficiency of safety equipment in the production of output $\left(\frac{\partial^2 R}{\partial s \partial \mu} > 0\right)$,

$W(\pi) \equiv$ the market wage function, observable to workers and firms, with $W' > 0$,

$p_s \equiv$ the price per-unit of safety measures (equipment),

$p_k \equiv$ the price per-unit of capital,

$P_b(\pi) \equiv$ the price per-unit (of the benefits) of workers' compensation insurance, $P_b' > 0$,

$b \equiv$ insurance benefits provided to workers if injured,

$V(\pi, e) \equiv$ the expected fine for violating safety and health standards with $\frac{\partial V}{\partial \pi} > 0$, $\frac{\partial V}{\partial e} \geq 0$, and $\frac{\partial^2 V}{\partial \pi \partial e} > 0$,

$e \equiv$ the level of government enforcement of safety and health regulations, and

$d \equiv$ the expected court award to a worker if injured.

By differentiating equation (23.1) with respect to $n$, $k$, and $\pi$, and rearranging terms, we can show that the optimal usage of each input occurs when

$$\frac{\partial R}{\partial n} = W(\pi)(1-\pi) + P_b(\pi)b, \quad (23.2)$$

$$\frac{\partial R}{\partial k} = p_k, \quad (23.3)$$

$$\frac{\partial R}{\partial S}\frac{\partial S}{\partial \pi} - \left(\frac{\partial W}{\partial \pi}(1-\pi) - w\right)n - \frac{\partial P_b}{\partial \pi}bn - \frac{\partial V}{\partial \pi}d = p_s\frac{\partial S}{\partial \pi}. \qquad (23.4)$$

Firms increase their use of labor and capital until the expected marginal revenue product of each input equals its expected marginal cost. In addition, firms reduce workplace hazards until the marginal benefits of greater safety—greater output,[1] lower wages,[2] lower insurance costs, smaller government fines for workplace hazards, and smaller court awards for damages from worker injuries—equal the marginal costs of supplying greater safety. Because the output effects of safety programs vary among workplaces, the marginal benefits of reducing work-related health hazards differ among firms, in turn causing the optimum level of safety to vary. Firms where safety equipment is highly productive reduce hazards more than firms where safety equipment is less productive.

Notice that, even in the absence of government programs geared toward improving workplace safety, equation (23.4) indicates that managers still have incentives to engage in safety efforts as a result of the reduction in wages associated with such efforts.[3] The government can augment these incentives by mandating insurance coverage for workplace injuries ($b$), clarifying the relationship between the price of workers' compensation insurance coverage and risk $\left(\frac{\partial P_b}{\partial \pi}\right)$, establishing and enforcing workplace safety and health standards $\left(\frac{\partial V}{\partial \pi}\right)$, and allowing workers to sue for work related illnesses and injuries ($d$).

Figure 23.1 provides another way to think about firms' decisions regarding workplace safety. The figure shows the market wage function ($W$) and the offer wage functions ($\Phi$) for two companies. Graphically, a firm's offer wage function (isoprofit curve) shows the trade-off between wages and workplace safety at a constant level of expected profit with capital and labor used in optimal quantities. To keep the same level of profit, wages must fall as workplace safety rises to compensate for the added cost of purchasing safety equipment. Offer wage functions slope upward. Firms with greater costs of producing a safe workplace require a greater wage reduction to improve safety than firms with smaller costs of producing a safe work environment, all else equal. The firm with the higher marginal cost of producing a safer workplace will have a more steeply sloped offer wage function at a given wage and injury rate than a firm with a lower marginal cost. Finally, profits rise as wages fall, implying that the lower the offer wage function the higher the profit.

At this stage $W(\pi)$ depicted in Figure 23.1 need not be an equilibrium wage function; firms and workers need only observe and make their decisions based on the relationship between wages and workplace risk. As can be seen, company A maximizes profit by offering workers job risk equal to $\pi^A$, the level where the offer wage function is just tangent to the market wage function. Because its costs of providing a safe work environment are greater, company B maximizes profit by offering a less agreeable job, $\pi^B$, but paying higher wages than company A to compensate workers for the less pleasant working conditions. With a sufficiently large number of diverse firms, each point on the market wage function represents a point of tangency for some company or companies. The

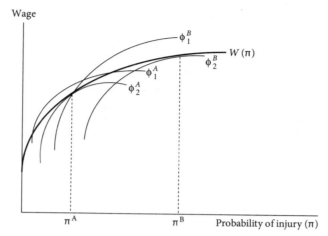

**FIGURE 23.1** Firm Equilibrium

market wage function represents an upper envelope of a family of offer wage curves that differ because of the variation in the technical abilities of firms to produce workplace safety. It slopes upward because firms are willing to pay higher wages to avoid bearing the added expenses of providing better working conditions.

The problem confronting a worker is to find the level of consumption and workplace safety that maximizes expected utility subject to the overall budget constraint. Algebraically, after substituting the income constraint into the utility functions for consumption goods, a worker's expected utility becomes

$$\bar{u} = (1-\pi)U(W(\pi)+y;\xi)+\pi\tilde{U}(b+d+y;\xi). \tag{23.5}$$

where $\bar{u} \equiv$ expected utility,

$U(\cdot) \equiv$ the worker's utility function if uninjured,

$\tilde{U}(\cdot) \equiv$ the worker's utility function if injured, $U > \tilde{U}$ and $U' > \tilde{U}'$,

$y \equiv$ nonlabor income, and

$\xi \equiv$ a parameter determining an individual's aversion to risk.

Expected utility is a weighted average of the utility if uninjured and the utility if injured with the weights equaling the probabilities of the two states. The formulation in equation (23.5) explicitly considers both monetary and nonmonetary losses from workplace injuries. The difference between $U(\cdot)$ and $\tilde{U}(\cdot)$, income held constant, represents the pain and suffering resulting from an injury or illness.

By differentiating expected utility with respect to $\pi$, setting the result equal to 0, and then rearranging, a worker's optimal level of risk (safety) occurs when

$$U'\frac{\partial W}{\partial \pi} = U(W(\pi)+y;\xi)-\tilde{U}(b+d+y;\xi). \tag{23.6}$$

The story here is the standard one: a worker weighs the marginal benefit of increased risk against the marginal cost. The left-hand side of equation (23.6) represents the marginal benefit, the added pay from a more risky job, while the right-hand side represents the marginal cost, the greater likelihood of an injury that lowers both income and the utility from income. Because people differ in their degrees of risk aversion, the perceived marginal gain and cost differ among people, in turn causing the optimal level of safety to vary. Workers with low risk aversion sort into high-risk jobs, and workers with high risk aversion sort into low-risk jobs.

Similar to the situation for firms, workers' decisions regarding risk can also be depicted graphically. A worker's acceptance wage function (indifference curve) illustrates the trade-off between wages and $\pi$ at a constant level of utility. Because risk reduces expected utility, wages must rise to compensate for bearing more risk. Acceptance wage functions slope upward. Additionally, more risk-averse workers require greater wage compensation for a given increase in $\pi$ than less risk-averse workers, all else equal, so the worker with the steeper acceptance wage function at a given $(W, \pi)$ is the more risk averse. Lastly, workers prefer higher wages to lower wages at any level of risk, so the higher the acceptance wage function the higher the utility. The choice of the optimal level of $\pi$ can be viewed similarly to the choice of the optimal purchase of commodities with the market wage function replacing the standard income constraint.

Figure 23.2 portrays acceptance wage functions ($\Theta$) for two workers in relation to a market wage function. We see worker C maximizing utility by selecting a job with the level of risk equal to $\pi^C$. The highest level of utility the worker can achieve occurs where the acceptance wage function is just tangent to the market wage curve. Although $\pi^C$

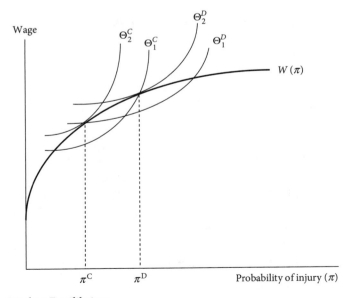

FIGURE 23.2 Worker Equilibrium

maximizes worker C's utility, it does not maximize worker D's utility; worker D requires a smaller increase in wages to accept a slight rise in workplace risk, utility held constant. Worker D maximizes utility by choosing a slightly more dangerous job, characterized by $\pi^D$, and earning a higher wage. With a sufficiently large number of diverse workers, each point on the hedonic wage function is a point of tangency for some group of workers. In technical language, the wage function represents the lower envelope of a family of acceptance wage curves, which differ because workers vary in their attitudes regarding $\pi$.

Firms supply a given type of workplace based on the market wage function and their ability to produce a safe work environment. Workers sort into a given job risk based on the market wage function and their preferences regarding safety. The market wage function equilibrates the supply and demand for labor along the entire job risk spectrum. A shortage of workers in high-risk establishments, for instance, will drive up wages, thereby enticing some workers away from safer employment. At the same time, the wage hike will encourage some firms to expand their expenditures on workplace safety to reduce labor costs. With workers moving toward greater $\pi$ and firms moving toward lower $\pi$, wages must rise in relatively safer workplaces. An excess demand for labor at any point along the job risk spectrum alters the delicate balancing of labor supply and demand everywhere. Wages adjust until the supply of labor equals the demand for labor along the entire spectrum. Because in equilibrium wages must rise to compensate workers for undesirable job characteristics such as poor workplace safety, the market wage function is referred to as a hedonic wage function (Rosen 1974).

## 23.3 THE VALUE OF A STATISTICAL LIFE

The theory of hedonic equilibrium provides the basis for the economic approach to evaluating the benefits of programs aimed at improving health and safety, which requires placing a monetary value on the potential lives saved or injuries avoided. The slope of the acceptance wage function measures the wage a worker is willing to sacrifice to lower his or her chance of injury by a small amount and, therefore, provides an implicit dollar estimate of a worker's willingness to pay for workplace safety. In equilibrium, the slope of the hedonic wage function equals the slope of the indifference curves, so for small improvements in safety, the drop in the market wage reflects the value workers place on the improvement. Say wages in Figure 23.3 fall by \$80 when the chance of a workplace fatality drops from 5 in 100,000 to 4 in 100,000. A typical worker is willing to sacrifice \$80 to reduce his or her chance of death by 1 in 100,000, meaning that, collectively, 100,000 workers would sacrifice \$8 million and, on average, one life would be saved. The saved life is not known beforehand, but in a sense is drawn randomly from the 100,000 workers at risk, so the \$8 million represents the value of a statistical life (VSL). An implicit value of injury can be found in a similar manner by dividing a market wage change for a small reduction in the probability of a workplace nonfatal injury or illness

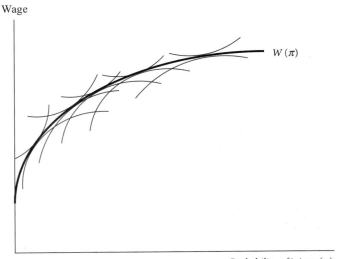

**FIGURE 23.3** Hedonic Labor Market Equilibrium

by the change in the probability of occurrence. The resulting calculation is known as the value of a statistical injury (VSI).

VSLs and VSIs do not represent the amounts that people would pay to avoid their own certain death or injury or that society would pay to rescue individuals from certain death or injury. Instead, the values allow policymakers to determine the benefits of actions that reduce risk by small amounts. The "value of mortality risk" may more accurately convey the true notion of what VSLs measure and may be a less emotionally charged term (US Environmental Protection Agency 2010b). VSLs and VSIs also do not accurately measure the values workers place on either large improvements or large reductions in safety. The wage change along an indifference curve is much smaller than the wage change along the hedonic wage curve for a substantial reduction in risk, and it is much greater than the wage change along the hedonic wage curve for a sizable increase in risk.

The typical approach to determining VSLs and VSIs is to estimate an equation such as,

$$\ln(w) = c + \sum_{i=1}^{m} \alpha_i \pi_i + \sum_{j=1}^{n} \beta_j X_j + \varepsilon, \qquad (23.7)$$

where $\ln(w)$ is the natural logarithm of wages, $\pi$s are measures of workplace risk, the $X_i$s are demographic variables (such as education, race, marital status, and union membership) and job characteristics (such as the wage replacement under workers' compensation insurance and industry, occupation, or geographic location indicators), $\varepsilon$ is an error term, and $c$, $\alpha_i$, and $\beta_j$ are parameters to be estimated. Many studies also include interaction terms between workplace risk and various $X$s to determine variation in risk compensation by type of worker (union/nonunion, white/black, native/immigrant, young/old) or by level of income replacement from workers' compensation insurance.

Viscusi (2004) provides a good example of how estimates of equation (23.7) can be transformed into a VSL calculation. He defines risk across 72 two-digit industries and 10 one-digit occupations to create 720 industry-occupation cells. He measures the number of fatalities in each industry-occupation cell using data from the Census of Fatal Occupational Injuries, a yearly report on workplace deaths generated by the Bureau of Labor Statistics based on information from death certificates, medical examiner reports, OSHA reports, workers' compensation records, and the number of full-time equivalent workers using data from the Current Population Survey (CPS). To reduce the importance of random changes in fatalities and the number of empty fatality risk cells, Viscusi averages fatalities and employees within each cell from 1992 to 1997. In the regression sample data the average fatality risk is 4/100,000 with the lowest risk level being 0.6/100,000 and the highest risk level about 25/100,000.

Viscusi then combines the fatal risk data with individual worker data from the 1997 merged outgoing rotation groups of the CPS. Sample individuals are nonagricultural full-time workers (usual weekly hours worked at least thirty-five) between the ages of eighteen and sixty-five. His estimate of equation (23.7) includes no interactions between fatal injury risk and other control variables and uses a linear relationship between log hourly wage and fatal injury risk. Consequently, with a fatality risk measure of deaths per 100,000 workers and a work year of 2000 hours, the value of a statistical life is VSL $= \alpha \times exp(\ln(w)) \times 100,000 \times 2000$.[4] Although the VSL function depends on the values of the right-hand side in (23.7), most commonly considered is the mean VSL. The VSL from his baseline regression of equation (23.7) for all workers is $12.5 million.[5]

VSL estimates can and do vary depending on the control variables included in the estimating wage equation. They also vary across populations. In the United States, union members have higher VSLs than nonunion workers (Viscusi and Aldy 2003); whites have higher VSLs than blacks (Viscusi 2003); and women have higher, but less statistically robust, VSLs than men (Leeth and Ruser 2003). VSLs for native workers are roughly the same as for immigrant workers, except for non-English-speaking immigrants from Mexico who appear to earn little compensation for bearing very high levels of workplace risk (Viscusi and Hersch 2010). VSLs vary by age, with values rising until the mid-40s and then very gradually falling (Kniesner et al. 2006; Aldy and Viscusi 2008). Finally, a substantial body of research discovers a very strong positive relationship between income and VSLs (Mrozek and Taylor 2002; Viscusi and Aldy 2003; Costa and Kahn 2004; Bellavance et al. 2009; Kniesner et al. 2010).

VSLs can vary across populations because of differences in risk preferences. Groups more willing to take risks will locate further to the right along the hedonic wage function, and if the wage function is concave from below as shown in Figure 23.3, the groups will have a smaller reduction in wage for a given increase in safety and, hence, a lower VSL. Alternatively, some populations may have a lower VSL because they are less careful than others and their lesser safety productivity causes the wage function they face to lie below and to be flatter (resulting in a lower VSL) than the wage function faced by others.

The lesser ability of some workers to produce safety makes it desirable for employers to offer them smaller wage premiums for accepting risk. Discrimination may also result in two separate hedonic wage functions, with the disadvantaged group facing not only lower wages at every level of risk but also smaller increases in wages for given changes in risk than for the advantaged group.

Viscusi and Hersch (2001) provide a test to determine if VSL differences between populations result from the groups locating at different places along the same hedonic wage function or from the groups facing different hedonic wage functions. In Figure 23.4 the group more risk tolerant locates at job risk $\pi_2$ and the less risk tolerant at job risk $\pi_1$. If the groups face the same hedonic wage function then the more risk tolerant, who bear more workplace risk, receive more compensation for risk than the less risk tolerant.[6] If the high-risk group earns a smaller risk premium than the low-risk group then the high-risk group must face a lower, flatter hedonic wage function such as the one labeled "Disadvantaged" in Figure 23.4. The risk premium for the low-risk group, $w^a(\pi_1) - w^a(0)$, in Figure 23.4 exceeds the risk premium of the high-risk group, $w^d(\pi_2) - (w^d(0)$, indicating that the two groups face different wage functions. Viscusi (2003) finds that blacks face a lower, flatter hedonic wage function for workplace fatalities than whites and Viscusi and Hersch (2010) find that non-English-speaking Mexican immigrants to the United States face a lower, flatter hedonic wage function for workplace fatalities than US natives.

The range of VSL estimates across studies is quite large, on the order of $0–$40 million (Mrozek and Taylor 2002; Viscusi and Aldy 2003; Bellavance et al. 2009). This variation creates a dilemma for policy makers. A proper evaluation of any program designed

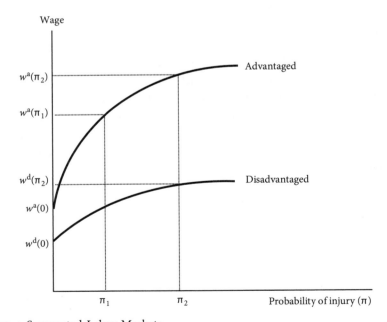

**FIGURE 23.4** Segmented Labor Markets

to improve health and safety requires an estimate of the benefits generated by the new standards imposed. A too-low VSL will underestimate the benefits of a mortality risk reduction, resulting in a rejection of desirable programs, while too high of a VSL will overestimate the benefits of mortality risk reduction, resulting in accepting undesirable (in a cost/benefit sense) programs. Still, a single immutable VSL is unlikely. Risk preferences, knowledge, safety productivity, income, or discrimination result in differences across countries, over time, or across demographic groups, and policy makers wishing to use estimated VSLs for cost/benefit analyses must be careful to choose a value appropriate for the group affected by the change in safety policy.

In general, government agencies consider the full range of VSL estimates in determining a value to place on small mortality risk reductions. For instance, the US Environmental Protection Agency (EPA) recommends using $8.3 million as the default VSL based on fitting a Weibull distribution to twenty-six separate VSL estimates (US EPA 2010a). The $8.3 million figure represents the central estimate (mean) of the fitted distribution. In a similar vein, the US Department of Transportation (DOT) issued a memorandum in 2008 specifying a $6.1 million VSL based on the mean value of five VSL studies, four of which were meta-analyses of many existing VSL studies (US DOT 2008).

Managers can also use VSLs and VSIs to determine possible wage savings from safety improvements. Say that a possible safety initiative will eliminate a potential hazard and drop the chance of a fatal accident by 0.5 per 100,000 workers. With 700 workers exposed to the hazard and an $8 million VSL, the firm should be able to lower wage expenses by $(0.000005 \times 8,000,000 \times 700 = \$28,000)$. VSL and VSI estimates vary across populations and managers should use an estimate appropriate for their workers. Moreover, as with any fringe benefit, workers chose to work at a particular firm because of the combination of wages and benefits that is offered. High-risk firms attract less risk-averse workers, who prefer higher wages to greater safety. Improvements in safety combined with wage reductions will result in turnover as the combination of wages and safety is no longer optimal for these less safety-conscious workers. In the other direction, new workers are less likely to be surprised at the hazards faced on the job, which should reduce quits and decrease recruiting and training expenses.

## 23.4 WORKERS' COMPENSATION INSURANCE

Workers' compensation is primarily a state-operated disability insurance program covering workers against losses caused by industrial accidents and some diseases. Regardless of who is at fault, employers must fully compensate employees for medical expenses and partially compensate them for lost wages caused by work-related injuries. Although standards for replacing lost wages vary, most states require employers to replace two-thirds of weekly wages up to a maximum benefit of two-thirds of the state's average weekly wage for more serious injuries. In return, employees forgo their rights to sue employers when injuries occur. Most states allow employers to provide workers' compensation coverage by either purchasing insurance with a private provider or by self-insuring after proof of financial ability to pay.

Before workers' compensation was introduced, employees had to prove that an injury was caused by the employer's negligence before they could recover damages. An employer could avoid a negligence ruling in court by demonstrating that the worker's injury resulted from his own actions, was an ordinary hazard of employment, or resulted from the carelessness of a coworker. Because legal defenses made damage recovery uncertain, the negligence system was viewed as providing insufficient compensation for injured workers and inadequate incentives for employers to provide reasonably safe work environments. In contrast, workers' compensation provides certain benefits for injured workers regardless of fault and, by shifting the financial costs of accidents to employers, provides an economic incentive for employers to reduce workplace hazards.

The impact of workers' compensation insurance on employer incentives to provide a safe working environment can be seen by examining the first-order conditions for the profit- maximizing use of safety equipment, equation (23.4). Assuming that expected court damage awards are negligible and the provision of insurance has no impact on wages, then the passage of workers' compensation and the expansion of benefits ($b$) increase the marginal benefit of greater safety, which should lead to fewer workplace injuries.

Unfortunately, the direct impact on the firm's incentives may be counteracted by other influences affecting employers and employees. First, it is not clear that expected court damage awards were small before passage of workers' compensation laws. Fishback and Kantor (1998) present evidence that changes in liability laws in the early 1900s and a series of court decisions limiting employers' defenses in liability suits, increased the likelihood that workers would prevail in court if injured on the job. The introduction of workers' compensation insurance, and the replacement of a negligence system for the award of damages with a strict, but limited, liability system, raised employers' incentives to provide a safe workplace through the increase in the payment of insurance benefits but lowered their incentives to provide a safe workplace by reducing expected court awards for worker injuries.

Wages will also change with the introduction of workers' compensation. Wages adjust not only for undesirable job characteristics, such as a high likelihood of injury, but also for desirable ones, such as generous insurance coverage. Employers are able to pass along some of the costs of higher insurance benefits through lower wages (Fishback and Kantor 1998; Moore and Viscusi 1989; Viscusi 2004). Additionally, workers' compensation benefits alter the relationship between wages and risk. By reducing income losses from injury, more generous workers' compensation benefits reduce the wage demanded by workers for accepting a more dangerous job. Greater ex post compensation for an injury lowers the ex ante compensation required for accepting a higher job risk and flattens the hedonic wage function, which reduces firms' incentives to provide a safe work environment.

Finally, because workers' compensation benefits reduce workers' economic losses from the injuries, they reduce (at least for less serious injuries) the marginal cost of a worker accepting greater risk. The difference in utility if uninjured and the utility if injured falls in equation (23.6), causing the worker to choose a higher risk job. More generous workers' compensation insurance may also entice workers to report more accidents and diseases (either legitimate or illegitimate) and file more claims for disability benefits. Even if workers' compensation insurance has no influence on workers' acceptance of risk, the stronger incentives to file workers' compensation insurance claims as benefits expand would likely cause a positive relationship between benefits and reported injuries. Most empirical studies find that larger benefits raise the number of reported nonfatal workplace injuries, suggesting a trade-off between safety and economic security (Ruser and Butler 2009).

Kniesner and Leeth (1989) separate reported injuries from actual injuries and show that the greater incentives to file claims for workers' compensation insurance can easily mask the measured impact of employers' actions that improve workplace safety. Reported injuries rise even when actual injuries fall. This so-called reporting effect may also explain why the number of claims jumps on Mondays, particularly claims for hard to diagnose muscular and skeletal injuries, such as sprains and lower back impairments (Smith 1990; Ruser 1998). By contrast, studies focusing on either fatal or extremely severe injuries, injuries unlikely to suffer from a reporting effect, discover that higher benefits improve safety. Moore and Viscusi (1989) find that a 10% increase in workers' compensation benefits reduces occupational fatalities by 2%. Based on their estimates, workplace fatalities are 22% lower now than they would be in the absence of workers' compensation insurance.

To create the optimal incentives for providing a safe workplace, the price of workers' compensation insurance must reflect firms' safety efforts. The larger is $\dfrac{\partial P_b}{\partial \pi}$ in equation (23.4), the more likely firms will expand safety as workers' compensation insurance benefits rise. In the parlance of insurance jargon, workers' compensation insurance premiums must be fully experience-rated to create the maximum incentives for safety. By experience rating, we mean the process of adjusting insurance prices to reflect individual versus group claims experience. As an example, car insurance is experience-rated. The more traffic accidents a person has, the more the individual driver will pay for car insurance. Currently, insurance providers completely experience-rate all workers' compensation insurance premiums only for the largest establishments. Very small firms are not experience-rated at all, which means that their individual safety records have no impact on the prices they pay for workers' compensation insurance.

This muted impact on small firms' insurance premiums implies that the incentives of smaller firms to invest in workplace safety are limited. Studies find that small, imperfectly experience-rated firms have the largest increase in total worker injuries and the smallest reduction in fatalities when workers' compensation benefits rise (Ruser 1985, 1991).

## 23.5 THE OCCUPATIONAL SAFETY AND HEALTH ADMINISTRATION

In 1970 Congress passed the Occupational Safety and Health Act, "to assure safe and healthful working conditions for working men and women." The Act created the National Institute for Occupational Safety and Health (NIOSH) and the Occupational Safety and Health Administration (OSHA). NIOSH gathers information and conducts scientific research into the causes of occupational injuries and illnesses, develops recommendations for improving safety and health in the workplace, disseminates information, and responds to requests to evaluate possible workplace health hazards. OSHA promulgates occupational safety and health standards, conducts worker education programs about workplace hazards, inspects work sites under its jurisdiction, investigates worker complaints about health and safety, and cites and fines employers for noncompliance with safety and health standards. If a work site is so hazardous that workers are in "imminent danger" of death or serious physical harm, the Secretary of OSHA can petition in US district court to shut down the work site until the danger has been removed.

The Occupational Safety and Health Act also established criminal sanctions for willful violations of OSHA standards, unauthorized notice of upcoming inspections, and falsifying business records required by OSHA. The law encouraged states to develop and operate their own workplace safety and health systems. State standards must be as effective at promoting worker health and safety as federal standards and most states with their own programs establish workplace standards identical to the federal standards. Currently, twenty-seven states and jurisdictions operate their own plans, but five cover only public sector workers.

OSHA health and safety standards come in a variety of forms. The most well-known are specification standards that mandate specific types of safety programs. Examples of specification standards include requirements that guards be affixed to machinery to prevent injuries from moving parts, engineering and work practice controls to eliminate or minimize employee exposure to blood borne pathogens, and requirements that machinery be shut down and locked/tagged to prevent restart during servicing. Perhaps, less well-known are performance standards that set maximum levels of exposures to particular hazards such as noise or dust but allow employers to decide how best to achieve the desired levels of exposure. Performance standards provide employers with the flexibility to reduce hazards in the most cost-efficient manner and to accommodate changing circumstances or technological breakthroughs. Additionally, OSHA requires employers to post warnings specifying potential dangers from operating equipment or using a product and detailing the appropriate precautions or procedures workers need to take to avoid these dangers.

The impact of new safety and health standards on firm profitability and worker welfare is uncertain. Tighter regulation may harm both parties. New standards raise production costs and lower profits, driving some firms out of business. At the same time, workers who chose to work at high-risk jobs consume greater safety but earn lower wages and for such workers the drop in earnings is valued more highly than the increase in safety. Alternatively, safety and health standards may help workers but harm firms. If workers are uninformed of the dangers faced on the job then they will not demand wages sufficient to compensate for the lack of safety. In such an information void, hazard warnings or safety and health standards may improve worker welfare by moving workers closer to their optimal levels of safety with full information. Even if workers are fully informed about job risks, safety and health standards may disrupt hedonic labor market equilibrium, causing wages across the risk spectrum to rise, and allowing at least some workers to gain at the expense of firm owners (Kniesner and Leeth 1995, chap. 2). Wages may also increase if standards raise capital costs more than labor costs. Miller (1984) argues that unions rationally support the imposition of engineering controls (such as noise enclosures) over personal protective devices (such earmuffs or earplugs) because engineering controls raise the cost of capital relative to the cost of labor, causing firms to substitute labor for capital. By reducing productivity and requiring additional workers to service equipment, engineering controls may further raise the demand for labor.

In some cases, the imposition of new health and safety standards may help both firms and workers. Maloney and McCormick (1982) derive a set of sufficient conditions for when regulations will raise market prices by more than they will raise costs, thereby increasing overall profitability. More generally, if firms have differing compliance costs then regulation may raise the profitability of some firms at the expense of other firms. Maloney and McCormick test their theory by examining the impact of OSHA's cotton dust standard on the monthly stock returns of fourteen textile firms traded on the New York Stock exchange. In developing the final standard, OSHA rejected reducing worker exposure to cotton dust by requiring workers to wear cotton masks or other protective devices in favor of very expensive engineering controls preferred by the textile union (Viscusi 1985). Maloney and McCormick find the cotton dust standard raised the average stock market value of textile manufacturers with the gains greatest for those firms relying most heavily on cotton production.[7]

Passage of safety and health standards does not assure that firms will comply with these standards. Firms observe safety standards for the same reason drivers observe speed limits; they fear they will be ticketed and fined. More firms will obey safety standards and more drivers will obey speed limits if the chance of being caught is fairly high. Likewise, holding the probability of detection constant, more firms will comply with safety standards and more drivers will obey speed limits if sanctions for violations are stiffer. Firms, like drivers, react not to the existence of the law but to the enforcement of the law as measured by the likelihood of detection and the penalty for noncompliance. The government can expand compliance by stepping up its enforcement efforts; it can increase the number of firms or products inspected, raise the number of violations found per inspection, or boost the average fine per violation. Firms establish new safety programs because enforcement efforts raise the financial incentives for reducing hazards.

OSHA is currently responsible for over 130 million workers at 8 million work sites with the help of only about 2200 health and safety inspectors (US Department of Labor 2012). Using the 2011 inspection rate, a typical American worker can expect to see an OSHA inspector once every 86 years.

Given the relatively small chance of an inspection, penalties for violations must be severe to assure compliance with costly regulations. OSHA fines tend to be relatively small. The Occupational Safety and Health Act established three violation categories: (1) nonserious, (2) serious, and (3) willful and repeated. OSHA inspectors do not need to penalize companies for nonserious violations of health and safety standards but must level fines for serious violations, infractions substantially increasing the likelihood of a worker being fatality or seriously injured, and for willful and repeated violations. Currently, the maximum penalty for a serious violation is $7,000 and for a willful and repeated violation is $70,000. In most cases, fines are much lower. The average OSHA penalty is about $1,000. Even in the case of a worker death, the penalty generally is small. In FY2007 the median initial proposed penalty where a worker died on the job was $6,400 (Michaels 2010).

With such a small chance of an inspection and such low fines when violations are discovered, it should not be too surprising that the vast majority of econometric studies examining OSHA's impact on workplace safety find no statistically significant reduction in the rate of fatalities or injuries due to OSHA (see Ruser and Butler 2009 for a review of the research). Supporters of OSHA generally cite work by Scholz and Gray (1990) and Gray and Scholz (1993) who find, using data from 1979 to 1985, that an OSHA inspection with an imposed penalty reduces lost-workday injuries by 15% to 22%. In a follow-up study, Gray and Mendeloff (2005) reestimate the impact across three time periods and find that an OSHA inspection resulting in a penalty reduces lost-workday injuries by about 19% in 1979–85, but by only 11% in 1987–91, and a statistically insignificant 1% in 1992–98. The authors cannot explain the overall decline in OSHA's effectiveness.

Mine safety is not regulated by OSHA, but instead by a separate government agency, the Mine Safety and Health Administration (MSHA). The law governing miner safety is more potent than the Occupational Safety and Health Act in that inspections are much more frequent and penalties for noncompliance with safety regulations more substantial. Still, despite purposely employing an econometric approach likely to overstate the efficacy of MSHA activities, Kniesner and Leeth (2004) find only small impacts on miner safety.

The Canadian regulatory system of worker protection is also stronger than the US system and offers another comparison to determine the likely impact of strengthening OSHA's enforcement powers. In Quebec, province workers can refuse hazardous tasks, firms must establish joint labor-management workplace safety committees, and firms are required to initiate accident prevention programs. The Commission de la Santé et de la Sécurité du Travail, Quebec's equivalent of OSHA, also spends over four times more per worker in prevention activities than OSHA. Even with more innovative safety measures and a much greater level of enforcement the Quebec system of workplace regulation has been no more successful than OSHA in improving worker safety and health (Lanoie 1992).

## 23.6 INFORMATION

Many proponents of the regulatory approach to improving occupational health and safety argue that people lack the basic knowledge necessary to make informed judgments. If people do not understand the hazards they face then they cannot choose between a safe and a risky employer. In the absence of information about hazards, labor markets will not establish compensating wage differentials for risk and firms will lack incentives to improve safety. Even if workers realize that hazards exist but they underestimate the risks they face, then compensating wage differentials will be too small and safety incentives will be too weak.

Evidence indicates that workers do consider risk when accepting employment. Many labor market studies show wages rising as the chance of a fatal or nonfatal injury or disease at work expands. All else equal, the typical US worker in a job with a likelihood of injury at about the labor market average earns 1% to 2% more than a person working in a totally safe job (Viscusi and Aldy 2003, 29). The positive relationship between wages and risk has been found in the United States and other industrial countries and also in less developed countries. Wages rise not only for accident risks but also for the risk of a long-term illness such as cancer (Lott and Manning 2000; Sandy and Elliot 2005).

Even when workers do not understand the risks they face initially, they reevaluate their beliefs relatively quickly. Evidence indicates that workers quit hazardous jobs more frequently than relatively safe jobs (Viscusi 1992, chap. 6). Increases in the probability of an accident also raise quit intentions and job searching, and reduce job tenure. Learning about job risks after accepting employment may be responsible for about one-third of all workers' quits (Viscusi 1979).

Viscusi and O'Connor (1984) directly examine how workers incorporate new information into risk assessments. When a group of chemical workers were told that they would soon be working with sodium bicarbonate, a safe chemical, they lowered their assessment of workplace hazards by 50%. When told that they would be working with either asbestos or TNT they raised their assessment of workplace hazards by 200%. No worker required extra compensation to handle the safe sodium bicarbonate but they did demand an extra $7,000 to $12,000 per year to handle the dangerous asbestos or TNT. No worker said that he/she would quit because of being required to handle sodium bicarbonate, but a majority of workers said they would quit because they would be handling asbestos or TNT.

Workers do react to information concerning health and safety risks, but because of the public goods aspect of basic research, the private market will underprovide health and safety information. The government therefore has a role to play in trying to uncover and disseminate information on the causes and consequences of health and safety hazards. NIOSH was explicitly created to gather information and conduct scientific research about workplace injuries and illnesses. Research by NIOSHA can be used to develop better workplace safety and health standards or production technologies and it can be conveyed to workers by posting hazard warnings.

A benefit of hazard warnings over health and safety standards is that they allow workers to make the cost/benefit calculations on the appropriate precautions to take based on their own circumstances and preferences. By clarifying job hazards, warnings increase the likelihood that workers demand compensating wage differentials for their exposure to risk. As can be seen in equation (23.4) an expansion in the compensation for risk $\left( \dfrac{\partial W}{\partial \pi} \right)$ raises managerial incentives to improve worker safety. Firms likewise will expand safety efforts to reduce labor turnover and the associated costs of recruitment and training. Accidents also generally do not happen in a vacuum, but instead are the result of the interaction of the user and the technological characteristics of the product. Simply specifying workplace characteristics may not address all of the contributors to deteriorating health and safety. Finally, in many situations, usage of a product is so decentralized that government monitoring of regulations dictating appropriate precautions is difficult, if not impossible. In these situations, hazard warnings or training programs on appropriate usage may be the only way to encourage workers to take suitable precautions (Viscusi 1991b, chap. 7).

For hazard warnings to be effective, they need to explain the degree of danger the person is facing, describe the appropriate precautions that should be taken, and indicate the particular risks that will be reduced by taking the specified precautions (Viscusi 1991b, chap. 7). Information overload can occur if precautionary labels present too much information or if too many products have precautionary labels. Warnings about small risks, such as the risk of cancer from silica (sand), may actually reduce safety by convincing people that warning labels are irrelevant. A proliferation of hazard warnings may also prove counterproductive if people are led to view all activities or products as equally dangerous.

## 23.7 Tort Liability

As can be seen in equation (23.4), the higher the expected court award to a worker injured on the job ($d$), the larger the marginal benefit of added workplace safety. Expected court awards increase when more workers prevail in court or the average award for damages rises. As discussed earlier, state workers' compensation laws prevent employees injured on the job from suing their employers for damages even if the employer is negligent. In some cases, workers have been able to overcome this limitation by suing other parties for damages under product liability laws. Instead of suing the employer for an injury from operating a backhoe, the worker sues the manufacturer of the backhoe. Litigation for illnesses arising from asbestos exposure is perhaps the most famous example of workers bypassing employers and suing product manufacturers for work-related damages.

Potential damage awards through tort liability can produce powerful incentives for firms to produce safe products. Litigation costs can be substantial. Firms can be forced to pay for economic losses, pain and suffering, and punitive damages if found liable for an injury or an illness. Originally, companies were liable for product-related injuries only if they failed to exercise the care of a reasonable person. Starting in the 1960s, strict liability increasingly became the norm, and producers were found liable for product-related injuries regardless of negligence. The courts believed that manufacturers could assume product risks and spread these risks across all consumers through higher prices (Viscusi 1991a).

A history of asbestos litigation in the United States provides an illustration on how product liability can spill over into occupational health and safety. The breathing of asbestos fibers can create a variety of diseases including two that are unique to asbestos exposure—asbestosis, a scaring of the lungs that reduces breathing capacity, and mesothelioma, a cancer of the pleural lining around the chest and abdomen—and others that can be produced either by asbestos exposure or other factors such as smoking (White 2004). The diseases have a long latency period making it difficult for workers to collect benefits through workers' compensation insurance. Although employers are strictly liable for workplace injuries, they can contest a claim for benefits if there is too long of a delay in filing the claim, the worker was injured while employed elsewhere, or the injury was not work-related. Many asbestos workers were employed by multiple companies over the twenty to forty years between exposure to asbestos and a diagnosis of disease, making it difficult to pinpoint the company liable for the payment of benefits and even if they were employed by only a single company, the short statute of limitations for filing a claim made many workers ineligible for benefits (White 2004). In the case of nonunique diseases, companies could also contest the work-relatedness of the disease making it more difficult for workers to collect. The workers' compensation system awards benefits to accident victims quite efficiently and, as suggested by research on workplace fatalities, provides incentives for firms to improve workplace safety. The system is far less effective in the area of occupational diseases.

The danger of asbestos-caused diseases was recognized as early as the 1920s and safer substitutes existed in many areas and yet, US consumption of asbestos expanded from 100,000 metric tons in 1932 to a peak of 750,000 metric tons in 1974 and then declined to 25,000 metric tons in 1994 (White 2004). Instead of providing incentives to improve workplace safety, workers' compensation may have led to greater use of asbestos because the exclusive remedy of workers' compensation prevented workers from suing their employers for damages and the long latency period and possible other causes of asbestos-related diseases made collecting workers' compensation benefits difficult. Regulatory efforts before 1970 either did little to prevent worker exposure to asbestos or in some areas, such building code requirements, increased it (White 2004).

With the creation of OSHA, the Consumer Product Safety Commission, and the EPA, worker protection expanded somewhat but was far from effective. Producers began substituting safer materials for asbestos, resulting in a much safer workplace, less because of regulatory efforts, and more because of the change in product liability standards. The move to strict liability beginning in the 1960s raised producer incentives dramatically to substitute safer materials for asbestos. Under strict liability, manufacturers are liable for damages to users if the products are unreasonably dangerous or users are inadequately warned of the hazards, standards easily met by workers exposed to asbestos (White 2004). The explosion of court awards in the 1980s for damages from asbestos has all but eliminated the use of asbestos in new products, and worker exposure to the material in the workplace today is largely from its removal from earlier uses.

Although exposure to asbestos fibers is potentially quite harmful, asbestos has saved a great many lives by preventing or reducing the spread of fire. Substitutes exist but in some uses asbestos is more effective and can be used virtually risk free (Sells 1994). Nevertheless, the proliferation of court awards for damages from asbestos exposure, in some cases awards to individuals with little or no evidence of any disability, has removed asbestos from the marketplace without any consideration of the potential benefits of the product or any sort of comparison of costs and benefits.

The ability of workers to sue manufacturers for product liability raises their incentives to produce safe equipment and provide suitable warnings of job hazards. In some areas the incentives may be too strong. Producers can be held liable for damages even for hazards unknown at the time of production. Legal uncertainties and potentially large damage awards for unknown hazards may prevent firms from marketing useful products (Viscusi 1991a). Attempts to minimize legal judgments may also cause firms to issue an overabundance of hazard warnings causing workers to ignore important information.

## 23.8  CONCLUSION

There are four forces conditioning how managers may guide the firm's workplace health and safety dimensions. Three are explicit and one is implicit. It is interesting that, according to the best economic evidence available, the less overt factor seems most important.

Programs or policies that overtly influence managers' decisions here are workers' compensation insurance, safety regulations, and tort lawsuits. Insurance, regulation, and lawsuits are direct economic influences on safety because workers' compensation premiums are designed to rise with injury claims and penalize hazardous firms, as do fines on firms found not to be in compliance with safety regulations. To the extent that workers successfully sue employers and the firms who make products or design processes that their employers purchase for the workplace that harm workers, then liability lawsuits encourage workplace safety too. We have seen, though, that workers' compensation premiums do not fully reflect the injury experiences of all firms purchasing the insurance and that it is not always possible to attribute diseases and illnesses to the workplace, so that they are not reflected in insurance premiums. Similarly, fines for noncompliance with regulations may be small or irregularly imposed and the regulations themselves may have little to do with removing what causes workers to become ill or injured. Although tort liability suits have come into play, they run counter to the desire to make injured or sickened workers "whole" without regard to fault and also run counter to the trend away from large damage claims in US liability cases more generally.

The economic evidence is that the most important financial incentive for workplace health and safety improvements is implicit, operating through the matching of workers and workplaces. The incentives for firms to adjust the health and safety aspects of the work site will be made evident by a difficulty in hiring new or replacing separated workers. A firm with too little safety will discover that spending to make a safer and healthier workplace will lower wage costs. Although managers will confront the costs of insurance, regulation, and lawsuits directly, they must also pay attention to the implicit voice of the labor market and the opportunities to trade-off expenditures on health and safety against lower wage costs and, in turn, achieve greater profitability.

In looking to the future, we all want safer workplaces, which is the driving force behind government regulations not yet proposed or conceived. It is also the case that new regulation will effectively occur via litigation of future damage claims for injuries from products and services such has been the case already for tobacco, firearms, or lead paint (Viscusi 2002). Ideally, regulations will be proposed that consider the benefits and inevitable opportunity costs. Even if we ignore the benefit side of a regulation on the workplace or product market for any reason, including the emotional objection to valuing life extension, there is the reality that a dollar spent on safety in one area is not being spent in another area. This is the so-called topic of risk-risk trade-offs (Graham and Wiener 1995), which should take on greater importance over time as part of a continuing push to make government policy not excessively economically onerous on firms. The difference in lives saved across possible regulations is, for want of a better word, astonishing. Tengs et al. (1995) document 500 programs and how some regulations save a life at the cost of virtually $0 while others have astronomical costs.

In considering a portfolio of future regulatory efforts, policymakers will confront several issues related to interpersonal differences. Does it matter what type of death is prevented or is a death a death? Is it better for society to prevent a death from a terrorist attack or from a natural disaster? How about an automobile accident versus a terrorist attack? Another interpersonal issue that will appear more in the future is that of forming regulations that take account of fairness concerns. A recent executive order by President Obama (Executive Order 13,563) reaffirms President Clinton's Executive Order 12,866 that agencies consider the values of equity and distributive impacts when developing new regulations, which will be the likely area of most immediate future interest to regulation scholars and policymakers.

## Notes

1. Safety programs may increase or decrease production. Viscusi (1979) argues that safety equipment increases output by diminishing the disruptive effects of injuries and by increasing the stability of the workforce. In the other direction, programs such as slowing the pace of the assembly line or installing cumbersome machine guards can interfere with the work process and decrease output. On net, which effect dominates is an unresolved

empirical question. For purposes of discussion, we assume that safety equipment is a productive factor. None of the conclusions of the analysis change if safety equipment reduces output.

2. Although wages fall for all workers, a reduction in the number of injuries means that a greater proportion of workers are paid for the full period. We assume that the wage reduction from greater safety swamps the wage bill increase from fewer accidents.

3. A more complete model would consider the firm's decision to purchase disability insurance in the absence of a government mandate. To simplify the discussion we assume that the required level of workers' compensation insurance coverage exceeds the level that would be chosen for profit maximization.

4. If $\alpha$ is small then $\alpha \times exp(\ln(w)) \approx \alpha w$.

5. All dollar figures have been adjusted for inflation to 2011 using the CPI-U.

6. For instance, along the upper wage function, labeled "Advantaged," the risk premium for the more risk-taking group would be $w^a(\pi_2) - w^a(0)$ and the risk premium for the less risk-taking group would be $w^a(\pi_1) - w^a(0)$.

7. Work by Hughes et al. (1986) calls into question the conclusion that the cotton dust standard raised textile firm profitability. They reexamine the issue using a larger sample of firms and daily stock price data and find the events leading up to the final rule, including the Supreme Court decision upholding the standard, lowered stock prices on average with losses greatest for larger firms and firms selling more cotton products. Their results are in line with the traditional view of regulation that argues expensive engineering controls lower firm profits because firms are unable to pass along to consumers through higher prices the full increase in costs.

# References

Aldy, Joseph E., and W. Kip Viscusi. 2008. "Adjusting the Value of a Statistical Life for Age and Cohort Effects." *Review of Economics and Statistics* 90 (3): 573–81.

Bellavance, Francois, Georges Dionne, and Martin Lebeau. 2009. "The Value of a Statistical Life: A Meta-Analysis with a Mixed Effects Regression Model." *Journal of Health Economics* 28 (2): 444–64.

Costa, Dora L., and Matthew E. Kahn. 2004. "Changes in the Value of Life, 1940–1980." *Journal of Risk and Uncertainty* 29 (2): 159–80.

Fishback, Price V., and Shawn E. Kantor. 1998. "The Adoption of Workers' Compensation in the United States, 1900–1930." *Journal of Law and Economics* 41:305–41.

Graham, John D., and Jonathan Baert Wiener, eds. 1995. *Risk vs. Risk, Tradeoffs in Protecting Health and the Environment.* Cambridge, MA: Harvard University Press.

Gray, Wayne B., and John M. Mendeloff. 2005. "The Declining Effects of OSHA Inspections on Manufacturing Injuries, 1979–1998." *Industrial and Labor Relations Review* 58 (4): 571–87.

Gray, Wayne B., and John T. Scholz. 1993. "Does Regulatory Enforcement Work? A Longitudinal Study of OSHA Enforcement." *Law and Society Review* 27 (1): 177–213.

Hughes John S., Wesley A. Magat, and William E. Ricks. 1986. "The Economic Consequences of the OSHA Cotton Dust Standards: An Analysis of Stock Price Behavior." *Journal of Law and Economics* 29 (1): 29–59.

Kniesner, Thomas J., and John D. Leeth. 1989. "Separating the Reporting Effects from the Injury Rate Effects of Workers' Compensation Insurance: A Hedonic Simulation." *Industrial and Labor Relations Review* 42 (2): 280–93.

———. 1995. *Simulating Workplace Safety Policy*. Boston, Dordrecht, and London: Kluwer Academic Publishers.

———. 2004. "Data Mining Mining Data: MSHA Enforcement Efforts, Underground Coal Mine Safety, and New Health Policy Implications." *Journal of Risk and Uncertainty* 29 (2): 83–111.

Kniesner, Thomas J., W. Kip Viscusi, and James P. Ziliak. 2006. "Life-Cycle Consumption and the Age-Adjusted Value of Life." *Contributions to Economic Analysis and Policy* 5. Accessed on January 15, 2013. http://www.bepress.com/bejeap/contributions/vol5/iss1/art4.

———. 2010. "Policy Relevant Heterogeneity in the Value of Statistical Life: New Evidence from Panel Data Quantile Regressions." *Journal of Risk and Uncertainty* 40 (1): 15–31.

Lanoie, Paul. 1992. "The Impact of Occupational Safety and Health Regulation on Risk of Workplace Accidents: Quebec, 1983–87." *The Journal of Human Resources* 27 (4): 643–60.

Leeth, John D., and John Ruser. 2003. "Compensating Wage Differentials for Fatal and Nonfatal Injury Risk by Gender and Race." *Journal of Risk and Uncertainty* 27 (1): 257–77.

Lott, John R., and Richard L. Manning. 2000. "Have Changing Liability Rules Compensated Workers Twice for Occupational Hazards? Earnings Premiums and Cancer Risks." *Journal of Legal Studies* 29 (1): 99–130

Maloney, Michael T., and Robert E. McCormick. 1982. "A Positive Theory of Environmental Quality Regulation." *Journal of Law and Economics* 25 (1): 99–123.

Michaels, David. 2010. "Testimony of David Michaels, Assistant Secretary for Occupational Safety and Heath, US Department of Labor." Presented before the Subcommittee on Workforce Protections, The Committee on Education and Labor, US House of Representatives, March 16, 2010. Accessed on January 15, 2013. https://www.osha.gov/pls/oshaweb/owadisp.show_document?p_table=TESTIMONIES&p_id=1062.

Miller, James C. 1984. "Is Organized Labor Rational in Supporting OSHA?" *Southern Economic Journal* 50 (3): 881–85.

Moore, Michael J., and W. Kip Viscusi. 1989. "Promoting Safety through Workers' Compensation: The Efficacy and Net Wage Costs of Injury Insurance." *Rand Journal of Economics* 20 (4): 499–515.

Mrozek, Janusz. R., and Laura O. Taylor. 2002. "What Determines the Value of Life? A Meta-Analysis." *Journal of Policy Analysis and Management* 21 (2): 253–70.

Rosen, Sherwin. 1974. "Hedonic Prices and Implicit Markets: Product Differentiation in Pure Competition." *Journal of Political Economy* 82 (1): 34–55.

Ruser, John W. 1985. "Workers' Compensation Insurance, Experience Rating, and Occupational Injuries." *RAND Journal of Economics* 16 (4): 487–503.

———. 1991. "Workers' Compensation and Occupational Injuries and Illnesses." *Journal of Labor Economics* 9 (4): 325–50.

———. 1998. "Does Workers' Compensation Encourage Hard to Diagnose Injuries?" *The Journal of Risk and Insurance* 65 (1):101–24.

Ruser, John, and Richard Butler. 2009. "The Economics of Occupational Safety and Health." *Foundations and Trends in Microeconomics* 5 (5): 301–54.

Sandy, Robert, and Robert F. Elliott. 2005. "Long-Term Illness and Wages: The Impact of the Risk of Occupationally Related Long-Term Illness on Earnings." *Journal of Human Resources* 40 (3): 744–68.

Scholz, John T., and Wayne B. Gray. 1990. "OSHA Enforcement and Workplace Injuries: A Behavioral Approach to Risk Assessment." *Journal of Risk and Uncertainty* 3 (3): 283–305.

Sells, Bill. 1994. "What Asbestos Taught Me about Managing Risk." *Harvard Business Review* March–April:76–90.

Smith, Robert S. 1990. "Mostly on Mondays: Is Workers' Compensation Covering Off-the-Job Injuries?" In *Benefits, Costs, and Cycles in Workers' Compensation*, edited by Philip S. Borba and David Appel, 115–28. Boston: Kluwer Academic Publishers.

Tengs, Tammy O., Miriam E. Adams, Joseph S. Pliskin, Dana Gelb Safran, Joanna E. Siegel, Milton C. Weinstein, and John D. Graham. 1995. "Five-Hundred Life-Saving Interventions and Their Cost-Effectiveness." *Risk Analysis* 15 (3): 369–90.

US Department of Labor. 2012. "Commonly Used Statistics." Accessed on January 6, 2012. http://osha.gov/oshstats/commonstats.html.

US Department of Transportation. 2008. "Memorandum: Treatment of the Value of Preventing Fatalities and Injuries in Preparing Economic Analyses." Accessed on July 1, 2011. http://ostpxweb.dot.gov/policy/reports/080205.htm.

US Environmental Protection Agency. 2010a. "Guidelines for Preparing Economic Analyses." Accessed on December 17, 2012. http://yosemite.epa.gov/ee/epa/eerm.nsf/vwAN/EE-0568-50.pdf/$file/EE-0568-50.pdf

——. 2010b. "Valuing Mortality Risk Reductions for Environmental Policy: A White Paper." Draft December 10. Accessed on January 15, 2013. http://yosemite.epa.gov/ee/epa/eerm.nsf/vwAN/EE-0563-1.pdf/$file/EE-0563-1.pdf

Viscusi, W. Kip. 1979. "Job Hazards and Worker Quit Rates: An Analysis of Adaptive Worker Behavior." *International Economic Review* 20 (1): 29–58.

——. 1985. "Cotton Dust Regulation: An OSHA Success Story?" *Journal of Policy Analysis and Management* 4 (3): 325–43.

——. 1991a. "Product and Occupational Liability." *Journal of Economic Perspectives* 5 (3): 71–91.

——. 1991b. *Reforming Products Liability*. Cambridge, MA: Harvard University Press.

——. 1992. *Fatal Tradeoffs: Public & Private Responsibilities for Risk*. New York: Oxford University Press.

——, ed. 2002. *Regulation through Litigation*. Washington, DC: Brookings Institution Press.

——. 2003. "Racial Differences in Labor Market Values of a Statistical Life." *Journal of Risk and Uncertainty* 27 (3): 239–56.

——. 2004. "The Value of Life: Estimates with Risks by Occupation and Industry." *Economic Inquiry* 42 (1): 29–48.

Viscusi, W. Kip, and Joseph E. Aldy. 2003. "The Value of a Statistical Life: A Critical Review of Market Estimates Throughout the World." *Journal of Risk and Uncertainty* 27 (1): 5–76.

Viscusi, W. Kip, and Joni Hersch. 2001. "Cigarette Smokers as Job Risk Takers." *Review of Economics and Statistics* 83 (2): 269–80.

——. 2010. "Immigrant Status and the Value of Statistical Life." *Journal of Human Resources* 45 (3): 749–71.

Viscusi, W. Kip, and Charles O'Connor. 1984. "Adaptive Responses to Chemical Labeling: Are Workers Bayesian Decision Makers?" *American Economic Review* 74 (5): 942–56.

White, Michelle J. 2004. "Asbestos and the Future of Mass Torts." *Journal of Economic Perspectives* 18 (2): 183–204.

# CHAPTER 24

# MERGER STRATEGIES AND ANTITRUST CONCERNS

## GREGORY J. WERDEN AND
## LUKE M. FROEB[1]

MERGERS and acquisitions can be attractive business propositions if they capture value. Horizontal mergers and acquisitions involve firms that compete with each other, or potentially could do so, and combining such firms can offer opportunities to capture substantial value by eliminating competition. The antitrust enforcement agencies, however, are concerned about capturing value from customers by eliminating competition and thereby raising prices.

Mergers and acquisitions also can be attractive business propositions if they create value. Vertical mergers and acquisitions involve firms that operate at adjoining levels of the supply chain, produce complementary products, or control complementary technologies, and combining such firms can offer opportunities to create substantial value by integrating complementary assets. Creating value in this way rarely concerns the antitrust enforcement agencies, and this chapter does not address exceptional cases when it does.

Although horizontal mergers and acquisitions can be of serious concern to the antitrust enforcement agencies, most are viewed as competitively benign. Moreover, some horizontal mergers and acquisitions are seen as procompetitive because their predominant effect is to combine complementary assets just as with vertical mergers. This chapter explains how the relatively few horizontal mergers and acquisitions that do violate the antitrust laws are identified (see generally ABA Antitrust Section, 2008).

As is often noted, merger analysis under the antitrust laws is highly fact-intensive. This chapter details how the analysis focuses on the precise competitive interaction between the parties and on the nature of the competitive environment in which they operate. Although the relevant laws and enforcement mechanisms differ significantly across countries, the basic competitive analysis of horizontal mergers and acquisitions does not, so the analysis described here for US antitrust law is much like that in other jurisdictions.

# 24.1  ANTITRUST TREATMENT OF HORIZONTAL MERGERS

## 24.1.1  The Structural Approach of the Supreme Court

Mergers and acquisitions are subject to US federal antitrust law, in particular section 7 of the Clayton Act, which prohibits mergers and acquisitions the effect of which "may be substantially to lessen competition." The US Department of Justice (DOJ) and the Federal Trade Commission (FTC) share responsibility for enforcing section 7. Both devote substantial resources to reviewing proposed mergers and acquisitions, and both investigate some consummated deals as well.

The Hart-Scott-Rodino Antitrust Improvements Act prohibits the consummation of certain mergers without prior notification of the enforcement agencies, but prior agency approval is not required. Rather, to block a deal, the US agencies file suit in federal court seeking an injunction. Nevertheless, merger litigation is uncommon. Faced with the prospect of litigation and a possible injunction, the parties proposing mergers and acquisitions often restructure deals to satisfy the objections of the federal enforcement agencies, and some deals are abandoned.

Relevant case law on the application of section 7 of the Clayton Act includes 1960s-era Supreme Court decisions. In *Brown Shoe* (1962, 332, 335), the Supreme Court observed that the application of section 7 "requires a prognosis of the probable *future* effect of the merger" and held that a proposed merger violates section 7 "if there is a reasonable probability that the merger will substantially lessen competition." As later restated by Judge Posner (*Hospital Corp. of America*, 1986, 1389):

> Section 7 does not require proof that a merger … caused higher prices in the affected market. All that is necessary is that the merger create an appreciable danger of such consequences in the future. A predictive judgment, necessarily probabilistic and judgmental rather than demonstrable … is called for.

Tools for making predictive judgments about the competitive effects of horizontal mergers were lacking in the 1960s, and the Supreme Court reasoned in *Philadelphia National Bank* (1963, 362) that the courts should avoid "complex and elusive" economic analysis and "simplify the test of illegality" to promote both "sound and practical judicial administration" and "business planning." In *Brown Shoe* (343n70), the Court looked to market shares as "a meaningful base upon which to build conclusions of the probable future effects of [a] merger," and in *Philadelphia National Bank* (363), the Court went further, holding that

> a merger which produces a firm controlling an undue percentage share of the relevant market, and results in a significant increase in the concentration of firms in

that market, is so inherently likely to lessen competition substantially that it must be enjoined in the absence of evidence clearly showing that the merger is not likely to have such anticompetitive effects.

Later Supreme Court decisions continued to apply this structure-based approach to assessing the legality of horizontal mergers and acquisitions, and a relatively recent appeals court decision (*H.J. Heinz*, 2001, 715 (citations omitted)) summarized the structural approach that is a legacy of 1960s Supreme Court decisions:

> First the government must show that the merger would produce a firm controlling an undue percentage share of the relevant market, and would result in a significant increase in the concentration of firms in that market. Such a showing establishes a presumption that the merger will substantially lessen competition. To rebut the presumption, the defendants must produce evidence that shows that the market-share statistics give an inaccurate account of the merger's probable effects on competition in the relevant market.

## 24.1.2  Market Share and Concentration Thresholds

For a half century, courts have asked whether mergers and acquisitions would result in "an undue percentage share" of the market without articulating a general rule indicating what market share is "undue." A few Supreme Court decisions from the 1960s suggested that a single-digit market share for the merged firm could be "undue," but, for more than two decades, the lower courts have not taken guidance from those decisions. Instead, many courts have cited the policy statements of the federal enforcement agencies, the latest of which is the edition of the *Horizontal Merger Guidelines* issued in 2010 by the DOJ and FTC (2010).

The *Guidelines* do not look to market shares as such, but rather to an index based on them. The Herfindahl-Hirschman Index (HHI) is derived by summing the squared shares of all participants in a market. In a market populated by four firms with shares of 40%, 30%, 20%, and 10%, the HHI is $40^2 + 30^2 + 20^2 + 10^2 = 1600 + 900 + 400 + 100 = 3000$. The agencies also focus on the increase in the HHI resulting from a merger, which can be computed directly as twice the product of the merging firms' shares $[(a + b)^2 - a^2 - b^2 = 2ab]$. The increase in the HHI from the merger of the firms with shares of 10% and 20%, thus, is 400.

The *Guidelines* (§5.3) state that mergers producing an increase in the HHI of less than 100 points "are unlikely to have adverse competitive effects and ordinarily require no further analysis." They further state that mergers resulting in an HHI above 2500 and that increase the HHI more than 200 points "will be presumed to be likely to enhance market power," and thus subject to challenge, absent "persuasive evidence showing that the merger is unlikely to enhance market power." Data compiled by the FTC and the DOJ (2003), however, indicate that they have rarely objected to mergers that increased the HHI just 200 points and that a substantial majority of their merger challenges involved increases in the HHI of over 500 points. These data suggest that a merger of two 15% firms normally would not be challenged, but a merger of two 25% firms typically would be.

Firms proposing mergers or acquisitions often cannot be sure in advance whether the US enforcement agencies would be concerned. One reason is that, as detailed below, factors other than market share are important in the agencies' assessment of proposed mergers. Perhaps even more importantly, the definition of the relevant market is rarely self-evident. The *Horizontal Merger Guidelines* (§4) warn that the US enforcement agencies define relevant markets that "are not always intuitive and may not align with how industry members use the term 'market.'" Finally, for a given market definition, market shares often could be assigned in several different ways (see Werden 2002).

## 24.1.3  Relevant Markets

The US enforcement agencies often define the relevant market much more narrowly than an industry as a whole. The *Horizontal Merger Guidelines* (§4) explain that the agencies generally find that "[m]arket shares … in narrowly defined markets" best "capture the relative competitive significance" of close substitutes combined by a merger and best "reflect competition between" those products. For example, the FTC defined a relevant market limited to superpremium ice cream (which has less air and more butterfat than either regular or premium ice cream) when both merging firms sold superpremium brands (*Nestlé Holdings*, 2003).

Defining a relevant market entails a determination of its product dimensions and its geographic dimensions. The product dimensions of the relevant market indicate the range of products that are included, and they normally are specified in terms of characteristics. For example, the DOJ defined the relevant market's product dimensions for the merger of two bakers as white pan bread (*Interstate Bakeries* 1995), which includes only white bread (e.g., not whole wheat and many other varieties) and only pan bread (e.g., not rolls or hearth-baked breads).

As explained in the *Guidelines* (§4), the US enforcement agencies determine the product dimensions of relevant markets on the basis of "demand substitution factors, i.e., on customers' ability and willingness to substitute away from one product to another in response to a price increase." The determination of the product dimension of a relevant market, therefore, is largely a matter of evaluating customer preferences, and many different sources of evidence can be informative.

The specification of a level of distribution is also usually associated with the product dimensions of the relevant market: For a merger of manufacturers, a relevant market normally is defined in a manner that specifies wholesale trade. Occasionally, the product dimensions of the relevant market are segmented on the basis of time or market conditions: For a merger of electric utilities, a separate market could be defined for summer peak demand conditions.

The geographic dimensions of the relevant market denote either of two quite different things: Either they identify the production facilities in the relevant market, or they identify the customers in the relevant market. The *Guidelines* (§4.2) explain that the US enforcement agencies define the market around customer locations when it is feasible for sellers to charge different prices (net of transportation cost) to customers at different locations, and they define the market around the locations of production facilities when that sort of geographic price discrimination is infeasible. In the bread case just mentioned, the DOJ defined metropolitan area markets on the basis that bakers could price differently in different metropolitan areas without fear that the price difference would be undermined by arbitrage between adjoining areas.

Just as different locations are treated as separate markets when distinct prices can be maintained, markets also can be segmented in other ways if a distinct competitive process sets a distinct price. When a product is sold to different customer groups at distinct prices (and arbitrage between customer groups is infeasible), the market might be segmented on the basis of particular customer groups apt to be harmed by the merger. The definition of the relevant market also can reflect the fact that a separate competitive process sets a distinct price for each transaction. For industrial equipment that is expensive, customized, and sold though a bidding process, a separate market might be defined for each transaction.

The details of the US enforcement agencies' approach to the definition of the relevant market are complex yet inessential to this chapter. That subject is discussed by Baker (2008) and Werden (1993, 1998, 2005). Werden (2003) documents the fact that the basic approach of the US agencies also is followed by US courts and enforcement agencies in other countries.

## 24.1.4  Unilateral Anticompetitive Effects

In the 1960s, the assessment of likely competitive effects of horizontal mergers typically did not go beyond an examination of market shares. A dissenting justice in one Supreme Court case (*Von's Grocery* 1966, 282, 295) observed that the majority had found the merger unlawful through "a simple exercise in sums" with "no effort to appraise the competitive effects" of the merger. Market shares remain important today, but they are now viewed as just the starting point for a fact-intensive analysis built around one or more theories describing how the merger could affect the competitive process. Theories are classed as unilateral if they posit that the merged firm strictly pursues its own self-interest both before and after the merger.

Unilateral effects theories posit that a merger is anticompetitive because it changes how self-interest is perceived. Prior to merging, the self-interest of firm A does not include the profits of firm B, but the self-interest of merged firm AB does, so AB accounts for effects on profits from B's products resulting from actions relating to A's products. In this way, the merger internalizes the competition between A and B, and that is the source of the unilateral anticompetitive effect. For example, in deciding whether to add something to firm A's product line, merged firm AB accounts for cannibalization effects on both firm A's products and firm B's products. This could cause merged firm AB to decide against introducing a new product that firm A would have introduced, considering only the cannibalization effects on its own products.

Unilateral anticompetitive effects potentially occur with respect to every competitive action merged firm AB could take, but the theories on which the US enforcement agencies most often rely relate directly or indirectly to pricing. Several distinct theories are employed, which differ depending on the competitive environment. The DOJ and FTC (2006, 25–36) published brief case histories of their unilateral effects analysis of actual proposed mergers, which they sorted into five categories. The category with the simplest analysis is that of merger to monopoly or near monopoly. To the extent that premerger competition keeps prices below monopoly levels, such a merger would eliminate that competition and raise prices. The four other categories mentioned by the agencies are discussed below.

Section 7 prohibits only mergers likely to produce a substantial lessening of competition, so the US enforcement agencies and courts must gauge the significance of likely unilateral effects. For many particular unilateral effects theories, economics provides a concrete basis for gauging quantitatively the impact of the internalization of competition resulting from the merger. This basis differs among the unilateral effects theories, and much of this chapter is devoted to the assessment of likely competitive effects in several distinct competitive environments.

## 24.1.5 Coordinated Anticompetitive Effects

Competitive effects theories are classed as coordinated if they posit that the merged firm does not strictly pursue its own self-interest. Coordinated effects theories instead posit that a merger is anticompetitive because it causes the competitors in a relevant market to begin pursuing their collective self-interest, at least to some extent, or if they already had been pursuing their collective self-interest, to do so more effectively. Coordination could take the form of an explicit agreement on the terms on which several competitors do business, although such an agreement would be subject to challenge under the antitrust laws and might constitute a crime. Coordination also could take the form of accommodative actions evolving through repeated interaction and without verbal communication among the competitors.

Because section 7 prohibits only those mergers likely to produce a substantial lessening of competition, it is necessary to gauge the significance of likely coordinated effects, and both quantitative and qualitative gauges are used. The quantitative gauges are the HHI after a proposed merger and the increase in the HHI from the merger, although the precise reading on neither gauge is important.

When the needle on either gauge is in the low range, the US enforcement agencies are very unlikely to be concerned about coordinated effects. When both needles are in the high range, the agencies typically are concerned, although consideration of other factors can allay their concerns. Past practice suggests that the agencies generally have had little concern with mergers after which at least four significant competitors would remain in the relevant market; the agencies sometimes were concerned with mergers that would reduce the number of significant competitors from four to three; and the agencies normally were concerned with mergers that would reduce the number of significant competitors from three to two.

The US enforcement agencies gauge coordinated effects more qualitatively than quantitatively. A threshold consideration is the ease with which new firms could enter the market and achieve an efficient scale of operations (or the ease with which small incumbents could do so through internal expansion). As indicated by the *Horizontal Merger Guidelines* (§9), coordinated effects concerns are allayed "if entry would be timely, likely, and sufficient in its magnitude, character, and scope to deter or counteract the competitive effects of concern."

Also as indicated by the *Guidelines* (§7), the agencies seek to determine whether the relevant market is vulnerable to coordinated conduct. This vulnerability largely comes down to whether competitive conditions suggest that some meaningful form of coordination would be simple enough to be arrived at without verbal communication and transparent enough that each competitor could know whether important rivals are acting in the coordinated fashion. Although the enforcement agencies' principal concern is the likely effect of a merger on prices, the coordination itself need not be on price. Even if coordination on price is infeasible, postmerger coordination nevertheless could raise prices significantly. For example, coordination that takes the form of abstention from poaching rivals' customers likely would produce significant price increases.

The agencies also examine premerger competition to determine whether the merged firm likely would prefer coordination when one or both merging firms did not. The agencies look, in particular, for signs that either of the merging firms had frustrated coordination prospects in the past. For example, a small competitor pursuing an aggressive growth strategy could frustrate a no-poaching arrangement, and the acquisition of such a firm by a much larger rival could end its aggressive posture. For more on coordinated effects, see Kühn (2008) or Ordover (2008).

## 24.1.6  Merger-Generated Efficiencies

Section 7 says nothing about efficiencies produced by mergers, and 1960s' Supreme Court decisions tended to view merger-generated efficiencies as either irrelevant or as a basis for thinking a merger would be anticompetitive. Appeals court decisions from the past quarter century, however, have consistently taken a contrary view, as have the US enforcement agencies. Hence, the fact that a horizontal merger creates value, as well as captures value, is potentially important. A controversy explored by Werden (1997, 2010) concerns precisely how efficiencies affect the legality of mergers. US courts (e.g., *University Health*, 1991, 1223) have held that efficiencies are relevant to the extent that they "ultimately would benefit competition, and hence, consumers," that is, to the extent that they mitigate or offset anticompetitive effects.

Efficiencies typically mitigate anticompetitive effects by countering the impact that the merger otherwise would have on incentives. An important manifestation of this mechanism arises with respect to pricing. The internalization of competition caused by a merger creates an incentive to raise prices, while merger-generated efficiencies reducing the marginal costs of production or distribution have just the opposite effect. Indeed, prices could decrease if the efficiencies of the proper sort are of sufficient magnitude. How efficiencies affect prices with unilateral effects theories depends both on the nature of the efficiencies (especially how they affect marginal costs) and on the nature of the competitive environment.

With coordinated effects theories, efficiencies can make substantial anticompetitive effects either less likely or more likely. If the merged firm achieves costs lower than those of its rivals, that could make effective coordination less likely either by creating a divergence of opinion on the preferred level of price or by inducing the merged firm to adopt a more aggressive competitive posture. Conversely, if the merged firm achieves costs closer to those of its rivals, the result could be to make effective coordination more likely.

With either unilateral or coordinated effects, merger-generated efficiencies could result in tangible consumer benefits unrelated to, but in the same market as, consumer harms from the anticompetitive effects. For example, the anticompetitive effects could stem from higher prices for existing products, while the consumer benefits could stem from the introduction of a new product facilitated by combining complementary assets. These opposing effects must be balanced, although no court has addressed such balancing.

A merger also could produce anticompetitive effects in some markets but procompetitive effects in others. This can occur when the merging firms operate in local or regional markets and have very different competitive positions across markets. This also can occur as a result of the US enforcement agencies' practice of defining narrow markets. Each merging firm might have a single factory producing many products, only a small fraction of which are within the relevant market defined by the agency, but merger-generated efficiencies could reduce costs common to all of the products. In such circumstances, the agency might credit consumer benefits from products outside the relevant market. The *Horizontal Merger Guidelines* (§9n14) state that the agencies "will consider efficiencies not strictly in the relevant market, but so inextricably linked with it that a partial divestiture or other remedy could not feasibly eliminate the anticompetitive effect in the relevant market without sacrificing the efficiencies in the other market(s)."

# 24.2 Unilateral Price Effects with Differentiated Consumer Products

## 24.2.1 The Nestlé–Dreyer's Merger

In 2002 Nestlé S.A. entered into an agreement to acquire Dreyer's Grand Ice Cream Inc. Both companies sold multiple brands of ice cream and other frozen desserts. The FTC was concerned that the proposed merger would result in substantial unilateral anti-competitive effects in the sale of superpremium ice cream. Nestlé, with its Häagen-Dazs brand, had a 37% share of US superpremium ice cream sales, and Dreyer's, with its Dreamery, Godiva, and Starbucks brands, had a share of 19%. The Ben and Jerry's brand accounted for nearly all of the rest. To resolve the FTC's concerns, the parties agreed to divest Dreyer's superpremium brands, while retaining all remaining Dreyer's and Nestlé brands (*Nestlé Holdings* 2003).

The substance of the FTC's analysis was not made public, but the FTC apparently took the view that the merger would internalize the competition between Häagen-Dazs and Dreyer's superpremium ice cream brands and thereby result in higher prices for all of them. Before merging, neither Nestlé nor Dreyer's cared whether sales gained when it cut its price came from the other, nor did either care whether sales lost when it hiked its price went to the other. Merging would change this pricing calculus. The merged firm would account for the effect of the Häagen-Dazs price on sales of the Dreyer's brands and the effects of the prices of the Dreyer's brands on sales of Häagen-Dazs. The merged firm would maximize profits by raising superpremium ice cream prices because some of sales lost by raising the Häagen-Dazs price would go to Dreyer's superpremium brands, and some sales lost by raising the prices of the Dreyer's superpremium brands would go to Häagen-Dazs.

## 24.2.2  Basic Analysis of Unilateral Effects

The analysis conventionally applied to differentiated consumer products is detailed by Werden (2008) and Werden and Froeb (2008a, 2011). This analysis posits that the merging firms and their rivals compete on the basis of price, with any other material aspects of rivalry invariant within the near term. The basic insights on unilateral price effects in this environment can be understood most easily by initially supposing that the merging firms sell a single product and compete only with each other.

In this competitive environment, the unilateral effects of a merger on prices are straightforward: the only competition affecting prices is that between the two merging products, and the merger eliminates that competition, so prices rise. The amounts of the price increases are determined mainly by the impact of an increase in the price of each merged product on the profits of the other merged product. This profit impact, in turn, is determined by the degree of substitutability between the merged products and by the price–cost margins earned on them.

The substitutabilities of pairs of products combined by the merger are characterized by diversion ratios. The diversion ratio from A to B is the fraction of the sales lost by A, due to an increase in its price, that goes to B. The two diversion ratios between a pair of products can be very different, resulting in highly asymmetric postmerger price increases. Tenn et al. (2010) estimated the diversion ratios between Nestlé and Dreyer's brands of superpremium ice cream at roughly 19% and 2%, so the merger likely would have resulted in highly asymmetric price increases. The merged firm's incentive to raise the price of A is determined by the diversion ratio from A to B multiplied by the margin earned on B. This multiplication, roughly speaking, yields the increment to profits from B produced by raising the price of A.

Thus far, we have considered only competition between the two merging firms. Accounting for competition with nonmerging rivals does not alter the analysis greatly, although it does require additional analytic machinery. Economic models of competition employ game theory, especially the concept of noncooperative equilibrium. In this context, a noncooperative equilibrium is a state in which each competitor is happy with its chosen action in view of the actions its rivals have chosen.

In the Bertrand model of oligopoly, the action of each competitor is the single price (for each product) it charges all of its customers. The Bertrand model is used widely to analyze competition among differentiated consumer products. Using this model, it is possible to account for pricing responses by nonmerging sellers of superpremium ice cream and for substitution from superpremium ice creams to other ice creams and other frozen desserts. Accounting for all of the substitution and rival responses does not alter the basic insight that the diversion ratios multiplied by the corresponding price–cost margins largely determine unilateral price effects.

Merger simulation (Werden and Froeb 2008a, 64–85) using the Bertrand model generates quantitative predictions of the likely unilateral price effects from differentiated consumer products mergers. A drawback of merger simulation is that predicted price effects are sensitive to assumptions that must be made relating to the curvature of demand curves for individual products (see Crooke et al. 1999). To eliminate the necessity of making any assumptions related to the curvature of demand, Werden (1996) characterized the extent of unilateral price effects for each merging product by how large a reduction in its marginal cost, stemming from merger-generated efficiencies, would be required to prevent a postmerger price increase. These are called the Compensating Marginal Cost Reductions (CMCRs). The curvature of demand curves does not affect these CMCRs because marginal cost reductions equal to the CMCRs prevent any postmerger movement along the demand curves. CMCRs also have the considerable advantage that they can be computed without any data relating to nonmerging firms.

Werden and Froeb (2011) derive simple yet accurate approximations to the CMCRs dubbed the aCMCRs. If the prices and price–cost margins of firms A and B are denoted $p_A$, $p_B$, $m_A$, and $m_B$, and the diversion ratio from A to B (B to A) is denoted $d_{AB}$ ($d_{BA}$), the aCMCRs are $d_{AB}m_B(p_B/p_A)$ for firm A and $d_{BA}m_A(p_A/p_B)$ for firm B. And when the premerger prices charged by the merging firms are the same, the aCMCRs are just the products of diversion ratios and margins. The CMCRs and aCMCRs can be expressed relative to premerger price or relative to premerger marginal cost, and these are relative to price.

CMCRs largely solve the problem of how to account for merger-generated cost reductions. As explained above, the case law holds that merger-generated efficiencies are relevant only to the extent that they benefit customers, which has led courts to demand evidence on the rate at which cost savings would be passed through. Werden et al. (2005) show that pass-through rates are determined by the curvature of demand, which typically cannot be gauged empirically. CMCRs obviate a separate pass-through inquiry because, as Froeb et al. (2005) demonstrate, the price effects of mergers with differentiated consumer products are determined by the same demand curvature properties that determine the pass-through rates.

Consider the diversion ratios presented above for the Nestlé–Dreyer's merger. If the wholesale gross margins of the companies had been about 50% (in the range typical for differentiated consumer products) and their prices roughly the same, the aCMCRs would have been roughly 10% and 1%. This means that merger-generated efficiencies could have offset the anticompetitive effect from internalizing competition only if marginal cost for one of the companies would have decreased by 10% of its price. With a 50% margin, that translates into a 20% reduction in marginal cost, which is quite large. The aCMCRs also provide a crude indication of the amount by which the internalization of competition would cause prices to increase absent merger-generated efficiencies—about half the aCMCRs. The price increases absent efficiencies are exactly half the CMCRs if demand is linear at the product level.

The foregoing conveys the basic insights on unilateral effects from differentiated consumer products mergers, but many additional issues arise in particular cases. Some of those issues are discussed presently. For an analysis of one particular DOJ case, see Werden (2000).

## 24.2.3  Extensions of the Basic Analysis

The field of marketing refers to the "Four Ps"—price, product, placement, and promotion. All four could be significant to the unilateral competitive effects of a consumer products merger, so an exclusive focus on price might undermine the utility of a merger analysis. Yet the important near-term competitive effects of mergers involving differentiated consumer products are most apt to be those involving prices, so treating product, placement, and promotion as fixed in the near term often yields reliable price-effect predictions.

Werden et al. (2004, 94) address when the basic differentiated products analysis of a merger should be viewed as reliable and advise that, at a minimum, "[a]ny model used to predict the effects of a merger must fit the facts of the industry in the sense that the model explains past market outcomes reasonably well." A model used to predict price levels over the next several years should explain price levels over the preceding several years. In addition, some consideration must be given to how product, placement, and promotion relate to price.

Product, in the case of ice cream, refers to brands, flavors, and recipes. The internalization of product competition resulting from a merger might be significant in the assessment of the merger's likely unilateral effects. The reason is that a merged firm might reduce cannibalization by repositioning products combined by the merger so they compete less directly. Doing so reduces the diversion ratios between the pairs of products separated this way and therefore reduces the incentive of the merged firm to raise price.

Gandhi et al. (2008) examine the effects of mergers within a simple model that characterizes a product by a point along a line segment, and that treats product repositioning as both costless and instantaneous. They find that the merger of adjoining products along the line would lead to product separation by the merged firm, and this repositioning could greatly reduce postmerger price increases. In the real world, however, repositioning significantly reducing cannibalization normally would be expensive, time-consuming, and risky. Consequently, unilateral effects analysis for consumer products mergers generally can safely hold all product attributes constant. Radio broadcasting is one of the rare exceptions to this general rule, and Sweeting (2010) finds that station reformatting commonly has occurred following mergers of radio stations.

Placement of consumer products like ice cream relates to their distribution, and distribution arrangements can be important in determining the retail price effects of differentiated products mergers. Basic differentiated products analysis ignores distribution, implicitly assuming that manufacturers sell directly to final consumers. The direct sale channel can be important, but for many consumer products, and ice cream in particular, consumers buy from retailers.

Ignoring the retail sector is harmless when retailers essentially apply fixed percentage markups. In that event, any change in a wholesale price results in the same percentage change in price at both the wholesale and retail levels. Consequently, the retail-level demand elasticities and diversion ratios, which commonly are estimated using scanner data, are exactly the same as the wholesale-level demand elasticities and diversion ratios, which govern manufacturers' pricing.

Froeb et al. (2007) analyze two other distribution scenarios. In one, retailers are monopolists and impose monopoly markups on the wholesale prices they pay to manufacturers. In this scenario, the effects of a manufacturer merger on retail prices are similar to those in the scenario in which retailers apply fixed percentage markups. The differences in retail price effects between the two scenarios depend on the curvature of the demand curves.

In the other scenario, manufacturers sell through contracts with a per-unit price optimally set at the wholesale marginal cost and a fixed fee that divides the value each retailer adds to the distribution chain between that retailer and the manufacturer. In this scenario, mergers of manufacturers affect the fixed fees but not the per-unit prices, and hence have no effect on retailers' prices. The retail-price effects of mergers are very different in this scenario than in the other two scenarios, but the difference most likely is not important under antitrust law. One court held a merger between manufacturers unlawful largely on the basis of likely effects of the merger on the fixed fees paid to retailers (*H.J. Heinz* 2001, 712, 718–19).

Promotion of a consumer product like ice cream entails advertising by both the manufacturer and the retailer, coupons, and in-store displays. The internalization of promotion competition resulting from a merger potentially is important to the assessment of the merger's likely price effects because changes in promotion affect the brand-level elasticities of demand and hence prices.

If promotion makes demand more elastic (e.g., by making consumers better informed and thus more sensitive to price changes), the internalization of promotion competition reinforces the price effects of the merger. In this case, the increase in prices from the merger reduces the preferred level of promotion, and less elastic demand results from reduced promotion, so higher prices maximize profits. For the Nestlé–Dreyer's merger, Tenn et al. (2010) found that promotion did make demand more elastic, so not accounting for promotion would have led to an underestimate of the unilateral price effects of the merger. Of course, the opposite would have been true had promotion made demand less elastic (e.g., by inducing brand loyalty and hence making customers less sensitive to price changes). In that case, not accounting for promotion would have led to an overestimate of the unilateral price effects of the merger.

# 24.3 UNILATERAL CAPACITY EFFECTS WITH HOMOGENEOUS PRODUCTS

## 24.3.1 The Altivity–Graphic Merger

In 2007 Altivity Packaging LLC and Graphic Packaging International, Inc., announced plans to combine their operations producing coated recycled boxboard (CRB), a paperboard made from recycled paper and then converted into products such as cereal boxes. Altivity was the largest CRB producer in North America with about 27% of total capacity, while Graphic was the fourth-largest with about 15% of capacity. The DOJ concluded that the merger likely would produce substantial unilateral anticompetitive effects in the production and sale of CRB in North America (*Altivity Packaging* 2008). To resolve the DOJ's competitive concerns, the parties agreed to divest two mills accounting for a total of 11% of CRB capacity.

As explained by Heyer and Hill (2008, 254–58), the DOJ concluded that the unilateral anticompetitive effects of this merger (and also the merger in the 2008 *Abitibi-Consolidated* case) would be brought about through permanent closure of paper mills, which would force up the price by restricting market supply. The DOJ explained (*Altivity Packaging* 2008, 19257) that

> the CRB market [was] operating at near capacity. Because of this condition and the fact that the proposed merger would substantially increase the capacity upon which the merged firm would benefit from a price increase, the merger would create incentives for a combined Graphic-Altivity to close one or more CRB mills ...

## 24.3.2 Analysis of Unilateral Effects Involving Permanent Capacity Closures

With homogeneous industrial products, competitive strategies tend to be much simpler than with differentiated consumer products. The actions potentially affected by mergers are mainly output and capacity decisions. By restricting output or withholding capacity, a merged firm might be able to increase the market price significantly. The ability and incentive of a merged firm to raise the market price depend primarily on (1) how large a portion of market output or capacity the firm accounts for, and (2) the extent of the excess capacity in the hands of rivals that can be economically brought into use. Also relevant is the elasticity of industry demand; the impact of restricting supply on market price is lower the more elastic is demand.

In some industries, permanently shutting down productive facilities may be the most profitable method of reducing supply following a merger. With some production processes, efficient utilization of capacity is achieved by operating essentially flat out. With these production processes, and with others, the cost savings from significantly reducing output is small compared with the cost savings from shutting down a block of capacity altogether. Permanently closing large blocks of capacity also can offer additional benefits from redirecting machinery, buildings, and land into other productive uses.

The plant-closing decision is familiar in the business world, but the usual profit calculus presumes that facilities are too small to affect total market supply materially. When the opposite is true, taking a significant portion of market capacity out of production offers every incumbent producer a benefit in the form of higher prices on the output from the remaining capacity. The profit calculus accounting for this added benefit could be affected significantly by a merger because the merged firm necessarily captures a larger portion than either merging firm alone of the total benefits from the higher price. If either merging firm has substantial marginal capacity, shutting down most or all of it could be highly profitable for the merged firm even though unprofitable absent the merger. Hill (2008) presents a simple model that determines whether a merged firm would shut down one or more plants combined by merger.

## 24.4  Unilateral Price Effects in Auctions

### 24.4.1  The Oracle–PeopleSoft Merger

In 2003 Oracle Corp. made a tender bid for PeopleSoft, Inc. They were rival vendors of software for automating accounting functions within large organizations. In February 2004, the DOJ filed suit, seeking an injunction and alleging that the acquisition would have substantial unilateral anticompetitive effects. The suit focused on human relations management (HRM) software, which deals with pay, benefit, and other employee matters, and financial management systems (FMS) software, which deals with receipts, accounts receivable, and the like. The DOJ argued that Oracle's acquisition of PeopleSoft would result in substantial increases in the license fees paid by customers finding the high-function HRM or FMS products of Oracle and PeopleSoft to be their two best options. After a three-week trial, the court rejected the challenge, and the merger was allowed to proceed (*Oracle* 2004).

The DOJ viewed the procurement process for this software much as an auction and maintained that the acquisition would eliminate PeopleSoft as a bidder, resulting in higher prices. Fundamental to the DOJ's unilateral effects theory was that each procurement of high-function HRM and FMS software constituted a separate competition, so the price charged by a vendor to any one customer was independent of its price to any other customer. McAfee et al. (2009) and Werden (2006) discuss both the DOJ's analysis and that of the court.

## 24.4.2  Analysis of Unilateral Effects in Bidding

The most familiar auction form is an oral ascending auction, often called an English auction. When the auctioneer sells something through an English auction, the level of bids ascends and bidding is open: Bidders shout out their bids or communicate them in some other way observed by the other bidders. The auction continues as long as the bidding advanced, and the selling price is the final bid. Consider an antiques auction in which the four bidders value a paperweight at $100, $110, $120, and $200. As the bidding progresses, the first bidder drops out at $100, the second at $110, and the auction ends when the third bidder drops out at $120. The winning bidder pays $120 or a small increment more.

In a reverse English auction, the auctioneer is a customer purchasing a good or service; the level of bids descends, rather than ascends, but the rest is just as in the paperweight auction. The winner of the auction is the bidder that can provide the good or service at the lowest cost, but the winning bid is the cost of the second-lowest-cost bidder or a small increment less. Procurement auctions serve two important functions: they match customers with the suppliers that can serve them at the lowest cost, and they set market prices for the transactions.

The unilateral effect of a merger in the context of a reverse English auction is simple when the merged firm maintains the separate facilities of the two merging firms and therefore the merged firm has the same costs that the merging firms had. The merged firm can supply each customer from either of its facilities at that facility's cost, but it bids just the lower of the two costs. If the merged firms' two facilities are the lowest- and second-lowest-cost sources of supply for a particular customer, the second-lowest bid, which sets the price, will no longer be the cost of the second-lowest-cost facility, but rather third-lowest-cost facility, because the merged firm submits only one bid.

A merger increases the price paid by the customer by whatever amount the cost of the third-lowest-cost facility exceeds that of the second-lowest cost facility, owned by the merged firm. With many suppliers with similar costs, the effect of the merger is slight, but with very few other suppliers with differing costs for supplying particular customers, the merger can produce a substantial unilateral anticompetitive effect.

The DOJ analyzed the procurement of high-function HRM and FMS software as a reverse English auction. The DOJ believed that the lengthy process in which software vendors worked with customers before submitting final bids allowed the vendors to learn the customers' preferences as well as the other vendors' offers. Moreover, as the DOJ (but not the court) saw things, only one other vendor—SAP AG—bid against Oracle and PeopleSoft for customers procuring high-function HRM and FMS software, and a significant number of the customers viewed SAP's products as inferior.

The DOJ's analysis predicted that the Oracle–PeopleSoft merger would have unilateral anticompetitive effects for customers that found the products of Oracle and PeopleSoft to be their two best options. The magnitude of the unilateral effect for each such customer would have been the difference between the value to that customer of the SAP product and the value to that customer of the Oracle or PeopleSoft product that was the customer's second choice. The merger could have had a substantial anticompetitive effect even if the group of unaffected customers (for which an SAP product was their first or second choice) was much larger than the group of harmed customers.

Unilateral effects from mergers in auctions are often likened to unilateral effects from mergers with differentiated consumer products, and the two can be quite similar. If software vendors in the Oracle–PeopleSoft case knew nothing about the preferences of individual customers, they would make the same offer to every customer, and the unilateral effects of the merger would have been just like with those with differentiated consumer products.

What often sets the auction context apart from differentiated consumer products is having price determined separately for each customer based on that customer's preferences. In the basic analysis of differentiated consumer products, prices are the same to all customers in a market. A merged firm's price increases are imposed market-wide and result in some customers switching away from the merged firm's products. With reverse English auctions (and some other auction forms), a merged firm does not lose any of the merging firms' customers despite raising prices to some of those customers.

Merger-generated efficiencies also have different effects with reverse English auctions than with differentiated consumer products. For an auction in which the merging firms would have been the two lowest bidders without the efficiencies, the winning bid would be unaffected by cost reductions. For an auction in which the merged firm wins only because merger-generated efficiencies reduced its costs, the winning bid decreases, and some of the cost reduction is passed through to customers. For an auction in which the merged firm is the second-lowest bidder and hence sets the price, the winning bid decreases, and some of the cost reduction is passed through. In a market with diverse customers and auctions of all three types, cost reductions do not prevent or even mitigate the price increases for any of the customers that experience them; instead, cost reductions cause price decreases for customers otherwise unaffected by the merger.

A more technical analysis of mergers in auction settings is presented by Werden and Froeb (2008a, 57–62; 2008b). Analysis of mergers with auction forms other than English auctions is provided by Froeb and Tschantz (2002) and Tschantz et al. (2000). A quantitative analysis of the effect of a hypothetical timber mill merger is presented by Brannman and Froeb (2000).

# 24.5  UNILATERAL PRICE EFFECTS WITH BARGAINING

## 24.5.1  The Evanston Northwestern–Highland Park Merger

In January 2000 Evanston Northwestern Healthcare Corp. (ENH), which operated two hospitals on the north side of Chicago, merged with Highland Park Hospital, another hospital on Chicago's north side. After the merger was consummated, the FTC examined its actual effects. Based on its preliminary findings, in February 2004 the FTC invoked administrative powers and commenced a formal proceeding to determine the legality of the merger. About a year later, an eight-week trial before an administrative law judge (ALJ), focused largely on the actual effects of the merger. The ALJ concluded that the merger violated section 7 by significantly increasing the reimbursement rates that the merged hospitals were able to negotiate with managed care organizations (MCOs). Haas-Wilson and Garmon (2011) present an empirical analysis consistent with this conclusion.

In August 2007, the FTC formally held that the merger violated section 7 (*Evanston Northwestern Healthcare* 2007). The remedy it subsequently imposed was not to undo the merger, but rather to require a separate contract negotiating team for Highland Park than for the pair of hospitals ENH owned before the merger. Having separate negotiating teams was intended to reestablish the premerger competition that moderated the reimbursement rates negotiated by the hospitals with MCOs.

## 24.5.2  Analysis of Unilateral Effects in Bargaining

A framework commonly used to analyze bargaining was developed by mathematician John Nash. His framework predicts that two bargaining parties evenly split the gains from reaching agreement, as measured relative to their outside alternatives if no agreement is reached. But the critical insight from this framework is not that gains are evenly split; rather, it is that the parties' outside alternatives determine the outcome of bargaining. By just saying no, either party can force both to accept those outside alternatives. This makes threatening to say no a powerful weapon for a party with a good outside alternative. And to improve its bargaining position, either party might be able to alter its outside option or that of the other party. In particular, the merger of either party with one of its rivals could worsen the other party's outside alternative.

Hospital mergers can produce unilateral anticompetitive effects by worsening an MCO's outside alternative and thus increasing its potential gains from reaching agreement with a merged hospital. Understanding why requires a bit of background. MCOs market health insurance plans to subscribers, who pay premiums, and they market their plans to health care providers, which receive reimbursements for services provided to subscribers. When heath care providers participate in an MCO's plan, they discount their regular charges but nevertheless benefit from participation because the MCO steers patients to participating providers. When a hospital bargains with an MCO, both understand that the hospital's participation in the MCOs network makes its plan more attractive to subscribers, but the incremental value of a hospital to the network is slight if other nearby hospitals of comparable quality already are in the network.

A simple example clarifies the mechanism of unilateral anticompetitive effects: An MCO is negotiating with the two hospitals in a town. The MCO must contract with at least one of the hospitals to market its health plan there successfully, but the MCO gains relatively little from adding the second hospital to its network. The MCO therefore simultaneously threatens each hospital with exclusion from its network, and the result is that both hospitals agree to terms favorable to the MCO. If the two hospitals merge, then offer the MCO both hospitals as a package, the MCO's outside alternative is much worse. Failing to reach agreement with the merged hospitals would create a substantial gap in its network and cause it to lose many subscribers. Hence, the MCO will agree to pay higher reimbursements.

An interesting feature of unilateral effects analysis in the bargaining context is how merger-generated efficiencies affect the bargaining outcome. If a merger reduces the marginal cost of supplying a customer, it increases the gain to the merged firm from striking a bargain with that customer, which causes marginal-cost reductions to be passed through to the customer at least partially. (Because gains are evenly split in the Nash framework, the resulting pass-through rate is 50%.) Contrary to the intuition developed from analyses of differentiated consumer products, fixed-cost reductions may be passed through partially in a bargaining context, even in the short term. If a customer is large enough that there is a recurring fixed cost associated with its particular account, merger-related reductions in that fixed cost are shared with the customer, just as reductions in marginal cost.

## 24.6  RECOMMENDATIONS FOR MANAGERS

As explained in detail in this chapter, whether a horizontal merger or acquisition violates the antitrust laws depends on the precise competitive interaction between the parties and on the nature of the competitive environment in which they operate. And what makes a merger or acquisition attractive as a business proposition can be what makes the deal unlawful under section 7 of the Clayton Act, which prohibits mergers that substantially lessen competition. Vertical mergers and acquisitions that create value by combining complementary assets rarely concern the US enforcement agencies, but horizontal mergers and acquisitions that capture value by lessening competition and raising prices often do concern them.

When the federal enforcement agency reviewing a proposed merger or acquisition has concerns, it conducts an investigation, which could delay consummation of the deal. Serious concerns likely result in an in-depth investigation and therefore could produce substantial delay. More importantly, serious concerns ultimately could lead to restructuring or even cancelling the deal. Abandoning deals might be very costly, because agreements typically provide for a significant breakup fee, and because business planning is disrupted.

When professionals with substantial experience in merger analysis identify a significant antitrust risk, it should be factored into planning. For example, the consummation date could be pushed back six months. If the antitrust risk is viewed as substantial, alternatives to the contemplated merger or acquisition should be considered. Abandoning merger plans early on might be better than committing time and money to a deal that might never be completed.

If the decision is made to proceed with a merger or acquisition despite significant antitrust risks, it is best to anticipate the enforcement agency's concerns and possibly even be proactive. Consideration should be given to presenting the deal to the enforcement agency with a remedy already in place. An acquiring firm can enter into an agreement to divest a business unit or a specific asset package (e.g., plants or brands) and thereby eliminate the competitive overlap that would be the source of the agency's concerns.

An approach often taken is to cooperate with the agency with the aim of either dissuading the agency from challenging the deal or negotiating with the agency a curative divestiture that preserves much of the deal's perceived benefits. This approach entails giving the agency the time it requires to fully assess the effect of the merger or acquisition on competition while expediting the review process by promptly providing information, perhaps even before it is requested. If the rationale for the deal is creating value, every effort should be made to explain this to the agency. The enforcement agencies have indicated, however, that they find statements and plans made in the course of negotiating mergers or acquisitions more persuasive than the arguments crafted later by people hired to persuade the agency (DOJ and FTC 2010, §2.2.1).

An approach rarely taken is to cooperate with the agency minimally with the aim of forcing it into a quick decision. This approach entails giving the enforcement agency no more time to investigate than the law requires. This approach increases the likelihood of a court challenge to the deal, but a favorable court decision might be achieved within a few months.

Finally, it is always possible to challenge the agency's analysis or perform an alternative analysis—revisiting the selection of analytic tools and reconsidering specific decisions made in applying those tools. How best to use economic theory and data analysis to assess proposed mergers is a subject of continuing research and policy debate, and the choices are best made in the specific context of each merger. As stressed by Werden et al. (2004), key issues to be considered are whether the tools and their application fit the facts at hand.

## Note

1. Gregory Werden is Senior Economic Counsel in the Antitrust Division of the US Department of Justice. The views expressed herein are not purported to reflect those of the US Department of Justice. Luke Froeb is William C. Oehmig Associate Professor in Entrepreneurship and Free Enterprise at the Owen Graduate School of Management, Vanderbilt University.

## References

ABA Section of Antitrust Law. 2008. *Mergers and Acquisitions: Understanding the Antitrust Issues*, 3rd ed. Chicago: American Bar Association.

*Abitibi-Consolidated Inc., United States v.* 2008. *Federal Register* 72:63187–97.

*Altivity Packaging LLC, United States v.* 2008. *Federal Register* 73:19250–59.

Baker, Jonathan B. 2008. "Market Definition." In *Issues in Competition Law and Policy*, edited by Wayne D. Collins, 1:315–52. Chicago: American Bar Association, Section of Antitrust Law.

Brannman, Lance, and Luke M. Froeb. 2000. "Mergers, Cartels, Set-Asides, and Bidding Preferences in Asymmetric Oral Auctions." *Review of Economics and Statistics* 82:283–90.

*Brown Shoe Co. v. United States.* 1962. 370 U.S. 294.

Crooke, Philip, Luke Froeb, Steven Tschantz, and Gregory J. Werden. 1999. "The Effects of Assumed Demand Form on Simulated Post-Merger Equilibria." *Review of Industrial Organization* 15:205–17.

*Evanston Northwestern Healthcare Corp.* 2007. 2007 WL 2286195, F.T.C., forthcoming.

Federal Trade Commission and US Department of Justice. 2003. *Merger Challenges Data, Fiscal Years 1999–2003.* Accessed on January 7, 2013. http://www.justice.gov/atr/public/201898.pdf.

Froeb, Luke, and Steven Tschantz. 2002. "Mergers among Bidders with Correlated Values." In *Measuring Market Power*, edited by Daniel J. Slottje, 31–46. Amsterdam: Elsevier.

Froeb, Luke, Steven Tschantz, and Gregory J. Werden. 2005. "Pass Through Rates and the Price Effects of Mergers." *International Journal of Industrial Organization* 23:703–15.

———. 2007. "Vertical Restraints and the Effects of Upstream Horizontal Mergers." In *The Political Economy of Antitrust*, edited by Vivek Ghosal and Johann Stennek, 369–81. Amsterdam: Elsevier.

Gandhi, Amit, Luke Froeb, Steven Tschantz, and Gregory J. Werden. 2008. "Post-Merger Product Repositioning." *Journal of Industrial Economics* 56:49–67.

Haas-Wilson, Deborah, and Christopher Garmon. 2011. "Hospital Mergers and Competitive Effects: Two Retrospective Analyses." *International Journal of the Economics of Business* 18:17–32.

Heyer, Ken, and Nicholas Hill. 2008. "The Year in Review: Economics at the Antitrust Division, 2007–2008." *Review of Industrial Organization* 33:247–62.

Hill, Nicholas. 2008. "Analyzing Mergers Using Capacity Closures." Economic Analysis Group Discussion Paper 08-8. Accessed on January 7, 2013. http://ssrn.com/abstract=1262317.

*H.J. Heinz Co., FTC v.* 2001. 246 F.3d 708 (D.C. Cir.).

*Hospital Corp. of America v. FTC.* 1986. 807 F.2d 1381, 1389 (7th Cir.).

*Interstate Bakeries Corp., United States v.* 1995. *Federal Register* 60:40195–204.

Kühn, Kai-Uwe. 2008. "The Coordinated Effects of Mergers." In *Handbook of Antitrust Economics*, edited by Paulo Buccirossi, 105–44. Cambridge, MA: MIT Press.

McAfee, R. Preston, David S. Sibley, and Michael A. Williams. 2009. "Oracle's Acquisition of PeopleSoft: *U.S. v. Oracle* (2004)." In *The Antitrust Revolution: Economics, Competition, and Policy,* edited by John E. Kwoka, Jr., and Lawrence J. White, 5th ed., 67–88. Oxford: Oxford University Press.

*Nestlé Holdings, Inc.* 2003. 136 F.T.C. 791.

*Oracle Corp., United States v.* 2004. 331 F. Supp. 2d 1098 (N.D. Cal.).

Ordover, Janusz A. 2008. "Coordinated Effects." In *Issues in Competition Law and Policy,* edited by Wayne D. Collins, 2:1359–83. Chicago: American Bar Association, Section of Antitrust Law.

*Philadelphia National Bank, United States v.* 1963. 374 U.S. 321.

Sweeting, Andrew. 2010. "The Effects of Mergers on Product Positioning: Evidence from the Music Radio Industry." *RAND Journal of Economics* 41:372–97.

Tenn, Steven, Luke Froeb, and Steven Tschantz. 2010. "Mergers when Firms Compete by Choosing both Price and Promotion." *International Journal of Industrial Organization* 28:696–707.

Tschantz, Steven, Philip Crooke, and Luke Froeb. 2000. "Mergers in Sealed vs. Oral Auctions." *International Journal of the Economics of Business* 7:201–13.

*University Health, Inc., FTC v.* 1991. 938 F.2d 1206 (11th Cir.).

US Department of Justice and Federal Trade Commission. 2006. *Commentary on the Horizontal Merger Guidelines.* Accessed on January 7, 2013. http://www.justice.gov/atr/public/guidelines/215247.pdf.

———. 2010. *Horizontal Merger Guidelines.* Accessed on January 7, 2013. http://www.justice.gov/atr/public/guidelines/hmg-2010.pdf.

*Von's Grocery Co., United States v.* 1966. 384 U.S. 270.

Werden, Gregory J. 1993. "Market Delineation under the Merger Guidelines: A Tenth Anniversary Retrospective." *Antitrust Bulletin* 38:517–55.

———. 1996. "A Robust Test for Consumer Welfare Enhancing Mergers among Sellers of Differentiated Products." *Journal Industrial Economics* 44:409–13.

———. 1997. "An Economic Perspective on the Analysis of Merger Efficiencies." *Antitrust* 11 (3): 12–16.

———. 1998. "Demand Elasticities in Antitrust Analysis." *Antitrust Law Journal* 66:363–414.

———. 2000. "Expert Report in *United States v. Interstate Bakeries Corp. and Continental Baking Co.*" *International Journal of the Economics of Business* 7:139–48.

———. 2002. "Assigning Market Shares." *Antitrust Law Journal* 70:67–104.

———. 2003. "The 1982 Merger Guidelines and the Ascent of the Hypothetical Monopolist Paradigm." *Antitrust Law Journal* 71:253–75.

———. 2005. "Beyond Critical Loss: Tailored Application of the Hypothetical Monopolist Test." *Competition Law Journal* 4:69–78.

———. 2006. "Unilateral Effects from Mergers: The *Oracle* Case." In *Handbook of Research in Trans-Atlantic Antitrust,* edited by Philip Marsden, 1–15. Cheltenham, UK: Edward Elgar.

———. 2008. "Unilateral Competitive Effects of Horizontal Mergers I: Basic Concepts and Models." In *Issues in Competition Law and Policy,* edited by Wayne D. Collins, 2:1319–41. Chicago: American Bar Association, Section of Antitrust Law.

———. 2010. "Consumer Welfare and Competition Policy." In *Competition Policy and the Economic Approach: Foundations and Limitations,* edited by Josef Drexl, Wolfgang Kerber, and Rupprecht Podszun, 11–43. Cheltenham, UK: Edward Elgar.

Werden, Gregory J., and Luke M. Froeb. 2008a. "Unilateral Competitive Effects of Horizontal Mergers." In *Handbook of Antitrust Economics,* edited by Paulo Buccirossi, 43–104. Cambridge, MA: MIT Press.

——. 2008b. "Unilateral Competitive Effects of Horizontal Mergers II: Auctions and Bargaining." In *Issues in Competition Law and Policy,* edited by Wayne D. Collins, 2:1343–57. Chicago: American Bar Association, Section of Antitrust Law.

——. 2011. "Choosing among Tools for Assessing Unilateral Merger Effects." *European Competition Journal* 7:155–78.

Werden, Gregory J., Luke M. Froeb, and David T. Scheffman. 2004. "A *Daubert* Discipline for Merger Simulation." *Antitrust* 18 (3): 89–95.

Werden, Gregory J., Luke M. Froeb, and Steven Tschantz. 2005. "The Effects of Merger Efficiencies on Consumers of Differentiated Products." *European Competition Journal* 1:245–64.

# CHAPTER 25

## ON THE PROFITABILITY OF CORPORATE ENVIRONMENTALISM

### THOMAS P. LYON AND JOHN W. MAXWELL

## 25.1 INTRODUCTION

In recent years, the environment has moved from a fringe concern on the corporate agenda to a mainstream part of management. By "corporate environmentalism," more specifically, we refer to environmentally beneficial actions undertaken by corporations that go beyond what is required by law. Because such actions benefit society as a whole, corporate environmentalism is often viewed as part of corporate social responsibility (CSR). The question of whether corporate environmentalism is profitable arises naturally from the ongoing debate over CSR that was started by Milton Friedman's (1970) famous article on the social responsibility of business.

In Friedman's view, the only social responsibility of a business is to increase its profits. He expressed disdain for corporate executives who sacrificed profits for the social good, likening the practice to "taxation without representation." For Friedman, an action counts as an act of CSR only if it is unprofitable. Socially beneficial actions that increase profits are merely "hypocritical windowdressing." Friedman opposed such "hypocrisy" because he felt it conveyed the notion that something was wrong with the pursuit of profit maximization.

Under our definition, corporate environmentalism can be profitable; all that matters is that the actions taken are not required by law. Friedman would not object to corporations taking such actions, although he might object to corporate executives attributing altruistic motives to them. The notion that corporations can undertake socially responsible actions that raise their profits is now generally accepted. To get a good sense of the evolution in the general perception of CSR, it is interesting to read articles on the topic in *The Economist* (2004, 2005, 2008).[1] While the first of these articles champions Freidman's view, the latter concludes that CSR is "just good business."

To better clarify the two views of CSR, Baron (2001) distinguishes CSR, which is driven by altruistic motives and is unprofitable, from "strategic CSR," which is profitable. Since the production and consumption of goods and services requires energy and generates pollution, it is often costly for firms to engage in actions that are "friendly" to the natural environment. Consequently, much of the theoretical work in this area focuses on strategic corporate environmentalism, explaining why profit-maximizing firms would engage in costly actions when they are not required to do so by law. While there has been some theoretical work on purely altruistic (unprofitable) corporate environmentalism, this area remains much less developed.[2] Empirical work has focused primarily on the drivers of corporate environmental actions, as well as assessing whether it pays to be green and, if so, under what circumstances.

This chapter examines three main drivers of corporate environmentalism: market forces, government regulation, and civil regulation. The key market forces driving corporate environmentalism include cost reduction, enhancement of consumer demand, access to capital, retention of employees, and management of supply chain pressures. It is sometimes the case that the quest to reduce costs can lead to innovations benefitting the environment, such as new production methods that require less input usage or reduce waste. These innovations are often labeled "win-win" in the literature. If consumer demand for green products is sufficiently large, businesses will find it profitable to satisfy this demand by supplying products with smaller environmental impacts. Firms may also find corporate environmentalism to be profitable if it helps attract and retain highly productive employees. Finally, firms that profit from being green might pressure their suppliers to engage in acts of corporate environmentalism to avoid the criticism that their concern for the environment is merely "greenwash."

Since we define corporate environmentalism as going beyond what is required by law, simple compliance with government regulations does not constitute an act of corporate environmentalism. Nevertheless, the desire to influence current or future government regulation can result in many actions and strategies that do fall under this label. Firms may voluntarily engage in pollution abatement to preempt stricter and more costly regulations from emerging. This could occur if the public observes the resulting reductions in pollution, or even if the public simply perceives that businesses are tackling the environmental problem. Sometimes a firm or subset of firms may be able to gain an advantage if environmental regulations are put in place. For example, the firm might be able to comply with a regulation at a lower cost than its rivals. In this case, an act of corporate environmentalism might be used to signal the regulator that the overall cost of the regulation is lower than she might have thought otherwise. Alternatively, the voluntary adoption of an abatement technology might constrain the regulator's ability to impose stricter rules simply because asking companies to abandon the technology they have just adopted would be too costly. If regulations are to be effective, they must be enforced. It is costly for business to prepare for environmental audits and there is always the possibility that those audits might result in penalties. A firm might find it profitable to invest *voluntarily* in abatement technologies that reduce the likelihood of noncompliance, thereby deflecting enforcement to other firms.

Government regulation is not the only form of regulation about which firms are concerned. Civil regulation, sometimes referred to as private politics, is increasingly important. With the rise of the Internet, activist NGOs have gained considerable clout in shaping firm activities—like-minded activists find meeting and organizing easier and they also find it easier to get their message out to the public. Sometimes these NGOs can be useful partners of firms, allowing them to convey credibly the quality of their environmentally friendly products to consumers willing to pay more for green products. Often, however, NGOs attempt to punish firms they see as environmentally irresponsible. In this setting, acts of corporate environmentalism can be profitable if they serve to deflect a costly NGO campaign towards another firm. In this way, the firm is able to preempt or perhaps shape civil regulations in much the same way it uses corporate environmentalism to deal with traditional government regulation.

The next section of this chapter lays out a theoretical framework for understanding when corporate environmentalism is profitable. While this section necessarily draws heavily on Lyon and Maxwell (2008), we focus our discussion on the most recent developments that contribute to advancing conceptual understanding of profitable avenues for corporate environmentalism. Section 3 then summarizes and critiques the empirical evidence relating corporate profitability to corporate environmentalism and identifying specific sources of "green" profits. In Section 4 we offer some concluding remarks concerning our views on the most valuable "lessons" for managers and the most promising areas for further scholarly research.

## 25.2 ADVANCES IN THE THEORY OF CORPORATE ENVIRONMENTALISM

The growing attention to corporate environmental initiatives by the business press strongly suggests that market forces in product, capital, and labor markets are increasingly powerful drivers of corporate environmental improvement. In this section, we begin by discussing how demand- and supply-side forces affect management decisions concerning the level of corporate environmentalism to undertake. Then we examine the role of two political forces in the promotion of corporate environmental actions. First, we review current understanding about the way traditional government regulation, or the threat of it, leads firms to undertake corporate environmental initiatives. Second, we explain how private politics, which involves activist NGOs promoting civil regulation, has grown to be a significant alternative to traditional government regulation.

### 25.2.1 Market Forces

The simplest explanation for managerial engagement in corporate environmental actions is that they arise naturally from profit-maximizing actions. Firms, in their quest to maximize profits, adopt production practices that are both more efficient and better for the environment. Porter and van der Linde (1995) provide numerous examples of firms that have increased their resource use efficiency, reducing pollution and production costs at the same time. The presence of waste does not mean that pollution abatement has been transformed into a strictly negative-cost activity, however. There is likely nothing unique about environmental efficiency improvements as a way to cut costs. Indeed, it is possible that businesses can reduce costs just as effectively by rooting out waste in human resources, outbound logistics, or any other business function as by improving environmental efficiency.[3] Nevertheless, when internal inefficiency is present, environmental regulations may cost firms less than they initially expect. Porter and van der Linde (1995) suggest that government regulations that raise the private cost of polluting the environment might spur innovation to such an extent that the resulting cost savings could more than cover any costs associated with the new regulation. This notion has been dubbed the Porter Hypothesis.

A second source of profitability in corporate environmental actions can arise from green consumerism. Production and sale of environmentally friendly products is a growth business, from organic food to organic cotton shirts to hybrid cars and solar energy. For example, US sales of organic food grew from $3.6 billion in 1997 to $21.1 billion in 2008 (Dimitri and Oberholtzer 2009). Similarly, US supply of alternative fuel vehicles rose from 234,000 in 1998 to 813,000 in 2009 (USDOE 2010). Arora and Gangopadhyay (1995) were the first to provide a rigorous economic explanation of this growth in green consumption, applying a standard model of vertical product differentiation to capture consumer heterogeneity in willingness-to-pay for environmental attributes. In this setting, one firm has incentives to increase its quality in order to reduce price competition with a rival. The assumption that green products command a price premium has since been incorporated into numerous other models that study additional aspects of corporate environmentalism.[4] As long as firms can extract enough of consumers' willingness to pay for enhanced environmental attributes to cover the additional cost of producing them, profits can be had from supplying these consumer wants. (We discuss the empirical evidence on consumer willingness to pay for green products in section 3.)

As one might expect, the level of competition in a market affects the amount of corporate environmentalism firms undertake. As shown by Bagnoli and Watts (2003), if the market for "brown" products is highly competitive, then their prices will be low, and fewer consumers will wish to buy "green" products. However, if the brown market exhibits market power, then prices will be high and consumers will switch to the green good.[5]

Uncertainty about standards weakens green consumer-motivated corporate environmental activities. Consumers often rely on product labels to determine the environmental quality of the products they purchase, but they do not necessarily know exactly what a label means. When there is uncertainty about the standard that lies behind a label, then consumers tend to give firms less credit for having a label, and may also give the benefit of the doubt to firms that do not have the label. Harbaugh et al. (2011) show that both of these factors reduce firms' incentives to label their products.

There has been much popular discussion of the role of green investors in driving companies to adopt greener practices. The amount of so-called "ethical" investing is on the rise. Theoretical work, however, is only beginning to explore this issue (Graff Zivin and Small 2005; Baron 2006b, 2007). In this research, investors allocate their wealth between savings, charitable donations, or shares of a socially responsible firm. If some investors prefer to make their social donations through investing in socially responsible companies (perhaps in order to avoid taxation of corporate profits), then corporate environmental actions can increase the value of the firm by attracting these investors. Baron (2006b) shows that the value of the firm is less than it would be without corporate environmentalism, but because its investors derive value from the firm's environmental actions, its shares trade at a price above what they would fetch if no investors cared about these actions. Thus, while the corporate environmental actions may not raise profits directly they provide investors with an investment-contribution bundle that they value. Baron (2007) goes on to show that when expenditures on green actions are fully anticipated by investors, the initial public offering of stock is at a price discount, with the cost borne by the entrepreneur who creates the firm, not shareholders.

A fourth market force driving corporate environmental actions arises from the labor market. Most employees want to feel good about the company where they work, and want to be able to tell their children they are working to make the world a better place. One way companies can attract and retain the best employees is by making environmental commitments that are aligned with these employees' environmental values. Frank (2003) surveyed Cornell University graduates and found that many are willing to accept substantially lower salaries from firms engaged in socially responsible activities. If such morally motivated employees are also less likely to shirk their job responsibilities, then companies can profitably screen for them by adopting socially responsible practices. Brekke and Nyborg (2008) find that if pollution abatement is inexpensive, the gains from labor market screening outweigh the costs of abatement. This may drive brown firms from the market, even when there is a substantial share of workers who have no moral motivation.

A final market force driving the adoption of corporate environmental actions stems from pressures on the supply chain. This is best seen in developing countries with weak regulatory systems. For example, Colombia is a major exporter of cut flowers to the United States and Europe. Customers in the European Union (EU) have begun to choose suppliers based in part on their practices concerning the use of pesticides. As a result, the flower industry in Colombia has created the Florverde program, which encourages members to adopt a set of environmentally friendly practices. By the end of 2006, Florverde had 137 member companies, exporting some 700 million flower stems per year.[6] Hence, the shift in market demand may well be playing a stronger role than the nation's incomplete and imperfectly enforced pesticide regulations. Similarly, when downstream retailers selling in developed countries require their suppliers in developing countries to achieve ISO 14001 certification, this can have a positive impact on environmental performance upstream.[7]

If all market participants had complete information about waste reduction opportunities and transaction costs were zero, then markets would bring about all socially beneficial pollution abatement without any government intervention. In practice, however, these conditions are unlikely to hold and market-driven emission reductions are unlikely to be sufficient to achieve the social optimum. As a result, politics and government regulation will remain key forces driving environmental improvement. It is to this subject that we now turn.

## 25.2.2  Political Forces—Government Regulation

Collective action is often required to solve environmental problems, and public politics remains the key venue for most collective action to protect the environment. The types of strategic corporate environmental action open to firms will often depend on whether a state of full information is assumed. We begin our discussion by assuming this state and then turn to an examination of corporate environmentalism when the assumption of full information does not hold.

One important reason industry invests in corporate environmental actions is to preempt advocacy groups from organizing to enter the political arena and press for regulation. Because organizing and lobbying is costly for advocacy groups, investing in activities such as pollution abatement may enable industry to preempt regulation with a lower level of abatement than would be required through the political process. Maxwell et al. (2000) formalize this notion and identify conditions under which firms can profitably preempt regulatory threats. When organizing and lobbying costs are low, preemption may be excessively costly. This is because advocacy groups may still enter the political process even after industry has made voluntary reductions in emissions. However, there is a point at which an advocacy group's organizing costs are high enough to make preemptive corporate environmental actions profitable. Beyond this point, voluntary abatement declines with organizing costs, but preemption remains profitable.

It is easy to see why industry and advocacy groups prefer to avoid the high costs of working within the regulatory system. Interestingly, regulators may share the desire to reduce the costs of regulation, and this opens up another opportunity for profitable corporate environmental activity. The regulator may negotiate "voluntary agreements" (VAs) with industry to circumvent the traditional regulatory process. Since industry is not required by law to participate in such programs, the actions they undertake in the agreement would correctly be considered corporate environmentalism.

When regulators bargain with industry, one might argue that the regulator could commit to blocking passage of threatened legislation if an agreement is reached. Segerson and Miceli (1998) present a model based on this notion, and find that both industry and government benefit from signing the agreement when the agreement has lower transaction costs than government regulation.[8]

Blackman et al. (2006) find that a voluntary agreement is socially desirable only when the probability of enforcing mandatory regulations is low. In the developing world, there may be considerable uncertainty regarding when regulators will have the capacity to enforce environmental laws that already are on the books. In cases where firms take this uncertainty into account, government may use a voluntary agreement to accelerate environmental improvement. However, Segerson and Miceli (1998) find that voluntary agreements are always socially desirable, regardless of the probability of enforcing mandatory regulation.

When industry groups negotiate voluntary environmental agreements with government, firms may disagree about how to allocate the burdens of the agreement. There is no consensus in the theoretical literature about how groups of firms resolve such disagreements. Nevertheless, in the area of corporate environmentalism, Dawson and Segerson (2008) and Manzini and Mariotti (2003) develop models of industry negotiation of VAs. Dawson and Segerson (2008) apply the approach of d'Aspremont et al. (1983) to argue that we should expect only a subset of the total population of the industry to enter into negotiated agreements, as is indeed often observed in practice. In contrast, if the negotiation process for some reason requires consensus among all firms in the industry, Manzini and Mariotti (2003) show that the outcome of the negotiations is controlled by the firm with the highest cost of abatement, which tends to produce low levels of green actions. In either case, however, the voluntary actions are profitable both for the firms that undertake them and for those that do not, in the sense that more costly regulation is avoided.

Most of the business/government partnerships offered by the US Environmental Protection Agency do not fit the foregoing analysis. These "public voluntary programs" are typically initiated by government when political conditions preclude any credible regulatory threat. Most of US climate policy to date has been conducted through these programs, which include the Energy Star program, Natural Gas Star, Climate Challenge, etc.[9] These programs typically offer firms technical assistance and favorable publicity if they adopt environmentally friendly practices. Hence, public voluntary programs offer industry small "carrots" (subsidies) when big "sticks" (regulatory threats) are unavailable.

Public voluntary programs are inherently weaker instruments than mandatory regulations such as environmental taxes, standards, or cap-and-trade programs (Lyon and Maxwell 2003). Since public voluntary programs involve only carrots, they cannot force inefficient, dirty firms out of business the way mandatory programs can. Additionally, unlike an environmental tax, public voluntary programs deplete public coffers, rather than contribute to them. Furthermore, if industry believes that a subsidy program might be forthcoming, it has greater incentives than usual to lobby against mandatory regulation. For these reasons, policy makers should have only modest expectations for public voluntary programs. Nevertheless, these programs may be useful when stronger measures are politically infeasible, and voluntary participation in them is profitable.

As these programs have grown in popularity over the past decade, they have attracted ever more attention from researchers. Ironically, despite the growing use of public voluntary programs, most empirical research has concluded that they are ineffective. Morgenstern and Pizer (2007) review many of the best known public voluntary programs, finding little evidence that participants achieved substantially more environmental improvement than nonparticipants. However, Lyon and Maxwell (2007) argue that most public voluntary programs should be viewed as information diffusion programs, whose goal is to change overall industry behavior, not just the behavior of participants. Thus, a successful public voluntary program would diffuse information about pollution reduction opportunities throughout an entire industry.

Despite industry's best efforts, not all environmental regulations can be preempted. Even so, corporate environmental actions can be profitable if they help firms shape the regulations that ultimately are implemented. In particular, corporate environmental investments can constrain the regulator's options, or send a signal about the costs of meeting new regulations.

Industrial organization teaches that a firm may make sunk investments that form strategic commitments constraining its subsequent actions or seizing first-mover advantages with the goal of altering the actions of its competitors. This insight applies to the regulatory arena as well. Lutz et al. (2000) show that corporate leaders may strategically commit to modest environmental improvements in order to constrain regulators' ability to set tough standards. For example, a firm's sunk investments may make it very costly to retool and achieve more substantial environmental gains. If the regulator cares about industry profits as well as environmental performance, she may set a weak standard so as not to dissipate profits too much. In this case, corporate environmentalism, while benefiting industry, does not necessarily have beneficial results for society.

Even after regulations are promulgated, they are unlikely to have much impact on corporate behavior unless government undertakes costly monitoring and enforcement activity. Enforcement agencies are chronically underfunded, which means that officials must carefully allocate their enforcement resources. As a result, companies (or plants) viewed by regulators as socially responsible are likely to be monitored less frequently. Harrington (1988) argued that regulators can leverage their enforcement resources by targeting firms with poor environmental performance records. If we assume that corporate environmental investments enhance a firm's environmental performance, then it is a small step to argue that regulators should target firms that invest less in compliance-related corporate environmentalism. Indeed, Maxwell and Decker (2006) show that if a firm voluntarily makes an observable investment in pollution control that lowers its marginal cost of abatement, then it is optimal for the regulator to monitor the firm less frequently, resulting in an increase in the firm's expected profits. Innes and Sam (2008) find empirical support for this theory with respect to toxic waste emissions.

Up to this point we have assumed a state of full information. We now consider corporate environmentalism as it relates to public politics, under incomplete information. When information is incomplete, firms can still use the familiar tools of campaign contributions and lobbying to influence future regulations, but other strategies, based on information provision, can also be used to influence legislation and regulation. To date, the relationship between corporate environmentalism and these tools of corporate public affairs management has not received much attention, but this may be changing. Beloe et al. (2007, 1) argue that because companies have not been sufficiently transparent about their public affairs activities, "other stakeholders—namely the mainstream investment community—are showing more involvement in assessing the public affairs activities of companies … and in some cases are now driving measurement of business activity in this area."[10]

When the public lacks full information about the state of the environment, environmental NGOs and firms can enhance their chances of influencing legislation by devoting effort to informing the public about the state of the natural environment. Complementarities between informing the public about the state of environment and direct political action are examined by Yu (2005). Yu assumes two stages of competition for legislative change: first, NGOs and firms invest resources in persuading the public to influence government policy and, second, the two groups directly lobby for change. Corporate environmental actions can be used as a tool to reduce the likelihood of legislation by convincing the public that the state of the environment is not as bad as they might be led to believe, or that firms are tackling the problem without the need for legislation.

Once legislation passes, regulations are written to implement it. In an ideal world, the regulator will attempt to balance the costs and benefits of proposed regulations in order to select the regulation that achieves the legislative goal with the maximum possible social welfare. When the regulator lacks information about the costs of alternative policies, corporate environmentalism can play an important informational role. For example, Denicolò (2008) provides a formal model in which a firm possessing a cost advantage in the use of a cleaner technology chooses voluntarily to adopt the cleaner process to signal to the imperfectly informed government regulator that compliance cost is low. The regulator, in balancing profits, consumer welfare, and environmental externalities, then finds it socially desirable to mandate the adoption of the clean technology, and the signaling firm thus successfully executes a raising rivals' cost strategy. Similarly, Innes and Bial (2002) show that firms can be induced to invest in new abatement innovations, and voluntarily reveal their existence to regulators, if they know that regulators will ratchet up standards in response. Moreover, they show that this mechanism can create excessive incentives for innovation, although optimal incentives can be restored if the new regulations impose less stringent requirements on rivals than on the innovator.

## 25.2.3  Political Forces—Civil Regulation

Activist NGOs are playing ever greater roles in corporate environmental actions. The Internet facilitates NGO activity by significantly lowering the internal and external communication costs of NGOs. More specifically, this translates into lower costs for bringing together like-minded individuals and groups to plot complex strategies that can bring attention to the group's concerns (internal communication). It also means lower costs for informing the public about objectionable corporate activities, and mobilizing the public for action (external communication).[11]

Unlike traditional government regulation—in which activists and firms interact with policymakers in an attempt to influence their actions—in civil regulation engagement between NGOs and firms is direct. David Baron coined the term "private politics" to describe this type of engagement. The literature on private politics, while fairly new, already provides interesting insights into the roles NGOs play in corporate environmentalism. This literature includes two distinct lines of work. The first focuses on the NGO as an adversary, inducing firms to engage in strategic acts of corporate environmentalism either as a preemptive measure or as a means of stopping NGOs from inflicting further harm on the firm. NGOs will generally desire a greater level of corporate environmental activity than even altruistic firms are likely to undertake voluntarily.[12] Therefore, altruistic firms are not immune to NGO threats, and may even represent more attractive targets than profit-maximizing rivals. The second line of research shows how NGOs can be corporate allies, using their reputations to certify firms' CSR activities. Indeed, NGOs with global reaches can be a very important source of endorsements since globalization has resulted in production and distribution across different governmental jurisdictions. These endorsements contribute directly to making acts of corporate environmentalism profitable.

Mitigation of an objectionable activity is presumably costly to the firm; otherwise the firm would simply comply with the mitigation request from the NGO. In order to induce compliance with its demands, the NGO may take an adversarial approach, threatening harm for noncompliance, or a cooperative approach, offering the firm a reward for compliance. As mentioned above, the firm might decide to self-regulate by taking voluntary actions in order to avoid a threat of harm. Alternatively, the NGO may participate in the firm's self-regulatory efforts, as part of the provision of a promised reward. In general, however, as shown by Baron and Diermeier (2007), NGOs prefer to threaten harm rather than to offer rewards, since harm reduces industry profits and discourages investment in the industry, thereby reducing the overall level of the targeted activity.

As with our discussion of traditional government regulation, we begin by assuming a state of full information. If the NGO chooses the adversarial path and the firm rejects the NGO's demand, the NGO will attempt to deliver its threatened harm (e.g., disseminating negative propaganda about the firm or launching a consumer boycott of the firm's products). These activities are designed to negatively impact sales, employee morale, corporate recruitment efforts, etc. These same tactics may also be used against the firm's suppliers to induce them to cease dealing with the firm, thus bringing about indirect pressure on the firm to step up its corporate environmental activities.

Resolution of the NGO's campaign can occur in three ways: 1) the firm remains intransigent but the NGO ceases its campaign anyway, 2) the firm acquiesces to the NGO's demands and the NGO ceases its campaign, or 3) the firm and the NGO negotiate a mutually acceptable level of CSR activity and the NGO ceases its campaign. Within this setting, actions that seem altruistic may be indistinguishable from strategic corporate environmentalism. Interestingly, even an altruistic firm that voluntarily undertakes the socially optimal level of mitigation is not necessarily protected against adversarial NGO demands. Because the NGO's focus is on improving environmental quality, it will pressure firms to reduce pollution beyond the level that balances the costs and benefits of abatement. In fact, in some cases, the altruistic firm may be a more attractive target for the NGO than a profit-maximizer, since it has less incentive to resist the NGO's demands.

Although the targeting strategies of NGOs are fascinating, and play a critical role in shaping strategic CSR behavior, they have just begun to receive attention from academic researchers. A pioneering example is the work of Baron and Diermeier (2007), who develop a theory of adversarial NGO campaigns.[13] They show that the NGO prefers to pick issues that have high social value and target firms that are likely to be responsive to the campaign (i.e., those that will incur low costs for complying with the NGO's demand), which reduces the resources needed to carry out a successful campaign. Consequently, NGOs do not necessarily target the worst social or environmental offenders, as these firms may be the most intransigent. As mentioned above, even firms that have undertaken some corporate environmental activities for altruistic or strategic reasons may find themselves targets of NGOs because they are viewed as softer targets.

The NGO prefers to target firms sequentially rather than targeting multiple firms simultaneously. Sequential targeting lowers the costs that consumers face for participating in the NGO's campaign, such as a boycott of the firm's products, allowing them to switch to a supplier of a similar product rather than giving up the product category altogether. Sequential targeting also reduces the NGO's campaign costs and allows it to use interim successes to raise additional funds.

Potential targets may use two very different strategies to deflect the NGO. First, they may increase their corporate environmental activities if the NGO will credibly commit never to retarget the firm after the requested improvements have been made. The NGO may agree to such a commitment if self-regulation by the firm makes the pursuit of an alternative firm more desirable. Second, firms may develop a reputation for being resistant to NGO demands in order to induce NGOs to target alternative (weaker) firms. This may have implications for public politics to the extent that intransigence in the public arena enhances a firm's general reputation for resisting social and environmental changes.

A product boycott is costly for the firm in terms of lost sales and for the NGO in terms of resources expended to conduct the campaign. This raises the question of why bargaining would not always preempt a boycott. Innes (2006) shows that an NGO may be willing to conduct a long-term boycott against a "dirty" firm in order to shift consumer demand towards a cleaner rival. The dirty firm may resist acquiescing to even a long-term boycott if the market gains from complying with the NGO's demands are small (e.g., if the dirty firm is small or if price competition between similar products would be too fierce). Thus, although a boycott is costly to the firm, it may arise in equilibrium because the alternative of undertaking the demanded corporate environmental activities is too costly.

Once we enter a world of incomplete information, the nature of the NGO–firm relationship can change, and this opens up a new set of corporate environmental strategies to the firm. A great deal of uncertainty may exist around the environmental impact of the firm's production processes and products. Because firms face a credibility problem in conveying information about their environmental impacts, NGOs are often considered to be more reliable sources of such information. In fact, one recent poll found that 55% of Americans trust NGOs, while less than 30% trust CEOs of major corporations.[14] If firms wish to obtain credit for their corporate environmental activities through increased prices or sales, or possibly even through heightened employee morale, public recognition is necessary. NGOs make excellent potential corporate allies, since they have more credibility with the public than does a typical corporation.

NGOs can use their credibility with the public to certify the existence of environmental or socially beneficial process changes. The literature has focused on two issues: 1) How NGOs can credibly convey information to the public and 2) How the presence of NGOs may affect government decisions to set minimum-quality standards for an industry.

Even though NGOs are generally viewed as trustworthy, they may not always be able credibly to vouch for the greenness of corporate offerings. Assuming that NGOs seek to minimize environmental damage, Feddersen and Gilligan (2001) show that they may prefer to discourage consumption across the board, rather than shifting consumption toward less damaging products. Thus, an NGO may be happy to label a few products in an industry as green, but it does not want to label all products as green (even if they are!) for fear of increasing overall demand and hence overall environmental impact.

Further complications arise when NGO certification and government-mandated minimum-quality standards may both be present in the marketplace. The NGO's voluntary label is more attractive to industry, since it allows higher-quality producers to distinguish themselves without forcing lower-quality producers to exit the industry, something a minimum-quality standard would do. Heyes and Maxwell (2004) show that if the NGO's label is seen as an alternative to government regulation, then its very existence may raise industry resistance to the government's minimum-quality standard, effectively weakening the standard in response to industry lobbying pressures. However, if the NGO's label is seen as a complement to government regulation, then industry will support their coexistence.

Harbaugh et al. (2011) have shown that a proliferation of labels, often developed by NGOs, can lead to consumer confusion, frustrating firms' attempts to convey information about the environmental qualities of their products. However, even in this setting, the authors show that there is a possible role for NGOs in enhancing the flow of information to the public by promoting the use of a single specific label as a signifier of environmental quality.

There is still the possibility of adversarial relationships between NGOs and firms in a setting of incomplete information. As time passes and firms face growing pressure from NGOs to undertake corporate environmental activities, they also face growing demands for transparency, that is, for full disclosure of their environmental profiles. This pressure is stronger when stakeholders are worried about environmental impacts and when an NGO boycott threatens to be very costly. Sinclair-Desgagne and Gozlan (2003) show that when the NGO wields a big threat it can induce green firms to distinguish themselves by issuing detailed Corporate Social Responsibility (CSR) reports. If the NGO threat is weak, however, then both green and brown firms release only moderately informative CSR reports. In this case, the NGO conducts its own audit of the firm, and initiates a boycott if the firm is found to be brown.

As firms increasingly strive to appear green, NGOs have become more vigilant about perceived corporate hypocrisy, which NGOs often label as "greenwash." Lyon and Maxwell (2011) develop a theory of greenwash as selective disclosure, in which an NGO may attack a firm for promoting green activities if it finds that the firm also suppressed information about environmentally harmful activities. Under this theory, firms with poor reputations fully disclose because they gain much from trumpeting a success and lose little by hiding a failure (since they are already expected to fail); in this case, there is little value in risking public backlash by refusing to disclose. At the other extreme, firms with excellent reputations disclose nothing because they gain little by disclosing successes (since they are already expected to succeed) and lose a lot by disclosing a failure; in this case, there is little value in risking public backlash by disclosing a success. For firms with moderate reputations, however, selective disclosure is attractive: disclosing a success can produce a significant improvement in public perception, and withholding information about a failure can prevent a significant negative public perception; thus, they are willing to risk public backlash by disclosing only partially.[15]

## 25.3 EMPIRICAL RESEARCH ON THE PROFITABILITY OF CORPORATE ENVIRONMENTALISM

As the previous section has shown, there are many ways in which corporate environmentalism can be profitable, at least in theory. Unfortunately, as Portney (2008) points out, it has proven surprisingly hard to establish empirically whether firms profit from being more socially and environmentally responsible. Indeed, scholars have debated whether better corporate social and environmental performance (CSEP) leads to better corporate financial performance (CFP) for years with remarkably limited success. In a meta-analysis of 167 academic studies, Margolis et al. (2007) conclude in their abstract that "Although the results suggest no financial penalty for CSP, they indicate at least as strong a link from prior CFP to subsequent CSP as the reverse. We conclude that if future research on the link persists, it should meet a number of minimum standards. Ideally, though, efforts to find a link should be redirected to better understand why companies pursue CSP, the mechanisms connecting prior CFP to subsequent CSP, and how companies manage the process of pursuing both CSP and CFP simultaneously." The methodological challenges of measuring the profitability of corporate environmentalism are substantial. Cross-sectional regressions are unlikely ever to resolve the puzzle of causality, because they cannot determine whether profitability preceded greening or vice versa. An alternative approach is to use panel data to identify intertemporal links between CSEP and CFP. If a change in CSEP in period $t$ is associated with a change in CFP in period $t$+1, but not vice versa, one can make a case that CSEP causes CFP. However, this approach inevitably confronts an array of methodological quandaries. First, it is hard to accurately control for all the factors that may affect a firm's CFP over time. Second, it is very difficult for the researcher to control for the autocorrelation of variables when seeking causal relations over time; thus, even time series data may not establish causal patterns. Third, it is very difficult to find instrumental variables that allow the researcher to predict CSEP independently of CFP and vice versa. As a result, even the literature on intertemporal links between CSEP and CFP is not conclusive.

## 25.3.1  Does It Pay to Be Green? Evidence from Event Studies

A more promising way of resolving the puzzle of causality is to focus on a discrete event that happens within a narrowly defined window of time, and that is expected to affect shareholder value. Work of this sort starts from the premise that financial markets have powerful incentives to incorporate all available information rapidly that may affect the future returns of listed companies. When news reaches the market, share prices will quickly reflect its effect on expected future returns (MacKinlay 1997). Such financial "event studies" can identify the impact on profitability of good or bad environmental news.

The challenges for an event study are quite different from those involved in estimating longitudinal correlations between CSEP and CFP. As long as the event itself is plausibly independent of firm profitability, the direction of causality is clear. For example, it is hard to argue that the timing and content of *Newsweek*'s Green Rankings are driven by the profitability of any of the firms in its sample. The biggest challenge in event studies is usually in identifying a well-defined event that occurs within a relatively narrow "event window" and for which the outcome could not be anticipated by informed insiders. Again, the *Newsweek* Green Rankings provide a good example: the release of the rankings is a well-defined event, and *Newsweek* has strong incentives not to leak the results of the ratings before publishing them.

The emerging literature on environmental event studies has already begun to establish some important empirical regularities. First, environmental problems that are likely to generate regulatory penalties or legal liability are generally punished by the capital markets, in both developed and developing countries (Muoghalu et al. 1990; Laplante and Lanoie 1994; Klassen and McLaughlin 1996; Lanoie et al.1998; Dasgupta et al. 2001; Karpoff et al. 2005; Capelle-Blancard and Laguna 2010). Second, emissions of toxic chemicals, even unregulated ones, by firms in the United States are penalized by investors (Hamilton 1995; Konar and Cohen 2001; Khanna et al. 1998; Bettenhausen et al. 2010). Third, negative ratings by third parties reduce stock prices significantly both in the United States and in India (Gupta and Goldar 2005; Beatty and Shimshack 2010; Lyon and Shimshack 2011). Thus, there appears to be an emerging consensus that stock markets punish bad environmental news. However, it remains an open question whether the reduction in shareholder value caused by bad environmental news is simply equal to the expected value of regulatory and legal penalties (Karpoff et al. 2005) or substantially greater than the value of such penalties (Muehlenbachs et al. 2011).

Much more controversial is the question of whether good environmental news is rewarded by financial markets. Dowell et al. (2000) divide US multinational firms into three groups: firms that default internationally to (less stringent) local environmental standards; firms that apply US environmental standards on an international scale; and firms that adopt more stringent standards than those required by US law. Their results suggest that firms adopting more stringent environmental standards have higher valuations, but they are unable to reject the possibility that this is simply because well-managed firms are both cleaner and more profitable. Some research finds that environmental good news is not valued by the market, or even meets with a negative response; this includes work examining corporate participation in environmental management systems (Wang and Yuan 2004; Alberton et al. 2009; Cañón-de-Francia and Garcés-Ayerbe 2009), and voluntary programs like the Carbon Disclosure Project (Kim and Lyon 2011) or Climate Leaders (Fisher-Vanden and Thorburn 2011). A neutral response may occur because external parties cannot distinguish "greenwash" (Lyon and Maxwell 2011) or "symbolic action" (Westphal and Zajac 1994; Delmas and Montes-Sancho 2010; Short and Toffel 2010) from substantive action, while a negative response may occur because firms are pressured into taking action, so that what appears to be "voluntary" is really coerced, and hence should not be expected to be profitable (Reid and Toffel 2009; Fisher-Vanden and Thorburn 2011).

Awards or rankings produced by credible third parties would appear to be a form of good news that is immune from the criticisms that it is simply greenwash on the part of firms trying to promote themselves, or the result of pressure from other stakeholders. Even in this situation, however, the empirical evidence is equivocal. *Newsweek*'s highly publicized Green Company Ratings had a significant impact on share prices, with firms in the top 100 earning abnormal returns nearly 1% higher than those in the bottom 400 (Lyon and Shimshack 2011). However, it is impossible to determine whether poor performers were being penalized, good performers being rewarded, or both.[16] In some cases, such as the climate ratings produced by the environmental group Climate Counts, performers rated highly received no positive abnormal returns (Beatty and Shimshack 2010). In other cases, environmental awards are greeted positively by the capital markets, both in the United States (Klassen and McLaughlin 1996) and in a number of developing countries (Dasgupta et al. 2001). In China, however, privately owned firms and firms in low-polluting industries suffered significant negative impacts from winning environmental awards (Lyon et al. 2011).

Even though the direct financial benefits of corporate environmentalism are unclear, empirical evidence suggests that voluntary environmental improvement generates an indirect bump in shareholder value by mediating the impact of external shocks. Several papers in the empirical accounting literature find that investors view firms with more extensive prior environmental disclosures as better prepared for possible future environmental regulations (Bowen et al. 1983; Hill and Schneeweis 1983; Blacconiere and Patten 1994; Blacconiere and Northcut 1997; Patten and Nance 1998; Freedman and

Patten 2004). Kim and Lyon (2011) study both the direct and the indirect impacts on share prices of corporate decisions to participate in the Carbon Disclosure Project (CDP). They find no direct impact on share prices, but when the threat of climate regulation increased (as a result of Russia ratifying the Kyoto Protocol), CDP participants earned larger returns than nonparticipants.

## 25.3.2   When Does It Pay to Be Green?

We turn now to the small body of empirical work that attempts to test specific hypotheses about when it pays to be green.

### 25.3.2.1   Market Forces

Perhaps the most common explanation for why corporate environmentalism is profitable is the notion that companies can both save money and reduce emissions by improving internal eco-efficiency. Anecdotes and case studies abound supporting this idea (Porter and Van der Linde 1995; Esty and Winston 2006; Hoffman 2007), but empirically robust evidence is surprisingly hard to find. Khanna and Damon (1999) find that chemical firms that participated in the EPA's 33/50 voluntary program (which encouraged reductions in toxic chemical emissions) suffered a short-term reduction in return on investment, but achieved a long-term gain as measured by excess value per unit of sales. In perhaps the best study of this kind, King and Lenox (2002) study a sample of 614 firms in a range of industries, and find that waste prevention is consistently profitable (as measured by Tobin's q, the firm's market value relative to assets), while other means of reducing pollution are not generally profitable.

Another simple market-driven explanation for why corporate environmentalism might be profitable is that firms can differentiate their products to sell to green consumers, earning higher margins in the process. There is a small literature that does indeed suggest that some consumers are willing to pay a price premium for some green products (Teisl et al. 2002; Kiesel and Villas-Boas 2007; Casadesus-Masanell et al. 2009; Elfenbein and McManus 2010). This literature has not focused on the profitability of green product differentiation, however. Since green products are likely to cost more to produce than brown products, there is no guarantee that they are more profitable.

### 25.3.2.2   Political Forces—Government Regulation

Maxwell, Lyon and Hackett (2000) find support for the theory of regulatory preemption, based on the empirical result that toxic emissions reductions were greater in states with high initial levels of emissions and a larger number of environmental group members per capita. Similarly, Innes and Sam (2008) find that firms were more likely to participate in the EPA's 33/50 Program in states with greater population densities of environmental group members.

Decker (2003) finds support for the theory that corporate environmentalism can deflect government enforcement efforts, based on the result that firms undertaking voluntary pollution abatement were granted permits for new plant construction and expansion of existing plants more quickly than other firms. In a related vein, Innes and Sam (2008) find that firms participating in the EPA's 33/50 Program were rewarded with relaxed regulatory scrutiny. In addition, Keohane et al. (2009) find that coal-fired electric generating units facing a greater likelihood of regulatory enforcement lawsuits reduced emissions more than other plants.

None of these papers directly estimate the profitability of the corporate strategies involved. However, revealed preference implies that the firms found the strategies to be profitable. In addition, Decker (2003) points out that for a large firm such as Intel, the cost of delay in building a new plant can be as high as $1 million per day; since one fewer environmental violation over a three-year period was associated with an eighty-one-day reduction in permitting time, the payoff to better environmental performance may be very high indeed.

### 25.3.2.3 *Political Forces—Civil Regulation*

The nascent empirical literature on private politics is very small but generally supportive of the theory described in Section 2.3. Lenox and Eesley (2009) find that firms with more cash on hand are less likely to acquiesce to activists' demands, as are firms with poor environmental performance. Activists adopt more aggressive campaigns against larger and dirtier firms, and firms with smaller capital reserves. In addition, they find that firms are more likely to be targeted by activists if they are larger, more profitable, more advertising-intensive, and dirtier; firms with large cash reserves are less likely to be targeted. Gupta and Innes (2009) also find that larger firms are more likely to be targeted by activists, and that targeting makes firms significantly more likely to adopt environmental management systems.

# 25.4 CONCLUSIONS AND FUTURE RESEARCH DIRECTIONS

The economics literature on corporate environmentalism has mushroomed over the past decade. Economic theory has identified numerous channels through which companies can profit from environmentally friendly actions that go beyond legal requirements. Cutting production costs, meeting the demands of green consumers, and shaping public and private politics—all offer the potential for shareholder gains. Although the first two of these channels are very similar to traditional aspects of managerial economics, the political dimension of corporate environmentalism is novel and has not traditionally been considered part of that field of study.

Work on the greening of the corporation has numerous implications for managers. First, it suggests that most companies have "twenty dollar bills" lying on the floor in the form of untapped opportunities for greater eco-efficiency. This means not only that corporate environmental initiatives will often cost very little, but that they may well have negative costs. Second, corporate environmentalism is both a market strategy (direct cost reduction and potential for topline growth) and a nonmarket strategy (influencing both public and private politics). This means that its full benefits are complex and easy to underestimate, since they include hard-to-quantify benefits in the forms of risk reduction, corporate reputation, employee retention, and preparedness for unexpected political events. Third, communicating about corporate environmental actions requires finesse, as firms may easily be accused of greenwash and risk failing to fully capitalize on their good works. In sum, corporate environmentalism as business strategy offers real benefits, but also requires more managerial expertise and care than some other types of strategies. It is not necessarily the right path for all companies, but can offer hard-to-imitate competitive advantages if executed well.

We can distinguish various types of corporate environmentalism according to their costs. Negative-cost, or win/win, actions are profitable in and of themselves, and a small additional push to action—from shareholders, employees, NGOs, or government—is often enough to bring them forth. There is also a set of low-cost actions that may be profitable, perhaps because they improve employee morale or supplier relations. These, too, can be seen as win/win investments in a broader perspective. Actions with moderate cost can be justified if they shape public policy or raise rivals' costs, though evaluating their profitability may be difficult. Finally, there is a set of high-cost actions that are unlikely to be undertaken absent explicit regulatory mandates; capturing and sequestering the carbon emitted by coal-fired power plants is one good example. For this last category, corporate environmentalism that adequately addresses the relevant social problem is unlikely.

From an empirical perspective, it is inherently hard to measure the profitability of corporate environmentalism. The benefits of negative-cost win/win opportunities are potentially measurable, as are the benefits of low-to-medium cost investments that pay off through improved employee morale and productivity. Higher-cost actions designed to preempt regulatory threats, influence legislation, and deflect enforcement are difficult to value, since the counterfactual is never observed. Thus, we largely concur with Margolis et al. (2007) that it is wise to redirect research into why companies pursue corporate environmentalism, why better financial performance brings forth better environmental performance, and how companies jointly manage financial and environmental performance. Indeed, assuming that companies pursue their own self-interest, their actions will reveal what forms of corporate environmentalism potentially are profitable.

Although companies have strong incentives to pursue profits, the mere fact that many win/win opportunities go unexploited for long periods of time calls into question the simplistic "black box" view of firms as perfect profit-maximizers that economists are sometimes accused of holding. Managers would benefit from reliable empirical research showing when it pays to be green. In our view, cleanly executed event studies are the most promising way forward in this regard. To date, the literature has been more successful in identifying situations where it is costly to be brown than situations where it pays to be green. There is a solid body of evidence that shareholder value drops when investors learn that a firm has increased its emissions of pollutants, or faces government regulatory penalties or legal liability. There is also evidence that pollution prevention can lower costs by improving upon inefficient production processes.

The evidence is mixed regarding whether shareholder value increases when firms receive environmental awards or other forms of favorable publicity. Some recent work has even identified situations where firms have taken actions in response to stakeholder pressure, and profits fell as a result—though we caution that they still may have been profitable relative to the unobserved alternative of taking no action! Even when firms do not receive a direct increase in share price from their environmental investments, greening can serve as a risk management tool, cushioning the firm against negative investor reaction when environmental accidents occur or when the risk of environmental regulation or litigation increases. In addition, corporate environmentalism can pay off by influencing the regulatory process—preempting or delaying new regulations, speeding the permitting process, and deflecting regulatory enforcement efforts towards other firms—even though it is almost impossible to measure these effects.

Many of the benefits of corporate environmentalism appear to come in terms of reputation building, and this is an area in which the economics literature is very thin. Reputation helps with lowering employee turnover, entering new markets, obtaining permits to build new plants, getting a "seat at the table" to influence future regulations, and many other aspects of strategic management. NGOs have learned that attacking corporate reputations can be a powerful strategy. Initial economic work in this area has been focused on firms developing false reputations for being green. In the domain of corporate environmentalism, such undeserved reputations are sometimes referred to as greenwash. Institutional theorists also use other terms for it, such as talking about symbolic action as opposed to substantive action. Much more work is needed to understand what goes into the building, maintenance, and destruction of corporate reputations. More work is also needed on the operations of the "NGO industry," so that we understand how NGOs leverage the fragility of corporate reputations for their own purposes. Interdisciplinary work on corporate reputations within business schools—linking economics to management, strategy, organizational behavior, and marketing—could be a very fruitful way of gaining deeper insight.

Corporate environmentalism is a relatively new dimension of managerial economics. The last two decades have seen great progress on both the theoretical and the empirical fronts. Nevertheless, much remains to be done. Research on relationships between NGOs and companies is still in its infancy. Corporate reputation is just beginning to attract attention from economists. Empirical evidence on the profitability of corporate environmentalism remains elusive. More work is needed on how firms link their environmental strategies with their broader market and nonmarket strategies. There is ample room for the next decade of research on corporate environmentalism to be just as productive as the last two.

## Notes

1. For details, see www.economist.com/node/2369912, www.economist.com/node/3555212, and www.economist.com/node/10491077.

2. Elhauge (2005) makes a compelling argument that, from a legal perspective, companies have considerable discretion to sacrifice profits in the public interest.

3. Even when there are no cost-reduction opportunities, Ahmed and Segerson (2011) show firms producing both brown and green products that are imperfect substitutes can profit by colluding to reduce their production of the "brown" products. Such collusion raises the price of brown products and consumer demand for green products, which increases prices and profits for both products. The authors assume that collusion on the green product would be a violation of antitrust laws, although competition policy in the European Union expressly exempts collusion of this type.

4. These include the political economy model of Lutz et al. (2000), the labeling models of Feddersen and Gilligan (2001) and Heyes and Maxwell (2004), and the private politics model of Baron and Diermeier (2007).

5. Comparatively low environmental standards in developing countries have raised concerns that multinational corporations may locate plants in developing countries to reduce costs. However, this "pollution haven" hypothesis has not been supported by empirical evidence (Christmann and Taylor 2002; Eskeland and Harrison 2003). Instead, studies show that multinationals profit more from self-regulating their environmental conduct, participating in global voluntary initiatives and proactively adopting internal environmental standards that are more stringent than those mandated by national governments (Dowell et al. 2000).

6. For further information, visit the website of the trade association Asocolflores at http://www.asocolflores.org/.

7. ISO 14001 is an environmental management certification system created by the International Organization of Standards. Prakash and Potoski (2006) offer a thorough discussion of the system.

8. In Segerson and Miceli (1998), the probability of legislation is exogenous. Glachant (2005) extends their analysis to determine this probability endogenously within the context of a political influence game played between industry and a green advocacy group. Like the earlier analysis, Glachant (2005) finds that a negotiated agreement enhances social welfare. Glachant (2007) extends the analysis further to the case where government observes industry compliance with the agreement but with a detection lag. This means that industry could use a voluntary agreement to delay compliance with threatened legislation.

9. See Lyon and Maxwell (2004a) for a thorough discussion of these programs.

10. One of the most egregious examples of opaque lobbying practices is "astroturf lobbying," in which companies covertly foot the bill to create artificial "grassroots" political lobbying organizations. Lyon and Maxwell (2004b) develop a model of this form of lobbying.

11. Lenox and Eesley (2009) provide one of the first empirical studies of the types of actions taken by NGOs, the types of firms they target, and the responses of these firms to being targeted.

12. The NGO's goal is perhaps best thought of as the optimization of environmental services subject to constraints, the most important of which is the need to retain the support of the general public, as this is the source of the NGO's power.

13. The findings we discuss in this and the next two paragraphs all derive from Baron and Diermeier (2007).

14. See http://www.euractiv.com/en/pa/ngos-top-public-trust-ratings-poll-shows/article-134675.

15. For empirical evidence on greenwashing by firms in the electric utility sector, see Kim and Lyon (2011).

16. The difficulty comes in selecting an appropriate market return benchmark against which to measure abnormal returns. Since *Newsweek* rates the 500 largest US firms, the S&P 500 does not provide an exogenous market benchmark; the Russell 4500 provides an independent benchmark, but because it comprises firms substantially smaller than those in the S&P 500 it is not necessarily an appropriate reference point.

## REFERENCES

Ahmed, Rasha and Kathleen Segerson. 2011. "Collective Voluntary Agreements to Eliminate Polluting Products." *Resource and Energy Economics* 33:572–88.

Alberton, A., N. C. Affonso da Costa Jr., L. M. de Souza Campos, and R. Marcon. 2009. "EMS Certification and Economic-Financial Performance: A Study on Brazilian Companies." Working Paper, Universidade do Vale do Itajai.

Arora, Seema, and Subhashis Gangopadhyay. 1995. "Toward a Theoretical Model of Voluntary Overcompliance." *Journal of Economic Behavior and Organization* 28:289–309.

Bagnoli, Mark, and Susan G Watts. 2003. "Selling to Socially Responsible Consumers: Competition and the Private Provision of Public Goods." *Journal of Economics & Management Strategy* 12:419–45.

Baron, David P. 2001. "Private Politics, Corporate Social Responsibility, and Integrated Strategy." *Journal of Economics and Management Strategy* 10:7–45.

——. 2006b. "The Positive Theory of Moral Management, Social Pressure, and Corporate Social Performance." Working Paper, Stanford University.

——. 2007. "Corporate Social Responsibility and Social Entrepreneurship." *Journal of Economics and Management Strategy* 16:683–718.

Baron, David P., and Daniel Diermeier. 2007. "Strategic Activism and Nonmarket Strategy." *Journal of Economics and Management Strategy* 16:599–634.

Beatty, T. K. M., and J. P. Shimshack. 2010. "The Impact of Climate Change Information: New Evidence from the Stock Market." *The B.E. Journal of Economic Analysis & Policy* 10 (1): art. 60. doi:10.2202/1935–1682.2374.

Beloe, Seb, Julia Harrison, and Oliver Greenfield. 2007. "Coming In From the Cold: Public Affairs and Corporate Responsibility." Research Report, BluePrint Partners, SustainAbility, Inc., and WWF-UK.

Bettenhausen, K., J. Byrd, and E. S. Cooperman. 2010. "Environmental Risk and Shareholder Returns: Evidence from the Announcement of the Toxic 100 Index." *International Review of Accounting, Banking and Finance* 2:28–45.

Blacconiere, W. G., and W. D. Northcut. 1997. "Environmental Information and Market Reactions to Environmental Legislation." *Journal of Accounting, Auditing and Finance* 12:149–78.

Blacconiere, W. G., and D. M. Patten. 1994. "Environmental Disclosures, Regulatory Costs, and Changes in Firm Value." *Journal of Accounting and Economics* 8:357–77.

Blackman, Allen, Thomas P. Lyon, and Nicholas Sisto. 2006. "Voluntary Environmental Agreements when Regulatory Capacity is Weak." *Comparative Economic Studies* 48:682–702.

Bowen, R. M., R. P. Castanias, and L. A. Daley. 1983. "Intra-Industry Effects of the Accident at Three Mile Island." *Journal of Financial and Quantitative Analysis* 18:87–111.

Brekke, Kjell Arne, and Karine Nyborg. 2008. "Attracting Responsible Employees: Green Production as Labor Market Screening." *Resource and Energy Economics* 30 (4): 509–26.

Cañón-de-Francia, J., and C. Garcés-Ayerbe. 2009. "ISO 14001 Environmental Certification: A Sign Valued by the Market?" *Environmental and Resource Economics* 44:245–62.

Capelle-Blancard, G., and M-A. Laguna. 2010. "How Does the Stock Market Respond to Chemical Disasters?" *Journal of Environmental Economics and Management* 59:192–205.

Casadesus-Masanell, Ramon, Michael Crooke, Forest Reinhardt, and Vishal Vasishth. 2009. "Households' Willingness to Pay for 'Green' Goods: Evidence from Patagonia's Introduction of Organic Cotton Sportswear." *Journal of Economics and Management Strategy* 18:203–33.

Christmann, Petra, and Glen Taylor. 2002. "Globalization and the Environment: Strategies for International Voluntary Environmental Initiatives." *Academy of Management Executive* 16:121–35.

Dasgupta, S., B. Laplante, and N. Mamingi. 2001. "Pollution and Capital Markets in Developing Countries." *Journal of Environmental Economics and Management* 42:310–35.

d'Aspremont, C.A., A. Jacquemin, J. J. Gabszewicz, and J. A. Weymark. 1983. "On the Stability of Collusive Price Leadership." *Canadian Journal of Economics* 16:17–25.

Dawson, Na Li, and Kathleen Segerson. 2008. "Voluntary Agreements with Industries: Participation Incentives with Industry-Wide Targets." *Land Economics* 84:97–114.

Decker, C. S. 2003. "Corporate Environmentalism and Environmental Statutory Permitting." *Journal of Law and Economics* 46:103–29.

Delmas, M. A. and M. J. Montes-Sancho. 2010. "Voluntary Agreements to Improve Environmental Quality: Symbolic and Substantive Cooperation." *Strategic Management Journal* 31:575–601.

Denicolò, Vincenzo. 2008. "A Signaling Model of Environmental Overcompliance." *Journal of Economic Behavior and Organization* 68:293–303.

Dimitri, Carolyn, and Lydia Oberholtzer. 2009. "Marketing U.S. Organic Foods: Recent Trends from Farms to Consumer." US Department of Agriculture, Economic Research Service, Economic Information Bulletin Number 58.

Dowell, G. A., S. Hart, and B. Yeung. 2000. "Do Corporate Global Environmental Standards Create or Destroy Market Value?" *Management Science* 46:1059–74.

Elfenbein, Daniel W., and Brian McManus. 2010. "A Greater Price for a Greater Good? Evidence that Consumers Pay More for Charity-Linked Products." *American Economic Journal: Economic Policy* 2:28–60.

Elhauge, Einer R. 2005. "Corporate Managers' Operational Discretion to Sacrifice Corporate Profits in the Public Interest." In *Environmental Protection and the Social Responsibility of Firms*, edited by Bruce L. Hay, Robert N. Stavins, and Richard H. K. Vietor, 13–76. Washington, DC: Resource for the Future Press.

Eskeland, Gunnar S., and Ann E. Harrison. 2003. "Moving to Greener Pastures? Multinationals and the Pollution Haven Hypothesis." *Journal of Development Economics* 70 (1): 1–23.

Esty, Daniel C., and Andrew Winston. 2006. *Green to Gold: How Smart Companies Use Environmental Strategy to Innovate, Create Value, and Build Competitive Advantage.* Hoboken, NJ: John Wiley & Sons.

Feddersen, Timothy J., and Thomas W. Gilligan. 2001. "Saints and Markets: Activists and the Supply of Credence Goods." *Journal of Economics & Management Strategy* 10:149–71.

Fisher-Vanden, K. and K. Thorburn. 2011. "Voluntary Corporate Environmental Initiatives and Shareholder Wealth." *Journal of Environmental Economics and Management* 62 (3): 430–45.

Frank, Robert H. 2003. *What Price the Moral High Ground? Ethical Dilemmas in Competitive Environments.* Princeton, NJ: Princeton University Press.

Freedman, M., and D. M. Patten. 2004. "Evidence on the Pernicious Effect of Financial Report Environmental Disclosure." *Accounting Forum* 28:27–41.

Friedman, Milton. 1970. "The Social Responsibility of Business is to Increase Profits." *The New York Times Magazine*, September 13. New York: The New York Times.

Glachant, Matthieu. 2005. "Voluntary Agreements in a Rent Seeking Environment." In *Handbook on Environmental Voluntary Agreements*, edited by E. Croci, 49–66. Dordrecht, Holland: Kluwer Academic Publishers.

———. 2007. "Non-Binding Voluntary Agreements." *Journal of Environmental Economics and Management* 54:32–48.

Graff Zivin, Joshua, and Arthur Small. 2005. "A Modigliani-Miller Theory of Altruistic Corporate Social Responsibility." *Topics in Economic Analysis and Policy* 5 (1): art. 10. doi:10.2202/1538-0653.1369.

Gupta, S., and B. Goldar. 2005. "Do Stock Markets Penalize Environment-Unfriendly Behavior? Evidence from India." *Ecological Economics* 52:81–95.

Gupta, S., and R. Innes. 2009. "Determinants and Environmental Impact of Private Politics: An Empirical Analysis." Working Paper, University of Arizona.

Hamilton, J. H. 1995. "Pollution as News: Media and Stock Market Reactions to the Toxics Release Inventory Data." *Journal of Environmental Economics and Management* 28: 98–113.

Harbaugh, Rick, John W. Maxwell, and Beatrice Roussillon. 2011. "Label Confusion: The Groucho Effect of Uncertain Standards." *Management Science* 57:1512–27.

Harrington, Winston. 1988. "Enforcement Leverage When Penalties are Restricted." *Journal of Public Economics* 37:29–53.

Heyes, Anthony G., and John W. Maxwell. 2004. "Private vs. Public Regulation: Political Economy of the International Environment." *Journal of Environmental Economics and Management* 48:978–96.

Hill, J., and T. Schneeweis. 1983. "The Effect of Three Mile Island on Electric Utility Stock Prices: A Note." *Journal of Finance* 38:1285–92.

Hoffman, Andrew J. 2007. *Carbon Strategies: How Leading Companies Are Reducing Their Climate Change Footprint.* Ann Arbor: University of Michigan Press.

Innes, Robert. 2006. "A Theory of Consumer Boycotts under Symmetric Information and Imperfect Competition." *The Economic Journal* 116:355–81.

Innes, Robert, and Joseph J. Bial. 2002. "Inducing Innovation in the Environmental Technology of Oligopolistic Firms." *Journal of Industrial Economics* 50:265–87.

Innes, Robert, and Abdoul Sam. 2008. "Voluntary Pollution Reductions and the Enforcement of Environmental Law: An Empirical Study of the 33/50 Program." *Journal of Law and Economics* 51:271–96.

Karpoff, P., J. Lott, and E. Wehrly. 2005. "The Reputational Penalties for Environmental Violations: Empirical Evidence." *Journal of Law and Economics* 48:653–75.

Keohane, Nathaniel O., Erin T. Mansur, and Andrey Voynov. 2009. "Averting Regulatory Enforcement: Evidence from New Source Review." *Journal of Economics and Management Strategy* 18:75–104

Khanna, M., and L. A. Damon. 1999. "EPA's Voluntary 33/50 Program: Impact on Toxic Releases and Economic Performance of Firms." *Journal of Environmental Economics and Management* 37:1–25.

Khanna, M., W. R. H. Quimio, and D. Bojilova. 1998. "Toxics Release Information: A Policy Tool for Environmental Protection." *Journal of Environmental Economics and Management* 36:243–66.

Kiesel, Kristin, and Sofia B. Villas-Boas. 2007. "Got Organic Milk? Consumer Valuations of Milk Labels after the Implementation of the USDA Organic Seal." *Journal of Agricultural & Food Industrial Organization* 5 (1): art. 4. doi:10.2202/1542-0485.1152.

Kim, E-H, and T. P. Lyon. 2010. "Strategic Environmental Disclosure: Evidence from the DOE's Voluntary Greenhouse Gas Registry." *Journal of Environmental Economics and Management* 61:311–26.

——. 2011. "When Does Institutional Activism Increase Shareholder Value?: The Carbon Disclosure Project." *The BE Journal of Economic Analysis and Policy* 11 (1): art. 50. doi:10.2202/1935-1682.2676.

King, Andrew A., and Michael J. Lenox. 2002. "Exploring the Locus of Profitable Pollution Reduction." *Management Science* 48:289–99.

Klassen, R. D., and C. McLaughlin. 1996. "The Impact of Environmental Management on Firm Performance." *Management Science* 42:1199–1214.

Konar, S., and M. A. Cohen. 2001. "Does the Market Value Environmental Performance?" *Review of Economics and Statistics* 83:281–89.

Lanoie, P., B. Laplante, and M. Roy. 1998. "Can Capital Markets Create Incentives for Pollution Control?" *Ecological Economics* 26:31–41.

Laplante, B., and P. Lanoie. 1994. "Market Response to Environmental Incidents in Canada." *Southern Economic Journal* 60:657–72.

Lenox, M. J., and C. E. Eesley. 2009. "Private Environmental Activism and the Selection and Response of Firm Targets." *Journal of Economics and Management Strategy* 18:45–73.

Lutz, Stefan, Thomas P. Lyon, and John W. Maxwell. 2000. "Quality Leadership When Regulatory Standards Are Forthcoming," *Journal of Industrial Economics* 48 (3): 331–48.

Lyon, T., Y. Lu, X. Shi, and Q. Yin. 2011. "How Do Shareholders Respond to Green Company Awards in China." Working Paper, University of Michigan.

Lyon, Thomas P., and John W. Maxwell. 2003. "Self-Regulation, Taxation, and Public Voluntary Environmental Agreements." *Journal of Public Economics* 87:1453–86.

——. 2004a. *Corporate Environmentalism and Public Policy*. Cambridge: Cambridge University Press.

——. 2004b. "Astroturf: Interest Group Lobbying and Corporate Strategy." *Journal of Economics and Management Strategy* 13 (4): 561–98.

——. 2007. "Environmental Public Voluntary Programs Reconsidered." *Policy Studies Journal* 35:723–50.

——. 2008. "Corporate Social Responsibility and the Environment: A Theoretical Perspective." *Review of Environmental Economics and Policy* 2:240–60.

——. 2011. "Greenwash: Corporate Environmental Disclosure under Threat of Audit." *Journal of Economics and Management Strategy* 20:3–41.

Lyon, Thomas P., and J. P. Shimshack. 2011. "How Does Environmental Disclosure Work?: Evidence from *Newsweek*'s Green Companies Rankings." Working Paper, Stephen M. Ross School of Business, University of Michigan.

MacKinlay, A. 1997. "Event Studies in Economics and Finance." *Journal of Economic Literature* 35:13–39.

Manzini, Paola, and Marco Mariotti. 2003. "A Bargaining Model of Voluntary Environmental Agreements." *Journal of Public Economics* 87:2725–36.

Margolis, J., H. A. Elfenbein, and J. Walsh. 2007. "Does It Pay to be Good? A Meta-Analysis and Redirection of Research on the Relationship between Corporate Social and Financial Performance." Working Paper, University of Michigan.

Maxwell, John W. and Christopher Decker. 2006. "Voluntary Environmental Investment and Regulatory Responsiveness." *Environmental and Resource Economics* 33:425–39.

Maxwell, John W., Thomas P. Lyon, and Steven C. Hackett. 2000. "Self-Regulation and Social Welfare: The Political Economy of Corporate Environmentalism." *Journal of Law and Economics* 43 (2): 583–618.

Morgenstern, Richard D., and William A. Pizer, eds. 2007. *Reality Check: The Nature and Performance of Voluntary Environmental Programs in the United States, Europe and Japan.* Washington, DC: RFF Press.

Muehlenbachs, Lucija, Elisabeth Newcomb Sinha, and Nitish Ranjan Sinha. 2011. "Hitting the Violators Where It Hurts? Stock Market Reaction to USEPA Press Releases." Working Paper, Resources for the Future, Washington, DC.

Muoghalu, M., H. D. Robinson, and J. Glascock. 1990. "Hazardous Waste Lawsuits, Stockholder Returns, and Deterrence." *Southern Economic Journal* 57:357–70.

Patten, D. M., and J. R. Nance. 1998. "Regulatory Cost Effects in a Good News Environment: The Intra-Industry Reaction to the Alaskan Oil Spill." *Journal of Accounting and Public Policy* 17:409–29.

Porter, Michael E., and Claas van der Linde. 1995. "Towards a New Conception of the Environment-Competitiveness Relationship." *Journal of Economic Perspectives* 9:97–118.

Portney, Paul R. 2008. "The (Not So) New Corporate Social Responsibility: An Empirical Perspective." *Review of Environmental Economics and Policy* 2:261–75.

Prakash, Aseem, and Matthew Potoski. 2006. *The Voluntary Environmentalists: Green Clubs, ISO 14001, and Voluntary Environmental Regulations.* Cambridge: Cambridge University Press.

Reid, E. and M. Toffel. 2009. "Responding to Public and Private Politics: Corporate Disclosure of Climate Change Strategies." *Strategic Management Journal* 30:1157–78.

Segerson, Kathy, and Thomas Miceli. 1998. "Voluntary Environmental Agreements: Good or Bad News for Environmental Protection." *Journal of Environmental Economics and Management* 36:109–30.

Short, Jodi L., and Michael W. Toffel. 2010. "Making Self-Regulation More Than Merely Symbolic: The Critical Role of the Legal Environment." *Administrative Science Quarterly* 55:361–96.

Sinclair-Desgagne, Bernard, and Estelle Gozlan. 2003. "A Theory of Environmental Risk Disclosure." *Journal of Environmental Economics and Management* 45:377–93.

Teisl, Mario F., Brian Roe, and Robert L. Hicks. 2002. "Can Eco-Labels Tune a Market? Evidence from Dolphin-Safe Labeling." *Journal of Environmental Economics and Management* 43:339–59.

*The Economist.* 2004. "Two-Faced Capitalism." January 22. Accessed January 20, 2013. www.economist.com/node/2369912.

*The Economist.* 2005. "The Good Company." January 20. Accessed January 20, 2013. www.economist.com/node/3555212.

*The Economist.* 2008. "Just Good Business." January 17. Accessed January 20, 2013. www.economist.com/node/10491077.

US Department of Energy, Energy Information Administration. 2010. "Historical Data: Alternative Transportation Fuels (ATF) and Alternative Fueled Vehicles (AFV)." Accessed January 20, 2013. http://www.eia.gov/cneaf/alternate/page/atftables/afv_hist_data.html

Wang, L., and Y. Yuan. 2004. "Effect on Stock Prices of Environment and Quality Management Certification." *Economic Science* 6:59–71.

Westphal, J. D., and E. T. Zajac. 1994. "Substance and Symbolism in CEOs' Long-Term Incentive Plans." *Administrative Science Quarterly* 39:367–90.

Yu, Zhihao. 2005. "Environmental Protection: A Theory of Direct and Indirect Competition for Political Influence." *Review of Economic Studies* 72:269–86.

# Name Index

# SUBJECT INDEX